The Hollywood Beauties

By James Robert Parish

As author:

The Fox Girls*
The Paramount Pretties*
The Slapstick Queens
Good Dames
Hollywood's Great Love Teams*
The Elvis Presley Scrapbook
The Great Movie Heroes
Great Child Stars
Film Directors Guide: Western Europe
Great Western Stars
The Jeanette MacDonald Story
The Tough Guys*
Film Actor's Guide: Western Europe

As co-author:

The Emmy Awards: A Pictorial History
The Cinema of Edward G. Robinson
The MGM Stock Company: The Golden Era*
The Great Spy Pictures
The George Raft File
The Glamour Girls*
Liza!
The Debonairs*
The Swashbucklers*
The Great Gangster Pictures
The Great Western Pictures
Film Directors Guide: The U.S.
Vincent Price Unmasked
Hollywood Players: The Forties*
Hollywood Players: The Thirties*
The All-Americans*
The Leading Ladies*
The Great Science Fiction Pictures
Hollywood on Hollywood

As editor:

The Great Movie Series
Actors Television Credits: 1950-72 & Supplement

As associate editor:

The American Movies Reference Book: The Sound Era
TV Movies

*Published by Arlington House

The Hollywood Beauties

James Robert Parish

with Gregory W. Mank & Don E. Stanke

Research Associates:

John Robert Cocchi   Richard Picchiarini

Peter Sanderson   Florence Solomon

Rainbow Books

CARLSTADT, NEW JERSEY

First Rainbow Printing, 1979

P 10 9 8 7 6 5 4 3 2 1

Book design by Pat Slesarchik

Library of Congress Cataloging in Publication Data

Parish, James Robert.
    The Hollywood beauties.

    Includes index.
    1. Moving-picture actors and actresses—United States—Biography. I. Title.
PN1998.A2P39176   791.43'028'0922 [B] 78-18306
ISBN O-89508-068-0

For Dr. Lawrence Charles Parish

Key to the Abbreviations

AA	Allied Artists Picture Corporation
AIP	American International Pictures
AVCO EMB	Avco Embassy Pictures Corporation
C	Color
BV	Buena Vista Distribution Co., Inc.
CIN	Cinerama, Inc.
COL	Columbia Pictures Industries, Inc.
EL	Eagle Lion Films, Inc.
EMB	Embassy Pictures Corporation (later part of Avco Embassy)
FN	First National Pictures, Inc. (later part of Warner Bros.)
FOX	Fox Film Corporation (later part of Twentieth Century-Fox)
LIP	Lippert Pictures, Inc.
MGM	Metro-Goldwyn-Mayer, Inc.
MON	Monogram Pictures Corporation
PAR	Paramount Pictures Corporation
PRC	Producers Releasing Corporation
RKO	RKO Radio Pictures, Inc.
REP	Republic Pictures Corporation
20th	Twentieth Century-Fox Film Corporation
UA	United Artists Corporation
UNIV	Universal Pictures, Inc.
WB	Warner Bros., Inc.

Acknowledgments

RESEARCH MATERIAL CONSULTANT:

Doug McClelland

RESEARCH VERIFIER:

Earl Anderson

Lillian Beck
DeWitt Bodeen
Richard Braff
Robert A. Evans
Morris Everett, Jr.
Filmfacts (Ernest Parmentier)
Film Favorites (Bob Smith, Charles Smith)
Films in Review
Focus on Film
Pierre Guinle
Hollywood Revue of Movie Memorabilia
Charles Hoyt
Ken D. Jones
René Jordan
Miles Kreuger
Edward S. Landreth
William T. Leonard

David McGillivray
Albert B. Manski
Alvin H. Marill
Mrs. Earl Meisinger
Jim Meyer
Peter Miglierini
Norman Miller
Howard Newman
Michael R. Pitts
Sal Rosa
Screen Facts (Alan G. Barbour)
Tony Slide
Mrs. Peter Smith
Charles K. Stumpf
T. Allan Taylor
Lou Valentino
Richard Wentzler

And special thanks to Paul Myers, curator of the Theatre Collection at the Lincoln Center Library for the Performing Arts (New York City), and his staff: Monty Arnold, David Bartholomew, Rod Bladel, Donald Fowle, Maxwell Silverman, Dorothy Swerdlove, and Betty Wharton, and Don Madison of Photo Services.

CONTENTS

A publicity pose for *Bird of Paradise* ('32).

CHAPTER 1

Dolores Del Rio

5'3½"
115 pounds
Black hair
Brown eyes
Leo

THERE HAS LONG been a strange dichotomy in the Hollywood attitude toward physical beauty. Of course, nothing has been so pursued by film producers eager to promote the magical image of the movies. Yet no aspect of the cinema has been so mocked and chastised by the movie colony and its fans. The more lovely the young lady or the more handsome the young man, the more reluctant are film judges to admit that the individual possesses talent. Perhaps this ambivalent attitude toward a comely countenance is a reaction to its impermanence. Beauty does not last, and it is heartbreaking to observe it fade.

A striking refutation to this "beautiful people" calumny is the legendary Dolores Del Rio. For over fifty years, she has matured in the public eye, aging so naturally and in so breathtaking a fashion that she suggests a hopeful antidote to the ravages of time. Now a septuagenarian, Dolores is not a varnished mannequin. Miss Del Rio has passed through the seasons of her life realistically, each era tinged with her remarkable loveliness.

In addition to her pulchritude, Dolores has always had acting talent potent enough to cause the more cynical of critics to applaud her even from her earliest starring days in movies. The combination should have made her a far bigger star than she eventually became in Hollywood. However, as the first Mexican girl to achieve success in the U.S. cinema, she utilized her American prestige to become the top female attraction of stage and screen in her native country. Still, her American film career, gliding from silents to the glorious Thirties and up to the McCarthy era, was filled with the romance and excitement befitting so epic a beauty. One can be grateful that she could defect to her adoring Mexico whenever professional and/or private problems stifled her Hollywood status.

Those familiar with Hollywood's treatment of Mexico can easily picture the characteristic touches of the ancient ranches, the proud, generation-tracing families, the convent educations, the festive family celebrations. It was just such a world into which Lolita Dolores Asunsolo y Martinez was born on Thursday, August 3, 1905, in Durango, Mexico. She was the only child of a bank president and semi-feudal land-owner who was the third generation from a Spanish-Basque family. Her mother traced her lineage to the Toltecs. A second cousin of Dolores' was Ramon Novarro. It was a wealthy, enviable way of life enjoyed by the Asunsolo family, though their lifestyle seemed threatened when Lolita was a youngster. As she would re-call, "I was only four when, in the middle of the night, my father, who was president of the bank of Durango, came and carried me out to a car-riage with my mother, and we fled to Mexico City. Pancho Villa was on his way to take over the bank and our home. We never returned."

Lolita was educated in cosmopolitan Mexico City, under the auspices of the French convent of Saint Joseph. She was an exceptionally lovely child and, with her schooling in such disciplines as singing and dancing, early in life she became a sight to behold and enjoy.

In 1919, Lolita joined her family on a Euro-pean tour and was presented to the King and Queen of Spain. Upon her return home, Lolita soon attracted the attention of Jaime Martinez del Rio, the scion of one of Mexico's oldest Castilian families. In 1921, fifteen-year-old Lo-lita became the bride of del Rio. Following a honeymoon in Madrid, the Pyrenees, and Paris, the couple settled on a northern Mexico ranch that had been in the groom's family for over 300 years.

This was the pattern acceptable to most wealthy young maidens of Mexico during the Twenties: marry a rich man, settle down on a sprawling estate, travel, and bear children. But Lolita was markedly different. She became rest-less with the pampered life of the idle rich, later commenting on "the teas, dinners, dances, and the same people—in winter the opera, in sum-mer the bullfights, the annual trips to Europe." Such a life might have appeared to be paradise to the peons begging for coins in the Rio Grande at the U.S. border, but Madame del Rio coveted more from life. Fortunately her spouse was equally restless, and the couple considered living in the Latin Quarter of Paris, specifically so he could develop his playwriting skills. However, fate would soon dictate forsaking the ranch for a locale further north—Hollywood.

With its romantic history, scenic beauty, and fast-marriage laws, Mexico was a haven for Hollywood citizens who desired to soothe their passions in quick, convenient matrimony. One such celebrity was director Edwin Carewe. As Dolores later recollected,

Edwin Carewe and his pretty wife, then Mary Akin, had come to Mexico to be married. They were spending a few days of their honeymoon in Mex-ico City.

One of the diplomatic corps intro-duced the Carewes to my family and one evening we tendered them a little dinner party at the home of my parents.

During the evening Mr. Carewe came to me and half smiling, half serious, mentioned the movies. Frankly, I was a movie fan, but few knew of it in my household. Not even my closest friends. When the director mentioned it, the very thought of my going to Hollywood and trying my luck under his care made me inwardly bubble with excitement.

The enthusiasm was largely confined to Do-lores. Her family at first took Carewe's career offer as a joke. They announced that such a life change was "simply out of the question." No Mexican girl of such ancestry had ever resorted to so unseemly an ambition as attempting to crash the glittery world of the cinema. Carewe, however, was determined and crafty. He plotted to lure Dolores to the studios by a more honorable route—her husband. The director informed the ambitious young man that the film industry boasted much opportunity for young people of style and intelligence, and persuaded him to visit Hollywood for several weeks to study the glory that could await him and his wife.

The approach worked. As Dolores would remember, "Fancy my surprise when, after he had been gone but a week, I received a cable from him telling me to pack and come to Hollywood. Again a storm of protest from family and friends. I left much against their will, it seemed." In fact, her family was totally aghast at her plans, and coldly intoned that no Mexican girl of aristocratic family had ever entered the seamy world of acting. Lolita's reply was, "Very well, I will be the first." With that, she left to meet her husband in Hollywood.

At that time, Hollywood was still only a small settlement amid the hills and groves of southern California. It was, in 1925, at the peak of its celebrated champagne-slipper decadence. Gloria Swanson, John Gilbert, Mae Murray, Lon Chaney, Douglas Fairbanks, Mary Pickford, John Barrymore, and Richard Dix were among the favorite stars who portrayed larger-than-life images to a celluloid-enraptured America. Movies vibrated with silent beauty and opulence. The seamy, naturalistic sides of life were a long way from attracting an audience. The fascinating beauty of the twenty-year-old Mexican lady who became Dolores Del Rio had found an appropriate showcase in this radiant atmosphere.

While Jaime sought a proper niche for himself in the cinema industry, preferably in the writing department, Dolores signed a personal contract with Carewe and was rushed into the project that he was then filming at First National in Burbank. *Joanna* (1925) starred Dorothy Mackaill and Jack Mulhall. Carewe cast his young discovery as a sleek society vamp named Carlotta de Silva who mistreats the heroine (Miss Mackaill). When the film premiered during the holiday season of 1925, a thrilled Dolores

managed to convince her many Mexican relatives and friends to attend the showing. She hoped the excitement of seeing her on the screen would dispel their initial disapproval. The disbelievers came, along with Dolores' new Los Angeles acquaintances—to witness a mere glimpse of the novice in the finished release print. Carewe had snipped most of her footage in the editing room. A dreadfully embarrassed Dolores seriously considered giving up her newfound ambition and reopening the del Rio Mexican ranch.

Carewe persuaded the determined novice to remain, but it was a tough job. The tenderly raised lady was uncomfortable with many aspects of life in the filmmaking world. Of her original screen test, she related, "What a day! It seemed as though the hours would never pass. I was nervous beyond words. I could hardly hear the director as he spoke to me from the camera lines. I remember how I felt when the publicity director asked me to pose for stills, telling me to look this way, smile, look down, look up—look every way. It seemed foolish. It was terrible— simply terrible." The fears had hardly diminished after *Joanna*. "I spoke very little English and had to have an interpreter on the set at all times to tell me what was being said and what Mr. Carewe wanted me to do. He was there morning, noon, and night."

Indeed, Edwin Carewe appeared totally enthralled by his protégée and, while Jaime still struggled to find his professional identity, the director carefully guided Dolores up the acting rungs. In *High Steppers* (1926), another First National release starring Mary Astor and Lloyd Hughes, Dolores was beautifully photographed by Robert Kurrle as Evelyn Iffield, the daughter of an English noblewoman. Though her role was brief, she made an impression. Carewe finally entrusted a leading role to her in First National's *Pals First* (1926), a melodrama, in which her leading man was Lloyd Hughes from *High Steppers*. Carewe was delighted when she proved to appeal to the preview audiences, and he wasted little time in loaning her to Universal to spice up an Edward Everett Horton comedy, *The Whole Town's Talking* (no relation to the John Ford 1935 comedy in which Edward G. Robinson performed a dual role).

In *High Steppers* ('26).

In 1926, Dolores' loveliness garnered a new accolade. Since 1922, the Western Association of Motion Picture Advertisers (abbreviated WAMPAS) yearly selected a bevy of starlets as the WAMPAS Baby Stars. These girls were predicted for top stardom and 1926 was a well-prophesied year. The selections included Mary Astor, Mary Brian, Joyce Compton, Dolores Costello, Fay Wray, Janet Gaynor, Joan Crawford, and Dolores Del Rio. Julie Lang Hunt would recall the following in a 1934 issue of *Photoplay* magazine about the evening of the WAMPAS Baby debut:

> The auditorium was jammed with thirty-five hundred cynically critical people. Reassuring applause had greeted each of the five starlets who preceded her on the stage. When Dolores Del Rio walked out to meet the wilderness of faces, a long silence fell. There was no applause. No indication of reassurance or acceptance. She turned, frightened and bewildered, to walk back into the shelter of the wings. Then the tension broke. Applause thundered. Half the audience was on its feet cheering. The master of ceremonies brought her back again and again to face the thousands who thundered their homage to her beauty for a full seven minutes.

The progress of Dolores' career had by this time won over her mother who came to Hollywood and counseled her daughter on investing her salary in real estate. "Hollywood, what a place it is!" the starlet commented in 1926. "It is so far away from the rest of the world, so narrow. No one thinks of anything but motion pictures, or talks of anything else. And I, too, am getting like the rest. I have not read anything for a year. I do not know what is happening in the world or what people are talking about, or even which revue is the favorite in Paris." This career preoccupation was having its deleterious effect on her marriage. Jaime del Rio still had not settled into a comfortable writing situation.

16

With William V. Mong, Edmund Lowe, Victor McLaglen, and August Tollaire in *What Price Glory* ('26).

The WAMPAS Baby Stars for 1926: Dolores Costello, Vera Reynolds, Mary Astor, Marceline Day, Edna Marion, Mary Brian, Fay Wray, Janet Gaynor, Sally Long, Joyce Compton, Dolores Del Rio, Sally O'Neill, and Joan Crawford.

17

Stardom now awaited Dolores. On Friday, September 5, 1924, *What Price Glory,* the war comedy of Laurence Stallings and Maxwell Anderson, had debuted at Broadway's Plymouth Theatre, playing over 400 performances and enticing the commercial interest of film producers. Fox Pictures finally solidified the offer, and their picture version of the acclaimed play became one of Hollywood's most discussed projects. Edmund Lowe and Victor McLaglen won the coveted roles of Sergeant Quirt and Captain Flagg (played on the stage by William "Stage" Boyd and Louis Wolheim), and director Raoul Walsh requested Dolores for the role of spitfire Charmaine. When the film premiered, the *New York Times* told its readers. . . . "The charmer of the movie, Charmaine, is impersonated by Dolores Del Rio, who, with no little abandon, gives an excellent characterization . . . in tune to the Mademoiselle D'Armentiers type." Released in the holiday season of 1926, *What Price Glory* garnered a smashing $2 million in box-office receipts, and Dolores won a new fleet of admirers, not just for her blossoming beauty, but for her increasing comfort as an actress. "Slowly I lost the fright of the clicking cameras and huge arc lights. I gradually learned to take direction and act at the same time, and found that acting was merely concentration on thoughts of my character."

Her prestige reaching its full flower, Dolores returned in triumph to star in United Artists' *Resurrection* (1927) for her old mentor Edwin Carewe. The Leo Tolstoy novel had been filmed several times before and would be reshot at least three times thereafter. Its turgid, tragic approach made it a natural for a four-handkerchief tearjerker of a film. Dolores portrayed Katusha, the Russian peasant girl seduced by a prince (Rod La Rocque). The latter soon discards her and, at a loss for means of survival, she turns to prostitution. The *New York Times* alerted its readers, "Few screen actresses have ever given as fine a performance in a role as difficult. Under the guidance of Mr. Carewe, Miss Del Rio lends life to this character. . . ."

The actress then returned to Raoul Walsh, who starred her as no less than Carmen in Fox's *Loves of Carmen* (1927), which boasted lavender-tinting as an audience enticement. As photographed by Lucien Andriot and John Marta, little wonder that Don José (Don Alvarado) was driven to ruin by her. The *New York Times* reported, "Miss Del Rio's characterization is apt to make the Carmens of the past appear relatively conservative."

Dolores remained at Fox for her next feature, *The Gateway of the Moon* (1928), in which she played Chela, the half-caste native girl, with a young Walter Pidgeon as her leading man. She then crossed the portals of MGM to play in *The Trail of '98,* a Clarence Brown-directed Western in which she replaced a seriously ill Renee Adoree as a dancehall girl named Berna. It was quite an action-filled oater, including an exciting brawl and well-mounted fire climax. Dolores appeared as at home in the rowdy adventure as she had gliding through her pulchritudinous paces in earlier motion pictures.

Edwin Carewe delivered Dolores to fully realized star status in *Ramona* (1928), the captivating love story based on Helen Hunt Jackson's very popular novel. It was already the third version of the story, but audience reaction was strongly whetted by a 78 rpm recording release in which Dolores sang the Mabel Wayne/ L. Wolfe Gilbert theme song. The tragic story was well played, with Dolores benefiting from an apt performance by Warner Baxter as Alessandro, the love-sick Indian who has a strong code of honor. For many, it would be the definitive version of Miss Jackson's book, far more effective than the 1936 Technicolor talkie version with Loretta Young and Don Ameche. The *New York Times* enthused, "Dolores Del Rio is an excellent choice for the part of Ramona. . . . [Her] interpretation of Ramona is an achievement. Not once does she overact. And yet she is perceived weeping and almost hysterical. She is most careful in all the moods of the character. Her beauty is another point in her favor." While *Ramona* won her some solid reviews, its success caused Fox to unleash a box-office dud entitled *No Other Woman* (1928), co-starring Don Alvarado, which had been filmed in 1926 but shelved as being too insipid for distribution.

In the meantime, with his wife becoming the object of idolatrous fan mail and increasing entreaties by film executives, Jaime del Rio felt even more acutely the pressure to become a suc-

In *Resurrection* (´27).

With Ralph Forbes in
The Trail of '98 (´28).

19

With Warner Baxter in *Ramona* ('28).

cess. Carewe's wife, Mary Akin, had by now begun divorce proceedings, and the rumor persisted in Hollywood that Dolores was his choice for the next Mrs. Carewe. Still deeply in love with his wife, Jaime had agreed to accept a job as a script clerk on his wife's productions just to be near her. If a decision by Dolores to shift her career ambitions to a lower gear could have aided the marriage, it was not tried. Mr. del Rio finally defected to New York to collaborate on a play, *From Hell Came a Lady*. The production failed to open on Broadway, and del Rio, crushed, could not face a return to dependency on his celebrated spouse. When he did not return, Dolores did what so many up-and-coming starlets have always done in show business—she began divorce proceedings to free herself from the unsuccessful husband who could do little for her career and was now becoming an embarrassment.

While Dolores' professional and romantic life was moving at fast speed in California, Jaime made a final attempt to attain his own identity. He accepted a chance to work for the American Play Company in Germany. The next bit of news

released about the pathetic young husband was that he had become critically ill and was at a Berlin sanitarium. The diagnosis made of his condition was that he had relinquished his will to continue living. Near the end, Dolores was informed of the gravity of his situation and she sent him a telegram. "Wish I were with you because I love you. God bless you. I love you." When he died of "blood poisoning following a minor operation," he was squeezing the cablegram in his hand.

Dolores' telegram and del Rio's demise caused some fan magazine rumbling and some nasty talk around Hollywood. However, it appeared that the star's status was sufficiently assured so that such unflattering remarks merely supplied notoriety rather than ruin.

Late that year (1928), Dolores appeared in yet another Edwin Carewe opus, *Revenge,* as Rascha, a whip-cracking gypsy girl eventually tamed to docility by James Marcus. A vacation followed. Dolores toured Europe with a Russian wolfhound, a German dachshund, an English pointer, an Irish setter, and a St. Bernard, and

20

With Rosita Marstini and Ben Bard in *No Other Woman* ('28).

21

was welcomed by the international set. Upon her return to America, she starred in what she later termed "my finest screen role and most pretentious picture." *Evangeline* (1929), a Carewe-produced/directed release for United Artists, boasted some sound sequences in which Dolores' character spoke a few lines of dialogue (the actress had been arduously perfecting her English), sang a French chansonette, and aged from young maiden to an old Sister of Mercy. For added box-office value, Carewe contracted Al Jolson to compose a song from the Longfellow poem for Dolores to perform. She sings the title tune at the film's close, as her long-lost lover (Roland Drew) lies dying. Some critics blamed her handling of the song for his demise, but the canard did not dent the film's success. Obviously Dolores must have been happy that she contradicted the statement she had issued in the wake of *The Jazz Singer*, "Never. Never will I make a talkie. I think they are terrible."

Then came a surprise in Dolores' personal affairs, a turn of events that no one expected. Now free to wed, it was believed that she and Carewe were en route to the altar and to a life of creatively stimulating each other in their film work. But again, the Del Rio ambition was underestimated. United Artists, producers of *Evangeline,* offered the actress an outstanding contract, promising her $9,000 each week she worked. To the shock of all, Dolores suddenly stopped seeing her beau of five years and signed the deal offered by United Artists executive Joseph Schenck. An agitated and embarrassed Carewe sued over the contract. But the case was settled out of court, no doubt with the aid of personal words between the director and actress. Dolores remained a United Artists product.

Her studio employers cast Dolores in *The Bad One* (1930), teaming her with Edmund Lowe and Don Alvarado. As Lita, the Marseilles bordello girl, she passes out keys to other rooms, and saves herself for the right man. The polished director George Fitzmaurice realistically captured a Marseilles atmosphere and Dolores was impressive in her first all-talking picture, combining dialogue, singing, and dancing (Irving Berlin's "To a Tango Melody") in a lovely package. Public response was enthusiastic and the critics found her diction adequate. Thus

Dolores Del Rio had become one of the great ladies of the U.S. screen in the new decade.

On July 23, 1930, Dolores denied the charges of her former attorney, Gunther Lessing, who was filing a divorce complaint against his wife, Loula, who had earlier filed a divorce complaint against him. Lessing charged that Dolores caused his home to break up by telling Loula that Gunther was an "ugly old man" and suggesting that Loula seek an outside romance "while a young and beautiful girl." Dolores' official reply was, "Mr. Lessing's charges are false and malicious and are made in an attempt to embarrass me and collect money which is not due him. There is absolutely no foundation in his ridiculous statements."

The trouble dated back to Dolores' divorce from Jaime del Rio, in which Lessing had successfully pleaded her case. In December of 1929 the lawyer sued Dolores for $31,000 worth of legal expenses in connection with the Mexican divorce, and Dolores refused to settle.

Regarding the matter, Loula Lessing stated, "Miss Del Rio, whom I am happy to consider one of my truest friends, had nothing to do with my decision to sue for divorce."

During this troublesome period, beautiful Dolores continued to fulfill her social obligations. At a party hosted by Marion Davies, she met Cedric Gibbons, the shy, gentlemanly art director responsible for supplying many of MGM's greatest pictures with their celebrated gloss. The pair became involved very quickly, and only a few weeks after their meeting, they were engaged. On Wednesday, August 6, 1930, at 5:40 P.M., she wed Gibbons in the old Franciscan Mission of Santa Barbara. There was a stumbling block to the marriage ceremony that was to be performed. Father Augustine stated he could not perform the wedding since Dolores was a divorced woman. However, her parish church in Hollywood supplied a letter in which it was explained that Jaime del Rio was dead and therefore the Church could allow the nuptials to take place. Dolores was twenty-five; her Dublin-born groom was ten years older. The couple honeymooned in Monterey and returned to Hollywood where Gibbons maintained two homes: one lost in the shade of Santa Monica Canyon, the other near the Culver City studio.

In *The Red Dance* ('28).

With Alec B. Francis
in *Evangeline* ('29).

23

While the aristocratic Gibbonses were celebrating their nuptials, a shattered Edwin Carewe returned to Mary Akin. While he was shooting a 1931 remake of *Resurrection,* with spitfire Lupe Velez in Dolores' old role, Carewe and Mary rewed. However, it was almost the end of the filmmaker who had been born in Gainesville, Texas, in 1883. As soon as Dolores left him, his film career began to slide. It was almost as if she had been his good luck charm. In a reversal of the Svengali-Trilby pattern, it was he who could not function when his Galatea was away. Carewe struggled some more years, finally producing and directing *Are We Civilized?* (1934) before obscurity swallowed him completely. He would end his life on January 22, 1940, a suicide.

Several weeks after her return to Hollywood from her honeymoon, Dolores fell very ill. The official diagnosis was acute pyelitis, but gossips insisted upon another one—a nervous breakdown. Since her arrival in Hollywood some five years earlier, Dolores had been involved closely with two men, one of whom was dead of a broken heart, the other who was suffering a career decline. Apparently some of the nasty whisperings of her detractors had filtered to her ears. Her intimates later claimed that it was this self-blame and remorse over her ambition that had made Dolores a very sick woman.

In actuality, while quite flirtatious and sexy, Dolores was never known to have spent nights out or shared dishonorable quarters. Reputedly, Carewe had expressed a desire to live with Dolores before their expected marriage, but her Latin honor made her decline. Thus, while Dolores was well known to utilize her beauty and charms to advance her career, she never compromised them.

Some years later, Dolores would have gathered sufficient perspective to speak of her nervous breakdown:

> All of my most frightful moments came while I was at the height of my career. Jaime was thrilled at first by my success. We both thought that he would achieve success, too, in pictures. But gradually he came to hate

24

With husband Cedric Gibbons (September 1930).

25

me because I had succeeded and he had not. It was terrible for both of us. . . . *Everything* happened to me! Things crashed around me. Tragic, terrifying things. I lived in a hotbed of intrigue, of politics, of lies and malice, of cross currents of human purposes. I was hurt so often, I was afraid to express myself!

Dolores would never publicly supplement these words with explanations, but her professional standing suffered greatly at this juncture. Medical examinations ruled out work and strain for an indefinite period of time. United Artists, all prepared to shoot *The Dove* with Dolores in the stellar spot, was unhappy. In fact, the studio had included in her contract a stipulation that if she were away from the lot for over one month for any reason, the contract would automatically expire. When her condition prevented her return, United Artists tore up the $9,000 weekly pact. The star was in no condition to accept any offers elsewhere. At this time, the worry of professional over-exposure was not great in Hollywood. Any luminary who went more than a year without a new release was considered in trouble. Hence at the close of 1931, Dolores was thought to be a twenty-six-year-old has-been, done in by her exalted beauty and ambition.

But she recovered. Husband Cedric Gibbons nursed her patiently. By late 1931 Dolores was in sufficiently good health to resume her career. RKO offered her a contract and she accepted. The first project on her new agreement was *Girl of the Rio* (1932), based on *The Dove* which RKO acquired from United Artists. It cast her in the title role as a cantina dancer and co-starred her with Leo Carrillo and Norman Foster. It was not an outstanding success, being a shallow remake of the 1928 Norma Talmadge version. It would be reshot by RKO in 1939 as the low-budget *The Girl and the Gambler,* featuring Steffi Duna, Leo Carrillo, and Tim Holt.

Her next project did far more to boost Dolores back to her former heights. This was *Bird of Paradise* (1932), the epic tale of the native girl Luana and the volcano into which she climactically descends. A curious project, it was packaged by producer David O. Selznick mainly as an exotic melodrama that would showcase the scantily clad bodies of Dolores and the then on-the-rise Joel McCrea. Enterprising Selznick reportedly told director King Vidor, "I don't care what story you use so long as we call it *Bird of Paradise* and Del Rio jumps into a flaming volcano at the finish."

The eighty-minute feature was a shallow but irresistible enterprise that cost over $1 million and reinstated Dolores as one of the most incandescent beauties of the American screen. It was also evident that she was beginning to be more like her old self during production. The fan magazines cryptically opined that a romance was brewing between her and McCrea. There was considerable speculation that she was more than professionally involved with producer Selznick, then the bridegroom of Louis B. Mayer's daughter, Irene. Once again, while Dolores was engaging in coquetry, she was always discreet and remained true to Gibbons during the lengthy production, much of it shot on location in Hawaii.

When the film debuted, the *New York Herald-Tribune* reported:

It is, as you must have seen in the advertisements, Miss Dolores Del Rio, the exquisite Latin, the bringer of more beauty from Mexico than Diego Rivera, who plays the tragic Luana of the story—a role which Miss Laurette Taylor once glorified. Miss Del Rio always seemed to me the most beautiful actress in the cinema—which, as you know, has often been rather handicapped by the prevalence of good-looking women—and I have always thought that she was a reasonably good actress.

In *Bird of Paradise,* she is perhaps no more skillful or experienced than usual, but her dusky, alien beauty fits in so effectively with her role that she is more admirable than ever, and succeeds in providing more loveliness for the film than director and cameraman managed, despite their million dollar budget.

With Stanley Fields and Leo Carrillo in *Girl of the Rio* ('32).

With Joel McCrea in *Bird of Paradise* ('32).

27

Posing with Gene Raymond for *Flying Down to Rio* ('33).

The less enthusiastic *New York Evening Post* printed, "Miss Del Rio and Mr. McCrea are simply Johnny Weissmuller and Maureen O'Sullivan in another setting, and the parallel with *Tarzan* cannot be ignored."

RKO had lavished a great deal of money on *Bird of Paradise,* and decided to next cast Dolores in a routine musical that could be economically shot but be depended on to be a large grosser. This became the classic *Flying Down to Rio* of 1933. Blond Gene Raymond was Dolores' leading man; Vincent Youmans, Edward Eliscu, and Gus Kahn produced tunes such as the title number, "Orchids in the Moonlight," "Music Makes Me," and "Carioca" (which was the name of the popular Latin American dance that was so delightfully showcased in the picture); and Fred Astaire and Ginger Rogers made their debut together as a dance team. When the black-and-white feature premiered at Radio City Music Hall in New York, Fred and Ginger were credited with stealing the picture, a fact not minded by Dolores who became good friends with the hoofers during production.

In his recent best seller, *Bring on the Empty Horses* (1975), David Niven, a friend of Astaire, recalls that he was introduced to Dolores by Fred and dispatched to try to learn some of the intriguing aspects of her marriage to Gibbons.

The Astaires took me down to Dolores Del Rio's house in a quiet street in Santa Monica. Dolores, a spectacular black-haired, dark-eyed Mexican beauty with skin whiter than a hen's egg, was married to a good-looking, military-moustached Cedric Gibbons, the head set designer at MGM studios. Their house was covered with climbing plants of various kinds, the choice of which perhaps contained a clue to the odd relationship of the two householders. Dolores had a large sunny room on the first floor containing a huge and inviting bed. Gibbons lived in comparative squalor in a small room immediately below. The only connection between these two rooms was by way of a stepladder which could be lowered only when a trapdoor in the floor of Dolores' room had been raised. There was a long stick in Gibbie's room with which, we conjectured, he signaled his intentions or hopes by rapping out signals on the floor of his wife's bedchamber.

Phyllis and Fred delegated me to find out more, but despite many happy hours spent in the company of Gibbie and Dolores, they declined to unravel the mystery.

Indeed, the beauty of Dolores, her personal charm, and her ability to enchant a man without dangerously exciting him made the star a great favorite in Hollywood social circles. Dolores found Hollywood in its heyday a wonderful and breathtaking experience.

You can't imagine what it was like—the parties that took weeks of planning, the great decorators like Billy Haines, who would redo a house for just one party, and the guests who were invited—the Jock Whitneys and Nelson Rockefeller, politicians from Washington, people from Europe. Indeed they were magnificent parties.

The Jack Warners gave some of the most wonderful parties. And Marion Davies once turned her beach house and patio into a circus tent. The guests came dressed as clowns, bareback riders, acrobats. Imagine Clark Gable, Norma Shearer, Marlene Dietrich dressed for a circus party. Marion Davies also gave gorgeous parties at San Simeon, that great palace of William Randolph Hearst's. They were incredible days, like a gorgeous, magnificent movie.

The Gibbonses themselves soon took a regal place among the more popular hosts of cinema social life. On Sunday afternoons they often hosted buffets and opened their pool and tennis courts on their Santa Monica estate to a horde of friends.

In the midst of this opulence, RKO dropped Dolores' option, a move that gave her little worry. Her fabled pulchritude was still much in demand. Jack L. Warner, patriarch of the desperately busy Burbank studio, had become enchanted with her at a party. Amidst rumors that the studio chief had romantic intentions toward Dolores, Warner signed her to a contract in late 1933, almost immediately after her RKO agreement had been officially terminated.

Although Metro-Goldwyn-Mayer was the class studio of Hollywood, Warner Bros. was the busiest. The lot averaged approximately sixty films a year, pictures of every genre directed by directors of every specialty and performers of every type. As 1934 opened, the studio boasted such directors as Michael Curtiz, Lloyd Bacon, William Wellman, Archie Mayo, and Busby Berkeley. Some of the lot's stars included Paul Muni, James Cagney, Edward G. Robinson, Dick Powell, George Brent, Joe E. Brown, Leslie Howard, Warren William, and Pat O'Brien; the females encompassed Kay Francis, Bette Davis, Joan Blondell, Ruby Keeler, and Mary Astor. Most of the personalities at Warner Bros. had an identifying trademark—Cagney's pugnacity, Francis' elegance, Blondell's vivaciousness, etc. It was decided immediately that Dolores' trademark would obviously be her beauty, with a slight assist from her singing and dancing skills. It was a decision that would not survive as long as most Jack L. Warner decisions.

Her first picture at Warner Bros., *Wonder Bar* (1934), was in many ways her best. It was a delightful musical that mixed Harry Warren/Al Dubin tunes with a hodgepodge of picaresque performances. Al Jolson received an offer of ten percent of the gross to play Al Wonder, owner of the club; Kay Francis, then the top-paid, most idolized star of the lot, was cast as Liane, a bitchy, unfaithful wife; Dick Powell was the nightclub crooner who warbles "Don't Say Goodnight" and "Why Do I Dream These Dreams?"; swarthy Ricardo Cortez oozed as a hateful featured dancer named Harry; and Dolores was a joy as Inez, Cortez's ill-treated partner. In the story, both Jolson and Powell are understandably smitten with Dolores, and after she stabs Cortez in an audience-pleasing climax, it is Powell who wins her love.

While it was star Al Jolson who received the most footage singing "Vive La France," "Wonder Bar," and the extravagantly mounted "Goin' to Heaven on a Mule" (performed in blackface), Dolores, in her slinky gowns and very sexy "Tango Del Rio" number with Cortez, almost matched his appeal when the film premiered in early 1934. This situation did not sit well with everybody, especially Kay Francis. Director Lloyd Bacon had scissored Kay's scenes to build up Dolores' role and the front office, annoyed by the demands and temperament of their top goddess, joyfully approved the changes. This made for a fiery set as Miss Francis stormed her disapproval and threatened to walk off the picture (which she later wished she had done). Be that as it may, Dolores had made a grand debut on the Warner lot and the studio was delighted with the response thundered by the fan mail and exhibitors.

Warner Bros. was famous for rushing its stars into one picture after another. Joan Blondell recalls that the studio once crammed her into "thirty-two pictures in twenty-seven months." However, Dolores escaped this frantic pace. Perhaps it was because of Warner's special personal interest in her; perhaps it was because the film company hoped she would bloom into another Garbo, whose vehicles were picked with exquisite care by the Metro production staff. Whatever the actual reason, while most Warner regulars fought to keep up the frantic pace of their work schedule, Dolores returned to her hostess interests as the studio searched for the proper follow-up.

The choice was not fortunate. *Madame Du Barry* (1934), which followed *Wonder Bar* by eight months, was a tedious period account of the celebrated Madame that drew mixed critical response and mild audience approval. William Dieterle, a Warner Bros. class director, made everything just a bit too cute, and the froth rested on the many gorgeous costumes and powdered wigs worn by the star. Dolores did reveal a flair for comedy in this effort, but her interpretation was a bit obnoxious—while a viewer might be easily dazzled by her charms, he could not fully stifle the urge to wring her deceitful neck. The *New York Times* wrote, "So earnest is it in its efforts to show how the tur-

With Ricardo Cortez in *Wonder Bar* ('34).

With Gino Corrado (left) and Victor Jory in *Madame Du Barry* ('34).

31

With Leo Carrillo in *In Caliente* ('35).

bulent wench took the French treasury for 100,000,000 livres that, although its intention is to accent her allure, its effect is to convince the spectator that the guillotine was much too good for her. In the decorative and brunette person of Dolores Del Rio, La Comtesse possesses all the visual glamour of a chorus girl, and the same murderous coy charm of person. Thus she fails rather definitively to come alive on the screen as the fascinating courtesan of history and you will not discover in this *Madame Du Barry* why she has excited the imaginations of the generations which followed her." *Madame Du Barry* did benefit from a very amusing performance by Reginald Owen as King Louis XV and by Anita Louise as a lovely Marie Antoinette.

When reaction to *Madame Du Barry* fell far short of expectation, Warner Bros. decided to tap Dolores' musical talents. The studio commissioned *Wonder Bar*'s director Lloyd Bacon and song writers Harry Warren and Al Dubin, along with Busby Berkeley, to create a new hit musical. *In Caliente* was a summer 1935 release that starred Dolores with Pat O'Brien. She was dancer Rita Gomez; he was a magazine editor

who scathingly criticizes her work and then falls in love with her. The film attracted an audience, but, again, the picture's best moments did not showcase Dolores. The famous "Lady in Red" number was delivered by Winifred Shaw with a comedy assist from wide-mouthed Judy Canova, and the gloriously art deco Busby Berkeley touches included a hotel patio being transformed into a bandit cave. There blazing fires, a pack of beautiful white horses, and a looming mountain range supplied the magic. Much of the minimal sparkle of this musical was due to the supporting cast—Leo Carrillo, Glenda Farrell, and Edward Everett Horton—who did much to allay the viewers' ennui.

Warners was not a studio noted for paternalism. When Dolores showed signs of not being all they hoped she would be at the box office, the company executives rapidly dismissed her as an asset. She was wasted as the leading lady of Everett Marshall, a one-time Metropolitan Opera performer, in *I Live for Love* (1935). Marshall sang the title tune, "Mine Alone," "I Wanna Play House with You," and other numbers, while Dolores looked on. She did what she

Glamour, 1935-style.

33

With Everett Marshall in
I Live for Love ('35).

With Warren William in *Widow from Monte Carlo* ('35).

could to color her thankless role, with the result being, according to the *New York Times,* that she "overacts alarmingly." Busby Berkeley directed the quickly forgotten feature.

She concluded her Warner tenure with *Widow from Monte Carlo* (1936), a minor melodrama in which she portrays Inez, a duchess plagued by a blackmailer. It flanked her with leading men Warren William and Colin Clive and was apathetically received by the press and public alike. On this note, Dolores vacated her Warner Bros. dressing room. With excellent judgment, she decided to escape the Burbank jungle, where actresses like Bette Davis and newcomer Olivia de Havilland would be waging nasty wars for suitable screen projects. Dolores' aristocratic bearing did not lend itself to foul squabbles with the front office that characterized displeased studio contract stars. She peacefully left to resume her career elsewhere.

It is unfortunate that Warner Bros. did not develop Dolores' screen persona more effectively. She was certainly different enough from Kay Francis or Bette Davis to attract her own type of scripts, and with the studio talent force properly channeled in her support, she could have been a great favorite, as proven by *Wonder Bar.*

Needing a change of scenery from her Hollywood surroundings, Dolores accepted an offer from England's United Artists-Criterion Studios and traveled to London to star with Douglas Fairbanks, Jr. in *Accused* (1936). The Thornton Freeland-directed picture was an agile whodunit. It offered Dolores a flamboyant role as Gaby Seymour, a volatile, knife-hurling dancer. It again displayed her dancing agility in a number she performed with Fairbanks.

Upon her return to California, Dolores considered trying her luck on the stage. She began studying with a drama coach to prepare herself for such a challenge. She had previously considered such a move in 1932, but signed with RKO instead. On the advice of her husband, she spoke to MGM drama coach Oliver Hinsdell and the latter sent writer DeWitt Bodeen to discuss two one-act plays he had written that might serve her purpose in a proposed vaudeville tour.

With Douglas Fairbanks, Jr. in *Accused* ('36).

At home with her bull terrier dog, "Faultless of Flighty" (December 1935).

Meeting Dolores in her Santa Monica home, Bodeen recalls being almost overwhelmed by "the extraordinary beauty *and* the intelligence and sense of humor" of the star. "She was extremely professional and had an outgoing personality and real warmth as a person. She was also intelligent, although when you met her and were having conversation with her, you couldn't help but keep telling yourself that this was one of the truly great flawless beauties of the screen."

Dolores was impressed by Bodeen's plays, but at this time she did not carry out her intentions to attempt the stage. Her life was still very movie-oriented: her husband was busy at Metro and friends such as Gary Cooper (his wife was Gibbons' niece), Clark Gable, Errol Flynn, and directors John Ford and King Vidor were just some of the cinema names who frequently visited the Gibbonses for those famous Sunday afternoon tennis matches and buffets. So rather than embark on the tour, Dolores surprisingly honored the contract offer of Columbia Pictures, then still very much a *B*-picture factory. The studio was overjoyed, and announced that a project entitled *Continental* would be the lady's first vehicle there. However, this idea was scrapped and instead she starred in a program film entitled *Devil's Playground* (1937). She had the role of Carmen, a taxi dancer who weds a deep sea diver and proceeds to seduce his best friend. Richard Dix and Chester Morris were co-starred. When the film won no more attention than it deserved, Dolores again decided to immediately terminate what seemed to be a bad situation and took measures to end her Columbia pact.

Evidently Columbia's legal department was no match for Dolores, and by the summer of 1937 she was a free agent again. However, with the ambition that so characterized her screen success, the star sought another film factory at which to base headquarters and to somehow regain the path to top stardom. Hardly had she left Columbia when she came to terms with Darryl F. Zanuck, head of the rapidly expanding Twentieth Century-Fox Studio. Zanuck had begun his producing career at Warner Bros. and brought to his Pico Boulevard studio the same accent on a strong contract roster. Leading men included Warner Baxter, Tyrone Power, Don Ameche, Victor McLaglen, the Ritz Brothers, Brian Donlevy, and newcomer George Sanders; leading distaff attractions listed Loretta Young, Shirley Temple, and Alice Faye, plus such *B* queens as Claire Trevor. Once again Dolores possessed a style unlike her studio competitors'; once again, her stay at the studio was a misfire.

Zanuck was fond of melodrama and decided that the swarthy sexiness of Dolores would best serve the lot in femme fatale roles. Her first appearance at Fox was in a guest cameo in *Ali Baba Goes to Town* (1937), a weird concoction that mixed the Arabian Nights with Eddie Cantor's comedy and Tony Martin's singing. Immediately afterward came *Lancer Spy* (1937), a thriller in which George Sanders—in his first good guy lead in a Hollywood film—disguises himself as a Hun to spy on the imperialistic fatherland. Elaborately made-up and costumed, Dolores had to choose between patriotism and love for George in the raucous plot, directed by Gregory Ratoff, which at one point has Dolores and George dancing to the "Blue Danube Waltz." An interesting cast included such intriguing personalities as Peter Lorre, Joseph Schildkraut, Virginia Field, and Lionel Atwill. But the film was little more than a routine program filler.

Her next project at Fox, *International Settlement* (1938), was much the same, a turgid melodrama in which she co-starred with Sanders again, this time as an agent assigned to kill him. This Sino-Japanese tale offered Dolores a little more than her previous effort, including a spot for her to sing "You Make Me That Way." However, the plot outcome was too predictable, besides being strangely repetitious of *Lancer Spy*, with Dolores falling in love with Sanders rather than slaying him.

After her two misguided efforts at Fox, Dolores rapidly took stock of her situation at the studio which had not done much to promote either film. In the brief time she had spent on the studio payroll, she had been far outshone by her competitors. Loretta Young had been given the major female role in the respectably budgeted *Four Men and a Prayer* to be directed by Dolores' good friend John Ford, and Alice Faye had triumphed in the stellar role of Belle Fawcett in the studio's roadshow epic, *In Old Chi-*

Posing with Chester Morris and Richard Dix for *The Devil's Playground* ('37).

38

With George Sanders in *International Settlement* ('38).

On the set of *Lancer Spy* ('37) with Joseph Schildkraut (left) and director Gregory Ratoff (third from left).

Her Throat Insured For $50,000.

DOLORES DEL RIO* tells why it's good business for her to smoke Luckies...

"That $50,000 insurance is a studio precaution against my holding up a picture," says Miss Del Rio. "So I take no chances on an irritated throat. No matter how much I use my voice in acting, I always find Luckies gentle."

They will be gentle on *your* throat, too. Here's why... Luckies' exclusive "Toasting" process expels certain harsh irritants found in all tobacco. This makes Luckies' fine tobaccos even finer... a *light* smoke.

Sworn records show that among independent tobacco experts—men who know tobacco and its qualities—Luckies have twice as many exclusive smokers as all other cigarettes combined.

WITH MEN WHO KNOW TOBACCO BEST IT'S LUCKIES—2 TO 1

Copyright 1935, The American Tobacco Company

*DOLORES DEL RIO STARRING IN THE 20th CENTURY-FOX PICTURE, "SHANGHAI DEADLINE"

Dolores Del Rio the spokeswoman ('37).

40

cago (1938). Predictably, by the spring of 1938, Dolores had left the Fox lot.

With such studio hopscotching, Dolores must have set a record for accumulated film contracts. Since arriving in Hollywood in 1925, she had been under personal contract to Edwin Carewe, and under studio contract to United Artists, RKO, Warner Bros., Columbia, and Twentieth Century-Fox.

Two years would pass before Dolores would make another film. Nearing her mid-thirties, she was still a great beauty, her loveliness paralyzing spectators whenever she entered a restaurant or attended a premiere. However, her wounded pride prevented her from accepting scripts that might tarnish her image any further. It was a long time before she summoned the courage to finally accept another motion picture offer. It came with *The Man from Dakota* (1940), an MGM Western in which she aided escaping Union soldiers Wallace Beery and John Howard and helped the forces of Ulysses Grant in the bargain. It was the only major woman's role in the picture, which must account for her accept-ing so unprestigious an offer. The combination of genteel, beautiful Dolores with crude, over-stuffed Beery was not exactly a box-office combination destined to set fans' hearts aflutter. At one point in the storyline, Beery's character says to Dolores' heroine, "Aw . . . I wouldn't let 'em hang youse—sugarplum. . . . That would be a crime." It was enough to make sensitive fans of Miss Del Rio shudder.

During this professional decline, Dolores' unique marriage to Gibbons also began to disintegrate. Whatever strange touches perplexed David Niven when he met the couple apparently reached a peak when they separated in March 1940. On Friday, January 17, 1941, Dolores appeared before Superior Court Judge Thurmond Clarke, asking for a divorce due to the "cold and indifferent" personality of her spouse, which she claimed made her nervous and ill. In her accustomed style, Dolores agreed to answer mainly only yes and no questions about the marriage. She was accompanied to the courtroom by her friend Fay Wray, who did most of the talking for her, telling again of the "cold and indifferent

With John Howard and Wallace Beery in *The Man from Dakota* ('40).

attitude" she had witnessed during frequent visits to the couple's home. Gibbons did not contest the suit. Both parties retained their own properties.

With the divorce came a social distinction that seemed to promise a new wave of popularity (or at least notoriety) for Dolores. She became the offscreen love of twenty-six-year-old Orson Welles. The flamboyant Welles was then in the midst of the controversy concerning his film *Citizen Kane*. Some called him a genius; others labeled him a blowhard. But everyone took notice of the enfant terrible who had supercharged the reputation of the Mercury Theatre and appeared destined to change the artistry of the American cinema. Dolores and Welles appeared everywhere together. Her friends insisted they had never seen her so glowing, and swore that the age difference between them was no handicap to the relationship.

The Welles-Del Rio love affair climaxed with the release of *Citizen Kane* in mid-1941. Welles later told the press:

I thought she was the most beautiful woman I had ever seen. I used to follow her around—at a discreet distance, of course—just to admire her. I followed her out of a nightclub once in New York and stood on the street admiring her as she waited for a cab. But I always thought she was a dumbbell. Didn't really want to meet her because I didn't want to spoil an illusion.

He further explained their likes and dislikes:

We have many things in common. We both love music, though we quarrel about it a lot. We do not agree on ballet . . . we are one on the theory of exercise. We do not take it and don't like to watch others exercise either. We both take massage to keep our circulatory systems fit. We both like to fish. . . .

On yet another occasion he explained:

She lives so graciously. Everyone around her loves her. She just inspires it. . . . We paint for hours with sometimes hardly a word passing between us for as much as half an hour. She is one girl you can be with and not feel the need for conversation. She has a mind full of talk, though, when she wants.

Dolores was obviously joyously in love with Welles, but in her usual tasteful fashion refused to discuss marriage with reporters (and with Orson). "Please! It would be very common of me to talk about such things until I am legally free to marry again." It turned out to be a romantically fatal discretion.

Welles' second follow-up to *Citizen Kane* was *Journey into Fear* (1942), a bleak espionage tale based on Eric Ambler's novel which Orson scripted with his good chum and co-star Joseph Cotten. Welles surprised no one when he contracted Dolores to play the leading female role. The RKO feature was stocked with Mercury Theatre veterans such as Ruth Warrick, Agnes Moorehead, and Everett Sloane. Norman Foster, with some assistance from Welles, directed, and the original version was supposed to have much promise. However, RKO so rapaciously edited the film after Welles left the project that the release print was a mess. The critics were unimpressed and Dolores was heartbroken.

There was more heartache to follow. At one of Cotten's dinner parties, Welles made the acquaintance of the most acclaimed new sex goddess in Hollywood, Rita Hayworth, another Latin-flavored woman of striking beauty. Rita was considered the greatest catch available in 1942 Hollywood, and soon twenty-seven-year-old Orson threw over thirty-seven-year-old Dolores in favor of twenty-four-year-old Rita. The couple wed on September 7, 1943, and the humiliation was the final blow to Dolores' crushing Hollywood downfall.

This time she planned not to simply desert a studio, but to return to Mexico. She informed the press, "I wish to choose my own stories, my own director and cameraman. I can accomplish this better in Mexico." With that, she left for Mexico

With Orson Welles at the New York premiere of *Citizen Kane* (May 1, 1941).

With Joseph Cotten in
Journey into Fear ('42).

With Pedro Armendáriz in *Flor Silvestre* ('43).

44

City, though she retained much prosperous real estate that her mother had purchased for her in the Los Angeles area.

Within a year of her defection, Dolores Del Rio had kept her word and had become the most celebrated actress of the Mexican cinema. She fully carried out her producing plans and in 1943 starred in *Flor Silvestre,* a drama in which she hired director Emilio Fernandez, cameraman Gabriel Figueroa, and leading man Pedro Armendáriz. She cast herself as Esperanza, a laborer's daughter who weds a landowner's son and becomes involved in a revolution. The film won Dolores an Ariel Award (the equivalent of the U.S. Oscar), did well in release engagements in South America and Europe (U.S. release was minimal), and was a wonderful boost to the lady's pride and reputation. The same leading man, director, and cinematographer (with Dolores they became known as Mexico's "Big Four") also collaborated on *Maria Candelaria,* a 1944 release filmed in the exquisite flower gardens of Mexico's Xochomilco. It was a tragic plot with Dolores as a persecuted Indian girl. MGM would release it in the United States with English subtitles as *Portrait of Maria.* At the 1946 International Exposition at Cannes, the film won the "World's Best" ribbon. *Bugambilia* (1944), another tragedy, found Dolores portraying a society girl smitten with a gambler. *Las Abandonadas* (1944), yet another weeper in the *Madame X* vein, cast Miss Del Rio as a betrayed girl who winds up a beggar. In the last reel she receives a peso from her successful son. *Las Abandonadas* won for her a second Ariel.

Dolores was understandably reluctant to return to Hollywood and concentrated on Mexican productions with repeated success. But after the release of *La Otra* (1946)* in which she played twin sisters, Hollywood finally made an offer she accepted. The reasons were obvious—the director was to be her close friend John Ford, and the production was to be shot entirely in Mexico.

*Warner Bros. would acquire the screen rights to the property and make it as *Dead Ringer* (1964) with Bette Davis in the dual role.

With Pedro Armendáriz in *Bugambilia* ('44).

45

This was *The Fugitive* (1947), an RKO Christmas release, with Henry Fonda as a hunted priest in a strange reworking of the Passion Play. Dolores played the Magdalene character, here an Indian who aids Fonda in his escape. The star enjoyed making the film, not only because of the good role, ideal filming conditions, and reacquaintance with Ford, but also because it offered Pedro Armendáriz a sizeable part as the government agent who attempts to capture Fonda. Reviewing the film, Bosley Crowther (*New York Times*) labeled it a "strange and haunting picture" and noted that Dolores "is a warm glow of devotion as an Indian Magdalene." *Variety* judged Del Rio to be "decorative and mutely impassioned as a devout victim of the law."

Shortly before the release of *The Fugitive,* reporter Louis Berg (*New York Herald-Tribune*) spoke with Dolores at the Papagayo Hotel in Cuernavaca, and later observed her as she went about her routines. "If she were to leave Mexico now it would cause something of a revolution. Her popularity there is unprecedented." Mexicans referred to her as "our Lolita," and called to her when she appeared on the streets, saying with reverence and warmth, "Buenas tardes, Lolita."

It was also noted that Dolores was very much the aristocrat, a very wealthy woman with a palatial home in Churubusco and a financial interest in her films. She moved freely, aided by her command of seven languages, in the mainstream of Mexican society life. She mixed with statesmen, artists, and writers. She entertained lavishly but, as ever, tastefully.

Also publicized at this time was Dolores' carefully led life, and her methods of maintaining so unlined a face and smooth a figure as she reached her middle years. Reported the *Herald-Tribune*: "She leads an almost religiously strict life. Some of the discipline is imposed upon her by society—the Mexican conventions for married or unmarried women of good family are rigid. Other restrictions are demanded by her career. The life of a professional beauty is not easy. Miss Del Rio may neither smoke nor drink. She adheres to a rigid diet. When she is not making a picture she lies in bed till noon. She makes no appointments before 2 P.M. She lives with her

mother. Her public appearances are chaperoned."

After *The Fugitive,* Dolores signed to appear in Abel Gance's *Giselle,* an intended epic to be shot in French, Spanish, and English, but plans fell through and no version was made. Instead, she went to Argentina and starred in *Historia De Una Mala Mujer* (1948), better known as Oscar Wilde's play *Lady Windermere's Fan.* The film was a great success in the Latin American countries, unlike Twentieth Century-Fox's *The Fan* (1949) which starred Madeleine Carroll and Jeanne Crain. Dolores continued her Mexican film career, starring in such pictures as *La Malquerida* (1949) which was another product of the "Big Four," *Doña Perfecta* (1951)* for which she won her third Ariel as a bitch who tries to destroy her daughter's happiness, and *El Nino Y La Niebla* (1953), for which she received her fourth Ariel as a concerned mother who fears the family history of insanity so much that she herself loses her mind.

In addition to the cinema triumphs which made Dolores "First Lady of the Mexican Cinema," she also became "First Lady of the Mexican Stage." She appeared in the Mexican theatre (where the pace is far rougher than in the States—matinees are every day) in such productions as *The Little Foxes, Ghosts,* and *Lady Windermere's Fan.* Especially remembered by her followers is her version of *Camille,* in which her beauty was showcased with almost legendary results among Mexican audiences.

Dolores' great success finally impressed Hollywood enough to again offer her a decent role. Twentieth Century-Fox was planning to remake *House of Strangers* (1949) as a Western, *Broken Lance* (1954), with Edward Dymytryk directing and Spencer Tracy starring. Fox attempted to contact Dolores to perform in it, but the McCarthy era of Communist investigations was just dying down. The U.S. State Department delayed her visa when it feared her association with Communists in the Mexican film industry. Dolores firmly stated that she was "delighted to say I am not a Communist and have never been a

*Del Rio was wise enough to frequently join with a leading screen rival in a film venture such as when she was paired with Miroslava in *La Casa Chica* (1949), Esther Fernandez in *Doña Perfecta* (1951), and Maria Felix in *La Cucaracha* (1958).

With Henry Fonda in *The Fugitive* ('47).

Communist. I love America and regard it as my very own." The State Department finally relented and granted Dolores a visa. But time had forced Twentieth Century-Fox to sign Katy Jurado to replace her.

However, Dolores did return to the United States in 1956 to appear in an East Coast summer stock tour of *Anastasia*. Critics and audiences found her beauty spellbinding and her acting far more impressive than the gloss of her Hollywood movies had allowed them to perceive. She stayed on to make two television appearances: on June 7, 1957, she appeared on the CBS-TV "Schlitz Playhouse of Stars" in the episode entitled *Old Spanish Custom;* and on April 23, 1958, she again worked for CBS-TV, this time on the "U.S. Steel Hour" in *The Public Prosecutor.* She still remembered her loyal Mexican audience and returned there, playing in *A Donde Van Neustros Hijos* (1958) and *La Cucaracha* (1958), the latter reuniting her with Emilio Fernandez (this time as a co-star) and Pedro Armendáriz, and cinematographer Gabriel Figueroa.

On Saturday, November 24, 1959, in New York, Dolores wed for a third time. The groom was Lewis A. Riley, a film producer who had been residing in Mexico for twenty years. She later commented: "The ideal marriage is to find a great companion. It is no mistake to marry someone in your own business. You can share each other's triumphs and failures with understanding, and avoid that cruel wall in marriage—indifference." The marriage has proven solid and has been beneficial to Dolores professionally as well as personally.

In 1960, Dolores finally returned to Hollywood, after an eighteen-year absence from feature-film making, to play the mother of Elvis Presley in Twentieth Century-Fox's *Flaming Star.* While some cynics scoffed that playing Elvis' ma was hardly a glorious return, Don Siegel directed so well and the script was surprisingly so good that the film was a critical as well as commercial success. As Dolores said, "It is a Western with some depth and humor. And Elvis is quite good in it. He acts well and is very Indian." In the offbeat film, nearly all the characters die, and Dolores has a lovely death scene in

which she wanders into the desert, stoically meeting her fate.

Columnists besieged her to tell them how she maintained her beauty. "I have never dieted in my life. I've kept my figure and never had to play golf to do it. Sometimes I walk. Sometimes I swim. But it is not a daily or a fixed thing. I never smoke or drink. I get plenty of rest whenever I can. Even women with children and with cares can find a time just to sit and think and not think. The thing is not to be bored."

Since her marriage to Riley, Dolores' career has been a fluctuating one. She has continued her stage work in Mexico and Latin America, and in 1961 appeared in a Spanish-speaking skit at the Los Angeles Million Dollar Theatre. She has starred in a number of Spanish films, including *La Dama Del Alba* (1966) as the "Lady of the Dawn." In *Casa De Mujeres* (1966), she appeared as, of all things, the madam of a whore house. In the Mexican drama *Rio Blanco* (1967), which delved into the killing of striking textile workers by government forces, Dolores had a focal role as a revolutionary character. The picture was shot in the environs of Vera Cruz.

Occasionally she returned to the United States for work. She played "the Spanish woman" in John Ford's *Cheyenne Autumn* (1964), a sprawling yarn about the U.S. mistreatment of the Indian. She appeared as the mother of Omar Sharif in the MGM-Carlo Ponti picture *C'era Una Volta,* released in an aborted, dubbed English-language version in the U.S. as *More Than a Miracle* (1967). In this example of royal whimsy, Sophia Loren had the pivotal female assignment. Dolores was slated to join the array of veteran stars for a cameo in 1970's *The Phynx,* but she wisely backed out of the project. She guest-starred on American television, appearing in the sixty-minute CBS drama *The Man Who Bought Paradise* (January 17, 1965), the *Return to Glory* episode (February 23, 1966) of NBC's "I Spy," and *The Ghost of Murietta* episode (March 20, 1966) of NBC's "Branded." Also, on ABC's "Marcus Welby, M.D.," she and Janet Blair played gravely ill women in *The Legacy* episode (January 27, 1970).

In 1974, Dolores received a gold medal from Mexican President Luis Echeverria for her work

With Carroll Baker and Gilbert Roland in *Cheyenne Autumn* ('64).

Advertisement for *Casa De Mujeres* ('66).

In *More Than a Miracle* ('67).

Arriving at Kennedy Airport (April 1968).

51

in the Mexican Actors Guild nursery. At the time, she said of her film career, "I enjoyed it while I was doing it, but now I have the nursery to occupy my time—and I feel that it is something very worthwhile." On April 22, 1975, Dolores won her fifth Ariel for "the prestige . . . [she has] brought to Mexico's cinematographic arts over the span of half a century." Luis Bunuel was similarly honored that evening. In May of 1975, the *Hollywood Reporter* announced that Quinn Martin Productions had signed Dolores to star in a two-hour CBS-TV movie special, *Who'll See to the Children?* The film began shooting on Mexican locations, but Dolores suffered a back injury and had to bow out. She was replaced by Carmen Zapata.

Today, in her seventies, Dolores is still the great beauty. She often adds a fall to her still raven-black hair, and her hands are not the hands of a young woman, but otherwise she is stunning. She and Riley live in a 200-year-old house, surrounded by a beautiful, lush garden in the exclusive Mexico City suburb of Coyocan.

She is still stage struck. She was anxious to star as Eleanor of Aquitaine in a Mexican stage production (to be produced by her husband) of *The Lion in Winter.* But instead she joined with Anthony Quinn and Katy Jurado in *The Children of Sanchez,* produced and directed by Hall Bartlett in mid-1977. When she accepted the guest-starring role and was asked if she were coming out of "retirement," the actress responded, "I have never retired. . . . The type of cinema they have been doing has just not been my style." The grande dame of Mexican cinema also has been rumored to be considering acting as a consultant in a planned remake of *Evangeline,* to be entitled *Caluna.* She might also play the heroine's mother in the production.

But there is far more to Dolores than her acting interests. She is intelligent, well-read, and civic-minded. She recently said, "My only regret is that I never had children." Shortly thereafter, she did take on her special project, the Estancia Infantail, a nursery for children of working actresses. "Our nursery is the first of its kind in the world. . . . Our doors never close. We are trying new ways of education and are getting wonderful results. The enormous advantage we have is the children live there for many weeks,

Visiting in Hollywood in early 1978 to promote *The Children of Sanchez.*

sometimes many months while their mothers are on location, and we have a chance to get at the child. Being [that they are] children of artists, we put an enormous emphasis on ballet, singing, music."

Not long ago, when Dolores was in Hollywood promoting the forthcoming release of *The Children of Sanchez,* she took the occasion to expound on a variety of subjects dealing with the acting profession:

Today's talent: "[They are] extremely lucky, especially when you compare the opportunities today with those facing actors who started in the Twenties and Thirties. For one thing they have TV, which we never had, of course. And the whole world has become kind of a motion picture industry, and it didn't exist that way at all when I began. In those days, when you worked in Hollywood, that was it. We didn't think of going to other countries to work. The theatre scared us to death, too. The only good theatre existed in New York, and only those trained on the stage would attempt it; studios often forbade it, as well. If you were a motion picture actor at that time, you had a circle to develop in that was about the size of a thimble, but today there is an entire world to grow in. Actors—if they *really* want to be actors—should take advantage of it and realize how lucky they are for the opportunity. They should never complain."

Show business survival: "You must have discipline. I think anyone who wants to be in this business should plan their career 'inside' discipline from the very beginning. Discipline will

"A great star, a great lady, a legend in our own time, returns to the screen." A HALL BARTLETT FILM "THE CHILDREN OF SANCHEZ"

Advertisement for *The Children of Sanchez* ('78).

help you not to have heartaches and run away when things go bad, and it will keep you from getting drunk when something goes wrong and you think you can't pull yourself together. There are 10,000 disappointments facing anyone who goes into this business, and discipline will give you the guts to get through them, to not let them destroy you, and to help you endure."

Dolores has very little interest in living in the past—little wonder, since the present offers her so much. She will not discuss her early Hollywood dramas. "I have a bad memory for bad memories," she recently said. "I want to live today and, as the years have gone by, I am more and more interested in today." Her faulty memory is quite thorough. Once John Gillett of the British Film Institute watched a revival of one of her Carewe-directed films and, unaware of the melodrama of her affair with the director, asked who the director was. Replied Dolores, "I can't remember. That was all so long ago."

She will discuss the Hollywood of old, but only to recall the glamour and lament the lack of style in that smog-filled establishment today. "I think the greatest difference is between the young players of today and the older players. The stars of today all look alike. In the days of Jean Harlow, Norma Shearer, and Greta Garbo, there was no resemblance. They were all distinct personalities. Ronald Colman, Clark Gable, and Gary Cooper were in no way alike. Yet all these young boys I see on the screen today are carbon copies of each other, and the singers all have a marked resemblance." At another time, she sighed, "Hollywood had glamour then but, like the world, Hollywood has changed enormously. There are still important writers there, but nobody gathers them any more. And the whole star system is dead. There are no Garbos, no Gables, no Dietrichs. Today, the stars are the directors."

The Dolores of today is happiest talking of today's world, especially the items closest to her. She vows that her beloved Mexico is fighting Communism "with all our strength," and that the modern Mexico is "a very important one. We are very much ahead of the rest of the Latin American countries. Mexico is already greatly respected in Latin America and they are following in our footsteps—financially, economically, educationally, and culturally." Her advice to women seeking to stay desirable is: "Take care of your inner beauty, your spiritual beauty, and that will reflect in your face. We have the face we created over the years. Every bad deed, every bad fault will show on your face. God can give us beauty and genes can give us our features, but whether that beauty remains or changes is determined by our thoughts and deeds."

With beauty, fame, and cultural interests, one might think that Dolores Del Rio has experienced a most satisfying life. However, she has never reached a point where she has seen or done enough. Still a very vital lady, she recently reflected, "There is so little time left and I still want to do so many things. There are so many things I want to accomplish, so many roles I still want to play, so many countries I still want to see, so much I must do in the time I have left. And my time has become very precious to me."

FILMOGRAPHY

JOANNA *(First National, 1925)* 7,762 feet

Presenter/director, Edwin Carewe; based on the book *Joanna, of the Skirts Too Short and the Lips Too Red and the Tongue Too Pert* by Henry Leyford Gates; screenplay, Lois Leeson; art director, John D. Schulze; assistant director, Wallace Fox; camera, Robert Kurrle, Al M. Greene; editor, Edward McDermott.

Dorothy Mackaill (Joanna Manners); Jack Mulhall (John Wilmore); Paul Nicholson (Frank Brandon); George Fawcett (Anthony Eggleson); John T. Murray (Lord Teddy Dorminster); Rita Carewe (Georgie Leach); Dolores Del Rio (Carlotta de Silva); Lillian Langdon (Mrs. Roxanna Adams); Edward Davis (Grayson); Bob Hart (The Chauffeur).

HIGH STEPPERS *(First National, 1926)* 6,136 feet

Presenter/director, Edwin Carewe; based on the novel *Heirs Apparent* by Philip Hamilton Gibbs; adaptor, Finis Fox; screenplay, Lois Leeson; camera, Robert Kurrle.

Lloyd Hughes (Julian Perryam); Mary Astor (Audrey Nye); Dolores Del Rio (Evelyn Iffield); Rita Carewe (Janet Perryam); John T. Murray (Cyril Buckland); Edward Davis (Victor Buckland); Alec B. Francis (Father Perryam); Clarissa Selwynne (Mrs. Perryam); Charles Sellon (Grandpa Perryam); John Steppling (Major Iffield); Emily Fitzroy (Mrs. Iffield); Margaret McWade (Mrs. Clancy).

PALS FIRST *(First National, 1926)* 6,843 feet

Presenter/director, Edwin Carewe; based on the novel and play by Francis Perry Elliott; adaptor, Olga Printzlau; screenplay, Lois Leeson; titles, Ralph Spence; camera, Robert B. Kurrle.

Lloyd Hughes (Richard Castleman/Danny Rowland); Dolores Del Rio (Jeanne Lamont); Alec Francis (Dominie); George Cooper (The Squirrel); Edward Earle (Dr. Harry Chilton); Hamilton Morse (Judge Lamont); George Reed (Uncle Alex); Alice Nichols (Aunt Caroline); Alice Belcher (Charley Anderson).

THE WHOLE TOWN'S TALKING *(Universal, 1926)* 6,662 feet

Presenter, Carl Laemmle; director, Edward Laemmle; based on the play by John Emerson and Anita Loos; screenplay, Raymond Cannon; camera, Charles Stumar.

Edward Everett Horton (Chester Binney); Virginia Lee Corbin (Ethel Simmons); Trixie Friganza (Mrs. Simmons); Otis Harlan (Mr. Simmons); Robert Ober (Donald Montallen); Aileen Manning (Mrs. Van Loon); Hayden Stevenson (Tom Murphy); Margaret Quimby (Sadie Wise); Dolores Del Rio (Rita Renault); Malcolm Waite (Jack Shields).

WHAT PRICE GLORY *(Fox, 1926)* 11,400 feet

Presenter, William Fox; director, Raoul Walsh; based on the play by Laurence Stallings and Maxwell Anderson; screenplay, James T. O'Donohue; titles, Malcolm Stuart Boylan; music, Erno Rapee; assistant director, Daniel Keefe; camera, Barney McGill, John Marta, John Smith.

Victor McLaglen (Captain Flagg); Edmund Lowe (Sergeant Quirt); Dolores Del Rio (Charmaine); William V. Mong (Cognac Pete); Phyllis Haver (Hilda of China); Elena Jurado (Carmen); Leslie Fenton (Lieutenant Moore); August Tollaire (French Mayor); Barry Norton (Private Lewisohn); Sammy Cohen (Private Lipinsky); Ted McNamara (Private Kiper); Mathilde Comont (Camille, the Cook); Pat Rooney (Mulcahy).

RESURRECTION *(Inspiration-United Artists, 1927)* 9,120 feet

Producer/director, Edwin Carewe; based on the novel by Leo Tolstoy; adaptors, Carewe and Count Ilya Tolstoy; screenplay, Finis Fox; titles, Tom Miranda; assistant director, Wallace Fox; literary advisor, Count Ilya Tolstoy; military advisor, Major General Michael N. Pleschkoff; camera, Robert Kurrle and Al M. Green; editor, Jeanne Spencer.

Rod La Rocque (Prince Dimitri Nekhludof); Dolores Del Rio (Katusha Maslova); Marc MacDermott (Major Schoenboch); Lucy Beaumont (Aunt Sophya); Vera Lewis (Aunt Marya); Clarissa Selwynne (Princess Olga Ivanovitch Nekhludof); Eve Southern (Princess Sonia Korchagin); Count Ilya Tolstoy (Old Philospher).

LOVES OF CARMEN *(Fox, 1927)* 8,538 feet*

Presenter, William Fox; director, Raoul Walsh, based on the novel by Prosper Merimée; screenplay, Gertrude Orr; titles, Katherine Hilliker, H. H. Caldwell; assistant director, Archibald Buchanan; camera, Lucien Andriot, John Marta; editors, Hilliker, Caldwell.

Dolores Del Rio (Carmen); Victor McLaglen (Escamillo); Don Alvarado (Don José); Nancy Nash (Michaela); Rafael Valverda (Miguel); Mathilde Comont (Emilia); Jack Baston (Morales); Carmen Costello (Teresa); Fred Kohler (Gypsy Chief).

THE GATEWAY OF THE MOON *(Fox, 1928)* 5,038 feet

Presenter, William Fox; director, John Griffith Wray; based on the novel *Upstream* by Clifford Bax; screenplay, Bradley King; titles, Katherine Hilliker, H.H. Caldwell; assistant director, A.F. Erickson; camera, Chester Lyons; editors, Hilliker, Caldwell.

Dolores Del Rio [Chela (Toni)], Walter Pidgeon (Arthur Wyatt); Anders Randolf (George Gillespie); Ted McNamara (Henry Hooker); Adolph Millar (Rudolf Gottman); Leslie Fenton (Jim Mortlake); Noble Johnson (Soriano); Virginia La Fonde (Indian Child).

THE TRAIL OF '98 *(MGM, 1928)* 8,799 feet

Director, Clarence Brown; based on the novel by Robert William Service; screenplay, Benjamin Glazer, Waldemar Young; adaptor, Glazer; titles Joe Farnham; art directors, Cedric Gibbons, Merrill Pye; music, David Mendoza, William Axt; song, Hazel Mooney, Evelyn Lyn, Axt; assistant

*Lavender-tinted.

director, Charles Dorian; wardrobe, Lucia Coulter; camera, John Seitz; editor, George Hively.

Dolores Del Rio (Berna); Ralph Forbes (Larry); Karl Dane (Lars Petersen); Harry Carey (Jack Ocasto); Tully Marshall (Salvation Jim); George Cooper (Samuel Foote, the Worm); Russell Simpson (Old Swede); Emily Fitzroy (Mrs. Bulkey); Tenen Holtz (Mr. Bulkey); Cesare Gravina (Berna's Grandfather); E. Alyn Warren (Engineer); Johnny Downs (Mother's Boy); Ray Gallagher and Doris Lloyd (Bits).

RAMONA *(United Artists, 1928)* 7,650 feet

Director, Edwin Carewe; based on the novel by Helen Hunt Jackson; screenplay and titles, Finis Fox; art director, Albert S. D'Agostino; sets, Tec-Art Studios; theme song, Mabel Wayne, L. Wolfe Gilbert; assistant directors, Leander De Cordova, Richard Easton; camera; Al M. Greene; editor, Jeanne Spencer.

Dolores Del Rio (Ramona); Warner Baxter (Alessandro); Roland Drew (Felipe); Vera Lewis (Senora Moreno); Michael Visaroff (Juan Canito); John T. Prince (Father Salvierderra); Mathilde Comont (Marda); Carlos Amor (Sheepherder); Jess Cavin (Bandit Leader); Jean (The Dog); Rita Carewe (Baby).

THE RED DANCE *(Fox, 1928)* 9,250 feet

Presenter, William Fox; director, Raoul Walsh; based on the novel *The Red Dancer of Moscow* by Henry Leyford Gates; adaptors, Pierre Collings, Philip Klein; story, Eleanor Browne; screenplay, James Ashmore Creelman; titles, Malcolm Stuart Boyland; music, S. L. Rothafel, Erno Rapee; song, Lew Pollack, Rapee; assistant director, Archibald Buchanan; camera, Charles Clarke, John Marta; editor, Louis Loeffler.

Charles Farrell (Grand Duke Eugen); Dolores Del Rio (Tasia); Ivan Linow (Ivan Petroff); Boris Charsky (Agitator); Dorothy Revier (Princess Varvara); Andres De Segurola (General Tanaroff); Demetrius Alexis (Rasputin).

NO OTHER WOMAN *(Fox, 1928)* 5,071 feet

Presenter, William Fox; director, Lou Tellegen; story, Polan Banks; screenplay, Jessie Burns, Bernard Vorhaus; titles, Katherine Hilliker, H. H. Caldwell; assistant director, A. F. Erickson; camera, Ernest Palmer, Paul Ivano; editor, J. Edwin Robbins.

Dolores Del Rio (Carmelita Desano); Don Alvarado (Maurice); Ben Bard (Albert); Paulette Duval (Mafalda); Rosita Marstini (Carmelita's Aunt); André Lanoy (Grand Duke Sergey).

REVENGE *(United Artists, 1928)* 6,541 feet

Producer/director, Edwin Carewe; based on the story "The Bear Tamer's Daughter" by Konrad Bercovici; screenplay/titles, Finis Fox; music, Hugo Riesenfeld; camera, Robert Kurrle, Al M. Greene; editor, Jeanne Spencer.

Dolores Del Rio (Rascha); James Marcus (Costa); Sophia Ortiga (Binka); LeRoy Mason (Jorga); Rita Carewe (Tina); José Crespo (Stefan); Sam Appel (Jancu); Marta Golden (Leana); Jess Cavin (Lieutenant De Jorga).

EVANGELINE *(United Artists, 1929)* 8,268 feet

Producer/director, Edwin Carewe; based on the poem by Henry Wadsworth Longfellow; screenplay/titles, Finis Fox; assistant director, Jack Boland; technical aide, Eugene Hornbostel; sets, Stephen Goosson; music synchronization, Hugo Riesenfeld; lighting engineer, C. P. Drew; camera, Robert B. Kurrle, Al M. Greene; editor, Jeanne Spencer.

Dolores Del Rio (Evangeline); Roland Drew (Gabriel); Alec B. Francis (Father Felician); Donald Reed (Baptiste); Paul McAllister (Benedict Bellefontaine); James Marcus (Basil); George Marion, Sr. (René La Blanc); Bobby Mack (Michael); Lou Payne (Governor General); Lee Shumway (Colonel Winslow).

THE BAD ONE *(United Artists, 1930)* 6,673 feet

Presenter, Joseph M. Schenck; supervisor, John W. Considine, Jr.; director, George Fitzmaurice; story, John Farrow; screenplay/dialogue, Carey Wilson, Howard Emmett Rogers; art directors, William Cameron Menzies, Park French; assistant director, Walter Mayo; costumes, Alice O'Neill; music arranger, Hugo Riesenfeld; sound, Frank Grenzbach; camera, Karl Struss; editor, Donn Hayes.

Dolores Del Rio (Lita); Edmund Lowe (Jerry Flanagan); Don Alvarado (Spaniard); Blanche Friderici (Madame Durand); Adrienne D'Ambricourt (Madame Pompier); Ullrich Haupt (Pierre Ferrande); Mitchell Lewis (Borloff); Ralph Lewis (Blochet); Charles McNaughton (Petey); Yola D'Avril (Gieda); John St. Polis (Judge); Henry Kolker (Prosecuting Attorney); George Fawcett (Warden); Victor Potel, Harry Stubbs, Tom Dugan (Sailors); Boris Karloff (Guard).

GIRL OF THE RIO *(RKO, 1932)* 78 min.

Director, Herbert Brenon, based on the play *The Dove* by Willard Mack; screenplay, Elizabeth Meehan; sound, John Tribby; camera, Leo Tover; editor, Artie Roberts.

Dolores Del Rio (Dolores); Leo Carrillo (Don Jose Tostado); Norman Foster (Johnny Powell); Lucille Gleason (The Matron); Ralph Ince (O'Grady); Edna Murphy (Madge); Stanley Fields (Mike); Frank Campeau (Bill); Roberta Gale (Mabelle).

BIRD OF PARADISE *(RKO, 1932)* 80 min.

Producer, David O. Selznick; director, King Vidor; based on the play by Richard Walton Tully; screenplay, Wells Root; adaptors, Leonard Praskins, Wanda Tuchock; choreography, Busby Berkeley; music, Max Steiner; song, Milia Rosa, Peter de Rose; camera, Clyde DeVinna.

Dolores Del Rio (Luana); Joel McCrea (Johnny Baker); John Halliday (Mac); Lon Chaney, Jr. (Thornton); Richard "Skeets" Gallagher (Chester); Bert Roach (Hector); Pukui (The King); Agostino Borgato (Medicine Man); Sophie Ortego (Old Native Woman); and: Wade Boteler.

FLYING DOWN TO RIO *(RKO, 1933)* 99 min.

Executive producer, Merian C. Cooper; associate producer, Lou Brock; director, Thornton Freeland; based on a play by Anne Caldwell from an original story by Brock; screenplay, Cyril Hume, H.W. Hanemann, Erwin Gelsey; art directors, Van Nest Polglase, Carroll Clark; music director, Max Steiner; choreography, Dave Gould; songs, Vincent Youmans, Edward Eliscu, Gus Kahn; costumes, Walter Plunkett; sound, P. J. Faulkner; camera effects, Vernon Walker; camera, J. Roy Hunt; editor, Jack Kitchin.

Dolores Del Rio (Belinha de Rezende); Gene Raymond (Roger Bond); Raoul Roulen (Julio Rubeiro); Ginger Rogers (Honey Hale); Fred Astaire (Fred Ayres); Blanche Friderici (Doña Elena); Walter Walker (Senor de Rezende); Etta Moten (Black Singer); Roy D'Arcy, Maurice Black, Armand Kaliz (The Three Greeks); Paul Porcasi (Mayor); Reginald Barlow (Banker); Eric Blore (Butterbass, the Head Waiter); Franklin Pangborn (Hammersmith, the Hotel Manager); Luis Alberni (Carioca Casino Manager).

WONDER BAR *(First National, 1934)* 84 min.

Producer, Robert Lord; director, Lloyd Bacon; based on the play by Karl Farkas, Robert Katscher, and Geza Herczeg; screenplay, Earl Baldwin; songs, Harry Warren, Al Dubin; music director, Leo F. Forbstein; music numbers staged by Busby Berkeley; camera, Sol Polito; editor, George Amy.

Al Jolson (Al Wonder); Dolores Del Rio (Inez); Ricardo Cortez (Harry); Kay Francis (Liane Renaud); Dick Powell (Tommy); Guy Kibbee (Simpson); Hugh Herbert (Pratt); Robert Barrat (Captain Von Ferring); Ruth Donnelly (Mrs. Simpson); Louise Fazenda (Mrs. Pratt); Fifi D'Orsay (Mitzi); Merna Kennedy (Claire); Henry Kolker (Mr. Renaud); Henry O'Neill (Richard); Kathryn Sergava (Ilke); Gordon De Main, Harry Woods (Detectives); Marie Moreau (Maid).

MADAME DU BARRY *(Warner Bros., 1934)* 77 min.

Director, William Dieterle; supervisor, Henry Blanke; story/screenplay, Edward Chodorov; art director, Jack Okey; dialogue director, Daniel Reed; choreography, Albertina Rasch Dancers; camera, Sol Polito; editor, Bert Levy.

Dolores Del Rio (Madame Du Barry); Reginald Owen (King Louis XV); Victor Jory (Duke D'Aiguillon); Osgood Perkins (Richelieu); Verree Teasdale (Duchess De Granmont); Henry O'Neill (Duc De Choiseul); Anita Louise (Marie Antoinette); Ferdinand Gottschalk (Lebel); Maynard Holmes (Dauphin); Dorothy Tree (Adelaide); Helen Lowell (Countess De Bearn); Joan Wheeler (Florette); Hobart Cavanaugh (De La Vauguyon); Jessie Scott (Zamore); Virginia Sale (Sophie); Camille Rovelle (Victoria); Nella Walker (Madame De Noailles); Halliwell Hobbes (English Ambassador); Arthur Treacher (Master of the Bedroom); Doris Lloyd (Madame); Mary Kornman (Felice); Robert Greig (Chef); Allan Cavan (Nobleman); Joan Barclay (Bit); Eula Guy, Victoria Vinton (Young Girls).

IN CALIENTE *(First National, 1935)* 84 min.

Director, Lloyd Bacon; story, Ralph Block, Warren Duff; screenplay, Jerry Wald, Julius J. Epstein; songs, Mort Dixon, Allie Wrubel; Al Dubin, Harry Warren; musical numbers staged by Busby Berkeley; camera, Sol Polito, George Barnes; editor, Jimmy Gibbons.

Dolores Del Rio (Rita Gomez); Pat O'Brien (Larry MacArthur); Leo Carrillo (Jose Gomez); Glenda Farrell (Clara); Edward Everett Horton (Harold Brandon); Phil Regan (Pat Casey); Winifred Shaw ("Lady in Red"); Dorothy Dare (Baby Blonde); Harry Holman (Biggs); Herman Bing (Mexican Florist); George Humbert (Mexican Photographer); William B. Davidson (Man); Luis Alberni (Magistrate); Soledad Jimenez (Maid); Olive Jones (Singer); Judy, Anne, Zeke, and Pete Canova, and Sally and Tony DeMarco (Specialty Numbers); John Hyams (Bob, the Reporter); Florence Fair (Miss G, Larry's Secretary); James Donlan (Swanson); Chris-Pin Martin, C. I. Dafau, Carlos Salazar, L. R. Felix (Mexican Quartet); Harry Holman (Man at Table in "Lady in Red" Number).

I LIVE FOR LOVE *(Warner Bros., 1935)* 63 min.

Producer, Byran Foy; director, Busby Berkeley; story/screenplay, Jerry Wald, Julius J. Epstein, Robert Andrews; songs, Allie Wrubel, Mort Dixon; camera, George Barnes; editor, Terry Morse.

Dolores Del Rio (Donna Alvares); Everett Marshall (Roger); Guy Kibbee (Henderson); Allen Jenkins (Jimmy McNamara); Hobart Cavanaugh (Morgan); Berton Churchill (Fabian); Don Alvarado (Rico Cesaro); Sam Shaw, Al Lee, Eddy Conrad (Musician Trio); Mary Treen (Clementine); Miki Morita (Toya); Frank DuFrane, Eddie Morgan (Actors); Gordon "Bill" Elliott (Friend); Emmett Vogan (Announcer); Ernest Van Pelt (Stage Director); Nick Copeland (Stage Manager); Betty Farrington, Bess Flowers, Mary Marsh, Gertrude Astor (Interviewers); Florence Fair (Dowager).

WIDOW FROM MONTE CARLO *(Warner Bros., 1936)* 63 min.

Producer, Bryan Foy; director, Arthur G. Collins; based on the story "Meet the Duchess" by Ian Hay and A.E.W. Mason; screenplay, F. Hugh Herbert, Charles Belden, George Bricker; camera, Warren Lynch; editor, Thomas Pratt.

Warren William (Chepstow); Dolores Del Rio (Inez); Louise Fazenda (Mrs. Torrent); Colin Clive (Eric); Herbert Mundin (Mr. Torrent); Warren Hymer (Dopey); Olin Howland (Eaves); E. E. Clive (Lord Holloway); Mary Forbes (Lady Holloway); Eily Malyon (Lady Maynard); Ann Douglas (Joan); Andre Cheron (Croupier); Charles Fallon (Foreigner); Billy Bevan (Officer); Norman Ainsley (Englishman); Charles Coleman (Barker, the Torrents' Butler); John G. Spacey (Kilted Man); Ferdinand Schumann-Heink (Chauffeur); May Beatty (Dowager); Boyd Irwin, Sr. (Desk Sergeant); Alphonse Martell (Emil); Olaf Hytten (Englishman).

ACCUSED *(United Artists, 1936)* 84 min.

Producer, Marcel Hellman; director, Thornton Freeland; story, Zöe Akins; screenplay, Akins, George Barraud; camera, Victor Arminese.

Douglas Fairbanks, Jr. (Tony Seymour); Dolores Del Rio (Gaby Seymour); Florence Desmond (Yvette Delange); Basil Sydney (Eugene Roget); John Roberts (Justice); Cecil Humphries (Prosecuting Counsel); Esme Percy (Morel); Edward Rigby (Alphonse); George Moor Marriot (The Concierge); Cyril Raymond (Guy Henry); Googie Withers (Ninette); Roland Culver (Henry Capelle).

DEVIL'S PLAYGROUND *(Columbia, 1937)* 74 min.

Director, Erle C. Kenton; story, Norman Springer; screenplay, Liam O'Flaherty, Jerome Chodorov, Dalton Trumbo; camera, Lucien Ballard; editor, Viola Lawrence.

Richard Dix (Dorgan); Dolores Del Rio (Carmen); Chester Morris (Mason); George McKay (Red); John Gallaudet (Wounded Soldier); Pierre Watkin (Commanding Officer of Submarine); Ward Bond (Sidecar Wilson); Don Rowan (Reilly); Francis McDonald (Romano); Stanley Andrews (Salvage Boat Commander); Gene Morgan (Orderly); Garry Owner (Radio Man); Jack Pennick (Gob); William J. Worthington (Vice Admiral); Buddy Roosevelt (Deck Officer); Wesley Hopper (Diver); Sammy Blum (Bartender); Ann Doran, Alma Chester, Beatrice Curtis (Women); Lutra Winslow (Marcia); Edward Hearn (Surgeon).

ALI BABA GOES TO TOWN *(Twentieth Century-Fox, 1937)* 84 min.

Producer, Darryl F. Zanuck; associate producer, Laurence Schwab; director, David Butler; story, Gene Towne, Graham Baker, Gene Fowler; screenplay, Harry Tugend, Jack Yellen; songs, Mack Gordon, Harry Revel; Raymond Scott; music director, Louis Silvers; art director, Bernard Herzbrun; set decorator, Thomas Little; assistant director, Ad Schaumer; costumes, Gwen Wakeley, Herschel; sound, Alfred Bruzlin; camera, Ernest Palmer; editor, Irene Morra.

Eddie Cantor (Ali Baba); Tony Martin (Yusuf); Roland Young (Sultan); June Lang (Princess Miriam); Louise Hovick [Gypsy Rose Lee] (Sultana); John Carradine (Ishak); Virginia Field (Dinah); Alan Dinehart (Boland); Douglass Dumbrille (Omar, the Rug Maker); Warren Hymer, Stanley Fields (Tramps); Ferdinand Gottschalk (Chief Councilor); the Peters Sisters, Jeni Le Gon, the Raymond Scott Quintet, the Pearl Twins (Themselves); Sidney Fields (Assistant Director); Jim Pierce (Captain of the Guards); Sam Hayes (Radio Announcer); Charles Lane (Doctor); Eddie Collins (Wife-Beating Arab); Marjorie Weaver (Beaten Wife); Francis McDonald (Peasant Ringleader); Douglas Fairbanks, Lady Sylvia Ashley, the Ritz Brothers, Ann Sothern, Victor McLaglen, Phyllis Brooks, Michael Whalen, Cesar Romero, Tyrone Power, Sonja Henie, Shirley Temple, Dolores Del Rio, Eddie Cantor (Celebrities in Premiere Newsreel).

LANCER SPY *(Twentieth Century-Fox, 1937)* 84 min.

Associate producer, Samuel G. Engel; director, Gregory Ratoff; based on the novel by Martha McKenna; screenplay, Philip Dunne; art director, Albert Hogsett; music director, Arthur Lange; camera, Barney McGill; editor, Louis Loeffler.

Dolores Del Rio (Fraulein Dolores Daria); George Sanders (Baron Kurt Von Rohback/Lieutenant Michael Bruce); Peter Lorre (Major Sigfried Gruning); Virginia Field (Joan Bruce); Sig Rumann (Lieutenant Colonel Gottfried Hollen); Joseph Schildkraut (Prince Ferdi Zu Schwarzwald); Maurice Moscovich (General Von Meinhardt); Lionel Atwill (Colonel Fenwick); Luther Adler (Schratt); Fritz Feld (Fritz Mueller); Lester Matthews (Captain Neville); Carlos de Valdez (Von Klingern); Greg-

ory Gaye (Captain Freymann); Joan Carol (Elizabeth Bruce); Holmes Herbert (Dr. Aldrich); Clyde Cook (Orderly); John Burton (Lieutenant); Herbert Evans (Sergeant); Kenneth Hunter (Commandant); Claude King (Captain); Olaf Hytten (Barber); Ian MacLaren (Plainclothesman); Elisabeth Frohlich (Farmer's Wife); Paul Weigel (Hotel Manager Schreiber); Bud Geary (Captain's Aide); Major Sam Harris (Officer at Party); Lynn Bari (Fenwick's Companion).

INTERNATIONAL SETTLEMENT *(Twentieth Century-Fox, 1938)* 75 min.

Producer, Sol M. Wurtzel; director, Eugene Forde; story, Lynn Root, Frank Fenton; screenplay, Lou Breslow, John Patrick; music director, Samuel Kaylin; songs, Sidney Clare, Harry Akst, Harold Spina; art directors, Bernard Herzbrun, Albert Hogsett; camera, Lucien Andriot; editor, Nick de Maggio.

Dolores Del Rio (Leonore); George Sanders (Del Forbes); June Lang (Joyce Parker); Dick Baldwin (Wally Burton); Ruth Terry (Specialty Song); John Carradine (Murdock); Keye Luke (Dr. Wong); Harold Huber (Joseph Lang); Leon Ames (Silvers); Pedro de Cordoba (Zabello); Bruce Wong (Bellboy); Walter Miller, Jeffrey Sayre (Gangsters); Creighton Hale (Clerk); James B. Leong, Russ Clark (Officers); Edwin Stanley (Doctor); Nora Cecil (English Woman); Rosina Galli (Italian Woman); Al Kikume (Doorman); James C. Morton (Bartender); Hal K. Dawson (Master of Ceremonies); Bert Roach (Lord Fauntleroy); Forbes Murray (Man).

THE MAN FROM DAKOTA *(MGM, 1940)* 75 min.

Producer, Edward Chodorov; director, Leslie Fenton; based on the novel *Arouse and Beware* by MacKinlay Kantor; screenplay, Laurence Stallings; art directors, Cedric Gibbons, Malcolm Brown; set decorator, Edwin B. Willis; men's costumes, Gile Steele; wardrobe, Dolly Tree; makeup, Jack Dawn; camera, Ray June; editor, Conrad A. Nervig.

Wallace Beery (Sergeant Barstow); John Howard (Oliver Clark); Dolores Del Rio [Eugenia (Jenny)]; Donald Meek (Mr. Vestry); Robert Barrat (Parson Summers); Addison Richards (Provost Marshal); Frederick Burton (Leader); John Wray (Carpenter); Gregory Gaye (Colonel Borodin); Frank Hagney (Guard); William Royle (Supervisor); Ted Oliver and Buddy Roosevelt (Officers); Hugh Sothern (General); Edward Hearn (Captain); John Butler (Voss); Tom Fadden (Driver); Francis Ford (Horseman).

JOURNEY INTO FEAR *(RKO, 1942)* 69 min.

Producer, Orson Welles; directors, Norman Foster and (uncredited) Welles; based on the novel by Eric Ambler; screenplay, Welles, Joseph Cotten; music director, C. Bakaleinikoff; art directors, Albert S. D'Agostino, Mark-Lee Kirk; special effects, Vernon L. Walker; camera, Karl Struss; editor, Mark Robson.

Joseph Cotten (Howard Graham); Dolores Del Rio (Josette Martel); Ruth Warrick (Stephanie Graham); Orson Welles (Colonel Haki); Agnes Moorehead (Mrs. Mathews); Jack Durant (Gogo); Everett Sloane (Kopekin); Eustace Wyatt (Dr. Haller); Frank Readick (Mathews); Edgar Barrier (Kuvetli); Jack Moss (Banat); Stefan Schnabel (Purser); Hans Conried (Magician); Richard Bennett (Ship's Captain); Robert Meltzer (Steward).

FLOR SILVESTRE *(Films Mundiales, 1943)* 96 min.

Producer, Agustin J. Fink; associate producer, Emilio Gomez Muriel; director, Emilio Fernandez; based on the novel *Sucedio Ayer* by Fernando Robles; adaptors, Fernandez, Mauricio Magdaleno; assistant director, Felipe Palomino; music, Francisco Dominguez; sound, Howard Randall, Fernando Barrera, Manuel Esperon; camera, Gabriel Figueroa; editor, Jorge Bustos.

Dolores Del Rio (Esperanza); Pedro Armendáriz (José Luis Castro); Miguel Angel Ferriz (Don Francisco); Mimi Derba (Doña Clara); Eduardo Arozamena (Melchor); Agustin Isunza (Nicaror); Armando Soto La Marina El Chicote (Reynaldo); Margarita Cortés (Sister of José Luis); Emilio Fernandez (Rogelio Torres); Manuel Donde (Ursulo Torres); Salvador Quiroz (Colonel Ruben Pena y Ber Langa); José Elias Moreno (Colonel Panfilo Rodriquez); Carlos Riguelme (The Priest); Raul Guerrero (Ursulo's Assistant); Pedro Galindo (Pedro); Hernan Vera (Blacksmith).

MARIA CANDELARIA *(a.k.a. XOCHIMILCO) (Films Mundiales, 1944)* 101 min.

Producer, Agustin J. Fink; associate producer, Felipe Subervielle; director/screenplay, Emilio Fernandez; adaptors, Fernandez, Mauricio Magdaleno; music, Francisco Dominguez; assistant director, Matilde Landeta; sound, Howard Randall, Jesus Gonzalez Gancy, Manuel Esperon; camera, Gabriel Figueroa; editor, Gloria Schoemann.

Dolores Del Rio (Maria Candelariá); Pedro Armendáriz (Lorenzo Rafael); Margarita Cortés (Lupe); Alberto Galán (El Pintor); Beatriz Ramos (Reporter); Manuel Inclán (Don Damian); Rafael Icardo (Senor Cura); Julio Ahuet (José Alfonso); Arturo Soto Rangel (Doctor); and Irma Torres.

U.S. release title: *Portrait of Maria.*

BUGAMBILIA *(Films Mundiales, 1944)* 98 min.

Producer, Felipe Subervielle; director, Emilio Fernandez; story, Fernandez, Mauricio Magdaleno; screenplay, Fernandez; wardrobe, Royer; music, Raul Lavista; assistant director, Zacarias Gomez Urquiza; sets, Manuel Fontanale, Estrella Boissevain; camera, Gabriel Figueroa; editor, Gloria Schoemann.

Dolores Del Rio (Amalia de los Robles); Pedro Armendáriz (Ricardo Rojas); Julio Villarreal (Don Fernando); Alberto Galán (Luis Felipe); Stella Inda (Zarca); Paco Fuentes (Don Enrique, the Judge); Arturo Soto Rangel (The Priest); Elba Alvarez (Mercedes); Concha Sanz (Nana Nicanora); Maruja Grifell (Mathilde); Roberto Cañedo (Alberto); Victor Velazquez (District Attorney); Lupe del Castillo (Rosenda); José Elias Moreno (Ricardo's Partner); and Hernan Vera, Armando Velasco, Oscar Ramos, Juan Urban, Cynthias Boissevain.

LAS ABANDONADAS *(Films Mundiales, 1944)* 95 min.

Producer, Armando Espinosa; director, Emilio Fernandez; story, Fernandez, Mauricio Magdaleno; screenplay, Fernandez; music, Manuel Esperon; assistant director,

Felipe Palomino; sets, Manuel Fontanals; makeup, Ana Guerrero; sound, Howard Randall, Jesus Gonzales Goncy, Manuel Esperon; camera, Gabriel Figueroa; editor, Gloria Schoemann.

Dolores Del Rio (Margarita Perez); Pedro Armendáriz (Juan Gomez); Victor Junco (Julio Cortazar/Margarito); Paco Fuentes (Judge); Arturo Soto Rangel (Lawyer); Lupe Inclan (Gualupita); Fanny Schiller (Ninon); Alfonso Bedoya (Gertrudis Lopez); Maruja Grifell (Francesa); Alejandro Cobo (Policeman); Armando Soto, La Marina, "El Chicote" (Photographers); Josefina Romagnoli (Marta Ramirez); Fernando Fernandez (Official).

LA SELVA DE FUEGO *(Dyana, 1945)* 100 min.

Producers, Jesus Grovas, Mauricio de la Serna; director, Fernando de Fuentes; based on the novel by Antonio Mediz Bolio; adaptors, Paulino Masip, de Fuentes; music, Max Urban; sets, Edward Fitzgerald; makeup Margarita Ortega; assistant director, Winfield Sanchez; camera, Agustin Martinez Solares; editor, Jorge Bustos.

With Dolores Del Rio, Arturo de Cordova, Miguel Inclán, Gilberto González, Luis Beristain, José Torvay, Manuel Donde, Daniel Herrera, Felipe Montoya, Juan José Laboriel, Paco Astol, Enrique Gonzalez Alonso.

LA OTRA *(Mercurio, 1946)* 98 min.

Producer, Mauricio de la Serna; director, Roberto Gavaldón; based on the novel *Dead Pigeon* by Rian James; screenplay, José Revueltas, Gavaldón; music, Raul Lavista; assistant director, Ignacio Villarreal; sets, Gunther Gerszo; makeup, Ana Guerrero; sound, James L. Fields, Nicolas de la Rosa, Galdino Samperio; camera, Alex Phillips; editor, Charles L. Kimball.

Dolores Del Rio (Magdalena Mendez/Maria Mendez); Agustin Irusta (Roberto Gonzalez); Victor Junco (Fernando); José Baviera (De la Fuente the Lawyer); Manuel Donde (Vilar); Conchita Carracedo (Carmela); Carlos Villarias (Felix Mendoza); Rafael Icardo (The Judge); and Daniel Pastor.

THE FUGITIVE *(RKO, 1947)* 104 min.

Producers, John Ford, Merian C. Cooper; associate producer, Emilio Fernandez; director, Ford; based on the novel *The Labyrinthine Ways* by Graham Greene; screenplay, Dudley Nichols; art director, Alfred Ybarra; set decorator, Manuel Parra; music/music director, Richard Hageman; orchestrator, Lucien Cailliet; assistant director, Jesse Hibbs; sound, José B. Carles, Galdino Samperio; camera, Gabriel Figueroa; editor, Jack Murray.

Henry Fonda (Fugitive); Dolores Del Rio (Indian Woman); Pedro Armendáriz (Lieutenant of Police); J. Carroll Naish (Police Informer); Leo Carrillo (Chief of Police); Ward Bond (El Gringo); Robert Armstrong (Sergeant of Police); John Qualen (Refugee Doctor); Fortunio Bonanova (The Governor's Cousin); Chris-Pin Martin (Organ-Grinder); Miguel Inclan (Hostage); Fernando Fernandez (Singer).

HISTORIA DE UNA MALA MUJER *(Argentine Sono, 1948)* 92 min.

Director, Luis Saslavsky; based on the play *Lady Winder-*

mere's Fan by Oscar Wilde; screenplay, Pedro Miguel Obligado; sets, Gori Munoz; music, Victor Slister; camera, Alberto Etchebechere; editor, Jorge Garate.

With Dolores Del Rio, Maria Duval, Francisco de Paula, Alberto Closas, Fernando Lamas, Amalia Sanchez Arino.

LA MALQUERIDA *(Calderon/Columbia, 1949)* 83 min.

Executive producer, Francisco de P. Cabrera; producer, Felipe Subervielle; director, Emilio Fernandez; based on the play by Jacinto Benavente; screenplay, Fernandez, Mauricio Magdaleno; music, Antonio Diaz Conde; sets Manuel Fontanals; interior decorators, Manuel Parra; makeup, Ana Guerrero; assistant director, Jaime L. Contreras; sound, José B. Carles, Galdino Samperio; camera, Gabriel Figueroa; editor, Gloria Schoemann.

Dolores Del Rio (Raimunda); Pedro Armendáriz (Esteban); Columba Dominguez (Acacia); Roberto Cañedo (Faustino); Julio Villarreal (Don Eusebio); Gilberto Gonzalez (Rubio); Mimi Derba (Dona Mercedes); Enriqueta Reza (Juliana); Trio Calaveras and Mariachi Vargas (Themselves); Carlos Riquelme (Norberto); Eduardo Arozamena (Pastor); Manuel Donde (Juez of Acordada); and Juis Aceves Castaneda, Rogelio Fernandez, Agustin Fernandez, Jaime Fernandez, Santiago Torres.

LA CASA CHICA *(Filmex, 1950)* 96 min.

Executive producer, Gregorio Walerstein; producer, Jacobo Derechin; Roberto Gavaldón; story, José Revueltas; adaptors, Revueltas and Gavaldón; dialogue, Mauricio Magdaleno and Edmundo Baez; assistant director, Ignacio Villarreal; music, Antonio Diaz Conde; sets, Jorge Fernandez; wardrobe, Armando Valdes Peza; makeup, Ana Guerrero; sound, Enrique Rodriguez; camera, Alex Phillips; editor, Rafael Ceballos.

Dolores Del Rio (Amalia); Robert Cañedo (Dr. Fernando Mendoza); Miroslava (Lucila del Castillo); Domingo Soler (Professor Alfaro); Maria Douglas (Mimi Gutierrez); José Elias Moreno (Carlos Villanueva); Julio Villarreal (Senor Del Castillo); Arturo Soto Rangel (Don Florencio Carrasco); Hector Mateos (Lawyer); and Nicolas Rodriguez, Enriqueta Reza, Manuel de la Vega, Rafael Torres, Hernan Vera, Humberto Rodriguez.

DESEADA *(Sanson, 1951)* 105 min.

Producers, Clemente Guizar Mendoza, José Baviera; director, Robert Gavaldón; based on the play *La Ermita, La Fuente y El Rio* by Eduardo Marquina; adaptors, José Revueltas, Antonio Mediz Bolio, Gavaldón, José Baviera; music, Eduardo Hernandez Moncado; wardrobe, Armando Valdes Peza; makeup, Armando Meyer; assistant director, Americo Fernandez; sound, Luis Fernandez; camera; Alex Phillips; editor, Carlos Savage.

With Dolores Del Rio, Jorge Mistral, José Baviera, Annabelle Gutierrez, Arturo Soto Rangel, Enriqueta Reza.

DOÑA PERFECTA *(Columbia, 1951)*

Producer, Adolfo Torres Portillo; director, Alejandro Galindo; based on the novel by Benito Perez Galdos; adaptors, Inigo de Martino, Francisco de P. Cabrera, Alejandro Galindo, Gunther Gerszo; assistant director, Jesus Marin; music, Gustavo Cesar Carrion; sets, Gunther Gerszo; ward-

robe, Armando Valdes Peza; makeup, Noemi Wallace; sound, Manuel Topete, Galdino Samperio; camera, José Ortiz Ramos; editor, Fernando Martinez.

Dolores Del Rio (Perfecta); Esther Fernández (Rosario); Carlos Navarro (Pepe Rey); Julio Villarreal (Don Inocencio); José Elias Moreno (Cristóbal Ramos); Natalia Ortiz (Dona Remedios); Ignacio Retes (Jacintito); Rafael Icardo (Don Cayetano); Manuel Arvide (Captain Pinzon); Maria Gentil Arcos (Librada); Bruno Marquez (José Juan Arciniegas); Salvador Quiroz (Don Pedro, the Judge); Hector Matcos (Chief Politician); and Hilda Vera.

REPORTAJE *(Periodistas Cinematograficos Mexicanos and Associancion Nacional de Actores, 1953)*

Director, Emilio Fernandez; story/screenplay, Fernandez, Mauricio Magdaleno; music, Antonio Diaz Conde; sets Salvador Lozano Mena; makeup, Elda Loza; assistant director, Americo Fernandez; sound, José B. Carles; camera, Alex Phillips; editor, Gloria Schoemann.

Arturo de Cordova (Bernardo); Dolores Del Rio (Maria Enriqueta), Jorge Negrete (Humberto Salazar); Maria Felix, Pedro Armendáriz, Maria Elena Marques (Guests); Roberto Cañedo (Aurelio); Pedro Infante (Damian); Carmen Sevilla (Eugenia Bazan); Joaquin Pardave (Bonifacio); Pedro Lopez Lagar (Senor Gamez Rivera); Victor Parra (Roberto Garibay); Julio Villarreal (Surgeon); Antonio Espino (Clavillazo); Amanda del Llano (Candida); Rebeca Iturbide, Miguel Angel Ferriz, Victor Manuel Mendoz (Chief Participants); Esther Fernandez (Nurse); Columba Dominguez (Petra); Luis Aldas (Gerardo Munoz); Fernando Soler (Ernesto del Valle); Manolo Fabregas (Rafael Galindo); Nini Marshall (Matilde Gamboa); Domingo Soler (Pedro Marquez); Sara Montiel (Esperanza); David Silva (Driver); and Carlos Orellana, Crox Alvarado, Queta Lavat, Beatriz Ramos.

EL NINO Y LA NIEBLA *(Grovas, 1953)* 111 min.

Producer, Ricardo Beltri; director, Roberto Gavaldón; based on the play by Rodolfo Usigli; adaptors, Gavaldón, Edmundo Baez; music, Raul Lavista; sets, Nauel Fontanals; makeup, Ana Guerrero; assistant director, Mario Llorca; sound, Manuel Topete; camera, Gabriel Figueroa; editor, Gloria Shoemann.

Dolores Del Rio (Marta); Pedro Lopez Lagar (Engineer Guillermo Estra); Eduardo Noriega (Engineer Mauricio de la Torre); Alejandro Ciangherotti, Jr. (Daniel); Miguel Angel Ferriz (Dr. Mancera); Carlos Riquelme (Professor); Tana Lynn (Club Singer); Lupe Inclan (Bit).

SEÑORA AMA *(Diana Films-Union Films-Fernando de Fuentes, Jr., 1954)*

Director, Julio Bracho; based on the story by Jacinto Benavente; adaptors, Enrique Llovet, Julio Bracho; music, Salvador Ruiz de Luna; sets, Eduardo Torre de la Fuente; sound, Jaime Torrens; camera, Ted Pahle; editor, Antonio Martinez.

Dolores Del Rio (Dominica); José Suarez (Feliciano); Maria Luz Galicia (Maria Juana); and Manuel Monroy, Rafael Luis Calvo, Josefina Bejarano, Casimiro Hurtado, Mercedes Cora, Matilde Munoz Sampedro, Maria de la Riva, Josefina Serratosa, José Capilla, Dolores Bremon,

Juan Manuel Ramirez, Juan Cordoba, Pepe Loza, Ernestina Siria, Maria Teresa del Rio, Angela Tamayo, Elisa Mendez.

TORERO *(Mexican, 1957)* 80 min.

Producers, Barbachano Ponce, Manuel Barbachano Ponce; associate producer, George Werker; director, Carlos Velo; screenplay, Hugo Butler; assistant directors, Alejandro Velasquez, Emilio Gonzales, Leonardo Santos, Giovanni Korporaal; music, Rodolfo Halffter; music director, Rosalio Ramirez; sound, Adolfo de la Riva; special sound effects, Giovanni Korporaal; camera, Ramon Munoz; editor, Miguel Campos; dialogue editor, Luis Sobreyra.

With Luis Procuna, Antonio Fayat, Paco Malgesto, Antonio Sevilla, Ponciano Diaz, Carlos Robles Gil, Manuel Rodriguez Manolete, Alfonso Ramirez Calesero, Lorenzo Garza, Carlos Arruza, Dolores Del Rio, Miroslava, Lorraine Chanel.

A DONDE VAN NUESTROS HIJOS *(a.k.a. MEDIO TONO)* *(Filmex, 1958)* C-95 min.

Producers, Francisco de P. Cabrera, Vicente Fernandez, Manuel Rodriguez; director, Benito Alazraki; based on the novel *Medio Tono* by Rodolfo Usigli; adaptors, Cabrera, Alazraki; music, Gonzalo Curiel; sets, Jorge Fernandez; wardrobe, Armando Valdes Peza; sound, Rodolfo Benitez, Enrique Rodriguez; camera, Agustin Martinez Solares, Francisco Gomez; editor, Rafael Ceballos.

Dolores Del Rio (Rosa); Tito Junco (Martin Sierra); Ana Bertha Lepe (Gabriela); Martha Mijares (Sara); Carlos Rivas (Eduardo Mendez); Carlos Fernandez (Julio); Rogelio Jimenez Pons (Martinito); Carlos Riquelme (Don Miguel); Hector Godoy (Alejandro); Leon Michel (Victor); Andrea Palma (Carlo's Mother); Luis Aragon (Joaquin); Armando Saenz (Carlos); Elaine Bruce (Gringo).

LA CUCARACHA *(Unifilms-Cimex, 1958)* C-90 min.

Producer/director, Ismael Rodriguez; screenplay, José Bolanos Prado, Rodriguez, José Luis Celis, Ricardo Garibay; art director, Edward Fitzgerald; music, Raul Lavista; sound, James L. Fields; camera, Gabriel Figueroa; editor, Ferdinand Martino.

Emilio Fernandez (Colonel Zeta); Maria Felix (La Cucaracha); Dolores Del Rio (Chabela); Pedro Armendáriz (Razo); Antonio Aguilar (Captain Ventura); and Ignacio Lopez Tarso, Flor Silvestre, Cuco Sanchez.

FLAMING STAR *(Twentieth Century-Fox, 1960)* C-101 min.*

Producer, David Weisbart; director, Don Siegel; based on the novel by Clair Huffaker; screenplay, Huffaker, Nunnally Johnson; music, Cyril J. Mockridge; music director, Lionel Newman; songs, Sherman Edwards and Sid Wayne; Sid Tepper and Roy Bennett; art directors, Duncan Cramer, Walter M. Simonds; set decorators, Walter M. Scott, Gustav Bernstsen; assistant director, Joseph E. Rickards; costumes, Adele Balkan; makeup, Ben Nye; orchestrator, Edward B. Powell; choreography, Josephine Earl; second unit director, Richard Talmadge; sound, E. Clayton Ward, Warren B.

*Cut to 92 min.

Delaplain; camera, Charles G. Clarke; editor, Hugh S. Fowler.

Elvis Presley (Pacer Burton); Barbara Eden (Roslyn Pierce); Steve Forrest (Clint Burton); Dolores Del Rio (Neddy Burton); John McIntire (Pa Burton); Rudolph Acosta (Buffalo Horn); Karl Swenson (Dred Pierce); Ford Rainey (Doc Phillips); Richard Jaeckel (Angus Pierce); Anne Benton (Dorothy Howard); L. Q. Jones (Tom Howard); Douglas Dick (Will Howard); Tom Reese (Jute); Marian Goldina (Ph'Sha Knay); Monte Burkhardt (Ben Ford); Ted Jacques (Hornsby); Rodd Redwing (Indian Brave); Perry Lopez (Two Moons); Sharon Bercutt (Bird's Wing); Ray Beltran (Indian); Barbara Beaird (Dottie Phillips); Virginia Christine (Mrs. Phillips); Griswold Green, Tom Allen, Guy Way, Joe Brooks, William Herrin (Men at Crossing); The Jordanaires (Vocal Accompaniment).

EL PECADO DE UNA MADRE *(Peliculas Nacionales, 1960)* 90 min.

Director, Alfonso Corona Blake; story, Fernando Galeania; screenplay, Julio Alejandro; camera, Jack Draper.

With: Libertad Lamarque, Dolores Del Rio, Pedro Geraldo, Enrique Rambal, Teresa Velazquez.

CHEYENNE AUTUMN *(Warner Bros., 1964)* C-156 min.

Producer, Bernard Smith; director, John Ford; associate director, Ray Kellogg; based on the novel by Mari Sandoz; screenplay, James R. Webb; music/music director, Alex North; art director, Richard Day; set decorator, Darrel Silvera; assistant directors, Wingate Smith, Russ Saunders; sound, Francis E. Stahl; camera, William H. Clothier; editor, Otho Lovering.

Richard Widmark (Captain Thomas Archer); Carroll Baker (Deborah Wright); Karl Malden (Captain Oscar Wessell); Edward G. Robinson (Carl Schurz); Sal Mineo (Red Shirt); Dolores Del Rio (Spanish Woman); Ricardo Montalban (Little Wolf); Gilbert Roland (Dull Knife); Arthur Kennedy (Doc Holliday); Patrick Wayne (Second Lieutenant Scott); Elizabeth Allen (Miss Guinevere Plantagenet); John Carradine (Major Jeff Blair); Victor Jory (Tall Tree); Judson Pratt (Mayor Dog Kelly); Mike Mazurki (Senior First Sergeant Stanislaus Wichowsky); Ken Curtis (Homer); George O'Brien (Major Braden); Shug Fisher (Trail Boss); Carmen D'Antonio (Pawnee Woman); Walter Baldwin (Deborah's Uncle); Nancy Hseuh (Little Bird); Chuck Roberson (Trail Hand); Nanomba "Moonbeam" Morton (Running Deer); John Qualen (Svenson); Sean McClory (Dr. O'Carberry); Walter Reed (Lieutenant Peterson); James Flavin (Sergeant of the Guard); Ben Johnson (Plumtree); Harry Carey, Jr. (Smith); Bing Russell (Telegrapher); Dan Borzage, Dan Carr, James O'Hara, David Miller, Ted Mapes, John McKee (Troopers); Charles Seel (Newspaper Publisher); Major Sam Harris (Newspaper Publisher); Carleton Young (Secretary to Schurz); Louise Montana (Woman); Philo McCullough (Man); William Henry (Infantry Captain).

LA DAMA DEL ALBA *(Films Rovira Beleta, 1966)* 105 min.

Director, Francisco Rovira Beleta; based on the play by

Alejandro Casona; screenplay, Manuel Maria Salo, Beleta; music arranger, Federico Martinez Tudo; set decorator, Alfonso de Lucas; camera, Pierre Montazei.

With Juliette Villard, Daniel Martin, Dolores Del Rio, Yelena Samarina, Jean Yonnel, Ana Maria Noe, Fernando Cebrian, Barta Barry.

CASA DE MUJERES *(Spanish, 1966)*

Producer, Carlos Amador; director, Julian Soler.

With Dolores Del Rio, Fernando Soler, Carlos Lopez Moctezuma, Enrique Alvarez Feliz.

C'ERA UNA VOLTA *(a.k.a. MORE THAN A MIRACLE) (MGM, 1966)* C-100 min.

Producer, Carlo Ponti; director, Francesco Rosi; story, Tonino Guerra; screenplay, Rosi, Guerra, Raffaele La Capria, Peppino Patroni Griffi; music, Piero Piccioni; song, Piccioni, Larry Kusik, Eddie Snyder; art director, Piero Poletto; costumes, Giulio Coltellacci; assistant directors, Camillo Teti, Dante Brini; camera, Pasquale de Santis; editor, Jolanda Benvenuti.

Sophia Loren (Isabella); Omar Sharif (Prince Ramon); Dolores Del Rio (Princess Mother); Georges Wilson (Monzu, the Chef); Leslie French (Brother Joseph); Carlo Pisacane (First Witch); Marina Malfatti (Devout Princess); Anna Nogara (Impatient Princess); Rosemary Martin (Vain Princess); Rita Forzano (Greedy Princess); Carlotta Barilli (Superstitious Princess); Fleur Mombelli (Haughty Princess); Anna Liotti (Infant Princess); Giovanni Tarallo (Elderly Monk); Renato Pinciroli (Prince's Chamberlain); Pietro Carloni (Village Priest); Chris Huerta (Spanish Groom).

RIO BLANCO *(Galindo Bros., 1967)*

Director, Roberto Gavaldón; screenplay, Gavaldón, Tito Davidson.

With Silvia Pinal, Ignacio Lopez Tarso, Dolores Del Rio, David Reynoso.

THE CHILDREN OF SANCHEZ *(Hall Bartlett, 1978)* C- min.

Producer/director, Hall Bartlett; based on the novel by Oscar and Ruth Lewis; screenplay, Cesare Zavattini.

With Anthony Quinn, Katy Jurado, Dolores Del Rio, Lupita Ferrer, Lucia Mendez, Hector Bonilla, Carmen Montejo, Armando Silvestre, Rebecca Silva, Patricia Reyes Spindola, Salvador Sanchez, Rodrigo Puebla, José Carlos Ruiz, Patricia Aspillaga.

In *Another Dawn* ('37).

64

CHAPTER 2

KAY FRANCIS

5'5"
112 pounds
Dark brown hair
Brown eyes
Capricorn

IN THE 1972 film *Cabaret,* vivacious Liza Minnelli models her new sleek coat to Michael York and gurgles, "I feel just like Kay Francis!" To a young lady of two generations ago, there could be no higher tribute. Tall, dark, sultry Kay Francis—with the famed widow's peak and lisp—was soap opera's most gallant heroine. In the Thirties she was the cinema's most celebrated clothes horse. While there was far more to Miss Francis than her opulent wardrobe, cinema aficionados have never been able to agree on the extent and quality of her talents.

Not the movies' most powerful thespian, or most ambitious, or most versatile, Kay Francis had a monopoly in one arena: she could suffer through a celluloid weeper with more chic, style, and sangfroid than any of her rouged confreres. Be she dying of heart disease, offering herself to one man to save the person she really loved, or serving as the understanding mistress to a lover saddled with a shrewish wife, Kay brought the perfect touch of class to the lachrymose pace of such films as *One Way Passage* (1932) and *I Found Stella Parish* (1935).

Sadly, Kay's reign (1930 to 1937) was brief before the public's changing taste, the actress' personal foibles, and her advancing age militated against her. The fall of the star from a vivacious, life-loving celebrity to a bitter recluse was a tragedy. When she died she willed that her body be cremated so that "no sign of my existence be left on this earth." It was the unhappy finale of a not always appreciated legend.

Kay Francis was born Katherine Edwina Gibbs on Friday the 13th of January 1899* in Oklahoma City. She was the daughter of Joseph Sprague Gibbs, a former Los Angeles businessman who was then a hotel manager, and Katherine Clinton Franks who was something of a name (as Katherine Clinton) on the stage. The Gibbs family moved about quite a bit: when Katherine was one year old, they relocated to Denver, then on to Santa Barbara, and later to Los Angeles. Because Mr. Gibbs was such a heavy drinker (Mrs. Gibbs also had a fondness for the bottle) and was so irresponsible, mother and child returned East when Katherine was three or four, and Mrs. Gibbs once again began performing on the stage up and down the Atlantic seaboard. What became of Mr. Gibbs remains a mystery. Even decades later Kay would have bitter words to offer regarding her errant father. As for Kay's mother, she and her movie-star daughter would always have a strained relationship. While the adult Kay would entertain her mother privately at home, Mrs. Gibbs was not allowed to mingle with Francis' movie colony friends or even to visit her daughter on the set of her films.

Years later, when Kay was at the height of her fame, fan magazines would report that as a youngster the movie actress had attended assorted fashionable East Coast boarding schools (such as the Holy Angels parochial school in Fort Lee, New Jersey, the Notre Dame School in Roxbury, Massachusetts, and the Holy Child of Jesus Academy in New York City). In reality, Kay endured a very unpleasant, tawdry childhood. One of her friends would recollect, "I know her mother [Katherine Clinton] had an awful lot of odd jobs. Some things Kay told me I wouldn't repeat. They were horrible. It was all very third-rate."

Somehow Mrs. Gibbs did manage to send Katherine to Miss Fuller's Girls Academy in Ossining, New York. George Eels, in his study of Miss Francis, refers to a rare public interview by Kay's mother in which she mentioned that Kay did not do well at Miss Fuller's: "I've always thought it ridiculous for an attractive woman to study such things as Latin and Greek. I wanted her to do well in piano. But what possible use would geometry be? [Kay failed that course.] She was like her father. He had this great personality. He was a clear thinker and possessed excellent judgment. Kay has that, too. And you must remember, Kay has the greatest gift in the world for an actor—personality. That's a star's most valuable asset." Later Kay would be transferred to the Cathedral School of St. Mary in Garden City, Long Island, New York. She was there for one academic year.

It was at Cathedral that she made her stage bow. The play, *You Never Can Tell,* was written by her classmate Katty Stewart. "Katty played the female lead because she was the author, and I played the leading male role because I was the tallest girl in the class."

Instead of completing her education at Cathedral, Kay entered the Katherine Gibbs Secretarial School in New York City. Her mother had decided that she should be prepared to make her own way in the world and that secretarial skills would be very useful. Later publicity implied that the Ms. Gibbs for whom the school was named was Kay's mother, but this was not so—there was no relation.

After completing her courses, she had a

*Kay, along with Ruth Chatterton, was one of the oldest of Hollywood's leading ladies of the Thirties, a fact of life she took pains to distort. Publicity usually gave Kay's year of birth as 1903, and later she went so far as to list 1906 and 1910.

The initial publicity about Kay in the "Answer Man" sections of the leading fan magazines, *Photoplay, Motion Picture, Picture Play,* etc., insisted that she was born on Friday the 13th and stated the year of birth was 1906. Then along came a studious sort who pointed out that Friday the 13th had fallen in 1899 and 1905, and if one were to believe the Friday the 13th part, it had to be either 1899 or 1905. Thereafter Kay maintained that the year was 1899.

In his fine book *Ginger, Loretta and Irene WHO?* (1976), George Eels, who did very extensive research on his Kay Francis biography chapter, states that her year of birth was 1905. He also adds that an inebriated Mr. Gibbs celebrated his daughter's birth by "riding his horse through the hotel lobby and up the big staircase leading to the room where his wife lay with their newborn daughter. . . ."

modest-paying post for two businessmen. Later she was a model, real-estate seller, publicity girl, and promotionalist. She also assisted Juliana Cutling in arranging debutante parties. In early January 1922, the tall, brown-eyed, striking, raven-haired beauty met James Dwight Francis, scion of a prominent Massachusetts family. He had attended Harvard, but never graduated. By the time he and Kay met, he was already a slick playboy who lived and drank well beyond his means. In late October they were engaged and early the next month they drove to Pittsfield, Massachusetts, to meet the Francis clan. On Wednesday, December 13, 1922, the couple was wed at St. Thomas' in New York City. It was the beginning of her matrimonial career, about which speculation has been great and facts have been very minimal. Her obituaries would claim that she was wed anywhere from three to five times, and the fan magazines of the Thirties and Forties carried tidbits of the "secret" husbands the actress had accumulated over the years.

At any rate, the marriage failed. Mr. Francis liked high living, but had no notions of where the income was to be derived. It remained for Kay to contribute to the household funds. Along the way she had an abortion, which left her emotionally shaken. Later, to economize, the couple moved to his parents' home in Pittsfield, a rural area that bored the outgoing Katherine. (By this point Dwight had also become physically abusive of his wife.) Before the union had endured three years, a divorce was in preparation. Warner Bros. producer David Lewis would later tell research writer George Eels, "She married several times and had many lovers but she never really recovered from that first marriage. The affection was still there." (Dwight Francis would later wed Lesley Frost, daughter of poet Robert Frost. That marriage also ended in divorce.)

Kay returned to New York City where she roomed with Virginia Farjeon, a Cathedral school pal. Kay was now in need of a job. Again, later publicity would distort the facts and claim that she became a social secretary for the wealthy. But Kay would deny this, stating, "I was a secretary to the two elderly ladies who handled income tax for Mrs. [Dwight] Morrow, Mrs. [W. K.] Vanderbilt, and other wealthy women. That was during the six-month period when I was getting my first divorce and I needed a job."

Once again, Katherine's exquisite beauty dictated secretarial work as too mundane for a career. Leo Mielziner, the artist who would later become Kay's father-in-law, was so taken by her exotic appearance that he offered to paint her portrait. The result was an acclaimed work of art that in 1926 was exhibited at the British Royal Academy.

Before her marriage to Francis, Katherine had become the intimate of Allan A. Ryan, Jr., of the wealthy Thomas Ryan family. The young couple had become engaged but then separated. During and after her marriage to Francis he remained a close friend. One of their more madcap moments occurred when he escorted her to New York's Cotton Club on the eve of his marriage to socially respected Eleanor Barry.

It was through Virginia Farjeon that Kay met William Gaston, a wartime flyer and the grandson of a former Massachusetts governor. Supposedly she wed the cafe society member when she thought she was pregnant by him. The couple decided to keep the wedding a secret until the child came. But it was a false alarm and he was soon begging her for a divorce. As with her first husband, Gaston faced a tragic matrimonial future. He later wed actress Rosamond Pinchot who had won such favor as the nun in Max Reinhardt's lavish *The Miracle*. After an estrangement from Gaston, Miss Pinchot garbed herself in ermine and killed herself by inhaling carbon monoxide in her closed car.

Among Kay's intimates at this time were Charles Baskerville, who reviewed and illustrated cabaret news under the pseudonym "Top Hat" at *New Yorker* magazine, and Lois Long, who was employed at *Vogue*. Long, Baskerville, and Kay would go to Paris the summer after her divorce from Gaston. Baskerville would recall their trek abroad:

> She was an extraordinary person. That summer she had no wardrobe, and neither of us had much money. But she took a paisley—gray, black, and white—Persian shawl and had it made into an evening wrap. Whenever we were going to any swell place,

she would put the paisley wrap over her gown, and she was a knock-out. She carried herself beautifully; her hair was cut as short as mine, and she wore no jewelry, only lipstick. No eyeshadow or anything; she didn't need it. People were stampeded by this creature. They thought she was an Indian. I don't mean an American Indian. They thought she was a maharani on the loose or something like that.

When they returned from Europe, Kay and Lois shared a small apartment at 140 East 39th Street in New York. The girls again became a staunch part of the supperclub scene, enjoying life to the fullest. Then events led Kay into stage work. Through Baskerville she met producer Edgar Selwyn who hired her to understudy Katharine Cornell in *The Green Hat,* which opened on Broadway in September of 1925. Kay, who was by no means ready for such complex stage work, was hired more for her resemblance to Miss Cornell than for any hidden thespian talents.

Selwyn again used Kay—who was billing herself as Katharine Francis—for his modern-dress production of *Hamlet.* The drama starred Basil Sydney as the Danish prince (he would later play Claudius in Laurence Olivier's 1948 cinema version), Helen Chandler as Ophelia, Adrienne Morrison (mother of Constance, Barbara, and Joan Bennett) as Gertrude the Queen Mother, Charles Waldron as Claudius, Walter Kingsford as the first gravedigger, and Kay as the Player Queen. The show opened at the Booth Theatre on Monday, November 9, 1925. The *New York Times* reported, "Neither the clothes nor the settings matter. In the worn and beaten-out phrase of Hamlet himself, 'the play's the thing.'" The reviewer praised Sydney's work and that of most of the leads. But Kay, who had made her Broadway bow, was *not* mentioned. The *Times* did note, however, that "some of the minor roles are not well-played."

"When I first went on the stage, I didn't know—just as I hadn't known at the start with secretarial work—whether it was to be merely a temporary way of earning my living or whether

it was to be something more. I just went at it calmly and to the best of my ability, not with any of the feverish, pushing anxiety of the usual stagestruck girl. Probably that's why I was lucky. Perhaps if I'd been all tied up in knots about it, I'd not have had half as easy a time. Things go that way, you know." *Hamlet* ran for eighty-eight performances. On another occasion, when she was asked how she had gotten this role, she responded, "By lying a lot . . . to the right people."

After it closed, Katherine decided a little more theatrical experience could not hurt, although it cut into her nightlife, and with the help of director James Light she joined the Stuart Walker stock company which played its repertory (including *Polly Preferred, Puppy Love,* and *Candida*) in Cincinnati, Dayton, and Indianapolis. Other members of the troupe were Peggy Wood, McKay Morris, and Elizabeth Patterson. As Kay would recall:

My real training in acting came with Stuart Walker. Sometimes, while I was playing in Cincinnati, I'd get up early to take a train to Dayton, rehearse the next week's bill, and get back to Cincinnati in time to appear that night. My parts were heavies, but I always wanted sentiment. Once, when I was begging for a weepy part, Stuart Walker actually shook me. "I'll shake some sense into you," he said. "If you learn to play heavies well, leads will come easy to you." I later found that this was true.

The Stuart Walker experience was no joy for Kay. Not only was she frustrated by being cast in unsympathetic roles, but she began a torrid romance with co-performer McKay Morris, nine years her senior. When she returned that fall to New York, Kay was suffering from a broken collarbone (no one was quite sure how the accident occurred) and she was encased in an uncomfortable plaster cast. She and McKay took up residence at the Hotel Marlton on Eighth Street. Since neither of them was working, Kay's friends took up a collection among the "gang" and donated $1,000 to her bank account. Pal Lois

Long would relate to historian Eels of McKay Morris, "He was a great actor and very handsome but impotent, which didn't really seem to make a great deal of difference to her. I don't think sex meant that much to her. I really don't." It was during this period of low finances that Kay became a very heavy drinker. And somehow—no one is just sure how—she managed to keep up with her cafe society friends on their expensive nights about town.

Fortunately, her stage career took a jolt for the better. Producer Al Woods hired her to play Marjorie Gray in *Crime,* which opened on Tuesday, February 22, 1927, at the Eltinge Theatre and ran for 186 performances. The drama starred Sylvia Sidney, Douglass Montgomery, and Chester Morris. The *New York Times* found the show, which had had more than its share of out-of-town tryout problems, to be a "spectacular and fast-moving melodrama." Once again, Kay—now billed as Katherine Francis—had a minor part, a role which won her no great critical notice. But it did provide her with more experience in her chosen craft.

Following this production, Kay went into *Amateur Anne* which closed before it could open. She then won a role in Rachel Crothers' *Venus* which did open on Monday, December 26, 1927, at the Masque Theatre. The offbeat, sophisticated comedy dealt with sex equality (and the reversal of male-female traits and desires) in the future. Kay was Diana Gibbs, an aviatrix who naturally tends "toward pure intelligence." The cast included Cecilia Loftus, Patricia Collinge, and Tyrone Power, Sr. The latter's wife died tragically only a few days before the opening. This almost caused a delay in the premiere, but Power insisted upon going on with the show which found him dancing a fandango and crying into his handkerchief. The unusual play could not find a sufficient audience and closed after only eight performances.

There followed a minor success for Katherine the next season. The play was *Elmer the Great* which premiered at the Lyceum Theatre on Monday, September 24, 1928. It starred Walter Huston and Nan Sunderland, with Kay again in support as Evelyn Corey. The comedy concerned baseball, with Huston as a blowhard pitcher and Katherine as one of his flames. It lasted a mere

forty performances. In 1933, First National would film the property with Joe E. Brown and Patricia Ellis starred and Claire Dodd in Kay's old role.

At this time, New York City was still a prominent location of silent film production. While the majority of movie industry personnel had settled in the splendor of Hollywood, some remained in New York. Paramount, in particular, had a lot located in Astoria, usually populated by stage actors between plays who were anxious to earn extra money. The facility had been closed in 1927 but re-opened in 1928 to film Florenz Ziegfeld's *Glorifying the American Girl,* and with the coming of talkies, it found a new prosperity.

One such thespian who made use of the proximity of the Paramount plant was Walter Huston. After *Elmer the Great* collapsed, he contracted with Paramount to star in *Gentlemen of the Press* (1929), a crackly newspaper story in the vein of the acclaimed *The Front Page* that had seared Broadway when it debuted in August 1928. The film required a vamp. Huston notified Kay that there just might be a possibility for her in the movies and arranged a meeting between her and director Millard Webb.*

"She fascinated me," recalled Webb, who had been reluctant to confer with the actress because the part called for a blonde menace. However, after viewing Katherine's screen test,** Webb realized that the blonde aspect could be forgotten and he cast her in her debut cinema role. She was to be Myra May, a sleek, beautifully adorned vampire who injects lethal seduction into the pressroom comedy/drama. When *Gentlemen of the Press* premiered in May of 1929 (released in both silent and sound versions,

---

*Writer Ward Morehouse, who worked on *Gentlemen of the Press* with Bartlett Cormack, would offer his version of how he and the co-creators of the film were desperate to fill the villainess role. Depressed, they abandoned their search temporarily and adjourned to Tony's Club. ". . . There, in the haze of that famous backroom . . . we found Kay Francis. She was resting comfortably behind a Tom Collins. She was tall, dark, and interesting-looking but had made far more appearances in Tony's than she had on the Broadway stage. She looked the part of Myra, all right. But the day of just looking it was gone forever. Could she act, and how was her voice? She was hustled over to Astoria. In the first test her voice came through strong and clear and vibrant. Her career began that very day."

**Regarding her screen test, Kay would relate, "My face was shiny, and I looked more like the devil."

starring Huston, Charles Ruggles, and Betty Lawford, with Brian Donlevy in a bit role), *Variety* assured the trade that the film "will create no tumult." It did note that with the presence of Katherine "as the seductive siren . . . photographing well and also recording, the major difficulty in casting this talker was over." The *New York Times* was of the opinion that Kay "overacts."

Delighted over his find, Webb rushed to the Paramount front office and exclaimed, "Her snake-like study of this part is absolutely fascinating. She can become the first great vamp of the audible screen." *Photoplay* magazine agreed, heralding Kay as having given "one of the most astonishing first performances in the history of motion pictures." As was predicted, the fan publication introduced her to readers as "the first great vamp of the talking pictures."

At this time, Paramount was not in the best of financial shape (the Depression would soon be upon the United States and the world), despite the maintenance of a top contract roster. The men included Gary Cooper, Charles "Buddy" Rogers, Richard Arlen, Clive Brook, George Bancroft, Richard Dix, and William Powell, and soon would include such stage converts as Fredric March, Jack Oakie, and Phillips Holmes, and imports like Maurice Chevalier. On the distaff side were Clara Bow, Nancy Carroll, Ruth Chatterton, ingenues Fay Wray and Mary Brian, and Broadway catches such as Jeanette MacDonald, Claudette Colbert, and Lillian Roth. Directors such as Ernst Lubitsch, Josef von Sternberg, Edmund Goulding, Rowland V. Lee, Edward Sutherland, Monta Bell, and Dorothy Arzner supplied their talents to the variety of formats tested by Adolph Zukor and Jesse L. Lasky's busy studio. Kay was signed to a studio contract at $500 weekly.

At first the Paramount brass decided to promote Kay as the vamp who had dazzled Webb. An important step in the process was to clarify her private life. It seems Katherine was married to (or, as some insisted, was living with) playwright/director/performer John Meehan, who had been the dialogue director on *Gentlemen of the Press*. While the studio attempted to dispense with this then delicate problem by counseling Kay to remain very quiet on the subject, she did retakes on *Gentlemen of the Press* and was assigned to her next picture.

This was 1929's *The Cocoanuts*, which contained the film premiere of none other than the four Marx Brothers. The wild foursome had played on Broadway in *The Cocoanuts* (which opened in December 1925 for a 377-performance run) with such hysterical results that they had won a Paramount contract. Although Kay was fortunate in not drawing the ingenue role of Polly (*Variety* insisted that with the zany Marxes cavorting about the screen, the juveniles "mean nothing"), her role was not that much better. She was the parasol-sporting Penelope, a luscious villainess out to snare the bracelet owned by Margaret Dumont. With music (including the popular theme song, "When Our Dreams Come True") and the mugging brothers, *The Cocoanuts* was a big box-office and critical success. This was in spite of the poor sound recording and very stagey proceedings and Groucho's fear during filming: "Sometimes I wondered what I was doing there."

As soon as this Long Island-made film comedy was completed, Paramount exported Katherine to Hollywood where she arrived before either of her Astoria-lensed pictures was released. There she reported to director Lothar Mendes for a featured role in a Clara Bow vehicle entitled *Dangerous Curves* (1929). Shot in both sound and silent versions, the film dealt with a young waif (Bow) who brings love to a dashing aerialist (Richard Arlen) who was cheated and heartbroken by his beautiful, heartless partner. Yes, this latter character was Katherine, who finally achieved her childhood ambition to be (or at least play at being) a circus performer. As the alluring Zara, she all but steals the picture from the pert Miss Bow. This hardly bothered the devil-may-care Clara. In fact, the effervescent screen star confided to Katherine during production that Miss Francis had what it takes to be a star. Therefore, she should shorten her name for easy access to marquees. Hence, Katherine Francis became Kay Francis.

It took some time for Kay to match the bid for attention supplied in her first Hollywood feature. Mendes again cast Kay in a circus picture, *Illusion* (1929), but her role was little more than a bit as Paramount favorites Charles "Buddy"

With William Powell and John Risso in *Street of Chance* ('30).

Rogers and Nancy Carroll won the opportunity to sing and dance as partners in a magic act. *The Marriage Playground* (1929), loosely based on Edith Wharton's *The Children,* won kudos for roster members Fredric March and Mary Brian. But, again, Kay was wasted oncamera, this time as a titled lady with marital problems. While the role of Zinnia La Crosse was a bit larger than her spot in *Illusion,* her billing dropped from fourth to fifth and some on the lot whispered that Kay Francis was a flash in the proverbial pan.

But already Kay was developing a reputation on the social scene. In the early Sixties, director/actor Frank Merlin would recall for this author about the days when Miss Francis had just come to Hollywood. From the start, he remembered, she was an avid partygoer and enjoyed liquor more than the usual offender in Prohibition-clad America.

While Kay was enjoying the California nightlife, her career took an upward swing with another lethal vamp role, this one in *Behind the Make-Up* (1930). In this weeper, she first worked with William Powell, he playing a magician whom Kay persuades to leave his "good dame" wife (Fay Wray). Kay then drives him to suicide. *Variety* found her wretchedness to be "subtly convincing," and Paramount rewarded her with a genuine lead in another Powell vehicle, *Street of Chance* (1930), one of the best of the early Thirties' crime capers. It was based on the career of gambler Arnold Rothstein, and was well-fictionalized by Oliver H. P. Garrett and well-directed by John Cromwell. It won for increasingly suave Powell his usual set of complimentary notices. It also boosted Kay's stock—for the first time, she not only had a lead role (as Alma Marsden), but a sympathetic part as well, as the wife who winces and weeps over her husband's addiction to gambling. Jean Arthur, top-billed next to Powell, had the other woman's role.

Paramount, realizing that Kay was indeed growing in popularity, included her in the all-star line-up of their marathon *Paramount on Parade* (1930), a hodgepodge of skits, songs, and musical numbers, with a few Technicolor sequences. Kay did not draw the sizable vignettes that were assigned to such established names as Chevalier, Powell, and Chatterton, but served

attractively in two spots, one as a Spanish beauty and another as a stooge for George Bancroft in a skit entitled "Impulses."

This inclusion in an all-star mélange was followed by another sign of increasing prestige in Hollywood—Kay was loaned out to another studio. Warner Bros. borrowed her to emote in a Billie Dove picture, *A Notorious Affair* (1930), which cloaked both Billie and Kay in breathtaking gowns by Edward Stevenson, but inspired critical malaise. The creaky plot saw Basil Rathbone driven to hysteria by a countess (Kay) who lures him from his wife (Billie) with *Variety* lamenting that "Billie Dove plots hardly vary the traditional .0005 of an inch." Still, Kay in her finery and lounging about her boudoir rubbing a long-stemmed rose against her cheek was a worthy sight to behold. *Variety* added, "Kay Francis, whose upward rise has been very rapid since last summer . . . sufficiently supports, merely by her presence, the story's suggestion of a seductive countess of definite nymphomaniacal tendencies. . . . Hers, not Miss Dove's, is the reason for the unwarranted title, *A Notorious Affair.*"

Paramount, preoccupied with its array of other contract stars, had nothing on tap for Kay after she left the Burbank lot so they willingly loaned her out again, this time to Samuel Goldwyn for the film that won her top celebrity status. The actress was teamed with the immensely popular Ronald Colman in the elegant sort of drawing room mirth that captivated audiences. *Raffles* (United Artists, 1930) was an appropriate follow-up to Colman's sound debut, *Bulldog Drummond* (United Artists, 1929). It allowed the dapper British matinee idol to display his resonant voice, smooth style, and impeccable decorum. As the gentleman thief Raffles, Colman falls madly in love with Lady Gwen (Kay) and eventually confides to her his dishonorable profession. Meanwhile he has been hounded by Scotland Yard's Inspector McKenzie (David Torrence). But the intrepid crook manages to elude the law (thanks to the use of a grandfather clock and a concealing cape for his escape) and to head for Paris where it is suggested he will rendezvous with his lady fair. *Variety* reported of Kay's Gwen. "In Kay Francis the caster has made a happy choice—an actress with the suggestion of reserve vitality that makes her stand out strongly in a part that is intrinsically pale." With this prestige feature to her credit, Kay returned to Paramount a full-fledged star who could bid farewell to her "other woman" roles in favor of consistent leading lady opportunities. By the time of this film, Kay had abandoned her boyish bob and replaced it with a more bouffant coiffure which she kept for the remainder of her career.

Meanwhile, Paramount had two other films featuring Kay ready for release. *For the Defense* (1930) reteamed her with William Powell. This time Kay tragically bore the neglect of her alcoholic lawyer husband. Then came an offbeat opportunity in 1930's *Let's Go Native*, in which Kay was shipwrecked with the unlikely starring duo of Jack Oakie and Jeanette MacDonald, the "iron butterfly" who had done so well in such sophisticated studio musicals as Ernst Lubitsch's *The Love Parade* (1929) and his *Monte Carlo* (1930). Despite her blossoming stardom, Kay was only sixth billed in this "ludicrous audible film hodgepodge" (*New York Times*) filmed earlier in the year. Audiences, however, found it rather amusing and enjoyed, among other sights, witnessing Kay sing a duet with the rotund comedian Oakie.

At any rate, *Let's Go Native* was a pleasant change of pace for Kay, who afterwards went back to tear-wringing in *The Virtuous Sin* (1930). Here as nurse Marya Ivanovna, Kay offers herself to gruff Russian officer Walter Huston to save her teacher-husband Kenneth MacKenna from prison. Upon his release, the husband tries to avenge his wife's honor by killing the general, only to learn she has fallen in love with her seducer! The result was maudlin indeed, although Paramount had high hopes for this class vehicle to which they assigned two directors, George Cukor and Louis Gasnier. In the book *On Cukor* (1972), the director confided to writer Gavin Lambert, "It wasn't much good. . . . I'd be in great shock if they [the archives] rescued this one. (I remember that I enjoyed working with Kay Francis and Walter Huston, though.)"

With James Hall and Jeanette MacDonald in *Let's Go Native* ('30).

With husband Kenneth MacKenna in 1931.

During the filming of *The Virtuous Sin,* which had more interesting scenery (Louise Long) than dialogue (Martin Brown), Kay had two professional pleasures: enjoying her reunion with stage and film co-lead Walter Huston, and becoming better acquainted with Kenneth MacKenna,* the stage and film actor. Although each partner would deny the romance to the press, it was an actuality. Here again, Kay revealed her cynical and practical nature. Just as she preferred to drive a simple Ford car ("It gets you there!" she snapped to one status-conscious friend who wondered why she did not have a Rolls Royce), so now she was weary of matrimonial involvements that would endanger her already burgeoning assets. She insisted that a legal agreement be drawn up between her and MacKenna which would counteract the Califor-

nia community property laws. In any event, the couple wed on Saturday, January 17, 1931, at Avalon on Catalina Island. MacKenna was the son of Leo Mielziner who had painted her portrait and the brother of stage set designer Jo Mielziner.

Kay concluded 1930 with yet another motion picture, this one made at MGM. It was *Passion Flower,* another sudsy romance, which was directed by Cecil B. DeMille's brother, William. In his autobiography, *Bulls, Balls, Bicycles, and Actors* (1965), outspoken Charles Bickford recalled this picture "as a dreadful piece of claptrap. . . . I threatened to walk out of the studio rather than play in the thing. . . . Of all the bad pictures I have appeared in, and there were many, *Passion Flower* takes the cake."

Actually, *Passion Flower,* based on Kathleen Norris' novel, was no better or worse than a lot of other turgid romances turned out by the studios in the early Thirties. It offered Kay Francis as the unpleasant cousin of Kay Johnson, the former craving the latter's stevedore-farmer husband (Bickford). In reviewing this Decem-

*Born Leo Mielziner, Jr. on August 19, 1899, in Canterbury, New Hampshire, he was educated in London and Paris and later at Columbia University. He debuted on Broadway in *At 9:45* in 1919, and later appeared in such shows as *Insect Comedy, What Every Woman Knows* (with Helen Hayes), and *You and I.* He made silent features at Paramount's Astoria studio in 1925-1926, and in 1929 was under contract to Fox Films.

With Kay Johnson and Dickie Moore in *Passion Flower* ('30).

ber 1930 release, the *New York Times* judged, "The good work of the players and the competent direction of William de Mille are somewhat vitiated by strained psychology, strangely vacillating characters, and uneven dialogue. The quality of subtlety is conspicuous by its absence...." But critic Mordaunt Hall of the *Times* noted, "Kay Francis does exceptionally well as the fashionably clad Dulce."

With Kay being seen on the screen in 1930 in such an array of impressively dressed if not well-scripted characterizations, it is little wonder that she rose to being one of the top Hollywood stars of the time. Exhibitors noted that her name on a marquee spelled top business, and fan magazines consistently featured her photo and requested interviews. Unfortunately, as it turned out for Kay, she had too little patience with the interest of her growing public, maintaining a right to her privacy and brandishing a "get lost" temperament with the press that would eventually militate against her. When *Photoplay* magazine first visited Kay in 1929 at her Hollywood bungalow (she was a very parsimonious creature despite the seeming opulence with which she entertained herself and others), she was flip and cursory during the interview.

> *Photoplay:* Do the camera and mike scare you?
> *Kay:* No! What is there in a mike to scare you after you are used to 1500 people?
> *Photoplay:* Do you miss the theatre?
> *Kay:* Yes, I miss it some, but this is a great chance for me, and everyone at Paramount is swell to me, and I'm happy. Will you have a dash more of that ginger ale?"

Even when accoladed at the time with the indubitable honor of being the screen's best-dressed woman, Kay replied cynically but truthfully, "I'm not well-dressed on the screen—I'm usually over-dressed."

Paramount did what it could to increase Kay's friendliness toward the public, and meanwhile rushed her into one 1931 release after another, scarcely allowing her sufficient time to change her clothes, freshen her makeup, and recomb her latest hairdo. In *Scandal Sheet,* directed by John Cromwell, George Bancroft and Clive Brook were the leading men, with Kay fluctuating between banker-husband Bancroft and embezzler-lover Brook. *Ladies' Man* benefited from Herman J. Mankiewicz's scenario and was a sophisticated offering. It showcased William Powell as the suave cad who makes his well-heeled livelihood from fleecing others. As Norma Page, Kay is the one true love of gigolo Powell, despite the presence of lovely, younger Rachel Fendley (Carole Lombard—offcamera she began dating Powell and they would wed later in 1931). Kay in every way proved to be Powell's equal as the world-weary out-of-towner who finds a new meaning to love in his embraces. But fate had cruel plans for her; Powell later falls to his death and she must carry on alone.

The Vice Squad matched Kay with Hungarian leading man Paul Lukas; *Transgression* (on loan to RKO) saw elegant Kay dallying with Ricardo Cortez while husband Paul Cavanagh is in India; *Guilty Hands* (on loan to MGM) found Lionel Barrymore prosecuting poor but well-groomed Kay for a crime that he committed; *24 Hours* reteamed her with Clive Brook as mutually cheating spouses (Miriam Hopkins, Kay's good friend, was the third co-star of this sixty-five-minute vehicle).

For her seventh and final 1931 release, Kay had the benefit of George Cukor as director, and a screenplay based on a Zöe Akins story. In *On Cukor,* Cukor reminisced, "On the screen, because of censorship, there was a kind of innocence about her [Akins'] tarts. They had lovely clothes and lots of money and a succession of rich men who were mad about them, but they always said 'Good night' at the door. Of course, the audience smelled something, they thought, 'Well, they may say "good night," but where the hell do they get all those clothes?'... How about Kay Francis? Wasn't she decorative?"

On Cukor writer Gavin Lambert had his comments on Kay during this period: "Kay Francis was always a bit schmaltzy—she wore clothes very well and managed to signal that her happiness wouldn't last, there'd be tears after the party. Almost like a silent movie heroine."

The fashionable star in 1931.

With Ricardo Cortez in *Transgression* ('31).

There is a good deal to recommend the sixty-six-minute *Girls About Town,* from the two contrasting, golddigging leading ladies (Kay and Lilyan Tashman) to the hero (Joel McCrea) and an engaging supporting cast (Eugene Pallette, Lucille Webster Gleason, Alan Dinehart, George Barbier, and Robert McWade). There are some very pleasant moments within the photoplay. One scene finds Kay and McCrea at the zoo, with the camera tracking them as they glide past the various cages, with the players' conversation interrupted as they stop to look at the animals. Another moment finds Kay stripping down to her skimpy lingerie and revealing a gem of a figure.

Kay continued her upward swing as a popular movie star. She was a woman not only desired by men who saw a challenge in her cool reserve and admired by women who envied her wardrobe and romantic triangles, but an actress coveted by other Hollywood studios. Unfortunately, Paramount was facing considerable financial woe. After Kay completed her contractual agreement with the studio via insipid roles in the weak films *The False Madonna* (1932) and *Strangers in Love* (1932) with Fredric March, the film company hesitated to renew her contract until it figured out how much it could afford to offer her.

The hesitation was a mistake Paramount would bitterly lament. Crafty Jack L. Warner, monarch of the Warner Bros.' Burbank lot, learned of the situation across town and called Myron Selznick (the foul-mouthed agent and brother of equally shrewd producer David O. Selznick) to plot strategy. Paramount had not only failed to re-sign Kay immediately, but also had left options open on such other premier attractions as William Powell and Ruth Chatterton.

MGM might have had more stars than in the heavens, but no leading producer in town placed more emphasis on maintaining a top contract roster than did Jack Warner. In 1931, his studio overworked James Cagney, who had blazed a pugnacious trail to stardom in *The Public Enemy;* laureated George Arliss, prestige star of the monocled school of elegant acting; detonated John Barrymore in two Grand Guignol entries, *Svengali* and *The Mad Genius;* built new character lead Edward G. Robinson, the powerful star of *Little Caesar* and *Five Star Final;* gave wide-mouthed Joe E. Brown reason to howl in comedies such as *Broadminded;* and, in general, put such popular workers as Loretta Young, Barbara Stanwyck, Constance Bennett, Dorothy Mackaill, Warren William, Joan Blondell, Aline MacMahon, Frank McHugh, and Marian Marsh through exhausting six-days-a-week, fifteen-hours-a-day paces. In 1931 alone, Warner Bros. had turned out sixty-three full-length releases. Its stable of actors prevented the studio from having to do much star borrowing from other film factories.

At any rate, under Warner's personal orders, Myron Selznick furtively approached Ruth Chatterton, William Powell, and Kay, making lucrative and solid contract offers. To the horror of Paramount, the trio of VIP players accepted the terms approved by Warner, placing three new feathers in J. L.'s producer cap and establishing the lusty Selznick as the top agent in the business. None of this delighted Paramount which hurried to court to attempt to reclaim its three attractions. The law had sympathy for Paramount and agreed to order Warner to loan Kay back to the lot at a time mutually agreeable. But for all intents and purposes, 1932 saw Kay Francis as a Warner Bros. star. (Ironically, had she remained with Paramount she would have enjoyed a salary increase on a fifty-two—not a forty—week basis, plus a $15,000 bonus, all told more money than the $4,000 weekly salary the brothers Warner were offering her at the start.)

Kay celebrated her changeover by renting the home of ex-Western star William S. Hart for two years. It was a step up from the six-room bungalow she had occupied on De Longpre Avenue when she first came to Hollywood. Her companion remained Ida, a black woman, who worked as Kay's maid and secretary. Once in the Hart abode, she also hired a gardener and cook.

The Burbank publicity department immediately ballyhooed Kay as a new member of the studio's impressive star line-up. Among the material the promotional releases turned out about her was such inside information as, "Has very tender vocal cords and is unable to scream when called upon to do so; to save her throat has someone else scream for her." Meanwhile, the studio propelled her into an exhausting regime, and by the end of April 1932, her fourth official month as a Warner star, she had already completed a quartet of films.

The first two were disappointments for the high-priced actress. *Man Wanted* starred her with soft but handsome David Manners, the young, self-effacing leading man whose quiet acting style and quiet temperament made him the ideal screen mate for actresses with loud acting styles.* Warner Bros. shivered when their teaming Kay with Manners backfired. *Variety* coyly noted, "Miss Francis . . . slightly suffers in comparison with Manners. His youth emphasizes a maturity in her screen personality which, charming as it is, should not be so endangered." *Street of Women*** went into distribution one month later, casting Kay as a beautifully gowned (by Orry-Kelly), understanding mistress. It bored most viewers and apparently failed to stimulate Kay herself, who was critiqued as being apathetic in her portrayal. Warners, who had stretched its budget to lure Kay to the lot, began to panic. However, her next film, *Jewel Robbery,* reteaming her with William Powell (she was a hasty replacement for Barbara Stanwyck), brought top results. In this William Dieterle-directed bit of frou-frou, Powell was a robber, Kay was the bored wife of a stodgy banker (Henry Kolker), and together the lovers make the picture a continental delight. This film, by the way, contained a scene in which a doped cigarette was passed about, captivating audiences then fascinated by the little-known topic of marijuana.

Then came the motion picture that boosted Kay to the popularity peak where Warner Bros. expected her to roost. This was the classic sudser *One Way Passage* (1932). Powell as a convict en route to the electric chair, Kay as a mature play-

*Recently David Manners spoke of *Man Wanted:* "Andy Devine and I behaved very badly in that. We were whooping it up one day and Kay Francis walked off the set. She sent back word that she'd return to work when those two 'apes' quieted down."

**In *Here's Looking at You, Kid* (1976) scenarist Mary McCall recollects: "I wasn't a very ardent fan of Miss Francis, and I didn't know that she had a speech impediment and couldn't pronounce words with 'r's in them. Every character in my script had an 'r' in their name. The grand climax came when she rang for her secretary, Sarah, and said, 'Sawah, I want to have my bwotha's woom wedecowated.'"

With David Manners in *Man Wanted* ('32).

In *Jewel Robbery* ('32).

On the set of *One Way Passage* ('32) with William Powell.

81

girl dying of heart disease, and an ocean voyage from Hong Kong to San Francisco during which the two fall blissfully in love were the ingredients which made this film one of the Thirties' great tearjerkers.

Tay Garnett, who also worked on the script, directed *One Way Passage*. In his memoirs, *Light Your Torches and Pull Up Your Tights* (1973), he recalls that Kay was almost *not* cast in the picture because Darryl F. Zanuck, then a top Warner Bros. producer, found her speech impediment too distressing.

> Zanuck's reaction to my treatment was, "Jeez, Tay, it's GREAT. How soon can you be ready to shoot?"
>
> I got a fast nod to my request for [Wilson] Mizner and [Joseph] Jackson [as scripters], so I tested my luck a little further. For leads I wanted Bill Powell and Kay Francis.
>
> "You had Powell before you came in," said Zanuck. "But what about Kay's speech impediment?"
>
> "I can write around that. All I have to do is duck any word beginning with R or L." (I remembered having heard Kay read the line, "It wouldn't be right, even if we are in love," as "It wouldn't be wight, even if we ah in wuv.")
>
> Darryl snapped, "It's *your* problem."

Still, Kay's first line in the film, as she bumps into smooth Powell in a crowded Hong Kong honky tonk, is "Oh! I'm so sowwy!" But why quibble? *One Way Passage* is a delight, with the stars matchless in their elegantly morbid paces, breaking champagne glasses, and receiving excellent support from such stock company regulars as Frank McHugh, Aline MacMahon,* and

---

*MacMahon would recall, "Warners engaged a broken-down iron boat for location shooting and sent the cast offshore, allowing us some fantastic sum like thirty-seven cents a day for food. It was an uncomfortable assignment and we were all pretty miserable. It was boiling hot. The food was terrible. The kids got drunk, and Tay Garnett took this occasion to be difficult. So the assistants were doing what work there was done—which wasn't much. Finally, the studio lost patience and brought us back to the lot to finish it. Through it all Miss Francis behaved with great dignity and did her work without complaint."

Warren Hymer. Powell and Kay handled some of the more sappy dialogue of their careers with perfect aplomb. For example, they jokingly sing the old hymn about the "Golden Gates . . . Keep those gates ajar," as they pass under the Golden Gate Bridge:

> *Powell:* I was born here in San Francisco. And when I was a youngster, I used to think they were singing about this Golden Gate. I thought it was the only one.
> *Kay:* I hope you were wrong.
> *Powell:* I hope so. . . .

Even the most cynical of audiences who chuckled at such romantics (and 1932 exhibitors reported that the film indeed drew its share of laughs in the wrong spots) were moved by the finale, when Kay bids goodbye to Powell, he being in police custody.

> *Kay:* Dan! . . . Goodbye, Dan!
> *Powell:* Not goodbye, dear! Auf Wiedersehen! Until New Year's Eve . . .
> *Kay:* Auf Wiedersehen. . . .

Later Kay has died and Powell has been executed. But on New Year's Eve, as mayhem breaks loose at midnight, two bartenders in the resort town of Agua Caliente accuse each other of breaking glasses at the bar. The camera zooms in, and there, in all its glorious schmaltz, are the crossed stems of two champagne glasses—provided by the lovers' ghosts, who have kept their New Year's date. It was truly one of the decade's most unabashedly tear-seducing finales.

One Way Passage was a box-office success. "By far the best movie that Kay Francis and William Powell have turned out as a team. . . . Swell stuff," reported *Photoplay*. The film won Kay great acclaim. Kay herself was pleased. Garnett recalls in his autobiography, "After the preview, Kay Francis rushed from the theatre weeping wildly. Throwing her arms around me, she sobbed, 'It's heartbweaking. It's the most moving film I've eveh seen.'" It was, however, the last film teaming of Kay and Powell. The debonair star soon became miffed at Warner

With Charles Ruggles and Edward Everett Horton in *Trouble in Paradise* ('32).

Bros. when the studio, in a patriotic depression move, cut his weekly paycheck from $6,000 to $4,000. Later he defected to MGM where he achieved his greatest cinema successes, especially when teamed with Myrna Loy. Warner Bros. would attempt to duplicate the profits of *One Way Passage* by remaking the story in 1940 as *'Til We Meet Again* with Merle Oberon and George Brent starred. It failed to live up to the original in any way.

Kay's popularity was rapidly rising. The studio softened her screen image, emphasizing even more her widow's peak, the most famous in movie annals until MGM's Robert Taylor came along in the mid-Thirties. In fact Kay was, with the release of *One Way Passage,* quickly gaining ground on the "Queen" of the Warner Bros. lot, Ruth Chatterton. No actress at the Burbank facility appeared to be any real competition for Kay. Certainly, in her worst nightmare, Miss Francis would have never imagined that a new, pop-eyed blonde contract player, Bette Davis, would soon begin a dizzying climb to fame that

would overthrow Kay's reign as royal mother of Burbank.

Meanwhile Paramount, despite the arrival of Mae West, was still combating bankruptcy threats and jumped now to order Kay back to the studio as their court victory warranted. Warner Bros. sent her across town, and promised Kay that, upon her return, a musical, *42nd Street,* would await her.

Upon her re-entry at the Paramount facility, Kay put on a rebellious, haughty manner; the film had forced her to cancel a planned four-month vacation. Also, Kay learned that her pal, volatile Miriam Hopkins, whom she had topped in billing in 1931's *24 Hours,* would *now* precede her in the billing of *Trouble in Paradise* (1932). Obviously, this was done out of deference to Miss Hopkins, who had the loyalty to stay on the floundering studio's payroll during its crisis.

Actually *Trouble in Paradise* emerged as a delightful comedy, produced and directed by the stylish Ernst Lubitsch (it is his favorite picture) with a flair that hides the fact that the tempestuous Miriam and explosive Kay were at complete odds with one another throughout the entire filming. The plot, in which Hopkins and polished Herbert Marshall plan to fleece wealthy widow Kay only to have Marshall fall for her, was heralded by *The Nation* as "thoroughly delightful," and the *New York Herald-Tribune* found Kay's performance to be "excellent." It was a charming, adult film, but the fact that Kay, potentially the cinema's most charming actress of sophisticated comedy, benefited from Lubitsch, the cinema's finest director of sophisticated comedy, made little impression on her. To mercurial Kay, *Trouble in Paradise* spelled canceled vacation and billing inequity. She would never make another film at Paramount.

Kay returned to Burbank in a mighty huff. Lubitsch, with his meticulous filming methods, had run over schedule on *Trouble in Paradise* and with the big-budgeted *42nd Street* all ready to start, Warner Bros. had to replace her with

Bebe Daniels. Kay was angry, and understandably so. The musical was a smash and would certainly have presented soigné Kay to huge audiences in a top production. (Granted Bebe Daniels' role as the actress replaced in the big show by younger Ruby Keeler was not the focal point, but it might have been with Kay's presence and a few scripting alterations.)

Kay made sure that the front office felt her wrath. In compensation, the studio lent her out again, this time to Samuel Goldwyn for his highly touted *Cynara* (1932). This King Vidor-directed romance again co-starred Kay with Ronald Colman, the man with the boudoir voice. It dealt with an attorney who becomes involved with a girl (Phyllis Barry) and with whom he has an affair while the wife (Kay) is away tending to an errant relative. The superbly done tragedy was acclaimed, but it was Colman, not Kay as the patient, well-groomed wife, who won a set of effusive notices.

By the close of 1932, Kay was indeed one of

With Ronald Colman, Florence Britton, and C. Montague Shaw in *Cynara* ('32).

the most worshipped stars* of the movies, a favorite of fan magazine covers, a prime target of fan mail writers, and a top-paid property. The actress, however, soon began to lose sight of the art of acting. Unlike Bette Davis, Katharine Hepburn, Barbara Stanwyck, and other stars who shrewdly planned their amazingly durable careers, Kay allowed herself to be dazzled by the fame and fortune. At the close of 1932, a *Photoplay* writer managed to be invited to (or, more realistically, placed at) a New Year's Eve party Kay and husband MacKenna hosted at New York's Chateau Elysee Hotel. Kay almost forgot about the journalist as she fluttered, caressed, and drank with the "dahling" set. Upon her return to Hollywood, the star did not place her emphasis on what the role would allow her to show onscreen. Instead, she was far more concerned with how she could wangle some vacation time to travel to Europe or what new bonus luxury she could enjoy from the pampering studio. Unlike most other highly-paid stars, Kay was not a free-spender, preferring to hoard her money for the proverbial rainy day. (She could be very generous, however, with friends in need.) But she was considered a festive adornment at any social gathering, and had no problem being invited to instead of hostessing the swankiest parties of the decade.

Meanwhile, the Warner Bros. contract roll was growing. George Brent had signed his services there, and Warners decided to team Kay with the stocky, well-bred Irishman, the actor who would have been her vis-à-vis in *42nd Street.* There was some irony in the situation since Brent had wed rival Ruth Chatterton in

1932. Kay and Brent's first joint vehicle was *The Keyhole* (1933). Studio workhorse Michael Curtiz directed this sixty-nine-minute diversion which had many flaws. Brent was forced to enact the unappealing role of a professional stool pigeon (a divorce detective) while Kay was allowed to be little more than a mannequin as she modeled her newest Orry-Kelly wardrobe.

Although the *New York Times* would lament that this Radio City Music Hall attraction "sways from the sublime to the mundane," it had a fair share of entertainment value.

The Robert Presnell scenario provided quite a bit of action. Kay is Anne Brooks, wed to wealthy, much older Schuyler Brooks (played by Henry Kolker, her frequent onscreen spouse). As it develops, Kay had a sordid past. She had been the blonde member of the dance team of Valentine and Maurice, and her ex-partner, slimy Maurice Le Brun (Monroe Owsley), is blackmailing her. She has already given him $10,000 and he wants $50,000 more. Her sister-in-law (Helen Ware) suggests that Kay go to Havana and once there lead Maurice on, while it is arranged for foreigner Le Brun to be denied re-entry into the country. Possessive Schuyler meanwhile believes that Kay is two-timing him and hires slick Neil Davis (Brent) to follow Kay and to learn the truth of her activities. As Brent smirkingly tells Schuyler, "You want me to find out something you don't even dare think."

No Thirties movie seemed complete without comedy relief, and *The Keyhole* was "blessed" with Allen Jenkins as Brent's dumb, crude, but likeable assistant and Glenda Farrell as the perennial golddigger. The comic interaction and asides were occasionally amusing but definitely distracting. There was one delicious moment, however, as Jenkins, putting on airs for the supposedly wealthy Miss Farrell, admits, "Every spring we go to the Falls; every fall we go the Springs."

And since a shipboard romance had worked wonders for Kay in *One Way Passage,* it cropped up again as she and Brent fall in love on their way from New York to Havana, aboard the *Santiago.* They exchange worldly thoughts: "Leaving champagne in the bottom of the glass is like leaving moonlight left untouched."

Once in Cuba, Brent becomes more reluctant

---

*A recurrent theme among interviews with the illustrious Miss Francis was that degree of aloofness which clung to her on the set. As one public relations man of the Thirties would rationalize this professional situation, "Kay was an original. She wasn't like some of the great beauties who never smiled because they might develop lines. She wasn't vain. She was warm and funny about herself if she trusted you. But that was on a personal level. She just didn't want to bother with publicity."

Costume designer Orry-Kelly would say of Kay, "In the beginning, she was very reserved but well mannered and knew exactly what she wanted. I designed simple unadorned evening gowns in velvet, chiffon, and crepe for *One Way Passage.* And I introduced what was the forerunner of the shirtmaker dress for evening.... At first, only those with sensitive taste were impressed. Luckily, Kay was the essence of good taste." [One does wonder, in retrospect, why designer Orry-Kelly always seemed to fashion gowns for Kay that zoomed to a lower cleavage point than with any other actress, especially since Miss Francis was so notoriously flat-chested.]

Clothes

SCREENLAND presents a new slant on screen fashions! Here we show you not only the star's dress, but how it looks in action

And here is Kay's gown in action. For kissable shoulders, this strap effect is strongly recommended! The pictures above and to the right show you Miss Francis with her leading man, George Brent, in scenes from "The Keyhole."

Here's Kay Francis posing for us in the Grecian-influence gown she wears in her latest film, "The Keyhole." Of ivory brocaded velvet, it has the flowing lines and even the corded girdle of its classic model. The shoulder treatment is particularly interesting.

Suggested for summer evenings: a frock of yellow chiffon with petalled flounce; and, if possible, a cape bordered with silver fox! Kay Francis, right, poses for you in this striking ensemble. Extreme right, the same costume in graceful action.

Photographs by Elmer Fryer, especially posed for SCREENLAND. Costumes by Orry-Kelly.

With George Brent in a fashion layout for *The Keyhole* ('33).

to inform on Kay's innocent activities, and wonders how to separate his job from his personal feelings. The film climaxes with Maurice's accidental death, and Kay's admission to Schuyler that she can never trust him again. ("After all," he has said to her, "I picked you up out of nothing; you can go back to nothing for all I care.") Wrapping up the tale, Brent admits, "I'm not a private detective anymore. . . . I'm not a sneak. . . . I am just someone who loves you."

But it is Kay's presence that gives the film class. Whether confronting Maurice in his cheap Manhattan hotel room ("The next time you try to kill yourself, let me know. I'd like to try and help you"), enduring her husband's crass ways, or romancing on a Cuban beach with Brent ("I found something here I've always longed for"), she makes the proceedings almost believable. Realistically, what can a star do with dialogue such as her final speech: "No one's to blame. It had to happen, I guess. . . . We worry and struggle to solve our little problems and it's over just like that."

While Warner Bros. wondered just what the correct Kay Francis film formula should be, they lent her out again. This time her temporary employer was MGM, where she again starred with Walter Huston in *Storm at Daybreak* (1933). Under Richard Boleslavsky's direction, the production values were expansive in this study of the revolution-torn Balkans, but the scenario was old-hat, and the formula of presentation too much like that of a silent melodrama. Huston was the cuckolded husband who goes to his death to save Kay and her lover (Nils Asther), his best friend.

Meanwhile, Kay's home studio had decided that Kay, along with being a soap-opera heroine par excellence, could also be a perfect "professional woman" onscreen. Hence, her next release was *Mary Stevens, M.D.* (1933), a Lloyd Bacon-directed film casting Kay as a professional woman in a soap opera. The weeper saw Kay sacrifice her illegitimate child to save a fleet of children during a shipboard epidemic. Lyle Talbot was the refined villain of the piece and Glenda Farrell provided enough expert comedy to keep things from getting too sticky. *Variety* noted of *Mary Stevens, M.D.* that it was "exceptionally good adult entertainment."

With George Arliss terminating his Warners' stay, the studio was newly promoting both Edward G. Robinson and Paul Muni as the "class" actors of the lot. In what must have been a clear case of an acting contest, the studio assigned both actors to almost identical plots: concerning the odd subject of meat packing. Muni starred in 1933's *The World Changes* and Robinson led the cast of *I Loved a Woman*, which beat Muni's showcase into release by one month. Kay played an opera singer with whom Robinson is enamored. Her brief singing interludes, mostly of popular material, were dubbed by Rose Dirman. In his memoirs, *All My Yesterdays* (1973), published after his death, Robinson wrote of the picture, "Let me give a small bow to Kay Francis. . . . She had that indefinable presence that somehow enabled her to be convincing as well as beautiful."

Nevertheless, *I Loved a Woman* gave a glimpse of the career problems Kay was to face at Warners. Three of her best scenes were deleted from the release print and, despite her lofty status, the studio gave her only featured billing. Genevieve Tobin as Robinson's wife, received equal screen time to Kay. There was another indelicacy at the Hollywood premiere of the film. Bette Davis, who was *not* involved with the picture at all, attended the festivities with all eight of the men that the columnists had been linking her with, upstaging all of the talents associated with the picture.

The mystery of why Warners treated Kay in so progressively a shabby manner has been the cause of much speculation. There were several reasons. Kay had indeed become a big attraction, but a large number of her films had not done good business at the theatres. The front office was very upset over this. They were paying Kay $4,000 weekly, second now on the lot only to Ruth Chatterton whose days as a $9,375-a-week star had just about collapsed due to box-office apathy. Then there was Kay's willingness to appear in almost any property the studio thrust at her. Years later, she would explain her (rather weak) rationale, "I don't think a star knows when a story is right for her—or him. We read a script with an eye to our own part, rather than to the story as a whole. The studios have done pretty well for me. They've made me an im-

With Walter Huston and Nils Asther in a pose for *Storm at Daybreak* ('33).

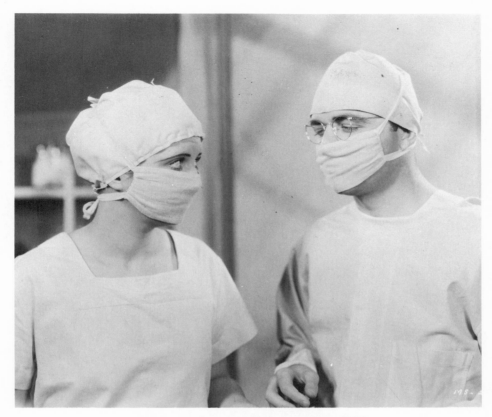

With Lyle Talbot in *Mary Stevens, M.D.* ('33).

portant star and they pay me good money. If they put me in poor stories they lessen my box-office value and the returns on their investment won't be so good. Why shouldn't I rely on their judgment?" This was a rather foolish laissez-faire attitude, to say the least, in the jungle known as Hollywood.

Another career problem for Kay was that her private life was in none-too-good shape. In June of 1933, Kay had confided to *Photoplay* on the subject of divorce, "It's pride that goads women on to an unforgiving attitude. They simply can't believe it. . . . Unless a marriage is just all wrong from the beginning, unless two people are hopelessly mismated, I do think a woman can plan her happiness. . . . It isn't necessary to dash into the divorce court and come out with a decree which eventually may tear her life to pieces."

This sermon had hardly left her lips when rumors of her growing discord with her husband were substantiated. The couple would separate "amicably" on December 20, 1933, and in late February 1934 she and MacKenna would divorce. She stated to the judge, "He continually

nagged and harassed me. He didn't like my selection of a home, my manner of dressing, or even my acting. He assumed an air of superiority and for months made slighting remarks about me."* Unmentioned by the gentlemanly Mac-Kenna was that when Kay would become drunk (as sometimes happened after a tough day on the set), she would become vicious in her denunciation of his Jewish background, and say anything that might goad him into a hoped-for retaliation. She could be quite brutal when under the influence of liquor.

The year 1933 ended professionally for Kay with the release of *The House on 56th Street,* directed by Robert Florey. Kay was a last-minute replacement for Ruth Chatterton who rejected

*Kenneth MacKenna would later wed actress Mary Phillips, who had once been wed to Humphrey Bogart. In the mid-Thirties he returned to stage acting. In 1937 he became New York story editor for MGM and two years later he was brought to Hollywood to be studio story editor; later he took over the control of the scenario department. From 1942 to 1946 he was a major in the Signal Corps, as director of the Morale Films Division. He returned to MGM in 1948. His final stage appearance was in Dore Schary's *The Highest Tree* (1959). MacKenna died on January 15, 1962, in California.

89

With Edward G. Robinson in *I Loved a Woman* ('33).

90

the role. In *The Great Romantic Films* (1974), author Lawrence J. Quirk generously judges this to be "Kay Francis' finest performance, in the type of role that made her a household name in the 1930s." The sixty-eight-minute feature covers the period 1905 to 1933 with Kay as a member of the New York Floradora Sextet who weds the scion (Gene Raymond) of Manhattan society. Later she is sent to prison for the manslaughter death of her ex-beau (John Halliday). Twenty years later, the middle-aged heroine is released from prison, but told by her in-laws (Raymond has died in World War I) to take a sum of money and never see her now-adult daughter. But Kay and her girl (Margaret Lindsay) are destined to meet. Kay, who has become an accomplished con artist, is placed in charge of the gaming rooms at a midtown speakeasy—yes, the old house on 56th Street. Lindsay later becomes embroiled in a manslaughter episode ("like mother like daughter") and is protected from discovery by Kay's boss, William "Stage" Boyd. Boyd's price is that restless Kay promise to stay in his employment "forever."

Writer Quirk has glowing regard for the film and Kay in his survey book *The Great Romantic Films.* "[It] is replete with poignant keynote scenes—the shot where she [Kay] looks up, after twenty years, at the house where all her lost happiness is buried; her first meeting with her daughter, now grown, who is unaware that the sad-eyed, sleek, chicly gowned woman is her mother; her cynical, hard-eyed stance and gestures that conceal a heart long broken but now freshly bleeding, as she deals expert blackjack in what was once her child's nursery. . . . The film does full credit to the distinctive talents of Kay Francis, one of the more underrated stars of her era. . . . Miss Francis made an ideal 'woman's picture' heroine, portraying the many ways of love with an eloquent sincerity and cool authority."

Next on Kay's agenda was another Ruth Chatterton hand-me-down, *Mandalay* (1934), stylishly directed by Michael Curtiz. The film is more highly regarded today than when it was released. Then came another Warner Bros. blow-up. Al Jolson, who had baptized the commercial talking screen, had been relatively inactive in

With Reginald Owen in *Mandalay* ('34).

91

With Ricardo Cortez, Dolores Del Rio, Al Jolson, and Dick Powell in a pose for *Wonder Bar* ('34).

Hollywood in the mid-Thirties. Warners, who had produced *The Jazz Singer* (1927), wooed the egomaniacal entertainer back to the fold (his wife Ruby Keeler was then a big studio star), promising him ten percent of the profits if he would star in a musical. Jolson agreed. The vehicle selected was *Wonder Bar* (1934), which he had played on Broadway and on tour. Since Jolson had been out of the cinemagoer's eye for a bit (his 1933 vehicle, *Hallelujah, I'm a Bum,* had not been a success), the studio safeguarded box-office stability by casting Kay and Dick Powell in the picture.

But once again the studio treated Kay unfairly, assigning her the role of Liane Renaud, the faithless wife of Henry Kolker. "It was a small, inconsequential part and I believe (and still believe) that I should not have been forced, by my contract, to play it," said Kay to *Silver Screen* magazine several months later. To compound the slight, the studio trimmed Kay's scenes to pad the parts of Jolson and a Mexican beauty named Dolores Del Rio. Rather than walk off

the film (as Bette Davis would have done) and tolerate a studio suspension, Kay instead stayed on, venting her pique at director Lloyd Bacon and giving an indifferent performance. *Variety* reported that "Miss Francis plays her faithless wife role with a superciliousness and condescension not in keeping with the assignment." In later years, Kay admitted that she wished she had walked out on the production that showcased so pleasantly the talents of Jolson, Del Rio, Powell, and even Ricardo Cortez (in his "Tango Del Rio" number with Dolores) while wasting her as a box-office insurance policy.

Shortly after the flames died down on this production, Warners cast Kay in the title role of *Dr. Monica* (1934) in which she delivers an illegitimate baby that turns out to be sired by her husband (Warren William). The embarrassment, heartache, and frustration of the situation leads Kay to inform her swank pal (Verree Teasdale), "I'm afraid to think. . . . I don't dare to talk." It was the usual operatics, but congenially handled by director William Keighley. Jean Muir as the husband-stealing aviatrix almost stole the picture.

But Kay's next, *British Agent* (1934), was a well-mounted, sweeping story of the Russian Revolution teaming Kay with top-billed Leslie Howard. (It was clearly his vehicle.) Kay is good Russian Elena, secretary to Lenin, and torn between her duty and love for Howard who functions as the title character. The stars made a nice team, and Kay was effective indeed in one of the best of her Warners' outings. Shortly afterwards, she explained her success in such roles: "I try to strike a balance, to make these women thoroughly rounded individuals. Professionally, they must be competent, but it mustn't make them hard or cold or destroy their appeal in their scenes of private life."

Meanwhile, Kay played real-life episodes in which she did destroy some of her appeal as a human being. In 1934, the press gave ample coverage to an incident at the Newark (New Jersey) airport where Kay "flew" at a news photographer who snapped her picture.

Offcamera, Kay had become the object of Maurice Chevalier's affection. His marriage to Yvonne Vallée had faltered, and he found the sultry Miss Francis—not to mention Marlene Dietrich and sundry others—welcome diversions from his depression. It was rumored in the press that the Frenchman and Kay would wed, once it was legally possible, but self-sufficient, independent Kay denied such possibilities. "Good friends" was how she termed her relationship with Chevalier. Director Robert Florey would recall, "When all was going well in his love affair [with Kay], he could be very gay; he would dance around and hum [Victor] Schertzinger tunes or some of his early songs. But then, when he was unhappy, I would find him despondent and talking about returning to Paris immediately. Charles Boyer has told me he used to witness the same kind of emotional outbursts."

By this point in Kay's career, Ruth Chatterton had left the Warner lot, a colossal disappointment to the studio which had expected her

With Jean Muir in *Dr. Monica* ('34).

93

With Maxine Doyle, Louella Parsons, and Phil Regan on radio in 1934.

appeal to build a whole new soundstage area for them. Officially (in salary terms) this made $4,000-per-week Kay the female superstar of the lot, a title unwarranted by her popularity. Far more attention caressed irrepressible Bette Davis whose performance on loan-out to RKO for *Of Human Bondage* (1934) won her many fans and the admiration of critics. Still, Kay saw no reason to worry. Bette's salary was not one-fifth of hers. Miss Francis allowed Warners to waste her throughout 1935 in a series of unworthy romantic dramas that kept her secure in her free-wheeling lifestyle. Unknown to her, she was rapidly tiring the public.

Before reteaming with George Brent for *Living on Velvet* and *Stranded*—made back-to-back in 1935—Kay took another European sojourn (she was traveling with scripter Delmer Daves,* but the press said she was chasing Chevalier), stopping in New York City upon her return and granting an interview to *Colliers'* magazine. In her usual unfriendly style, Kay took pot shots at her fans, claiming that if acting "looks like a life of ease, let any business girl try it." She went on to detail a typical Kay Francis working day:

> I get up in the morning at a quarter of six if I'm going to wear an evening dress [oncamera]. That sentence sounds a little ga-ga, doesn't it? But never mind. An evening dress means body makeup. It takes time. Otherwise, I get fifteen minutes more sleep. By nine I am at the studio, made up, and on the set for work. We stop usually at six-thirty in the afternoon. Then comes a talk, probably

with the director and the leading man, sometimes with others, so that we'll be ready with everything thoroughly understood for the next day. After that, we see the rushes of the day's take. At about eight, it's time to go home. I jump into a bath, and am glad to have dinner on a tray in bed. If I don't get to sleep before eleven, I have only seven hours. Just let anyone try to persuade me to go out any evening except Saturday! It can't be done when I'm working.

> This round-the-clock schedule goes on for four or six weeks at a stretch. It makes a long business day in the office feel like a vacation. I have seen switchboard operators plugging long telephone cords in and out in so complicated and rapid a maze that it looked as though they were knitting something, but plugging your own emotions in and out at the same rate all day is infinitely more wearing.

Kay went on to say that acting is a "business-art—neither one separately, but both intermixed," and she paid a weak tribute to her craft with, "I'm like everyone else in every other business—I wouldn't advise anyone to go into it, and nothing could drag me out of it. I've no desire to go back to the stage. I'm happy right where I am. It's never monotonous—it's always interesting—and when you do get a vacation, it's long enough to let you really do things."

Back at the studio, Kay and Brent (who had freed himself of wife Chatterton) did some of their best tandem work in *Living on Velvet* (1935), he as a bitter wastrel, she as a socialite with a heart. The *New York Times* noted that "Mr. Brent's performance is excellent, and Miss Francis displays not merely a new collection of gowns (which had the female members of the audience cooing) but a somewhat surprising talent for comedy in the earlier sequences." Three months later there issued another Francis-Brent vehicle, *Stranded*, incorporating newsreel footage of the construction of the Golden Gate Bridge with the usual problem-plagued romance and the topical subject of

*Thirty-one-year-old Delmer Daves was working at Warner Bros. at the time and was sent by Hal B. Wallis to help eliminate troublesome words from the script of *Stranded* so Kay would not be plagued so badly with her tell-tale lisp. As Daves would recall, ". . . [I] went to her house, introduced myself and the object of my visit . . . and it became . . . 'one of those things,' for we hit it off so well I never left, and we were devoted to each other solely for the next three years, traveling between films. . . . During those years Hedda and/or Louella (both close friends of ours and very tactful in their reportings of our wanders, etc.) would make us Best Bets in their annual Matrimonial Derby columns."

On another occasion (for Lyn Tornabene's biography of Clark Gable, *Long Live the King,* 1976), Daves would recollect: "Kay was a free spirit like Carole [Lombard], and Clark [Gable] loved women who could make him laugh. Carole would invite Kay and me up to dinner."

strikes. Audiences of the day could not readily accept the glamourous Kay delivering a passionate plea to the proletariat ("Never lose your arrogance"). Then, three months after this film, came *The Goose and the Gander,* marketed as a Francis/Brent love teaming, but wisely offering equal time to Genevieve Tobin and Claire Dodd, respectively, as would-be adulteress and a smart-mouthed jewel thief. *Variety* phrased it well, "Miss Francis is pleasant but not outstanding. . . . Misses Tobin and Dodd share the honors."

These screen releases maintained Kay's popularity level but did not increase it, and enraged Warners by not doing brisk box-office business. However, her last 1935 release salvaged the year. *I Found Stella Parish* was a smash hit directed by Mervyn LeRoy who invested the picture with the full four-handkerchief treatment "in the cadence of a graveyard procession" *(New York Times).* Again the plot borrows freely from *Madame X,* with Kay as the famed actress Stella Parish, who does her level best to prevent her daughter (Sybil Jason, touted as "the new five-year-old sensation") from learning of her

sordid lineage. The effort takes Kay from the spotlight of London's most legitimate stages to burlesque and vaudeville, where she does "true confession" exploitation playlets eight times daily. "Wife—Mother—Idolized Darling of the Stage—and Then the Adoring World Found Out She Had Once Been Something Else! . . . A Resplendent Actress Finds Her Perfect Role," decreed the advertisements. Audiences found Kay, immersed in a weepy plot and two leading men (Ian Hunter and Paul Lukas), impossible to resist. It really did not matter to most contemporary audiences that the *New York Times'* reviewer sneered, "Miss Francis's unfortunate lisp continues to plague this corner; it makes even more unbelievable the notion that London could regard her Stella as the Duse of the day."

In late 1935, Kay laughed to interviewer Gladys McVeigh about what Hollywood prophets ominously called "the five-year jinx." With complete assurance and unusual good humor (at least for an interview), she attested, "Of course, everybody knows that a good many players begin to go downhill in prestige after

With Dell Henderson in *I Found Stella Parish* ('35).

they have been before the public for five years. That has happened to a number of very good friends of mine, whom I won't mention. . . . We never stand still in this life. We either go forward or we go backward. That seems to be an eternal law of nature, and I'm going forward!" Ironically, Kay was about to become one of the most tragic and totally sacrificed victims of the "five-year jinx."

By 1936, Paul Muni was indeed the "class" actor of Warner Bros., and of all Hollywood for that matter. Against total front-office opposition, Muni, director William Dieterle, and producer Henry Blanke had pressured Jack L. Warner to allow them to make *The Story of Louis Pasteur*. The screen biography went on to win an exultant international reception, provide Muni with an Oscar, and reap for the studio the huzzahs of the world for turning out so humanitarian an opus. As a result, Warners was now on a full-fledged movie-biography cycle. In considering great lives to adapt to the film medium, the name of Florence Nightingale arose. Her heroic life story was chosen and the studio assigned a task force of top-level talent, including director Dieterle* and producer Blanke, to repeat the *Pasteur* formula. Kay had won praise from a few for supplying so complimentary a picture of the American female, so Warners decided to cast her as the legendary nurse (a part far more suited to the likes of contractees Bette Davis or Josephine Hutchinson).

The selection of Kay for the prestigious production delighted Delmer Daves, still a Warners' screenwriter. It was he who reputedly "sold" her on the idea of tackling the offbeat assignment. With solid class and hands-clasped reverence, Warners inflicted on the public in the summer of 1936 one of the greater celluloid disasters of the decade (even with sixteen minutes cut from the running time).

"KAY FRANCIS as FLORENCE NIGHTINGALE in THE WHITE ANGEL." So read the marquees, with the advertising intoning, "While The Cheers For *Pasteur* Still Echo, Warner Bros. Screens The Story Of Another Great Hero Of Humanity!" The good intentions withered due to a juvenile script (adapted from Lytton Strachey's well-regarded biography), a misgauged release date (summer, when school vacation prevented the classroom ballyhoo that the studio intended to employ), and Kay's inappropriate performance. As *Variety* examined the situation. "There may be a quarrel about Kay Francis in the title role. She handles herself well and the part might ordinarily be considered a plum for any actress. But there seems too much restraint. A more passionate attitude towards the inefficiency and clumsy brutality of mid-Victorian hospitals, a less poised bearing in the face of the military bureaucracy might have made for greater emotional voltage from the spectator's viewpoint." *The Journal of the American Medical Association* summed up Kay's work in one succinct word, "antiseptic."

The White Angel inflicted a permanent wound in the Francis-Warner Bros. relationship. The studio powers reasoned that if Kay could not succeed in a picture in which the best studio talents were supporting her, she was hardly worth her keep. (It was an attitude augmented when Paul Muni's *The Life of Emile Zola* did so wonderfully the following year.) By the time *The White Angel* was released and Kay was collecting consistently dismal notices, Bette Davis had won her first Oscar for Warner Bros.' *Dangerous*.

So it was back to glorified soap opera for Kay, with *Give Me Your Heart* (1936) once again matching her with placid George Brent. It was a well-mounted rehash of that old *Madame X* theme: Kay dips into shattering scandal, then does her all to keep her daughter from learning the sordid truth. It was based on the Joyce Carey play *Sweet Aloes* that had enticed West End audiences but had bored Broadway. The *New York Herald-Tribune*'s evaluation of Kay was becoming more and more characteristic of the critics' attitude towards that aging "clotheshorse with the lisp." As the paper viewed it, "The best-dressed woman in the cinema capital is a well-

---

*Director William Dieterle would later say: "That was a beautiful story but it was, shall I say, written by the wrong people—they wanted to be so correct with the English. We had so much trouble with the English censor; in the end it almost killed the story. . . . The film itself could have been a lot better, but one of the things that we had to face at Warners, a mark, a shadow upon us, was that we hardly ever made a retake after a preview. . . . At Warners the attitude was 'Just let it go, it will sell.' We never really took care. Once Wallis liked it, it was okay."

As Florence Nightingale in *The White Angel* ('36).

98

groomed and handsome decoration to the proceedings but no ornament to its histrionics." For Kay Francis devotees, these were harsh but realistic words.

Ironically, Kay emerged from 1936 as the highest paid employee at Warner Bros. Her salary was reported to the government as $227,500 for forty weeks of work. This was said to be a contributing factor to the faltering studio popularity of the star. No producer on the lot earned such a salary, and certainly Delmer Daves' $39,000 yearly income as a studio scripter paled in comparison. Undoubtedly this must have been one of the reasons for the breakup of Kay and Daves who at various times were reported engaged or secretly wed.

To be fair, the studio still tried to make Kay a marquee lure. *Stolen Holiday* (1936) had found her beautifully adorned as a Parisian model entranced with an elegant swindler (Claude Rains). This version of the Stavisky affair was far more entertaining than the 1974 French edi-

tion with Jean-Paul Belmondo. *Confession** (1937), shot under the title of *One Hour of Romance,* was a remake of *Mazurka* (1936) which starred Pola Negri. Warners had acquired the U.S. distribution rights to Miss Negri's comeback film and shelved it so it would not compete with their version.

In *Confession,* a rampant tearjerker, Kay's one-night indiscretion with a roué (Basil Rathbone) results in husband Ian Hunter walking out and taking their child with him. When Kay later traces her grown daughter (Jane Bryan), she discovers the girl is being lured down that primrose path by the ever-lascivious Rathbone. What else is there to do? Kay shoots the scoundrel.

*William K. Everson in a reappraisal of the film for *Films in Review* (1976) judges, ". . . Kay Francis is surprisingly good in a role that seems to have been deliberately downplayed to take it out of the 'vehicle' category. She is talked about and *heard* before she is seen; her initial appearance is almost casual by the standards of the bravura entrances normally concocted for Francis. For once it's a role for an actress rather than a personality, and she does well with it. . . ."

With Alison Skipworth in *Stolen Holiday* ('36).

99

With Ben Welden in *Confession* ('37).

Regarding the film, *Screenland* magazine reviewed, "Having laughed until we cried at several of the movies this month, I suppose that it is only fair that we should have at least one film to make us cry until we laughed." Kay actually had such dialogue embarrassments as "Someone's at the door! I must go and see who it is!"

Confession's soundstage was the arena for an emotional brawl between Kay and her director, in this case German import Joe May. The European was so fond of the 1936 film original that he decided to duplicate it exactly, using a stop watch to insure that each scene ran exactly as long as the original's! Jane Bryan would later recall the whole mess as "ridiculous," and explained, "We were all marching through the film like sleepwalkers. There was absolutely no spontaneity." While Kay had some strong moments in the film, all were dashed in the closing reels when she appeared singing (courtesy of a dubbed voice) in a sleazy cabaret in a tacky outfit and a frizzy blonde wig so at odds with her well-groomed image that audiences laughed along with the critics.

Another Dawn (1937) was a strange meeting of talent. It united fast-rising Errol Flynn with fast-fading Kay. The hero was a full decade younger than his leading lady. Using sets from Flynn's *The Charge of the Light Brigade* (1936), the desert triangle saw Kay as the sophisticated wife of British colonel Ian Hunter. But she becomes fascinated with Errol, a captain in the service, who reminds her of her lost lover from World War I. In the finale, Hunter flies off on a death mission, allowing his wife and her lover to have "another dawn" together. It was all very gallant, very civil, and extremely well photographed (Tony Gaudio). The cast, especially Frieda Inescort as Flynn's sister, was sterling. A strange policy decision on the part of the studio involved clipping a fifteen-minute desert battle from the feature before general release. Apparently the company realized that pairing Kay with their new male superstar had done little for either party's career.

As in 1935 and 1936, Kay's artistic profit column for 1937 was shaping up more red than black. With her contract up for renewal, Warners seriously considered dropping her. How-

With Anita Louise in *First Lady* ('37).

ever, just before the lapse, Kay began work on the promising *First Lady* (1937), a version of the George Kaufman-Katharine Dayton comedy that had run for two seasons on Broadway with Jane Cowl in the stellar spot. As the White House-seeking spouse of Secretary of State Preston Foster and the granddaughter of a former President, Kay was later hailed by *Variety* as being "splendid and witty," but another critic wrote, "The difference between the stage and screen version of *First Lady* is approximately the difference between Jane Cowl and Kay Francis." The actress herself would remark, "Fans expect sincerity from me, a certain warmth, and if they don't get it, they howl. They didn't like me in *First Lady* worth a cent. They told me so by the hundreds." Nevertheless Warners felt there was still box-office mileage in the star.

The renewed option was announced to the press with much honesty. Kay admitted that her recent screen failures had been "real-stinkeroos," and blamed her problems on the staleness of scripts. "Even if it was me the public so kindly went to see, there was a limit to the number of times a certain type of story or motif could be repeated." Producer Hal B. Wallis, a top Warner Bros. executive, added, "It is the producer's business to gauge his public; it is the star's business to trust the producer's judgment. Kay Francis is possibly the only star in the entire history of Warners who has realized this fact and who has been ready to meet us more than half-way."

Despite this faith-filled public chatter, both star and studio were maintaining private opinions that were not so friendly. Wallis knew that Kay's nature did not dictate fighting over scripts, roles, and directors even though she would battle for vacation time and a bigger salary. On her part, Kay knew that Warners had occasionally allowed her a different type of story (*The White Angel*) and that they might or might not show duplicity in the future about looking out for her proper welfare. Still, both parties seemed happy. Warners announced that Kay was now reaping a $5250-per-week salary, and would soon star in two vehicles especially purchased for her: *The Sisters* and *Tovarich*.

Sadly, Kay paid her employers too high a compliment by trusting their word. While she *believed* that she would be fairly treated, Bette Davis and relative newcomer Olivia de Havilland were *fighting* for the scripts, directors, cameramen, etc., that would insure the longevity of their careers. Kay meanwhile turned her attention to her private luxuries. About this time she purchased a three-story home in Coldwater Canyon which she filled with a menagerie of pets, including two dogs, two cats, goldfish, frogs, a parrot, a rabbit, and a canary.

Variety had called the failure of *The White Angel* the "final crusher" in the decaying Warner-Francis tandem. However, it would be *Tovarich* that would be the proverbial straw that broke the camel's back. The sophisticated comedy had been playing since October 1936 at the Plymouth Theatre on Broadway with Marta Abba and John Halliday starring as the displaced royalty forced to labor as domestic help. Kay was delighted when she read the role of Tania and was particularly pleased that her basic costume in the film—a black satin maid's uniform—would be so nice a change of pace from the usual overdressed chores. However, only two weeks after Warners promised Kay the property as an incentive to sign a new three-year pact, the studio changed its mind and announced that the role of Tania would go to Claudette Colbert, whom they would borrow from Paramount to star opposite Charles Boyer.

Kay was understandably incensed. She recognized the recasting as both dishonest and demeaning. All Hollywood knew that Warner Bros. had acquired this valuable property especially for her. On Friday, September 3, 1937, she summoned her bosses to court, demanding she be released from her freshly signed contract. The press was openly unsympathetic to the star who had so often snubbed their requests for comments and photo poses. Newsmen issued such unfavorably slanted reports as, "Kay was so angry that she wants to throw up her $5,250 per week job—honest!—and find work somewhere else."

But Kay did not break her contract. Whatever arbitration went on behind closed doors among the star, her agent, and the studio evidently angered the woman to the point where she dropped her suit and planned to stay with the studio out of pure spite. This greatly intimidated the front office. Due to Kay's "advanced" age, poor profit showing, battles with the bosses, unfriendly press relations, tyrannical set behavior, rumored sexual aberrations, and alleged heavy drinking, the studio regretted its decision to re-sign Kay. It then tried to shame her into breaking her pact. In an unprecedented announcement that shocked exhibitors, fans, and all of Hollywood itself, Warners heralded that Kay Francis whose earnings in 1937 were $209,100 (topping Hal B. Wallis' $208,083 and Dick Powell's $176,249) would serve out her contract in *B* programmers. Not since MGM and John Gilbert had a studio so garishly given a former star the kiss of death.

The titilated press swarmed to Kay, ready for the expected news of a walk-out. Instead, a scarcely composed Kay swore that she would honor her contract and collect every cent of the $5,250 weekly salary due her, "even if they put me in a bathing suit and have me walk up and down Hollywood Boulevard!"

The studio never went quite this far, but they came close. They suggested she star with the Mauch twins in *A Prayer for My Sons* and actually cast her in a series of dismal potboilers that insulted not only Kay herself, but her sizeable number of still-loyal fans. She was assigned to a project coyly entitled *This Woman Is Dangerous,* which was released as *Women Are Like That* (1938). This, the first of Kay's B's, had photography and lighting that could not have been more unflattering. The difference between Kay here and in the *A* films was startling, and it had nothing to do with her screen performance.

Miserable as Kay was on the set, she did get along well with co-star Pat O'Brien, the extroverted Irishman. He would recall of Kay in his optimistic memoirs, *The Wind at My Back* (1964):

> One of the most glamorous leading ladies I played opposite was Kay Francis. Not only was she a big dark beautiful creature, but she was endowed with a wonderful sense of humor. I saw Kay a few years ago when I was playing in Falmouth,

With Ralph Forbes in *Women Are Like That* ('38).

Massachusetts. She and Eloise [Mrs. O'Brien] and I dined together and I reminded her how completely uninhibited she was. "Whenever you played love scenes, you always took off your shoes." "I was taller than most of the men I played with."

It more than enhanced her grace. She was a statuesque beauty. . . .

Still *Women Are Like That,* with Kay wed to drunk Pat, did nothing for the striking beauty. As *Photoplay* groaned, "Poor Kay Francis certainly got a dirty deal in this. Unbelievably gauche and tiresome. . . . Maybe we'd better pretend we didn't know about it." Equally offensive was the John Farrow-directed *My Bill* (1938), which had Kay in the glamourless role of a penniless widow with several offspring. *Secrets of an Actress* (1938) reteamed her with George Brent, stuck her with dialogue like "I love you, Peter, but I'm not in love with you," and earned the canard from *Variety,* "It involved no secret other than why it was made." That same review

took a swipe at the studio for wasting Kay, "It's no use hitching race horses to milk wagons."

But there followed *Comet over Broadway* (1938) which, even trimmed to sixty-five minutes, was a too-distilled version of a mawkish Faith Baldwin story. Bette Davis had refused adamantly to make the project. It was directed by Busby Berkeley and starred Kay for the seventh and final occasion with Ian Hunter.

Kay had seen *The Sisters* made in 1938 without her, teaming Bette Davis, Jane Bryan, and Anita Louise with Errol Flynn and Ian Hunter. It would have been a nice showcase for Kay. Miss Francis did at one point break down and virtually beg Warners to cast her as Empress Carlotta in the studio's *Juarez* (1939) with Paul Muni in the title spot. Kay should have known better than to ask—the assignment would go to Bette Davis.

It seemed that even this severe professional punishment was not enough to satisfy the vindictive studio, which unwillingly paid her $224,000 in 1938. Knowing very well how sensitive the actress was about her age, Warners sent out a publicity release on Kay's new romance

103

With Bobby Jordan, Bernice Pilot, and Bonita Granville in *My Bill* ('38).

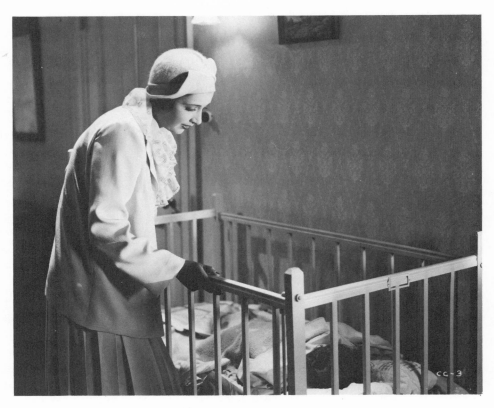

In *Comet over Broadway* ('38).

104

With Gilbert Roland and
Delmer Daves in 1938.

Publicity pose in 1938.

SEE THE SCORCHING STORY OF GANGDOM'S LAST STAND!

WARNER BROS.
HUMPHREY BOGART
KING OF THE UNDERWORLD

KAY FRANCIS   JAMES STEPHENSON   JOHN ELDREDGE   Directed by LEWIS SEILER   A WARNER BROS. PICTURE

Advertisement for *King of the Underworld* ('39).

with alleged aircraft manufacturer Baron Raven Erik Angus Barnekow, claiming that nuptials would soon be approaching for the forty-six-year-old baron and the thirty-nine-year-old star. Long ago the studio had been warned to use 1905 as the birthdate year. If it erred on purpose to annoy the actress, it succeeded. Kay unwittingly raised a ruckus, which only spawned such snide headlines as "Kay Francis Is Not 39, Nor 35. She's Only 33."

The indignities continued. In 1935 Warner Bros. had tricked Paul Muni into making a film called *Dr. Socrates* by informing him that rival Edward G. Robinson was determined to win the role. Muni had regretted making the gangster picture ever since. Someone had the notion of exhuming the property, transforming the doctor into a female, and casting Kay in the lead role. Director Lewis Seiler could not hold the unfortunate project together, and it was temporarily shelved. Later scenes were added and it was released in 1939 as *King of the Underworld*. To show how far the mighty had fallen, the studio

top-billed Humphrey Bogart who was still a studio character player, changed the title to describe *his* character, and demoted Kay to mere feature billing.

Soon the suffering would cease. Kay's last Warner Bros. feature was *Women in the Wind* (1939), a totally undistinguished account of a powder-puff air derby. Not only was Kay billed below the title, but most of the posters revealed her garbed in flying smock and a pilot's cap, rendering her unrecognizable. Before this quickie was even completed, Kay had removed all her belongings from her lavish studio bungalow to make way for its new occupant, Miss Bette Davis.

While *Women in the Wind* limped to completion, Kay consented to talk with *Photoplay*. She made no secret about her ignominious treatment at Warners:

Perhaps I'd have been better off if I had fought for better stories, but the end didn't justify the means. I'd have been suspended, and the time I was under suspension would have been added to the end of my contract. This problem was solved when Olivia de Havilland waged a long, costly court battle against Warner Bros. in 1943 on just this point. So, instead of being free now, I would probably have had another year to go. And, even then, I'd have had no guarantee the stories I picked would have been any better. Even if they had been, the only difference would have been that I would be retiring in a blaze of glory instead of more or less inconspicuously—and this is the way I want it. I'll be forgotten quicker this way.

I have never brandished a sword for the Little Theatre Movement. I have never kidded myself about Art for Art's sake. I went into this business because I thought I could make more money in it than in any other.

On some occasions Kay was very tough and cool about her downfall at the studio, claiming that money had been her only guideline while scrambling up the Hollywood ladder. As she told Bryan Foy when her career was sagging, "Look, as long as they pay me my salary, they can give me a broom and I'll sweep the stage." Years later, when she encountered Bette Davis in Ogunquit, Maine, Davis asked Kay why she had put up with the crass treatment she'd gotten from Jack L. Warner. "I didn't give a damn," Kay responded. "I wanted the money." Davis felt to the contrary, "I didn't. I wanted the career." Yet back in early 1939 Kay privately admitted that the deal administered by Warner Bros. "almost broke my heart." She was indeed a very human, complex—although often cross-purposed—creature.

Kay was more eager to talk to the press about her coming marriage to Erik Barnekow. In 1938 it was a positive subject in a time of bad happenings for her. She claimed she looked forward to a life of ease. But it was all camouflage coming

With Victor Jory and William Gargan in *Women in the Wind* ('39).

from a crushed woman. Barnekow alienated many of Kay's friends—who felt he was a bounder and maybe even an Axis spy. The situation caused her to temporarily sever relationships with her closest pals, Jessica and Richard Barthelmess. In October of 1938 Kay was in San Juan alone (Barnekow had made one of his sudden trips back to Germany). She told the press she was now a "former film star."

Throughout the earlier parts of 1939 Kay and Barnekow feuded in public and private, but she seemed desperately attached to him. At one point, fearful he might be imprisoned as an enemy alien, she suggested they depart for Hawaii and that she would take care of their financial future (a rash act of love on the part of money-conscious Kay!). He refused and soon left for New York. When England announced on September 3, 1939, that it was at war with Germany, Barnekow was back in Germany and Kay knew that their relationship was over. As she wrote in her diary, "Oh, dear God. Goodbye, Erik."

Meanwhile Kay had made one of her best films. It was all at the insistence of her pal Carole Lombard who was to star in RKO's *In Name Only* (1939) with Cary Grant. The role of the villainess was open and Carole negotiated for Kay to get the meaty assignment. (How long ago it must have seemed when, during the making of Paramount's *Ladies' Man,* Carole had become engaged to William Powell and Kay was miffed when the ensuing hoopla outdid the interest in her then-recent marriage to Kenneth MacKenna.)

In Name Only proved to be one of the soundest love stories of the decade, directed with total control by John Cromwell who allowed no posturing and no clichés. Since he had no fondness for Miss Francis as an actress, he worked her especially hard on the project. The film dealt with wealthy Alec Walker (Grant) married for his money by Maida (Kay) who gave up her true love to gain security. Her former lover committed suicide when she wed Alec. When Alec learns the truth, he descends into boorishness until he meets Julie Eden (Lombard), a widow with a young daughter (Peggy Ann Garner). He falls deeply in love with Julie, but cannot convince his money-lusting mate to divorce him.

As Maida Walker, Kay was the perfect soap-opera villainess. The *New York Times* found her to be "a model cat, suave, superior, and relentless." She was also a bit too old to deserve Cary Grant. At one point in the story, Peggy Ann Garner asks Lombard about the departing Kay, "Was that Alec's *mother?*" Kay's final showdown with Lombard, outside a hospital room where Grant lies seriously ill from pneumonia, fascinated audiences:

> *Lombard:* Please don't go in there. . . .
> *Kay:* How dare you!
> *Lombard:* Alec is very ill. He may not live. But if he does live, it will be because he believes he'll never see you again.
> *Kay:* And how did you manage that, Miss Eden?
> *Lombard:* I've told him that you won't fight us anymore. We can be married.
> *Kay:* What makes you think it's as simple as that?
> *Lombard:* Oh, you needn't worry. His father was there. He knew it was a lie. Everyone knew it was a lie, except Alec.
> *Kay:* You've handled this very skillfully, Miss Eden. You've made it look as if Alec's life depends on you. I admire your ingenuity. But it won't work!
> *Lombard:* You'd rather see him dead than with me, wouldn't you?
> *Kay:* Yes, I would!
> *Lombard:* You don't love him. You don't love anybody except yourself.
> *Kay:* I gave up love for what I've got. Do you think I'm going to let you or anyone else get it away from me?
> *Lombard:* All you can possibly get from Alec is money; he'll give you that!
> *Kay:* If Alec gave me every cent he has, it still wouldn't be enough. But someday, his father is going to die. . . .

Unfortunately for Kay, Alec's father (Charles Coburn) overhears this last statement. Immediately he informs the money-loving daughter-in-law, "You might as well take what you can get from Alec—because you won't get anything from me!" Kay is left behind as the hospital door closes for a promising, teary finale.

With Kay billed above the title in the third stellar spot, *In Name Only* rescued a great deal of her respect. It appeared that a new future as a bitch par excellence was hers. But despite flattering reviews and top business, the picture only temporarily halted Kay's descent into cinema limbo.

During this period Kay's weight fluctuated from her standard 112 up to 140 and back down again, aggravated by over-drinking, over-eating, and a general listlessness. She was also plagued by increasing ill health, an assortment of maladies that singly might not have bothered her, but, compounded, added to her overall state of depression. Unlike other fading cinema stars who had yanked themselves back to the top via a comeback role, Kay seemed too disinterested.

When better offers failed to materialize after *In Name Only,* Kay moved over to Universal City to co-star with the lot's top attraction, Deanna Durbin, in *It's a Date* (1940).* Predictably, she played plump Miss Durbin's mother, one who realizes that her daughter has stage aspirations and, as a former stage star herself, gives her some clever clues as how to best attract attention.

Kay stayed at Universal for a complete change of pace—her first Western. It must have been an ordeal for she hated the sound of guns. It was not in the same league with the studio's *Destry Rides Again* (1939), directed by George Marshall, which had given Marlene Dietrich a new lease on cinema life, but *When the Daltons Rode* (also helmed by Marshall) was crisp and had a colorful batch of actors. There were Broderick Crawford, Brian Donlevy, Stuart Erwin, Frank Albertson, and Mary Gordon, as well as wonderful stunt work, and trustworthy Randolph Scott as the hero. The lively eighty-one-minute entry was crammed with "plenty of action, excitement, and gunplay" according to *Variety,* though Kay, as Scott's girlfriend, was

the one player who did not seem to be enjoying the rowdy proceedings. It was another comedown for Kay to be playing a corseted second fiddle to brawls and bloodshed.

The downward trend continued as Kay accepted decent salaries, invested the money carefully, and bitterly swore that she had not been heartbroken by fickle Hollywood. She was top-billed in RKO's *Little Men* (1940), noted by the *Hollywood Reporter* as "a real surprise package of sheer entertainment." Yet the modest film which co-starred her with two other ex-Paramount celebrities (George Bancroft and Jack Oakie) wasted Kay as a school head. Elsie, the celebrated Borden Company cow, made her film bow here and received better camera angles than Kay. Remaining at RKO, Kay starred in *Play Girl* (1940), a *B* waste of time, as an over-seasoned golddigger now instructing young girls in the larcenous, seductive trade.

Universal then recalled Kay for *The Man Who Lost Himself* (1941), a comedy showcasing Brian Aherne in a dual role and landing mainly double-bill engagement playdates. Continuing to free-lance, she paid her first visit to Darryl F. Zanuck's Twentieth Century-Fox to join in the shenanigans of *Charley's Aunt* (1941). One of the year's top grossers, it was yet another screen version of the Brandon Thomas stage hit. Jack Benny played the leading role of the Oxford graduate who poses in white wig and woman's attire as his aunt from Brazil—"where the nuts come from." As the actual Madame Lucia from Brazil, who turns out to be lovely and hardly decrepit, Kay was fetchingly gowned and photographed. But the straight role was lost in the shuffle.

Kay's last 1941 film returned her to Culver City for MGM's *The Feminine Touch,* a fine, sophisticated comedy that assembled a nice cast (Don Ameche, Van Heflin, Henry Daniell), but was primarily a vehicle for the increasingly popular Rosalind Russell. The plot placed Kay as a publishing executive who helps Ameche issue a book theorizing that women want men to retain caveman touches.

Then, the surprise came: Kay returned to Warner Bros. The film was *Always in My Heart* (1942). Her role was that of an unfaithful wife, and her leading man was Walter Huston, who

*Remade at MGM in 1950 as *Nancy Goes to Rio,* with Ann Sothern and Jane Powell as mother and daughter respectively.

had induced the studio to accept Kay. She had forgiven the studio. "I buried . . . [the hatchet] over here on my way out," she told company executives, "and if you want me to work for you again, here I am."

The movie developed into a sloppy mixture of comedy, melodrama, and song—it introduced young Gloria Warren with Borrah Minevitch and his Harmonica Rascals accompanying her in song at the least provocation. Despite her brave front, Kay was understandably ill at ease during the making of the film. Perhaps that accounts for her weak performance. As the *New York Times* reported, "Mr. Huston plays the father with such ease and sincerity that the defects of his associates—especially Kay Francis—and the script stand out in embarrassing prominence when he is not on the screen."

Again, Kay trekked back to Universal, where she was cast as another mother. This time, Diana Barrymore was her daughter. *Between Us Girls* (1942)* was to be Miss Barrymore's make-or-break assignment on the lot. Unfortunately for Diana, her illustrious father, John, fell fatally ill during the shooting, and neither director Henry Koster's coaching nor the encouragement of Kay could bolster the distracted girl. *Between Us Girls,* a vehicle for Diana, was quickly dismissed and forgotten. Two years would pass before Kay would make another film. In this period, she was plagued by insomnia, brought on by her general unhappiness. It made life in her new home—in the foothills of Santa Monica—hellish.

During her absence from the screen, Kay donated some of her free time to the USO and traveled to North Africa and various other combat zones to buoy the spirits of the U.S. fighting man. It was a rugged experience: twice she was bombed by the Germans in Algiers. But the warm reception she received from troops wherever she appeared did much to reassure her that she was a *star*. Kay loved the experience and recalled of her khaki admirers, "They would have been perfectly happy if all you said was 'boo' to them."

In between overseas tours, Kay made some radio broadcasts, including a reteaming* on "Lux Radio Theatre" with George Brent in *The Lady Is Willing* in 1943. She was not adverse to poking fun at her famed lisp and on a comedy show would now and then allow the scripters to play up the well-publicized speech defect.

Twentieth Century-Fox decided to film an account of the USO's work and to showcase the studio's roster at the same time. As a result, four of Hollywood's most generous performers on USO tours (Kay, Carole Landis, Martha Raye, and Mitzi Mayfair) became the *Four Jills in a Jeep,* as that 1944 release dubbed them. With Jimmy Dorsey and his band, Phil Silvers, and Dick Haymes, along with special appearances by Betty Grable, Carmen Miranda, and Alice Faye warbling tunes from recent Fox musicals, *Four Jills* was intended simply to be a potpourri of warm entertainment, not an artistic triumph. Critical reaction to the frolic was mixed, at best. Phil Silvers in his recent autobiography, *The Laugh's On Me* (1973), took a potshot at Kay Francis. He recalled that Kay really had to *act* in the storyline to pretend that she was in love with a soldier.

By 1945, Kay was rapidly losing the firm looks that had once been her professional fortune. While still quite a striking woman, she was not aging well. She was putting on weight again and the puffiness about her face was attributed to years of heavy drinking. With offers dwindling to nothing reasonable, Kay made a last bid for a film comeback by bypassing the need for a producer. Along with Jeffrey Bernerd, she formed her own producing company. Unfortunately, the company was headquartered at Monogram Studios, poverty row's most consistent producer of celluloid junk.

Be that as it may, Kay co-produced and starred

*In *Charles Laughton: An Intimate Biography* (1976), author Charles Higham records an anecdote involving Laughton and Kay when Kay was filming *Between Us Girls* for director Henry Koster: "Kay was in the middle of a scene when the lights on the set suddenly went out and guns began to go off. Kay, who hated guns, was horrified, screamed, and grabbed Koster's arms saying, 'Somebody's shooting.' Then the lights went up and Charles came down the stairs in a long nightgown and nightcap he had worn in *It Started with Eve,* singing 'Happy Birthday, Dear Henry!' accompanied by the entire cast and crew. Koster, who had completely forgotten his own birthday, was astounded, while Kay Francis ran off the set in tears."

*Kay previously had been on the "Lux Radio Theatre" in *One Way Passage* (with William Powell) on March 6, 1939; *In Name Only* (with Carole Lombard and Cary Grant) on December 11, 1939; *The Rains Came* (with George Brent) on March 18, 1940; and *My Bill* (with Warren William) on March 3, 1941.

With Broderick Crawford and Mary Gordon in *When the Daltons Rode* ('40).

in three dismal cheapies, filmed in black-and-white and later waggishly dubbed "The Monogram Trilogy."* The first, *Divorce* (1945), starred Kay as a four-time divorcee who fractures the marriage of a former flame before the man realizes his error. Her co-stars were Bruce Cabot and Helen Mack. Later in 1945 came *Allotment Wives,* which concerned the original plot theme of a mobster syndicate using loose females to wed soldiers to get their federal paychecks. It was the only one of Kay's three Monogram pictures to rate a *New York Times* critique. As usual, it was not favorable: "As the co-producer of the picture and its distaff Fagin and mob chief, Kay Francis wears an assortment of impressive gowns and accessories and appears far too genteel for her job." They kindly did not mention that some unflattering camera shots revealed that Kay had a slight double chin. Her last entry at Monogram was *Wife Wanted*

Divorce was shown on TV as *The Hillsboro Story*. *Allotment Wives* was also released as *Woman in the Case,* and *Wife Wanted* as *Shadow of Blackmail*.

(1946) in which she played an on-the-wane film star (again very curious casting) who learns her real estate holdings are actually a front for lonely heart swindlers. It was a sad, lower-half of the double-bill ending for Kay Francis' film career. She would never make another feature film.

It was a lonely time for Kay and the thought of life without some form of work was, for the moment, intolerable. She had told an interviewer in the Thirties that a woman "may lose the love of her husband, but she can make up for some of that in other interests such as children, or work, or her home, or something she can be terribly interested in."

With the film industry having discarded her, Kay returned to the stage in *Windy Hill,* written by former silent screen star Patsy Ruth Miller and staged/produced by Kay's one-time Warners' rival Ruth Chatterton. The show opened in New Haven on September 20, 1945, and closed in Chicago on May 25, 1946. The leading man was Roger Pryor, and Eileen Heckart had a supporting role. The tour was haunted by produc-

With Jimmy Lydon in *Little Men* ('40).

With George P. Huntley and Mildred Coles in *Play Girl* ('40).

With Jack Benny in *Charley's Aunt* ('41).

With Don Ameche, Rosalind Russell, and Van Heflin in *The Feminine Touch* ('41).

With Sidney Blackmer and Gloria Warren in *Always in My Heart* ('42).

With John Boles on the set of *Between Us Girls* ('42).

tion and cast problems. George Eels reported that when the show played Pittsburgh, one troublesome performance found Kay unable to cope any further with the unintended mayhem on stage. "... The curtain fell on pandemonium. A moment later it inexplicably rose to reveal the elegant Kay, arms akimbo, stamping her tiny foot and screaming, 'Damn this production!' "

In September of 1946 she returned to Broadway for the first time in eighteen years to replace Ruth Hussey as Mary Matthews in the Pulitzer Prize-winning *State of the Union*. The eight-shows-a-week schedule wore on Kay, but for a time saved her from indulging in the drinking and dissipation that rumors insisted she was practicing. The warmth of an appreciative live audience was also good for her morale. After the Broadway run, Kay toured in the Howard Lindsay/Russel Crouse comedy for two seasons.

There were unhappy episodes. In January of 1948 the newspapers reported that Kay was in a Columbus, Ohio, hospital after taking an over-dose of sleeping pills and collapsing against a radiator, suffering intense leg burns. After a long and painful recuperation, she told the press that it was simply the strain of the tour that caused her to "accidentally" misgauge the dosage of pills.

After *State of the Union*, Kay remarked in one of her increasingly rare public statements that she was not through with films. "I have not left Hollywood for good. But I don't know when I'll go back." However, they were through with her. Gradually, Kay began to slip from the public eye. She had long ago given up her Hollywood home and was residing on Manhattan's fashionable East Side. At this time—in the late Forties and early Fifties—she embarked on summer stock tours* in such vehicles as *The Last of Mrs. Cheyney, Let Us Be Gay, Favorite Strangers, Goodbye, My Fancy,* and a hoped for pre-Broadway trek in *The Web and the Rock*. Then there was *Mirror, Mirror,* which horrified its playwright George Oppenheimer. "She pronounced all six r's in the title as w's," he would say later. As for the show, "The play wasn't a very good play, and the result was chaos. She

wasn't the greatest person to work with because she couldn't remember lines easily. She was drinking in those days, too. She always claimed that she never drank when she worked, but she'd quit at eight and start again at eleven....She was a good scout—a good scout and a bad actress."

As stage manager Hap Graham and actor Joel Ashley had been her romantic interests in recent stock seasons, so actor/director Dennis Allen became her constant companion in 1951 when he and Kay worked together in Winter Park, Florida, and elsewhere in a version of Somerset Maugham's *Theatre*. The show enjoyed quite a successful run in the straw-hat circuit. Infrequently Kay would appear on television, as on November 7, 1950, when she guest-starred on the CBS-TV "Prudential Playhouse" series in the episode *Call It a Day*. But that medium was too exhausting and the camera proved too revealing of her age.

In late 1951 she purchased a cooperative apartment at 32 East 64th Street. It was the start of a new chapter in her life. Dennis Allen remained her lover, but she hardly ever saw her pals from Hollywood or from the New York years. Among her new crowd of intimates were her lawyer, L. Arnold Weissberger, and his mother Anna, actor Paul Lipson, stage director/producer Richard Barr, New Orleans businessman Clay Shaw (later involved in a John F. Kennedy assassination plot), Hilda Coppage who operated an inn near Falmouth (Cape Cod), Massachusetts, art gallery owners Allan and Priscilla Brandt, hospital administrator Eva Patton, and an assortment of here-today-gone-tomorrow acquaintances from the nightclub circuit.

Over the next years, only Greta Garbo exceeded Kay's notoriety for shunning cameras, refusing reporters, and weaving a web of secrecy around her private life.* She divided her time between a guest cottage at Hilda Coppage's inn and her off-Fifth Avenue apartment. She turned

---

*In the spring of 1951, the Summer Stock Managers Association voted her "Most Cooperative Actress." What a nice surprise considering her Warner Bros. reputation a decade earlier.

*This book's author had occasion to speak with Kay Francis in 1963 on Cape Cod. At that time she was convinced no one could care less about her past; she was still bitter at the treatment she received from Warner Bros., and was still sensitive about her age. When we met briefly, she looked remarkably fit in her white tennis outfit, tall and regal. Her hair had turned grayish and her teeth were no longer capped; but she was the same vibrant if brusque personality as before.

With Carole Landis, Martha Raye, and Mitzi Mayfair in *Four Jills in a Jeep* ('44).

With Bruce Cabot and Helen Mack in *Divorce* ('45).

116

With Paul Cavanagh in *Wife Wanted* ('46).

up in Hollywood in 1960 with Dennis Allen. It was falsely rumored that they had wed. In 1961, Kay and Allen went their separate ways. "The whole thing was psychologically bad and I honestly believe that she broke off with me because she realized that otherwise I'd sit there and dedicate my life to her. I loved her deeply, and I think in the beginning she loved me." Allen added, "If we'd continued, I could never have had a life other than sitting around holding the hand of a sick old lady."

Ill health continued to plague Kay. She had a lung and kidney surgically removed. She endured several back injuries, fractured an ankle bone, and suffered through assorted other ailments. And she continued to be a heavy, raucous drinker, a situation that alienated most of her remaining friends. It had reached the point where she could not go out for a social evening without causing some sort of disturbance.

In 1966 producer Ross Hunter allegedly offered the overweight Kay the role of Lana Turner's chic mother-in-law in *Madame X,* but Kay was unable to accept and Constance Bennett took the part.

At about this time it was discovered that Kay had breast cancer. A mastectomy was performed, but her illness continued. Thereafter she hardly went out at all, remaining in bed where she watched television, read, drank, and talked to her few acquaintances on the phone. One of her friends to remain loyal, Stephie Wiman, would recall of Kay's final years:

> . . . She was so alone. There was no family. And . . . when she was so sick, she'd get frightened at times. She'd call, and I'd go down there at three or four in the morning. She had my private unlisted number in my bedroom. I'd get up, leave a note for the maid where I was and go down there. It was just awful, having her die there alone.

In the summer of 1968, film trade papers mentioned briefly that the actress was ill and that well-wishers could contact her at New York Hospital. On Saturday, August 24, 1968, she was released by the hospital. Two days later, on

117

August 26, Kay Francis died in her apartment at an age reported to be anywhere from sixty-three to sixty-nine.

The publicity concerning Kay's last wishes shed ample light on the extreme bitterness that shrouded her final, degenerating years. Her seven-page will, dated March 1967, left bequests amounting to $18,350 to twelve individuals;* the remainder of her nearly $2 million estate went to Seeing Eye, Inc., of Morristown, New Jersey, to train guide dogs for the blind. (According to Kay's attorney, the gesture resulted from the star's belief that losing one's sight was the biggest tragedy in life.) Kay had long before lost touch with her father and in her will stated that she had *no* living relatives.

*Among them, her lawyer, L. Arnold Weissberger, received a drawing by Leo Mielziner, Sr. and two drawings by Jo Mielziner; Priscilla Brandt was bequeathed Picasso's "Guitar Player," her emeralds went to Stephie Wiman, and Helen Morgan of Needham, Massachusetts, received $2,000, two pieces of sculpture, and Kay's dog. The Museum of the City of New York received Francis' collection of press notice books, diaries, film stills, etc.

Most sadly, Kay left instructions that there be no funeral service and that her remains be cremated and the ashes be simply disposed of, but not scattered to the winds or interred. It was her wish that no trace of her existence be left on earth.

The obituaries for Kay all eulogized her as one of the Thirties' most alluring glamour girls; most praised her for her representation of the American woman as a poised, intelligent, and admirable person. However, all marveled at the flood of bitterness that cascaded from the pages of her will, the dammed-up emotion of three decades of hurt.

Had Kay Francis' remains been honored by a memorial—her will dictated that absolutely no marker or memorial of any kind was to be created—it would have probably born the epitaph that titled a 1939 interview with *Photoplay,* written at the time that Kay Francis was beginning her exile from her glories into thirty years of festering bitterness: "I can't wait to be forgotten."

FILMOGRAPHY

As Katherine Francis:

GENTLEMEN OF THE PRESS (*Paramount, 1929*) 75 min.

Director, Millard Webb; based on the novel by Ward Morehouse; screenplay, Bartlett Cormack; dialogue director, John Meehan; camera, George Folsey; editor, Morton Blumenstock.

Walter Huston (Wickland Snell); Katherine Francis (Myra May); Charles Ruggles (Charlie Haven); Betty Lawford (Dorothy Snell); Norman Foster (Ted Hanley); Duncan Penwarden (Mr. Higgenbottom); Lawrence Leslie (Red); Harry Lee (Copy Desk Editor); Brian Donlevy (Bit).

THE COCOANUTS (*Paramount, 1929*) 90 min.

Producer, Monta Bell; associate producer, James R. Cowan; director, Bell; numbers directed by Joseph Santley and Robert Florey; based on the play by George S. Kaufman and Irving Berlin; adaptor, Morris Ryskin; song, Berlin; camera, George Folsey.

Groucho Marx (Hammer); Harpo Marx (Harpo); Chico Marx (Chico); Zeppo Marx (Jamison); Mary Eaton (Polly); Oscar Shaw (Bob); Katherine Francis (Penelope); Margaret Dumont (Mrs. Potter); Cyril Ring (Yates); Basil Ruysdael (Hennessey); Sylvan Lee (Bell Captain); Alan K. Foster Girls, Gamby Hall Girls (Dancing Bellhops); Barton MacLane (Bather).

As Kay Francis:

DANGEROUS CURVES (*Paramount, 1929*) 73 min.

Supervisor, B. F. Zeidman; director, Lothar Mendes; story, Lester Cohen; screenplay, Donald Davis, Florence Ryerson; dialogue, Viola Brothers Shore; titles, George Marion, Jr.; camera, Harry Fischbeck; editor, Eda Warren.

Clara Bow (Pat Delaney); Richard Arlen (Larry Lee); Kay Francis (Zara Flynn); David Newell (Tony Barretti); Anders Randolf (Colonel P. P. Brock); May Boley (Ma Spinelli); T. Roy Barnes (Pa Spinelli); Joyce Compton (Jennie Silver); Charles D. Brown (Spider); Stuart Erwin, Jack Luden (Rotarians); Oscar Smith (Black Porter).

ILLUSION (*Paramount, 1929*) 80 min.

Producer, B. P. Schulberg; director, Lothar Mendes; based on the play by Arthur Chesney Train; adaptor/dialogue, E. Lloyd Sheldon; titles, Richard H. Digges, Jr.; song, Larry Spier; sound, Harry M. Lindgren; camera, Harry Fischbeck; editor, George Nichols, Jr.

Charles "Buddy" Rogers (Carlee Thorpe); Nancy Carroll (Claire Jernigan); June Collyer (Hilda Schmittlap); Regis Toomey (Eric Schmittlap); Knute Erickson (Mr. Jacob Schmittlap); Kay Francis (Zelda Paxton); Eugenie Besserer (Mrs. Jacob Schmittlap); Maude Turner Gordon (Queen of Dalmatia); William Austin (Mr. Z); Emilie Melville (Mother Fay); Frances Raymond (Mrs. Y); Catherine Wallace (Mrs. Z); J. E. Nash (Mr. X); William McLaughlin

(Mr. Y); Eddie Kane (Gus Bloomberg); Michael Visaroff (Equerry); Paul Lukas (Count Fortuny); Richard Cramer (Magus); Bessie Lyle (Consuelo); Colonel G. L. McDonell (Jarman, the Butler); Lillian Roth (A Singer); Harriet Spiker (Midget); Anna Magruder (Fat Lady); Albert Wolffe (Giant).

THE MARRIAGE PLAYGROUND (*Paramount, 1929*) 70 min.

Director, Lothar Mendes; based on the novel *The Children* by Edith Wharton; screenplay, J. Walter Ruben; adaptor/dialogue, Doris Anderson; sound, M. M. Paggi; camera, Victor Milner.

Mary Brian (Judith Wheater); Fredric March (Martin Boyne); Lilyan Tashman (Joyce Wheater); Huntley Gordon (Cliffe Wheater); Kay Francis (Zinnia La Crosse); William Austin (Lord Wrench); Seena Owen (Rose Sellers); Philippe De Lacy (Terry Wheater); Anita Louise (Blanca Wheater); Little Mitzi Green (Zinnie); Billie Seay (Astorre Wheater); Ruby Parsley (Beatrice [Beechy]); Donald Smith (Chipstone [Chip] Wheater); Jocelyn Lee (Sybil Lullmer); Maude Turner Gordon (Aunt Julia Langley); David Newell (Gerald Omerod); Armand Kaliz (Prince Matriano); Joan Standing (Miss Scopy); Gordon De Main (Mr. Delafield).

BEHIND THE MAKE-UP (*Paramount, 1930*) 65 min.

Director, Robert Milton; based on the story "The Feeder" by Mildred Cram; adaptors/dialogue, George Manker Watters, Howard Estabrook; songs, Leo Robin, Sam Coslow, Newell Chase; sound, Harry D. Mills; camera, Charles Lang; editor, Doris Drought.

Hal Skelly (Hap Brown); William Powell (Gardoni); Fay Wray (Marie); Kay Francis (Kitty Parker); E. H. Calvert (Dawson); Paul Lukas (Boris); Agostino Borgato (Chef); Jacques Vanaire (Valet); Jean De Briac (Sculptor).

STREET OF CHANCE (*Paramount, 1930*) 76 min.

Director, John Cromwell; story, Oliver H. P. Garrett; dialogue, Lenore J. Coffee; adaptor, Howard Estabrook; titles, Gerald Geraghty; sound, Harry D. Mills; camera, Charles Lang; editor, Otto Levering.

William Powell (John B. Marsden [Natural Davis]); Jean Arthur (Judith Marsden); Kay Francis (Alma Marsden); Regis Toomey ("Babe" Marsden); Stanley Fields (Dorgan); Brooks Benedict (Al Mastick); Betty Francisco (Mrs. Mastick); John Risso (Tony); Joan Standing (Miss Abrams); Maurice Black (Nick); Irving Bacon (Harry); John Cromwell (Imbrie).

PARAMOUNT ON PARADE (*Paramount, 1930*) 101 min.*

Supervisor, Elsie Janis; directors, Dorothy Arzner, Otto Brower, Edmund Goulding, Victor Heerman, Edwin H.

*Technicolor sequences.

119

Knopf, Rowland V. Lee, Ernst Lubitsch, Lothar Mendes, Victor Schertzinger, Edward Sutherland, Frank Tuttle; songs, Janis and Jack King; Ballard MacDonald and Dave Dreyer; Leo Robin and Ernesto De Curtis; L. Wolfe Gilbert and Abel Baer; Richard A. Whiting and Raymond B. Eagan; Whiting and Robin; David Franklin; Sam Coslow; dance/ ensemble director, David Bennett; set designer, John Wenger; camera, Harry Fischbeck and Victor Milner.

With: Iris Adrian, Richard Arlen, Jean Arthur, Mischa Auer, William Austin, George Bancroft, Clara Bow, Evelyn Brent, Mary Brian, Clive Brook, Virginia Bruce, Nancy Carroll, Ruth Chatterton, Maurice Chevalier, Gary Cooper, Cecil Cunningham, Leon Errol, Stuart Erwin, Henry Fink, Kay Francis, Skeets Gallagher, Edmund Goulding, Harry Green, Mitzi Green, James Hall, Phillips Holmes, Helen Kane, Dennis King, Abe Lyman & His Band, Fredric March, Nino Martini, Mitzi Mayfair, Marion Morgan Dancers, David Newell, Jack Oakie, Warner Oland, Zelma O'Neal, Eugene Pallette, Joan Peers, Jack Pennick, Russ Powell, William Powell, Charles "Buddy" Rogers, Lillian Roth, Rolfe Sedan, Stanley Smith, Fay Wray.

A NOTORIOUS AFFAIR (*First National, 1930*) 70 min.

Producer, Robert North; director, Lloyd Bacon; based on the play by Audrey Carter and Waverly Carter; adaptor/ dialogue, J. Grubb Alexander; set designer, Anton Grot; assistant directors, John Daumery, Irving Asher; costumes, Edward Stevenson; sound, Oliver S. Garretson; camera, Ernest Haller; editor, Frank Ware.

Billie Dove (Patricia Hanley Gherardi); Basil Rathbone (Paul Gherardi); Kay Francis (Countess Balakireff); Montagu Love (Sir Thomas Hanley); Kenneth Thomson (Dr. Allen Pomroy); and Philip Strange, Gino Corrado, Elinor Vanderveer.

RAFFLES (*United Artists, 1930*) 70 min.

Producer, Samuel Goldwyn; directors, Harry D'Abbabie D'Arrast, George Fitzmaurice; based on the novel *The Amateur Cracksman* by Ernest William Hornung and the play *Raffles, the Amateur Cracksman* by Hornung and Eugene Wiley Presbrey; screenplay, Sidney Howard; assistant director, H. Bruce Humberstone; technical directors, Gerald Grove, John Howell; art director, William Cameron Menzies; sound, Oscar Lagerstrom; camera, George Barnes, Gregg Toland; editor, Stuart Heisler.

Ronald Colman (Raffles); Kay Francis (Lady Gwen); Bramwell Fletcher (Bunny); Frances Dade (Ethel); David Torrence (Inspector McKenzie); Alison Skipworth (Lady Melrose); Frederick Kerr (Lord Melrose); John Rogers (Crawshaw); Wilson Benge (Barraclough).

FOR THE DEFENSE (*Paramount, 1930*) 62 min.

Director, John Cromwell; story, Charles Furthman; screenplay/dialogue, Oliver H. P. Garrett; sound, Harold M. McNiff; camera, Charles Lang; editor, George Nichols, Jr.

William Powell (William Foster); Kay Francis (Irene Manners); Scott Kolk (Defoe); William B. Davidson (District Attorney Stone); John Elliott (McGann); Thomas Jackson (Daly); Harry Walker (Miller); James Finlayson (Parrott); Charles West (Joe); Charles Sullivan (Charlie);

Ernest Adams (Eddie Withers); Bertram Marburgh (Judge Evans); Edward Le Saint (Judge).

LET'S GO NATIVE (*Paramount, 1930*) 75 min.

Director, Leo McCarey; screenplay/dialogue, George Marion, Jr., Percy Heath; songs, Richard A. Whiting, Marion, Jr.; dances/ensembles director, David Bennett; sound, Harry D. Mills; camera, Victor Milner.

Jack Oakie (Voltaire McGinnis); Jeanette MacDonald (Joan Wood); Skeets Gallagher (Jerry); James Hall (Wally Wendell); William Austin (Basil Pistol); Kay Francis (Constance Cook); David Newell (Chief Officer Williams); Charles Sellon (Wallace Wendell); Eugene Pallette (Creditor's Man).

THE VIRTUOUS SIN (*Paramount, 1930*) 80 min.

Directors, George Cukor, Louis Gasnier; based on the play *A Tabornok (The General)* by Lajos Zilahy; screenplay, Martin Brown; scenery, Louise Long; sound, Harold M. McNiff; camera, David Abel; editor, Otto Levering.

Walter Huston (General Gregori Platoff); Kay Francis (Marya Ivanovna); Kenneth MacKenna (Lieutenant Victor Sablin); Jobyna Howland (Alexandra Stroganov); Paul Cavanagh (Captain Orloff); Eric Kalhurst (Lieutenant Glinka); Oscar Apfel (Major Ivanoff); Gordon McCleod (Colonel Nikitin); Youcca Troubetzkoy (Captain Sobakin); Victor Potel (Sentry).

PASSION FLOWER (*MGM, 1930*) 78 min.

Director, William de Mille; based on the novel by Kathleen Norris; adaptor/dialogue, Martin Flavin; additional dialogue, Laurence G. Johnson, Edith Fitzgerald; art director, Cedric Gibbons; gowns, Adrian; sound, J. K. Brock, Douglas Shearer; camera, Hal Rosson; editor, Conrad A. Nervig.

Kay Francis (Dulce Morado); Kay Johnson (Katherine Pringle Wallace); Charles Bickford (Dan Wallace); Winter Hall (Leroy Pringle); Lewis Stone (Antonio Morado); ZaSu Pitts (Mrs. Harney); Dickie Moore (Tommy).

SCANDAL SHEET (*Paramount, 1931*) 77 min.

Director, John Cromwell; story, Oliver H. P. Garrett; screenplay, Vincent Lawrence, Max March; sound, J. A. Goodrich; camera, David Abel; editor, George Nichols.

George Bancroft (Mark Flint, the Editor); Clive Brook (Noel Adams, the Banker); Kay Francis (Mrs. Flint); Gilbert Emery (Franklin, the Publisher); Lucien Littlefield (McCloskey, the City Editor); Regis Toomey (Regan, the Reporter).

British release title: *The Dark Page*.

LADIES' MAN (*Paramount, 1931*) 70 min.

Director, Lothar Mendes; story, Rupert Hughes; screenplay, Herman J. Mankiewicz; sound, H. M. Lindgren; camera, Victor Milner.

William Powell (James Darricott); Kay Francis (Norma Page); Carole Lombard (Rachel Fendley); Gilbert Emery (Horace Fendley); Olive Telly (Mrs. Fendley); Martin Burton (Anthony Fendley); John Holland (Peyton Weldon); Frank Atkinson (Valet); Maude Turner Gordon (Therese Blanton).

THE VICE SQUAD (*Paramount, 1931*) 80 min.

Director, John Cromwell; story, Oliver H. P. Garrett; sound, E. C. Sullivan; camera, Charles Lang.

Paul Lukas (Stephen Lucarno); Kay Francis (Alice Morrison); Helen Johnson [Judith Wood] (Madeleine Hunt); William B. Davidson (Magistrate Morrison); Rockliffe Fellowes (Detective Sergeant Mather); Esther Howard (Josie); Monte Carter (Max Miller); G. Pat Collins (Pete); Phil Tead (Tony); Davison Clark (Doctor); Tom Wilson (Court Attendant); James Durkin (Another Magistrate); William Arnold (Prosecutor); Lynton Brent (Court Clerk).

TRANSGRESSION (*RKO, 1931*) 72 min.

Director, Herbert Brenon; story, Kate Jordan; screenplay, Elizabeth Meehan; dialogue, Benn W. Levy; sound, John Tribby; camera, Leo Tover.

Kay Francis (Elsie Maury); Paul Cavanagh (Robert Maury); Ricardo Cortez (Don Arturo); Nance O'Neal (Honora Maury); John St. Polis (Serafin); Adrienne d'Ambricourt (Julie); Cissy Fitzgerald (Countess Longueval); Doris Lloyd (Paula Vrain); Augstino Borgato (Carlos).

GUILTY HANDS (*MGM, 1931*) 71 min.

Director, W. S. Van Dyke II; story/screenplay, Bayard Veiller; camera, Merritt B. Gerstad; editor, Anne Bauchens.

Lionel Barrymore (Richard Grant); Kay Francis (Marjorie West); Madge Evans (Barbara Grant); William Bakewell (Tommy Osgood); C. Aubrey Smith (Reverend Hastings); Polly Moran (Aunt Maggie); Alan Mowbray (Gordon Rich); Forrester Harvey (Spencer Wilson); Charles Crockett (H. G. Smith); Henry Barrows (Harvey Scott).

24 HOURS (*Paramount, 1931*) 65 min.

Director, Marion Gering; based on the novel by Louis Bromfield and the play by William C. Lengle, Lew Levenson; screenplay, Louis Weitzenkorn; camera, Ernest Haller.

Clive Brook (Jim Towner); Kay Francis (Fanny Towner); Miriam Hopkins (Rosie Dugan); Regis Toomey (Tony Bruzzi); George Barbier (Hector Champion); Adrienne Ames (Ruby Wintryingham); Lucille La Verne (Mrs. Dacklehorse); Wade Boteler (Pat Healy).

GIRLS ABOUT TOWN (*Paramount, 1931*) 66 min.

Director, George Cukor; story, Zöe Akins; screenplay, Raymond Griffith, Brian Marlow; camera, Ernest Haller.

Kay Francis (Wanda Howard); Joel McCrea (Jim Baker); Lilyan Tashman (Marie Bailey); Eugene Pallette (Benjamin Thomas); Alan Dinehart (Jerry Chase); Lucille Webster Gleason (Mrs. Benjamin Thomas); Anderson Lawler (Alex Howard); George Barbier (Webster); Robert McWade (Simms); Judith Wood (Winnie).

THE FALSE MADONNA (*Paramount, 1932*) 70 min.

Director, Stuart Walker; based on the story "The Heart Is Young" by May Edginton; screenplay, Arthur Kober, Ray Harris; dialogue, Kober; camera, Henry Sharp.

Kay Francis (Tina); William "Stage" Boyd (Marcy); Conway Tearle (Grant Arnold); John Breeden (Phillip

Bellows); Marjorie Gateson (Rose); Charles D. Brown (Peter); Almeda Fowler (Mrs. Swanson).

STRANGERS IN LOVE (*Paramount, 1932*) 76 min.

Director, Lothar Mendes; based on the novel *The Shorn Lamb* by William J. Locke; screenplay, Grover Jones, William Slavens McNutt; camera, Henry Sharp.

Fredric March (Buddy and Arthur Drake); Kay Francis (Diana Merrow); Stuart Erwin (Stan Kenney); Juliette Compton (Muriel Preston); George Barbier (Mr. Merrow); Sidney Toler (McPhail); Earle Foxe (J. C. Clark); Lucien Littlefield (Professor Clark); Leslie Palmer (Bronson); Gertrude Howard (Snowball); Ben Taggart (Crenshaw); John M. Sullivan (Dr. Selous).

MAN WANTED (*Warner Bros., 1932*) 60 min.

Director, William Dieterle; story, Robert Lord; screenplay, Charles Kenyon; camera, Gregg Toland; editor, James Gibbon.

Kay Francis (Lois Ames); David Manners (Tom Sheridan); Andy Devine (Andy Doule); Una Merkel (Ruth Holman); Kenneth Thomson (Fred).

STREET OF WOMEN (*Warner Bros., 1932*) 60 min.

Supervisor, Hal B. Wallis; director, Archie Mayo; based on the novel by Polan Banks; screenplay, Charles Kenyon, Mary McCall, Jr.; dialogue, Brown Holmes, Kenyon; settings supervised by W. and J. Sloane; music director, Leo F. Forbstein; camera, Ernest Haller; editor, Jim Gibbons.

Kay Francis (Natalie Upton); Alan Dinehart (Larry Baldwin); Marjorie Gateson (Lois Baldwin); Roland Young (Link Gibson); Gloria Stuart (Doris Baldwin); Allen Vincent (Clarke Upton); Louise Beavers (Mattie, the Maid); Adrienne Dore (Frances); William Burress (Doctor); Wilbur Mack (Mayor).

JEWEL ROBBERY (*Warner Bros., 1932*) 68 min.

Director, William Dieterle; based on the play by Ladislaus Fodor; screenplay, Erwin Gelsey; camera, Robert Kurrle; editor, Ralph Dawson.

William Powell (The Robber); Kay Francis (Baroness Teri von Horhenfels); Hardie Albright (Paul); Andre Luguet (Count Andre); Henry Kolker (Baron Franz von Horhenfels); Spencer Charters (Johann Christian Lenz); Alan Mowbray (Fritz); Helen Vinson (Marianne); Lawrence Grant (Professor Bauman); Jacques Vanaire (Manager); Harold Minjur (Clark); Ivan Linow (Chauffeur); Charles Coleman (Charles, the Butler); Ruth Donnelly (Berta, the Maid); Clarence Wilson (The Commissioner); Leo White (Assistant Robber); Donald Brodie, Eddie Kane (Robbers); Gordon "Bill" Elliott (Girl-Chasing Gendarme).

ONE WAY PASSAGE (*Warner Bros., 1932*) 69 min.

Director, Tay Garnett; story, Robert Lord; screenplay, Wilson Mizner, Joseph Jackson; camera, Robert Kurrle; editor, Ralph Dawson.

William Powell (Dan Hardesty); Kay Francis (Joan Ames); Frank McHugh (Skippy); Aline MacMahon (Betty [The Countess]); Warren Hymer (Steve Burke); Frederick Burton (Doctor); Douglas Gerrard (Sir Harold); Herbert Mundin (Steward); Wilson Mizner (Singing Drunk); Mike

Donlin (Hong Kong Bartender); Roscoe Karns (Bartender on Ship); Dewey Robinson (Honolulu Contact); Bill Halligan (Agua Caliente Bartender); Stanley Fields (Captain); Willie Fung (Curio Dealer); Heinie Conklin (Singer); Allan Lane, Ruth Hall (Friends); Harry Seymour (Ship's Officer).

TROUBLE IN PARADISE (*Paramount, 1932*) 81 min.

Producer/director, Ernst Lubitsch; based on the play *The Honest Finder* by Laszlo Aladar; screenplay, Grover Jones, Samson Raphaelson; gowns, Travis Banton; song, W. Franke Harling, Leo Robin; camera, Victor Milner.

Miriam Hopkins (Lily Vautier); Kay Francis (Mariette Colet); Herbert Marshall (Gaston Monescue [LaValle]); Charlie Ruggles (The Major); Edward Everett Horton (Francois Filiba); C. Aubrey Smith (Adolph Giron); Robert Greig (Jacques, the Butler); George Humbert (Waiter); Rolfe Sedan (Purse Salesman); Luis Alberni (Annoyed Opera Fan); Leonid Kinskey (Radical); Hooper Atchley (Insurance Agent); Nella Walker (Madame Bouchet—Francois' Friend); Perry Ivins (Radio Commentator); Larry Steers (Guest); Tyler Brooke (Singer).

CYNARA (*United Artists, 1932*) 78 min.

Producer, Samuel Goldwyn; director, King Vidor; based on the novel *An Imperfect Lover* by Robert Gore-Brown, and the play by H. M. Harwood, Gore-Brown; adaptors, Frances Marion, Ivan Starling; camera, Ray June; editor, Hugh Bennett.

Ronald Colman (Jim Warlock); Kay Francis (Clemency Warlock); Phyllis Barry (Doris Lea); Henry Stephenson (John Tring); Viva Tattersall (Milly Miles); Florine McKinney (Gorla); Clarissa Selwyn (Onslow); Paul Porcasi (Joseph); George Kirby (Mr. Boots); Donald Stewart (Henry); Wilson Benge (Merton); C. Montague Shaw (Constable); Charlie Hall (Court Spectator).

Reissue title: *I Was Faithless.*

THE KEYHOLE (*Warner Bros., 1933*) 69 min.

Director, Michael Curtiz; based on the story "Adventuress" by Alice D. G. Miller; screenplay, Robert Presnell; dialogue director, Arthur Greville Collins; art director, Anton Grot; gowns, Orry-Kelly; music director, Leo F. Forbstein; camera, Barney McGill; editor, Ray Curtiss.

Kay Francis (Anne Valee Brooks); George Brent (Neil Davis); Glenda Farrell (Dot); Allen Jenkins (Hank Wales); Monroe Owsley (Maurice Le Brun); Helen Ware (Portia Brooks); Henry Kolker (Schuyler Brooks); Ferdinand Gottschalk (Brooks' Lawyer); Irving Bacon (Grover, the Chauffeur); Clarence Wilson (Weems, the Head of the Detective Agency); George Chandler (Joe, the Desk Clerk); Heinie Conklin (Departing Guest); Renee Whitney (Cheating Wife); John Sheehan (Bartender); Gordon "Bill" Elliott (Dancing Extra); George Humbert, Gino Corrado (Waiters); Maurice Black (Salesman); Leo White (Porter).

STORM AT DAYBREAK (*MGM, 1933*) 82 min.

Director, Richard Boleslavsky; based on the play *Black-Stemmed Cherries* by Sandor Hunyard; adaptor, Bertram Millhauser; music, Dr. William Axt; camera, George Folsey; editor, Margaret Booth.

Kay Francis (Irina Dushan); Nils Asther (Geza); Walter Huston (Mayor Dushan); Phillips Holmes (Csaholyi); Eugene Pallette (Janos); C. Henry Gordon (Panto); Louise Closser Hale (Militza); Jean Parker (Danitza); Charles Halton, Leonard Kinskey (Villagers); Akim Tamiroff (Gypsy Fiddler); Mischa Auer (Assassin); Frank Conroy (Archduke Franz Ferdinand).

MARY STEVENS, M.D. (*Warner Bros., 1933*) 71 min.

Supervisor, Hal B. Wallis; director, Lloyd Bacon; based on the novel by Virginia Kellogg; adaptors, Rian James, Robert Lord; dialogue director, William Keighley; gowns, Orry-Kelly; music director, Leo F. Forbstein; camera, Sid Hickox; editor, Ray Curtiss.

Kay Francis (Mary Stevens, M.D.); Lyle Talbot (Don Andrews); Glenda Farrell (Glenda); Thelma Todd (Lois Rising); Una O'Connor (Mrs. Simmons); Charles Wilson (Walter Rising); Hobart Cavanaugh (Alf Simmons); Harold Huber (Tony); George Cooper (Pete); John Marston (Dr. Lane); Christian Rub (Gus); Reginald Mason (Hospital Superintendent); Walter Walker (Dr. Clark); Ann Hovey (Miss Gordon); Constantine Romanoff (Dynamite Schultz); Harry C. Myers (Nervous Patient); Grace Hayle (Wealthy Lady); Ed Gargan (Cop); Sid Miller (Nussbaum); Wilfred Lucas (Barry); Lloyd Ingraham (Ship's Captain); Harry Seymour (Ship's Officer); Wallace MacDonald (Purser).

I LOVED A WOMAN (*First National, 1933*) 90 min.

Director, Alfred E. Green; based on the book by David Krasner; screenplay, Charles Kenyon, Sidney Sutherland; camera, James Van Trees; editor, Bert Levy.

Edward G. Robinson (John Hayden); Kay Francis (Laura McDonald); Genevieve Tobin (Martha Lane Hayden); J. Farrell MacDonald (Shuster); Henry Kolker (Sanborn); Robert Barrat (Charles Lane); George Blackwood (Henry); Murray Kinnell (Davenport); Robert McWade (Larkin); Walter Walker (Oliver); Henry O'Neill (Farrell); Lorena Layson (Maid); Sam Godfrey (Warren); E. J. Ratcliffe (Theodore Roosevelt); Paul Porcasi (Hotel Proprietor); William V. Mong (Bowen).

THE HOUSE ON 56TH STREET (*Warner Bros., 1933*) 68 min.

Supervisor, James Seymour; director, Robert Florey; based on the novel by Joseph Santley; screenplay, Austin Parker, Sheridan Gibney; art director, Esdras Hartley; dialogue director, William Keighley; gowns, Orry-Kelly, Earl Luick; camera, Ernest Haller; editor, Bud Bretherton.

Kay Francis (Peggy); Ricardo Cortez (Bill Blaine); Gene Raymond (Monte Van Tyle); John Halliday (Lindon Fiske); Margaret Lindsay (Eleanor Burgess); Frank McHugh (Hunt); Sheila Terry (Dolly); William "Stage" Boyd (Bonelli); Hardie Albright (Henry Burgess); Phillip Reed (Freddy); Philip Faversham (Gordon); Henry O'Neill (Baxter); Walter Walker (Dr. Wyman); Nella Walker (Mrs. Van Tyle).

MANDALAY (*Warner Bros. 1934*) 65 min.

Associate producer, Robert Presnell; director, Michael Curtiz; based on the story by Paul Hervey Fox; adaptors, Austin Parker, Charles Kenyon; art director, Anton Grot;

costumes, Orry-Kelly; camera, Tony Gaudio; editor, Thomas Pratt.

Kay Francis (Tanya); Ricardo Cortez (Tony Evans); Lyle Talbot (Dr. Gregory Burton); Warner Oland (Nick); Ruth Donnelly (Mrs. Peters); Reginald Owen (Commissioner); David Torrence (Captain); Etienne Girardot (Mr. Abernathie); Rafaela Ottiano (Countess); Lucien Littlefield (Mr. Peters); Halliwell Hobbes (Colonel Dawson Ames); Bodil Ann Rosing (Mrs. Kleinschmidt); Herman Bing (Professor Kleinschmidt); Lillian Harmer (Louisa Mae Harrington); Torben Meyer (Mr. Van Brinken); Harry C. Bradley (Henry P. Warren); James Leong (Ram Singh); Shirley Temple (Betty); Leonard Mudie (Lieutenant); Frank Baker (First Mate); Olaf Hytten (Cockney Purser); Eric Wilton (English Agent); Otto Frisco (Fakir); George Huerrera (Steward); Desmond Roberts (Sergeant).

WONDER BAR (*First National, 1934*) 84 min.

Producer, Robert Lord; director, Lloyd Bacon; based on the play by Karl Farkas, Robert Katscher, and Geza Herczeg; screenplay, Earl Baldwin; songs, Harry Warren, Al Dubin; music director, Leo F. Forbstein; musical numbers staged by Busby Berkeley; camera, Sol Polito; editor, George Amy.

Al Jolson (Al Wonder); Dolores Del Rio (Inez); Ricardo Cortez (Harry); Kay Francis (Liane Renaud); Dick Powell (Tommy); Guy Kibbee (Simpson); Hugh Herbert (Pratt); Robert Barrat (Captain Von Ferring); Ruth Donnelly (Mrs. Simpson); Louise Fazenda (Mrs. Pratt); Fifi D'Orsay (Mitzi); Merna Kennedy (Claire); Henry Kolker (Mr. Renaud); Henry O'Neill (Richard); Kathryn Sergava (Ilke); Gordon De Main, Harry Woods (Detectives); Marie Moreau (Maid); Emil Chautard (Concierge); Pauline Garon (Operator); Alphonse Martel (Doorman); Jane Darwell (Buxom Grand Dame); Gordon "Bill" Elliott (Norman); Michael Dalmatoff (Count); Renee Whitney, Amo Ingraham, Rosalie Roy (Chorus Girls); Alfred James (Night Watchman); Clay Clement, William Stack (Businessmen); Grace Hayle (Fat Dowager).

DR. MONICA (*Warner Bros., 1934*) 75 min.

Director, William Keighley; based on the play by Marja Morozowiez Szczepokowska; screen story, Charles Kenyon; adaptor, Laura Walker Mayer; art director, Anton Grot; costumes, Orry-Kelly; music director, Leo F. Forbstein; camera, Sol Polito; editor, William Clemens.

Kay Francis (Dr. Monica Braden); Warren William (John Braden); Jean Muir (Mary Hathaway); Verree Teasdale (Anna Littlefield); Phillip Reed (Burton); Emma Dunn (Mrs. Monahan); Herbert Bunston (Mr. Pettinghill); Ann Shoemaker (Mrs. Hazlitt); Virginia Hammond (Mrs. Chandor); Hale Hamilton (Dr. Brent); Virginia Pine (Louise); Pauline True, Leila McIntyre, Norma Drew (Maids); Edward McWade (Janitor); Harry Seymour (Taxi Driver); Eric Wilton (Butler); Gordon "Bill" Elliott (Rutherford); Reginald Pasch (Mr. Swiegart); Marion Lessing (Mrs. Swiegart); Helen Jerome Eddy (Miss Gelsey); Louise Beavers (Mary Hathaway's Maid).

BRITISH AGENT (*First National, 1934*) 75 min.

Director, Michael Curtiz; suggested by the novel by R. H.

Bruce Lockhart; screenplay, Laird Doyle; art director, Anton Grot; music director, Leo F. Forbstein; camera, Ernest Haller; editor, Tom Richards.

Leslie Howard (Stephen Locke); Kay Francis (Elena); William Gargan (Medill); Phillip Reed (Gaston LaFarge); Irving Pichel (Pavlov); Walter Byron (Stanley); Cesar Romero (Tito Del Val); J. Carrol Naish (Commissioner for War); Ivan Simpson (Evans); Gregory Gaye (Kolinoff); Halliwell Hobbes (Sir Walter Carrister); Arthur Aylesworth (Farmer); Mary Forbes (Lady Treherne); Doris Lloyd (Lady Carrister); Alphonse Ethier (Devigny); Paul Porcasi (Romano); Addison Richards (Zvododu); Marina Schubert (Maria); George Pearce (Lloyd George); Tenen Holtz (Lenin); Thomas Braidon, Basil Lynn, Fred Walton, Winter Hall (Cabinet Members); Olaf Hytten (Undersecretary); Frank Lackteen, Robert Wilber, Lew Harvey (Suspects); Frank Reicher (Mr. X).

LIVING ON VELVET (*First National, 1935*) 77 min.

Supervisor, Edward Chodorov; director, Frank Borzage; story/screenplay, Jerry Wald, Julius Epstein; art director, Robert M. Haas; gowns, Orry-Kelly; music director, Leo F. Forbstein; camera, Sid Hickox; editor, William Holmes.

Kay Francis (Amy Prentiss); Warren William (Walter "Gibraltar" Pritcham); George Brent (Terrence Clarence Parker); Helen Lowell (Aunt Martha Prentiss); Henry O'Neill (Thornton); Samuel S. Hinds (Henry L. Parker); Russell Hicks (Major); Maude Turner Gordon (Mrs. Parker); Martha Merrill (Cynthia Parker); Edgar Kennedy (Counterman); Austa (Max, the Dachshund Dog); Lee Shumway (Officer); Sam Hayes (Announcer); Walter Miller (Leader); Emmett Vogan (Officer); May Beatty, Mrs. Wilfrid North (Dowagers); Frank Dodd (Minister); David Newell (Smalley); Bud Geary (Aunt Martha's Chauffeur); William Wayne (Butler); Gordon "Bill" Elliott (Commuter).

STRANDED (*Warner Bros., 1935*) 76 min.

Supervisor, Sam Bischoff; director, Frank Borzage; based on the story "Lady with a Badge" by Frank Wead, Ferdinand Reyher; screenplay, Delmer Daves; additional dialogue, Carl Erickson; assistant director, Lew Borzage; art directors, Anton Grot, Hugh Reticker; gowns, Orry-Kelly; music director, Leo F. Forbstein; camera, Sid Hickox; editor, William Holmes.

Kay Francis (Lynn Palmer); George Brent (Mack Hale); Patricia Ellis (Velma Tuthill); Donald Woods (John Wesley); Barton MacLane (Sharkey); Robert Barrat (Stanislaus Januaschek); June Travis (Jennie Holden [Mary Rand]); Henry O'Neill (Mr. Tuthill); Ann Shoemaker (Mrs. Tuthill); Frankie Darry (Jimmy Rivers); William Harrigan (Updyke); Joseph Crehan (Johnny Quinn); John Wray (Mike Gibbons); Edward McWade (Tim Powers); Gavin Gordon (Jack); Mary Forbes (Grace Dean); Emmett Vogan (Officer on Ferry); Sam McDaniel (Porter); Joan Gay (Diane Nichols); Edwin Mordant (Surgeon); Wilfred Lucas (Pat, a Worker); Mia Liu (Japanese Girl); Rita Rozelle (Polish Girl); Louise Seidel (Danish Girl); Frank LaRue (Doctor); Philo McCullough (Immigration Officer); Adrian Morris (Rivet Boss); Milton Kibbee (Pat, the Timekeeper); Vesey O'Davoren (Butler).

THE GOOSE AND THE GANDER (*Warner Bros., 1935*) 65 min.

Supervisor, James Seymour; director, Alfred E. Green; story/screenplay, Charles Kenyon; art director, Robert M. Haas; gowns, Orry-Kelly; music director, Leo F. Forbstein; assistant director, Chuck Hansen; camera, Sid Hickox; editor, Bert Leonard.

Kay Francis (Georgiana Summers); George Brent (Bob McNear); Genevieve Tobin (Betty Summers); John Eldredge (Lawrence Thurston); Claire Dodd (Connie Thurston); Helen Lowell (Aunt Julia Hamilton); Ralph Forbes (Ralph Summers); William Austin (Arthur Summers); Spencer Charters (Winklesteinbergher); Eddie Shubert (Sweeney); John Sheehan (Murphy); Charles Coleman (Jones); Wade Boteler, Davison Clark, Nick Copeland, Cliff Saum, Glen Cavender (Detectives); Al Woods (Bellboy); Milton Kibbee (Garageman); Jack Richardson (Jack, the Baggageman); Edward McWade (Justice of Peace); Jan Buckingham (Mrs. Burns); Gordon "Bill" Elliott (Teddy); Olive Jones (Miss Brent).

I FOUND STELLA PARISH (*First National, 1935*) 84 min.

Producer, Harry Joe Brown, director, Mervyn LeRoy; story, John Monk Saunders; screenplay, Casey Robinson; music director, Leo F. Forbstein; art director, Robert M. Haas; gowns, Orry-Kelly; camera, Sid Hickox; editor, William Clemens.

Kay Francis (Stella Parish); Ian Hunter (Keith Lockridge); Paul Lukas (Stephen Norman); Sybil Jason (Gloria Parish); Jessie Ralph (Nana); Joseph Sawyer (Chuck); Eddie Acuff (Dimmy); Walter Kingsford (Reeves); Robert Strange (Jed Duffy); Ferdinand Munier (Andrews); Rita Carlyle, Shirley Simpson, Elspeth Dudgeon, Tempe Pigott (Women); Charles Evans (Old Actor); Lotus Liu (Mabel); Olaf Hytten (Butler); Elsa Buchanan (Maid); Vesey O'Davoren (Deck Steward); Lotus Thompson (Secretary); Milton Kibbee (Costumer); John Dilson (Producer's Assistant); Harlan Briggs (Theatre Manager); Alice Keating (New York Operator); Marie Wells (Hotel Operator); Phyllis Coghlan (London Operator); Emmett Vogan, Lew Harvey, Gordon "Bill" Elliott (Reporters); Crauford Kent (Lord Chamberlain); Edward Cooper (Caligula); Hugh Huntley (Cemellus); Ralph Bushman [Francis X. Bushman] (Erik); Vernon Downing, Vernon Steele (Slaves); Mary Treen (Sob Sister); Barton MacLane (Clifton Jeffords); Harry Beresford (James).

THE WHITE ANGEL (*First National, 1936*) 75 min.

Producer, Henry Blanke; director, William Dieterle; based on the biography by Lytton Strachey; screenplay, Michel Jacoby, Mordaunt Sharp; dialogue director, Stanley Logan; music director, Leo F. Forbstein; camera, Tony Gaudio; editor, Warren Low.

Kay Francis (Florence Nightingale); Ian Hunter (Fuller); Donald Woods (Charles Cooper); Nigel Bruce (Dr. West); Donald Crisp (Dr. Hunt); Henry O'Neill (Dr. Scott); George Curzon (Sir Sidney Herbert); Phoebe Foster (Elizabeth Herbert); Charles Croker King (Mr. Nightingale); Georgia Caine (Mrs. Nightingale); Billy Mauch

(Tommy); Lillian Kemble-Cooper (Parthe Nightingale); Ara Gerald (Mrs. Elda Stevens); Montagu Love (Mr. Bullock); Halliwell Hobbes (Lord Raglan); Frank Conroy (Mr. LeFroy); Eily Malyon (Sister Columbo); Egon Brecher (Fieldner); Barbara Leonard (Minna); Gaby Fay (Queen Victoria); Ferdinand Munier (Soyer, the Cook); Tempe Pigott (Mrs. Waters, the Nurse); Daisy Belmore, Alma Lloyd, May Beatty, Kathrin Clare Ward (Nurses); Lawrence Grant (Colonel); Nelson McDowell (Superintendent of Hospital); Eric Wilton (Servant); Robert Bolder, James May, Arthur Turner Foster (Doctors).

GIVE ME YOUR HEART (*Warner Bros., 1936*) 87 min.

Supervisor, Robert Lord; director, Archie Mayo; based on the play *Sweet Aloes* by Jay Mallory (Joyce Carey); screenplay, Casey Robinson; gowns, Orry-Kelly; music director, Leo F. Forbstein; camera, Sidney Hickox; editor, James Gibbon.

Kay Francis (Linda Warren); George Brent (Jim Baker); Roland Young (Tubbs Barrow); Patric Knowles (Robert Melford); Henry Stephenson (Edward, Lord Farrington); Frieda Inescort (Rosamond Melford); Helen Flint (Dr. Florence Cudahy); Halliwell Hobbes (Oliver); Zeffie Tilbury (Esther Warren); Elspeth Dudgeon (Alice Dodd); Russ Powell (Cab Driver); Edgar Norton (Servant); Dick French, Ethel Sykes (Guests); Bruce Warren (Young Man); Elsa Peterson (Young Woman); Wayne and Teske (Dance Team); Toekie Trigg (Edward, the Baby); Helena Grant (Nurse).

STOLEN HOLIDAY (*Warner Bros., 1936*) 76 min.

Producer, Hal B. Wallis; associate producer, Harry Joe Brown; director, Michael Curtiz; story, Warren Duff, Virginia Kellogg; screenplay, Casey Robinson; music director, Leo F. Forbstein; art director, Anton Grot; dialogue director, Jo Graham; gowns, Orry-Kelly; special effects, Fred Jackman; camera, Sid Hickox; editor, Terry Morse.

Kay Francis (Nicole Picot); Claude Rains (Stefan Orloff); Ian Hunter (Anthony Wayne); Alison Skipworth (Suzanne); Alexander D'Arcy (Anatole); Betty Lawford (Helen Tuttle); Walter Kingsford (Francis Chalon); Charles Halton (LeGrande); Frank Reicher (Ranier); Frank Conroy (Dupont); Kathleen Howard (Madame Delphine); Wedgewood Nowell (Borel); Robert Strange (Prefect of Police); Egon Brecher (Deputy Bergery).

CONFESSION (*Warner Bros., 1937*) 91 min.

Producer, Hal B. Wallis; associate producer, Henry Blanke; director, Joe May; based on the screenplay *Mazurka* by Hans Rameau; English adaptors, Julius J. Epstein, Margaret LeVino; art director, Anton Grot; gowns, Orry-Kelly; music director, Leo F. Forbstein; music, Peter Kreuger; songs, Kreuger, Jack Scholl; dialogue director, Stanley Logan; camera, Sid Hickox, editor, James Gibbon.

Kay Francis (Vera); Ian Hunter (Leonide Kirow); Basil Rathbone (Michael Michailow); Jane Bryan (Lisa); Donald Crisp (Presiding Judge); Dorothy Peterson (Nurse); Laura Hope Crews (Stella); Mary Maguire (Hildegarde); Robert Barrat (Prosecuting Attorney); Ben Welden (Defense Attorney); Veda Ann Borg (Xenia); Helen Valkis

(Wanda); Anderson Lawler (Reporter); Michael Mark (Russian Interpreter); Sam Rice, Albert Lloyd, Perc Teeple, Jack Richardson (Men at Station); Lyle Moraine (Usher at Theatre); Ferdinand Munier (Bald Man at Theatre); Peggy Keys, Jewel Jordan (Autograph Fans); Sam Ash (Waiter); Edward Keane (Cabaret Manager); Pierre Watkin (Lawyer); Dawn Bender (Lisa as a Baby); Janet Shaw, Jody Gilbert, Evelyn Mulhall, Symona Boniface, Elsa Peterson (Actress Friends); Edward Price, Jeffrey Sayre, John Mather, Lane Chandler, Jack Davidson, Maurice Brierre (Actor Friends); Lawrence Grant (Doctor).

ANOTHER DAWN (*Warner Bros., 1937*) 73 min.

Executive producer, Hal B. Wallis; associate producer, Harry Joe Brown; director, William Dieterle; screenplay, Laird Doyle; dialogue director, Stanley Logan; art director, Robert Haas; gowns, Orry-Kelly; music, Erich Wolfgang Korngold; orchestrators, Hugo Friedhofer, Milan Roder; assistant director, Frank Heath; sound, Robert B. Lee; camera, Tony Gaudio; editor, Ralph Dawson.

Kay Francis (Julia Ashton); Errol Flynn (Captain Denny Roark); Ian Hunter (Colonel Wister); Frieda Inescort (Grace Roark); Herbert Mundin (Wilkins); G. P. Huntley, Jr. (Lord Alden); Billy Bevan (Hawkins); Clyde Cook (Sergeant Murphy); Richard Powell (Henderson); Kenneth Hunter (Sir Charles Benton); Mary Forbes (Mrs. Benton); Eily Malyon (Mrs. Farnold); Charles Austin (Yeoman); Joseph Tozer (Butler); Ben Welden (Mr. Romkoff); Spencer Teakle (Fromby); David Clyde (Campbell); Charles Irwin (Kelly); Reginald Sheffield (Wireless Operator); Martin Garralaga (Ali); George Regas (Achaben); Jack Richardson (Lang); Edward Dew (Glass); R. M. Simpson (Lloyd); Will Stanton, Neal Kennedy (Caddies); Major Sam Harris (Guest); Stefan Moritz (Arab Horseman).

FIRST LADY (*Warner Bros., 1937*) 82 min.

Producer, Hal B. Wallis; associate producer, Harry Joe Brown; director, Stanley Logan; based on the play by George S. Kaufman, Katharine Dayton; screenplay, Rowland Leigh; art director, Max Parker; music director, Leo F. Forbstein; gowns, Orry-Kelly; assistant director, Sherry Shourds; camera, Sid Hickox; editor, Ralph Dawson.

Kay Francis (Lucy Chase Wayne); Anita Louise (Emmy Paige); Preston Foster (Stephen Wayne); Walter Connolly (Carter Hibbard); Victor Jory (Senator Keane); Verree Teasdale (Irene Hibbard); Louise Fazenda (Mrs. Greevey); Marjorie Gateson (Sophie Prescott); Marjorie Rambeau (Belle Hardwick); Eric Stanley (Tom Hardwick); Henry O'Neill (George Mason); Lucille Webster Gleason (Mrs. Ives); Sara Haden (Mrs. Mason); Harry Davenport (Charles); Gregory Gaye (Gregoravitch); Olaf Hytten (Bleacker); Jackie Morrow (Boy); Jack Mower (Halloran); Elizabeth Dunne, Lillian Harmer (Women); Joseph Romantini (Senor Ortega); Robert Cummings, Sr., Wedgewood Nowell (Men).

WOMEN ARE LIKE THAT (*Warner Bros., 1938*) 78 min.

Director, Stanley Logan; story, Albert Z. Carr; adaptor, Horace Jackson; art director, Max Parker; gowns, Orry-Kelly; music director, Leo F. Forbstein; sound, Charles Lang; camera, Sid Hickox; editor, Thomas Richards.

Kay Francis (Claire Landin); Pat O'Brien (Bill Landin); Ralph Forbes (Martin Brush); Melville Cooper (Mainwaring); Thurston Hall (Claudius King); Grant Mitchell (Mr. Snell); Gordon Oliver (Howard Johns); John Eldredge (Charles Braden); Herbert Rawlinson (Avery Flickner); Hugh O'Connell (George Dunlap); Georgia Caine (Mrs. Amelia Brush); Joyce Compton (Miss Hall); Sarah Edwards (Mrs. Snell); Josephine Whittell (Miss Douglas); Loia Cheaney (Miss Perkins); Edward Broadley (Holliwell); Sam McDaniel (Porter).

MY BILL (*Warner Bros., 1938*) 65 min.

Director, John Farrow; based on the play *Courage* by Tom Barry; screenplay, Vincent Sherman, Robertson White; art director, Max Parker; gowns, Orry-Kelly; sound, Charles Lang; camera, Sid Hickox; editor, Frank Mayo.

Kay Francis (Mark Colbrook); Dickie Moore (Bill Colbrook); Bonita Granville (Gwen Colbrook); John Litel (Mr. Rudlin); Anita Louise (Muriel Colbrook); Bobby Jordan (Reginald Colbrook); Maurice Murphy (Lynn Willard); Elisabeth Risdon (Aunt Caroline); Helena Phillips Evans (Mrs. Crosby); John Ridgely (Florist); Jan Holm (Secretary); Sidney Bracy (Jenner); Bernice Pilot (Beulah).

SECRETS OF AN ACTRESS (*Warner Bros., 1938*) 70 min.

Producer, David Lewis; director, William Keighley; based on the screen story "Lovely Lady" by Milton Krims, Rowland Leigh, Julius J. Epstein; screenplay, Krims, Leigh, Epstein; art director, Anton Grot; gowns, Orry-Kelly; music director, Leo F. Forbstein; sound, Charles Lang; camera, Sid Hickox; editor, Owen Marks.

Kay Francis (Fay Carter); George Brent (Dick Orr); Ian Hunter (Peter Snowden); Gloria Dickson (Carla Orr); Isabel Jeans (Marian Plantagenet); Penny Singleton (Miss Reid); Dennie Moore (Miss Blackstone); Selmer Jackson (Thompson); Herbert Rawlinson (Harrison); Emmett Vogan (Spencer); James B. Carson (Carstairs).

COMET OVER BROADWAY (*Warner Bros., 1938*) 65 min.

Associate producer, Bryan Foy; director, Busby Berkeley; based on the story by Faith Baldwin; screenplay, Mark Hellinger, Robert Bucker; music director, Leo F. Forbstein; music, Heinz Roemheld; gowns, Orry-Kelly; art director, Charles Novi; sound, Charles Lang; camera, James Wong Howe; editor, James Gibbons.

Kay Francis (Eve Appleton); Ian Hunter (Bert Ballin); John Litel (Bill Appleton); Donald Crisp (Joe Grant); Minna Gombell (Tim Adams); Sybil Jason (Jacqueline Appleton); Melville Cooper (Emerson); Ian Keith (Wilton Banks); Leona Maricle (Janet Eaton); Ray Mayer (Tim Brogan); Vera Lewis (Mrs. Appleton); Nat Carr (Burlesque Manager); Chester Clute (Willis); Edward McWade (Harvey); Clem Bevans (Lem); Dorothy Comingore (Miss McDermott); Jack Mower (Hotel Manager); Edgar Edwards (Waiter); Lester Dorr (Performer); Alice Connor, Fern Barry, Susan Hayward (Amateur Actors); Owen

King (Actor); Janet Shaw (Woman); Kay Gordon, Jessie Jackson (Chorus Girls); Frank O'Connor (Officer); Henry Otho (Baggage Man); Frank Orth (Cab Driver); Sidney Bracy (English Porter); Jimmy Conlin (Comic); Charles Seel (Jury Foreman); Mitchell Ingraham (Court Clerk); Raymond Brown (Judge); Emmett Vogan (Prosecutor); Ed Stanley (Doctor); Howard Mitchell (Court Officer).

KING OF THE UNDERWORLD (*Warner Bros., 1939*) 69 min.

Associate producer, Bryan Foy; director, Lewis Seiler; based on the serialized novel *Dr. Socrates* by W. R. Burnett; screenplay, George Bricker, Vincent Sherman; music, Heinz Roemheld; dialogue director, Sherman; assistant director, Frank Heath; art director, Charles Novi; gowns, Orry-Kelly; technical adviser, Dr. Leo Schulman; sound, Everett A. Brown; camera, Sid Hickox; editor, Frank Dewar.

Humphrey Bogart (Joe Gurney); Kay Francis (Carole Nelson); James Stephenson (Bill Forrest); John Eldredge (Niles Nelson); Jessie Busley (Aunt Margaret); Arthur Aylesworth (Dr. Sanders); Raymond Brown (Sheriff); Harland Tucker (Mr. Ames); Ralph Remley (Mr. Robert); Murray Alper (Butch); Charles Foy (Eddie); Joe Devlin (Porky); Elliott Sullivan (Mugsy); Alan Davis (Slick); John Harmon (Slats); John Ridgely (Jerry); Richard Bond (Intern); Paul MacWilliams (Anesthetist); Richard Quine (Student); Stuart Holmes (Doorman); Vera Lewis (Woman); William Gould (Chief of Police); Clem Bevans, Carl Stockdale, Nat Carr (Villagers); Jack Mower, John Harron (G-Men); Sherwood Bailey (Boy); Jimmy O'Gatty, Frank Bruno, Paul Panzer, Cliff Saum, Doc Stone (Gangsters); Sidney Bracy, Lottie Williams (Farmer Couple); Tom Wilson, Glen Cavender (Deputies).

WOMEN IN THE WIND (*Warner Bros., 1939*) 63 min.

Producer, Mark Hellinger; associate producer, Bryan Foy; director, John Farrow; based on the novel by Francis Walton; screenplay, Lee Katz, Albert De Mond; assistant director, Marshall Hageman; art director, Carl Jules Weyl; dialogue director, Jo Graham; technical advisor, Frank Clark; music director, Leo F. Forbstein; gowns, Orry-Kelly; camera, Sid Hickox; editor, Thomas Pratt.

Kay Francis (Janet Steele); William Gargan (Ace Boreman); Victor Jory (Doc); Maxie Rosenbloom (Stuffy McInnes); Sheila Bromley (Frieda Boreman); Eve Arden (Kit Campbell); Eddie Foy, Jr. (Denny Carson); Charles Anthony Hughes (Bill Steele); Frankie Burke (Johnnie); John Dilson (Sloan); Spencer Charters (Farmer); Vera Lewis (Farmer's Wife); Sally Sage, Alice Connors, Marian Alden, Iris Gabrielle, Diana Hughes (Aviatrixes); John Harron (Process Server); John Ridgely, Nat Carr, Richard Bond, Jack Mower, Frank Mayo (Salesmen); Lucille Denver, Marie Astaire (Women); Steven Darrell, David Kerman (Photographers); Emmett Vogan (Radio Announcer); Frank Faylen (Mechanic); George O'Hanlon (Bellboy); Eddie Graham (Microphone Man); Milton Kibbee (Bartender).

IN NAME ONLY (*RKO, 1939*) 94 min.

Executive producer, Pandro S. Berman; producer, George Haight; director, John Cromwell; based on the novel *Memory of Love* by Bessie Brewer; screenplay, Richard Sherman; music, Roy Webb; art directors, Van Nest Polglase, Perry Ferguson; set decorator, Darrell Silvera; Miss Lombard's gowns by Irene; other gowns, Edward Stevenson; assistant director, Dewey Starkey; sound, Hugh McDowell, Jr.; special effects, Vernon L. Walker; camera, J. Roy Hunt; editor, William Hamilton.

Carole Lombard (Julie Eden); Cary Grant (Alec Walker); Kay Francis (Maida Walker); Charles Coburn (Mr. Walker); Katharine Alexander (Laura); Jonathan Hale (Dr. Gateson); Maurice Moscovich (Dr. Muller); Nella Walker (Mrs. Walker); Peggy Ann Garner (Ellen); Spencer Charters (Gardener); Alan Baxter (Charley); Harriet Mathews, Sandra Morgan (Women on Boat); Harold Miller (Man on Boat); John Dilson, Doug Gordon (Stewards); James Adamson, Tony Merlo (Waiters); Frank Puglia (Manager); Alex Pollard (Butler); Charles Coleman (Archie Duress); Florence Wix, Clive Morgan, Major Sam Harris, Kathryn Wilson (Party Guests); Grady Sutton (Escort); Bert Moorhouse (College Man); Gus Glassmire (Hospital Attendant); Mary MacLaren (Nurse); Robert Strange (Hotel Manager); Jack Chapin, Allan Wood, Harold Hoff (Bellhops); John Laing (Chauffeur); Frank Mills (Bartender); Byron Foulger (Owen); Arthur Aylesworth (Farmer on Truck).

IT'S A DATE (*Universal, 1940*) 103 min.

Producer, Joseph Pasternak; director, William A. Seiter; story, Jane Hall, Frederick Kohner, Ralph Block; screenplay, Norman Krasna; songs, Pinky Tomlin and Harry Tobias; Ralph Freed and Frank Skinner; Eddie Cherkose, L. Belasco, and Jacques Press; camera, Joseph Valentine; editor, Bernard Burton.

Deanna Durbin (Pamela Drake); Kay Francis (Georgia Drake); Walter Pidgeon (John Arlen); Samuel S. Hinds (Sidney Simpson); S. Z. Sakall (Carl Ober); Lewis Howard (Freddie Miller); Cecilia Loftus (Sarah Frankenstein); Henry Stephenson (Captain Andrews); Eugene Pallette (Governor); Joe King (First Mate); Fritz Feld (Headwaiter); Charles Lane (Horner); John Arledge (Newcomer); Romaine Callender (Evans); Virginia Brissac (Holden); Leon Belasco (Captain); Anna Demetrio (Cook); Mary Kelley (Governor's Wife); Eddie Acuff (Ship's Steward); Johnny Day (Sleepy-Eyed Blonde); Fay McKenzie, Linda Deane, Phyllis Ruth, Virginia Engels (Young Girls); Eddie Polo (Quartermaster); Mary Shannon (Wardrobe Mistress); Mark Anthony (Officer).

WHEN THE DALTONS RODE (*Universal, 1940*) 81 min.

Director, George Marshall; based on the book by Emmett Dalton, Jack Jungmeyer, Sr.; screenplay, Lester Cole, Stuart Anthony, Harold Shumate; art director, Jack Otterson; assistant director, Vernon Keays; camera, Hal Mohr; editor, Ed Curtiss.

Randolph Scott (Tod Jackson); Kay Francis (Julie King); Brian Donlevy (Grat Dalton); George Bancroft (Caleb Winters); Broderick Crawford (Bob Dalton); Stuart Erwin (Ben Dalton); Andy Devine (Ozark); Frank Albertson

(Emmett Dalton); Mary Gordon (Ma Dalton); Harvey Stephens (Rigby); Edgar Dearing (Sheriff); Quen Ramsey (Wilton); Dorothy Grainger (Nancy); Bob McKenzie (Photographer); Fay McKenzie (Hannah); Walter Soderling (Judge Swain); Mary Ainslee (Minnie); Erville Alderson (District Attorney Wade); Sally Payne (Annabelle); June Wilkins (Suzy); William Gould (Deputy on Train); Jack Clifford (Deputy); Pat West (Pete, the Restaurant Owner); Dorothy Moore (Girl); George Guhl (Deputy in Baggage Car); Robert Dudley (Juror Pete Norris); Ed Brady (Deputy); Walter Long (Deputy on Train); Bob Reeves (Henchman); Kernan Cripps (Freight Agent); Tom London (Lyncher); Mary Cassidy (Girl); Lafe McKee (Doctor); Russ Powell (Engineer); John Beck (Native); James Morton (Juror Ed Pickett).

LITTLE MEN (*RKO, 1940*) 84 min.

Producers, Gene Towne, Graham Baker; associate producer, Donald J. Ehlers; director, Norman Z. McLeod; based on the novel by Louisa May Alcott; screenplay, Mark Kelly, Arthur Caesar; art directors, Van Nest Polglase, Al Herman; music, Roy Webb; camera, Nicholas Musuraca; editor, George Hively.

Kay Francis (Jo); Jack Oakie (Willie); George Bancroft (Major Burdel); Jimmy Lydon (Dan); Ann Gillis (Nan); Carl Esmond (Professor); Richard Nichols (Teddy); Casey Johnson (Robby); Francesca Santoro (Besa); Johnny Burke (Silas); Lillian Randolph (Asia); Sammy McKin (Tommy); Edward Rice (Demi); Anne Howard (Daisy); James Zaner (Jack); Bobbie Cooper (Adolphus); Schuyler Standish (Nat); Paul Matthews (Stuffy); Tony Neil (Ned); Fred Eaton (Emmett); Douglas Rucker (Billy); Donald Rackerty (Frank); William Demarest (Constable); Sterling Holloway (Reporter); Elsie (Buttercup, the Cow); Isabel Jewell (Stella); Bud Jamison (Cop); Sarah Edwards (Landlady); Duke York (Poker Player); Howard Hickman (Doctor); Stanley Blystone (Bartender).

PLAY GIRL (*RKO, 1940*) 76 min.

Producer, Cliff Reid; director, Frank Woodruff; story/screenplay, Jerry Cady; camera, Nick Musuraca; editor, Harry Marker.

Kay Francis (Grace Herbert); James Ellison (Tom Dice); Mildred Coles (Ellen Daley); Nigel Bruce (Bill Vincent); Margaret Hamilton (Josie); Katharine Alexander (Mrs. Dice); George P. Huntley (Van Payson); Charles Quigley (Lock); Georgia Carroll (Alice Sawyer); Kane Richmond (Don Shawhan); Stanley Andrews (Joseph Shawhan); Selmer Jackson (Fred Dice); Dick Hogan (Bellhop); Ralph Byrd (Doctor); Cecil Cunningham (Dowager); Larry Steers (Cafe Extra); Charles Arnt (Grady, the Private Detective); Marek Windheim (Dr. Alonso Corvini, the Orchestra Conductor).

THE MAN WHO LOST HIMSELF (*Universal, 1941*) 72 min.

Producer, Lawrence W. Fox, Jr.; director, Edward Ludwig; based on the novel by H. DeVere Stagpoole; screenplay, Eddie Moran; camera, Victor Milner.

Brian Aherne (John Evans and Malcolm Scott); Kay Francis (Adrienne Scott); S. Z. Sakall (Paul); Henry Stephenson (Frederick Collins); Eden Gray (Venetia Scott); Wilson Benge (Butler); Nils Asther (Peter Ransom); Sig Rumann (Dr. Sims); Marc Lawrence (Frank DeSoto); Henry Kolker (T. J. Mulhausen); Janet Beecher (Mrs. Milford); Dorothy Tree (Mrs. Van Avery); Russell Hicks (Mr. Van der Girt); Frederick Burton (Mr. Milford); Selmer Jackson (Green); Henry Roquemore (Bartender); Sarah Padden (Mrs. Cummings, the Maid); Ethel Clifton (Maid); Paul Bryar (Bar Waiter); Irene Colman (Office Girl); Cyril Ring (Relative); Frank O'Connor (Cab Driver); Lloyd Whitlock (Attendant); Billy Benedict (Messenger Boy); Billy Engle (News Vendor).

CHARLEY'S AUNT (*Twentieth Century-Fox, 1941*) 81 min.

Producer, William Perlberg; director, Archie Mayo; based on the play by Brandon Thomas; screenplay, George Seaton; music, Alfred Newman; art directors, Richard Day, Nathan Juran; set decorator, Thomas Little; costumes, Travis Banton; camera, Peverell Marley; editor, Robert Bischoff.

Jack Benny (Babbs); Kay Francis (Donna Lucia); James Ellison (Jack Chesney); Anne Baxter (Amy Spettigue); Edmund Gwenn (Stephen Spettigue); Reginald Owen (Redcliff); Laird Cregar (Sir Francis Chesney); Arleen Whelan (Kitty Verdun); Richard Haydn (Charley Wyckham); Ernest Cossart (Brassett); Morton Lowry (Harley Stafford); Lionel Pape (Babberly); Claude Allister, William Austin (Spectators); Russell Burroughs, Gilchrist Stuart, John Meredith (Teammates); Bob Conway, Bob Cornell, Basil Walker, Herbert Gunn (Students); Will Stanton (Messenger); C. Montague Shaw (Elderly Man); Maurice Cass (Octogenarian).

THE FEMININE TOUCH (*MGM, 1941*) 97 min.

Producer, Joseph L. Mankiewicz; director, W. S. Van Dyke II; screenplay, George Oppenheimer, Edmund L. Hartmann, Ogden Nash; music, Franz Waxman; art director, Cedric Gibbons; special effects, Warren Newcombe; camera, Ray June; editor, Albert Akst.

Rosalind Russell (Julie Hathaway); Don Ameche (John Hathaway); Kay Francis (Nellie Woods); Van Heflin (Elliott Morgan); Donald Meek (Captain Makepeace Liveright); Gordon Jones (Rubber-Legs Ryan); Henry Daniell (Shelley Mason); Sidney Blackmer (Freddie Bond); Grant Mitchell (Dean Hutchinson); David Clyde (Brighton).

ALWAYS IN MY HEART (*Warner Bros., 1942*) 92 min.

Producers, Walter MacEwen, William Jacobs; director, Joe Graham; suggested by a play by Dorothy Bennett, Irving White; screenplay, Adele Comandini; music, Heinz Roemheld; music director, Leo F. Forbstein; orchestrator, Frank Perkins; camera, Sid Hickox; editor, Thomas Pratt.

Kay Francis (Marjorie Scott); Walter Huston (MacKenzie Scott); Gloria Warren (Victoria Scott); Patty Hale (Booley); Frankie Thomas (Martin Scott); Una O'Connor (Angie); Sidney Blackmer (Philip Ames); Armida (Lolita); Frank Puglia (Joe Borelli); Anthony Caruso (Frank); Elvira Curci (Rosita); Herbert Gunn (Dick); Harry Lewis (Steve);

John Hamilton (Warden); Borrah Minevitch and The Rascals (Blackie and His Musicians); Leon Belasco (Violinist); Cliff Saum (Trusty); Lester Sharpe (Tuba Player); Frank Mayo (Pianist); Hank Mann (Truck Driver); Lon McCallister (Boy); Jean Ames, Juanita Stark, Mary Brodel (Girls); Frank Lackteen (Pedro); Bob Stevenson (Fisherman); Pat O'Malley (Cop).

BETWEEN US GIRLS (*Universal, 1942*) 89 min.

Producer, Henry Koster, associate producer, Philip P. Karlstein (Phil Karlson); director, Koster; based on the play *Le Fruit Vert* by Regis Gignoux, Jacques Thery; adaptor, John Jacoby; screenplay, Myles Connolly, True Boardman; art directors, Jack Otterson, Richard Riedel; gowns, Vera West; music director, Charles Previn; camera, Joe Valentine; editor, Frank Gross.

Diana Barrymore (Caroline Bishop); Robert Cummings (Jimmy Blake); Kay Francis (Christine Bishop); John Boles (Steven Forbes); Andy Devine (Mike Kilinsky); Ethel Griffies (Gallagher); Walter Catlett (Desk Sergeant); Guinn "Big Boy" Williams (Father of the Boys); Scotty Beckett (Leopold); Andrew Tombes (Doctor); Peter Jamerson (Harold); Mary Treen (Mary Belle); Lillian Yarbo (Phoebe); Irving Bacon (Soda Dispenser); Aileen Pringle, Charles Coleman, Virginia Engels (Guests); Edgar Dearing (Cop); Jack Mulhall, Leon Belasco (Waiters); Billy Lenhart (Boy); Bennie Bartlett (Kid); Walter Woolf King (Duke); Ed Gargan (Cab Driver); Edgar Licho (Ambassador); Bobby Barber (Waiter).

FOUR JILLS IN A JEEP (*Twentieth Century-Fox, 1944*) 89 min.

Producer, Irving Starr; director, William A. Seiter; story, Froma Sand, Fred Niblo, Jr.; screenplay, Robert Ellis, Helen Logan, Snag Werris; songs, Jimmy McHugh, Harold Adamson; music numbers staged by Don Loper; music directors, Emil Newman, Charles Henderson; art directors, James Basevi, Albert Hogsett; set decorators, Thomas Little, Al Orenbach; camera, Peverell Marley; editor, Ray Curtiss.

Kay Francis, Carole Landis, Martha Raye, Mitzi Mayfair (Themselves); Jimmy Dorsey & His Band (Themselves); John Harvey (Ted Warren); Phil Silvers (Eddie); Dick Haymes (Lieutenant Dick Ryan); Alice Faye, Betty Grable, Carmen Miranda (Guest Stars); George Jessel (Master of Ceremonies); Glenn Langan (Captain Stewart); Lester Matthews (Captain Lloyd); Miles Mander (Colonel Hartley); Frank Wilcox (Officer); Paul Harvey (General); Mary Servoss (Nurse Captain); B. S. Pulley, Dave Willock (Soldiers); Ralph Byrd (Sergeant); Renee Carson (French Maid); Edith Evanson (Swedish Maid); Betty Roadman (Housekeeper); Mary Field (Maid); Mel Schubert (Pilot); Winifred Harris (Lady Carlton-Smith); Crauford Kent (British Officer); Frances Morris (Surgical Nurse); James Flavin (M.P.); Jimmy Martin (Aide).

DIVORCE (*Monogram, 1945*) 71 min.

Executive producer, Trem Carr; producers, Jeffrey Ber-

nerd, Kay Francis; director, William Nigh; story, Sidney Sutherland; screenplay, Harvey H. Gates, Sutherland; music director, Edward J. Kay; art director, Dave Milton; set decorator, Vin Taylor; assistant director, Richard Harlan; sound, Tom Lambert; camera, Harry Neumann; editor, Richard Currier.

Kay Francis (Dianne Hunter Carter); Bruce Cabot (Bob Phillips); Helen Mack (Martha Phillips); Jerome Cowan (Judge Jim Driscoll); Craig Reynolds (Bill Endicott); Ruth Lee (Liz Smith); Jean Fenwick (Joan Endicott); Mary Gordon (Ellen, the Housekeeper); Larry Olsen (Michael Phillips); Johnny Calkins (Bobby Phillips); Jonathan Hale (Judge Conlon); Addison Richards (Plummer, the Lawyer); Leonard Mudie (Harvey Hicks); Reid Kilpatrick (Dr. Andy Cole); Virginia Wave (Secretary); Napoleon Simpson (Train Porter); Pierre Watkin (John B. Carter).

TV title: *The Hillsboro Story*.

ALLOTMENT WIVES (*a.k.a. WOMAN IN THE CASE*) (*Monogram, 1945*) 83 min.

Producers, Jeffrey Bernerd, Kay Francis; director, William Nigh; story, Sidney Sutherland; screenplay, Harvey H. Gates, Sutherland; art director, Dave Milton; set decorators, Vin Taylor, Charles Thompson; assistant director, Richard Harlan; sound, Tom Lambert; camera, Harry Neumann; editor, William Austin.

Kay Francis (Sheila Seymour); Paul Kelly (Colonel Pete Martin); Otto Kruger (Whitey Colton); Gertrude Michael (Gladys Smith); Teala Loring (Connie Seymour); Bernard Nedell (Spike Malone); Matty Fain (Louie Moranto); Anthony Warde (Agnew); Jonathan Hale (General Gilbert); Selmer Jackson (Deacon Sam); Evelynne Eaton (Ann Farley).

WIFE WANTED (*a.k.a. SHADOW OF BLACKMAIL*) (*Monogram, 1946*) 73 min.

Producers, Jeffrey Bernerd, Kay Francis; director, Phil Karlson; suggested by the novel by Robert Callahan; screenplay, Caryl Coleman, Sidney Sutherland; art director, Dave Milton; assistant director, Doc Joos; music director, Edward J. Kay; sound, Tom Lambert; camera, Harry Neumann; editor, Richard Currier.

Kay Francis (Carole Raymond); Paul Cavanagh (Jeffrey Caldwell); Robert Shayne (Bill Tyler); Veda Ann Borg (Nola Reed); Teala Loring (Mildred Hayes); John Gallaudet (Lee Kirby); Barton Yarborough (Walter Desmond); Selmer Jackson (Lowell Cornell); Bert Roach (Arthur Mayfield); John Hamilton (Judge); Jonathan Hale (Philip Conway); Anthony Warde (Man); Sara Berner (Agnes); Charles Marsh, Claire Meade (Tenants); Will Stanton (Squint); Paul Everton (Toland); Buddy Gorman (Newsboy); Shelby Payne (Secretary); Mabel Todd (Florist); Tim Ryan (Bartender); Barbara Wooddell (Miss Sheldon); Maurice Prince, Bob Alden (Messengers); Valerie Ardis (Nurse); Wilbur Mack (Doctor); Bud Fine (Cop); Joe Greene (Hector).

As Victoria Jones in *Bhowani Junction* ('56).

130

CHAPTER 3

AVA GARDNER

5' 4"
110 pounds
Black hair
Green eyes
Capricorn

"I'M JUST A plain, simple girl off the farm," Ava Gardner has said, and she wants the public to believe that she wishes she had never left. Moviemaking, she claims, bores her. As far as she is concerned, her films, many of them classics, were only the easiest means of making money. Her performances range from surprisingly moving to embarrassingly mediocre, but she despises them all. She once told columnist Rex Reed, "My sister Dee Dee can't understand why after all these years I can't bear to face a camera. But I never brought anything to this business and I have no respect for acting. . . . I never did anything to be proud of." On another occasion she admitted, "Maybe I should have stayed in North Carolina, married some nice simple guy, and raised a big family." In case anyone does not think Ava is serious about that remark, she adds, "Go ahead and laugh, everybody laughs, but how great it must be to tramp around barefoot and cook for some great goddamn s.o.b. who loves you the rest of your life."

The Ava of today—who resides in London—is no longer a barefoot contessa. She is very different from the country girl transformed into a reckless international celebrity. Gone are her celebrated bouts of abandon as she sought one new adventure and/or conquest after another. Now she is far more withdrawn. Perhaps she is equally at loose ends and is still

131

searching for emotional satisfaction, but there are far fewer occasions these years to examine her intriguing behavioral patterns. As her close pal and hair stylist Sydney Guilaroff explains, "Ava was never born to be exposed. She's shy. No one gets to her anymore because she's been burned so many times." (She abhors most of the press who she believes has repeatedly betrayed her confidences.)

A few years ago Ava commented on her state of life to columnist Vernon Scott: "I am really an uncomplicated person. . . . Writers attribute all sorts of things to me that don't exist. Even now. I'm sorry, but I simply cannot relax. And after all these years I don't even try anymore."

Ava Lavinia Gardner was born on Sunday, December 24, 1922. Many articles about her state Smithfield, North Carolina, as her birthplace. Still others claim that she was born in an outlying area of Smithfield called Grabtown. Gardner's former publicist and personal manager David Hanna wrote that Ava decided to say that she was born in Smithfield because it sounded better. She herself told Rex Reed, "They used to write in my studio bios that I was the daughter of a cotton farmer from Chapel Hill. Hell, baby, I was born on a tenant farm in Grabtown. How's that grab ya?" It did not seem to faze her more recent biographer Charles Higham. In his book *Ava* (1974), he states that she was born in a small nearby settlement named Brogden.

Her father, Jonas Bailey Gardner, was by Ava's account a sharecropper but nevertheless had a 300-acre farm on which he principally raised tobacco. He had a sawmill and a cotton gin on his property as well. Ava was the last of seven children: five girls and two boys. (One of the boys died at the age of two when the child accidentally fired his dad's rifle; the other survived and eventually became a member of the North Carolina state legislature.) When Ava was ten, Jonas Gardner was forced to sell the farm because of the fall in the price of tobacco caused by the Depression. Ava's family life had been happy until then, but when the farm was sold her mother, Mary Elizabeth ("Molly"), left her husband and took Ava and her sister Myra with her. Molly became a matron at a Smithfield boarding house for teachers. Jonas died two years later.

In her childhood there were incidents that scarred Ava both physically and emotionally. When she was six, her sister Myra accidentally hit her under the right eye with a hoe, leaving a tiny scar that never disappeared. Decades later,

Ava would again injure her face and the fears that this first incident produced would rise to the surface once more. The on-again-off-again years of poverty left Ava ever fearful of never having enough money, eventually pushing her into a career for which she felt ill-equipped.

Her mother seems to have hated men, especially after Jonas' death. She did not want Ava to go out on dates and flew into a rage when she once caught her daughter embracing a boy. As a result, the woman who one day would be famous for her romances grew up afraid of the opposite sex. When she went on her first date in high school, she later recalled, "I couldn't think of a thing to say, so we just sat." When the boy tried to kiss her at the doorstep, she ran off in panic. A sister of Ava's remembered that "sometimes when boyfriends came to call, Ava would beg us to go to the door and tell them to go home." She was, of course, beautiful even then and had plenty of male admirers.

Where Ava went to school depended on where her mother was running a boarding house at the time. She attended Brogden Elementary School, Newport News High School (when they moved to Virginia), Smithfield High School (when they moved back), and Atlantic Christian College in Wilson, North Carolina (when Molly got a new job in nearby Rock Ridge). While at Atlantic Christian College, Ava studied to be a secretary and achieved a shorthand speed of 120 words per minute. At the time she was a rather unhappy young woman. "I never had any ambitions to be anything but dead in those days. I didn't have any interests, and there was nothing I wanted to do."

But then fate changed Ava's entire future. Her oldest sister, Beatrice ("Bappie"), who was in her late twenties, was living in New York City with her photographer husband, Larry Tarr. When Ava went to visit them in the summer of

At the age of twelve.

At age fifteen with
her mother.

1941 to look for a secretarial job, Tarr needed a model for photographs to be put in window displays at the Fifth Avenue shop where he worked. He convinced Ava to pose for the shots. Later Barney Duhan, an errand clerk in MGM's legal department, spotted the pictures in the store window. He phoned the shop to find out who the model was, intending to ask her out for a date. Beatrice answered the call, and Duhan said that he wanted to find out about Ava because he was an MGM talent scout. By this time Ava had left for North Carolina but Beatrice said she would send her back. Duhan, thinking fast, said that would not be necessary; all he would need were the pictures.

Duhan sent sixty copies of Ava's photos around the MGM offices where Martin Schenck, in charge of talent there, and publicity head Howard Dietz had Duhan and the Tarrs summon Ava back to New York for a screen test. Although Ava's Southern accent was impossibly thick at the time and she had no ideas about acting or proper poise, she possessed natural beauty. The filmmakers gave her a silent test, with the best possible lighting, and sent the results out to Hollywood. There George Sidney, later a director, reviewed it. He told an assistant, "Tell New York to ship her out! She's a good piece of merchandise!"

Ava went to Hollywood with Beatrice to endure another screen test, this time one with sound. When MGM studio head Louis B. Mayer witnessed the audition, he exclaimed, "She can't act, she can't talk, she's terrific." With that, Ava was given a standard contract for potential starlets, joining the studio where Greta Garbo, Norma Shearer, Joan Crawford, Hedy Lamarr, Judy Garland, and Greer Garson were queens, and young, luscious Lana Turner was the latest sex goddess on the lot. Ava was then seventeen years old.

At the time, the biggest male star on the Metro lot was not Clark Gable, Spencer Tracy, or Robert Taylor, but twenty-year-old, 5'3" Mickey Rooney. As the multi-talented performer would remark in his autobiography, _I. E._ (1965), "The more successful I was, the more successful I had to become. I'd acted, sung, danced, drunk, gambled. I'd met President Roosevelt and Henry Ford. My face was postered all over America.

What was there left for me at twenty? What was there left for me to do? Try marriage. That was where my drive pushed me next. My drive and the beauty of Ava Gardner."

Their first encounter was hardly a propitious one. Ava had just signed her contract and was being shown around the lot as was customary for the new starlets. On the tour she encountered Rooney who was dressed up as Carmen Miranda for a scene in _Babes on Broadway_. "I was conservative in those days," Rooney would write. "It was all of five seconds before I told myself I had seen the girl I was going to marry." What intrigued Mickey about Ava as he grew to know her was that, unlike most of the other girls he dated, she did not appear to be impressed by his fame. Moreover, once they began dating seriously, MGM executives and Mickey's parents jointly decided they did _not_ want him to get married at this juncture in his career. It might damage the professional future of the screen's Andy Hardy. So Ava became a challenge to the youth who felt driven to prove that he could do most anything. She was, in his words, "a new world to conquer."

"This girl, whom I wanted, didn't seem to want me," reports Rooney. "Well, by God, she was going to want me. I'd show her. I'd get her. The hook was baited." Mickey drove the newcomer to the studio every morning and took her out practically every night. He continually took her to nightclubs, restaurants, and his family's Encino home. He constantly tried to impress her with his jokes, stories, drum playing, and impersonations. "There wasn't a minute," says Ava, "when he wasn't on stage."

If Ava really was not impressed by Mickey, why did she let this situation continue and magnify? Columnist Ruth Waterbury observed, "There was probably a good deal of ambition mixed up in her motives. After all, for an obscure starlet to make it with the biggest star would have been a tremendous coup for her."

Mickey coached her for her first walk-on part in a feature in Norma Shearer's _We Were Dancing_ (1942),* got her the best acting and voice

*Earlier she had appeared in a Pete Smith comedy short, _Fancy Answers_ (1941), and some insist that she had a bit in Mickey Rooney-Judy Garland's _Babes on Broadway_. In 1942, she did appear in the Our Gang comedy _Mighty Lak a Goat_, playing a theatre cashier.

With husband Mickey Rooney in 1942.

coaches he could, and pressured Metro into giving her more parts. Thus she was seen in bits in *Joe Smith—American* (1942), *Sunday Punch* (1942), *This Time for Keeps* (1942), *Kid Glove Killer* (1942), *Pilot No. 5* (1943), *Hitler's Madman* (1943)*, and many others at the Metro lot, including a loan-out to Monogram for the Bowery Boys/Bela Lugosi quickie film *Ghosts on the Loose* (1943). But if ambition was her chief reason for dating (and then wedding) Mickey, she must have been disappointed, for all her roles were bit parts. *Reunion in France* (1943), for example, gave her only one line of dialogue. She resented her roles and herself for performing them.

By all accounts, however, Ava was truly attracted to the pint-sized Mickey. As she later told Joe Hyams, "He had a powerful effect. He was the original laugh-a-minute boy. . . ." Rooney cautions those suspicious of Ava's motives that then she was "rather naive and unpossessed of fierce ambition. . . . We were a couple of kids, not conspirators." At first during their courtship Ava would reply to Mickey's constant proposals, "Marry you, Mickey? I hardly know you. Please don't start that again." Later it became, "I don't want to marry anyone until I'm positive it will work out." She did not wait long enough.

After Ava accepted Rooney's newest marriage offer, Louis B. Mayer realized he had no choice but to go along with the wedding plans. Press agent Les Peterson was assigned to make sure that the ceremony received as little publicity as possible: he was to select a faraway place for the wedding and a home for the couple where they would not be bothered. He was to shield them from the general press during their honeymoon.

On Saturday, January 10, 1942, the wedding party, consisting of Ava and Mickey, Beatrice, Mickey's father Joe Yule, Sr., and his mother Nell Pankey and stepfather, drove from Los Angeles to Carpinteria, California, which is near Santa Barbara. After obtaining a marriage license, they drove to nearby Ballard. There, in a small white church, the two were married by the

Reverend Glenn H. Lutz. Ava could not afford the white wedding gown she had wanted and so had to settle for a blue dress and a corsage of orchids. After the ceremony, the couple went to Monterey. Mickey had nearly dropped the ring from nervousness during the service; that night he became entangled in his pajamas while trying to put them on. Ava had her maternal heritage to make her nervous. It was an inauspicious beginning.

Ava had feared before the marriage that Mickey would not change his way of life. He frequented the race track and elsewhere with his cronies and nagged Ava into attending parties when she preferred to stay at home and be with him. Ava would later tell Joe Hyams, "We had no idea that marriage involved a meeting of minds. That it involved sharing of problems, planning together, making a life together." Rooney would write that he "thought that marriage was a small dictatorship. . . . What should a husband do? Precisely what he wants to do. What should a wife do? Precisely what the husband wants, also."

Once an angered Ava walked out on Mickey while he was having a good time at the Palladium. When he finally returned home three or four days later drunk, she threw an inkwell at him that just missed its mark. Another time he took her to dinner and then allowed her to go home alone while he stayed to have a few drinks. When he did return, he found she had cut the furniture with a knife. Once she developed stomach pains; he could not be bothered. It turned out to be appendicitis. Rooney realized their marriage was "inevitably, inescapably doomed" the night that his wife threatened, "If I ever get pregnant, I'll kill you."

Writer James Darson in *Modern Screen* magazine (July 1949) would place the blame for the marriage breakup in part on Ava's "disappointment at not being recognized for herself." According to Darson, "An incident at a luncheon one day with several of her studio associates threw this attitude of hers into bold relief. As they were leaving the restaurant, she noticed that several people at the next table had their heads together, whispering. She was sure they were talking about her. Out of earshot, she turned to one of her friends and asked anxiously,

---

*This cheapie film entry had been lensed during one week in mid-1942 as an independent production; it was acquired by MGM who had director Douglas Sirk re-shoot some scenes in October–November 1942. There are many (unintentional) similarities between this taut minor feature and Fritz Lang's *Hangmen Also Die* (1943) released by United Artists.

Cheesecake pose, 1944-style.

With Van Johnson in
Three Men in White
('44).

With Roland Dupree, Ann Sothern, Cliff Clark (at desk), Paul Cavanagh, and Marta Linden in *Maisie Goes to Reno* ('44).

'Weren't they talking about me? What were they saying?' 'They were saying,' he replied drily, 'that there goes Mrs. Mickey Rooney.'" "No marriage can last," Mr. Darson intoned, "when a woman is not willing to be known as her husband's wife." But Ava claims she tried her best to let her husband have his way. In any event, nothing worked. One day she threw him out of their Bel Air home. He thought she would beg him to return, but she was a woman of her word. She moved back to the apartment near Westwood that they had shared following the wedding. Later the couple reconciled for a few weeks, but then parted permanently. Ava received her first divorce on Friday, May 21, 1943, in the Los Angeles courtroom of Superior Judge Thurmond Clarke. That same day Ava's mother died of breast cancer.

After the divorce Ava dated numerous men, single and otherwise, including Peter Lawford and Robert Walker. Then finally Metro gave her a decent part. In fact, she received fifth billing in *Three Men in White* (1944), one of the post-Lew Ayres *Dr. Kildare* film entries. Van Johnson was the handsome young doctor in this episode, and Marilyn Maxwell was the other woman in the story. Metro tested Ava's screen charm in another film series, casting her as Tom Drake's spouse in *Maisie Goes to Reno* (1944), starring flippant, pretty Ann Sothern as Miss Fix-It. Surviving this testing ground, Ava was given the second female lead in a minor MGM effort entitled *She Went to the Races* (1945), starring Frances Gifford and James Craig. Ava was cast as the scheming brunette, Hilda Spotts. Of the cast's work in this silly opus, the *New York Post* sympathized, "They all do as well as possible under the circumstances."

Meanwhile maturing Ava found a new boyfriend. From the cinema's biggest star, she moved on to one of the world's richest men, Howard Hughes. The bashful billionaire set up a dinner party as a means of meeting Ava. Thereafter he dated her quite frequently, presented her with gifts, and took her to Mexico on many occasions. A friend of Ava's would later recall, "One time she requested a tub of orange ice cream—certainly a way of making him prove his love for her, as at that stage in the War even a President would have had difficulty getting orange ice cream. Within two hours of the request an enormous limousine arrived at her front door and a uniformed chauffeur stepped out with a wastebasket-sized container of the best orange ice cream. Ava screamed!" But Ava tired of Hughes, although she allowed the persistent beau to continue to squire her about town.

Ava had an affair with scenarist Philip Yordan, a writer who wanted her for his film *Whistle Stop* (1946) at United Artists. The picture starred George Raft and Victor McLaglen with Ava cast as Mary, the center of the love triangle. Director Leonide Moguy soon discovered that Ava's abilities as an actress were still nascent, but she did possess tremendous sexual magnetism. The *New York Sun* labeled the crime melodrama a "second-rate thriller" and accused Ava of looking "like a Hollywood show girl." The *New York Times* was less kind, insisting that she "brings nothing but appearance to the role. . . . " But at least she was being noticed by the critics and the public, forcing MGM to re-evaluate her box-office potential.

Whistle Stop, in itself a forgettable product, did lead to Ava's first major part, as Kitty Collins in the *film noir* classic *The Killers* (1946). This was columnist/producer Mark Hellinger's first film for Universal and was based on the famous Ernest Hemingway short story. In the brutal narrative, two murderers come to town to kill The Swede (Burt Lancaster) while their victim waits in his room, knowing he is a doomed man. The remainder of the picture is laced with flashbacks as an insurance investigator (Edmund O'Brien) probes into the reasons for the killing. Lancaster, in his first screen role, turns out to be a boxer on his way down, involved with criminals and double-crossed by Miss Gardner. *News-*

---

*In his article, "Villains and Victims," in *Film Comment* (November 1974), Mitchell S. Cohen labels Ava's Kitty the "apotheosis" of the beautiful but dangerous woman of the Forties crime film. "For much of the film, Gardner hardly speaks, but her gestures and the moody *mise-en-scène* mark her as narcissistic, self-confident, and unprincipled. When she does speak, it is to frame the man who loves her, or to beg the dying husband to swear to her innocence. Kitty Collins is certainly among the most thoroughly wanton women in *film noir*—female duplicity incarnate—and Gardner meets the rather one-dimensional demands of the character with an assurance that is lacking in many of her other performances. She lets her voluptuous body and a scintillating expression carry her through the film; and (in a role in which she is, until the last twenty minutes or so, a supporting character) that is very nearly enough."

With Burt Lancaster in *The Killers* ('46).

With Tom Conway, George Raft, and Victor McLaglen in *Whistle Stop* ('46).

140

With Howard Hughes at a prize fight in 1947.

week commended the film as "one of Hollywood's top-flight thrillers" which also "achieves a credibility in dialogue and characterizations that is all too rare in its class." Ava, wrote Bosley Crowther in the *New York Times*, was "sultry and sardonic."*

Obviously, the German director Robert Siodmak in *The Killers* had worked wonders with Ava. He had perceived her potential and taught her to communicate her particular charisma to the camera. *The Killers* provided Ava with her first indirect contact with two people who would become great friends of hers in later years: John Huston, who was an uncredited collaborator on the screenplay, and Ernest Hemingway, who admired Ava's performance.

After her *The Killers* success, MGM finally had to start treating Ava well. Moreover MGM was worrying about their prima donna, Lana Turner. As one Hollywood observer phrased it, "It's no longer a secret that Lana had been her studio's prime headache for more years than Hollywood cares to remember. When it finally began to appear that her drawing power at the box office might eventually be harmed by the unfortunate publicity that Lana seems to attract . . . studio executives began to cast about for insurance—insurance in the form of a new and stellar name." And it was decided that Ava was just that insurance.

Thus she was given the part of the singer Jean Ogilvie in *The Hucksters* (1947),* a then biting indictment of the advertising industry. Ava did not have the female lead—that went to Britisher Deborah Kerr in her American screen debut—but she had a love scene with Clark Gable.** Under Jack Conway's direction, the cast, which also included Sydney Greenstreet and Adolphe Menjou, turned in superlative performances, and Ava provided one of her best. Young, pretty, and vivacious, she demonstrated that she could be a most appealing ingenue. As *Newsweek* magazine noted, she "walks off with a good portion of the footage as a smalltime singer waiting for a chance at the big time."

In her personal life Ava was equally active. She finally terminated her relationship with Hughes. It was becoming too disconcerting to continue seeing the demanding man. On one occasion he flew into town to see her, carrying with him a shoe box containing $250,000 in thousand-dollar bills that he would give her as a bonus if she would make a motion picture for him. "I told him to lump it," Ava later revealed. She then added, "If he wanted to make a deal with me he'd have to talk with my agent like everybody else. That I wasn't touching that kind of money—not now—not ever. Not if I starve." On another occasion Hughes had a quarrel with Ava regarding her continued interest in Mickey Rooney. Hughes slapped her; she knocked him unconscious with a copper-based ashtray. Exit Mr. Hughes for the time being.

By now Ava had developed into a woman who loved parties and night life. While at a club before *Whistle Stop* started production, Van Heflin's wife, Frances, a close pal of Ava's, introduced her to Artie Shaw, famed as a clarinet player, a bandleader, and former husband of four women (including Lana Turner). Ava and Shaw had a whirlwind courtship and decided to marry. But one element seemed a stumbling block. Shaw was obsessed with the need to educate and refine his women. Ava was certainly not the right woman for him at this time. The only book she had ever read completely was *Gone with the Wind*. He presented her with a variety of books to read. When she did not understand them, he grew infuriated. To accommodate him, she began taking courses in English literature and economics at UCLA.

On Wednesday, October 17, 1945, they were married by Judge Stanley Mosk at his house in Beverly Hills, with Frances Heflin as the bridesmaid. Ava wore a blue outfit with an orchid corsage. While Mickey Rooney had turned his honeymoon with Ava into a golf tournament, Shaw converted the occasion into a crash literary course. He brought Tolstoy's *War and Peace*, Marx's *Das Kapital*, and Thomas Mann's *The Magic Mountain* along for his wife to read.

---

*Years later, Arthur Hornblow would reminisce, "I suggested that they use Ava Gardner in *The Hucksters*. She was a beautiful, dedicated actress and never any trouble, but later on she became cynical by her lifestyle and demoralized by it and now does not see the good things she did."

**Ava had long had a crush on the "King," but it seemed that whenever they worked together either she or he was then currently wed.

With husband Artie Shaw
in 1946.

The Gardner-Shaw union survived one year, long enough, state some observers, for Ava "to realize that there were other things in life besides nightclubs, glamour, and adulation. . . . She learned that home, not Hollywood, was the true center of a woman's life." But Shaw apparently had no conception of how to cope with Ava. He would continually embarrass her in public and was constantly berating her for her alleged stupidity. It got so bad that Ava's friends suggested she take an I.Q. test to prove to herself she was not dumb. She did and it turned out that she possessed a high intelligence quotient. Yet she thought something must be wrong with the test. Shaw had managed to totally destroy her confidence in herself. They stopped sleeping together, but it was Ava who had to spend the nights on the couch. Finally she moved in with the agent Minna Wallis (sister of producer Hal B. Wallis). Considering the status of her personal life, the unhappy Ava was contemplating leaving acting and earning a doctorate at the University of California in Los Angeles. "What good will money and fame do me if I have no happy home?" she asked the *Los Angeles Times.*

"And money and fame are all that the studios and my agent, who persuade me to stay in pictures, promise me." On Friday, October 25, 1946, Superior Court Judge Henry R. Archibald granted Ava a divorce. Shaw would go on to other wives, including his present spouse, actress Evelyn Keyes.

A discouraged but determined Ava now continued her social life with a vengeance. She again was escorted by Peter Lawford and Robert Walker on her nights about town. But more important, while she was in New York promoting *The Killers,* she met Universal contract player Howard Duff. This relationship lasted from the fall of 1947 through 1949 and was marked by raging quarrels and equally intense good times. Duff would later relate that on their first date, "Quickly I understood how mercurial and changeable she was, maddening, exasperating one minute, adorable the next. . . . We had a restless, volatile relationship. . . . The main difference between us was that I liked to live fairly quietly whereas she always wanted to be doing something so she wouldn't have to sit still, and think. . . . Gradually I came to understand that although she thought she wanted one husband, one home, for a long period, in fact she wasn't meant to devote her life to one person at all."

Another acquaintance of Ava's at this time, speaking of Gardner's wish to have children, had a harsher analysis of the actress. "Years ago I told Ava that if she couldn't have a child, she ought to adopt. She wouldn't listen. And I think I know the reason: It would have tied her down, and that's something Ava won't let anyone do. Deep down, you see, she is really rather selfish."

Ava was a last-minute replacement in a Universal melodrama called *Singapore* (1947), directed by John Brahm and co-starring her with Fred MacMurray. It was all shot on the studio's back lot, adding to the artificial look of the production. It was made in a rush and unfortunately showed it. *Time* magazine noted that at the film's New York premiere "the first hundred women to get to the box office were awarded one string of pearls each. The pearls were synthetic. So was the picture." As Linda, the amnesiac fiancée of MacMurray, Ava was described by the *New York Times* as being "sultry and empty-headed as the script demands."

Remaining on loan to Universal, Ava next made the film version of *One Touch of Venus* (1948), the Broadway musical by S. J. Perelman, Ogden Nash, and Kurt Weill which had starred Mary Martin. This William A. Seiter-directed feature is a typical example of how Hollywood can vitiate the qualities of a property, making viewers wonder why people had enthused so much about the stage-show original. Bosley Crowther (*New York Times*) would point out in his review, "No more than three of the original sixteen Kurt Weill songs are used, and these are tossed off, incidentally, with new lyrics. . . . A second-rate brand of slapstick has replaced the musical's gossamer style." Crowther was particularly annoyed with Ava who here portrays a statue of Venus whom department store employee Robert Walker brings to life with a kiss. Crowther insisted that Ava walked across the screen "with the customary coyness and swagger of a strip-teaser about to go into her act." With the aid of offscreen dubbing, Ava had the opportunity to sing Weill's "Speak Low."

Finally Metro recalled Ava to the home lot. There had been plans of teaming her with Lana Turner, Robert Walker, and Van Heflin in a film version of *Raintree County,* but it was decided that the Civil War epic would be too costly to produce, and the project was shelved until 1957 when it was produced with Elizabeth Taylor, Eva Marie Saint, and Montgomery Clift in the lead parts. (Another project that was constantly on the boards was a talkie version of Greta Garbo's silent, *Flesh and the Devil*, 1927, to be produced and directed by Clarence Brown. The latter dropped the idea eventually.) Instead, Ava was cast in *The Bribe* (1949). Its cast, which included Robert Taylor, Charles Laughton, Vincent Price, and John Hodiak, was promising. But under Robert Z. Leonard's direction the project faltered, unaided by the Marguerite Roberts scenario. As *Newsweek* magazine analyzed it, the black-and-white feature proved to be "an essay on the nonremunerative qualities of crime so bad that it's funny." Taylor is cast as Rigby, an undercover federal agent whose duty is to jail Hodiak, the latter involved in smuggling airplane engines belonging to our armed services. But Taylor does not want to implicate Hodiak's sexy wife, Elizabeth Hintten (Ava). So, will he just chuck the whole job? No. Ava seemed to sleepwalk through her role, which was in keeping with the tone of the whole production.

At this time it is said that Ava became pregnant and allegedly had an abortion performed without an anesthetic by an unqualified doctor. The physician cut her womb so badly that according to one Ava Gardner biographer, Charles Higham, "It probably would have been very difficult [thereafter] for her to have [had] any children. The event so traumatized her that she never fully recovered from the shock, and never had a child."

One would have thought that the next of Ava's features, *The Great Sinner* (1949), would have been an artistic success. The MGM film was based on Dostoevsky's classic short novel *The Gambler,* about a man who destroys himself through his passion for gambling. The screenplay was co-written by the great novelist Christopher Isherwood and Ladislas Fodor. The film had seasoned performances by Walter Huston, Ethel Barrymore, Agnes Moorehead, and Melvyn Douglas, and a wonderful one by Frank Morgan. But it was merely an average movie.

With Robert Walker
in *One Touch of Venus*
('48).

With Charles Laughton and Robert Taylor in *The Bribe* ('49).

Isherwood objected to having Gregory Peck and Ava cast as the gambler and the Russian general's daughter he loves. Under Robert Siodmak's direction, Ava was good enough as Pauline Ostrovski, but Peck was his ever-wooden, lanky self. According to *Time* magazine, "The rich, exuberant flow of dialogue, incident, and atmosphere characteristic of the Russian master has been choked to a pedestrian trickle. Dostoevsky's brilliant insights into the tortured motives and emotions of his lovers have paled into kleig-lighted stereotypes. Much of the time Peck and Miss Gardner act as if they had been stranded at a sedate costume party. In other scenes, when they try for a truly Slavic intensity, they seem to be acting out a burlesque on the whole school of Russian novelists."

Ava's next, her third 1949 release, *East Side, West Side,* did not fare well at the hands of the critics. "Frankly," declared the *New York Times,* "we thought that films like this one had been put on the dud-list years ago." Indeed, the plot does seem unpromising, despite its adult slant. Barbara Stanwyck is a socialite of New York's East Side whose husband (James Mason) is having an affair with West Sider Isabel Lorrison (Ava). Stanwyck turns to a friend (Van Heflin) for comfort but does not allow the relationship to become anything deeper. Then Gardner is murdered and Heflin tracks down the killer, who, by the way, is neither Mason nor Stanwyck. Thanks to the excellent performances of Stanwyck and Heflin and the direction of Mervyn LeRoy, the film is an enjoyable experience. In fact, the melodrama ends with Miss Stanwyck deciding to separate from Mason, quite an advance for a Forties film. Unfortunately Ava's attentions were not on filmmaking and she gave a very bad performance in this opus.

While MGM was reluctant to loan out their beautiful Lana Turner to other studios, they had no such reluctance about Ava. She next traveled over to RKO, the studio now owned by Howard Hughes. The project was *My Forbidden Past* (also known as *Carriage Entrance*) and co-starred Robert Mitchum and Melvyn Douglas. After it was completed, Hughes kept the film on the shelf for well over a year, finally releasing it in April 1951. The costumed melodrama was passed off as "a cloyingly saccharine saga" (*New York Times*). Ava played Barbara Beaurevel, a New Orleans turn-of-the-century belle, who witnesses the man (Mitchum) she loves marry another woman (Janis Carter). So she employs her disreputable cousin (Melvyn Douglas) to seduce the wife. Unfortunately he accidentally murders her and Mitchum is accused of the crime. Ava confesses what she has instigated, but through a plot contrivance finally gets to wed Mitchum. The critics remarked on Ava's beauty as highlighted by the film's low-cut costumes.

Every so often over the years Ava had encountered Frank Sinatra, but she did not care for him at all. Ava's friend Ruth Schechter stated, "Ava disliked Frank intensely. She kept saying that she found him conceited, arrogant, and overpowering. They had an instant hostility." But it did not last. In 1950, Ava attended the premiere of the stage musical *Gentlemen Prefer Blondes* in New York and encountered Sinatra in the lobby. She suddenly realized she had an overpowering attraction to and for him. The next day their meeting was the talk of New York. They met again two weeks later (in February) at a Palm Springs party. He drove her home that evening, stopping along the way to croon to her under the cover of a palm tree. Ava now decided the singer/actor was *the* man for her.

Seemingly it was essential to the Ava-Sinatra relationship that she be the dominant one. Her career, despite the long list of inferior films, was thriving. Sinatra's voice, however, had temporarily declined and his career had gone downhill with it. Ava always claimed she wanted children; a husband whose professional life was going all wrong was the next best thing. According to David Hanna, Ava "set less score on her own success than on the happiness of mothering Sinatra, talking him out of his moods of deep depression, bolstering his courage, and reassuring him that he was the world's best singer." It certainly helped matters that Ava and Frank were both night people who required very little sleep, loved sporting events, were highly emotional, and adored Italian food and hard liquor.

Sinatra's emotional dependence on Ava at this period of his life is shown most powerfully by an infamous incident at New York's Hampshire House. Frank, despite a severe throat infection,

With Douglas Kennedy and James Mason in *East Side, West Side* ('49).

With Gregory Peck in *The Great Sinner* ('49).

was singing at the Copacabana club. It was a very important engagement for his comeback plans. But he was not establishing a rapport with his audiences. Ava, always anxious to avoid unpleasant situations, decided to avoid sitting ringside at the Copacabana, and instead went out to another club with some friends, including Artie Shaw. When Sinatra found out, he and Ava had a furious quarrel during which she threatened to leave him. Frank, holding a gun, responded by threatening to commit suicide. As Ava stalked out through the door, Sinatra fired the gun out of the window twice. He thought that would make Ava return. It did not.

But Ava was equally possessive of Frank. "I was so jealous every minute he was away from me," she once confessed. "When I couldn't get him on the telephone right away at Las Vegas or wherever he was, I wanted to kill myself. It was stupid, I suppose."

Gardner and Frank had another problem, a major one. Frank was married, had three children, and was Catholic. Louis B. Mayer tried to reason with Ava, fearful that an open scandal would ruin the studio's investment in her. But her employer's disapproval only intensified Ava's desire to be seen in public with Sinatra. Ava's refusal to be discreet about the Sinatra affair was a determined defiance of public standards of morality. She had certainly gone to the opposite extreme from her lonely solitude in North Carolina.

During this tumultuous period in her life, Ava welcomed the chance to leave Sinatra for a while to shoot *Pandora and the Flying Dutchman* (1951)* in Spain. It was her first color film. This $1.25 million feature (a big budget for 1951) was written, directed, and co-produced by Metro's Albert Lewin. The filmmaker wrote the part of Pandora Reynolds especially for Ava and worked hard with her on the role. In the 123-minute feature, the Flying Dutchman, portrayed by James Mason, is the ghost of a seaman from the seventeenth century. Wrongly suspecting his wife of adultery he killed her and blasphemed against God. As a punishment he

*In 1951 MGM planned to shoot *The Lonesome Gal* about a real-life lady disc jockey with a very sexy voice. Studio head Dore Schary stated either Lana Turner or Ava would star in the vehicle, "depending on which one is free." Neither did, nor was the film project ever realized.

was condemned to wander the seas until he could achieve salvation by finding a woman who would give up her life for him. Mason's character arrives in Spain in 1930 and becomes one of Pandora's lovers. It is she who ends his wanderings by dying.

Pandora and the Flying Dutchman is a very mature, artistic production, which failed to find an audience in its day. Not only did cinematographer Jack Cardiff illuminate the story with a flair of excellence (especially in the storm sequence) but director Lewin managed to make Ava both radiant and credible as a performer. The critics of the day who acknowledged Lewin's intelligent effort were not enthusiastic about the film. The same ambiguous tone was present in their evaluation of Ava's presence. The *New York Times* reported: "Ava Gardner . . . never looked lovelier as Pandora" but "somehow never seems to epitomize or project the character of the American singer, loved by many, but who, for no solid reason, gives both her heart and life to the troubled stranger."

While filming *Pandora,* Ava discovered the beauties of Spain and its vigorous bullfighters. She formed a relationship with matador Mario Cabre, who played her bullfighter beau in *Pandora.* Sinatra became intensely jealous of this casual (at least on Ava's part) alliance and flew to Spain to be with her. After several spats— Sinatra flew back to the States—the couple were reunited that July in London where Sinatra was to appear at the Palladium and Ava was to finish work on *Pandora.* That September, Nancy Sinatra won her separate maintenance suit from Frank and received custody of their children and the family home in Holmby Hills.

In 1927, *Show Boat,* Jerome Kern and Oscar Hammerstein II's musical adaptation of Edna Ferber's novel, opened on Broadway and became a great hit. It was filmed in 1929 and 1936 by Universal and later purchased by MGM as a starring vehicle for Jeanette MacDonald and Nelson Eddy. But the MacDonald-Eddy team never made the musical together and it was shelved until 1950 when it went into production under the direction of George Sidney. When Judy Garland proved incapable of accepting the role of Julie Laverne, Sidney decided that he wanted Ava for the color film.

148

With James Mason
in *Pandora and the
Flying Dutchman*
('51).

With Robert Sterling in *Show Boat* ('51).

149

"Everybody thought I was crazy to buy *Show Boat*," Sidney would state. "And even crazier when they heard I was going to cast Ava as Julie, the tragic half-caste that Helen Morgan played originally. . . . I can still remember Hedda Hopper and Louella Parsons calling me and begging me not to cast her. The studio top brass was dead against it. But I was determined. I *knew* she would be Julie."

The role of Julie required singing and Ava was extremely nervous about the challenges of the part. Singing coach Phil Moore would relate that Ava was "absolutely petrified of singing—into a microphone." But she wanted to sing in *Show Boat* and so she had to make a demonstration record using a microphone. Moore says, "I turned the lights off in the studio so she wouldn't have to look at the mike. That did the trick. She sang in the dark without any tension."

Although Ava recorded her songs ("Can't Help Lovin' Dat Man" and "Bill") for the film, Metro was nervous about using her voice on the soundtrack. Thus they had Annette Warren dub Ava's songs for the release print (although on the soundtrack album it is Ava's singing that is heard). The critics were mixed in their opinion of Ava's performance: "Ava Gardner, if occasionally out of her dramatic depth, has no trouble looking her part as the sensuous Julie" (*Time* magazine). "Ava Gardner does surprisingly well as the mulatto, Julie" (*Newsweek* magazine). "In the role of Julie, the singer who is found to have Negro blood, Miss Gardner is much more 'dramatic' than even a showboat soubrette should be, which, along with poor cutting and too much close-up, ruins particularly her 'Can't Help Lovin' Dat Man.' Likewise, a big 'heart' scene, written for Julie along toward the end by scriptwriter John Lee Mahin, is something you'll just have to suffer through."

But the public endorsed Ava's performance and proved that Sidney had been correct in his hunch. He explained to Charles Higham why he wanted Ava for the picture: "She was a 'second best' girl, she felt that, and she had a terrific inferiority complex. I knew that Helen Morgan had had the same sense of insecurity. And then, Ava was a Southern girl; she had a lilting accent that suited Julie perfectly. Ava went back to her North Carolina voice, and it was almost beautiful."

Ava had worked very hard at her interpretation of Julie; it was one of the first films she really cared about. She wanted to prove that in musical comedy she could be as effective as her co-stars: Kathryn Grayson, Howard Keel, and Marge and Gower Champion. But she was and still is tremendously annoyed at MGM's lack of faith in her. "I really tried in *Show Boat*," she told Rex Reed years later, "but that was MGM crap. Typical of what they did to me there. I wanted to sing those songs—hell, I've still got a Southern accent—and I really thought Julie should sound a little like a Negro since she's supposed to have Negro blood. Those songs like 'Bill' shouldn't sound like an opera. So what did they say? 'Ava, baby, you can't sing. You'll hit the wrong keys. You're up against real pros in this film, so don't make a fool of yourself.' Pros! . . . I still get royalties on the . . . records I did."

With the success of *Show Boat*, Ava's MGM contract was now renewed for another seven years. Under the new Dore Schary bureaucracy at Metro, she was to receive a $50,000 yearly salary but could be suspended if she refused to take a part that was assigned to her. Unlike Lana Turner, MGM still felt they could get along quite nicely with or without Ava's presence in the star stable.

Ironically, her next part was that of a newspaperwoman (and she despised the press who always went out of their way to report every exaggeration about her activities) in *Lone Star* (1952). Her co-star was Clark Gable and the film was a distortion of how Texas became part of the United States. Lionel Barrymore growled his way through the role of President Andrew Jackson who uses Texas cattleman Devereaux Burke (Gable) to help persuade Sam Houston (Moroni Olsen) that Texas, which has just declared its independence from Mexico, should be annexed to the United States. But Gable has to contend with Thomas Craden (Broderick Crawford), the would-be tyrannical president of Texas, and newspaperwoman Martha Ronda (Ava) who supports him. The critics were not impressed by this oversized, childish Western, nor by Ava's performance. "Miss Gardner . . . is decorative but not much more as the lady who is torn by love and political affiliations" (*New York Times*).

If Clark Gable, suffering from ill health and fears of growing old, had envied Ava's youth and vitality during the filming of *Lone Star,* Sinatra was now determined to consolidate his relationship with Ava. The singer and Ava left for a Mexican vacation, with the press besieging them all the way. Sinatra continually lost his temper with the pursuing fourth estaters, who managed to always find out just where he and Ava might be at any given moment. By the time they had returned to the States and Sinatra had gone to Reno, Nevada, he could admit, "I got sore because I got pretty rough handling from a couple of guys. They were the exceptions to the rule, though, for the press has done a lot for me."

While in Reno, Frank made arrangements for his divorce which was finally granted on November 2, 1951. The next day Frank and Ava obtained their marriage license in Judge Charles Klein's chambers in the Philadelphia City Hall; they had decided to hold the wedding at the Philadelphia home of Sinatra's pal Lester Sacks. The law required them to wait seventy-two hours before holding the marriage ceremony. Thus on Friday, November 7, the couple were wed. Among those present were Sinatra's parents, his arranger Dick Jones, his conductor Axel Stordahl with his wife June, Frank's partner Ben Barton, and Ava's sister Beatrice. Stordahl filmed the proceedings. Ava wore a Howard Greer-designed cocktail-length dress of mauve-hued marquisette.

They honeymooned for two days in Cuba and then went to New York where Frank did a TV show. When the press proved demanding, Sinatra became rambunctious, exhibiting his old flair for bad publicity. After some time in Los Angeles, they went to London for Frank's appearance at the Royal Command Variety Performance.

Ava enjoyed her new role as Frank's wife. "I thought I was going to be blasé . . . but now when people call me Mrs. Sinatra, I break out into a fit of giggles." On another occasion, she told *Movieland* magazine, "So many stories have made Frank sound like a holy terror and he's *not.* He's the gentlest, sweetest, warmest person I've ever known and I must say that most people are prepared for something else and are shocked when they meet him—good and shocked." She also told the press that she and Frank wanted to have children as soon as possible and that she and Frank wanted to make a film together. So content was Ava to be Mrs. Sinatra that she allowed the studio to suspend her when she refused to leave Frank to make a film in Mexico.

Meanwhile Darryl F. Zanuck, head of Twentieth Century-Fox, finally decided to film a project he had long planned, a version of Ernest Hemingway's story "The Snows of Kilimanjaro." Scripter Casey Robinson admitted, "I had written the part of Cynthia, that lost Twenties girl, for Ava. I'd known her when she was young. . . . All of the qualities I saw in her when she was young had developed in just the right way for Cynthia." Not only did Robinson want her for the film, but so did Hemingway himself. The part might have gone to Fox contractee Anne Francis, but the actress playing Cynthia had to look enough like Susan Hayward, who played the hero's (Gregory Peck) wife, to make credible the scene in which Peck mistakes his wife for Cynthia.

Ava wanted* to do the film, but Sinatra did not want her to, for he had to fly to New York and wanted her at his side. To oblige Ava, director Henry King rearranged the shooting schedule so that Ava only had to spend ten days on the soundstages. However, at the end of the period, King realized that to shoot Ava's final scenes he would have to film at night, which would have been financially prohibitive. He made Ava stay another day for daytime shooting, which infuriated Miss Gardner and Sinatra.

The critics were none too kind about *The Snows of Kilimanjaro,* which was released in the early fall of 1952. *Time* magazine insisted that it was "likely to remind most adult males of their more lurid adolescent daydreams." Scripter Casey Robinson describes the script as "one-

*On the home lot, Ava had rejected the role of Rebecca of York in *Ivanhoe* (1952), feeling the role was too "unimportant." Elizabeth Taylor was substituted. Plans for Ava to co-star with Clark Gable in *Sometimes I Love You* fell through because of Gable's unhappiness with the MGM regime. It was Ava who rejected *Sombrero* (1953) opposite Ricardo Montalban; she was replaced by Pier Angeli.

151

With spouse Frank Sinatra on their wedding day (November 7, 1951).

third Hemingway, one-third Zanuck, and one-third myself" which probably accounts for the pat, happy ending. Ava turned in a fairly decent performance and received good reviews. "Ava Gardner is surprisingly effective in the early scenes in Paris" (*Time* magazine). The *New York Times* thought her "pliant and impulsive as the charmer he [Peck] can't forget." *Variety* endorsed, "She makes the part of Cynthia a warm, appealing standout." Ava herself was enthralled by the role. "I really felt comfortable in that part. I could understand the girl I played so well. It wasn't like some other parts I've had. This girl wasn't a tramp or a bitch or a really smart cookie. She was a good average gal with normal impulses. I didn't have to pretend." But Ava was honest enough to say, "You won't like it, not if you're a Hemingway fan. They changed a lot of things around, including the ending."

MGM, still under Dore Schary's regime, did not seem to care about Ava's good reviews, and they cast her in another box-office dud entitled *Ride, Vaquero!* (1953),* which at best was an interesting variation on the old horse-opera formula. Ava was Cordelia Cameron, the wife of a cattleman besieged by outlaws. Her co-stars in this entry were Robert Taylor and Howard Keel. Adding insult to injury, the John Farrow-directed feature was shot in a dreary small town in Utah during 120° F temperatures.

But then Metro finally assigned Ava to a good picture, John Ford's *Mogambo* (1953). (The title means "passion" in Swahili.) This was a remake of the classic *Red Dust* (1932), moved from the Malay peninsula to Africa where Ford made good use of the wildlife. Ava was cast in Jean Harlow's old part and Clark Gable repeated his assignment from the earlier version, this time as a mighty white hunter. Grace Kelly, soon to become the biggest box-office attraction in Hollywood, had the third major role, as the very British, cool wife of Donald Sinden. Ava, in the storyline, must compete with Miss Kelly for Gable's affections; Ava wins.

Many feel that *Mogambo* is the first (and only) film which reveals the actress' real-life personality. As her sister Inez would say, "I knew when I saw it that the director had let her improvise some of the dialogue. Some of the expressions I had often heard her use in family conversation." Ava took full advantage of the opportunities the picture gave her and the critics rewarded her for it. *Newsweek* stated that "Ava Gardner, encouraged to suggest a jazzy cafe society queen rather than her usual smoldering passion flower, is very fetching whether she is shooing a large household snake called Joe out of her bed, patting a small elephant, or calculating her chances against the anthropologist's wife." The *New York Times* insisted, "She easily steals the show" and is "as enticing as any calculated vampire can be." Ava would win her only Oscar nomination to date for her role in *Mogambo,* but she lost out in the Academy Award sweepstakes to Audrey Hepburn (*Roman Holiday*).

That Ava produced such a polished performance in *Mogambo* was a tribute to her natural instincts, for she had a good deal to cope with during the on-location production. As John Ford would remark, "She was a real trouper. She was unhappy over Sinatra, but she worked...just the same. I loved her." At first Ava and Ford did not get along professionally but then he called her aside and told her, "You're damned good. Just take it easy." After that they got along beautifully together.

Before *Mogambo* started shooting, Ava and Sinatra had been fighting over his visits to his ex-wife's house to see the children. Ava, possessive as always, feared that he would return to Nancy. But despite their problems, Sinatra's career was on an upswing and the growing success made him more self-confident and far less needy of Ava's moral support. The tension exploded when Ava was in the audience for one of Frank's performances at the Fort Lee, New Jersey, Riviera nightclub and saw him singing "All of Me" in the direction of an old flame, Marilyn Maxwell. Ava flew back to Los Angeles and mailed her wedding ring to him. He managed to patch it up, but then a month later,

*Another potential MGM project that did not materialize was *My Most Intimate Friend,* which would have teamed Lana Turner and Ava as two female TV commentators vying for audience ratings and the love of the same man. However, for producer Arthur Freed, Ava made a cameo appearance as "The Movie Star" in the sophisticated musical *The Band Wagon* (1953), a cinema moment studio head Dore Schary would have preferred to have been given to Esther Williams. It seemed that Schary had very little appreciation for Gardner's screen presence.

With Gregory Peck in *The Snows of Kilimanjaro* ('52).

With Kurt Kasznar,
Howard Keel, and
Robert Taylor in
Ride, Vaquero! ('53).

154

On African location with director John Ford for *Mogambo* ('53).

in October, it was Frank who became enraged. He returned home to find Ava and Lana Turner together allegedly discussing and comparing Frank's sexual prowess with that of Artie Shaw. Sinatra refused to go on location with Ava to Africa, but then changed his mind. But by this time, Ava, now living apart from her husband, had changed her phone number (as she habitually did) and Sinatra had to apologize to her through Earl Wilson's newspaper column. The reconciliation was effected and the couple went to Africa in November.

Also during this time Frank had been making it known that he was ready and willing to play the role of Maggio in the projected Columbia film version of *From Here to Eternity,* no matter what the salary might be. Before leaving for Africa, Ava pleaded with Columbia Pictures mogul Harry Cohn to give Sinatra at least a screen test. Ava's intervention made Columbia take the idea seriously. The suspense Frank felt over whether or not he would get the role, combined with the hardships of location shooting in Africa, led to further quarreling with Ava during the *Mogambo* filming. (Co-stars Gable and Miss Kelly were then enjoying their own special romantic relationship.)

Then in the midst of the *Mogambo* lensing, Sinatra received a cable from Columbia offering him a screen test and he departed for three weeks. During this time, Ava, who was pregnant, went to London supposedly with a case of anemia. But she told John Hyams that it was really a miscarriage. "All of my life I had wanted a baby and the news that I lost him (I'm sure that it was a boy) was the cruelest blow I had ever received. Even though my marriage to Frank was getting shakier every day, I didn't care. I wanted a baby by him." But cinematographer Robert Surtees insisted, "Ava hated Frank so intensely by this stage she couldn't stand the idea of having his baby. She went to London to have an abortion. I know, because my wife went to London to be at her side at all times through the operation and afterward, and to bring her back on the plane."

When Ava returned to the filming site, she was ill, felt guilty, and found no enjoyment in her work. Then a very cheerful Frank returned; he had gotten the *Eternity* role. Within a few weeks Sinatra returned to California to begin his movie comeback. Ava went on to London to finish interior scenes for *Mogambo* and to begin production on her next, *Knights of the Round Table* (1954), Metro's first film in CinemaScope. En route, Ava, Grace Kelly, and Robert Surtees stopped over in Rome where Ava and Grace insisted Surtees take them on a round of Italian whorehouses.

Metro hoped that *Knights* would be a follow-up to its *Ivanhoe.* In fact, it used the same producer, director, and male lead for the new film: Pandro S. Berman, Richard Thorpe, and Robert Taylor, and employed the same castle set, built on a back lot of MGM's British studio. Ava played Queen Guinevere and did not care for the part; it showed in her performance. *Newsweek* found her "overly placid" while the *New York Times* rated her "luxurious and posey." *Time* magazine offered the snide comment, "Ava Gardner, as proud Guinevere, leans from a casement in a way that explains a lot of things the ancient lays left unexplained." Producer Berman explained why Ava was so bored with the role: "We were trying for a down-to-earth mass entertainment picture. It seemed more appropriate to use a beautiful woman than use someone who was a better actress but mightn't have the mass sex appeal Ava had by that time. And she didn't have such a huge part that it would have been beyond her."

Toward the end of the *Knights* shooting, Ava got a few days off, which she hoped to spend in Madrid. Sinatra, however, who had been staying with Ava in London during the filming, wanted her to come with him to Atlantic City for his new nightclub engagement. A fight ensued and Ava went off to a nightclub with Walter Chiari, the actor who was to become a post-Sinatra swain.

After wrapping up *Knights,* Ava flew back to New York where she and Frank endured several squabbles. They did attend the premiere of *Mogambo* together and jointly returned to Hollywood. But then, three weeks later, MGM issued a statement announcing that Ava would seek a divorce from Frank. The union had lasted twenty-three months and twenty days. It was to be Ava's last marriage to date.

Metro was planning to cast Ava in *Green Fire* (1954), but instead Grace Kelly was stuck with

On location with Robert Taylor for *Knights of the Round Table* ('53).

that dreadful film, set in the jungles of South America. Ava had a much better offer. Producer/director Joseph L. Mankiewicz had scripted a Hollywood exposé entitled *The Barefoot Contessa* (1954). Although the focal character was based on Rita Hayworth, Mankiewicz wanted Ava to play the part and had written the screenplay with her in mind. He had already signed Humphrey Bogart for a major role in this United Artists release. Then Metro, sensing a profit to be made, gave Mankiewicz a good deal of trouble over the loan of Ava's services. Finally an agreement was reached, with Metro receiving $200,000 plus ten percent of the gross after the first million dollars the film made. Bogart was receiving only $100,000 for the project, and as it developed Metro in turn had to pay Ava only $50,000 to $70,000 for her participation.

Arriving at the *Contessa* location in Rome, Ava informed Mankiewicz that she had not read the script. "But I read the outline. Anyhow, I just had to play it. You know I've got pretty feet. . . . Hell, Joe, I'm not an actress, but I think I understand this girl. She's a lot like me." Bogart was not fond of his co-star, feeling she was too self-centered and that, besides, she was not a good actress. "She gives me nothing," he complained. "I have to lift her every time." Bogart had the annoying habit of making sure that anytime a newspaper made an unkind remark regarding her and Sinatra or her and Luis Miguel Dominguin, her new matador boyfriend, it came to her attention. She accepted the unfriendly treatment with "rare good humor."

Meanwhile Ava continued to date Walter Chiari and was frequently escorted by Dominguin, who was a millionaire as well as a bullfighter. Frank Sinatra turned up in Rome over New Year's, but his visit must have been a disappointing one. He had to stay inside with Ava because she had developed a case of German measles.

Shot under grueling conditions (bad weather plagued the location filming), *The Barefoot Contessa* (1954) is a mixed bag of treats. Critic Pauline Kael would later evaluate that the film is "a trash masterpiece" about a Hollywood "where the men aren't men and the women are magnificent, frustrated animals. . . . It's hard to believe Mankiewicz ever spent an hour in Hollywood; the alternative supposition is that he spent too many hours there." *Time* magazine agreed, "But even the neat lines, Bogart's expert delivery, and some effectively acid scenes fail to make *Contessa* much more than an international-set soap opera."

The story is told via flashbacks from the funeral of the Contessa, Maria Vargas (Ava). Maria is only a flamenco dancer in the Madrid slums until she is discovered by an American millionaire (Warren Stevens) and his sycophantic lackey of a press agent (Edmond O'Brien). Stevens runs a movie studio and has an alcoholic has-been director (Bogart) give her a screen test in Rome. Bogart becomes her friend. She becomes a major film star and is romantically pursued by both Stevens and a South American playboy (Marius Goring). She winds up wedding an Italian count (Rossano Brazzi) who proves to be impotent. In the focal role, Ava failed to impress many critics. Bosley Crowther (*New York Times*) chided, "[She] fails to give it plausibility or appeal. . . . She is good in one or two moments—when she tells of a childhood in Madrid, and when she seeks the solace of her old friend, the director, in her terminal scene. But, for the most part, she is coldly ornamental. They say she emits electric charm. They say people fall for her at first sight. But she doesn't do anything to prove it. This is an evasion in the film."

After *Contessa* was finished, Ava went to Madrid where she had an extremely painful attack of gallstones that hospitalized her. Dominguin one night brought back a very famous Gardner fan to distract the ailing actress. It was Ernest Hemingway. Allegedly Ava told the celebrated author, "I love this damn hospital so much I almost don't want to pass this goddamn stone. Sit here on the bed, Papa, and talk to me. I'm absolutely floored you could come." She and Hemingway became good friends.

MGM then suspended Ava for refusing to play torch-singer Ruth Etting in the biographical *Love Me or Leave Me* (1955),* opposite James Cagney. "What are you trying to do to me?" she screamed at her bosses. "I stand there mouthing words like a great goldfish while

*Twentieth Century-Fox considered borrowing Ava or Lana Turner for *The Magnificent Matador* (1955). Maureen O'Hara was the actress to play the role opposite Anthony Quinn.

With Humphrey Bogart in *The Barefoot Contessa* ('54).

With beau Luis Miguel Dominguin in New York (October 1954).

you're piping in some goddamn dubbed voice." Doris Day did accept the role and nearly won an Oscar nomination for her efforts.

The suspension gave Ava a good deal of free time, which she spent dating first Dominguin and then Howard Hughes in America, and then touring South America and the Orient promoting *Contessa*. Ava had not obtained her divorce from Sinatra but insisted she would do so eventually. Meanwhile Sinatra was very depressed over losing her. For nearly a year after their separation he roomed with composer Jule Styne in a bachelor maisonette. He spent a good deal of time dating Ava Gardner look-alikes. He was quoted as saying, "Man, if I could only get her out of my plasma!" Ava and Frank did date several times during the shooting of *Guys and Dolls* (1955), in which he had a major role, but nothing happened. Ava began referring to Frank as "Mr. Sinada," "nada" being the Spanish word for "nothing." But, despite everything, the couple still retained a healthy respect for one another.

It was nearly two years before Ava was onscreen again, this time in the lavishly produced *Bhowani Junction* (1956),* based on the John Masters best seller. But the film was plagued with problems, from the laundered script to director George Cukor not being initially pleased with the choice of Ava's co-star, Stewart Granger. Then there was the nightmarish location filming in humid, intensely hot Pakistan. As producer Pandro S. Berman later recalled, "It was horrendous. I don't know how we got through it alive." Director Cukor would later admit, "Ava was a gem. She was marvelously punctual and never complained even when it was clear the poor darling was *exhausted*. She was wonderful in the part."

Bhowani Junction united Ava with a man who would become one of her few close friends, the great woman's director, George Cukor. The picture also provided her with a role different from any other in her career. She portrayed Victoria Jones, a "chee-chee," half English and half Indian, living in India during the last days of British rule there in 1947. As a half-breed she is an outcast from both races, but she tries to find a way to fit into society. Finally she becomes the lover of British officer Stewart Granger. Although Victoria's story occupies the picture's foreground, Cukor made sure audiences would be very much aware of the raging revolutionary passions of the time.

Under Cukor's guidance Ava came off surprisingly well in a difficult part. "As the Anglo-Indian lady, Ava Gardner has moments of staggering power, especially when she expresses the violence of the lady's social sentiments. Otherwise, she is mostly Ava Gardner being sorely oppressed and finding it difficult to be nice to Stewart Granger . . . or Francis Matthews. . . ." (*New York Times*). *Time* magazine on the other hand criticized, "The shape of Asia is almost obscured by the shape of Ava! Ava in costly saris, Ava in bloody rags, Ava in tight-fitting blouses, Ava bound and gagged in the villain's power, Ava clenched in the hero's arms, Ava in a temple, Ava in bed."

After completing *Bhowani Junction*, which had very respectable box-office results, Ava settled in a house some ten miles north of Madrid. She insisted she would return to America only to make movies. She excitedly looked forward to Frank Sinatra's arrival in Spain in the spring of 1956 for the filming of Stanley Kramer's *The Pride and the Passion*. But when the Academy Award-winning (*Eternity*) actor arrived, he was with his new girlfriend, actress Peggy Connolly. Ava was infuriated, but did consent to see him in private. There were no tries for any reconciliation.

Before Sinatra's arrival in Spain, Ava had gone to Rome to make *The Little Hut* (1957). She hated the script but it was the least of the evils of the projects offered her by Metro, to whom she owed three more years of service. *The Little Hut* would at least give her the chance to work with beau Walter Chiari and pal David Niven. "I'd play Little Eva if they wanted," Ava admitted. "Anything to get through this lousy deal fast."

*When Gregory Peck agreed to star with Lauren Bacall in *Designing Woman* (1957), part of the agreement—made in mid-1956—was that his independent producing company would acquire the services of Ava for a forthcoming Peck film to be entitled *Thieves' Market* at United Artists. The project did not come to fruition. Regarding Ava, with whom he would co-star in a total of three films, Peck has admitted, "As a person she has always been a close friend, and as an actress she is my favorite leading lady."

In Rome with sister
Bea in January 1957.

In a time when movies were being made in exotic locations, *The Little Hut,* which was set on a desert island, was filmed in a studio. The color feature was directed by Mark Robson, and Stewart Granger was the other co-star. "I hated it, that's all. Every minute of it," Ava later admitted to David Hanna. "It was a lousy story. I shouldn't have done it. The director was awful. It's not going to be much but what could I do? If I took another suspension, they would keep me at Metro the rest of my life."

The Little Hut was a triumph for Hollywood's hyperactive censors, but not for anyone else. The plot had Granger, his wife (Ava), and her foremost admirer (Niven) all marooned together on an island. In the Andre Roussin play, on which the film was based, the two men shared the woman's favors. In the movie, however, nothing happens. In fact, Granger's character is not even interested in her sexually. Niven talks (endlessly) about setting up a *ménage à trois,* but that is as far as he gets, being continually thwarted in his plans by a puritanical canine. Summing up the misfire, the *New York Times* noted, "It's

like a lame joke told in front of children, with the mildly naughty words spelled out."

Walter Chiari, who played a native with a limited vocabulary in *The Little Hut,* was still Ava's man of the moment. "I was obsessed with her" but "I don't believe she ever totally and committedly loved me as I loved her," he would later bemoan. "I think she felt I was riding on her coattails, that I was using her to improve my chances of professional success." Ava evidently believed the less charitable interpretation of Chiari's affection for her, and at one point was sure that "he was in league with the press in a conspiracy to persecute her." In actuality, Chiari proved to be her most devoted admirer, frequently risking his career to take a few days off from film and TV shooting to be at her beck and call wherever she might be at the moment.

Ava wanted to do another Ernest Hemingway film story and had long toyed with the idea of begging MGM to purchase the rights to *A Farewell to Arms* from Paramount. Instead, she agreed to go on loan to Twentieth Century-Fox for their rendition of *The Sun Also Rises*

161

With David Niven in *The Little Hut* ('57).

162

(1957).* Her *Kilimanjaro* director, Henry King, thought only she could play the part of Lady Brett Ashley. Since she never wanted to be the sole star of a motion picture and risk the box-office burden, she insisted on Tyrone Power for the male lead, rather than accept some lesser-known actor. When she disapproved of the initial scenario for the picture, she brought the draft to Hemingway, who threatened to sue the studio unless a new version was composed pronto.

The critics were enthusiastic about *The Sun Also Rises*. *Time* magazine raved that it was "real Hemingway almost all the way" and claimed, "In its best sequences, *Sun* shines more brilliantly than anything of Hemingway's ever filmed before." However, *Time* was discouraged by the unconvincing hopeful ending tacked onto the book's somber finish. At least in this plot, Ava ended up getting the man, despite her playing still another loose woman.

She is Lady Brett Ashley, a nymphomaniac chasing every man in sight because she cannot have the one (Power) she really wants, whom a battle wound has rendered impotent. Ava and Power play their story out against the background of the lost generation of the Twenties living in Paris and Spain. Lady Brett has much in common with the traditional fictional seductress: she loves men and destroys them.

Ava received mixed reviews. *Newsweek* wrote that she "seems a little distant" for Lady Brett. *Time* magazine, in contrast, felt that "as man-crazy Lady Ashley, Ava Gardner turns in the most realistic performance of her career." The *New York Times* acknowledged, "Miss Gardner, with an occasional look of real, fleeting anguish, excellently pegs her predatory aspects. She simply doesn't, or can't, convey the lady's innate, poignant air of breeding, for all Brett's promiscuity." Some critics chided the producers for using such a mature cast to play the young leads and suggested that Errol Flynn as the drunken Mike Campbell stole the show. For present day viewers, the film is execrable: the pacing is dull, the acting is non-existent, the

directing is mediocre, and the storyline seems improbable.

It was at this time that Ava engulfed herself in needless problems. In October 1957, about the time she and Sinatra split, she went to the ranch of Spanish bull-breeder Angelo Peralta, accompanied by Walter Chiari and some friends. Some of the people present dared Ava, who had no idea of how to ride a horse much less fight a bull, to try her luck at the sport. Peralta gave her one of his best horses and a special lance with a rubber tip to taunt the snorting bull. She agreed. In the process her horse reared and she was thrown off. The bull charged and she was thrown into the air, striking one of her cheeks in the process. As a result, she was left with a hematoma (swelling caused by a blood clot) on her right cheek.

Eventually the swelling went down so that the lump was invisible unless one set out to look for it. But no one could convince her of that. Ava was terrified. She feared her beauty might be marred and that her career might be irretrievably damaged. She flew to London to consult with the famed plastic surgeon Sir Archibald McIndoe who suggested that all they could do was to wait for the swelling to subside. Thereafter Ava became terrified of photographs and public attention. Her childhood dread of facial injury had returned with doubled force. She now felt driven to make as much money as she could while she was still in demand. She was thirty-six years old and fearful of the future.

In a fit of bad judgment, Ava agreed to star in *The Naked Maja* (1959) at United Artists. The title refers to the famed painting Francisco Goya did of his mistress, the Duchess of Alba, capturing her figure in the nude. Ava played the daring Duchess. Anthony Franciosa invested a good deal of hard work into his role as Goya, but his effort doesn't show in the Henry Koster-directed debacle. Ava turned in one of her worst performances; she virtually sleepwalks through the part. As *Newsweek* concluded of this highly publicized feature, "A stinker, and that's the naked truth."

"The one decent thing about this job," Ava told the *New York Times* concerning *The Naked Maja*, "is that it's my last picture under the Metro contract. I'll be free in September."

---

*Twentieth Century-Fox in 1957 released the David O. Selznick remake of *A Farewell to Arms* starring his wife Jennifer Jones and Rock Hudson. It was an artistic disaster.

In *The Naked Maja* ('59).

During the filming of *Maja* in Rome, where confusion reigned with the European producers, Ava invited Sinatra to come to Italy. But then she read about his new companion, an Englishwoman named Lady Beatty. When she finally saw him in Rome, she gave him back her wedding ring and told him to give his new girlfriend the ring. She later regretted her action, but by then Sinatra had hurriedly departed for New York.

Many believe producer/director Stanley Kramer to be gifted but misguided in his preachy attempts to liberalize the world through his films. One of his more subdued studies was *On the Beach* (1959), the film version of Nevil Shute's novel about the end of life on earth through nuclear warfare. The story focuses on survivors in Australia and their last days of life. Ava was cast as Moira Davidson, a disheartened woman who finds fulfillment with submarine commander Gregory Peck who has lost his wife and family in the assorted holocausts.

As *Time* magazine decided, *On the Beach* "turns out to be a sentimental sort of radiation romance, in which the customers are considerately spared any scenes of realistic horror, and are asked instead to accept the movie notion of what is really horrible about the end of the world: boy (Gregory Peck) does not get girl (Ava Gardner). . . . But what could any actor make of a script that imagines the world's end as a scene in which Ava Gardner stands and wistfully waves goodbye as Gregory Peck sails sadly into the contaminated dawn?" Yet the public and many critics found *On the Beach* to be a grim but absorbing melodrama, filled with intriguing casting, such as having Fred Astaire as a nuclear scientist who finds escape in alcohol and car racing. *Newsweek* judged the film "an extraordinary movie" and a "low-keyed . . . hair-raiser." Many were enthralled by Ava's decidedly unglamorous portrayal as a woman who had lived too hard and looked it.* Other less kind souls insisted it was merely type-casting for the aging sex symbol. *Newsweek* approved, "Miss

Gardner has never looked worse or been more effective."

Although Ava had finished her obligations to MGM, she found herself in a Metro release for 1960, *The Angel Wore Red*. She accepted the offer from director/scripter Nunnally Johnson, an old friend. She played Soledad, a Spanish cabaret girl who falls in love with a priest (Dirk Bogarde). The *New York Times* lambasted the picture, including its sensationalized title: "The shade of the heroine's wardrobe, whether scarlet or cherry-blossom pink, hardly matters when the film is released in standard black and white." The leads' love affair, which was considered highly controversial in 1960, was set against the background of the Spanish Civil War. The few who saw the film were unimpressed with its histrionics and its politically oriented message.

Years later Nunnally Johnson would recall of Ava, "She would cry a lot. She had no confidence in herself. She felt she couldn't act. She had no home, no base, no family. She missed them terribly. She felt she'd missed out on life. It was hard to believe her unhappiness." After the filming of *The Angel Wore Red*, Ava became a more erratic, hyper-tense creature, bouncing about from place to place. She still continued to see Walter Chiari, but nothing came of it. She would give dinner parties in Madrid that lasted up to twenty-four or thirty-six hours. Yet in her periods of great self-doubt she could still be generous. When Mickey Rooney was broke, she gave him a monthly stipend.

Philip Yordan, who long ago had put Ava in *Whistle Stop*, now offered her the principal female role in producer Samuel Bronston's epic *55 Days at Peking* (1963). Despite its Chinese setting, it was to be shot in Spain, with 1,500 Chinese flown in for the filming. Ava only did the movie for the money, and her mediocre performance and erratic behavior on the set showed it. Yordan would reveal, "Her manner had grown disdainful, bitter, superior, contemptuous. All through the picture she was constantly drunk. . . . She would remain in her dressing room, terrified by the thousands of extras, and her double appeared in endless over-the-shoulder shots. In many scenes . . . when [Charlton] Heston . . . begged her to join him . . .

*Before leaving for Australia to film *On the Beach*, Ava had Dr. McIndoe perform a minor operation, which lasted less than a minute, to help her cheek resume its natural look. No problems were encountered.

On location in Australia for *On the Beach* ('59).

166

With Gregory Peck in *On the Beach*.

With Dirk Bogarde in
The Angel Wore Red
('60).

167

she again hid, drank, and sulked. The real reason was fear: she was terrified of the competition from the major British stars, David Niven and Dame Flora Robson, appearing in the film and terrified also of the mob."

In addition, she was paranoid about her by now invisible facial injury. Once an actor playing a bartender took a picture of her. He was fired but she walked off the set for the rest of the day anyway. A fourteen-year-old boy who loaded the big cameras had to be transferred to a job in the photo lab because Ava was sure he was another secret photographer. Once there were two still photographers on the set who had agreed to show the actress the pictures they took, relying on her approval. But things still went wrong. She saw them talking and giggling and decided they must be making fun of her, so she ordered them off the set.

Ava was high-strung, to say the least, when she did appear on the set. Often she threw a temper tantrum and stalked off the soundstage. She did not fraternize with anyone on the set and retreated to her dressing room when she was not needed. On the set she would down a shot glass

of liquor after every take. But she never missed a day of shooting due to drinking. She would look beautiful on arriving in the morning, but as the day wore on the effects of those shot glasses took their toll on her looks and her temper. She did not get along with director Nicholas Ray. She had not wanted Heston in the film and had made her feelings known. Whenever she was on the set, she radiated a faint hostility toward everyone.

Artistically, *55 Days* did nothing to help her career and surely the outrageous stories of her behavior must have damaged her reputation within the industry. As a matter of fact, scripter Philip Yordan killed her off early in the storyline because he was so dissatisfied with her behavior during the shooting. Her reviews were rather unflattering. "Ava Gardner, as an ill-fated tarnished Russian baroness with whom Mr. Heston falls in love, appears to be merely haggard and tired in a role that could stand some elaboration."

Ava was next supposed to join with David Niven and Robert Wagner in the comedy *The Pink Panther* (1964), but she made such exces-

168

sive demands that she was dropped from the roster. The revamped casting included Capucine and Claudia Cardinale.

She did appear in United Artists' *Seven Days in May* (1964), based on the Fletcher Knebel-Charles W. Bailey II novel. She portrays Eleanor Holbrook, a Washington party hostess who has had an affair with General Scott (Burt Lancaster) who is out to overthrow the U.S. government headed by good President Fredric March. Colonel Casey (Kirk Douglas), in an attempt to foil his plot, tries to obtain Scott's love letters from Ava. As the distraught abandoned mistress, Ava gave a solid performance with no little thanks due to director John Frankenheimer. She was, of course, once again playing the beautiful other woman, but this time the audience's sympathies are on her side. Despite the brevity of the part, it was a key role and was bound to stand out since it was the film's only important female character. Ava was upset at the way the film's black-and-white photography made her look old, but she was satisfied with her reviews and felt that for once she had been in a motion picture with something important to say.

Old friend John Huston flew to Madrid to convince Ava to assume the role of Maxine in his upcoming filming of *The Night of the Iguana* (1964). The idea of playing a part written by Tennessee Williams (which had been performed on the stage by Bette Davis and Shelley Winters) terrified Ava. But Huston was determined. "She was—is—a very fine actress, though she thinks she's lousy. I knew she had the kind of random, gallant, wild openness Maxine had along with the 'other side' of Ava, which is very 'close' and almost secretive." Like Honey Bear in *Mogambo* and Eleanor Holbrook in *Seven Days,* two of her better roles, Maxine Faulk was a woman who was in certain ways similar to Ava herself. In this case the similarity was in her sadness as well as in her exuberance and Southern background. Ava eventually gave in to Huston's pleading and signed the contract, although she later tried to renege, fearing she was inadequate for the job.

The set of *The Night of the Iguana* was highly charged with the press covering all the activities with minute, world-wide attention. Star Richard Burton was accompanied by his then-fiancée Elizabeth Taylor, and observers predicted that there would be flare-ups of jealously between Taylor and Sue "Lolita" Lyon and/or Deborah Kerr. But the cast acted with decorum and dispatch, even though Ava admitted that Richard Burton was a man after her own heart and that Deborah Kerr's husband, writer Peter Viertel, was a former beau.

Ava found one of her finest screen vehicles in *Iguana. Time* magazine enthused, "In ten wild weeks at sunny places for shady people on Mexico's spectacular west coast, Huston and company put together a picture that excites the senses, persuades the mind, and even occasionally speaks to the spirit—one of the best movies ever made from a Tennessee Williams play." *Newsweek* commented that "Ava Gardner would be an improbable Maxine, except that Huston has had her get rid of what he calls her 'MGM English' and return to her original North Carolina drawl. Her vowels are wind-blown, like her hair, and she is all high blood and blowziness." Bosley Crowther (*New York Times*) substantiated that "appropriate, however, is Ava Gardner as the owner and mistress of the hotel, which she personally imbues with a raucous and blowzy decadence. Her loose-jointed sweeps across the premises, her howling gibes at the clattering guests, and her free deportment with a couple of glistening beach boys does help to steam the atmosphere."

Gardner's friendship with Huston involved her in *Iguana,* but it also led her into participating in *The Bible (. . . In the Beginning)* (1966), produced by Dino de Laurentiis for Twentieth Century-Fox with a screenplay by Christopher Fry. The critics unanimously concurred about this costumed epic—it was appalling. Brendan Gill, then the *New Yorker*'s film critic, wrote that "it has something in it to offend everybody" and that the movie "has been made on a scale and with an opulence that signal 'Epic!' 'Epic!' 'Epic!' and 'Money!' 'Money!' 'Money!' from one gorgeously bedaubed and bedizened sequence to the next."

Ava portrayed Sarah, Abraham's (George C. Scott) barren wife who miraculously, at an advanced age, bears him a son, Isaac. Bosley Crowther (*New York Times*) was convinced that Ava and Scott "play the couple as though

With Kirk Douglas in *Seven Days in May* ('64).

170

they were posing for monuments." "Ava Gardner's Sarah," reported *Newsweek,* "though she hardly looks ninety, makes a moving display of time-ravaged beauty." Indeed, although Ava is undercut by her weak, emotionless voice, she gives a solid performance. It is quite remarkable that an aging but still very impressive beauty like her would play a role requiring her to wear so much unflattering old-age makeup.

During the filming of the $18 million *The Bible,* George C. Scott fell passionately in love with Ava and followed her from Rome to London after they finished the picture. Scott found himself in a very vulnerable position. Ava was not in love with him and he was not in control of his extremely volatile emotions. In London he made his way to the Savoy Hotel where she was staying and not only broke down the door to her room, but brutalized her. According to John Huston, "He [Scott] began chasing her clear across the map—he even made a terrible scene after he had followed her to Hollywood and tracked her down to the Beverly Hills Hotel. When he found she was there he went up to her room and kicked the door down and molested her. At one stage in all of this he had to be put away in a nursing home." Even though Ava stopped seeing Scott for a time, they would have several meetings in 1971 while Ava was acting in Huston's *The Life and Times of Judge Roy Bean* and Scott was making his directorial debut in *Rage,* both shooting in Arizona.

For a while there were rumors that Ava would star in a film biography of Cervantes, playing an expensively kept woman. Vincent Sherman was scheduled to direct, but the project was later abandoned. Jackie Gleason in 1967 announced that he wanted Lana Turner and Ava to join with him in a film version of Peter Viertel's book *How Do I Love Thee?* It was eventually picturized with Gleason, Maureen O'Hara, and Shelley Winters.

To demonstrate that time was leaving Ava in its wake, for the third film version of *Mayerling* (1969) she was cast not as Omar Sharif's leading lady, but as his *mother,* Empress Elizabeth of Austria. But all was not lost, for Sharif's character, Prince Rudolf, has an Oedipal crush on his mother. Ava came off very well in this costumed picture released by MGM and co-starring Catherine Deneuve as Sharif's ill-fated love. "The surprise of the picture is Ava Gardner, as the enigmatic Empress of Austria, a roving sportswoman who champions her son's happiness. With an uncertain smile and a husky voice, this beautiful lady is the most beguiling character in the movie. She movingly underplays her few scenes, especially one encounter with Miss Deneuve." Ava interacted well with James Mason (as Emperor Franz-Josef) but she did not get along with Egyptian-born Sharif. He recently had unkind words about Ava: "Her drinking caused her to miss lines and cues. That's frustrating when one is working long hours in miserable, cramped locations." He claimed that her imbibing led her "to play practical jokes that no one appreciated—such as throwing glasses of water at the actors in their period costumes."

In 1969, Ava consented to play the title role in *The Devil's Widow* for her friend Roddy McDowall, who directed it. The movie was shot in London and Scotland and underwent several name changes. (It was also known as *Tamlin* and *Toya* before it got its final tag.) It was eventually acquired for distribution by American International in 1972 but shunted off to television rather than for any substantial theatrical playdates. Gardner biographer Charles Higham called it "a thoroughly ridiculous example of camp Gothic."

In an industry that prizes youth and beauty, Ava found it increasingly difficult to find film roles that would not totally embarrass her or the public. There was talk that she and Lana Turner would co-star in *Shocking!,* based on a story by Henry "What Ever Happened to Baby Jane?" Farrell. It concerned two glamorous sisters who seek to kill one another. The project was never made. But she did agree to a cameo part in John Huston's *The Life and Times of Judge Roy Bean* (1972). Paul Newman was cast as the legendary lawman who has a passion for actress Lily Langtry. In the episodic Western, Lily (Ava) does not appear until the final scene when she visits the Western town named after her, which is now no more than a railroad way station. It required Ava's services for only three days, but Huston paid her $50,000 for her time.

As the Seventies proceeded, Ava became far

With James Mason in *Mayerling* ('69).

With *Mayerling* producer M. Shaw in 1969.

With director Roddy McDowall on the set of *The Devil's Widow* ('69).

less of a gadabout, settling down to a more reclusive London life. She still keeps in touch with Mickey Rooney and Artie Shaw and is "very close" to Sinatra (having patched differences occurring when she accused his then wife-to-be, Mia Farrow, of looking like a boy). It is known that Sinatra provides Ava with considerable financial assistance (the gift of money, the loan of his Mexican villa, etc.) at a moment's notice.

Regarding her return to Hollywood to film the disaster picture *Earthquake* (1974), Ava commented: "To be honest, I needed a paid vacation. It wasn't [producer] Jennings Lang or the script. And it wasn't for a large salary, either. I wasn't paid that much. I was just ready for a change of scenery."

She was reunited on the Universal soundstages with co-star Charlton Heston and *The Little Hut* director Mark Robson. This time she got along well with both. Heston would graciously say after completing the filming, "In this picture she had a difficult part, and she was very good in it."

Universal spent $25,000 decorating a dressing room in Ava's favorite shades of green. Although the plush days of Hollywood's golden era were gone, Ava tried to revive a fragment of them, inviting co-workers and pals to luncheons in her dressing room. However, she hardly seemed like the Ava of old. Except for having wine, she did not drink much during the filming.

She seldom went out, preferring to stay home nights at her sister Beatrice's house. The only major events she attended during her California sojourn were a charity function benefiting the residents of the Watts ghetto and an exercise in nostalgia (the premiere of MGM's *That's Entertainment!*). For the latter event, she was accompanied by hair stylist Sydney Guilaroff, her long-time friend. Like many cinema stars, she has always been frightened of big crowds. When the fans spotted Ava at the premiere and began chanting her name, she panicked. "I've never seen Ava so frightened," reported Guilaroff. "She gripped my arm so tightly it hurt." In one way, Ava had become eccentric: her passion for animals had increased tremendously. Allegedly she would telephone her London flat just to hear her own dog barking.

During production of *Earthquake*, Ava was

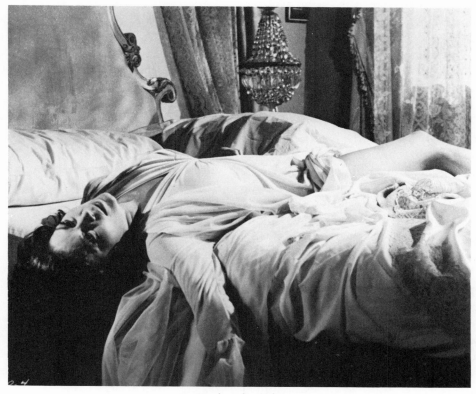

In *Earthquake* ('74).

some fifteen to twenty pounds heavier than of old and it caused one particularly embarrassing moment. A scene required a group of survivors to be lifted through a concrete hole drilled by rescuers. When it came time for Ava to be passed through the opening, she could not fit. Everyone expected the star to burst into a tantrum, but surprisingly she remained calm, saying, "Let's try that until we get it right."

Regarding her performance in *Earthquake,* she would insist to writer Vernon Scott, ". . . Charlton Heston and I play a scene in the middle of a raging torrent. At one point the water actually ripped off the wig I was wearing. It was realistic enough, God knows. I felt the bruises for a week. But I don't think you could call that acting. No, I'm not an actress." She also told Scott, "If studios and producers are willing to pay me to appear in their pictures, that's their business. And I enjoy the people on the set. I like other performers."

Earthquake offered viewers spectacular special effects on the screen as well as some earth tremors of their own via the new "Sensurround" process. The basic storyline was a hodgepodge of soap opera geared to make use of the assorted guest stars, ranging from George Kennedy to Marjoe Gortner to Richard Roundtree. Lorne Greene as Ava's father looked younger than the actress; in fact, she looked her best without the unflattering makeup as she struggled in the flooding sewer. Some of her dialogue as Heston's self-willed wife was embarrassingly trite. At one point early in the narrative she shouts at him, "Don't you lower your voice to me." Her role must have been an ironic change for her. After years of playing the other woman, now she was portraying Heston's jealous spouse opposite the other (younger) woman, Genevieve Bujold. *Earthquake,* while a big moneymaker at the box office, was definitely not one of the finer disaster epics.

Filming for Ava's next two films, *Permission to Kill* (1975) and *The Blue Bird* (1976), began in January 1975. Ava flew from London to Vienna, where *Permission to Kill* was to be shot, only to announce that unless she got top billing (over co-star Dirk Bogarde) she would turn right around and go back. She had pulled a similar stunt in *Earthquake.* Bogarde observed, "She can have the billing—I'll take the reviews." When the Avco Embassy Picture was released in November 1975 Bogarde had the top billing spot.

The story of the shooting of the new movie version of Maurice Maeterlinck's 1908 fantasy, *The Blue Bird,* has already become legendary. On paper the project seemed viable. It was to be the first American-Russian co-production, to be directed by George Cukor, with a cast including Elizabeth Taylor (in roles of Light, Mother, Witch, and Maternal Love), Jane Fonda (as Night), and Cicely Tyson (as Cat). Ava would play, appropriately enough, the part of Luxury. But everything began going wrong once shooting started in Russia. "The first word I learned here was problems," a harassed George Cukor informed *Newsweek.* Actor James Coco had to undergo surgery and was replaced in the film. The Russians refused to work overtime. Local cuisine made the Americans sick, so food had to be flown in from London. The Russians did not have up-to-date filming equipment available for the project and there was difficulty shipping proper substitutions from Hollywood. The Kirov Ballet withdrew from the film. The Russian cameraman was fired because he did not know how to work with color film and was making the scenes look too dark.

During filming Ava and Cukor got along well, quite pleased with the technical work of cinematographer Freddie Young. But the usual Ava Gardner shyness and temperament did emerge. On occasion she would lock herself in her dressing room and at another time she left Russia during the lengthy location shooting for an unscheduled trip to appease her ego.

The film, a simple story about two woodcutters' children looking for the Blue Bird of Happiness, ran over budget to a cost of $8 million. For a time the "epic" was suspended. Finally *The Blue Bird* was completed and, despite severe pre-release jitters, the film was distributed in time for the 1976 Easter season. There were few enthusiasts for the production. *Time* magazine snipped, "It is probably the first movie in history made because a country was available." The same journal termed the final results, "A cultural casualty." Howard Kissel (*Women's Wear Daily*) was more caustic, judg-

With Frederic Forrest in *Permission to Kill* ('75).

As "Luxury" in *The Blue Bird* ('76).

178

ing the picture "unnatural, static, and clumsy." He thought all "the high-priced talent" was wasted. "There is no way they can breathe life into the stilted, leaden dialogue and the dreary visual style does not enhance their natural screen presence." The much ballyhooed project was rather quickly withdrawn from release, probably to show up as a two-part TV special in some future season.

Meanwhile *Permission to Kill* was thrust into release and suffered critical barbs and public indifference. "Freddie Young's lensing is the only element which makes this film bearable. . . . [It] is a boring, talky, and dramatically flaccid European espionage meller. . . ." (*Daily Variety*). The disgruntled reporter continued, "It's sad to report that even Freddie Young can't do much to make Ava Gardner look good. She should play character roles and abandon the pretense of glamour." Within the ninety-six minutes of silliness, Dirk Bogarde is a phony intelligence agent who hopes to bring political exile Bekim Fehmiu out into the open so he can be killed. To accomplish this Fehmiu's ex-mistress (Ava) is drawn into the story. The *Hollywood Reporter* summed up the picture as "tripe." Ava had one bit of delicious dialogue. At one point a character is reciting expository statements to her and she chirps back, "I don't need to be told my life story. I happened to have lived it."

Thereafter Ava returned to London* where her escorts about town and on treks to Monte Carlo included twenty-eight-year-old black singer Freddie Davies and Spanish financier Riccardo Sicre (a great pal of Prince Rainier of Monaco). After visiting her family in North Carolina and Los Angeles, Ava returned to Europe to begin her role in *The Cassandra Crossing* (1977), a Sir Lew Grade/Carlo Ponti co-production starring Sophia Loren and Richard Harris, with guest performances by Burt Lancaster, Ava, Ingrid Thulin, O. J. Simpson, and Lee Strasberg. As the *Hollywood Reporter* noted of this V.I.P.-studded entry, it "is truly a disaster film. It concerns one and is one."

*She originally had a five-story house in Park Street, but recently moved to Ennismore Gardens, purchasing a second-floor flat. She has transformed the spacious area into an elegant home—very regal, very Edwardian. Her bed is a decorator's delight, a relic from the Napoleonic era.

The plotline was preposterous (a terrorist boards the Geneva-to-Stockholm Express, exposing the train passengers to a deadly virus), the acting was ludicrous, and the tension was non-existent (except for those viewers debating if they should leave the theatre and waste their admission fee). While a very mature Sophia Loren tried to act girlish and used the benefit of filtered photography to aid in the illusion of youth, Ava was far more natural as Nicole, the wife of a millionaire German arms manufacturer, traveling with her bored young gigolo (Martin Sheen). Ron Pennington (*Hollywood Reporter*) wrote, "Ava Gardner comes off as Ava Gardner (which is not necessarily a bad way to come off). . . ."

Director Michael Winner displayed a tinge of sentimentality when he hired Gardner for *The Sentinel*. "I cast her as the realtor [Miss Logan] . . . because every time I rent an apartment in New York, I get it from a realtor who looks just like Ava. She keeps saying she's a lousy actress, but she's very good. She's a recluse. She lives near me in an old Victorian house in London [actor Charles Gray is another Kensington neighbor of Ava's] and hardly ever goes anywhere or sees anyone. She hardly leads a film star's life, to put it mildly."

Regarding her *The Sentinel* stint, the star announced, "It should be a scream to do." However, the resultant demon-cycle film failed to

As Miss Logan in *The Sentinel* ('77).

charm the critics. "[It] is a grubby, grotesque excursion into religioso psychodrama," exhorted *Variety.* "[It] is notable for uniformly poor performances by a large cast of familiar names." Ava was "subdued, matter-of-fact" in her brief appearances (three scenes only) as the mysterious Brooklyn Heights realtor. To her credit, she looked more svelte than recently, although a bit too plumpish. In its quick playoff engagements, *The Sentinel* made back its costs but brought no glory to anyone involved.

A favorite gambit of yellow journalists is to keep tabs on aging glamour stars and to interpret the least little mishap that befalls them into a grand tragedy, slanted to show how they cannot cope with advanced middle age. Rita Hayworth has been a prime target and so has Ava; but the latter is far more self-contained.

She claims, "I don't mind growing old. I'd like to live to be 150. . . . I'll even have a fellow then. If I have to go before my time, this is how I'll go—cigarette in one hand, glass of scotch in the other."

Regarding drinking: "I'm not the great big boozer the press makes me out to be. I'm really rather a sneaky drinker. I'll pretend I have a lot more than I actually have. . . . I love parties and staying up late, but I believe that nothing must interfere with your work. If you can't get out of bed the next morning, or go straight from the party to work, then you should knock it off."

About London: "I like to live simply and out of the public eye. I can do these things in England. I am left alone there. My friends and I have dinner at our homes or go to parties in public places without being disturbed. That isn't too much to ask. It is easier for me in that respect than it is [in the United States]. The press refuses to believe that."

On the subject of her career, she admits, "I've always felt uncomfortable with stardom. My acting was never that hot. I felt it even when my directors assured me I was great."

One of her favorite topics still is Frank Sinatra. "I'm very happy for him that he's married to Barbara Marx. I sincerely wish them both the very best of everything. I want him to be happy." On one other occasion, she remarked, "We often run into one another. I know I can turn to him whenever I need him for something. . . . Often, when I've forgotten the time difference between England and California, I've awakened him in the middle of the night just to chat with him. . . . They're not mighty long conversations, but just enough to know the link is still there. It's a very good, friendly relationship that's important to both of us. . . . He'll always be that very special person to me."

Whatever myths circulate about the Ava of today, it is known that she is a much milder version of her former reckless self. Not that long ago, she was sitting in a famous bar in Rome and was asked by the owner to join him and some notables at a special table. But the one-time sex goddess refused. She lamented, "I'm not the playgirl I used to be. I prefer to be alone."

FILMOGRAPHY

WE WERE DANCING (*MGM, 1942*) 94 min.

Producers, Robert Z. Leonard, Orville Dull; director, Leonard; based in part on the play *Tonight at 8:30* by Noël Coward; screenplay, Claudine West, Hans Rameau, George Froeschel; art director, Cedric Gibbons; costumes, Adrian; sound, Douglas Shearer; camera, Robert Planck; editor, George Boemler.

Norma Shearer (Vicki Wilomirsky); Melvyn Douglas (Nicki Prax); Gail Patrick (Linda Wayne); Lee Bowman (Hubert Tyler); Marjorie Main (Judge Sidney Hawkes); Reginald Owen (Major Tyler-Blane); Alan Mowbray (Grand Duke Basil); Florence Bates (Mrs. Vanderlip); Sig Rumann (Baron Prax); Dennis Hoey (Prince Wilomirsky); Heather Thatcher (Mrs. Tyler-Blane); Connie Gilchrist (Olive Ransome); Florence Shirley (Mrs. Charteris); Paul Porcasi (Manager of Duquesne); John Piffle (Dutchman); Lionel Pape (Englishman); Philip Ahn (Chinaman); George H. Reed (Butler at Blane's House); Ottola Nesmith (Mrs. Quimby); Mary Forbes (Mrs. Sandys); Thurston Hall (Senator Quimby); Douglas Wood (Colonel Sandys); Alan Napier (Captain Blackstone); Bryant Washburn, Sr. (Mr. Lambert); Florence Wix (Sporting Woman); Alfred Hall (Butler); Betty Hayward (Debutante); Duncan Renaldo (Sam Estrella); Russell Hicks (Bryce-Carew); Harry Hayden (Clerk); Norma Varden (Mrs. Bryce-Carew); Tim Ryan (Traffic Cop); Ian Wolfe (Reggie); Henry Roquemore (Mr. Ransome); Charles Sullivan (Train Announcer); Ava Gardner (Girl).

JOE SMITH—AMERICAN (*MGM, 1942*) 63 min.

Producer, Jack Chertok; director, Richard Thorpe; story, Paul Gallico; screenplay, Allen Rivkin; art director, Cedric Gibbons; camera, Charles Lawton; editor, Elmo Vernon.

Robert Young (Joe Smith); Marsha Hunt (Mary Smith); Harvey Stephens (Freddie Dunhill); Darryl Hickman (Johnny Smith); Jonathan Hale (Blake McKettrick); Noel Madison (Schricker); Don Costello (Mead); Joseph Anthony (Conway); William Forrest (Gus); Russell Hicks (Mr. Edgerton); Mark Daniels (Pete); William Tannen (Eddie); Ava Gardner (Girl).

British release title: *Highway to Freedom.*

SUNDAY PUNCH (*MGM, 1942*) 70 min.

Producer, Irving Starr; director, David Miller; story, Fay and Michael Kanin; screenplay, Allen Rivkin, the Kanins; art director, Cedric Gibbons; camera, Paul Vogel; editor, Albert Akst.

William Lundigan (Ken Burke); Jean Rogers (Julie); Dan Dailey, Jr. (Olaf Kensen); Guy Kibbee (Pops Muller); J. Carroll Naish (Bassler); Connie Gilchrist (Ma Gulestrom); Sam Levene (Roscoe); Leo Gorcey (Biff); Rags Ragland (Killer); Douglass Newland (Baby Fitzsimmons); Anthony Caruso (Cucci); Tito Renaldo (Jose); Michael Browne (Al); Dane Clark (Bill); Dick Wessel (Moxie);

Dave Willock (Milkman); Lester Matthews (Smith); Alfred Hall (Butler); Floyd Shackleford (Doorman); Duke York, Sammy Shack (Fighters); Edward Earle (Clerk); Marcia Ralston (Blonde); Pat West (Announcer); Robin Raymond (Vivian); Ava Gardner (Ringsider).

THIS TIME FOR KEEPS (*MGM, 1942*) 73 min.

Producer, Samuel Marx; director, Charles Riesner; screenplay, Muriel Roy Bolton, Rian James, Harry Ruskin; camera, Charles Lewton; editor, Frederick Y. Smith.

Ann Rutherford (Katherine White); Robert Sterling (Lee White); Virginia Weidler (Harriett Bryant); Guy Kibbee (Harry Bryant); Irene Rich (Mrs. Bryant); Henry O'Neill (Arthur Freeman); Dorothy Morris (Edith Bryant); Richard Crane (Eustace Andrews); Connie Gilchrist (Miss Nichols); Joe Strauch, Jr. (Milton); Tim Ryan (Professor Diz); John "Buddy" Williams (Porter); Ken Christy (Conductor); Ava Gardner (Girl in Car); George Noisom (Caddy); Robert Emmett Keane (Mr. Reiner); Frank Hagney (Linesman); Doris Day (Freeman's Secretary); Bess Flowers (Saleslady); Babe London (Fat Lady); Regina Wallace (Mrs. Lornow).

KID GLOVE KILLER (*MGM, 1942*) 74 min.

Producer, Jack Chertok; director, Fred Zinnemann; story, John C. Higgins; screenplay, Allen Rivkin, Higgins; music, David Snell; art director, Cedric Gibbons; camera, Paul Vogel; editor, Ralph Winters.

Van Heflin (Gordon McKay); Marsha Hunt (Jane Mitchell); Lee Bowman (Gerald I. Ladimer); Samuel S. Hinds (Mayor Daniels); Cliff Clark (Captain Lynch); Eddie Quillan (Eddie Wright); John Litel (Matty); Catherine Lewis (Bessie Wright); Nella Walker (Mrs. Daniels); Ava Gardner (Carhop).

PILOT NO. 5 (*MGM, 1943*) 70 min.

Producer, B. P. Fineman; director, George Sidney; screenplay, David Hertz; art directors, Cedric Gibbons, Howard Campbell; set decorators, Edwin Willis, Glen Barner; assistant director, Sanford Roth; music, Lennie Hayton; sound, J. S. Burbridge, James Z. Flaster; special effects, Arnold Gillespie, Don Jahraus; camera, Paul Vogel; editor, George White.

Franchot Tone (George Sundersall); Marsha Hunt (Freddie); Gene Kelly (Vito Allesandro); Van Johnson (Everett Arnold); Alan Baxter (Winston Davis); Dick Simmons (Henry W. Clavens); Steven Geray (Major Eichel); Howard Freeman (Hank Durbin); Frank Puglia (Nickola); Edward Fielding (Dean Barrett); Frank Ferguson (Tully); William Tannen (American); Carl Saxe (Dutch Boy); Peter Lawford (Englishman); Jack Gardner (Mechanic); Sara Haden (Landlady); James Davis, Cliff Danielson (Military Police); Jacqueline White (Party Girl); Hobart Cavanaugh (Boat Owner); William Halligan (Bartender); Kay Medford (Secretary); Billy Wayne, Eddie Acuff (Cameramen);

Marie Windsor, Betty Jaynes, Marilyn Maxwell (Party Girls); William Bishop, Leigh Sterling (Cadets); John Dilson (Defense Instructor); Harry Semels (Barber); Ava Gardner (Girl).

HITLER'S MADMAN (*MGM, 1943*) 85 min.

Producer, Seymour Nebenzal; associate producer, Rudolph Joseph; director, Douglas Sirk; based on the story by Emil Ludwig and Albrecht Joseph and the story "Hangman's Village" by Bart Lytton; screenplay, Peretz Hirschbein, Melvin Levy, Doris Malloy; art directors, Fred Preble, Edward Willens; music, Karl Hajos; assistant director, Mel De Tay; camera, Jack Greenhalgh, Eugen Shuftan; editor, Dan Milner.

John Carradine (Heydrich); Patricia Morison (Jarmilla); Alan Curtis (Karel); Ralph Morgan (Hanka); Howard Freeman (Himmler); Ludwig Stossel (Mayor Bauer); Edgar Kennedy (Nepomuk); Jimmy Conlin (Dvorak); Blanche Yurka (Mrs. Hanka); Jorga Rollins (Clara Janek); Al Shean (Priest); Elizabeth Russell (Maria); Victor Kilian (Janek); Johanna Hofer (Mrs. Bauer); Wolfgang Zilzer (Colonel); Tully Marshall (Teacher); Ava Gardner (Katy Chotnik); Frances Rafferty (Eliza Cormak); Natalie Draper (Julia Petschek); Betty Jaynes, Celia Travers (Nurses); Lionel Royce (Captain Kleist); Dennis Moore (Orderly); Lester Dorr (Sergeant); Budd Buster (Conductor); Dick Talmadge (Chauffeur); Chet Brandenburg (Linesman); Ernst Hausman, Sam Waagenaar (Sentries).

GHOSTS ON THE LOOSE (*Monogram, 1943*) 65 min.

Producers, Sam Katzman, Jack Dietz; director, William Beaudine; screenplay, Kenneth Higgins; assistant director, Arthur Hammond; art director, David Milton; music director, Edward Kay; sound, Glen Glenn; camera, Mack Stengler; editor, Carl Pierson.

Leo Gorcey (Muggs); Huntz Hall (Gimpy); Bobby Jordan (Danny); Bela Lugosi (Emil); Ava Gardner (Betty); Ric Vallin (Jack); Minerva Urecal (Hilda); Wheeler Oakman (Tony); Stanley Clements (Stash); Billy Benedict (Barney); Sammy Morrison (Sorina); Bobby Stone (Dave).

YOUNG IDEAS (*MGM, 1943*) 77 min.

Producer, Robert Sisk; director, Jules Dassin; screenplay, Ian McLellan Hunter, Bill Noble; music, George Bassman; music director, David Snell; art directors, Cedric Gibbons, Leonid Vassian; set decorators, Edwin B. Willis, Mac Alper; assistant director, George Rhein; sound, John A. Williams; camera, Charles Lawton; editor, Ralph E. Winters.

Susan Peters (Susan Evans); Herbert Marshall (Michael Kingsley); Mary Astor (Jo Evans); Elliott Reid (Jeff Evans); Richard Carlson (Tom Farrell); Allyn Joslyn (Adam); Dorothy Morris, Frances Rafferty (Co-eds); George Dolenz (Pepe); Emory Parnell (Judge Kelly); Ava Gardner (Girl).

THE LOST ANGEL (*MGM, 1943*) 91 min.

Producer, Robert Sisk; director, Roy Rowland; screen idea, Angna Enters; screenplay, Isobel Lennart; music, Daniele Amfitheatrof; art directors, Cedric Gibbons, Lynden Sparhawk; set decorators, Edwin B. Willis, Helen Conway; assistant director, George Rhein; sound, J. S. Bur-

bridge; camera, Robert Surtees; editor, Frank E. Hall.

Margaret O'Brien (Alpha); James Craig (Mike Regan); Marsha Hunt (Katie Mallory); Philip Merivale (Professor Peter Vincent); Keenan Wynn (Packy); Alan Napier (Dr. Woodring); Henry O'Neill (Professor Pringle); Sara Haden (Rhoda Kitterick); Donald Meek (Professor Catty); Elisabeth Risdon (Mrs. Pringle); Kathleen Lockhart (Mrs. Catty); Walter Fenner (Professor Endicott); Howard Freeman (Professor Richards); Bobby Blake (Jerry); Bobby Driscoll (Boy on Train); Jack Lambert (Lefty Moran); Naomi Childers (Matron); Kay Medford, Gloria Grafton (Operators); Edward McWade (Old Man); Russell Gleason, William Bishop, Lee Phelps, Edward Hearn (Reporters); Mike Mazurki (Fighter); Allen Wood (Tough Kid); Ava Gardner (Hat Check Girl); Al Hill (Mug); Joe Yule (Tenant).

SWING FEVER (*MGM, 1943*) 80 min.

Producer, Irving Starr; director, Tim Whelan; story, Matt Brooks, Joseph Hoffman; screenplay, Nat Perrin, Warren Wilson; music directors, Georgie Stoll, David Snell; music arranger, Earl Brent; choreography, Ernst and Maria Matray; art directors, Cedric Gibbons, Stephen Goosson; set decorator, Edwin B. Willis; assistant director, Marvin Stuart; sound, Frank B. MacKenzie; camera, Charles Rosher; editor, Ferris Webster.

Kay Kyser (Lowell Blackford); Marilyn Maxwell (Ginger Gray); William Gargan (Waltzy Malone); Nat Pendleton (Killer Kennedy); Maxie Rosenbloom (Rags); Curt Bois (Nick); Morris Ankrum (Dan Conlon); Andrew Tombes (Clyde L. Star); Lou Nova (Kid Mandell); Clyde Fillmore (Mr. Nagen); Ish Kabbible (Ish); Pamela Blake (Lois); Lena Horne, Merriel Abbott & Her Abbott Dancers (Specialties); Kay Kyser's Orchestra featuring Sully Mason, Julie Conway, Trudy Irwin (Themselves); Harry Babbitt (Harry); Katharine [Karin] Booth, Kathleen Williams, Ava Gardner (Girls); Mike Mazurki, Sammy Stein (Wrestlers); Mantan Moreland (Woodie); William Bishop (Soldier); Dan Tobey (Announcer); Murray Alper (Burly Attendant); Charles Sullivan (Cop).

THREE MEN IN WHITE (*MGM, 1944*) 85 min.

Director, Willis Goldbeck; based on characters created by Max Brand; screenplay, Martin Berkeley, Harry Ruskin; art directors, Cedric Gibbons, Harry McAfee; set decorator, Edwin B. Willis; music, Nathaniel Shilkret; assistant director, Al Raboch; sound, John F. Dullam; camera, Ray June; editor, George Hively.

Lionel Barrymore (Dr. Leonard Gillespie); Van Johnson (Dr. Randall Adams); Marilyn Maxwell (Ruth Edley); Keye Luke (Dr. Lee Wong How); Ava Gardner (Jean Brown); Alma Kruger (Molly Byrd); Rags Ragland (Hobart Genet); Nell Craig (Nurse Parker); Walter Kingsford (Dr. Walter Carew); George H. Reed (Conover); Patricia Barker (Mary Jones); Sam McDaniel (Black Phone Operator); Billy Cummings (Boy on Street); Addison Richards (Mr. Brown); George Chandler (Attendant); Byron Foulger (Technician).

MAISIE GOES TO RENO (*MGM, 1944*) 90 min.

Producer, George Haight; director, Harry Beaumont;

based on characters created by Wilson Collison; story, Harry Ruby, James O'Hanlon; screenplay, Mary C. McCall, Jr.; music, David Snell; song, Sammy Fain and Ralph Freed; art directors, Cedric Gibbons, Howard Campbell; set decorators, Edwin B. Willis, Helen Conway; assistant director, Charles O'Malley; sound, P. R. Stevens; camera, Robert Planck; editor, Frank E. Hull.

Ann Sothern (Maisie Ravier); John Hodiak (Flip Hannahan); Tom Drake (Bill Fullerton); Marta Linden (Winifred Ashbourne); Paul Cavanagh (Pelham); Ava Gardner (Gloria Fullerton); Bernard Nedell (J. E. Clave); Roland Dupree (Jerry); Chick Chandler (Tommy Cutter); Bunny Waters (Elaine); Donald Meek (Parsons); James Warren (Dr. Hanley Fleeson); Douglas Morrow (Master of Ceremonies); William Tannen (Lead Man); Edward Earle (Clerk); Byron Foulger (Dr. Cummings); Leon Tyler (Boy); Noreen Nash (Goodlooking Girl); Dallas Worth, Lynn Arlen, Ethel Tobin, Elizabeth Dailey, Katharine [Karin] Booth (Girls at Party).

SHE WENT TO THE RACES (*MGM, 1945*) 86 min.

Producer, Frederick Stephani; director, Willis Goldbeck; story, Alan Friedman, De Vallon Scott; screenplay, Lawrence Hazard; music, Nathaniel Shilkret; art directors, Cedric Gibbons, Preston Ames; set decorator, Edwin B. Willis; assistant director, Al Raboch; sound, Douglas Shearer; camera, Charles Salerno; editor, Adrienne Fazon.

James Craig (Steve Canfield); Frances Gifford (Dr. Ann Wotters); Ava Gardner (Hilda Spotts); Edmund Gwenn (Dr. Pecke); Sig Rumann (Dr. Gurke); Reginald Owen (Dr. Pembroke); J. M. Kerrigan (Jeff Habbard); Charles Halton (Dr. Collyer); Frank Orth (Bartender); Chester Clute (Mason); Buster Keaton (Bellboy); Matt Moore (Duffy); John Dehner (Announcer); Johnny Forrest (Usher).

WHISTLE STOP (*United Artists, 1946*) 85 min.

Producer, Seymour Nebenzal; director, Leonide Moguy; story, Maritta M. Wolff; screenplay, Philip Yordan; choreography, Jack Crosby; music/music director, Dmitri Tiomkin; art directors, Rudi Feld, George Van Marter; set decorator, Alfred Kegerris; assistant director, Milton Carter; dialogue director, Leon Charles; sound, Corson Jowett; special camera effects, R. O. Binger; camera, Russell Metty; editor, Gregg Tallas.

George Raft (Kenny); Ava Gardner (Mary); Victor McLaglen (Gillo); Tom Conway (Lew Lentz); Jorja Curtright (Fran); Florence Bates (Molly Veech); Jane Nigh (Josie); Charles Judels (Sam Veech); Jimmy Ames (The Barker); Charles Drake (Ernie).

THE KILLERS (*Universal, 1946*) 105 min.

Producer, Mark Hellinger; director, Robert Siodmak; based on the story by Ernest Hemingway; screenplay, Anthony Veiller and (uncredited) John Huston; art directors, Jack Otterson, Martin Obzina; set decorators, Russell A. Gausman, E. R. Robinson; music, Miklos Rosza; assistant director, Melville Shyer; sound, Bernard B. Brown, William Hedgcock; special camera, D. S. Horsley; camera, Woody Bredell; editor, Arthur Hilton.

Burt Lancaster (Swede); Ava Gardner (Kitty Collins);

Edmond O'Brien (Riordan); Albert Dekker (Colfax); Sam Levene (Lubinsky); John Miljan (Jake); Virginia Christine (Lilly); Vince Barnett (Charleston); Charles D. Brown (Packy); Donald MacBride (Kenyon); Phil Brown (Nick); Charles McGraw (Al); William Conrad (Max); Queenie Smith (Queenie); Garry Owen (Joe); Harry Hayden (George); Bill Walker (Sam); Jack Lambert (Dum Dum); Jeff Corey (Blinky); Wally Scott (Charlie); Gabrielle Windsor (Ginny); Rex Dale (Man); Harry Brown (Paymaster); Howard Freeman (Police Chief); Reverend Neal Dodd (Minister); Noel Cravat (Lou Tingle); Charles Middleton (Farmer Brown); Ernie Adams (Little Man); Wally Rose (Bartender).

THE HUCKSTERS (*MGM, 1947*) 115 min.

Producer, Arthur Hornblow, Jr.; director, Jack Conway; based on the novel by Frederic Wakeman; screenplay, Luther Davis; adaptors, Edward Chodorov, George Wells; art directors, Cedric Gibbons, Urie McCleary; set decorators, Edwin B. Willis, Jack D. Moore; music, Lennie Hayton; assistant director, Sid Sidman; sound, Douglas Shearer; special effects, Warren Newcombe, A. Arnold Gillespie; camera, Harold Rosson; editor, Frank Sullivan.

Clark Gable (Victor Albee Norman); Deborah Kerr (Kay Dorrance); Sydney Greenstreet (Evan Llewellyn Evans); Adolphe Menjou (Mr. Kimberly); Ava Gardner (Jean Ogilvie); Keenan Wynn (Buddy Hare); Edward Arnold (Dave Lash); Aubrey Mather (Valet); Richard Gaines (Cooke); Frank Albertson (Max Herman); Clinton Sundberg (Michael Michaelson); Douglas Fowley (Georgie Gaver); Gloria Holden (Mrs. Kimberly); Connie Gilchrist (Betty); Kathryn Card (Regina Kennedy); Lillian Bronson (Miss Hammer); Vera Marshe (Secretary); Ralph Bunker (Allison); Virginia Dale (Kimberly Receptionist); Jimmy Conlin (Blake); George O'Hanlon (Freddie Callahan); Ransom Sherman (George Rockton); Tom Stevenson (Paul Evans); John Hiestand (Radio Announcer); Robert Emmett O'Connor (Doorman); Marie Windsor (Girl); Richard Abbott (Elevator Starter); Anne Nagel (Teletypist); Joan Valerie (Receptionist); Almeda Fowler (Woman in Elevator); Byron Morgan (Radio Soundman); Tiny Jones (Flower Woman).

SINGAPORE (*Universal, 1947*) 79 min.

Producer, Jerry Bresler; director, John Brahm; story, Seton I. Miller; screenplay, Miller, Robert Thoeren; art directors, Bernard Herzbrun, Gabriel Scognamillo; set decorators, Russell A. Gausman, Oliver Emert; music, Daniele Amfitheatrof; music arranger/orchestrator, David Tamkin; assistant director, Harold Herman; sound, Charles Felstead, Jack A. Bolger, Jr.; special effects, David Horsley; camera, Maury Gertsman; editor, William Hornbeck.

Fred MacMurray (Matt Gordon); Ava Gardner (Linda); Roland Culver (Michael Van Leyden); Richard Haydn (Chief Inspector Hewitt); Thomas Gomez (Mr. Mauribus); Spring Byington (Mrs. Bellows); Porter Hall (Mr. Bellows); George Lloyd (Sascha Barda); Maylia (Ming Ling); Lal Chand Mehra (Mr. Hussein); H. T. Tsiang (Sabar); Rudy Robles (Desk Clerk); Frederic Worlock

(Cadum); Holmes Herbert (Reverend Barnes); Philip Ahn (Bartender); Reginald Sheffield (Travel Agent); Richard Abbott (Maitre d'); Edith Evanson (Miss Barnes); Monica Winckel, Cha-bing (Native Women); Norman Ainsley (Immigration Official); Curt Conway (Pepe); Don Escobar (Night Desk Clerk).

ONE TOUCH OF VENUS (*Universal, 1948*) 82 min.

Producer, Lester Cowan; associate producer, John Beck; director, William A. Seiter; based on the musical play by Kurt Weill, S. J. Perelman, Ogden Nash; suggested by the novel *The Tinted Venus* by F. Anstey; screenplay, Harry Kurnitz, Frank Tashlin; art directors, Bernard Herzbrun, Emrich H. Nicholson; set decorators, Russell A. Gausman, Al Fields; music/new lyrics, Ann Ronell; choreography, Billy Daniels; music director, Leo Arnaud; assistant director, William Holland; costumes, Orry-Kelly; sound, Leslie I. Carey, Joe Lapis; special effects, David Horsley; camera, Franz Planer; editor, Otto Ludwig.

Robert Walker (Eddie Hatch); Ava Gardner (Venus, Goddess of Love/Venus Jones); Dick Haymes (Joe); Eve Arden (Molly Grant); Olga San Juan (Gloria); Tom Conway (Whitfield Savorny); James Flavin (Corrigan); Sara Allgood (Mrs. Gogarty, the Landlady); Hugh Herbert (Mercury); Arthur O'Connell, Kenneth Patterson, Anne Nagel, Mary Benoit, Russ Conway, Jerry Marlowe (Reporters); George J. Lewis, Eddie Parker (Detectives); Pat Shade (Newsboy); Helen Francell, Harriett Bennett (Women).

THE BRIBE (*MGM, 1949*) 98 min.

Producer, Pandro S. Berman; director, Robert Z. Leonard; based on the short story by Frederick Nebel; screenplay, Marguerite Roberts; art directors, Cedric Gibbons, Malcolm Brown; set decorators, Edwin B. Willis, Hugh Hunt; music, Miklos Rozsa; song, Nacio Herb Brown and William Katz; assistant director, Bert Glazer; makeup, Jack Dawn; Miss Gardner's costumes, Irene; sound, Douglas Shearer, Fred MacAlpin; special effects, Warren Newcombe, A. Arnold Gillespie; camera, Joseph Ruttenberg; editor, Gene Ruggiero.

Robert Taylor (Rigby); Ava Gardner (Elizabeth Hintten); Charles Laughton (A. J. Bealer); Vincent Price (Carwood); John Hodiak (Tug Hintten); Samuel S. Hinds (Dr. Warren); John Hoyt (Gibbs); Tito Renaldo (Emilio Gomez); Martin Garralaga (Pablo Gomez); Pepe Hernandez (Bellboy); Nacho Galindo (Clerk); Walter A. Merrill, Frank Mayo (Americans); Marcel de la Brosse, Albert Pollet (Frenchmen); Albert Morin (Jose, the Waiter); Felipe Turich (Clerk); Jerry Pina (Juggler); Harry Vejar (Indian).

THE GREAT SINNER (*MGM, 1949*) 110 min.

Producer, Gottfried Reinhardt; director, Robert Siodmak; based on the novel *The Gambler* by Fedor Dostoevsky; story, Ladislas Fodor, Rene Fulop-Miller; screenplay, Fodor, Christopher Isherwood; art directors, Cedric Gibbons, Hans Peters; set decorators, Edwin B. Willis, Henry W. Grace; music, Bronislau Kaper; music director, Andre Previn; assistant director, Marvin Stuart; makeup,

Jack Dawn; costumes, Irene, Valles; technical advisor, Paul Elbogen; special effects, Warren Newcombe; camera, George Folsey; editor, Harold F. Kress.

Gregory Peck (Fedor Dostoevsky); Ava Gardner (Pauline Ostrovski); Melvyn Douglas (Armand De Glasse); Walter Huston (General Ostrovski); Ethel Barrymore (Granny); Frank Morgan (Aristide Pitard); Agnes Moorehead (Emma Getzel); Ludwig Stossel (Hotel Manager); Ludwig Donath (Doctor); Erno Verebes (Hotel Valet); Curt Bois (Jeweler); Martin Garralaga (Maharajah); Antonio Filauri (Senor Pinto); Frederick Ledebur (De Glasse's Secretary); Jean Del Val (Croupier); Vincent Renno (Casino Inspector); William H. Hawes (Nervous Englishman); Andre Charlot (Distinguished Man); Sam Scar (Turk); John Piffle (Fat Man); Ann Sturgis (Pretty Brunette); Lorraine Crawford (Pretty Blonde); Victor Denny, Daniel De Johnge (Valets); Lisa Golm (Elderly Lady); John Cortay (Inspector); Dick Simmons (Voice); Eloise Hardt (Young Girl); Martha Bamattre (Woman Fountain Attendant); Wheaton Chambers (Priest).

EAST SIDE, WEST SIDE (*MGM, 1949*) 108 min.

Producer, Voldemar Vetluguin; director, Mervyn LeRoy; based on the novel by Marcia Davenport; screenplay, Isobel Lennart; art directors, Cedric Gibbons, Randall Duell; set decorators, Edwin B. Willis, Arthur Krams; music, Miklos Rozsa; assistant director, Howard Koch; makeup, Jack Dawn; costumes, Helen Rose; sound, Douglas Shearer, A. N. Fenton; special effects, A. Arnold Gillespie; camera, Charles Rosher; editor, Harold F. Kress.

Barbara Stanwyck (Jessie Bourne); James Mason (Brandon Bourne); Van Heflin (Mark Dwyer); Ava Gardner (Isabel Lorrison); Cyd Charisse (Rosa Senta); Nancy Davis (Helen Lee); Gale Sondergaard (Nora Kernan); Beverly Michaels (Felice Backett); Raymond Greenleaf (Horace Ellcott Howland); Douglas Kennedy (Alec Dawning); Tom Powers (Owen Lee); Lisa Golm (Josephine); Stanley Waxman (John); Peter Thompson (Jock Ardley); Stanley Orr (Bourne's Chauffeur); William Conrad (Lieutenant Jacobi); William Frawley (Bill, the Bartender); Jack Gargan (Doorman); Paula Raymond (Joan Peterson); Tom P. Dillon (Dan, the Old Policeman); Jewel Rose (Hat Check Girl); Sandra Spence (Cigarette Girl); Wesley Bly (Club Attendant); Wilson Wood, Ralph Montgomery, Fred Hoose, Roger Moore, Betty Taylor (Reporters); Ernest Anderson (Redcap); Harry Strang (Fred, the Doorman); Frank Meredith (Cop); Wheaton Chambers (Doorman); Ferike Boros (Grandma Sistina).

MY FORBIDDEN PAST (*RKO, 1951*) 81 min.

Producers, Robert Sparks, Polan Banks; director, Robert Stevenson; based on the novel *Carriage Entrance* by Banks; adaptor, Leopold Atlas; screenplay, Marion Parsonnet; art directors, Albert D'Agostino, Alfred Herman; music director, C. Bakaleinikoff; camera, Harry J. Wild; editor, George Shrader.

Robert Mitchum (Dr. Mark Lucas); Ava Gardner (Barbara Beaurevel), Melvyn Douglas (Paul Beaurevel); Lucile Watson (Aunt Eula); Janis Carter (Corinne); Gordon

Oliver (Clay Duchesne); Basil Ruysdael (Dean Cazzley); Clarence Muse (Pompey); Walter Kingsford (Coroner); Jack Briggs (Cousin Phillipe); Will Wright (Luther Toplady); Watson Downs (Hotel Clerk); Cliff Clark (Horse Vendor); John B. Williams (Fishmonger); Louis Payne (Man); Johnny Lee (Toy Vendor); George Douglas (Deputy); Ken MacDonald (Police Lieutenant); Everett Glass (Elderly Doctor); Barry Brooks (Policeman); Daniel DeLaurentis (Candle Boy).

PANDORA AND THE FLYING DUTCHMAN (*MGM, 1951*) C-123 min.

Producers, Albert Lewin, Joseph Kaufman; director/ story/screenplay, Lewin; music, Alan Rawstherne; music director, Dr. Hubert Clifford; art director, Tim Hopewell-Ash; set decorator, John Hawkesworth, sound, Harry Miller; camera, Jack Cardiff; editor, Ralph Kemplen.

James Mason (Hendrick van der Zee); Ava Gardner (Pandora Reynolds); Nigel Patrick (Stephen Cameron); Sheila Sim (Janet); Harold Warrender (Geoffrey Fielding); Mario Cabre (Juan Montalvo); Marius Goring (Reggie Demarest); John Laurie (Angus); Pamela Kellino (Jenny); Patricia Raine (Senora Montalvo); and: La Pillina, Abraham Sofaer, Francisco Igual, Guillermo Beltran, Lila Molnar, Phoebe Hodgson, Gabriel Carmona, Antonio Martin.

SHOW BOAT (*MGM, 1951*) C-108 min.

Producer, Arthur Freed; associate producer, Ben Feiner, Jr.; director, George Sidney; based on the musical *Show Boat* by Jerome Kern and Oscar Hammerstein II from the novel by Edna Ferber; screenplay, John Lee Mahin (uncredited), George Wells, Jack McGowan; music director, Adolph Deutsch; musical numbers staged/directed by Robert Alton; songs, Hammerstein II and Kern; Kern, Guy Bolton, and P. G. Wodehouse; orchestrator, Conrad Salinger; vocal arranger, Robert Tucker; Technicolor consultants, Henri Jaffa, James Gooch; art directors, Cedric Gibbons, Jack Martin Smith; set decorators, Edwin B. Willis, Alfred Spencer; makeup, William J. Tuttle; costumes, Walter Plunkett; special effects, Warren Newcombe; special montage director, Peter Ballbusch; camera, Charles Rosher; editor, Albert Akst.

Kathryn Grayson (Magnolia Hawks); Ava Gardner (Julie Laverne); Howard Keel (Gaylord Ravenal); Joe E. Brown (Captain Andy Hawks); Marge Champion (Ellie May Shipley); Gower Champion (Frank Schultz); Robert Sterling (Stephen Baker); Agnes Moorehead (Parthy Hawks); Adele Jergens (Cameo McQueen); William Warfield (Joe); Leif Erickson (Pete); Owen McGiveney (Windy McClain); Frances Williams (Queenie); Regis Toomey (Ike Vallon, the Sheriff); Frank Wilcox (Mark Hallson); Chick Chandler (Herman); Emory Parnell (Jake Green); Sheila Clark (Kim); Ian MacDonald (Drunken Sport); Fuzzy Knight (Piano Player); Norman Leavitt (George, the Calliope Player); Anne Marie Dore, Christian Lind, Lyn Wilde, Marietta Elliott, Joyce Jameson, Bette Arlen, Helen Kimbell, Tac Porchon, Mitzie Uehlein, Judy Landon, Nova Dale, Mary Jane French, Marilyn Kinsley, Alice Markham (Showboat Cast Girls); Michael Dugan, Robert Fortier,

George Ford, Cass Jaeger, Boyd Ackerman, Roy Damron, Joseph Roach (Showboat Cast Boys); George Lynn (Dealer); Louis Mercier (Dabney); Lisa Ferraday (Renee); Anna Q. Nilsson (Seamstress); Ida Moore (Little Old Lady); Alphonse Martell (Headwaiter).

LONE STAR (*MGM, 1952*) 94 min.

Producer, Z. Wayne Griffin; director, Vincent Sherman; based on the story by Borden Chase; screen story, Howard Estabrook; screenplay, Chase; music, David Buttolph; art directors, Cedric Gibbons, Hans Peters; camera, Harold Rosson; editor, Ferris Webster.

Clark Gable (Devereaux Burke); Ava Gardner (Martha Ronda); Broderick Crawford (Thomas Craden); Lionel Barrymore (Andrew Jackson); Beulah Bondi (Minniver Bryan); Ed Begley (Senator Anthony Demmett); William Farnum (Senator Tom Crockett); Lowell Gilmore (Captain Elliott); Moroni Olsen (Sam Houston); Russell Simpson (Senator Maynard Cole); William Conrad (Mizette); James Burke (Luther Kilgore); Ralph Reed (Bud Yoakum); Ric Roman (Curau); Victor Sutherland (President Anson Jones); Jonathan Cott (Ben McCulloch); Charles Cane (Mayhew); Nacho Galindo (Vincente); Trevor Bardette (Sid Yoakum); Harry Woods (Dellman); Dudley Sadler (Ashbel Smith); George Hamilton (Noah); Roy Gordon, Stanley Andrews, William E. Green (Men); Earle Hodgins (Windy Barton); Warren Macgregor (Rancher); Rex Lease, Davison Clark (Senators); Chief Yowlachie (Indian Chief); Emmett Lynn (Josh); Tony Roux (Chico).

THE SNOWS OF KILIMANJARO (*Twentieth Century-Fox, 1952*) C-117 min.

Producer, Darryl F. Zanuck; director, Henry King; based on the novel by Ernest Hemingway; screenplay, Casey Robinson; music, Bernard Herrmann; choreography, Antonio Triana; art directors, Lyle Wheeler, John De Cuir; set decorators, Thomas Little, Paul S. Fox; special camera effects, Ray Kellogg; camera, Leon Shamroy; editor, Barbara McLean.

Gregory Peck (Harry); Susan Hayward (Helen); Ava Gardner (Cynthia); Hildegarde Neff (Countess Liz); Leo G. Carroll (Uncle Bill); Torin Thatcher (Johnson); Ava Norring (Beatrice); Helene Stanley (Connie); Marcel Dalio (Emile); Vincente Gomez (Guitarist); Richard Allan (Spanish Dancer); Leonard Carey (Dr. Simmons); Paul Thompson (Witch Doctor); Emmett Smith (Molo); Victor Wood (Charles); Bert Freed (American Soldier); Agnes Laury (Margot); Monique Chantel (Georgette); Janine Grandel (Annette); John Dodsworth (Compton); Charles Bates (Harry at Age Seventeen); Lisa Ferraday (Vendeuse); Maya Van Horn (Princess); Ivan Lebedeff (Marquis); Salvador Baguez, George Navarro (Stretcher Bearers); George Davis (Servant).

RIDE, VAQUERO! (*MGM, 1953*) C-90 min.

Producer, Stephen Ames; director, John Farrow; story/ screenplay, Frank Fenton; art directors, Cedric Gibbons, Arthur Lonergan; camera, Robert Surtees.

Robert Taylor (Rio); Ava Gardner (Cordelia Cameron); Howard Keel (King Cameron); Anthony Quinn (Jose

Esqueda); Kurt Kasznar (Father Antonio); Ted de Corsia (Sheriff Parker); Charlita (Cafe Singer); Jack Elam (Barton); Walter Baldwin (Adam Smith); Joe Dominguez (Vincente); Frank McGrath (Pete); Charles Stevens (Vaquero); Rex Lease, Tom Greenway (Deputies); Paul Fierro (Valero); Percy Helton (Storekeeper); Movita Castenada (Hussy); Almira Sessions (Woman); Monte Blue (Bartender); Kay English (Woman in Park); Stanley Andrews (General Sheridan); Joey Ray (Croupier).

THE BAND WAGON (*MGM, 1953*) C-112 min.

Producer, Arthur Freed; associate producer, Roger Edens; director, Vincente Minnelli; story/screenplay, Betty Comden, Adolph Green; dances and music numbers staged by Michael Kidd; songs, Howard Dietz, Arthur Schwartz; music director, Adolph Deutsch; music numbers designer, Oliver Smith; orchestrators, Conrad Salinger, Skip Martin, Alexander Courage; color consultants, Henri Jaffa, Robert Brower; art directors, Cedric Gibbons, Preston Ames; set decorators, Edwin B. Willis, Keogh Gleason; makeup, William Tuttle; costumes, Mary Ann Nyberg; sound, Douglas Shearer; special effects, Warren Newcombe; camera, Harry Jackson; editor, Albert Akst.

Fred Astaire (Tony Hunter); Cyd Charisse (Gaby Berard); Oscar Levant (Lester Marton); Nanette Fabray (Lily Marton); Jack Buchanan (Jeffrey Cordova); James Mitchell (Paul Byrd); Robert Gist (Hal Benton); Thurston Hall (Colonel Tripp); Ava Gardner (The Movie Star); LeRoy Daniels (Shoe Shine Boy); Jack Tesler (Ivan); Dee Turnell, Elynne Ray, Peggy Murray, Judy Landon (Girls in Troupe); Jimmie Thompson, Bert May (Boys in Troupe); John Lupton (Jack, the Prompter); Owen McGiveney (Prop Man); Sam Hearn (Agent); Herb Vigran, Emory Parnell (Men on Train); Ernest Anderson (Porter); Frank Scannon, Stu Wilson, Roy Engel (Reporters); Al Hill (Shooting Gallery Operator); Paul Bradley (Dancer in Park/Waiter); Bobby Watson (Bobby, the Dresser); Lotte Stein (Chambermaid); Smoki Whitfield (Chauffeur); Dick Alexander, Al Ferguson (Stagehands); Betty Farrington (Fitter); Bess Flowers (Lady on Train in "Girl Hunter" Number).

MOGAMBO (*MGM, 1953*) C-115 min.

Producer, Sam Zimbalist; director, John Ford; based on the play by Wilson Collison; screenplay, John Lee Mahin; art director, Alfred Junge; costumes, Helen Rose; second unit directors, Richard Rosson, Yakima Canutt, James C. Havens; assistant directors, Wingate Smith, Cecil Ford; camera, Robert Surtees, Frederick A. Young; editor, Frank Clarke.

Clark Gable (Victor Marswell); Ava Gardner (Eloise Y. Kelly); Grace Kelly (Linda Nordley); Donald Sinden (Donald Nordley); Philip Stainton (John Brown Pryce); Eric Pohlmann (Leon Boltchak); Laurence Naismith (Skipper); Denis O'Dea (Father Joseph); Asa Etula (Young Native Girl); Wagenia Tribe of Belgian Congo, Samburu Tribe of Kenya Colony, Bahaya Tribe of Tanganyika, M'Beri Tribe of French Equatorial Africa (Themselves).

KNIGHTS OF THE ROUND TABLE (*MGM, 1954*) C-115 min.

Producer, Pandro S. Berman; director, Richard Thorpe;

based on *Le Morte D'Arthur* by Sir Thomas Malory; screenplay, Talbot Jennings, Jan Lustig, Noel Langley; art directors, Alfred Junge, Hans Peters; music, Miklos Rozsa; camera, Freddie Young, Stephen Dade; editor, Frank Clarke.

Robert Taylor (Lancelot); Ava Gardner (Guinevere); Mel Ferrer (Arthur); Anne Crawford (Morgan Le Fay); Stanley Baker (Modred); Felix Aylmer (Merlin); Maureen Swanson (Elaine); Gabriel Woolf (Percival); Anthony Forwood (Gareth); Robert Urquhart (Gawaine); Niall MacGinnis (Green Knight); Ann Hanslip (Nan); Jill Clifford (Bronwyn); Stephen Vercoe (Agravaine).

THE BAREFOOT CONTESSA (*United Artists, 1954*) C-128 min.

Director/screenplay, Joseph L. Mankiewicz; assistant director, Pietro Mussetta; art director, Arrigo Equini; gowns, Fontana; music, Mario Nascimbene; sound, Charles Knott; camera, Jack Cardiff; editor, William Hornbeck.

Humphrey Bogart (Harry Dawes); Ava Gardner (Maria Vargas); Edmond O'Brien (Oscar Muldoon); Marius Goring (Alberto Bravano); Valentina Cortesa (Eleanora Torlato-Favrini); Rossano Brazzi (Vincenzo Torlato-Favrini); Elizabeth Sellars (Jerry); Warren Stevens (Kirk Edwards); Franco Interlenghi (Pedro); Mari Aldon (Myrna); Bessie Love (Mrs. Eubanks); Diana Decker (Drunken Blonde); Bill Fraser (J. Montague Brown); John Parrish (Mr. Black); Jim Gerald (Mr. Blue); Gertrude Flynn (Lulu McGee); John Horne (Hector Eubanks); Carlo Dale (Chauffeur).

BHOWANI JUNCTION (*MGM, 1956*) C-110 min.

Producer, Pandro S. Berman; director, George Cukor; based on the novel by John Masters; screenplay, Sonya Levien, Ivan Moffat; art directors, Gene Allen, John Howell; music director, Miklos Rozsa; costumes, Elizabeth Haffenden; camera, Freddie Young; editors, Frank Clarke, George Boemler.

Ava Gardner (Victoria Jones); Stewart Granger (Colonel Rodney Savage); Bill Travers (Patrick Taylor); Abraham Sofaer (Surabhai); Francis Matthews (Ranjit Kasel); Marne Maitland (Govindaswami); Peter Illing (Ghanshyam); Edward Chapman (Thomas Jones); Freda Jackson (The Sadani); Lionel Jeffries (Lieutenant Graham McDaniel); Alan Tilvern (Ted Dunphy).

THE LITTLE HUT (*MGM, 1957*) C-78 min.

Producers, F. Hugh Herbert, Mark Robson; director, Robson; based on the play by Andre Roussin and the English stage adaptation by Nancy Mitford; screenplay, Herbert; art director, Elliott Scott; music, Robert Famon; song, Eric Maschwitz, Marcel Stellman, and Peggy Cochrane; costumes, Christian Dior; assistant director, David Middlemas; camera, Freddie Young; editor, Ernest Waller.

Ava Gardner (Lady Susan Ashlow); Stewart Granger (Sir Philip Ashlow); David Niven (Henry Brittingham-Brett); Walter Chiari (Mario); Finlay Currie (Reverend Brittingham-Brett); Jean Cadell (Mrs. Brittingham-Brett); Jack Lambert (Captain MacWade); Henry Oscar (Mr. Trollope); Viola Lyel (Miss Edwards); Jaron Yaltan (Indian Gentleman).

THE SUN ALSO RISES (*Twentieth Century-Fox, 1957*) C-129 min.

Producer, Darryl F. Zanuck; director, Henry King; based on the novel by Ernest Hemingway; screenplay, Peter Viertel; art directors, Lyle R. Wheeler, Mark-Lee Kirk; music, Hugo Friedhofer; music director, Lionel Newman; orchestrator, Edward B. Powell; camera, Leo Tover; editor, William Mace.

Tyrone Power (Jake Barnes); Ava Gardner (Lady Brett Ashley); Mel Ferrer (Robert Cohn); Errol Flynn (Mike Campbell); Eddie Albert (Bill Gorton); Gregory Ratoff (Count Mippipopolous); Juliette Greco (Georgette); Marcel Dalio (Zizi); Henry Daniell (Doctor); Bob Cunningham (Harris); Danik Patisson (The Girl); Robert J. Evans (Pedro Romero); Rebecca Iturbi (Frances Cohn); Eduardo Noriega (Mr. Braddock); Jacqueline Evans (Mrs. Braddock); Carlos Muzquiz (Montoya); Carlos David Ortigos (Manager of Romero); Lilia Guizar (English Girl); Lee Morgan (American at Bullfight).

THE NAKED MAJA (*United Artists, 1959*) C-111 min.

Producer, Goffredo Lombardo; directors, Henry Koster, Mario Russo; story, Oscar Saul, Talbot Jennings; screenplay, Norman Corwin, Giorgio Prosperi; assistant directors, Paolo Cavara, Mimola Girosi; art director, Piero Filipponi; set decorators, Gino Brosio, Emilio D'Andria; costumes, Dario Cecchi, Maria Baroni; makeup, Euclide Santoli, Franco Freda, Alma Santoli, Alfio Meniconi; choreography, Alberto Lorca; music, Angelo Francesco Lavagnini; camera, Giuseppe Rotunno.

Ava Gardner (Duchess of Alba); Anthony Franciosa (Francisco Goya); Amedeo Nazzari (Manuel Godoy); Gino Cervi (King Carlos IV); Lea Padovani (Queen Maria Luisa); Massimo Serato (Sanchez); Carlo Rizzo (Juanito); Renzo Cesana (Bayeu); Audrey MacDonald (Anita); Patrick Crean (Enrique); Tonio Selwart (Aranda); Peter Meersman (Dr. Peral); Yemiko Fulwood (Maria de la Luz); Carlo Giustini (Jose); John Karlsen (The Inquisitor); Renata Mauro, Pina Bottin (Majas); Amru Sani (The Singer); Carmen Mora (The Ballerina); Clayton Hall (Goya's Assistant); Stella Vitelleschi (Maria Josefa).

ON THE BEACH (*United Artists, 1959*) 134 min.

Producer/director, Stanley Kramer; based on the novel by Nevil Shute; screenplay, John Paxton; music, Ernest Gold; song, Marie Cowan and A. B. Paterson; production designer, Rudolph Sternad; art director, Fernando Carrere; makeup, John O'Gorman, Frank Prehoda; technical advisor, Vice Admiral Charles A. Lockwood, USN (Ret.); Miss Gardner's wardrobe, Fontana Sisters; assistant director, Ivan Volkman; sound, Hans Wetzel; sound effects, Walter Elliott; special effects, Lee Zavits; camera, Giuseppe Rotunno; editor, Frederic Knudtson.

Gregory Peck (Dwight Towers); Ava Gardner (Moira Davidson); Fred Astaire (Julian Osborn); Anthony Perkins (Peter Holmes); Donna Anderson (Mary Holmes); John Tate (Admiral Bridie); Lola Brooks (Lieutenant Hosgood); Guy Doleman (Farrel); John Meillon (Swain); Harp McGuire (Sundstrom); Ken Wayne (Benson); Richard Meikle

(Davis); Basil Buller-Murphy (Froude); Paddy Moran (Port Man); Grant Taylor (Morgan).

THE ANGEL WORE RED (*MGM, 1960*) 99 min.

Producer, Goffredo Lombardo; director, Nunnally Johnson; based on the novel *The Fair Bride* by Bruce Marshall; screenplay, Johnson; music, Bronislau Kaper; music director, Robert Armbruster; art director, Piero Filippone; set decorators, Gino Brosio, Nedo Azzino; costumes, Maurizio Chiara; assistant directors, Mario Russo, Carlo Lastricati; sound, Mario Messina; camera, Giuseppe Rotunno; editor, Louis Loeffler.

Ava Gardner (Soledad); Dirk Bogarde (Arturo Carrera); Joseph Cotten (Hawthorne); Vittorio De Sica (General Clave); Aldo Fabrizi (Canon Rota); Arnoldo Foa (Insurgent Major); Finlay Currie (The Bishop); Rossano Rory (Mercedes); Enrico Maria Salerno (Captain Botargas); Robert Bright (Father Idelfonso); Franco Castellani (Jose); Bob Cunningham (Mac); Gustavo De Nardo (Major Garcia); Nino Castelnuovo (Captain Trinidad); Aldo Pini (Chaplain).

55 DAYS AT PEKING (*Allied Artists, 1963*) C-154 min.

Producer, Samuel Bronston; director, Nicholas Ray; screenplay, Philip Yordan, Bernard Gordon; additional dialogue, Robert Hamer; music/music director, Dmitri Tiomkin; song, Tiomkin, Paul Francis Webster; art directors/costumes, Veniero Colasanti, John Moore; title paintings, Don Kingman; wardrobe, Gloria Mussetta; makeup, Mario Van Riel; assistant directors, Jose Lopez Rodero, Jose Maria Ochoa; camera, Jack Hildyard; second unit camera, Manuel Berenguerr; special effects, Alex Weldon; sound, David Hildyard, Gordon K. McCallum; editors, Robert Lawrence, Magdalena Paradell.

Charlton Heston (Major Matt Lewis); Ava Gardner (Baroness Natalie Ivanoff); David Niven (Sir Arthur Robertson); Flora Robson (Dowager Empress Tzu Hsi); John Ireland (Sergeant Harry); Harry Andrews (Father de Bearn); Leo Genn (General Jung-Lu); Robert Helpmann (Prince Tuan); Ichizo Itami (Colonel Shiba); Kurt Kasznar (Baron Sergei Ivanoff); Phillipe Leroy (Julliard); Paul Lukas (Dr. Steinfeldt); Lynne Sue Moon (Teresa); Elizabeth Sellars (Lady Sarah Robertson); Jacques Sernas (Major Bobrinski); Joseph Furst (Hanselman); Alfredo Mayo (Spanish Minister); Eric Pohlmann (Baron Von Meck); Mitchell Kowal (U.S. Marine); Nicholas Ray (American Minister).

SEVEN DAYS IN MAY (*Paramount, 1964*) 120 min.

Producer, Edward Lewis; director, John Frankenheimer; based on the novel by Fletcher Knebel, Charles W. Bailey II; screenplay, Rod Serling; art director, Cary Odell; set decorator, Edward Boyle; music, Jerry Goldsmith; assistant director, Hal Polaire; sound, Joe Edmondson; camera, Ellsworth Fredricks; editor, Ferris Webster.

Burt Lancaster (General James M. Scott); Kirk Douglas (Colonel Martin "Jiggs" Casey); Fredric March (President Jordan Lyman); Ava Gardner (Eleanor Holbrook); Edmond O'Brien (Senator Raymond Clark); Martin Balsam (Paul Girard); George Macready (Christopher Todd); Whit Bissell (Senator Prentice); Hugh Marlowe (Harold Mc-

Pherson); Bart Burns (Arthur Corwin); Richard Anderson (Colonel Murdock); Jack Mullaney (Lieutenant Hough); Andrew Duggan (Colonel "Mutt" Henderson); John Larkin (Colonel Broderick); Malcolm Atterbury (Physician); Helen Kleeb (Esther Townsend); John Houseman (Admiral Barnswell); Colette Jackson (Bar Girl).

THE NIGHT OF THE IGUANA (*MGM, 1964*) 125 min.

Producer, Ray Stark; director, John Huston; based on the play by Tennessee Williams; screenplay, Anthony Veiller, Huston; music/music director, Benjamin Frankel; associate director, Emilio Fernandez; assistant director, Tom Shaw; art director, Stephen Grimes; costumes, Dorothy Jeakins; makeup, Jack Obringer, Eric Allwright; sound, Basil Fenton-Smith; camera, Gabriel Figueroa; editor, Ralph Kemplin.

Richard Burton (Reverend T. Lawrence Shannon); Ava Gardner (Maxine Faulk); Deborah Kerr (Hannah Jelkes); Sue Lyon (Charlotte Goodall); James Ward (Hank Prosner); Grayson Hall (Judith Fellowes); Cyril Delevanti (Nonno); Mary Boylan (Miss Peebles); Gladys Hill (Miss Dexter); Billie Matticks (Miss Throxton); Fidelmar Duran (Pepe); Roberto Leyva (Pedro); C. G. Kim (Chang); Eloise Hardt, Thelda Victor, Betty Proctor, Dorothy Vance, Liz Rubey, Bernice Starr (Teachers).

THE BIBLE (. . . IN THE BEGINNING) (*Twentieth Century-Fox, 1966*) C-174 min

Producer, Dino De Laurentiis; associate producer, Luigi Luraschi; director, John Huston; "The Creation" sequence directed by Ernst Haas; adapted from episodes from the Old Testament; screenplay, Christopher Fry; music, Toshiro Mayuzumi; music director, Franco Ferrara; art directors, Mario Chiari, Stephen Grimes; set decorators, Enzo Eusepi, Bruno Avesani; choreography, Katherine Dunham; costumes, Maria De Matteis; makeup, Alberto De Rossi; sound, Fred Hynes, Basil Fenton-Smith, Murray Spivack, Leslie Hodgson; camera, Giuseppe Rotunno; editor, Ralph Kemplen.

Michael Parks (Adam); Ulla Bergryd (Eve); Richard Harris (Cain); John Huston (Noah/Narrator); Stephen Boyd (Nimrod); George C. Scott (Abraham); Ava Gardner (Sarah); Peter O'Toole (The Three Angels); Zoe Sallis (Hagar); Gabriele Ferzetti (Lot); Eleanora Rossi Drago (Lot's Wife); Franco Nero (Abel); Pupella Maggio (Noah's Wife); Alberto Lucantoni (Isaac); Luciano Conversi (Ishmael); Robert Rietty (Abraham's Steward); Adriana Ambesi, Grazia Maria Spina (Lot's Daughters); and: Claudie Lange, Peter Heinze, Gabriella Pallotta, Rosanna De Rocco.

MAYERLING (*MGM, 1969*) C-140 min.

Executive producers, Eugene Tuckerer, Marcel Hellman; producer, Robert Dorfmann; associate producer, Maurice Jacquin; director, Terence Young; based on the novel by Claude Anet, the novel *The Archduke* by Michael Arnold, and historical documentation; screenplay, Young; additional dialogue, Denis Cannan, Josef Kessel; music, Francis Lai; theme, Aram Khatchaturian; production designer, Georges Wakhevitch; art directors, Maurice Colasson, Tony Roman; assistant director, Christian Raoux; sound,

Jacques Carrere, Jo De Bretagne; camera, Henri Alekan; editor, Benedik Rayner.

Omar Sharif (Crown Prince Rudolf); Catherine Deneuve (Baroness Marie Vetsera); James Mason (Emperor Franz-Josef); Ava Gardner (Empress Elizabeth); James Robertson Justice (Edward, Prince of Wales); Genevieve Page (Countess Larisch); Ivan Desny (Count Josef Hoyos); Andrea Parisy (Crown Princess Stephanie); Fabienne Dali (Mizzi Kaspar); Maurice Teynac (Moritz Szeps); Moustache (Bratfisch); Bernard Lajarrige (Loschek); Veronique Vendell (Lisl Stockau); Charles Millot (Count Taafe); Roger Pigaut (Count Karolyi); Mony Dalmes (Baroness Helen Vetsera); Lyne Chardonnet (Hannah Vetsera); Howard Vernon (Prince Montenuevo); Fred Vellaca (Lawson); and: The Grand Ballet Classique De France.

THE DEVIL'S WIDOW (a.k.a. TAMLIN) (*American International, 1972*) C-107 min.

Executive producers, Henry J. Weinstein, Anthony B. Unger; producers, Alan Ladd, Jr., Stanley Mann; associate producer, Dennis Holt; director, Roddy McDowall; screenplay, William Spier; music, Stanley Myers; songs, The Pentagles; production designer, Don Ashton; camera, Billy Williams; editor, John Victor Smith.

Ava Gardner (Michaela); Ian McShane (Tom); Stephanie Beacham (Janet); Cyril Cusack (Vicar); Richard Wattis (Elroy); David Whitman (Oliver); Madeline Smith (Sue); Fabia Drake (Miss Gibbons); Sinead Cusack (Rose); Jennie Hanley (Caroline); Joanne Lumley (Georgia); Pamela Farbrother (Vanna); Bruce Robinson (Alan); Rosemary Blake (Kate); Michael Bills (Michael); Peter Henwood (Guy); Heyward Morse (Andy); Julian Barnes (Terry); Oliver Norman (Peter); Virginia Tingwell (Lottie).

THE LIFE AND TIMES OF JUDGE ROY BEAN (*National General, 1972*) C-124 min.

Producer, John Foreman; associate producer, Frank Caffey; director, John Huston; screenplay, John Milius; music/music director, Maurice Jarre; song, Jarre, Marilyn and Alan Bergman; art director, Tambi Larsen; set decorator, Robert Benton; animal trainer, Ron Oxley; stunt coordinator, James Arnett; makeup, William Tuttle, Monty Westmore; costumes, Edith Head; assistant director, Mickey McCardle; sound, Keith Stafford, Larry Jost, Richard Portman; special camera effects, Butler-Glouner; camera, Richard Moore; editor, Hugh S. Fowler.

Paul Newman (Judge Roy Bean); Jacqueline Bisset (Rose Bean); Ava Gardner (Lily Langtry); Tab Hunter (Sam Dodd); John Huston (Grizzly Adams); Stacy Keach (Bad Bob); Roddy McDowall (Frank Gass); Anthony Perkins (Reverend LaSalle); Victoria Principal (Marie Elena); Ned Beatty (Hector Crites); Anthony Zerbe (Hustler); Jim Burk (Bart Jackson); Matt Clark (Nick, the Grub); Steve Kanaly (Whorehouse Lucky Jim); Bill McKinney (Fermel Parlee); Karen Carr (Mrs. Grubb); Stan Barrett (Killer).

EARTHQUAKE (*Universal, 1974*) C-129 min.*

Executive producer, Jennings Lang; producer/director,

*When shown on U.S. network television, outtakes and additional footage were used to expand the running time another 21 minutes.

Mark Robson; screenplay, George Fo.., Mario Puzo; production designer, Alexander Golitzen; art director, E. Preston Ames; set decorator, Frank McKelvy; costumes, Burton Miller; assistant directors, Fred K. Simpson, Murray Schwartz; miniatures, Glen Robinson; music, John Williams; stunt coordinator, John Daheim; sound, Melvin McMetcalfe, Sr., Ronald Pierce; special camera, Clifford Stine; special camera effects, Albert Whitlock; matte camera, Ross Hoffman; camera, Philip Lathrop; editor, Dorothy Spencer.

Charlton Heston (Stuart Graff); Ava Gardner (Remy Graff); George Kennedy (Lew Slade); Lorne Greene (Sam Royce); Genevieve Bujold (Denise Marshall); Richard Roundtree (Miles Quade); Marjoe Gortner (Jody); Barry Sullivan (Stockle); Lloyd Nolan (Dr. Vance); Victoria Principal (Rosa); Walter Matthau (Drunk); Monica Lewis (Barbara); Gabriel Dell (Sal); Pedro Armendariz, Jr. (Chavez); Lloyd Gough (Cameron); John Randolph (Mayor); Kip Niven (Walter Russell).

PERMISSION TO KILL (*Avco Embassy, 1974*) C-96 min.

Executive producers, Heinz Lazek, Robert Jungbluth; producer, Paul Mills; director, Cyril Frankel; screenplay, Robin Estridge; production designer, Elliot Scott; makeup, George Partleton; wardrobe, Peppi Wanke, Emmi Minnich; Miss Gardner's wardrobe, Franka; camera, Freddie Young; editor, Ernest Walter.

Dirk Bogarde (Alan Curtis); Ava Gardner (Katina Peterson); Bekim Fehmiu (Alexander Diakim); Timothy Dalton (Charles Lord); Nicole Calfan (Melissa Lascade); Frederic Forrest (Scott Alexander); Alf Joint (MacNeil); Peggy Sinclair (Lily); Anthony Dutton (Jennings); Klaus Wildbolz (Muller); John Levene (Adams); Dennis Blanch (Brewer); Vladimir Popovic (Kostas); Ratislav Plamenac (Pavlos); Peter Garell (Carlo); Ermin Von Gross (Hotel Manager); Bob Sessions (Pete); Dr. Francois Baudet (French Doctor).

THE BLUE BIRD (*Twentieth Century-Fox, 1976*) C-100 min.

Producer, Paul Maslansky; executive producer, Edward Lewis; co-producers, Lee Savin, Paul Radin; director, George Cukor; based on the novel by Maurice Maeterlinck; screenplay, Hugh Whitemore, Alfred Hayes, Alexel Kapler; production designer, Brian Wildsmith; art director, Valery Urkevich; set decorator, Yevgeny Starikovitch, Edward Isaev, Tamara Polyanskoya; assistant directors, Mike Gowans, Yevgeny Tatarsky, Liliana Markova, Stirlin Harris; music, Irwin Kostal, Lionel Newman; lyrics, Tony Harrison; sound, Theodore Soderberg, Gordon Everett, Gregory Elbert, John Bramaill; camera, Freddie Young, Jonas Gritzus; editors, Ernest Walter, Tatyana Shapiro, Stanford C. Allen.

Elizabeth Taylor (Mother / Witch / Light / Maternal Love); Jane Fonda (Night); Ava Gardner (Luxury); Cicely Tyson (Cat); Robert Morley (Father Time); Harry Andrews (Oak); Todd Lookinland (Tyltyl); Patsy Kensit (Mytyl); Will Geer (Grandfather); Mona Washbourne (Grandmother); George Cole (Dog); Richard Pearson (Bread); Nadejda Pavlova (The Blue Bird); George Vitzin (Sugar); Margareta Terechova (Milk).

THE CASSANDRA CROSSING (*Avco Embassy, 1977*) C-126 min.

Producers, Sir Lew Grade, Carlo Ponti; executive producer, Giancarlo Pettini; director, George Pan Cosmatos; story, Robert Katz; screenplay, Tom Mankiewicz, Katy Cosmatos; music, Jerry Goldsmith; art director, Aurelio Crugnola; costumes, Andriana Berselli; assistant director, Antonio Gabrielli; sound, Carlo Palmieri; special camera, Tazio Secciaroli; camera, Ennio Guarnieri; editors, Francois Bonnot, Robert Silvi.

Sophia Loren (Jennifer); Richard Harris (Chamberlain); Ava Gardner (Nicole); Burt Lancaster (Mackenzie); Martin Sheen (Navarro); Ingrid Thulin (Elana); Lee Strasberg (Kaplan); John Phillip Law (Stack); Ann Turkel (Susan); O. J. Simpson (Father Haley); Lionel Stander (Conductor); Raymond Lovelock (Tom); Alida Valli (Mrs. Chadwick); Lou Castel (Driver).

THE SENTINEL (*Universal, 1977*) C-91 min.

Producers, Michael Winner, Jeffery Konvitz; director, Winner; based on the novel by Konvitz; screenplay, Winner, Konvitz; production designer, Philip Rosenberg; set decorator, Ed Stewart; costumes/wardrobe, Peggy Farrell; assistant director, Charles Okun; music, Gil Melle; sound, Hugh Train, Les Lazarowitz; special camera effects, Albert Whitlock; camera, Dick Kratina; editors, Bernard Gribble, Terence Rawlings.

Chris Sarandon (Michael Lerman); Cristina Raines (Alison Parker); Martin Balsam (Professor); John Carradine (Halliran); Jose Ferrer (Robed Figure); Ava Gardner (Miss Logan); Arthur Kennedy (Franchino); Burgess Meredith (Chazen); Sylvia Miles (Gerde); Deborah Raffin (Jennifer); Eli Wallach (Gatz); Christopher Walken (Rizzo); Jerry Orbach (Director); Beverly D'Angelo (Sandra); Hank Garrett (Brenner); Robert Gerringer (Hart); Nana Tucker (Girl at Finale); Tom Berenger (Man at Finale); Gary Allen (Malcolm Stinnett); Kate Harrington (Mrs. Clark); Jane Hoffman (Lillian Clotkin); Elaine Shore (Emma Clotkin); Sam Gray (Dr. Aureton); Reid Shelton (Priest); Fred Stuthman (Alison's Father); Lucie Lancaster (Alison's Mother); Anthony Holland (Party Host).

CITY ON FIRE (*Sandy Howard-Astral Bellevue Pathe, 1979*) C-min.

Executive producers, Sandy Howard, Harold Greenberg; producer, Claude Heroux; associate producer, Howard Lipson; director, Alvin Rakoff; production designer, William McCrow; art director, Claude Marchand; assistant directors, Charles Braive, Daniel Haussman; makeup, Michele Dion; sound, Patrick Rousseau; special effects, Cliff Wenger, Carol Lynn; camera, Rene Verzier.

With: Henry Fonda, Susan Clark, Ava Gardner, Barry Newman, Shelley Winters, Leslie Nielsen, Richard Donat.

As Eadie in *The Girl from Missouri* ('34).

190

CHAPTER 4

JEAN HARLOW

5'3½"
109 pounds
Blonde hair
Gray-blue eyes
Pisces

THE NAME "JEAN HARLOW" is Hollywood legend. No other star so obviously suggested the gloriously blonde, black-negligeed, spike-heeled, beauty-marked brand of Thirties-style cinema sex. No other luminary is so synonymous with suffering—just note her confrontations with parasitic guardians, her three disastrous marriages, and her early death which made her the tragic heroine of Hollywood lore. And most sad, no other star has had her talent so cruelly overshadowed by exploited personal problems.

Due to her untimely death in 1937 and the later demise of her intimates, Harlow would become one of the most fantasized-about figures of the cinema. So many quick-dollar writers cashed in on her name with specious intent that it is almost difficult to now regard her as a non-fictional character. Every medium has participated in dragging forth the "lurid" story of Jean Harlow for public enjoyment and poor Jean has become perhaps the most maligned victim of the Hollywood industry.

Jean was an unusual girl—impulsive, unrealistic, unable to "rise above her material" in three brief marriages. But she was also a very hard-working professional, who gave a great deal of effort to improving herself as an actress. Away from her personal problems, she emerges onscreen as an amazing performer. It is almost impossible to believe that the shapely mannequin who was so pathetically seductive in *Hell's Angels* (1930) and *The Public Enemy* (1931) was the same comedienne who was so wonderful in MGM's *Red Dust* (1932) and *Bombshell* (1933). While Harlow could thank her chassis and platinum glory for her original film discovery, she certainly could have thanked her native talent for her dizzying popularity as she became one of the most fascinating stars in the MGM heavens.

Her exploited life began on Friday, March 3, 1911, in Kansas City, Missouri, where she was christened Harlean Carpenter.* Her father, Montclair Carpenter, was a prominent dentist; her mother, nee Jean Harlow, was an unstable housewife of grandiose intents. From her infancy, Harlean was smothered in attention, showered not only by her parents but also by her maternal grandparents. With the latter she spent summers in Bonner Springs, Missouri. "My grandparents were about two of the most doting grandparents that ever lived. I was a small pampered tyrant. All throughout my childhood Grandfather and I were boon companions."

Dr. Carpenter believed in private education, and Harlean attended a succession of expensive and exclusive institutions. She studied at Kansas City's Barstow School from the first to sixth grades. The parents were overjoyed when she began to show signs of being an intelligent and quiet child. "You could never imagine Harlean the child and Jean Harlow the actress as being one and the same person," ambiguously stated her grandmother many years later.

When Harlean was ten, her parents divorced. The girl was sent to live with her grandparents who decided, along with the doctor, that she should remain at Barstow. Her mother in the meantime went to Chicago to find work. Instead she found a new husband. The man was Marino Bello, a swarthy, moustached, majestically groomed life-gazer who eked out a living as a waiter, a salesman, a hawker of unlisted stocks, or whatever other line of work struck his fancy. Mr. Harlow was outraged at the match and for a time forbade his daughter to bring her Latin charmer to the family house. He was determined to keep Harlean away from her stepfather, but Bello's inability to find steady work resulted in the couple moving in eventually with the Harlows.

It was in 1925, the middle of the Roaring Twenties, that Harlean Carpenter first visited Hollywood. On the money provided by Dr. Carpenter, Mrs. Bello escorted her daughter to the film capital, enrolled her in a private school for girls at Hollywood Boulevard and La Brea Avenue (later to become the site of the Hollywood Women's Club), and hoped her beautiful child would attract the attention of some movie mogul. Movie star Joel McCrea would later recall that the young Jean Harlow joined him at this time in making the daily calls to Central Casting. McCrea states that they landed some bit roles together, but he cannot remember the titles. He relates that most casting directors were not impressed by the twenty-year-old boy or the fourteen-year-old girl. "One of them told both of us we'd never get anywhere," says the now very wealthy McCrea. "He said we'd never be stars. Our noses were all wrong, he claimed."

With the motion picture industry too myopic for Mama Jean's expansive plans, mother and daughter returned to the Midwest, where Marino Bello was still incapable of finding a worthy job. Dr. Carpenter continued to provide for the girl, and she was enrolled at Miss Bigelow's private girls' school. By now, the peccadilloes of his flighty ex-wife had unnerved Dr. Carpenter and he decided to send his daughter away to school, for her own good. The sanctuary chosen was Ferry Hall School for Girls in Lake Forest, Illinois. But Dr. Carpenter's plan backfired— Harlean's enrollment in the posh school would result in a return for good to Hollywood where she would become one of the more tarnished of cinema sex queens.

*Studio publicity, which always presented Jean's early life as aristocratic, changed her last name to Carpentier, and the inaccuracy has been constantly repeated. The name "Harlean" was a feminization of the "Harlow" that the parents had planned to name the child had it been a boy.

At a school dance, attractive Harlean met Charles Fremont McGrew III, a twenty-one-year-old society product worth almost half a million dollars. Unhappy at Ferry Hall, where she was only an average student and was constantly reprimanded for not wearing a brassiere, Harlean fell in love with the silver-spooned McGrew who soon wanted to marry her. Both sets of parents disapproved, but the couple eloped to Waukegan, Illinois, where sixteen-year-old Harlean lied about her age and married McGrew before a justice of the peace on Wednesday, September 21, 1927. Years later Jean would laughingly recall, "Just to give you an idea of the solemnity of our wedding, a radio next door to the justice's office was blaring 'St. Louis Blues' as we listened to the words that made us man and wife."

In *Harlow: An Intimate Biography* (1964), Irving Shulman reports that the marriage lasted one night. "That's just not so!" insisted Mrs. Montclair Carpenter, the doctor's second wife, in 1964. "They were married over two years. They went out to Hollywood together. We've got letters from Harlean telling her dad all about her life out there, and how happy they were." In actuality, the marriage was rather dreamy. They honeymooned on a cruise through the Panama Canal en route to Los Angeles, where McGrew set himself up as a California realtor. The couple moved to Beverly Hills, rented a house not far from the "It Girl," Clara Bow, and began living a fast, blank-check lifestyle. Mama Jean and Marino soon made their pilgrimage to Hollywood, living for the most part on the charity of their fortunate daughter.

Vivacious, good-humored, and devil-may-care Harlean began looking for a constructive way to occupy her time. Her exquisite beauty suggested a cinema career. Mama Jean was in full agreement. The meddling mother, sporting a butch hairstyle, signed herself up as a film extra and pleaded with her daughter to follow suit. When friends agreed that her blonde pulchritude was just what the motion pictures were seeking, Harlean became a film extra, delighting her mother by adopting Jean as her professional first name. Since Jean/Harlean regarded her film-making as a lark, she never kept track of her screen credits. It is believed that her first

appearance was with her mother in a Fox silent film in 1928, the title of which has unfortunately not yet surfaced.

In 1928 Jean visited Paramount Studios, playing a bit in *Moran of the Marines* (1928), a Richard Dix vehicle. Her curvaceous figure and glorious blonde hair next attracted the eye of producer/director Hal Roach who employed Jean in a few comedy shorts, including Laurel and Hardy's very funny *Double Whoopee* (1929). This short has enjoyed considerable play; it contains the memorable sequence in which Jean emerges from a luxury car dressed to the nines, only to have the comics shut the car door on the train of her frock and off comes the gown. Jean then unknowingly enters the hotel clad only in her skimpy black lingerie, oblivious to the enraptured stares of the onlookers. Jean recalled fondly: "Stan and 'Babe' [Hardy] realized my ignorance and did everything in their power to make me feel at ease." The film delighted audiences but shocked Grandfather Harlow who threatened to write Harlean out of his will if such public shenanigans continued.

Grandfather's outrage slowly infected Charles McGrew as well. While his fun-loving wife continued to romp through bits as decorative background in such 1929 films as Paramount's *Close Harmony* and *The Love Parade,* United Artists' *New York Nights* and *City Lights* (the Charlie Chaplin feature not released until 1931), and Al Christie comedy shorts like *Bacon Grabbers* and *Weak but Willing,* the young half-a-millionaire became resentful of his wife's time-consuming hobby. In mid-1929 the couple separated and Jean established residence with her welcoming mother and stepfather on North Maple Drive in Beverly Hills.

It was not until January of 1931 that Jean and McGrew finally obtained a divorce. The husband lamented that Jean had embarked on a career of her own without consulting him, and that his spouse once posed for cheesecake photographs "with scarcely a stitch of clothes on." Jean would deny this. Her testimony regarding McGrew's drunkenness and cruelty influenced the court to award her a trust fund of $100,000 and alimony of $375 per month from her spouse of three and one-half years. Jean accepted, but had second thoughts. "I gave McGrew back his $100,000

With Stan Laurel and Oliver Hardy in *Double Whoopee* ('29).

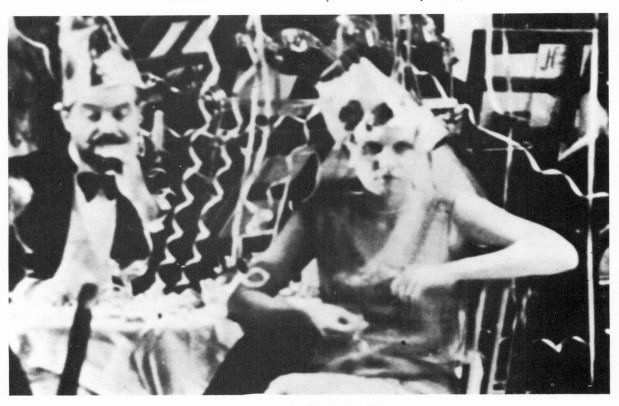

As an extra in *City Lights* ('31).

194

With Jean Arthur, Clara Bow, and Leone Lane in *The Saturday Night Kid* ('29).

trust fund; I'd rather have his good will, and I can make my own way, anyhow."

So Jean continued to seek acting roles. In the summer of 1929 she won the small featured role of Hazel, a department-store salesgirl in Paramount's *The Saturday Night Kid,* a Clara Bow vehicle that also featured Jean Arthur, James Hall, and Edna May Oliver. In the film's closing credits, Jean's name had eleventh billing. Both Jean and pal Joel McCrea tested at Pathé for small roles in *Holiday* (1930) starring Ann Harding, but neither landed a part. Still, Jean survived, saving Mama Jean from her occasional money-earning exploits as a dime-store clerk or a door-to-door saleslady, and keeping Marino from ever having to consider full-time employment.

Meanwhile, at the soundstage of Metropolitan Studios in Hollywood, a disaster was brewing—a picture called *Hell's Angels.* Since the summer of 1927, multi-millionaire boy-wonder Howard Hughes had invested some $2 million in his new-found hobby, Caddo Company, producing a feature film that had fantastic aerial

combat scenes, a miserable story line, and an "English" leading lady with an overly thick Swedish accent. The actress was $2,500-per-week Greta Nissen, a fatal casualty of the incoming sound era. Since it would cost Hughes another million dollars to reshoot the story with dialogue, the plucky rich man was in despair.

Unwilling to write off the costly venture, Hughes sought to rescue the venture from failure. Although he retained director credit, Hughes hired reedy young Englishman James Whale to direct the new version. Whale was in Hollywood preparing to shoot *Journey's End* at Tiffany and took the humble job to learn about the cinema in a brutally firsthand manner. Hughes borrowed MGM scripter Joseph Moncure March to refashion the war story. Miss Nissen was paid to make a graceful exit, and a new actress was sought to play the Limey tart Helen who seduces innocent soldiers with the immortal line, "Pardon me while I slip into something more comfortable!"

How Jean Harlow landed the plum role is, like so much of Hollywoodiana, passed down in sev-

With James Hall and Ben Lyon in *Hell's Angels* ('30).

With Ben Lyon in *Hell's Angels*.

196

eral conflicting versions. In *that* biography of Miss Harlow, it is stated that agent Arthur Landau, then the scurrying partner of the Small-Landau Agency and the ten-percenter of the unfortunate Greta Nissen, tried to provide client Dorothy Mackaill as a substitute. But her studio, Warner Bros., vetoed the deal. In his despondency to solve the casting matter, Landau visited the Hal Roach studio, calling on Laurel and Hardy. In the conversation, Stan and Ollie pointed out a blonde extra, and, incongruous as it seems, hypothesized as to whether or not she was wearing a brassiere. Landau took his cue and arranged a screen test for that unbridled blonde with Hughes' Caddo Company.

Taking strong exception to this account of Jean's discovery was Ben Lyon, who played Monte in *Hell's Angels*. "Landau only became her manager after her career began," he stated in 1964. "He didn't discover her. I did. . . . We were filming on a rented stage at the old Metropolitan Studios. One morning I wandered over to another rented stage where Al Christie was making one of his two-reel comedies. They were shooting a ballroom scene with about 200 extras. Suddenly, my eyes riveted on a girl in the middle of the crowd—a blonde in a tight-fitting black satin gown. It was obvious that she filled it without artificial aids." Lyon, who later in his career became a respected talent scout, claims that he arranged the test, introducing Jean to Hughes and coaching her late that afternoon after Jean finished her extra stint for Christie. Lyon is very insistent that he is telling the truth—peculiar, since his agent at the time was Arthur Landau. Jean herself never offered a definitive answer. "I still don't know how I got that role. I suppose Howard Hughes was just so sick of looking at blondes he was in the mood to give up."

At any rate, Jean's discovery and test came all in the same exhausting day. It was after 5:30 p.m. when scheduled shooting finally ceased and Whale aimed the cameras for a test of "the new girl." As writer March recalls of the would-be starlet, "She had almost albino blonde hair, a puffy, somewhat sulky little face, and she was dressed in what appeared to be an evening gown that fitted her tightly in the bodice and hips." Eyeing her flaring hips and narrow waist, the writer was moved to make a disparaging remark to the director. He said, " 'My God, she's got a shape like a dustpan.' . . . Most of us did not even know that the girl's name was Jean Harlow."

The test was a disaster; the gown was not right, Jean's makeup was garish, and a second test was shot after the nervous candidate was regroomed. It was almost as bad. Nevertheless, Whale, whose Swiftian humor and bizzare taste blossomed brilliantly in the horror films he would direct at Universal, saw just what he wanted in the lacquered Jean. After all, he himself pictured Helen as a "pig," an insight that was not announced to Jean when she ecstatically learned that she had won the part.

At this point, Arthur Landau was indubitably in the midst of the action, and confronted Hughes when making terms for his new client. The Texas millionaire's offer was almost insulting: a three-year contract with Caddo, $1,500 for her emergency fill-in in *Angels,* $250 a week thereafter when she worked and $200 a week when she did not. There would be a $50-a-week increase in the second and third years of the contract. Landau recognized that nothing better was in sight and Jean thus became an asset in the twenty-four-year-old tycoon's diversified empire.

Working in *Hell's Angels* was a sharp contrast to Jean's early extra work in pictures. Her life-of-leisure marriage had evaporated, and she now needed the income, not only for herself, but also for her luxury-loving guardians. Besides, the film was of epic proportions, and suddenly she had to act in front of the camera, instead of just decorating the background. The pressure wracked the nineteen-year-old starlet. "Harlow was quite aware of her deficiencies," recalled March, "and a lot of the time it must have seemed like a nightmare to her. Even her ability to be seductive was questioned, and in one scene which demanded considerable allure, she could not seem to please Mr. Whale. 'Tell me,' she said with desperate earnestness, 'tell me exactly how you want me to do it.' Mr. Whale, his patience sorely tried, said, 'My dear girl, I can tell you how to be an actress but I cannot tell you how to be a woman.' "

Nevertheless, filming came to a close and Jean survived the ordeal, due largely to the encouragement of Lyon, co-star James Hall, and other sympathetic set members. Hughes quickly patched the reels together and on Tuesday, June 3, 1930, *Hell's Angels* enjoyed a gala premiere at Grauman's Chinese Theatre, which Jean attended in lavish finery. She also was on hand for the dual Broadway openings at the Criterion and Gaiety Theatres. Most critics rejoiced over the film's action sequences, with the acting drawing mixed comments from the press across the nation. The *New York Times* lamented, "... So soon as the producer forgets Helen, the flaxen-haired creature, and takes to war, his film is absorbing and exciting. But while she is the center of attention, the picture is a most mediocre piece of work." The *New York Daily Mirror,* on the other hand, called Jean "a beauty with plenty of allure," and *Variety* exclaimed of Harlow, "It doesn't make much difference what degree of talent she possesses here, for the boys are apt to go into an uproar over this girl who is the most sensuous figure in front of a camera in some time. She'll probably always have to play these kind of roles, but nobody ever starved possessing what she's got."

Seen today, or actually viewed at any time in the annals of film criticism, Jean's work in *Hell's Angels* is quite dreadful. Her oncamera lovemaking is certainly fine, and her tussling with Lyon is realistic indeed. But the uncertain, frightened girl could not capture for the celluloid the breezy, heartless whore she was playing. Jean was one actress who just did not click as a screen bitch. As the public would observe, Harlow's acting technique improved when the roles allowed room for humor and heart to mix with the spice that won her film stardom.

After the exhausting production of *Hell's Angels,* Hughes had no picture planned for Jean. The new star was sent on the road to promote the film via personal appearances. In the initial engagements, Jean's live act was rancid and she usually retreated backstage from the crowd's boos in near hysterics. With new writers rushed in to patch up her act, the stage appearances improved dramatically. The press, delighted with the risqué act, began dubbing her "sexquisite." Theatres paid $3,500 for Jean's show, a sum that went directly to the Caddo Company while Jean continued to draw her $250 weekly salary.

Back in Hollywood, other film studios were anxious to employ the new favorite, Jean Harlow. Landau begged Hughes to sell Jean's contract to another producing company, but the crafty millionaire realized that his pact with the most celebrated sex find in Hollywood was a producer/businessman's dream. Rather than part with the contract, Hughes began loaning Jean's services to other studios, reaping from $1,500 to $1,750 per week while his 34-25-35 platinum blonde discovery received her usual allowances of about $300 per week. This exploitation, which Hughes conducted for some eighteen months, hardly made for a personal romance between employer and employee, as some gossipers to this day insist existed between Howard and Jean. Hollywood newspaperwoman/writer Adela Rogers St. John was right when she said, "They were friends—never anything more."

The first studio to nibble at the Hughes blonde bait was Metro-Goldwyn-Mayer. The Culver City lot had discovered to their amazement that audiences loved violence. Clark Gable had walloped Norma Shearer so thrillingly in *A Free Soul* (1930) that the lot had prepared another bullet spitter in the vein of the recent gangster epics *Doorway to Hell* and *Little Caesar,* both from Warner Bros.' Burbank lot. This was *The Secret Six,* a gangland thriller, which for the first time would unite Harlow with Gable. Jean plays Anne Courtland, a typically tacky moll, with Gable as Carl Luckner, a smirking reporter who advises the blonde, "Listen, if you're goin' t' fall for anybody, make it me. I'm dependable." Jean's plotline romance here, however, develops more with Johnny Mack Brown, Gable's rival journalist pal.

Gable and Harlow had little to discuss on the set. It was only later, when each was in the upper echelon of cinema stardom, that they became solid, wisecracking friends. Jean's relationship with Wallace Beery, who played her "keeper" in the film, came more quickly to a boil. The surly, no-nonsense actor immediately angered the actress and they soon began to despise one another—Beery resenting the young happy girl, and Jean not understanding the bear-like old grouch. Certainly the best reading of Jean's performance occurs when, asked on the witness

With Johnny Mack Brown and Wallace Beery in *The Secret Six* ('31).

stand if she really loves gangster Beery who is indulging her in diamonds, limousines, and a $20,000 flat, she swears with passion, "No! I loathe him and despise him!"

The *New York Daily Mirror* graciously found Jean's performance "plausible," as it was "softened by love," and Hughes farmed Jean out again, this time to Universal for *Iron Man* (1931). Again, Jean played a bitch, named Rose, a money-grubber who walks out on her boxer husband (Lew Ayres—then Universal's top-drawing card). Without a softness or humor to her characterization, her performance was severely criticized. The *New York Times* sneered, "It is unfortunate that Jean Harlow, whose virtues as an actress are limited to her blonde beauty, has to carry a good share of the picture."

The gangster craze was still searing box offices and Warners' director William A. Wellman swore to producer Darryl F. Zanuck, "I'll make the toughest of them all!" Many feel he succeeded with *The Public Enemy* (1931) which bolted James Cagney, as snarling Tom Powers, to stardom. Jean played another blonde charmer,

this one called Gwen, whom Cagney attains after grinding a grapefruit into Mae Clarke's face. Jean's performance in this classic film is, unfortunately, laughable, especially when she fights through a speech to Cagney defining his pugnacity. "You don't give, you take. . . . Oh Tommy, I could love ya' to death." Her best moments in the film include the one in which Wellman has the camera linger on her undulating derriere as she dances with compact Cagney, and the scene in which she heaves a piece of bric-a-brac at the wall after Cagney is called from her lair in an emergency. The ever-unimpressed *New York Times* noted, "The acting throughout is interesting, with the exception of Jean Harlow. . . ."

Despite these critical quips, the "slut" parade continued for Jean. Fox met Hughes' asking price to co-star her with Spencer Tracy in *Goldie* (1931) as a golddigging carnival high diver whom Tracy walks out on in a crowd-pleasing finale. "She is a decorative person but lacks the spark needed to make her shine as a personality," claimed the *New York Daily News*. Then at Columbia Jean played the title role of Frank

With Lew Ayres and Robert Armstrong in *Iron Man* ('31).

With James Cagney in *The Public Enemy* ('31).

With Spencer Tracy in *Goldie* ('31).

Capra's *Platinum Blonde* (1931), miscast as a society snob and forsaken in the final reel by hero Robert Williams for heroine Loretta Young. "For all her top billing, Jean Harlow has very little to do," reported the *New York American,* while the *New York Herald-Tribune* found her "competent, but not much more." Capra commented, "No one has ever realized Jean Harlow's potentialities. . . . Here is a personality which will be more intriguing and more dominating if it is not exaggerated by makeup and costuming."

The fact that the critics regarded her as a statuesque joke hurt Jean considerably. While agent Landau told her to be happy she was working and her parents continued to drain her weekly paycheck (moving into a lavish home on fashionable Club View Drive and dressing like stars themselves), Jean complained, "I've played a series of abandoned wretches whose wickedness is never explained, never condoned, never accounted for. How can I expect audience sympathy when I have none for the parts I've been forced to play? . . . A sordid heroine can be sympathetic only when she is clearly a victim of circumstances." It would not be the last time that Jean's innate intelligence and eloquence would take Hollywood by surprise, a town so willing to regard her only with a dirty smirk.

Back at Columbia—where Landau had negotiated a two-picture deal between Caddo and the studio—Jean was Cassie Barnes, one of the *Three Wise Girls* (1932), the other two being Mae Clarke and Marie Prevost. *Variety* noted that Jean played "the girl who keeps straight. She does her best to suggest the innocent young thing and does better than might be expected," though the reviewer noted that Mae Clarke, as a suicidal beauty, claimed the acting honors.

Finally, Hughes wore down. He had certainly received fat dividends on his investment in Jean. When MGM offered to purchase her contract for $60,000, Hughes capitulated.* The new Culver City contract called for Jean to receive $1,250

*According to Fay Wray, who played Ann Darrow in the classic *King Kong* (1933), Harlow was the original choice for the screaming heroine. When Jean became unavailable due to her change-over to MGM, RKO slapped a blonde wig on brunette Miss Fay and the rest is history.

With Spencer Tracy and Warren Hymer in *Goldie*.

With Robert Williams in *Platinum Blonde* ('31).

weekly the first year. While this did not compare to other star salaries,* it was paid on a fifty-two-weeks-per-year schedule rather than the usual forty. The pay would increase to $5,000 over a seven-year period, with options for an eighth and ninth year at the same top salary. The studio would provide for a secretary, hairdresser, and maid, and make available to Jean the studio limousine and wardrobe. Besides his $60,000 fee, Hughes retained the right to use Jean in two films over the next five years at her Metro price (he never exercised the option). Landau's delight with the terms he arranged for his Platinum Blonde shattered when Metro coldly informed him that since Jean was now with MGM, her affairs would be handled by the Orsatti Brothers Agency. Grateful Jean nevertheless told "Pops," as she dubbed her five-foot-tall impresario, not to worry and continued to pay him ten percent of her salary, which he unabashedly collected until her death.

* William Powell and Ruth Chatterton received $6,000 weekly at Warner Bros.; John Barrymore earned $150,000 per film at MGM.

In the winter of 1931-1932, Jean, with beaming Mama Jean and posturing Marino in tow, made a fabulously successful personal appearance tour, telling the news reporters of her new employers, "I'm crazy about MGM . . . especially Mr. Mayer, Mr. Thalberg, and Mr. Bern. I love making movies and I'm getting twelve-fifty a week. Hundreds, not dollars. And if a man with kids is getting twenty-five bucks a week, he's pretty lucky."

In 1932, MGM—whose roster included such luminaries as Marie Dressler, Greta Garbo, Joan Crawford, Norma Shearer, Clark Gable, John, Lionel, and Ethel Barrymore, Helen Hayes, and Wallace Beery—was reaching far afield in its array of studio product. Tod Browning was allowed to film the notoriously sickening *Freaks*; *Tarzan and the Ape Man* not only unleashed a new series but had about as much nudity as had ever legitimately been shown in movies; and *The Mask of Fu Manchu,* starring Boris Karloff, revealed new twists in imaginative, wild tortures of heroes and heroines. It was also the same year that the studio boosted Jean Harlow to superstardom. If the parallel seems uneven today, it was not then.

Metro-Goldwyn-Mayer was a bastion of *class*. When albino-haired, whiny-voiced, beauty-marked Jean joined the ranks of the stable's dazzlers, studio grapevines could not fathom who it was on the executive force who wanted Jean among the Metro constellation.

Certainly the hierarchy at MGM had no basic love for the famous girl. Louis B. Mayer was, among other things on the surface, a solid believer in the sanctity of womanhood, and his libido yearned for women of style (over the years, such redheaded ladies as Jeanette MacDonald, Myrna Loy, and Greer Garson were said to be his favorite intended conquests). Irving Thalberg, the workhouse junior boss of the studio, shared Mayer's preferences for "ladies"—after all, his wife was Norma Shearer. Only Paul Bern, Thalberg's charming righthand man, managed to greet Jean on their few early meetings with anything approaching friendship.

Still, now that she was "one of us," as Mayer would say of his lot of employees, the studio did its all to hone Jean into a performer who would make Culver City proud. Her first film under the pact was *The Beast of the City* (1932), yet another cops 'n' robbers bullet festival with Jean as Daisy the tart, deservedly extinguished by a police bullet. She drew second billing, flanked in the credits by Walter Huston and Wallace Ford, with Charles Brabin supplying the sort of expert direction that secured MGM's reputation. Brabin's coaching paid off, for her performance drew, of all things, enthusiastic and deserved raves. The *New York Post* lauded it as "excellent." The *New York Daily News* enthused, "Yes, the platinum blonde baby really acts in this one, mighty well." And even the *New York Times* managed to print, "Jean Harlow, the first of the platinum blondes, is a distinct asset to the film."

Those reviews succeeded in winning Jean slightly better treatment on the Metro lot, as did the fact that she was beginning to date the studio's most eligible "bachelor"—Paul Bern,*

*He was born in Wandsbeck, Germany, on December 3, 1889, to Henriette Hirsch and Julius Levy. The family moved to New York where he was educated in the public schools and then studied at the American Academy of Dramatic Arts. Later he was an actor, stage manager, and director in some theatrical productions (1911-1915). Among the films he directed were *The North Wind's Malice* (1920), *Worldly Goods* (1924), *Tomorrow's Love* (1925), and *Grounds for Divorce* (1925). The dapper 5'6", brown-haired, hazel-eyed man was an executive with MGM from November 1926 to August 1928. Then he moved over to Pathé in a similar capacity, returning to MGM in 1930 as a supervisor.

With Walter Byron and Mae Clarke in *Three Wise Girls* ('32).

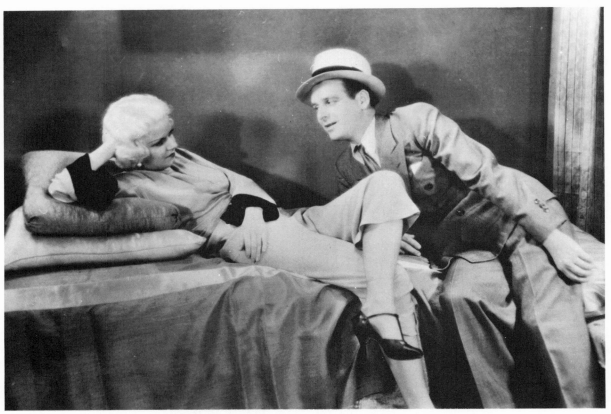

With Wallace Ford in *The Beast of the City* ('32).

posthumously described by *Time* magazine as "handsome, slender, melancholy, brilliant, and distinguished by his profound sympathy for other people's troubles. . . . 'A motion picture Christ.' " He did indeed have many disciples. His intelligence, wit, and uncanny insight into dramatic material had made him Thalberg's most trusted co-worker and friend. Mayer himself, though not comfortable around the intellectual Bern, admired his abilities. Bern was entrusted with the care of all the Garbo pictures and most of the top products that the studio was then developing. Personally he was one of the lot's best-liked people, always courteous and, away from his office, reputedly one of the finest romancers in Hollywood, specializing in appealing to the "spiritual" side of his protégées by reading poetry to them or playing classical records.

Unfortunately, Paul Bern is remembered today not so much for his considerable executive talent but for becoming one of the cinema's most colorful suicides. Had the sensitive, quixotic Bern known that he would be written about in

film history as a cross between Ernest Hemingway's Jake of *The Sun Also Rises* and the Marquis de Sade, he might have ended his life a lot earlier then he did. As it was, in 1932, he was, as an associate viewed it, "hell-bent on finding someone to make over and fall in love with." The fact that Jean Harlow was receiving a frosty treatment from the Metro bosses drew his sympathy to her. It was a situation that developed into a romance. His transcendental approach worked. Jean's more trustworthy biographers quote her as saying of the courtship, "My God, he wants to take me to the opera!" and "Here was *the* man who could distinguish between Jean Harlow and Harlean Carpenter!"

Something Bern did talk of was Harlow's potential talent and his listener was Irving Thalberg. Production of *Red-Headed Woman* (1932), an adulterous tale based on the popular Katharine Brush novel was drawing near. Norma Shearer had refused the role of Lil Andrews, the scarlet-headed tramp who triumphantly manages to break up a family of dolts, becomes mistress to a nobleman, and retains her sexy French

With Chester Morris in *Red-Headed Woman* ('32).

lover as a chauffeur. After Shearer dropped out of the running, ex-Paramount star Clara Bow and then Anita Page were considered for the part. As time went on, Thalberg continued to test such a wide selection of actresses for the part that one day hefty dowager Marie Dressler jokingly arrived for a test sporting a red wig. Thalberg had finally chosen Joan Crawford to play the part, but at the last minute, the rags-to-riches star refused it and Metro honored the increasingly popular actress' decision. Ultimately, Thalberg agreed to Bern's insistence that Jean be entrusted with the part and Jack Conway (whom others would later dispute as a man of talent or taste) was assigned to direct the vehicle.

In a flame-colored wig (although the film was shot in black and white) Jean occupied the top-billing spot over Chester Morris and studio favorite Lewis Stone. The film, scripted by Anita Loos in the pre-production Code days, intended from start to finish to mix Jean's sultriness with her natural good humor and personality. Perceptive Thalberg realized that such a slant would prevent the property from becoming a tasteless exercise in bawdiness. When the film debuted in June of 1932, audiences were wide-eyed when Jean showed Chester Morris her garters and were equally convulsed at her ribald antics, particularly with Charles Boyer (pre-stardom, but as Frenchy as ever) as her on-the-side playmate. "This shapely beauty gives a performance that will amaze you," stated the *New York Daily Mirror*, "out-Bowing the famed Bow as an exponent of elemental lure and crude man-baiting technique." Bern's judgment paid off. MGM began receiving hefty sacks of fan mail for the new star, and she was touted as the most lustrous nova of the Washington Avenue heavens.

Red-Headed Woman did not appeal to everybody. Censorial figures were aghast and Will Hays, former Postmaster General and the budding head of the industry's self-created Code Office, took the cue to sternly warn the trade that "adultery, sometimes necessary plot material, must not be explicitly treated, or justified, or presented attractively." Nor was Thalberg impressed by the immensely improved Harlow acting that was winning over the most dyspeptic of

207

critics. When asked after the premiere of *Red-Headed Woman* how Jean Harlow was in the picture, he responded, "Well, you know that girl's so bad she might just be good."

Perhaps part of Thalberg's animosity stemmed from the fact that Jean and Paul Bern were engaged to be married. The producer did not approve of the match, and much of Hollywood made the usual jokes about a nearly forty-three-year-old man of experience wedding the fabled blonde half his age. The engagement announcement also brought Jean piles of pornographic mail from "fans," titillated by the idea of the latest sex goddess facing a wedding night.

At this point Jean was making personal appearances at Loew's Theatre in Hollywood to promote *Red-Headed Woman,* dressed to the hilt and wearing the red wig from the film. Bern was immersed in studio matters. Thus the wedding plans were cursory. On the evening of Saturday, July 2, 1932, Mr. and Mrs. Louis B. Mayer, Mr. and Mrs. Irving Thalberg, Mr. and Mrs. David O. Selznick, John Gilbert and wife Virginia Bruce, Arthur Landau, and a select group of associates, relatives, and friends witnessed the evening wedding ceremony performed by Judge Leon Yanwitch between Bern and Jean at the bride's home. Gilbert was Bern's best man; Jean picked no bridesmaids to avoid slighted feelings. The brief, tasteful ceremony was marred only by the stepfather of the bride flamboyantly reading congratulatory telegrams from people whose names he considered impressive. The guests left soon thereafter and Paul escorted his bride to his Bavarian-style house on Easton Drive in Benedict Canyon.*

The ensuing weeks have been the subject of much speculation in cinema annals. In actuality, the marriage was a good one. The couple attended premieres together and a few parties, appearing quite happy. Bern continued his exec-

utive chores and Jean began working on *Red Dust* (1932), co-starring with Clark Gable, now a big MGM name. The second lead of the film was Mary Astor who in her book, *A Life on Film* (1971), recalls that Jean's marriage was solid. She cited Bern as "a gentle person who filled her [Jean's] dressing room daily with flowers and little presents like hand-embroidered handkerchiefs."

Monday morning, Labor Day, September 5, 1932, was the beginning of one of the great Hollywood scandals. John Carmichael, Bern's butler, approached his master's bedroom to awaken him. On the floor was Bern's naked body, drenched in Jean's perfume; beside him was a .38 caliber revolver and a gruesome pile of Bern's brains. On the dresser was the fabled note:

> Dearest Dear,
> Unfortunately this is the only way to make good the frightful wrong I have done you and to wipe out my abject [some accounts stated frightful] humiliation. I love you.**
> Paul
> You understand that last night was only a comedy.

In beholding the gruesome spectacle, Carmichael fainted. Bern's black gardener, Clifton Davis, entered the house, led by instinct to the bedroom, and ran to Mrs. Carmichael, telling her of finding two bodies in the boudoir. By this time Carmichael had revived, run downstairs, and done just what he had always been instructed to do in an emergency: Do not call the police—call MGM!

The servants also telephoned Jean. She was not in the house that night; she had spent the past two evenings at her parents'. While she wilted, unaided by her mother who became equally hysterical, Louis B. Mayer called Thalberg, studio police chief Whitey Hendry, studio publicist Ralph Wheelwright, and, of course, Metro's publicity chief, Howard Strickling. The contingent descended on the tragic scene in Benedict Canyon. For two hours, the MGM task

---

*In the Shulman biography, the author assures the reader that Bern beat his wife on their wedding night after she failed to raise his manhood, that Jean telephoned Landau after Bern passed out drunk, that she spent the night at Landau's, and that agent and actress returned to Easton Drive the next morning to awaken Bern and put him in shape for the scheduled reception that day.

This was disproved by Blanche Williams, maid to Jean, who spent that night right down the hall and surely would have heard any carryings-on, had they actually occurred. She also recalled serving breakfast to the newlyweds the next morning at 7 a.m., even remembering that Bern asked for "orange juice with an egg in it" and that the couple seemed perfectly happy and collected.

**Strangely, the words "I love you" have been discounted from the note in many accounts of the suicide.

On the set of *Red Dust* ('32) with Donald Crisp, Clark Gable, and Mary Astor.

force milled about the body *before* the police were notified, obscuring facts that have come to light only recently.

MGM had never had such a messy scandal in its lair and was determined to bypass one now. When the law enforcers did arrive, Mayer pocketed the suicide note, returning it only after Strickling warned him of the consequences of withholding evidence. The key note would thereafter disappear again, found this time in the pocket of a *Herald Express* reporter, one of the horde of press people who soon flooded the house. Studio officials were relieved to learn that Jean was not in the house that night, but horrified to learn that her stepfather, Marino, was away on a fishing trip with Clark Gable. Frightened of the potential taint to Gable's persona, the studio stationed a team of sisters from the publicity department at the intersection by the Bello home to prevent Gable and Bello from unknowingly driving into the mass of reporters and prurient bystanders gawking about the house. They succeeded. Gable dropped Bello off down the street and hurried away while Bello

reached the sanctuary of his home by climbing over the back fence. Unfortunately, Bello could not resist the opportunity to perform for the press, posing for pictures and flamboyantly defending his stepdaughter from defamation that nobody had yet even printed.

Upon their arrival the MGM Powers-That-Be learned from gardener Davis and neighbors that the voice of a woman—not Jean—was heard arguing behind the garden wall with Bern that night while his wife was away. Mayer was horrified by the thought that the great studio sex symbol was apparently forcing her husband to find sexual satisfaction elsewhere. As a result, Mayer had studio physician Edward B. Jones leak the rumor that Bern was a victim of infantile genitalia. The morgue released a statement claiming the deceased possessed "a physical deficiency that would have precluded marital happiness." As reported in *Mayer and Thalberg* (1975) by Samuel Marx, then head of the studio's scenario department, Jean, still under heavy sedation, was devastated by these reports. She protested vehemently to her bosses that "nothing was wrong with our marriage. It was a wonderful marriage. I loved him dearly."

While the newspapers reveled in the impotency rumors, the real reason for the Bern suicide began to make news. Letters to a Dorothy Millette were discovered, written by Bern to a lady who had been his common-law wife. Miss Millette was mentally ill and Bern had spent a good portion of his $1,500 weekly paycheck to afford her sanitarium aid and keep her discreetly away from Hollywood. Bern had not bargained on Dorothy, whom he had not seen in almost a year and with whom he had not co-habited for nearly a decade, becoming incensed when he wed Harlow (much in the tradition of *Jane Eyre*). Fitting together the pieces of clues provided by neighbors and gardener Davis (with whom Bello performed a laughable gaffe when he told him, in the hearing range of the reporters, to "keep your mouth shut"), it can be seen that Bern staged an argument with Jean about her parents, correctly assuming she would return home to her parents in a huff. She did and the house was clear for a scheduled visit from vengeful Dorothy. The neighbors' testimony of a strange female voice shouting in the yard and the arrival at the house of a veiled woman in a limousine all support evidence of her visit—as did her own suicide when she leaped off a Sacramento riverboat shortly after the news of Bern's suicide was published in newspapers.

Hence in Bern's oft-published suicide note the "frightful wrong" referred to his bigamy, and the "comedy" referred to the staged fight. Shulman's book and two motion picture biographies of Jean Harlow falsely suggest that the odd but loving, idealistic, protective Bern, who took his life to save Jean from career-wrecking headlines, was the most pathetic pervert since Fatty Arbuckle.*

Although there were wild rumors that Jean might be implicated in Bern's possible murder, she was never indicted and not even required to

*Perhaps the most complete pricking of the impotency theory occurred in 1964 when Irving Shulman appeared on a Chicago TV talk show to tout his book. Also on the program that day was famed fan dancer Sally Rand, who allegedly had had an affair with Bern shortly before he began dating Harlow. When it was mentioned that Bern was supposedly impotent, Ms. Rand laughed, insisting that Paul Bern was not only a wonderful man, but also a magnificent lover, and that she knew so by firsthand experience. The audience was stunned and Shulman was momentarily speechless.

testify at the inquest. The funeral was held at Inglewood Cemetery, a rabbi spoke of Bern's almost childishly helpful nature, Irving Thalberg wept bitterly, Louis B. Mayer sat stonefaced, and Bern's sister, who had come from the East with brother Henry, became hysterical. Black-draped Jean arrived, assisted by Marino, and cried uncontrollably throughout the services. Afterward, the flower-smothered casket was removed from the chapel and Bern's remains were cremated.

Jean Harlow never publicly commented on the reasons for Bern's suicide. Whatever she knew of the sordid scandal accompanied her to the grave five years later.

Bern left his insolvent estate to Dorothy Millette—he had not had time to alter his will—and Jean moved back with her parents. A week after the funeral, she returned to MGM to resume work on the jungle drama *Red Dust.* The cast and crew were kind, with Gable and Astor welcoming her back with hugs and director Victor Fleming posting a "No Visitors" sign to keep the morbidly curious at a safe distance.

The first few days back on the soundstage, Jean fluffed her lines and possessed little stamina. Fleming lamented privately, "How am I supposed to get a performance out of her with that look in her eyes?" However, Jean soon sparked up and amazed the production team with the performance she began to give as easy-virtued Vantine. Clark Gable stated sincerely, "She's got more courage than anyone I ever saw. That's a great girl."

Metro was very worried during the completion of *Red Dust,* fearful that the scandal would ruin the film's potential at the box office. But when the picture opened in October of 1932, Jean Harlow emerged a bigger star than ever, and deservedly so. As the most colorful third of a love-inflamed triangle that included Dennis Carson (Gable), surly operator of a tropical rubber plantation, and Barbara Willis (Astor), a frustrated newlywed with an ailing husband (Gene Raymond), Harlow won fully the stardom that her earthy appeal had previously denied her.

"What'ya been eating? Cement?" cracks Jean while cleaning the cage of a domesticated parrot. "Scrub my back," she purrs to Gable while taking that famous bath in a rain barrel. Perfectly blending humor with sex, Jean inspired the *New York Herald-Tribune* to report, "The flagrantly blonde Miss Harlow, who hitherto has attracted but intermittent enthusiasm from this captious department, immediately becomes one of its favorites by her performance in *Red Dust* . . . she proves herself a really deft comedienne. . . . In addition, however, to being amusing, she manages to create a credible character and to make the girl she plays a most engaging and sympathetic person." *Time* magazine found it necessary to inflict a put-down, cracking of "Harlot Harlow": "Audiences at *Red Dust* watched her face for traces of tragedy, found none."

Still, MGM was kinder now that Jean was a top draw, though her acting ability was still not the talk of the lot. The studio next cranked out another Gable-Harlow wisecracker, *Hold Your Man* (1933), which was geared to duplicate the formula of *Red Dust*, right down to Jean taking a bath in view of Gable (with the location switched from a rain barrel to an actual tub). Once again Jean was sexy, funny, and quite appealing. This time around, however, Jean's best shot revealed her acumen as a boxer! In a confrontation with Jean, co-player Dorothy Burgess inflicts a sharp face slap. Jean retaliates with a wicked left to the chin that, as the *New York Daily News* put it, "looks like a stunner!" The verbal exchanges were also stunners:

> *Gable:* Wait 'til you see how I'll grow on ya!
> *Jean:* Yeah . . . like a carbuncle!

Meanwhile, Metro had enjoyed an enormous success in 1932 with *Grand Hotel*, the all-star mélange that brought the Barrymores, Garbo, Wallace Beery, and Joan Crawford together with heralded results. Mayer wanted to repeat the all-star act, and the vehicle selected to showcase the stars was *Dinner at Eight*, a cinematization of the witty Broadway play by George S. Kaufman and Edna Ferber. David O. Selznick, Mayer's son-in-law, whose ambition and talent were a vast annoyance to his feisty father-in-law, was producing and George Cukor was to direct. MGM easily tapped their wide-ranging reser-

voir to fill the colorful roles. Carlotta Vance, aging actress, went to Marie Dressler; Larry Renault, boozehound ex-matinee idol, naturally went to John Barrymore; Oliver Jordan, shipping magnate dying of heart trouble, was assigned to brother Lionel; Dan Packard, big business blowhard, was given to Wallace Beery; and such Culver City names as Billie Burke, Lee Tracy, Karen Morley, Edmund Lowe, Phillips Holmes, and Madge Evans filled other major roles.* The role of Packard's cuckolding wife, Kitty, remained uncast.

The MGM hierarchy thought immediately of Harlow for the role, but Mayer smirked that she could never hold her own with such legitimate talent. Jean, as he phrased it, was merely a "freak whore." Selznick agreed, though more delicately. Cukor felt differently. "I'd seen her in *Public Enemy* and *Hell's Angels,* where she was so bad and self-conscious it was comic. She got laughs when she didn't want them," related Cukor. "Then I saw *Red Dust*—and there she was, suddenly marvelous in comedy. A tough girl, yet very feminine, like Mae West. They both wisecrack, but they both have something vulnerable, and it makes them attractive. Harlow was very soft about her toughness." Jean was signed for the role, receiving fourth billing under Dressler, John Barrymore, and old adversary Wallace Beery.

Dinner at Eight was the proverbial turning point in Jean's screen career. In a film where John Barrymore strutted as only he could as a drunken ham, Marie Dressler savored a mugging field day, and Wallace Beery inimitably bellowed, Jean topped all the seasoned scenestealers and stole the limelight. "Among a congress of stars doing their best, she is quite the hit of the evening," wrote the *New York Herald-Tribune,* a publication that only two years earlier had panned her "artificial qualities" and accused her of nearly ruining *Public Enemy.*

As Kitty Packard, Harlow appears as *the* Harlow everyone remembers: the wisecracking sexpot who languished in bed all day, testing new negligees, munching bonbons, narcissistically posing in her newest chapeau in front of

*Joan Crawford and Clark Gable were originally slated for the roles that because of secondary size went to Madge Evans and Edmund Lowe.

With Clark Gable in
Hold Your Man ('33).

With Clark Gable in
Hold Your Man.

As Vantine in *Red Dust* ('32).

213

her hand mirror, and blissfully topping her loud-mouth spouse. Still, for all this Epicureanism, Kitty is the heroine, saving Lionel Barrymore from the machinations of tycoon Beery. Her Olympian insult battles with Beery are gems. At one point she threatens Beery that if she reveals only some of his dirty dealing, "You couldn't even get in the men's room at the Astor!"

On another occasion, she and Beery battle as follows:

> *Beery:* . . . I'm the works around here, and I'll give you orders what to do!
> *Jean:* Who do ya' think you're talkin' to, that first wife of yours out in Montana?
> *Beery:* Now you leave her out of this . . .
> *Jean:* That poor mealy-faced thing with her flat chest that didn't have nerve enough to talk up t' ya? . . .
> *Beery:* Shut up!
> *Jean:* Washin' out your greasy over-alls and cookin' and slavin' in some lousy mining shack? No wonder she died!
> *Beery:* Hey, I'll sock you in a minute!
> *Jean:* Well, ya' can't get me that way. You're not gonna step on my face to get where ya' wanna go, ya' big wind-bag!

The closing sequence of *Dinner at Eight* is one of the best remembered exchanges of the Thirties:

> *Jean:* I was reading a book the other day. . . .
> *Dressler:* (mammoth double take) Reading a book?
> *Jean:* Yes, it's all about civilization or something—a nutty kind of a book. Do you know that the guy says that machinery is going to take the place of every profession?
> *Dressler:* Oh, my dear! That's something *you* need never worry about!

As Kitty Packard in *Dinner at Eight* ('33).

With Wallace Beery in *Dinner at Eight*.

Dinner at Eight was a smash hit and also reflects the trouper spirit of Hollywood in those days. Production began March 16, 1933; the 110-minute feature, despite star egos and Cukor's painstaking direction, was completed on April 17, 1933.

Jean's leviathan improvement in acting, unusual composure in coping with the Bern suicide, and consistently good-natured, down-to-earth personality had won her many friends on the Metro lot, from co-stars like Gable to crew members with whom she would frequently shoot craps at lunchtime. Ralph Wheelwright, an MGM publicity expert, saw her often and well described the Jean MGM knew: "She had—with all the gaudiness of her Hollywood role—*class*. To me, Jean was not The Baby [Mama Jean always referred to Jean as "The Baby," as did most of the Metro lot]. She was Jake. I don't know quite where the name Jake came from, but I reserved it for girls I particularly liked—Mabel Normand and Marion Davies, for instance. Jake meant to me a good kid. Garbo, much as I admired—and admire—her, could never be a Jake.

Neither could Norma Shearer. Maybe you can see the difference." In later years, when Shulman's book portrayed Jean as an oversexed harpy, picking up bellboys and spitting out obscenities, the honest Wheelwright stated, "Harlow knew all the words—could use them—but she never fell into gutter dialogue.... She was not exactly a lady—certainly not the girl next door—but neither was she a bawd. She was the sexiest-looking girl I've ever seen. Yet I believe her problem—if you could call it that—was that she was undersexed personally. She had all the equipment, but little of the desire."

Still, it must be stated that Jean did not cope with stardom with total sobriety. Even Kay Mulvey, an MGM publicist during the Thirties, admits that "success did fascinate her," and that "while money meant nothing to her as money, she did want to live as she thought a star should." This weakness delighted her parents and agent Landau, who personally supervised her purchase of a choice piece of property on Beverly Drive near the east gate of Bel Air. There Jean had built a mansion described by a columnist as "an ice cream confection in the sky," a white temple with, of course, a pool, where Jean now and then would risk sunburn. While Jean enjoyed her money, studio chores and continual publicity activities kept her busy, allowing Marino and Mama Jean nearly free reign to exhaust the bulk of the star's Metro paychecks. The fact that Bello incensed Metro officials and stars by approaching them incessantly for money to invest in his "mines," and that Mama Jean was ever present at interviews and personal appearances with her daughter, made Jean something of a joke in many Hollywood circles. So did the fact that Landau continued to draw commissions and to advertise Jean Harlow as his most dazzling client. The film industry did not understand or appreciate a soft touch like Jean.

The tragicomic aura of this personal situation served as the basis for Jean's next film—*Bombshell* (1933), which later was retitled *Blonde Bombshell* since promoters feared the public might think it a war movie. The script, a glorious inside joke that incensed Landau and her parents while delighting Jean, dealt with Lola Burns, adored sex star who is weary of her come-hither image and wearier yet of her merciless agent (Lee Tracy) and exploiting father (Frank Morgan). The Hollywood satire also featured Ted Healy and Una Merkel as other family members, Pat O'Brien as a smitten director, and Franchot Tone as a lovelorn actor hired to play a society boy saddled with trite dialogue as "I'd like to run barefoot through your hair."

Jean played Lola Burns with understandable identity. The *New York Herald-Tribune* praised the film because " . . . it provides the first full-length portrait of this amazing young woman's increasingly impressive acting talent . . . another step in Miss Harlow's brilliant career." Many feel that the film is marvelously hilarious, but few viewers seem to recognize it as also reflecting a pathetic part of a celebrity's life. Jean Harlow, like *Bombshell* counterpart Lola Burns, would never free herself from the web of sponging friends who would dominate her life. *Bombshell,* like Jean Harlow's life, is more tragedy than comedy.

Gradually Jean the widow had resumed dating. She was seen about town with director W. S. Van Dyke II and rumored to be romancing boxer Max Baer then acting at MGM in *The Prizefighter and the Lady* (1933) being directed by Van Dyke.* While filming *Bombshell,* impetuous Jean fell in love again. The beau was Hal Rosson, a Metro cameraman and an extremely capable craftsman, usually selected to film the best MGM products. Wags noted that Rosson resembled Bern not only in intellect, but also in appearance, being short and moustachioed, with a receding hairline. He was also sixteen years older than Jean. By the time *Bombshell* had completed production, the couple were a steady item. On Monday, September 18, 1933, they eloped to Yuma, Arizona. Upon their return, the newly-weds naturally posed with Mama Jean and Marino, who now had the run of the Beverly Drive home to themselves since Jean and Rosson occupied an apartment at Chateau Marmont. "He is just old enough to enable him to be my mentor," said Jean to the eager press. "I know that ours is one Hollywood marriage that will last. I am as confident of him as a husband as I am that he is the best cameraman in the world."

Unfortunately, once again the odds were against the success of the marriage. One intruding factor was Louis B. Mayer. The mogul was outraged that Jean had eloped and was disgusted that Jean, a Gentile, had married a Jew (until associates assured him that Rosson was in fact a Christian). Still, Mayer took every opportunity to snub his money-earning platinum blonde. On Saturday, September 30, 1933, at the Hollywood premiere of *Bombshell* at Grauman's Chinese Theatre,** the audience cheered the film and mobbed Jean in the lobby to bubble their praise. Then Mayer approached Jean, and the mob cleared for what they expected to be a bouquet of congratulatory verbiage. Instead, Mayer walked up to the beaming Jean, grinned widely, and said, "God, Lee Tracy's lines were great!" With that, he left. Mama Jean happened to be nearby (naturally) and was so outraged that she tele-

*Actually the married Max Baer and Jean had never dated. The fighter had visited the Harlow home, but at the invitation of Bello who hoped to become Baer's manager.

**On September 29, 1933, the evening before the *Bombshell* premiere Jean placed her hand and high-heel prints into the celebrated cement of Grauman's Chinese Theatre. Her inscription: "To Sid—with sincere appreciation—Jean Harlow."

With Lee Tracy in *Bombshell* ('33).

gramed Landau to do something about the crassness of her daughter's employer.

Four weeks after Jean's marriage, an event occurred which foreshadowed the star's untimely death. Stomach pains began troubling the actress and her mother refused to let her see a doctor, placing her trust in Science of the Mind. Rosson proved no match for the stifling Mama Jean and it took a mandate from Mayer, informed of his property's condition by a contact, to maneuver Jean to the Good Samaritan Hospital, where she underwent an emergency appendectomy. When another emergency operation was needed to save Jean's life three years later, Mayer's command for hospitalization would come too late.

Although Jean's health was now assured—for the time being—all was not well between the star and her studio. She was outraged when Mayer vetoed her honeymoon trip by assigning Rosson to shoot *Viva Villa!* in Mexico. (The executive later changed his decision.) Nor was she delighted with marriage publicity ordered by L.B., such as a *Los Angeles Times* item which

dismissed her bridegroom with, "He's no Apollo; his best friends wouldn't call him a lady killer, but he obviously reeks of lure," and quoted Jean as saying, "The physical means nothing to me." More concretely Jean was unhappy with her salary. When the script for her next projected film, *Living in a Big Way,* arrived, Jean returned it and took a studio suspension which lasted some six months.

The lay-off was no immediate financial burden to Jean as Rosson was still drawing a considerable salary ($50,000 per year) from the studio. To pass the time, she worked on a novel, *Today Is Tonight,* with friend Carey Wilson (a close acquaintance of Rosson and Bern). Wilson's widow, Carmelita, recalls, "The book was her idea. It was purely fictional. She wrote it with the idea that she would play it and MGM would produce." But the literary scene was not Jean's forte, nor was the intellectual company that her husband enjoyed keeping. Jean began escaping to Agua Caliente to gamble lavishly, irking her husband with her debts, and maintained an exasperating loyalty to her parents. After eight months of marriage, Jean planned divorce proceedings against Rosson.* The announcement came, of all places, at the wedding of Carey Wilson and Carmelita at which Jean was a bridesmaid!

Jean returned to her parents at the Beverly Drive palace. They greeted her return enthusiastically. In filing her reasons for divorce, Jean cited that his "ungenerous character constituted, in effect, continuous brutality." Jean also unwittingly noted that her husband angered her because "he read in bed." The press adored this item and played it to the hilt. To salvage her respect, Jean wrote a letter to the readers of *Screen Book* magazine,

> To my *Screen Book* friends:
>   I regret more than I can say that my marriage with Hal Rosson did not work out. Believe me, this is no frivolous matter— but the only way out for both of us. We are uncongenial and while there is no ill feeling between us, we realize that it is best for us to separate.
>
>   Jean Harlow

Meanwhile, Jean had returned to the Metro fold, receiving a slight pay increase and being assigned to star as Eadie, the money-hungry chorine title character of *The Girl from Missouri* (1934). Upon her return to the lot, the studio was shocked at her appearance. Away from the expert dieticians and hair stylists of MGM, Jean had gained many unflattering pounds and had destroyed her hair with personally applied bleachings and cuttings. The studio furtively ordered wigs made for Jean, which the actress thereafter had to wear whenever in the public eye. Affecting her wig and squeezed into a girdle, Jean still impressed *Photoplay* as a "gorgeous eyeful" and the magazine hailed the film as: "Noisily defiant, rip-snorting, and raucous in spots . . . hilarious. . . ." Franchot Tone and Lionel Barrymore helped keep the proceedings looking fresh, although it was a rather predictable

*Shortly after the divorce proceedings began, Rosson contracted polio. This caused a reconciliation, but the divorce did go through as planned. Rosson recovered quickly and resumed his filmmaking career.

vehicle packaging Jean in her usual sassy style. Almost needless to say, Hal Rosson was no longer assigned to film Jean's motion pictures.

With Jean's appearance and personal life more of a worry to the studio, publicity boss Howard Strickling assigned a young lady named Kay Mulvey to serve as a watchdog for Jean, keeping her in shape and clarifying any remarks that Jean might make to the press. Miss Mulvey and Jean became very close friends. The star spent hours playing with her advisor's child, engaging in children's games and mud-pie making, and Miss Mulvey states that she rarely saw Jean Harlow happier than during these playtimes. She remembers Jean as a very simple girl, bright but sentimental. "Jean played with only one doll in her whole life. She was given scores of others—but she put them away in drawers 'to sleep' as she called it. The one doll she loved had been her mother's when she was a little girl, and in that oldfashioned manner, it had a china head and a cloth body. One day, Jean accidentally broke it. She wrapped the pieces in tissue and she still had them when she died. She was sentimental over many things in this manner."

Late in 1934, MGM planned to star the lustrous Joan Crawford in a musical of epic proportions. David O. Selznick was to produce, Victor Fleming to direct, Jerome Kern and Oscar Hammerstein II and H. Burton Lane (among others) to write songs, Carl Randall and Chester Hale to choreograph, and William Powell, Franchot Tone, and Rosalind Russell to co-star. The project took the name *Reckless,* after the Kern-Hammerstein II tune, and took its plot loosely from the life of Broadway star Libby Holman.

From the start, *Reckless* had problems. Selznick offended Kern at the first meeting by saying, "Jerry, how about playing one of your tunes? You see, I'm not too familiar with your work." To which Kern replied, "Mr. Selznick, I'm sorry, but I don't give away free samples," and thereafter performed only token effort on the film. Joan Crawford also caused grief, not liking the script and refusing the assignment. Hence, for the second time (and not the last), Jean was offered and accepted a Crawford hand-me-down.

With Jean in the dancing/singing stellar role,

With Ben Bard and Charles C. Wilson in *The Girl from Missouri* ('34).

With Franchot Tone in *The Girl from Missouri*.

219

With William Powell in *Reckless* ('35).

220

there were still problems. It seems that Miss Holman had a husband, Zachary Smith Reynolds II, the Duke tobacco heir, who had coincidentally shot himself in July of 1932 under mysteriously sordid circumstances. Jean bridled at the parallel to her own life.

Additional problems arose when Jean did not take well to the choreography, and Randall and Hale had to rehearse her brutally to achieve the desired end. Finally, it was decided that Jean's voice could never do the music any sort of justice. The singing voice that came from her lips actually belonged to dubber Virginia Verrill, whose rich mezzo was totally unlike Jean's voice, making ridiculous Metro's claim that Jean did her own singing in this entry.

Her relationship with William Powell at this time balanced these problems for Jean.* The suave actor was in 1935 one of MGM's top attractions, and had just been in the classic *The Thin Man* (1934) with chic Myrna Loy. Twice married, Powell had recently divorced Carole Lombard. Jean and Powell's dating won the approval of Hollywood, which took the attitude that the actress was finally dating an attractive man who was more to her style. Actually Powell was very much (at least physically) like Bern and Rosson. He was nineteen years older than Jean, and his 5'6" stature and thinning hair invariably disappointed fans who saw him offcamera.

Maureen O'Sullivan** recalled of the Harlow-Powell match, "She was very much in love with Bill . . . and talked about him constantly. She respected him because of his intelligence. She was always anxious to increase her knowledge, and she felt she could learn a lot from Powell." Unlike Bern and Rosson, Powell also had a great sense of fun, joining Jean at gala film premieres and taking her on camping trips.

*He was born William Horatio Powell on July 29, 1892, in Pittsburgh, Pennsylvania. He was first married to Eileen Wilson (divorced) by whom he had a son and then to Carole Lombard (also divorced). He subsequently married Diana Lewis in 1940 to whom he remains wedded as of this writing. For a detailed study of his career and life see *The Debonairs* (Arlington House, 1975).

**Maureen O'Sullivan also became a close friend to Jean. She reminisces that she and Jean had roomed together on a vacation jaunt to Lake Arrowhead. "She was a fresh air fiend," says Miss O'Sullivan. "She never wore a nightgown, and worried about what the maids would say in the morning." Hence Jean would borrow a nightie from Miss O'Sullivan, crumple it up, and toss it on her bed each morning so that the maids would not gossip about her sleeping in the nude!"

Shortly after completing *Reckless,* Jean celebrated her twenty-fourth birthday, traveling with her parents and two friends to Agua Caliente. The papers reported how Jean placed a $2 bet on a craps table, let it ride through eight straight passes, and left the casino with $10,240!

The following month, *Reckless* premiered. "Good popular entertainment and the Harlow fans will applaud it enthusiastically," stated the *New York Daily Mirror.* Jean's fans applauded, but the star had too many problems meeting the standards of a musical comedy performer to encourage a follow-up song-and-dance film. Instead, Jean went into *China Seas* (1935), an all-star melodrama starring Clark Gable, Wallace Beery, Rosalind Russell, and Lewis Stone. Once again, brassy Jean was back in her element playing "China Doll," Gable's discarded mistress, loaded with sex appeal and wisecracks.

China Seas was crammed with box-office allure. Gable plays a hard-drinking captain, Beery a rascally pirate, Russell a British society dame engaged to Gable, Stone a cowardly ex-officer who redeems himself in the explosive last reel. Spicing up the proceedings is a plot featuring gold-laden ships in treacherous pirate waters of the Orient. The production was personally supervised by Irving Thalberg, who chose the property with the remark, "To hell with art this time. I'm going to produce a picture that will make money!"

The production was not without incident. Thalberg took too close an interest in the film, visiting the set daily and personally coaching the actors until director Tay Garnett threatened to quit. There also were a number of stunts performed that almost resulted in death. In one scene, Gable was to carry Jean to safety across a water-filled promenade, just before a flood of water cascaded behind them. The special effects crew mistimed the action and dumped fifty tons of water too early, washing Gable's and Jean's doubles (Chick Collins and Loretta Rush) off the stage and onto a mesh of water-soaked cables, where they just barely escaped electrocution. In another scene, Gable insisted on dodging—without aid of a stuntman—a five-ton steamroller that was to break loose and roll about a slick deck. He narrowly avoided being crushed.

With Wallace Beery and Clark Gable in *China Seas* ('35).

Nevertheless, *China Seas* was completed on schedule without any major mishaps.

Drinking Beery under the table, aiding the villain in his machinations out of spite for Gable, and warning Gable against wedding snooty Russell with a vicious "You can't quit me any more than I can quit you, and you can kiss a stack of cookbooks on that," Jean was delightful as China Doll. *Time* magazine not only heralded her as "the most ingratiating member of its cast," but treated Jean to a cover story.

On August 19, 1935, Jean Harlow appeared on the *Time* cover adorned in feathers, lounging in a plush chair, brandishing a hand mirror, and seductively staring into the camera. The feature replayed most of the studio-prepared biography, made a few cutting remarks about her stepfather, and unpleasantly credited Mama Jean as the power responsible for Jean's stardom. The feature noted, "If there is any fly in the scented ointment of Jean Harlow's current celebrity, it is her occasional dissatisfaction with the character with which her appearance and her mother, by a sort of conspiracy of nature and circumstance, have built up for her. . . .

"Last week at a party, when she made what she considered a bright remark, the person to whom she was speaking asked: 'Whom did you hear say that?' Jean Harlow paused bitterly before making another remark which was both brighter and indubitably her own: 'My God, must I always wear a low cut dress to be important?' "

To be a *Time* cover personality was indeed an honor. *Time* had in its twelve-year history featured only thirty women on the covers of over six hundred issues, and only a dozen movie figures (three of them actresses) had enjoyed this accolade. Unfortunately, many thought Jean Harlow was hardly an artist worthy of such treatment, and *Time* received a barrage of letters: e.g.,"I was completely shocked to see the picture of Jean Harlow on the front cover of the August 19 issue in such an undignified position" and "What a shock it was to receive *Time* . . . and find Jean Harlow's picture (dis)gracing the front cover." The magazine's official reply, "As in the past, *Time* will continue to depict on its front cover newsworthy cinema actresses when they make news."*

*Ironically, Jean had made the *back* cover of *Time* on October 19, 1931, by seductively endorsing Lucky Strike cigarettes.

Posing with Clark Gable for *China Seas*.

Another honor that came to Jean at this time was her own bungalow on the Metro lot. Mayer ordered custom-made cottages especially designed for such favorites as Myrna Loy, Jeanette MacDonald, Joan Crawford, and of course Garbo. Jean's cottage, completely decorated in white, was very close to the red and white bungalow of the elusive Greta. Garbo became very much aware of her platinum neighbor; as soon as Jean would arrive each morning, Harlow had her maid Blanche Williams stack records on her Victrola which could be heard blaring all around the bungalow. When the Metro bosses, coddling the famed Garbo temperament, asked the Swede if they should reprimand Jean for her noisy habit, Garbo was said to shrug, smile, and say, "I used to play happy music all the time, too."

In September of 1935, Mama Jean divorced Marino Bello, filing a slew of charges, all under the heading of cruelty: abusing and threatening her, Jean, and the servants, causing her anguish and humiliation in public places, and brandishing a wicked temper and foul language. It also was obvious to all who knew Jean that her flamboyant stepfather was the main cause of her insolvency—spending wildly on clothes and luxuries for himself. With Marino gone, Jean freed herself of the money-draining Beverly Glen Drive domain, selling it to Nat Levine of Republic Studios for $125,000. With Mama Jean, the actress moved into a small hacienda at 512 North Palm Drive in Beverly Hills, not far from the home of Ruth Chatterton and the home of Jean's old mentor, Hal Roach.

So popular was the screen love team of Harlow and Gable that MGM tried to reunite them professionally at any possible occasion. In August 1935 they recreated their *China Seas* parts on radio's "Hollywood Hotel," and there was talk of reactivating the projected screen version of Robert Sherwood's ribald play, *Road to Rome,* with George Cukor directing. It came to naught. (In 1955 MGM would transform it into the Esther Williams' musical *Jupiter's Darling,* with Howard Keel as Hannibal.)

The year 1936 proved to be a banner one for Jean, while her heftier, older counterpart, Mae West, was already suffering career reversals at Paramount. In a twelve-month period, Jean starred in four highly touted MGM features.

By now Thalberg had come to realize that Harlow was both a star *and* a talent. To promote her further, he chose *Riff-Raff* (1936), the story of a fishermen's strike. (The project had been originally geared for Gloria Swanson.) It was a change of pace from Jean's usual sultry melodramas. The producer assigned Spencer Tracy, a new Metro acquisition, as her co-star, with the belief that teaming the actor with sexy partners would also give the supposedly aloof Tracy some silver screen allure. Also, with Thalberg sensitive over the fact that Jean's famed blonde trademark was not her own, he ordered that she become a "brownette" in the picture, hoping to downplay her platinum trademark. He succeeded. Her secret swapping of a platinum wig for a honey-brown one was received enthusiastically by her fans.

Yet *Riff-Raff* appeared to be a doomed production. Tay Garnett refused to direct the picture. He felt that Jean as Hattie, the melancholy tuna cannery worker, was completely out of her element. "Harlow is the most famous courtesan in the world; people know her as a loveable tramp. Now you're trying to put her in the role of a madonna."* Thalberg argued that he was merely attempting to give the actress' career "a new dimension," but Garnett was adamant and his Metro contract was canceled. J. Walter Ruben took over the directing post, and the film was rushed to frantic completion to meet Thalberg's unalterable deadline. This pace became devastatingly apparent at the preview in Whittier, California. The swift cutting of the picture resulted in the second reel of celluloid breaking, and after "repairs" were hastily made, Tracy's dialogue was coming out of Harlow's mouth and vice versa. This set-up amused the audience but paralyzed the studio executives at the screening. The latter were further disheartened when they learned that the third reel had been left at the studio in the haste to rush the feature to the studio. (Thalberg simply ordered that the fourth reel be shown.) By the time that *Riff-Raff* went into national release, the product was more carefully assembled. The *New York Daily Mirror*

*On a personal level, Garnett felt quite differently about Jean. In his memoirs, *Light Your Torches and Pull Up Your Tights* (1973), he wrote, "I knew Jean Harlow very well. In person she was just a happy-go-lucky actress whose morals would have stood up against those of any devastatingly pretty girl in any large American city."

With Una Merkel in *Riff-Raff* ('36)

labeled it "lively, daring, meaty, and rough...the best film Jean Harlow has made for a long time." Jean and Tracy, he as an egotistical fisherman, worked together splendidly, and Tracy would recall Jean as "a square shooter if ever there was one."

Jean next went to work on her fifth film with Gable, *Wife vs. Secretary* (1936),* which added Myrna Loy to the snappy proceedings. Jean was billed under Gable but above Loy who in 1937 would be voted "The Queen of Hollywood" (with Gable elected "King"). The plot cast Jean as Whitey Wilson (the MGM wigmakers would be kept busy for the rest of Jean's stay there, providing her with whatever color coiffure the script dictated), the perfect secretary to the perfect boss (Gable) who happens to have the ideal wife (Loy). The charisma of the stars, abetted by Clarence Brown's nearly flawless direction and Metro's high-calibre production values, boosted

*In 1934 RKO had purchased the screen rights to the project *The Gorgeous Hussy* for Katharine Hepburn; then MGM acquired the property intending Harlow to play Peggy O'Neal, the innkeeper's daughter in 1830s Washington, D.C. But persuasive Joan Crawford convinced the MGM hierarchy that she should have the pivotal role in this costumed melodrama.

a rather trying film that had Loy cattily wondering if her husband had an off-hours yen for his secretary. Audiences adored the feature, especially the scene where the three stars took to ice skates.

Jean's likeability was immense in this picture. She was warm and amusing, and the absence of come-hither sexiness in her performance gave further illustration of her acting capabilities. The *New York Herald-Tribune,* which had become the most boisterous enthusiast of the Harlow talent, exuded, "The one joy of the film is Miss Harlow...she is so straightforward and human and pleasant to observe that she is of inordinate value to a film that certainly does require her gifts."

Just for the record, Jean's love interest in *Wife vs. Secretary* was lanky, drawling James Stewart, a fresh inductee on the Metro payroll. As Dave, he persuades Whitey to forsake the business world for marriage. Stewart today still laughs at how much in awe he was of the famed Harlow, recollecting their kissing scene with a beaming, "There were six rehearsals!"

There followed *Suzy* (1936), a spy yarn that

With Myrna Loy and Clark Gable in *Wife vs. Secretary* ('36).

With Myrna Loy in *Wife vs. Secretary.*

teamed Jean with Cary Grant and united her for the fourth time with dapper Franchot Tone. The script was interesting espionage film fare, and enough music was injected (Jean as the title character is a showgirl) to make the film appealing to the masses. The plot finds Jean bouncing from flighty Grant to dependable Tone, and an offbeat finish finds Jean and Grant placing Tone's body in a wrecked plane so that it will appear he died a hero—when he actually has been killed by his mistress' henchman. In the midst of the hectic proceedings, Jean "sings" "Did I Remember?" which is refrained by droll Grant himself. (The sequence is included in several compendium films, including the recent *That's Entertainment!*, 1974.) Critical reaction to the George Fitzmaurice-directed feature was mixed. The *New York Daily Mirror* termed Jean "a bewitching and loveable Suzy," but the *New York Post* observed, "She's a swell comedienne, and not too adept at drama, especially tragedy."

MGM promptly decided to place Jean back into comedy, and she adored the result—*Libeled Lady* (1936), a wonderfully screwball comedy

that not only gave her a nifty role (as Gladys Benton), but also presented William Powell as a leading man. However, while Jean in the story-line becomes smitten with Powell's character, she winds up in the arms of Spencer Tracy, and Powell embraces Myrna Loy in the final clinch. Jean led the cast in billing (followed in order by Powell, Loy, and Tracy).

Libeled Lady remains a polished gem today, a story where such stereotypes as a spoiled heiress (Loy), ne'er do-well charmer (Powell), dumb reporter (Tracy), and smart-mouthed blonde (guess who?) all jell perfectly. The four stars interact admirably, and the story of a libel expert trying to charm a rich girl out of suing a newspaper for printing romance rumors would later be remade by MGM as *Easy to Wed* (1946).

Hilarious scenes abound in *Libeled Lady*—examples include Powell dousing himself madly in a stream while trying to pass himself off as a fisherman, and Jean storming into the press room in a wedding gown after again being forsaken at the altar by Tracy who is preoccupied with the big scoop. Particularly memorable is

227

With Cary Grant and Lewis Stone in *Suzy* ('36).

the vignette where Jean marries Powell (as part of the libel defense plan) while real fiancé Tracy looks on in growing annoyance. The dialogue crackles:

> *Tracy:* Oh, come now! You mustn't fight!
> *Powell:* Why not? We're married!
> *Tracy:* Well, you're supposed to be *happily* married. You're supposed to be crazy in love with each other!
> *Jean:* Yeah! Well I must've been crazy to let you marry me off to another guy. But, let me tell you this, Warren Haggerty. From now on, you've got to forget the paper and take me places!
> *Tracy:* Well, darling, I can't take you places. You've got to stay home, you've got to stay in the apartment. You can sew, and sleep, and play the radio.
> *Powell:* Maybe you could learn to read!

"Miss Harlow, heaven be praised, is again a luminous comedienne," raved the *New York Telegraph*. Jean loved making the film because her romance with Powell was at its peak. Columnists constantly wanted to validate marriage rumors, but the stars refused to acquiesce. "Don't talk to me about love," replied Powell. "I know nothing about it—having failed at it twice." Jean, however, sadly told Louella Parsons, "I had thought I was in love before, but I never knew the meaning of the word until I met Bill. I never thought it would really happen to me. I'm afraid of it . . . I am so constantly trying to be what Bill wants me to, but I know we have a feeling that we will never be married."

Metro, meanwhile, kept Jean busy as she went into 1937, the climactic year in which her salary would reach a top $5,000 per week. While the salary escalated, the variety of screen roles did not. The studio had dynamite on their hands in the form of Robert Taylor* who had just reached a new high in masculine attractiveness as

---

*On December 14, 1936, Jean starred with Robert Taylor on the "Lux Radio Theatre" broadcast of *Madame Sans-Gene*.

With Cary Grant in *Suzy*.

Armand in Garbo's *Camille* (1936). Hence, Jean played her familiar golddigger (Crystal Wetherby) to Taylor's well-bred Englishman (Robert Dabney) in *Personal Property* directed by Jean's old beau W. S. Van Dyke II. The film did little more than treat both stars to flattering camera angles, thanks to ace cinematographer William Daniels. Still, the *New York Times* noted that there was enough within the film to please the throngs, reporting of the Manhattan opening that the Capitol Theatre "is ringing with feminine coos and delighted soprano laughter. . . . Miss Harlow—sweeping or flouncing through expensive sets in that negligee of hers—is positively the indignant lady of a Peter Arno drawing."

At the time of production, Taylor (then keeping very steady company with Barbara Stanwyck) and Jean headed east to join a gala birthday party for President Franklin D. Roosevelt to raise funds for the Warm Springs Foundation. There were many publicity stops en route to Washington, and usually the crowds consisted of female fans mobbing Taylor, with Jean left clear to pose for and talk to the press. The trek took a physical toll on the sex symbol. The press noted that she looked peaked, and that her weight was again ballooning. One Chicago journalist sneered that Jean was actually in town to buy a reducing machine. Jean replied, "That's very silly." Once in Washington, Jean not only appeared at the party on January 20, 1937, but also made side trips, such as the one to the U.S. Naval Academy in Annapolis, Maryland. In addition to ceaseless smiling for photographers, Jean had to endure three full-lipped kisses from Senator Robert Rice Reynolds of North Carolina, whose four marriages had earned him the accolade of being the then sexiest U.S. Senator. Photographs of the jaunt reveal a very worn Jean Harlow (on the train trip she had contracted influenza).

The California sunshine somewhat revived Jean's spirits. So did Powell who presented her with a 150-carat sapphire ring and had begun remodeling his English Tudor Beverly Hills home, winking to friends, "It will be just big enough for two." But things were not progress-

229

Posing with Spencer Tracy for *Libeled Lady* ('36).

With Robert Taylor in a publicity shot for *Personal Property* ('37).

In *Personal Property.*

ing entirely well for Jean. Powell and Jean could not quite bring themselves to finalize wedding plans. Jean began dating Donald Friede, a New York publisher allegedly interested in her novel. Jean's intimates noted that she was depressed and in poor health, and Jean told Louella Parsons, "I've been worn out since that personal appearance tour to Washington."

Life however went on at Metro and when Joan Crawford refused *Saratoga,* Mayer tossed the assignment at Jean. For the fifth time she would co-star with Gable (who had just suffered a career reversal with *Parnell*); Frank Morgan, Lionel Barrymore, Walter Pidgeon, and Una Merkel filled other major roles. The horse-racing tale got off to a poor production start, and once again director Jack Conway found himself desperately racing against time to complete the project.

Part of the film's pacing problem derived from Jean. Her health was deteriorating, her romance with Powell was shaky, and her dissatisfaction toward taking another Crawford reject added to her general unhappiness. Jean needed a

rest, but there was none in sight. In the midst of the *Saratoga* filming, MGM proudly announced that Jean would be lent to Twentieth Century-Fox to star as Belle Fawcett in that studio's epic *In Old Chicago,* with Tyrone Power and Don Ameche. (Eventually the part would go to Fox's own Alice Faye.) A vicious circle began to tragically develop: the more her appearance wilted, the earlier Jean had to report to the Metro make-up wizards each morning. The more fatigued she became, the later she had to stay each evening for retakes. In the storm of studio pressure to complete the costly picture, nobody realized, including Jean, that she was contracting fatal uremic poisoning.

"I'm perfectly well. There's nothing wrong with me," insists Jean Harlow's Carol Clayton in *Saratoga,* a film in which she ironically undergoes a medical examination, and kneels beside her dying father with tear-filled eyes. Finally, on Saturday, May 29, 1937, with a week of shooting left, Jean's collapse on the soundstage interrupted a scene she was playing with Gable, and the rattled director sent her home to rest.

232

What happened thereafter is essentially still a mystery. It is widely believed that Jean spent nearly a full week of retching in bed while Mama Jean, out of loyalty to her Science of the Mind religion, refused to call for a doctor. Another account claims that Jean resisted hospitalization, and refused to consider an operation. At any rate, on Wednesday, June 3, Mama Jean told the press that "this baby of mine" is better, weeping that "I feel like the whole world has been lifted from my shoulders." It was not so. On June 6, at the dictates of Louis B. Mayer and William Powell, Jean was rushed to Los Angeles' Good Samaritan Hospital. Powell and Mama Jean hovered at her bedside through the night while her physician, Dr. Fishbaugh, winced at the extremity of the star's condition. He wondered, like everyone else, why somebody had not rushed the girl to treatment sooner. "It's so hopeless," said Fishbaugh as he tried every possible means to discharge the poisons from her system.

Finally the next morning, Fishbaugh called the Los Angeles fire department to administer oxygen to Jean. But it was so hopeless that at 11:37 a.m. on Monday, June 7, 1937, Jean Harlow died. While Mama Jean collapsed, Powell ran sobbing from the room to the consoling presence of long-time pal Warner Baxter, crying "Oh God! Why did this have to be? I loved her! I loved her! Why, oh why must she die? It's terrible, terrible, Warner."

The shock with which Jean Harlow's death hit Hollywood and the world was immense, comparable to the later death of Marilyn Monroe or Judy Garland. MGM staff writer Harry Ruskin related, "The day 'the baby' died there wasn't one sound in the commissary for three hours. Not one goddamn sound!" Newspapers throughout America gave the tragedy front-page treatment, replaying her tragedies, and running photos of Bern's suicide note.

The MGM executives quickly released statements of condolence. Louis B. Mayer: ". . . I have lost a friend. The world has lost a ray of sunshine. . . . She was one of the most charming, thoughtful, and reasonable players with whom I have been associated. . . ." Nicholas Schenk: "She was a marvelous girl and a great actress. I feel terribly sorry and sympathize with all of her friends, of which there were many." Eddie Mannix: "A sweet child has passed from us. . . . She was not only a great artist, she was a wonderfully sincere, honest human being."

Unexpectedly, one of the most moving tributes came from a man who was not noted for his gregariousness—Lionel Barrymore. "She was the most gallant lady I ever knew," said the crusty actor. "She won my heart by her courage—her humor—and above all, by her dignity. It was not easy to have dignity sometimes in the spots Jean was put in." Of course, the celebrity all the press awaited in hopes for a comment was William Powell. The only remark he would make was a whimpered, "Please leave me alone!" from behind the closed door of his mansion.

All was *not* tasteful in Jean's death. The more prurient openly called into question the mysteriousness of the star's death and demanded full details of her demise. Rumors quickly sprouted that severe dieting and/or hair bleachings had killed Jean Harlow. There was even the notion that a botched abortion had done in MGM's high-priced luminary.

While the scuttlebutt continued and the corpse rested at Pierce Brothers Mortuary, funeral plans were made. Marino Bello appeared on the scene to inform the press, "Funeral services will be private because her mother wishes it so. She wants Jean to remain in the memory of her fans as she was in life, so her body will not lie in state." This remark spawned wild rumors that Jean's body was bloated and hideous, so the family decided Jean would be viewed. Pierce Brothers' finest embalmers, studio beauticians, and the actress' personal makeup artist, Violet Denoyer, worked through the night to prepare the sickness-ravaged body for what promised to be a morbidly critical public eye.

The greats of Hollywood entered the Tennyson Room of Pierce Brothers where lay Jean Harlow's body. In the pink gown she had worn in *Libeled Lady,* a honey-brown wig with luxuriant curls, and silver and white sandals, the body rested beneath a portrait of Tennyson and beside a table holding a book of the poet's works, opened to "Crossing the Bar." William Powell paced the room, sobbing bitterly to friends, "I don't know how I'll go on without my baby." The

With Clark Gable in *Saratoga* ('37).

mourners took for granted that the single gardenia held in the corpse's hand, with the note "Goodnight My Dearest Darling," was from Powell; the lack of signature and trembling penmanship made this a favorite bit of speculation among the visitors.

As nearly all the world tried to outdo one another in tributes to the beloved star, perhaps it was the MGM crew—messengers, prop people, and electricians among them—who offered the most touching service. The night before the funeral, the devoted co-workers stood watch outside of the mortuary with the explanation, "The baby didn't like to be alone in the dark."

On Wednesday, June 9, 1937, the funeral was held at the Wee Kirk of the Heather at Forest Lawn. There were 250 invited guests, and the Forest Lawn security force posted men throughout the cemetery to protect the solemnity of the occasion from the public that had been thronging at the star's home since her death, cheering and rushing for autographs as celebrities called to express sympathy to Mrs. Bello. Pallbearers included Eddie Mannix, producer Hunt Strom-

berg, directors Jack Conway and W. S. Van Dyke II, cameraman Ray June, and Clark Gable who attended with his future wife, Carole Lombard. The pallbearers bore the $5,000 burnished copper casket which displayed a reproduction of Jean's own signature into the Wee Kirk, and Dr. Carpenter, Charles McGrew, and Hal Rosson joined the celebrated mourners. William Powell, wearing smoke-colored glasses, was aided by his mother, and sat with Mrs. Bello in a special alcove of the chapel. Mrs. Genevieve Smith, a Christian Science Reader, led the service, Jeanette MacDonald sang an inappropriate but beautiful "Indian Love Call," and Nelson Eddy concluded the service with "Ah, Sweet Mystery of Life." Except for Barbara Brown, Harlow's stand-in, becoming hysterical and having to be removed from the chapel, the funeral was quiet. But as soon as the casket was removed and the mourners departed, a barrage of fans overran the grounds, stripping the chapel of the $15,000 worth of flower arrangements and milling about the very spot where the casket had just rested.

At first, the casket reposed in the Sanctuary of

With Clark Gable in *Saratoga*.

Benediction, a Romanesque mausoleum where the remains of Will Rogers, Marie Dressler, Lon Chaney, Florenz Ziegfeld, Wallace Reid, and many other cinema notables were interred. However, two days after the funeral, William Powell purchased a $25,000 crypt for Jean with spaces for three caskets: Jean's, her mother's, and an undisclosed one. The crypt adjoined the room of Irving Thalberg, whose funeral Jean had attended only the year before. Powell and Mama Jean visited the tomb at least once a week, bringing fresh flowers and strengthening the suspicion that the third receptacle in the crypt was to hold the body of Powell.

Meanwhile, at MGM, Mayer had announced that *Saratoga* would be scrapped. However, Culver City representatives soon sensed that there might be box-office magic in the last film of Jean Harlow if it could somehow be completed. Mary Dees, a blonde chorine, was selected to double for Jean in the remainder of scenes to be shot, and Paula Winslow dubbed in the voice. (Originally MGM had toyed with the idea of reshooting all of Harlow's scenes with studio newcomer Rita Johnson; the actress refused.) The technicalities of this task, with Miss Dees photographed from the back under a floppy hat or from behind binoculars, greatly upset the cast who were all terribly relieved when the production ended. In July 1937 the film was released. The *New York Herald-Tribune* noted of Jean, "Looking ill much of the time and striving gallantly to inject her performance with characteristic vigor and vibrancy, the result, in view of subsequent events, is grievous." Such notices only served to lure the public who thrived on the mini-game of trying to spot when the real Jean Harlow was or was not oncamera. *Saratoga* became a big grosser of the year!

There were many plans to erect a memorial to Jean Harlow, including a campaign to place a statue of her in New York City's Rockefeller Center. However, the indelicacies of her life and some news items that appeared after her death dampened such concepts. Mama Jean wrote a magazine story, "Jean Harlow Is Not Dead," that included a picture of the soundstage mother posing before an enormous painting of Jean in ethereal robes and eternal light, waving to the viewers. It provided the most callous reader with a bad case of the shivers. Also there was considerable publicity over the fact that Jean's estate totaled only $41,000 (not the million that originally was announced) and that this amount was subject to a lien by Mrs. Harriet Breese, owner of the Palm Drive home Jean had rented. Mrs. Breese filed a claim for damages of $618 and unpaid rent of $820. The Internal Revenue put in a claim for $10,244 in unpaid taxes. All was paid, and Mama Jean managed to sell MGM the rights to Jean's novel, *Today Is Tonight*, for $5,000 and a pension of $500 a month for life.

Jean's tragic demise naturally cancelled the extensive plans MGM held in reserve for her: the loanout to Twentieth Century-Fox for *In Old Chicago* (she was replaced by Alice Faye); *Tell It to the Marines* (a remake of the Lon Chaney 1927 silent which was to co-star her with Robert Taylor and Spencer Tracy); *The Best-Dressed Woman in Paris* (to have been produced by Edgar Selwyn); *Maiden Voyage* and *Spring Tide* (both to have been produced by Hunt Stromberg); *The Four Marys*; and *U.S. Smith*. The death of Harlow was a tremendous loss to her studio and to the world's cinema audiences. While MGM would try now and then to recapture the Harlow magic in such performers as Lana Turner and Ann Sothern, there was and will be only one Jean Harlow. As Clark Gable eulogized about the fun girl who could have become the screen's most precious comedienne, "She didn't want to be a star. She only wanted to be happy."

Gradually the name of Jean Harlow became more and more forgotten. In 1955, Marino Bello died and was buried at Forest Lawn; in 1958, Mama Jean succumbed to a heart condition and was entombed beside her daughter whose jewelry she had played with almost daily. Louis B. Mayer passed away in 1957, having been exiled by a new regime at MGM. William Powell had retired to Palm Springs with wife Diana Lewis, where they still reside. All the scandal and all the sensationalism that had marred Jean's life appeared finally still.

Actually, an exposé of the late star was fast approaching. In 1955, Arthur Landau contracted cancer of the larynx. In a costly and grueling operation his vocal cords were removed, a resonating chamber was inserted, and he learned to speak all over again. The medical treatments depleted all his savings. In 1961, the seventy-three-year-old agent was finished professionally and survived on social security and the income from his wife's work as a dressmaker. Desperate for funds, he looked over his roster of former clients, recalled the hysteria that surrounded Jean Harlow's career, and discussed with Bantam Books editor Saul Davis his idea of exhuming Jean's tragedies for public consumption.

"Landau had some marvelous stories to tell of the old Hollywood days, particularly of Jean Harlow," recalled editor Davis. "I thought they would make an interesting best seller. I got him together with a writer, Irving Shulman." Shulman was a colorful novelist, whose books included *The Amboy Dukes,* which became the movie *City Across the River,* and *Children of the Dark,* filmed as *Rebel Without a Cause.* Shulman met with Landau, later orated that he was attracted to what was the story of "a woman and her time" and a deal was made with Bernard Geis Associates. The publishers guaranteed Shulman and Landau $20,000, gave the desperate Landau $3,500 immediately, and followed this with subsequent advances.

Landau had, strangely enough, kept files on Jean, recording conversations he had had with her. *Some* of these dialogues recorded in large ledgers he showed to Shulman. The novelist spent three years composing the book, saw Landau allegedly only four times during that period, and on other occasions sent questionnaires to the ex-agent, some of which Landau ignored. By 1964 the work was done—*Harlow: An Intimate Biography.* Among the cast of villains in the book were Mama Jean and Marino Bello, Paul Bern the impotent sadist, the lecherous Louis B. Mayer, and so forth. People like Howard Hughes, Harold Rosson, and William Powell—all still alive and capable of suing—were presented neutrally. Sadly the worst fault of the exploitative book was that Jean Harlow was painted as a trashy, untalented nymphomaniac who swore, seduced bellboys, and maintained her popularity solely through the public's fascination with tawdry sex.

Harlow: An Intimate Biography soared to the top of the best-sellers chart. *Films in Review* called it "pandering to the prurient." *Time* magazine commented how "the only seemingly sympathetic person in this thoroughly unpleasant book is Harlow's agent, Arthur Landau, who appears as the tormented girl's friend, confidant, moneylender, sometime savior, and sole defender. Don't be fooled. Landau, now seventy-six, and living in Hollywood, is the one who spilled all the dirt to author Shulman. What they didn't know between them, they improvised." But the book continued to sell.

Some of Hollywood was aghast at the Harlow character assassination. Howard Strickling, Metro publicity chief, who knew everything there was to know about all the stars on the lot, insisted, "I knew Jean Harlow as well as, if not better than, Arthur Landau. I'm prepared to take the witness stand in open court and testify that much of the Shulman biography is factually false. . . . The book is one of the most nasty, filthy, sordid, vulgar, untrue hatchet jobs I've ever read. Anyone who thinks it tells the truth about Jean Harlow is being taken in." Robert Taylor stated, "I don't understand how anyone could do something like this to such a warm, generous human being as Jean Harlow." Franchot Tone attested, "Where did that man get that dialogue? No one ever heard Jean talk that way." And close friend Kay Mulvey insisted, "Jean was a highly educated girl and a lady always."

Jean's few remaining intimates were deeply hurt by the book. Her father, Dr. Montclair Carpenter, eighty-four and living in retirement in Kansas City, planned a $3 million lawsuit against the authors and had his second wife call Maureen O'Sullivan to thank her for defending his daughter when Irving Shulman visited the "Today" program. William Powell refused to honor the book with too many comments, but did say sadly, "This book is a scurrilous piece of writing, a compilation of inaccuracies on what it calls the 'secret files' of Arthur Landau, an agent who knew virtually nothing about Jean's private life. The entire book reveals no knowledge of Jean's character. Thank God that Jean herself cannot be hurt at all. She is sleeping very peacefully in Forest Lawn Cemetery. But the living who loved her are suffering and it is deplorable that any writer would do this just to make a fast buck."

Strangely, one of the most surprising defenders of Jean after the book's publication was Arthur Landau. While Shulman insisted that the titillating tidbits came from Landau's notes and reminiscences, Landau remarked to columnists that he had hardly seen Shulman while *Harlow* was in the works. He said that he had not read a word of copy until publication, and at one point now recalled of Jean, "I never knew her to use a dirty word. . . . She was not promiscuous. . . . I had no idea the book was to be written in that kind of language." Landau also stated, "He [Shulman] never met the girl. For me to say that it was inaccurate wouldn't be fair. . . . Some things . . . are exaggerated or shown wrong, I think. But it was Mr. Shulman's job as a writer to use the items I gave him as he saw fit. He is a fine writer and did a fine job. The book is selling very well." Indeed it did! Landau earned at least $150,000 from the sale of it.

Along with the hoopla over the book came Harlow capes, lingerie, shoes, and platinum wigs, and the announcement of at least two film versions of Jean's life. (Earlier Twentieth Century-Fox had planned to produce Harlow's life story with Marilyn Monroe, Jayne Mansfield, or Natalie Wood starred, with a script by Adela Rogers St. John, but the project was dropped.) Mogul Joseph E. Levine bought the exclusive film rights to the Shulman/Landau tome, then made some peculiar statements to the press in a speech in Toronto. "If anyone uses parts of the book which we own and if they use lies from the book then we've got them because we know they copied them from the book!" Levine chose Carroll Baker, a shapely bleached blonde to play Jean and posed with her in publicity shots, with Ms. Baker grotesquely lacquered to suggest Jean's famous *Time* magazine cover shot.

At the same time that Paramount's Shulman/Landau-inspired production went before the cameras, Magna Film Corporation decided to shoot their version of the Jean Harlow story. Carol Lynley was selected to portray Jean, and the film was shot in television style to beat Levine's Paramount picture into circulation.

The results were two rotten pictures. Levine's *Harlow* was slick, colorful, and phony. A strange cast included Peter Lawford as a hilariously miscast Paul Bern, Michael Connors as an actor apparently patterned after Gable, and Red Buttons as a saintly Arthur Landau. Angela Lansbury and Raf Vallone were fine as Mama Jean and Marino, and perhaps the most interesting acting job was provided by Leslie Nielsen as a Howard Hughes-type producer who has a wrestling match with Jean in his super bedroom. Ms. Baker's performance was not well-praised, but over the years has earned a special cult following for some unknown reason.

Magna's *Harlow* was a mess, although sparked by intriguing performances by Ginger Rogers (replacing Judy Garland) as Mama Jean, Barry Sullivan as Marino, and Hurd Hatfield as a flamboyantly pathetic Paul Bern. Jack Kruschen played Louis B. Mayer in reptile-like fashion, Efrem Zimbalist, Jr. played a William Powell-type,* and the less stated about Ms. Lynley's marshmallow performance, the better. This dismal picture was almost as ridiculous as it was vulgar. Deservedly, both productions did unpromising box-office business and the Harlow craze quickly burned out—for a time.

Another decade passed before films again tackled the subject of Harlow. In the independent production, *Hughes & Harlow: Angels in Hell,* Victor Holchak and Lindsay Bloom (who starred recently as *Six-Pack Annie*) portray filmmaker and actress in the Larry Buchanan-directed film. Shooting was accomplished in early 1977 at the Culver City studios, and on locations in the Los Angeles area, Redlands, and assorted airports. William B. Silberkleit was executive producer.

Fortunately, Jean Harlow has somehow survived all this debunking. Her films still find a wide audience on the late show circuit. Some viewers, familiar with her vulgarized legend, are amazed in watching *Red Dust, Dinner at Eight,* or *Libeled Lady* to observe that the lady was a most appealing actress. Others, unexposed to the Harlow myth, view her for the first time and can enjoy with full appreciation the warm, funny, delightful Jean unhampered by detracting myth.

Still it cannot be denied that life—and posterity—was savagely cruel to a girl who had the insight and trust to state shortly before her

*Powell had quietly yet firmly stated that any use of his name in connection with the movies would warrant an immediate law suit.

tragic demise, "I have learned to control myself, to sit quietly—and wait—and to utilize time to the best advantage. The world can get along without any individual, but that individual cannot get along without the world."

Carroll Baker as *Harlow* ('65).

FILMOGRAPHY

MORAN OF THE MARINES *(Paramount, 1928)* 5,444 feet

   Director, Frank Strayer; story, Linton Wells; screenplay, Agnes Brand Leahy; scenario, Sam Mintz, Ray Harris; titles, George Marion; camera, Edward Cronjager; editor, Otto Levering.

   Richard Dix (Michael Moran); Ruth Elder (Vivian Marshall); Roscoe Karns ("Swatty"); Brooks Benedict (Basil Worth); Captain E. H. Calvert (General Marshall); Duke Martin (The Sergeant); Tetsu Komai (Sun Yat); Jean Harlow (Bit).

FUGITIVES *(Fox, 1929)* 5,356 feet

   Presenter, William Fox; supervisor, Kenneth Hawks; director, William Beaudine; based on the story by Richard Harding Davis; screenplay, John Stone; titles, Malcolm Stuart Boylan; assistant director, Thomas Held; camera, Chester Lyons.

   Madge Bellamy (Alice Carroll); Don Terry (Dick Starr); Arthur Stone (Jimmy); Earle Foxe (Al Barrow); Matthew Betz (Earl Rand); Lumsden Hare (Uncle Ned); Edith Yorke (Mrs. Carroll); Jean Laverty (Mame); Hap Ward (Scal, the Rat); Jean Harlow (Bit).

CLOSE HARMONY *(Paramount, 1929)* 6,271 feet

   Directors, John Cromwell, Edward Sutherland; story, Elsie Janis, Gene Markey; adaptor, Percy Heath; dialogue, John V. A. Weaver, Heath; songs, Richard A. Whiting and Leo Robin; sound, Franklin Hansen; camera, Roy Hunt; editor, Tay Malarkey.

   Charles "Buddy" Rogers (Al West); Nancy Carroll (Marjorie Merwin); Harry Green (Max Mindel); Jack Oakie (Ben Barney); Richard "Skeets" Gallagher (Johnny Bey); Matty Roubert (Bert); Ricca Allen (Mrs. Prosser); Wade Boteler (Kelly, the Cop); Baby Mack (Sybil, the Maid); Oscar Smith (George Washington Brown); Greta Granstedt (Eva Larue); Gus Partos (Gustav); Jesse Stafford and His Orchestra (Themselves); Jean Harlow (Extra).

THE LOVE PARADE *(Paramount, 1929)* 110 min.

   Director, Ernst Lubitsch; based on the play *Le Prince Consort* by Leon Xanrof, Jules Chancel; film story, Ernest Vajda; libretto, Guy Bolton; dialogue director, Perry Ivins; art director, Hans Dreier; songs, Victor Schertzinger, Clifford Grey; sound, Franklin Hansen; camera, Victor Milner; editor, Merrill White.

   Maurice Chevalier (Count Alfred); Jeanette MacDonald (Queen Louise); Lupino Lane (Jacques); Lillian Roth (Lulu); Edgar Norton (Master of Ceremonies); Lionel Belmore (Prime Minister); Albert Roccardi (Foreign Minister); Carlton Stockdale (Admiral); Eugene Pallette (Minister of War); Russell Powell (Afghan Ambassador); E. H. Calvert (Ambassador); Andre Cheron (Le Mari); Yola D'Avril (Paulette); Winter Hall (Priest); Ben Turpin (Cross-Eyed Lackey); Anton Vaverka, Albert De Winton,

William von Hardenburg (Cabinet Ministers); Margaret Fealy, Virginia Bruce, Josephine Hall, Rosalind Charles, Helene Friend (Ladies in Waiting); Jean Harlow (Extra in Theatre Box).

THE SATURDAY NIGHT KID *(Paramount, 1929)* 63 min.

   Director, Edward Sutherland; story, George Abbott, John V. A. Weaver; screenplay, Ethel Doherty; dialogue, Lloyd Corrigan, Edward E. Paramore, Jr.; titles, Joseph L. Mankiewicz; adaptor, Lloyd Corrigan; camera, Harry Fischbeck; editor, Jane Loring.

   Clara Bow (Mayme); James Hall (Bill); Jean Arthur (Janie); Charles Sellon (Lem Woodruff); Ethel Wales (Ma Woodruff); Frank Ross (Ken); Edna May Oliver (Miss Streeter); Hyman Meyer (Ginsberg); Eddie Dunn (Jim); Leone Lane (Pearl); Jean Harlow (Hazel); Getty Bird (Riche Ginsberg); Alice Adair (Girl); Irving Bacon (McGonigle, the Sales Manager); Mary Gordon (Reducing Customer); Ernie S. Adams (Gambler).

NEW YORK NIGHTS *(United Artists, 1929)* 81 min.

   Presenter, Joseph M. Schenck; supervisor, John W. Considine, Jr.; director, Lewis Milestone; based on the play *Tin Pan Alley* by Hugh Stanislaus Stange; adaptor, Jules Furthman; song, Al Jolson, Ballard MacDonald, Dave Dryer; sound, Oscar Lagerstrom; camera, Ray June; editor, Hal Kern.

   Norma Talmadge (Jill Deverne); Gilbert Roland (Fred Deverne); John Wray (Joe Prividi); Lilyan Tashman (Peggy); Mary Doran (Ruthie Day); Roscoe Karns (Johnny Dolan); Jean Harlow (Extra); Landers Stevens (Gang Chief); Stanley Fields (Hood).

HELL'S ANGELS *(United Artists, 1930)* 135 min.

   Producer/director, Howard Hughes; story, Marshall Neilan, Joseph Moncure March; screenplay, Harry Behn, Howard Estabrook; dialogue, March; dialogue director, James Whale; art directors, Julian Boone Fleming, Carroll Clark; music, Hugo Riesenfeld; assistant directors, Reginald Callow, William J. Scully, Frederick Fleck; camera, Gaetano Gaudio, Harry Perry; editors, Douglas Biggs, Perry Hollingsworth, Frank Lawrence.

   Ben Lyon (Monte Rutledge); James Hall (Roy Rutledge); Jean Harlow (Helen); John Darrow (Karl Arnstedt); Lucien Prival (Baron von Krantz); Frank Clark (Lieutenant von Bruen); Roy Wilson (Baldy); Douglas Gilmore (Captain Redfield); Jane Winton (Baroness von Krantz); Evelyn Hall (Lady Randolph); William B. Davidson (Staff Major); Wyndham Standing (RFC Squadron Commander); Lena Malena (Gretchen); Carl von Haartmann (Zeppelin Commander); Stephen Carr (Elliott); Hans Joby (Von Schieben); Pat Somerset (Marryat); Marilyn Morgan [Marian Marsh] (Girl Selling Kisses); F. Schumann-Heink (First Officer of Zeppelin); William von Brincken (Von Richthofen).

CITY LIGHTS (*United Artists, 1931*) 87 min.

Producer/director/screenplay, Charles Chaplin; assistant directors, Harry Crocker, Henry Bergman, Albert Austin; music, Chaplin; camera R. H. Totheroh, Gordon Pollock, Mark Marklatt.

Charlie Chaplin (The Tramp); Virginia Cherrill (The Girl); Harry Myers (The Eccentric Millionaire); Florence Lee (Grandmother); Allan Garcia (The Butler); Hank Mann (A Prizefighter); Jean Harlow (Extra).

THE SECRET SIX (*MGM, 1931*) 83 min.

Director, George Hill; story/screenplay, Frances Marion; wardrobe, Rene Hubert; sound, Robert Shirley; camera, Harold Wenstrom; editor, Blanche Sewell.

Wallace Beery (Louis Scorpio); Lewis Stone (Richard Newton); John Mack Brown (Hank Rogers); Jean Harlow (Anne Courtland); Marjorie Rambeau (Peaches); Paul Hurst (Nick Mizoski, the Gouger); Clark Gable (Carl Luckner); Ralph Bellamy (Johnny Franks); John Miljan (Smiling Joe Colimo); DeWitt Jennings (Chief Donlin); Murray Kinnell (Dummy Metz); Fletcher Norton (Jimmy Delano); Louis Natheaux (Eddie); Frank McGlynn (Judge); Theodore Von Eltz (District Attorney); Tom London (Hood).

IRON MAN (*Universal, 1931*) 72 min.

Producer, Carl Laemmle, Jr.; associate producer, E. M. Asher; director, Tod Browning; based on the novel by W. R. Burnett; screenplay, Francis Edwards Faragoh; sound, C. Roy Hunter; camera, Percy Hilburn; supervising editor, Maurice Pivar; editor, Milton Carruth.

Lew Ayres (Kid Mason); Robert Armstrong (George Regan); Jean Harlow (Rose Mason); John Miljan (Paul H. Lewis); Eddie Dillon (Jeff); Mike Donlin (McNeil); Morrie Cohan (Rattler O'Keefe); Mary Doran (The Show Girl —Rose's Pal); Mildred Van Dorn (Gladys DeVere); Ned Sparks (Riley); Sam Blum (Mandl); Sammy Gervon (Trainer); Tom Kennedy (Bartender); Bob Perry (Referee); Wade Boteler (Reporter); Claire Whitney (Louise Lewis).

THE PUBLIC ENEMY (*Warner Bros., 1931*) 84 min.

Director, William A. Wellman; based on the story "Beer and Blood" by John Bright; screenplay, Kubec Glasmon, Bright; adaptor/dialogue, Harvey Thew; art director, Max Parker; music director, David Mendoza; costumes, Earl Luick; makeup, Perc Westmore; camera, Dev Jennings; editor, Ed McCormick.

James Cagney (Tom Powers); Jean Harlow (Gwen Allen); Edward Woods (Matt Doyle); Joan Blondell (Mamie); Beryl Mercer (Ma Powers); Donald Cook (Mike Powers); Mae Clark (Kitty); Mia Marvin (Jane); Leslie Fenton (Nails Nathan); Robert Emmett O'Connor (Paddy Ryan); Murray Kinnell (Putty Nose); Ben Hendricks, Jr. (Bugs Moran); Rita Flynn (Molly Doyle); Clark Burroughs (Dutch); Snitz Edwards (Hack); Adele Watson (Mrs. Doyle); Frank Coghlan, Jr. (Tommy as a Boy); Frankie Darro (Matt as a Boy); Robert E. Homans (Officer Pat Burke); Dorothy Gee (Nails' Girl); Lee Phelps (Steve, the Bartender); Helen Parrish, Dorothy Gray, Nanci Price (Little Girls); Ben Hendricks III (Bugs as a Boy); George

Daly (Machine Gunner); Eddie Kane (Joe, the Headwaiter); Charles Sullivan (Mug); Douglas Gerrard (Assistant Tailor); Sam McDaniel (Black Headwaiter); William H. Strauss (Pawnbroker); Landers Stevens (Doctor); Bob Reeves (Poolroom Customer).

British release title: *Enemy of the Public.*

GOLDIE (*Fox, 1931*) 68 min.

Director, Benjamin Stoloff; screenplay/dialogue, Gene Towne, Paul Perez; camera, Ernest Palmer; editor, Alex Troffey.

Spencer Tracy (Bill); Warren Hymer (Spike); Jean Harlow (Goldie); Jess DeVorska (Gonzales); Leila Karnelly (Wife); Ivan Linow (Husband); Lina Basquette (Constantina); Eleanor Hunt (Russian Girl); Maria Alba (Dolores); Eddie Kane (Barker); George Raft (Man at Carnival).

PLATINUM BLONDE (*Columbia, 1931*) 88 min.

Producer, Harry Cohn; director, Frank Capra; based on the story by Harry E. Chandlee, Douglas W. Churchill; adaptor, Jo Swerling; continuity, Dorothy Howell; dialogue, Robert Riskin; camera, Joseph Walker; editor, Gene Milford.

Loretta Young (Gallagher); Robert Williams (Stew Smith); Jean Harlow (Anne Schuyler); Louise Closser Hale (Mrs. Schuyler); Donald Dillaway (Michael Schuyler); Reginald Owen (Dexter Grayson); Walter Catlett (Bing Baker); Edmund Breese (Conroy, the Editor); Halliwell Hobbes (Smythe); Claud Allister (Violinist); Bill Elliott (Dinner Guest); Harry Semels (Waiter); Olaf Hytten (Radcliffe); Tom London, Hal Price, Eddy Chandler, Charles Jordan (Reporters); Dick Cramer (Speakeasy Proprietor); Wilson Benge (Butler).

THREE WISE GIRLS (*Columbia, 1932*) 68 min.

Director, William Beaudine; story, Wilson Collison; adaptor, Agnes C. Johnson; dialogue, Robert Riskin; camera, Ted Tetzlaff; editor, Jack Dennis.

Jean Harlow (Cassie Barnes); Mae Clarke (Gladys Kane); Walter Byron (Jerry Dexter); Marie Prevost (Dot); Andy Devine (Chauffeur); Natalie Moorhead (Ruth); Jameson Thomas (Arthur Phelps); Lucy Beaumont (Cassie's Mother); Katherine C. Ward (Mrs. Kane); Robert Dudley (Lem); Marcia Harris (Landlady); Walter Miller (Manager of Store); Armand Kaliz (Andre).

THE BEAST OF THE CITY (*MGM, 1932*) 90 min.

Director, Charles Brabin; story, W. R. Burnett; screenplay, John Lee Mahin; camera, Barney McGill; editor, Ralph Dawson.

Walter Huston (Jim Fitzpatrick); Jean Harlow (Daisy); Wallace Ford (Edward Fitzpatrick); Jean Hersholt (Sam Belmonte); Dorothy Peterson (Mary Fitzpatrick); Tully Marshall (Michaels); John Miljan (District Attorney); Emmett Corrigan (Chief of Police); Warner Richmond (Tom); Sandy Roth (Mac); J. Carroll Naish (Cholo); Edward Coppo (Fingerprint Expert); George Chandler (Reporter); Nat Pendleton (Abe Gorman); Arthur Hoyt (Witness); Julie Haydon (Blonde); Clarence Wilson (Coroner); Charles Sullivan (Cop in Hall); Morgan Wallace (Police Captain); Mickey Rooney (Mickey Fitzpatrick).

RED-HEADED WOMAN *(MGM, 1932)*

Producer, Paul Bern; associate producer, Al Lewin; director, Jack Conway; based on the novel by Katharine Brush; screenplay, Anita Loos; camera, Harold G. Rosson; editor, Blanche Sewell.

Jean Harlow (Lil Andrews); Chester Morris (Bill Legendre); Lewis Stone (William Legendre, Sr.); Leila Hyams (Irene Legendre); Una Merkel (Sally); Henry Stephenson (Gaersate); May Robson (Aunt Jane); Charles Boyer (Albert); Harvey Clark (Uncle Fred).

RED DUST *(MGM, 1932)* 83 min.

Producer/director, Victor Fleming; based on the play by Wilson Collison; screenplay, John Mahin; camera, Harold G. Rosson; editor, Blanche Sewell.

Clark Gable (Dennis Carson); Jean Harlow (Vantine); Gene Raymond (Gary Willis); Mary Astor (Barbara Willis); Donald Crisp (Guidon); Tully Marshall (McQuarg); Forrester Harvey (Limey); Willie Fung (Hoy).

HOLD YOUR MAN *(MGM, 1933)* 88 min.

Producer/director, Sam Wood; story, Anita Loos; screenplay, Loos, Howard Emmett Rogers; title song, Arthur Freed, Nacio Herb Brown; art directors, Cedric Gibbons, Merrill Pye; set decorator, Edwin B. Willis; gowns, Adrian; camera, Harold G. Rosson; editor, Frank Sullivan.

Jean Harlow (Ruby Adams); Clark Gable (E. Huntington Hall [Eddie]); Stuart Erwin (Al Simpson); Dorothy Burgess (Gypsy); Muriel Kirkland (Bertha Dillon); Garry Owen (Slim); Barbara Barondess (Sadie Kline); Paul Hurst (Aubrey Mitchell); Elizabeth Patterson (Miss Tuttle); Theresa Harris (Lily Mae Crippen); Inez Courtney (Maizie); Blanche Friderici (Mrs. Wagner); Helen Freeman (Miss Davis); George Reed (Reverend Crippen); Louise Beavers (Maid); Jack Cheatham, Frank Hagney (Cops); Jack Randall (Dance Extra); G. Pat Collins (Phil Dunn); Harry Semels (Neighbor); Nora Cecil (Miss Campbell, the Sewing Instructress); Eva McKenzie (Cooking Teacher).

DINNER AT EIGHT *(MGM, 1933)* 110 min.

Producer, David O. Selznick; director, George Cukor; based on the play by George S. Kaufman, Edna Ferber; screenplay, Frances Marion, Herman J. Mankiewicz; additional dialogue, Donald Ogden Stewart; art directors, Hobe Erwin, Fred Hope; camera, William Daniels; editor, Ben Lewis.

Marie Dressler (Carlotta Vance); John Barrymore (Larry Renault); Wallace Beery (Dan Packard); Jean Harlow (Kitty Packard); Lionel Barrymore (Oliver Jordan); Lee Tracy (Max Kane); Edmund Lowe (Dr. Wayne Talbot); Billie Burke (Millicent Jordan); Madge Evans (Paula Jordan); Jean Hersholt (Jo Stengel); Karen Morley (Lucy Talbot); Louise Closser Hale (Hattie Loomis); Phillips Holmes (Ernest De Graff); May Robson (Mrs. Wendel, the Cook); Grant Mitchell (Ed Loomis); Phoebe Foster (Miss Alden); Elizabeth Patterson (Miss Copeland); Hilda Vaughn (Tina, Kitty's Maid); Harry Beresford (Fosdick); Edwin Maxwell (Mr. Fitch, the Hotel Manager); John Davidson (Mr. Hatfield, the Assistant Manager); Edward Woods (Eddie); George Baxter (Gustave, the Butler); Herman Bing (The Waiter); Anna Duncan (Dora, the Maid).

BOMBSHELL *(a.k.a. BLONDE BOMBSHELL)* *(MGM, 1933)* 91 min.

Associate producer, Hunt Stromberg; director, Victor Fleming; based on an unproduced play by Caroline Francke, Mack Crane; screenplay, Jules Furthman, John Lee Mahin; gowns, Adrian; art director, Merrill Pye; set decorator, Edwin B. Willis; camera, Chester Lyons, Harold G. Rosson; editor, Margaret Booth.

Jean Harlow (Lola Burns); Lee Tracy (Space Hanlon); Frank Morgan (Pop Burns); Franchot Tone (Gifford Middleton); Pat O'Brien (Jim Brogan); Una Merkel (Miss Mac); Ted Healy (Junior Burns); Ivan Lebedeff (Marquis di Binelli); Isabel Jewell (Junior's Girl); Louise Beavers (Loretta); Leonard Carey (Winters); Mary Forbes (Mrs. Middleton); C. Aubrey Smith (Mr. Middleton); June Brewster (Alice Cole).

THE GIRL FROM MISSOURI *(MGM, 1934)* 75 min.

Producer, Bernard H. Hyman; director, Jack Conway; screenplay, Anita Loos, John Emerson; music, Dr. William Axt; camera, Ray June; editor, Tom Held.

Jean Harlow (Eadie); Lionel Barrymore (T. B. Paige); Franchot Tone (Tom Paige); Lewis Stone (Cousins); Patsy Kelly (Kitty); Alan Mowbray (Lord Douglas); Clara Blandick (Miss Newbery); Russell Hopton (Bert); Hale Hamilton (Charles Turner); Henry Kolker (Senator Titcombe); Nat Pendleton (Lifeguard); Marion Lord (Wardrobe Mistress); Carol Tevis (Baby Talker); Desmond Roberts (Butler); Bert Roach (Willie); Norman Ainsley (Second Butler); Howard Hickman (Senator); James Burke, Lee Phelps (Policemen); Alice Lake (Manicurist); Lane Chandler (Doorman); Richard Tucker (Office Manager); Gladys Hulette (Secretary); Charles C. Wilson (Lieutenant); Charles Williams, Fuzzy Knight (Cameramen); Dennis O'Keefe (Dance Extra); Larry Steers (Extra in Stateroom); William "Stage" Boyd (Eadie's Stepfather).

British release title: *One Hundred Percent Pure.*

RECKLESS *(MGM, 1935)* 96 min.

Producer, David O. Selznick; director, Victor Fleming; story, Oliver Jeffries; screenplay, P. J. Wolfson; songs, Jerome Kern and Oscar Hammerstein II; Jack King, Edwin Knopf, and Harold Adamson; Con Conrad and Herbert Magidson; choreography, Chester Hale, Carl Randall; camera, George Folsey; editor Margaret Booth.

Jean Harlow (Mona Leslie); William Powell (Ned Riley); Franchot Tone (Bob Harrison); May Robson (Granny); Ted Healy (Smiley); Nat Pendleton (Blossom); Robert Light (Paul Mercer); Rosalind Russell (Jo); Henry Stephenson (Harrison); Louise Henry (Louise), James Ellison (Dale Every); Leon Ames (Ralph Watson); Man Mountain Dean (Himself); Farina (Gold Dust); Allan Jones (Allan); Carl Randall, Nina Mae McKinney (Themselves).

CHINA SEAS *(MGM, 1935)* 89 min.

Producer, Albert Lewin; director, Tay Garnett; based on the novel by Crosbie Garstin; screenplay, Jules Furthman, James Kevin McGuinness; song, Arthur Freed, Nacio Herb Brown; costumes, Adrian; art directors, Cedric Gibbons, James Havens, David Townsend; set decorator, Edwin B. Willis; camera, Ray June; editor, William Levanway.

Clark Gable (Captain Alan Gaskell); Jean Harlow (China Doll [Dolly Portland]); Wallace Beery (Jamesy MacArdle); Lewis Stone (Tom Davids); Rosalind Russell (Sybil Barclay); Dudley Digges (Dawson); C. Aubrey Smith (Sir Guy Wilmerding); Robert Benchley (Charlie McCaleb); William Henry (Rockwell); Live Demaigret (Mrs. Volberg); Lilian Bond (Mrs. Timmons); Edward Brophy (Wilbur Timmons); Soo Yong (Yu-Lan); Carol Ann Beery (Carol Ann); Akim Tamiroff (Romanoff); Ivan Lebedeff (Ngah); Hattie McDaniel (Isabel McCarthy); Donald Meek (Chess Player); Emily Fitzroy (Lady); Pat Flaherty (Second Officer Kingston); Forrester Harvey (Steward); Tom Gubbins (Ship's Officer); Charles Irwin (Bertie, the Purser); Willie Fung (Cabin Boy); Ferdinand Munier (Police Superintendent); Chester Gan (Rickshaw Boy); John Ince (Pilot).

RIFF-RAFF *(MGM, 1936)* 89 min.

Associate producer, David Lewis; director, J. Walter Ruben; story, Frances Marion, H. W. Hanemann, Anita Loos; screenplay, Marion; music, Edward Ward; wardrobe, Dolly Tree; art directors, Cedric Gibbons, Stanwood Rogas; camera, Ray June; editor, Frank Sullivan.

Jean Harlow (Hattie); Spencer Tracy (Dutch); Joseph Calleia (Nick); Una Merkel (Lil); Mickey Rooney (Jimmy); Victor Kilian (Flytrap); J. Farrell MacDonald (Brains); Roger Imhof (Pops); Baby Jane "Juanita" Quigley (Rosie); Paul Hurst (Belcher); Vince Barnett (Lew); Dorothy Appleby (Gertie); Judith Wood (Mabel); Arthur Housman (Ratsy); Wade Boteler (Bert); Joe Phillips (Al); William Newell (Pete); Al Hill (Speed); Helen Flint (Sadie); Lillian Harmer (Mrs. McCall); Robert Perry (Lefty); George Givot (Markis); Helene Costello (Maisie); Rafaela Ottiano (Head Matron); King Mojavea, Al Herman, Philo McCullough, Sherry Hall, Jack Byron, Stanley Price, Herman Marx, Eddie Sturgis, John George (Fishermen); Ivor McFadden (Moving Man); Mary Wallace (Fisherman's Wife); Wally Maher (Newsreel Cameraman); Marshall Ruth (Agitator).

WIFE VS. SECRETARY *(MGM, 1936)* 85 min.

Producer, Hunt Stromberg; director, Clarence Brown; based on the story by Faith Baldwin; screenplay, Norman Krasna, Alice Duer Miller, John Lee Mahin; costumes, Adrian; art director, Cedric Gibbons, music, Herbert Stothart, Edward Ward; camera, Ray June; editor, Frank E. Hull.

Clark Gable (Van Stanhope); Jean Harlow (Helen "Whitey" Wilson); Myrna Loy (Linda Stanhope); May Robson (Mimi); Hobart Cavanaugh (Joe); James Stewart (Dave); George Barbier (Underwood); Gilbert Emery (Simpson); Margaret Irving (Edna Wilson); William Newell (Tom Wilson); Marjorie Gateson (Eve Merritt); Leonard Carey (Taggart); Charles Trowbridge (Hal Harrington); John M. Qualen (Mr. Jenkins); Hilda Howe (Mary Conners); Mary MacGregor (Ellen); Gloria Holden (Joan Carstairs); Tommy Dugan (Finney); Jack Mulhall (Howard); Frank Elliott (Mr. Barker); Greta Meyer (German Cook); Aileen Pringle (Mrs. Barker); Frank Puglia (Hotel Clerk); Myra Marsh (Miss Clark); Holmes Herbert (Frawley); Frederick Burton (Trent); Harold

Minjir (Williams); Maurice Cass (Bakewell); Tom Herbert (Businessman); Guy D'Ennery (Cuban Waiter); Niles Welch (Tom Axel); Richard Hemingway (Bridegroom); Paul Ellis (Raoul); Tom Rowan (Battleship); Edward Le Saint, Helen Shipman (Bits); Clay Clement (Herbert); Tom Mahoney (Policeman); Nena Quartaro (Telephone Operator); Charles Irwin (Information Clerk); Andre Cheron (Frenchman); Eugene Borden (Ship's Officer); Hooper Atchley (Postal Clerk); Lucille Ward (Scrub Woman); Clifford Jones [Philip Trent] (Elevator Boy).

SUZY *(MGM, 1936)* 99 min.

Producer, Maurice Revnes; director, George Fitzmaurice; based on the novel by Herbert Gorman; screenplay, Dorothy Parker, Alan Campbell, Horace Jackson, Lenore Coffee; song, Harold Adamson, Walter Donaldson; music, Dr. William Axt; camera, Ray June; editor, George Boemler.

Jean Harlow (Suzy Trent); Franchot Tone (Terry Moore); Cary Grant (Andre Charville); Benita Hume (Madame Diane Eyrelle); Lewis Stone (Baron Charville); Reginald Mason (Captain Barsanges); Inez Courtney (Maisie); Greta Meyer (Mrs. Schmidt); David Clyde (Knobby McPherson); Elspeth Dudgeon (Mrs. Boggs); Tyler Brooke (Raoul, the Airman); Robert Livingston (Pierre, the Officer); Dennis Morgan (Lieutenant Charbret); Christian Rub (Pop Gasparol, the Pianist); Ferdinand Gottschalk (Pommot, the Proprietor); George Spelvin (Gaston); Charles McNaughton (Peter); Una O'Connor (Mrs. Bradley, the Landlady); Forrester Harvey, John Rogers (Countermen); Hugh Huntley (Adjutant); Bob Adair (London); Drew Demarest (Aviator).

LIBELED LADY *(MGM, 1936)* 98 min.

Producer, Lawrence Weingarten; director, Jack Conway; story, Wallace Sullivan; screenplay, Maurice Watkins, Howard Emmett Rogers, George Oppenheimer; art directors, Cedric Gibbons, William A. Horning; set decorator, Edwin B. Willis; music, Dr. William Axt; wardrobe, Dolly Tree; sound, Douglas Shearer; camera, Norbert Brodine; editor, Frederick Y. Smith.

Jean Harlow (Gladys Benton); William Powell (Bill Chandler); Myrna Loy (Connie Allenbury); Spencer Tracy (Warren Haggerty); Walter Connolly (James B. Allenbury); Charley Grapewin (Hollis Bane); Cora Witherspoon (Mrs. Burns-Norvell); E. E. Clive (Evans, the Fishing Instructor); Bunny Lauri Beatty (Babs Burns-Norvell); Otto Yamaoka (Ching); Charles Trowbridge (Graham); Spencer Charters (Magistrate McCall); George Chandler (Bellhop); Greta Meyer (Connie's Maid); William Benedict (Joe); Hal K. Dawson (Harvey Allen); Fred Graham (Press Man); William Stack (Editor); Selmer Jackson (Adams, Editor of the Washington *Chronicle*); William Newell (Divorce Detective); Duke York (Taxi Driver); Pat West (Detective); Ed Stanley (Clerk); Wally Maher (Photographer); Tom Mahoney (Alex); Libby Taylor (Tiny, Gladys' Maid); Myra Marsh (Secretary); Howard Hickman (Cable Editor); Charles King, Dennis O'Keefe, Jack Mulhall, Richard Tucker (Barkers); Ines Palange (Fortune Teller); Charles Croker King (Charles Archibald, the Lawyer); Jay Eaton, Ralph Brooks (Dance Extras).

PERSONAL PROPERTY *(MGM, 1937)* 88 min.

Producer, John W. Considine, Jr.; director, W. S. Van Dyke II; based on the play *Man in Possession* by H. M. Harwood; screenplay, Hugh Mills, Ernest Vajda; music, Franz Waxman; art directors, Cedric Gibbons, Henry McAfee; set decorator, Edwin B. Willis; wardrobe, Dolly Tree; sound, Douglas Shearer; camera, William Daniels; editor, Ben Lewis.

Robert Taylor (Robert Dabney); Jean Harlow (Crystal Wetherby); Reginald Owen (Claude); Una O'Connor (Clara); E. E. Clive (Mr. Dabney); Henrietta Crosman (Mrs. Dabney); Cora Witherspoon (Mrs. Burns); Barnett Parker (Arthur Trevalyn); Forrester Harvey (Bailiff); Marla Shelton (Katherine Burns); Lionel Braham (Lord Carstairs); William Stack (Policeman); Jimmy Aubrey, Leyland Hodgson, Douglas Gordon (English Cabbies); Arthur Stuart Hull, Charles Requa (English Businessmen); Tom Ricketts (Elderly Man); Billy Bevans (Frank, the Waiter).

British release title: *The Man in Possession.*

SARATOGA *(MGM, 1937)* 94 min.

Producer, Bernard H. Hyman; associate producer, John Emerson; director, Jack Conway; story/screenplay, Anita Loos, Robert Hopkins; art directors, Cedric Gibbons, John Detlie; set decorator, Edwin B. Willis; music, Edward Ward; songs, Walter Donaldson, Bob Wright, Chet Forrest; wardrobe, Dolly Tree; sound, Douglas Shearer; camera, Ray June; editor, Elmo Vernon.

Clark Gable (Duke Bradley); Jean Harlow (Carol Clayton);* Lionel Barrymore (Grandpa Clayton); Walter Pidgeon (Hartley Madison); Frank Morgan (Jesse Kiffmeyer); Una Merkel (Fritzi O'Malley); Cliff Edwards (Tip O'Brien); George Zucco (Dr. Beard); Jonathan Hale (Frank Clayton); Hattie McDaniel (Rosetta); Frankie Darro (Dixie Gordon); Carl Stockdale (Boswell); Henry Stone (Hard-Riding Hurley); Ruth Gillette (Mrs. Hurley); Charley Foy (Valet); Robert Emmett Keane (Auctioneer); Edgar Dearing (Medbury, the Trainer); Frank McGlynn, Sr. (Kenyon); Margaret Hamilton (Maizie); Lionel Pape, Pat West, John Hyams (Horse Owners); Sam Flint (Judge); Harrison Greene (Clipper); Irene Franklin, Bill Carey, Ernie Stanton, Franklyn Ardell, John "Skins" Miller, Hank Mann, Nick Copeland, Bert Roach (Train Passengers); Forbes Murray (Pullman Steward); George Reed, Billy McLain (Butlers); Si Jenks (Gardener); George Chandler, Drew Demarest (Cameramen); Mel Ruick (Tout); Fred "Snowflake" Toones (Train Porter); Gertrude Simpson (Bit).

*After Harlow's death, Mary Dees was substituted for long shots and backviews so that the film could be completed. The speaking voice of Paula Winslow was utilized to approximate that of the late star.

The star, MGM-style ('54).

CHAPTER 5

GRACE Kelly

5'6"
115 pounds
Blonde hair
Blue eyes
Scorpio

TODAY GRACE DE MONACO, Duchess de Valentinois, Marquise de Baux, Comtesse de Carlade—and assorted other titles—has established herself as one of the most written-about celebrities of the international social world. With her husband and three children she shares a palace in Monaco, an apartment in Paris, and a chalet in the ski resort of Gstaad, Switzerland. Beyond her continuous efforts to further enhance the respect and revenue of her "adopted" country of Monaco, she is deeply involved in the establishment of a ballet school and assorted charities in Europe and the U.S. More recently, she joined the board of Twentieth Century-Fox, hoping to guide the once great film company—and Hollywood—into a more decorous future.

If she is a dazzling personality of the 1970s, she was an equally vibrant luminary in the Hollywood of the Fifties. The Oscar-winner of Paramount's *The Country Girl* (1954) was considered the most potent box-office magnet of that time. Ironically, her home lot, Metro-Goldwyn-Mayer, had little idea what to do with the regal, cool beauty, and spent most of her contract period loaning her screen services to other studios.

The qualities that attracted audience interest to Grace the actress were multi-faceted. Her aura of self-confidence was impressive. One-time agent Jay Kanter would say recently, "I don't think she ever had any concern about not making it." Her *Rear Window* co-star, Jimmy Stewart, would analyze, "What impressed me was the wonderful confidence she had in her work. I tried to figure it out. . . . I felt that Grace had wanted to learn the craft [and did]."

Many writers have dissected her considerable beauty (admitting the flaw of her too-square jaw), but it would be Alfred Hitchcock—on Princess Grace's 1977 TV documentary—who would best explain the visual magnetism which lay beneath her "elegance" and "outside purity":

> I think the subtlety of her sex appeals to me. I think that Grace as a motion picture performer conveyed much more sex than the average sex pot. With Grace you've got to find it out, you've got to discover it.

Adding to this discussion, co-star Cary Grant would praise her "laughing style."

William Holden, who was teamed with Grace in *The Bridges at Toko-Ri* (1954) and *The Country Girl,* would conclude, "Grace is not a calculating or shrewd person, but I think that Grace's career was the best calculated career in the history of the motion pictures."

"In Philadelphia, the Kellys are about as conspicuous as the Thirtieth Street Station" (*Time* magazine, January 31, 1955). To this beautiful family named Kelly, Grace Patricia was born on Friday, November 12, 1929. She was the third child and the second daughter of John Brendan and Margaret Majer Kelly. She had been preceded in birth by sister Margaret (Peggy) and brother John, Jr. (Jack or Kell); she was to be followed by another sister who would be named Lizanne.

Grace's father, one of nine sons of an immigrant Irish farmer from County Mayo, had been a laborer/bricklayer by trade. But by 1919 he had transformed a $7 thousand loan from his brother Walter into a contract construction business that would eventually be worth a reputed $18 million. Her mother, a former magazine cover girl and model, was an advocate of the importance of physical fitness and was the first woman to teach physical education at the University of Pennsylvania. Among Grace's relatives were uncles George Kelly, the recipient of a Pulitzer Prize for his play *Craig's Wife,* and Walter C. Kelly, a famous vaudevillian known as the "Virginia Judge."

Her father was also recognized for his political activities (he made an unsuccessful bid in 1935 as the Democratic candidate for Philadelphia's mayor) and for his athletic contributions. As a proficient sculler (oarsman) he was eliminated from the 1920 regatta competition at Henley, England, because his manual labor trade did not qualify him as a gentleman. But that same year he entered the Olympics at Antwerp where he defeated the Henley champion. In 1947 and 1949, son Jack would revenge his father's bad treatment at Henley with victories for his school, the University of Pennsylvania.

Grace was a shy, quiet little girl whose childhood was marred by a seemingly endless head cold. The Kelly home, located five miles across the Schuylkill River from Philadelphia in East Falls, was a red-brick, fifteen-room mansion with sprawling lawns and space devoted to a tennis court, children's swings, and a large sandbox. Along with physical fitness, Catholicism was also a major interest of Mrs. Kelly's and she guided her youngsters to church on a daily basis. The Kellys' summers were spent frolicking at their home on the New Jersey shore at Ocean City, about thirteen miles down the coastline from Atlantic City.

From the age of six to fourteen the future star attended Ravenhill, a convent school. There she made her stage bow at the age of six. Not long

At the age of two with brother Jack and sister Peggy.

ago, Sister Elizabeth Mary Blint, one of her former teachers, would recall:

> I never imagined a first grader could display such talent. She portrayed the Blessed Mother in the school's annual nativity play and she looked like an angel . . . dressed in a long, flowing white dress.
>
> She gave a superb performance. Her poise, dignity, and the way she projected her strong little voice amazed everyone. . . . At the end of the performance, she curtsied to a standing ovation.

However, for Grace, her biggest childhood thrill occurred when she was seven and actor Douglas Fairbanks, Jr. visited the family and "He kissed me goodnight. I was never going to wash again."

According to some past instructors, Grace was not always angelic at Ravenhill. Sister Marie

Dorothy has memories of the future princess when she was twelve and thirteen:

> I can still picture her sitting at the back of the class, laughing, giggling, and telling her classmates dirty jokes while I was trying to teach.
>
> I often scolded her three or four times before she settled down and paid attention. Once she and another girl were pushing a three-foot-tall statue of Christ up and down the classroom aisles as a joke when I was out. But the prank backfired. They accidentally pushed the statue against a desk and broke off its arm.

When Grace was eleven, she was cast in a production offered by the Academy Players of Philadelphia. There her stage mother forgot her lines of dialogue. Grace professionally ad-libbed a bit of business concerned with her handbag while she whispered the proper words to the older woman. It was then that John Kelly observed with surprise, "We've got a trouper on our hands!"

Sister Peggy often directed plays at the Kelly home, using her sisters and brothers as cast members, along with neighborhood kids. It was during these amateur presentations that Grace lost her timidity while hiding behind the mask of make-believe.

Sister Marie Dorothy would also recall that before Grace departed Ravenhill she had discovered the opposite sex: "She had lots of boyfriends by the time she was fourteen and I remember her drawing hearts in her schoolbooks and putting in her name and those of her boyfriends." After leaving Ravenhill Grace completed her secondary education at Stevens Academy in Chestnut Hill, Pennsylvania. According to one teacher at the school, Mrs. Agnes Bergen, "Grace was an average student but with a little effort she could've been an 'A' student. However, she really wasn't interested in scholastic achievement—she gave priority to drama and boys."

Grace's mother would have her own recollections of the teenager from the age of fourteen to sixteen:

> . . .[She] was nothing but a gaggly somebody with a high nasal voice, the result of a long head cold throughout the winters. Her enjoyment of food gave her a little extra weight and she had to wear glasses.
>
> Despite all this, every young man who knew her from the time she was fifteen wanted to take care of "Gracie." Every last boy who ever went out with her fell a little in love with her.

One Stevens classmate would recall, "She was always out on dates and was never a wallflower at parties. She became most sophisticated for her age." Another would recollect Grace's chaperoned weekend treks: "I remember her standing there at the train station every Friday afternoon, ready to go off on another date. She wore a beautiful dress, high heels, pearls, and white gloves. The girls were jealous of Grace's beauty and they expressed nasty little remarks about her which she hated."

For Grace her most important date was Harper Davis, a friend of her older brother, Jack. When she was thirteen and still at Ravenhill they had gone to a basketball game together. In 1946 he would contract muscular dystrophy and would die at the age of twenty-two. Seventeen-year-old Grace was heartbroken. That year she graduated from Stevens where it was predicted beneath her yearbook picture, "She is very likely to become a stage and screen star."

Her parents thought that their well-bred daughter should attend college. However, she was rejected by Bennington College for women in Vermont when she failed to pass the math portion of the entrance examination. Instead, after a European sojourn, she announced to her parents that she intended to move to New York City and enroll at the American Academy of Dramatic Arts. Neither John Kelly nor his wife condoned her daring decision; he was to say, "Those movie people lead pretty shallow lives," while Mrs. Kelly admitted, "We'd hoped she would give it up." Nevertheless, it was agreed that they would pay Grace's tuition through one year of dramatic pursuit, after which she would have to be on her own.

Her Manhattan residence was the Barbizon Hotel for Women where she received her monthly financial care package from home and where she studiously watched her weight, a problem that had haunted her through childhood. She took dramatic lessons seriously although she doubted that she would ever sparkle on the stage. Instructors and students alike were impressed with her voice which hinted of English ancestry and her bearing which was indicative of sophistication and good breeding.

In 1948, to pay tuition for her second year at the American Academy, Grace found employment as a photographer's model. At first, the jobs presented themselves on an irregular basis, one of which was modeling hats for photographer Edward Ozern. He recently recalled, "She was very pleasant to work with, but I don't remember her as anything spectacular. To tell the truth," he went on, "I can remember the hats she posed in more than I do her." Grace's hourly fee was $7.50 but within a few months she was earning $400 a week posing as the exponent of such diversified products as Schaefer beer, Bridgeport Brass insecticides, Remington typewriters, Ipana toothpaste, Electrolux vacuum cleaners, and Old Gold cigarettes. (At one point Grace was used for three different beer company advertisements; she never drank the beverage offcamera.)

Another photographer, Ruzzie Green, admitted to *Time* magazine in 1955, "She's not a top model and never will be. She's the girl next door. No glamour, no oomph, no cheesecake. She has lovely shoulders but no chest." She was hired as the Old Gold "convention girl" for which she received $2,000 but refused to be photographed wearing a short skirt, nor would she attend any conventions outside New York because the travel might interfere with her regimen of acting instruction. Richard Leeds, president of Thomson-Leeds advertising agency which promoted the Old Gold gimmick, recalled, "She wasn't friendly with the customers because she didn't want men jollying and pinching her." William Disesa, then the ad manager of Bridgeport Brass Company, has said, "From the moment you looked at her and heard her speak you realized she didn't have to be posing with a spray can for a living."

Six times during this period, she made the covers of nationally distributed magazines (such as *Redbook* and *Cosmopolitan*) and has admitted, "The money was very nice and that's what makes it all worthwhile." When not modeling before a still camera, she dressed in tweed suits, hats with veils, and shoes with sensible heels (some had flaps in front). Before leaving the Academy, she was offered a $250-per-week movie contract by Twentieth Century-Fox, but she rejected it because she did not feel that she was prepared for Hollywood movies.

Instead, she gained experience with featured roles* in television plays, usually as a rosy-cheeked ingenue. She estimates, "I did quite a few—oh, sixty or eighty." She also did television commercials and played summer stock. The latter endeavor took her to the Bucks County Playhouse at New Hope, Pennsylvania, where she had small parts in *The Heiress* and *The Torchbearers* (written by Uncle George), and to Denver, Colorado's Elitch Gardens. There "we did a different play every week for ten weeks." On Wednesday, November 16, 1949, she opened at the Cort Theatre on Broadway playing the "angelic" and beloved daughter to Raymond Massey's* title role in *The Father,* a revival of August Strindberg's tragedy about a Swedish cavalry officer who loses his mind after twenty years of marriage to a shrewish woman (Mady Christians). Grace received some encouraging reviews: "Miss Kelly is a young actress of quality. She is worth watching" (*New York Daily Mirror*). "Grace Kelly gives a charming, pliable performance of the bewildered and broken-hearted daughter" (*New York Times*). But the production proved to be too maudlin for both critics and audiences and it closed after sixty-nine performances on January 7, 1950.

This turn of events sent Grace back to pounding her sensibly heeled shoes against the Manhattan sidewalks in search of work. She read for the ingenue part in *The Country Girl,* presented on Broadway in 1950 with Uta Hagen and Paul Kelly, but failed to get it. She has claimed, "I wasn't really the ingenue type and didn't have name enough for a lead." (The role played by Phyllis Love would be omitted from Paramount's 1954 film.)

In early autumn of 1950 Grace was selected by director Henry Hathaway as one of those in-

---

*She would be tremendously active in the video medium during the early Fifties, a time when the TV industry was blossoming in New York City. She appeared on many of the better dramatic (live) anthology shows, including "Studio One," "Philco Playhouse," "Lux Playhouse," and "Robert Montgomery Presents," and appeared in such series as "Big Town," The Web," "Danger," and "Suspense."

Several years before Grace would star in MGM 1950s' version of *The Swan,* she played in the Molnar vehicle on "The Play's the Thing" (CBS-TV, June 9, 1950). One of her important video as-

signments was joining with Eli Wallach and Eva Marie Saint in the much-touted version of F. Scott Fitzgerald's *The Rich Boy* presented on "TV Playhouse" on February 10, 1952. During one thirteen-day stretch Grace would perform three different roles in three different TV shows: she was a college girl, a rich miss, and a backwoods school marm.

Perhaps the most nerve-wracking TV assignment for Grace was her live appearance on Ed Sullivan's Sunday night variety show in 1953 when she and Ralph Meeker performed the French song from *Good News.* The combination of singing and dancing frightened the usually confident actress.

*On the 1977 TV documentary concerning Grace Kelly, Massey would assess, "Some actors have that quality you have to look for. . . . I thought to myself here's one who has it. . . . I have never been so impressed with anyone at first sight as I was with this girl. . . . She had serenity. I wish she'd stayed on the stage a little longer because she is a wonderful stage actress. . . ."

251

In England with brother Jack and sister Peggy at the Diamond Sculls championship races in 1947.

volved in three subplots calculated to supply tension relief in the semi-documentary drama *Fourteen Hours* (1951). Most of the Twentieth Century-Fox feature was shot in New York City, but Grace's indoor scenes were photographed in-studio and she was whisked off to California. The picture was based on a true 1938 news event. The John Paxton screenplay has Richard Basehart as a mentally disturbed, suicidal young man who perches all day on the seventeenth floor ledge of a downtown Manhattan hotel. Paul Douglas is an Irish policeman who tries to talk him back into the hotel room, and Agnes Moorehead is his mother who seems to have more problems than the son.

As Mrs. Fuller, a conservatively dressed young woman in her lawyer's office across the street from the unbalanced man, Grace talks divorce while watching Basehart through the lawyer's window. "I don't understand it," she says to the lawyer as her eyes move from his face to the figure hugging the concrete wall of the building across the way. "Issue one . . . Issue two . . . You make it sound dirty [with reference to her two children]. I can't remember who is the defendant, who is the plaintiff. It's more difficult than being married." She cancels her divorce plans,

realizing that her marital problems are minimal compared to those of the man on the ledge.

The script followed closely the true drama of the man who *does* commit suicide. But the ending of the film was altered after the suicide of the daughter of Fox executive Spyros Skouras. Skouras insisted that the entire film be permanently shelved, but Hathaway and other Fox decision-makers chose to save it by revising the ending wherein Basehart is rescued by the police after he comes perilously close to accidentally plummeting to his demise. Had Skouras' decision gone unchallenged, Grace Kelly's screen debut might never have occurred.

After the release of *Fourteen Hours* (on March 1, 1951) Grace was again offered a Twentieth Century-Fox contract, but again she refused to join the ranks of Betty Grable, Marilyn Monroe, and Mitzi Gaynor at the Fox lot. Stanley Kramer* then came forth with the fifth-billed role of the ex-marshal's Quaker wife in his proposed screening of "The Tin Star," a story by John W. Cunningham. This she accepted be-

*In 1977 Stanley Kramer would admit that it was "arrogance" on his part to give such a demanding role to such a newcomer. "I think she was miscast for the part [in *High Noon*]. She was really too young to play opposite Gary Cooper."

252

With George MacQuarrie
in *Fourteen Hours* ('51).

cause it would give her the opportunity of working with actor Gary Cooper and director Fred Zinnemann in a sophisticated Western. The black-and-white film was released through United Artists in April 1952 as *High Noon.*

As Amy, the proponent of pacifism, Grace is the very picture of round-cheeked wholesomeness. She is married to older Will Kane (Cooper) at 10:30 on a quiet, sun-drenched morning in the frontier town of Hadleyville. All is serene and her future appears to be pretty much cut and dried as she and her husband, who has given up his marshal's star for her, prepare to embark on their honeymoon. Just then, word filters into town that a pardoned convict named Frank Miller (Ian MacDonald) will arrive on the noon train to even the score with Kane who caused his incarceration five years earlier. Amy convinces Will that their plans to leave Hadleyville should not be altered and they drive out of town. But Kane's principles will not permit him to run away and he turns back, much to Amy's displeasure.

From then on, the film's stars are Cooper and the town's clocks as he races against time to muster help from the townsfolk, who all turn their backs on him out of fear of the younger Miller and his sinister henchmen (Lee Van Cleef, Bob Wilke, and Sheb Woolley). Left alone to face the four killers, Kane plays a waiting game as the clocks approach high noon and the tension mounts as the camera swings from his worried face to that of his young bride to those of the townspeople who huddle in the church and saloon. At noon, Miller arrives and Kane faces the men in the hot, dusty street where, with the last-minute help of Amy, he kills them all. Without further ado, he and Amy get into their buckboard and drive out of town. She knows that it was his final challenge as a lawman.

Prior to the film's release, Grace agreed to help promote it with a guest spot on Louella Parsons' radio show emanating from Hollywood. In *Tell It to Louella* (1961), Miss Parsons recorded Grace's presence on radio with, "Her beauty literally lit up our broadcasting studio. There are some women who are beautiful on the screen but lose a part of that loveliness off it. Not Grace."

253

With Gary Cooper in *High Noon* ('52).

Although Louella raved about Grace's beauty, she could not do the same about her on-the-air talkativeness. After getting nowhere with either personal talk or a comparison between Broadway and Hollywood ("Wouldn't that be silly?" said Grace. "I'm not an authority on either—and I'm in love with both"), the two ladies simply discussed Grace's role in *High Noon*. Miss Parsons added, "Frankly, the 'material' I got from Grace was far from being my scintillating radio interview."

High Noon became a box-office draw because of its non-Western flavor and music by Dmitri Tiomkin, theme song "Do Not Forsake Me, Oh, My Darlin' " (music by Tiomkin, lyrics by Ned Washington), cinematography by Floyd Crosby on location at Wyoming's Grand Tetons, and over-all capable supporting cast including Thomas Mitchell, Lon Chaney, Jr., Katy Jurado, and Otto Kruger. Bosley Crowther, in his *New York Times* critique, included Grace's name when he accoladed Gary Cooper's co-players as being "the best in key roles."

Nevertheless, Grace was not convinced that she could act. "With Gary Cooper, everything is so clear," she explained. "You look into his face,

and see everything he is thinking. I looked into my own face, and saw nothing. I knew what I was thinking, but it didn't show." With her mind made up to learn more about acting, she returned to New York where she became a student of Sanford Meisner's at the Neighborhood Playhouse. She tried out for a play in Albany, New York, where she lost a role to Betsy von Furstenberg, but bared her legs as a music hall entertainer who bedeviled men into murderous acts in an episode on NBC-TV's suspense series, "Lights Out," hosted by Jack La Rue. On CBS-TV's "Danger," she starred in the episode entitled *The Soldier and the Doll* in which she grew breathless from escaping the guillotine of the French revolutionaries.

Beginning on Wednesday, April 23, 1952, she was featured in William Marchant's play, *To Be Continued,* at New York's Booth Theatre.* Starring Dorothy Stickney, Jean Dixon, and Neil

*Earlier in the year she had dropped out of the cast of *Dear Barbarians,* a play by Lexford Richards. During the out-of-town tryout in Albany, New York, Grace and co-player Leatrice Joy decided the show did not have a chance on Broadway and they left the production. Grace was replaced by Betsy von Furstenberg and Miss Joy by Violet Heming. *Dear Barbarians* would open on Broadway on February 21, 1952, and close after four performances.

In a publicity shot with Katy Jurado, Gary Cooper, and Lloyd Bridges for *High Noon*.

Hamilton, it was the comedic story of a man who was faithful to a wife as well as to a mistress for twenty-six years. Grace received mixed notices: "Then, there is Grace Kelly, who is an exceptionally attractive young actress and obviously has far more talent for the theater than her one brief scene as the daughter of the legal marriage allows her to display" (*New York Post*). "Miss Kelly is tall and easy on the eyes. She acts with sincerity, but could learn a thing or two about the art from her distinguished uncle, George" (*New York Daily Mirror*). The play failed to generate interest beyond May 3, 1952, when it closed after having received generally unfavorable notices.

In the summer of 1952, director Gregory Ratoff summoned Grace, on behalf of Twentieth Century-Fox, to take a screen test for *Taxi* (1953), a film he was preparing that had a New York background. It was to be a tale of a hard-boiled New York cabbie who succumbs to the naivete of an immigrant Irish girl. Grace affected an Irish brogue and Ratoff exclaimed, "She's perfect! . . . What I love about this girl, she's not pretty." Ratoff's bosses in California did not agree that she was "perfect" for the role and she lost out to Fox contractee Constance Smith. (Dan Dailey played the cab driver.)

Meanwhile, out in Hollywood, Grace's value as a potential movie actress received an unexpected boost when Gary Cooper was voted the Best Actor of 1952 by the members of the Academy of Motion Picture Arts and Sciences for his acting job in *High Noon*. The film took a total of four Oscars, including Best Scoring of a Drama or Comedy (Tiomkin); Best Song (Tiomkin and Washington); and Best Film Editing (Elmo Williams and Harry Gerstad). Movie fans who had missed seeing *High Noon* in its initial release, almost a year earlier, now went out of their way to discover for themselves what all the hoopla had been about. *High Noon* is now considered a classic in the Western genre, along with *Stagecoach* (1939) and *Shane* (1953).

Among those in Hollywood who re-evaluated Grace Kelly was veteran director John Ford. He reviewed her *Taxi* test and, thinking she was British, offered her the third-billed role of Linda Nordley in Sam Zimbalist's MGM remake of *Red Dust* (1932), now entitled *Mogambo* (1953). The studio liked her and drew up a seven-year contract starting at $750 a week, but she held off signing until it was agreed that she could have a year of freedom every two years to return to New York for stage work. MGM granted the request. Grace was to say a few years later, "I wanted *Mogambo* for three things: John Ford, Clark Gable, and a free trip to Africa."

In the John Lee Mahin scenario (he had also scripted *Red Dust*), Grace took on the part played in the original version by Mary Astor. Gable is the hero, as he was in the 1932 edition, and Ava Gardner is the sultry temptress who was earlier enacted by Jean Harlow. A change of scenery has occurred (from French Indo-China to Africa) and character names are altered, but the plot is essentially the same. As Victor Marswell, Gable is a mighty white hunter who has taken up with Honey Bear (Gardner), an American entertainer in Africa to get away from it all. Into this cozy love scene walks Donald Nordley (Donald Sinden), a British anthropologist, and his lovely but stuffy wife, Linda (Grace). Victor and Linda are immediately attracted to each other, but the husband is too naive to see it. Honey Bear is very attuned to the situation and emphasizes the facts to everyone. During a safari, Victor almost tells Nordley the truth, but the Englishman's unabashed respect for him makes him change his mind and he even saves the man from being mauled by a gorilla. Later, back at camp, Victor rejects Linda by informing her that their relationship existed only because he enjoys variety. He once again turns to Honey Bear. After a bit of self-recrimination when she believes she wants to shoot Victor, Linda leaves Africa with Nordley, who is none the wiser about his wife's adventures.

While in Africa—with Ava Gardner busy consoling and irritating Frank Sinatra—Gable became more than mildly interested in Grace when she joined him on an offscreen safari. She plunged into the thicket with him without complaining of bug bites, scratches, heat, or the lack of comfort. Grace's twenty-fourth birthday occurred during production and it was Gable, along with MGM unit publicist Morgan Hudgins, who arranged a surprise party for the Philadelphian.

According to one member of the *Mogambo* crew, "Quite obviously Gable liked her. Who wouldn't? She was always quietly there and

With Donald Sinden, Clark Gable, and Ava Gardner in a mock-up pose for *Mogambo* ('53).

never got in the way. It was probably the first time in his life that he had ever met a woman like Grace. He was obviously fascinated and seeing her in that setting cast a kind of spell over them both."

Neither Kelly nor Gable would admit to the inquiring press whether their relationship had any substance. He claimed, "I'm old enough to be her father." On another occasion, he said, "Such a sweet well-brought-up girl." When Grace was asked later by columnist Earl Wilson how often she had dated Gable, she skirted the issue, "Oh, I never counted. I wasn't the only girl he dated and he wasn't the only guy I went out with."

When Gable and Kelly (she stopped over in England first) returned to California, they continued dating. He was a frequent caller at the Bel Air Hotel where she was staying. When she was later nominated in the Best Supporting Actress category for her English lady portrayal in *Mogambo,* it was Gable who accompanied her to the Pantages Theatre in Los Angeles on the evening of Thursday, March 25, 1954. It was he who consoled her when the Supporting Actress

Oscar went to Donna Reed for her change-of-type dramatics in *From Here to Eternity*. As a gesture of friendship, Grace gave Gable a Mexican burro tagged "Ba." On his part, Clark intended to co-star Kelly in his first independent production after leaving MGM.

The Gable-Kelly romance would fade away. He would later wed Kay Williams by whom he had a son named John. Grace would tell reporters of the relationship, "Perhaps it would have been different, if it weren't for the difference in our ages."

Mogambo, beyond the Gable rapport, had helped to escalate Grace's film career. When the film had opened in September 1953, *Newsweek* magazine had observed, "Grace Kelly makes one of the loveliest patricians to appear on the screen in a long time. Her particular quality is the suggestion that she is well born without being arrogant, cultivated without being stuffy, and highly charged emotionally without being blatant." *Look* magazine, largely on the basis of her *Mogambo* performance, would name her the Best Actress of 1953. By 1978, *Mogambo* would

With Clark Gable and Ava Gardner in *Mogambo*.

have grossed almost $5 million in theatrical rentals.

Grace was now being judged by filmmakers other than those at MGM. While her contract studio was in doubt as to what to do with her, Alfred Hitchcock, long known for his penchant for blonde leading ladies, viewed her *Taxi* test. His verbal response was, "You could see Grace's potential for restraint. I always tell actors: Don't use the face for nothing. Don't start scribbling over the sheet of paper until we have something to write. We may need it later. Grace has this control. It's a rare thing for a girl at such an age [twenty-four]." He summed up his opinion of her by saying that she possessed "sexual elegance." Hitchcock borrowed her to co-star in his directorial assignment of Frederick Knott's screen adaptation of his own play, *Dial M for Murder* (presented on the New York stage in 1952 with Maurice Evans and Gusti Huber). MGM's reported loan figure for Grace's services was $20,000 which did not affect her $750-per-week salary.

Grace's cinematic star was rising, but it was said that her traveling bags were never fully unpacked because of her plans to one day return to New York. She moved to a small apartment on Sweetzer Avenue in West Hollywood while continuing to maintain rental payments on a Manhattan apartment on Sixty-Sixth Street. She weighed 115 pounds, measured 5'6" tall, had blue eyes which were nearsighted, a soft voice with a very refined accent, and she professed, by way of MGM's publicity expert, Rupert Allen, to have interests in skiing, swimming, piano, riding, and sketching in pastels. That same department of publicists moaned over her lack of personal anecdotes. "I don't think Grace would allow an anecdote to happen to her," said a friend. Newspaper writers referred to Grace as a "porcelain doll" and "icy goddess."

In 1953-1954, in order to compete against the enormous popularity of at-home television, the film industry (re)introduced such gimmicks as CinemaScope and the process known as "3-D" (three-dimensional). *Dial M for Murder* was shot in the latter, but was released as a standard film when viewing of the final form revealed that it could survive quite nicely on quality, color, and its acting performances. Grace is Margot Wendice, the beautiful wife of Britisher Tony Wendice (Ray Milland). Jealous of the attention his wife gives to (Robert Cummings) and anxious to inherit her fortune, Tony arranges that she should die at the hands of a hired killer (Anthony Dawson).

The murder plans are upset when the plucky girl manages to stab her would-be assailant with a pair of scissors. Tony carefully schedules himself to be away for the appointed hour among many people who might later testify to his exact whereabouts. He telephones Margot at the set hour when the attacker will be inside the flat. She answers the phone, but he does not reply. He is then able to hear the struggle as the murderer comes upon her from behind. As the hired killer lies dead at her feet, she picks up the telephone to call the police and Tony responds. "Oh, Tony. . . . Tony, thank God," she cries.

"Come back at once. . . . I can't explain now. . . . Come quickly, please."

In a sweet voice Tony inquires what has happened. "A man attacked me," she replies tearfully. "He tried to strangle me." Tony is unable to keep the curiosity out of his next question, "Did he get away?" but Margot is too upset to notice. "No, he's dead," she cries.

Tony later devises the story that she willingly killed the man, allegedly one of her suitors. She is utterly baffled by the events, never once considering that her husband might have engineered the whole thing for the ultimate prize— her wealth. The key to the proceedings is an actual key to the door of the couple's flat which the smooth, likeable police chief, Inspector Hubbard (John Williams), finally uncovers.

The film is in typically suspenseful Hitchcock style and one which must be viewed from the beginning and followed closely. According to Bosley Crowther in his *New York Times* review, "In the pliant hands of Alfred Hitchcock, past master at the job of squeezing thrills, the

With Robert Cummings in *Dial M for Murder* ('54).

With Robert Cummings and Ray Milland in *Dial M for Murder.*

With Robert Cummings and John Williams in *Dial M for Murder.*

coils twine with sleek and silken evil. . . ." The *Times'* critic also decided that Grace "does a nice job of acting the wife's bewilderment, terror, and grief." On the other hand, *Time* magazine weighed that she "is not required to do much more than look beautiful and vulnerable, and she accomplishes both with patrician distinction."

In *Tell It to Louella,* Miss Parsons wrote, "And then came into being a romance which never should have been." Grace fell in love with Ray Milland, long respected as one of Hollywood's more stable, dependable married men. Although Milland and his wife, Malvina, had had a few skirmishes during their twenty-four-year marriage, they were nothing compared to the separation induced by his relationship with Grace. He moved into an apartment of his own from where he courted his blonde co-star, but the affair cooled after Grace learned that Malvina did not intend divorcing the forty-seven-year-old Milland. It wasn't long after that she stopped seeing Milland and Grace was paired with designer Oleg Cassini, the ex-

husband of heiress Merry Fahrey and actress Gene Tierney, and another so-called romance was quickly publicized by the press and fan magazines.

For her fifth film Grace was again borrowed by Alfred Hitchcock to portray the in-love model who helps unravel a murder mystery in Paramount's *Rear Window* (1954). As Lisa Fremont, she wants to wed her action photographer boyfriend, Jeff Jeffries (James Stewart), who is temporarily confined to his lower Fifth Avenue apartment due to a broken leg which is encased by plaster from his toes to his thigh. From his back window, Jeff takes to passing the dull recuperation period by visually eavesdropping on his assorted neighbors. One of these is Lars Thorwald (Raymond Burr), an oversized salesman whom Jeff suspects has done away with his invalid wife (Irene Winston).

The key to this mystery is the missing woman's wedding ring which Lisa finds during a surreptitious visit to Thorwald's apartment while Jeff watches from his window. It is Lisa's

With frequent date Oleg Cassini in Hollywood (August 1954).

261

In 1954.

262

heads-up contention that no woman would "go away" without her wedding ring and she pockets it as evidence. As Jeff watches, Thorwald approaches the apartment where Lisa searches, neither knowing of the other's presence. This is where Hitchcock's tension works at full force. Lisa manages to escape, but the audience suffers it out with Jeff until she is safely out of danger— for the time being.

Released on July 13, 1954, *Rear Window* went on to garner more than $5.7 million in distributors' domestic film rentals, and ensured Grace's position as a star. In some American cities, theatre owners ignored both Stewart and Hitchcock by placing on their marquees Grace's name alone, above the film's title. Otis L. Guernsey, Jr. of the *New York Herald-Tribune* wrote of Grace, "She has never looked more lovable, and that is saying a great deal." (Audiences of the day were titillated to learn that Grace's character carries a scant negligee in her purse when visiting Stewart for overnight sojourns.)

Grace's mother went to California to visit her daughter during the Milland episode in an effort to re-instill the Roman Catholic ideal that a girl should remain virtuous until marriage. When Grace switched from Milland to Cassini* to French actor Jean-Pierre Aumont ("I'm crazee about her"), Grace's father spoke up with, "I don't like that sort of thing much. I'd like to see Grace married. These people in Hollywood think marriage is like a game of musical chairs." At the same time, her brother's comments included, "I don't generally approve of these oddballs she goes out with. I wish she would go out

*Cassini was quite anxious to wed Grace. However, Kelly's parents were disinclined toward him, judging him "a very poor risk for a marriage." Even Cassini's friend, Joseph Kennedy, father of the future president, reportedly told the actress of Oleg, "He's a wonderful guy but it wouldn't work." Grace and Cassini would continue to date through 1955 when she informed him of her pending marriage to Prince Rainier.

With James Stewart in *Rear Window* ('54).

263

With Thelma Ritter in *Rear Window*.

As Lisa Fremont in *Rear Window*.

With Bing Crosby at the Mocambo Club in Hollywood (May 1954).

with the more athletic type, but she doesn't listen to me anymore." Conversely, Grace maintained that she was unchanged and observed aloud, "It took a long time to learn that everyone is as shy as I am." It would seem that most every male in filmdom was after Grace's favors; the next one to make overtures was Robert Wagner (one year her junior) resulting in a Philadelphia rendezvous which his studio, Twentieth Century-Fox, took pains to hush up when Cassini exerted pressure.

Loaning Grace to Paramount was becoming a habit: her next film for that studio was *The Bridges at Toko-Ri* (1954). It is a man's action film, concerned with the bombing of strategic supply bridges in North Korea during the Korean "police action" of 1952. Based on the James Michener novel, it was directed by Mark Robson and co-produced by William Perlberg and George Seaton.

William Holden is Lt. Harry Brubaker, a carrier-based jet pilot, who is sent by his commander, Rear Admiral Tarrant (Fredric March), on the mission of destroying "certain bridges,"

an assignment which is dangerous for less-than-daring pilots. Grace, as Nancy Brubaker, visits her husband in Tokyo before the big mission when a week is to represent the remainder of their lifetimes together. For the first time, Grace was photographed in bed with a man (Holden) where the love scenes were sweet, almost innocent, but talky. The script also afforded Holden an opportunity to bare his chest in a Japanese family bath, while Grace's fair skin excited those male audience members who feast on such an observance.

Grace has two major scenes. In one, March warns her of what is ahead and she states, "If I can't face the reality now, then there won't be much hope for me afterward—if anything should happen." The other is in bed with Holden when they frankly discuss the future of their daughters (Nadene Ashdown and Cheryl Lynn Callaway). Other than these two sequences, her role is perfunctory with Holden receiving most of the celluloid footage during air action sequences.

William K. Zinsser of the *New York Herald-*

With steady escort Jean-Pierre Aumont in Paris (May 1955).

Tribune gave Grace a flattering pat on the back with, "Everybody knows how nice it is to have *her* around," while Bosley Crowther of the *New York Times* found her to be "briefly bewitching."

While Grace was on the Paramount soundstages, it was learned that Jennifer Jones' pregnancy would prevent her from appearing in the studio's *The Country Girl* (1954). Producer William Perlberg was so pleased with Grace's work in *Toko-Ri* that he decided she should play Georgie Elgin (performed on Broadway in 1950 by Uta Hagen). However, MGM was against loaning out her services again. Determined to have the role, Grace contacted the MGM hierarchy and informed them that she wanted to be sent to Paramount for *The Country Girl.* She threatened to leave films, telling them, "I'll send you my address, so you'll know where to send my Christmas card." No one doubted her seriousness. The studio reluctantly agreed to the loan-out, this time for $50,000.

The Country Girl, made after *Toko-Ri,* would be released before that picture. Under the guidance of director George Seaton, Grace would give her most dramatic film performance. Gone were the glamorous gowns, opulent sets and Technicolor that had distinguished her past hits.

As Georgie, Grace is just plain drab. She is wed to alcoholic, has-been singer/actor Frank Elgin (Bing Crosby) who tries for a stage comeback at the prodding of Bernie Dodd (William Holden), a well-known Broadway director. Frank confides a parcel of lies to Bernie, Georgie, and himself in an effort to mask his own weakness, and Bernie believes him. Bernie is determined to lead Georgie away from her husband to cut him off from the evil influence she projects. Bernie believes that he hates the woman but in a confrontation wherein he orders her to stay away from Frank, he learns the truth. In actuality she is the strong one of the two. She explains that Frank chose alcohol as a defense when their young son was hit and killed by a car. Frank has blamed himself for the boy's death. With the revelation that Frank has been lying to him, Bernie realizes that he loves Georgie and takes her into his arms and kisses her. "How could you

With William Holden in a pose for *The Bridges at Toko-Ri* ('54).

With Cheryl Lynn Callaway, Nadene Ashdown, and William Holden in *The Bridges at Toko-Ri*.

With William Holden in *The Bridges at Toko-Ri*.

With makeup artist Wally Westmore on the set of *The Country Girl* ('54).

be so angry with someone you didn't even know?" she asks softly. They now work together to make Frank's comeback a success and he becomes self-sufficient and respects himself. Bernie asks Georgie to leave Frank now that he has found strength again. But in the final scenes, she decides that she will stay with Frank and make a go of their marriage.

According to *Look* magazine, "Crosby and Miss Kelly play this human tragedy with a compassion and psychological insight reaching the best traditions of dramatic skill." *Cue* magazine applauded the three stars with, "The Crosby-Kelly-Holden team comes just about as close to theatrical perfection as we are likely to see on-screen in our time." Adapted by Seaton from Clifford Odets' play, the film has gone on to register more than $6.5 million in distributors' domestic rentals.

Director/writer Seaton has said about his star actress, "Grace doesn't throw everything at you in the first five seconds. Some girls give you everything they've got at once, and there it is—

there is no more. But Grace is like a kaleidoscope: one twist and you get a whole new facet." At the start, Crosby voiced his apprehension about working with her, untried as a dramatic actress, but before the picture was completed, he said, "Never let me open my big mouth again." By this point he and Grace were dating socially.

On December 29, 1954, one day after the official release of *The Bridges of Toko-Ri,* the public was treated to seeing Grace in the glorious Technicolored arms of Stewart Granger. MGM selected *Green Fire* as her sixth film since signing her to a contract (but only the second at the home studio). It is, she has claimed, the only one of her movies she dislikes. The "green" of the title refers to emeralds, those buried in abandoned South American (Colombia) mines, the very thought of which draws the presence of two avaricious and adventurous parties (Granger and Paul Douglas). Granger is attacked by the local banditos and left for dead but he finds his way through the jungle to the spacious ranch run by Grace and her brother (John Ericson). She

With director George Seaton and William Holden rehearsing *The Country Girl.*

prefers that the emeralds—if there are any—remain buried, but the brother joins forces with the miners and is later killed. Granger re-routes the river which then threatens to engulf Grace's land and only after Douglas joins her team and the banditos reappear does Granger turn humane and dynamite the mountain top. His action forever obliterates the emerald hoards, but saves the ranch from flooding. A touch of suspense occurs when no one is sure that Granger has survived the blast. Then Grace sees his figure in the distance and runs to him. The whole affair is pure hokum, reminiscent of **dozens of class B** plots, and whatever gratuities were realized at the box office were due to the presence of Grace and Granger, both at the peak of their drawing power. To help promote the feature, exhibitors were asked to display a cut-out poster of Grace's face set atop the bosomy body of another girl wearing a green drape. "It makes me so mad," Grace said, "and the dress isn't even in the picture."

Clark Gable wanted Grace as his co-star in Twentieth Century-Fox's *Soldier of Fortune* (1955), but MGM vetoed the idea on the grounds that the schedule they had established for her provided no time for outside acting jobs. (Susan Hayward was given the role opposite Gable.) Grace's next assignment was Metro's *The Cobweb* (1955), which she refused to do and that part eventually went to Lauren Bacall (after Lana Turner also turned it down). Next, Miss Kelly was handed the script of *Quentin Durward* (1955) with Robert Taylor as co-star, to be filmed at MGM's England facility. She read the script and rejected it, explaining, "All the men can duel and fight, but all I'd do would be to wear thirty-five different costumes, look pretty and frightened. . . . The stage directions on every page of the script say: 'She clutches her jewel box and flees.' I just thought I'd be bored." (Kay Kendall replaced Grace in the role.) Grace also rejected *Diane* (1956) which Lana Turner would accept at Metro; and it would be Dana Wynter who would play opposite Rock Hudson in MGM's long-planned filming of Robert Ruark's *Something of Value* (1957). Another project that never came to fruition for Grace was *Bannon*, in which MGM had planned to star her opposite Montgomery Clift and Spencer Tracy.

On December 28, 1954, the New York Film Critics chose Grace as the year's Best Actress for her performances in *The Country Girl, Rear Window,* and *Dial M for Murder.* (Marlon Brando was selected as Best Actor for *On the Waterfront,* and that picture was named Best of the Year.)

On February 12, 1955, when the Oscar nominees were announced for the previous year's honors, no one was surprised when Grace's name appeared on the Best Actress list for *The Country Girl.* Her closest contender was Judy Garland for *A Star Is Born,* considered to be the sentimental favorite and the "shoo-in" winner. At the Academy Award festivities on Wednesday, March 30, 1955, at the Pantages Theatre, the Best Actor of 1954, William Holden (*Stalag 17*) announced the winner as Grace Kelly. Garland enthusiasts swore and pouted for months; some are still doing so. On the verge of tears, Grace's acceptance speech included, "The thrill of this moment keeps me from saying all I'd like to. I can only say thank you with all my heart to all those who made it possible for me."

Within four years Grace had risen from the status of a featured player in *Fourteen Hours* to the most celebrated actress in American films. She was pronounced the top feminine attraction in movies for the 1954-1955 season by Motion Picture Exhibitors and, on the very eve of the Oscar ceremonies, was suspended by MGM for having refused a third assignment. She was scheduled to begin *Jeremy Rodock,* a Western with Spencer Tracy, but she failed to report for work because, as she reportedly told her pals, she did not want to play opposite Tracy's "minor key style." (The property was released in 1956 as *Tribute to a Bad Man* with James Cagney rather than Tracy in the lead, and with Irene Papas, in her first American film, as his co-star.)

In April 1955 MGM announced the purchase of *The Swan* (originally a play by Ferenc Molnar) from Paramount in which Grace would portray the princess who momentarily falls in love with a commoner. It had been previously filmed in 1925 with Frances Howard and again in 1930 with Lillian Gish; Grace had played in a TV version of the work back in 1950.

The following month, while in France, Grace attended the Cannes Film Festival where she

As Georgie Elgin in *The Country Girl*.

Advertisement for *Green Fire* ('54).

With Paul Douglas in *Green Fire*.

275

Relaxing on the set of *Green Fire* with John Ericson.

Oscar-winning Grace Kelly cutting the celebration cake at Paramount (March 30, 1955).

was one of the major attractions. Also at Cannes were Olivia de Havilland and her husband, Pierre Galante, an editor of *Paris-Match* magazine. Galante wished to do a story layout on Grace and, because, as Louella Parsons had once said, Grace was "notoriously bad copy" due to "her restrained manner" and since she was "certainly no prospect for that stand-by of picture magazines—leg pictures," he devised the idea of a story based on the meeting of Hollywood royalty and the royal Prince Rainier III of Monaco.

The meeting took place in Monaco on Friday May 6, 1955, after which the marriageable Prince confided to his palace chaplain, Father Tucker, "I've met somebody. I think she is the one." The Prince, age thirty-one, a man of twenty-four titles (His Serene Highness, The Prince of Monaco, Duke of Valentinois, Prince of Chateau-Porcien, Count of Belfort, Baron of St. Lo, etc.), was soft-spoken, brown-haired, thick-waisted, and handsome. His subjects were the 22,000 Monegasque natives who lived on the small nation's 370 acres (less than one-half the size of New York City's Central Park) and whose army numbered 69 soldiers. The Prince, one of the world's most eligible bachelors, resided in a 200-room palace, attended by his 100 servants.

Prior to the Cannes Film Festival, Grace had worked with Cary Grant (his first film in two years) in Paramount's *To Catch a Thief* (1955), her third for Alfred Hitchcock. Touted as a mystery-comedy, it fails to contain the suspense of earlier or later Hitchcock products, but in VistaVision and rich Technicolor, and with Grant and Kelly starring, no one seemed to care very much. The picture went on to collect more than $4.5 million in distributors' domestic rentals.

In the ninety-seven-minute feature, Grant is John Robie, a retired cat burglar who is basking on the Riviera when several burglaries are committed in the style that had been established by Robie throughout his career. Also on the Riviera is the American Mrs. Stevens (Jessie Royce Landis), an earthy, outspoken soul who is blatantly hunting a spouse for her seemingly frigid, selective daughter, Frances (Grace). While Robie, with the help of insurance man H. H. Hughson (John Williams), sets out to clear

himself of suspicion of the recent thefts, Frances becomes more and more attracted to him but is not certain that he is really innocent. "Why should I steal?" he asks her. "I'm rich." She rejoins with "How did you become rich?" to which he replies quickly, "By stealing."

A masterful scene wherein fireworks fill the tropical night sky has the screen stars kissing insatiably which culminates with Grace's line, "Give me back my mother's jewels." He solicits her body along with her help in tracking down the actual cat burglar who turns out to be a girl (Brigitte Auber), the daughter of his ex-partner. Mrs. Stevens' search for a son-in-law ends as Frances and Robie fall in love.

Although *Variety* honestly labeled the film a "disappointment" and "[it] won't enhance the prestige of either the stars or the producer-director," the *Los Angeles Times'* Philip K. Scheuer found it to be "a high-polish job, a kind of reversion to the urbanities of a gentleman Raffles, with Cary Grant and Grace Kelly ideal in the romantic leads."

Hitchcock's comments regarding Grace included, "She is that rare thing in movies, a lady. She is a real actress. Not in the histrionic sense, but in a deeper sense. She's one of those people who fit into any leading-lady part. She has a youthful appearance photographically, but she is no child or juvenile in any sense. Ingrid Bergman has the same quality. It suggests intelligence."

On Grace's return to the United States, MGM revealed many of its cinematic plans for her. In July 1955 it was announced that Tennessee Williams' play *Cat on a Hot Tin Roof* (on Broadway that year with Barbara Bel Geddes and Ben Gazzara) had been purchased for Grace. (When it was filmed, three years later, it was with Elizabeth Taylor and Paul Newman.) It was planned that Grace should star as Mary Haines in the studio's musical remake of *The Women* (1939), entitled *The Opposite Sex* (1956), but June Allyson ultimately took the role. Grace was scheduled to portray Elizabeth Barrett Browning in the remake of *The Barretts of Wimpole Street* (1957), but Jennifer Jones would be the actress to play that harassed poetess. Warner Bros. asked for her screen services as the girl from Virginia who marries a brash and rich Texan in *Giant* (1956), but that Edna Ferber-written

With Cary Grant in *To Catch a Thief* ('55).

With Jessie Royce Landis in *To Catch a Thief*.

characterization eventually went to Elizabeth Taylor and clinched major stardom for her. In August 1955 Grace was set to star opposite James Stewart in *Designing Woman* (1957) at Metro, but once again she reneged, as did Stewart, and the leads were eventually played by Lauren Bacall and Gregory Peck.

In December 1955 Grace was at home in Philadelphia for the Christmas holidays when who should arrive on the scene but Prince Rainier of Monaco. After a brief period of getting reacquainted, the Prince, through his chaplain, asked John Kelly for his daughter's hand in marriage. On Thursday, January 5, 1956, the engagement was officially announced to the press when Grace, wearing a champagne-colored brocade dress, appeared beside her Prince at her parents' home for photographs. Mrs. Kelly proudly informed the newspeople, "Here I am a bricklayer's wife, and now my daughter is marrying a prince." John Kelly said, "We're not impressed by royalty. We're impressed by the man. Marriage is not a game of musical chairs with us. We play for keeps." (Decades later Grace would admit of this life-changing decision to wed the Prince, "I had reached a point in my life where I was able to make my own decision on it. . . . I acted more on instinct, but then I always have. I have good instincts, I think.")

It was revealed that the Prince's annual salary was fifty-two million francs, or $148,571, and that a 1918 treaty between Monaco and France dictated that the small principality should become French territory in the event that the ruling prince (Rainier had held the throne since 1949) failed to produce a male heir. Prince Rainier, a shy man, spoke fluent English and confessed that his interests (aside from finding a suitable wife) included reading, ballet, and Beethoven. The evening after their engagement announcement, the couple attended a ball at Manhattan's Waldorf-Astoria Hotel. Wearing a Dior-fashioned gown with low-heeled shoes so she would not stand above Rainier who was 5'9", Grace danced with her betrothed until four the next morning.

On April 11, 1956, MGM released *The Swan* which had been filmed on location near Asheville, North Carolina, the previous autumn. Grace is the Princess Alexandra of a make-believe Ruritanian nation whose family is facing financial ruin. It is left to her to save the clan by marrying the wealthy Prince Albert (played by Alec Guinness, a replacement for Rex Harrison and Joseph Cotten, each of whom had been announced as Grace's co-star). The princess' family (Jessie Royce Landis, Leo G. Carroll, Estelle Winwood, and Brian Aherne as the clergyman) suffers a case of collective fright when their savior temporarily sways from her destiny by pitching visual woo to the palace's handsome tutor, Dr. Agi (Louis Jourdan).

Wrote Bosley Crowther in the *New York Times,* "The experience is a bit like eating the food at a wedding reception and sipping the light champagne, but that should be no discouragement to Miss Kelly's vast multitude of fans, who will no doubt welcome the opportunity to do just that with her."

Grace arrived at Monaco aboard the 23,000-ton liner *Constitution,* at which time planes and helicopters flew overhead, the palace guns saluted her, sirens sounded, and Prince Rainier's personal yacht sailed out to meet her. On Wednesday, April 18, 1956, they were married in a sixteen-minute civil ceremony required by Monaco law. But the next day they were solemnly united in Catholic ceremonies at St. Nicholas Cathedral by the bishop of Monaco. At 10:35 a.m. a thin Grace (she had lost ten pounds before the wedding) entered the cathedral on the arm of her father while in the congregation sat Egypt's ex-king Farouk, the Aga Khan and his Begum, author Somerset Maugham, Randolph Churchill, and U.S. President Dwight Eisenhower's representative, Conrad Hilton. Also on hand, among others, was MGM's representative, Ava Gardner. One of the bridesmaids was actress Rita Gam. Present were 1,600 reporters representing worldwide publications.

Grace's wedding gown consisted of 25 yards of silk taffeta, 100 yards of silk net, and 300 yards of lace; the Prince wore a full-dress uniform. As crowds lined the walks outside (they began lining up as early as six in the morning), Grace Patricia Kelly of Philadelphia became Her Serene Highness Princess Grace of Monaco by saying, "Oui, je veux" to the eternal question put forth in French by the bishop. If a commoner, she would have been just Mrs. Rainier Louis

Henri Maxence Bertrand Grimaldi. The bride was twenty-six; the groom was thirty-two. (Among the many media events spawned by the wedding of the decade was an Ethel Merman Broadway musical entitled *Happy Hunting,* about a rich but gauche Philadelphian who is not invited to the festivities.)

Prior to embarking for Monaco and a new life, Grace had taken over the old Katharine Hepburn role of Tracy Lord in MGM's musical remake of *The Philadelphia Story* (1940). The modernized version emerged on July 17, 1956, as *High Society,* with the locale switched from Philadelphia to Newport, Rhode Island, to allow for the inclusion of Louis Armstrong and references to the Newport Jazz Festival. As the extremely rich and very spoiled Tracy Lord (played both on Broadway in 1938 and in the screen rendition by Katharine Hepburn), Grace is professionally reunited with Bing Crosby and with her behind-the-*Mogambo*-scenes acquaintance, Frank Sinatra. Garbed in Helen Rose creations, Grace epitomizes the rich young woman who does not always get what she bar-

gained for in life. Everyone is on hand for Tracy's wedding to stuffy George Kittredge (John Lund), including her ex-husband, C. K. Dexter-Haven (Crosby), and a pair of friendly reporters (Sinatra and Celeste Holm). C. K. is still very much in love with her but is unable to persuade her that he is sincere even with the help of Cole Porter's "True Love" which they sing in duet (Grace does her own singing). The night before the ceremony is scheduled to take place, Tracy gets drunk with the help of the reporters at which time she dives into the family swimming pool. The plunge seems to permanently clear her mind because the next morning she jilts the expectant Kittredge by re-marrying likeable, fun-loving C. K.

Variety, in its review of this, Grace's last film to date, asserted, "Miss Kelly impresses as a femme lead with pleasantly comedienne overtones. This is perhaps her most relaxed performance." The *Hollywood Reporter* labeled her "very good, and she plays with Crosby and Sinatra in a relaxed and delightful way."

Prince Rainier and his Princess Grace made

With Louis Jourdan in *The Swan* ('56).

With Alec Guinness in a pose for *The Swan*.

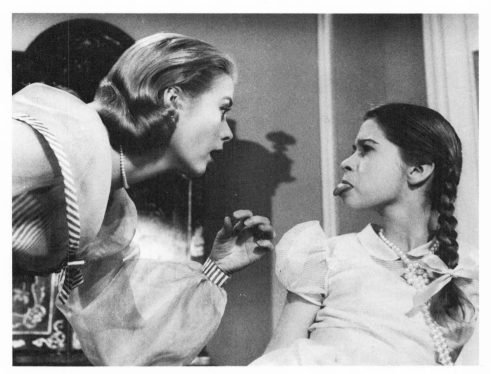

With Lydia Reed in *High Society* ('56).

With Frank Sinatra in *High Society*.

their first public appearance since their marriage by attending a July 4, 1956, Mass at the cathedral. Later, they watched a boys' cadre drill and when the Prince was respectfully questioned regarding the possibility of Grace being pregnant, he replied carefully, "Not for the moment." According to Hedda Hopper in *The Whole Truth and Nothing But* (1962), Prince Rainier took a "back seat" while Grace "reigned as regally as Queen Victoria in the comic-opera palace at Monaco, with its toy-soldier guards parading solemnly outside like bit players in an old Mack Sennett movie." Miss Hopper conceded that this was the impression derived during the early days of Grace's marriage and that later she became a much warmer monarch. Whenever asked for her autograph, it was written "Grace de Monaco."

In September 1956 it was admitted that Grace was expecting a child the following February. The royal couple arrived in Manhattan that month for a two-month visit in the United States. By November, Grace had gained twenty-six pounds which, she said, could be blamed on spaghetti and noodles as well as on her pregnancy. Both Rainier and Grace hoped for a boy and when asked if a name had been selected she replied, "I love the name Henry, but the Prince doesn't."

Back in Monaco in January, Elaine, the principality's single legal fortune teller, predicted that Grace would give birth to a boy child. By tradition, if this proved true, it would be signaled by a 101 salvo salute from two naval cannons pointing across Monaco Bay. If a girl, the news would be telegraphed by twenty-one salvos. On January 20, 1957, the visiting Sultan of Morocco was welcomed with a twenty-one gun salute which prematurely sent the natives of Monaco and newshounds scurrying to verify the birth of a daughter. At Monte Carlo, gamblers placed seven to five wagers that the baby would be a boy while Grace offered a complete set of baby clothes to all born in Monaco the same day as her child. At the same time, Prince Rainier offered to open a savings account for each child. It was further revealed that the average daily birth rate in Monaco was two or three.

On Wednesday, January 23, 1957, Grace gave birth to an eight-pound, three-ounce girl at Grimaldi Palace, the ancestral home for 700 years. The dark-haired, blue-eyed baby girl was named Caroline Louise Marguerite although the baptism would not occur until February. All of Monaco (except the casino croupiers) celebrated the holiday with champagne, folk dancing, and bands playing in the red-and-white festooned public square. The next day it was reported to the world that mother and daughter were "in excellent condition" and that Grace had nursed her baby and was "delighted" over the return of her "trim figure." To build her strength, she was given a glass of beer with each of her meals, as prescribed by her physician, Emile Hervet. The baby was registered as the heiress-presumptive to the throne of Monaco but it was determined that she would yield the precedence in the event of the birth of a son. The United States State Department declared that Caroline was born American as well as Monegasque but that she would lose her U.S. nationality if she failed to visit the United States before age twenty-three and remain there for at least five years.

With Grace's apparent abdication from the world of movies, all Hollywood studios sought replacements to fit the vacated mold of the cool, detached blonde lady. Among those screen starlets who were groomed to fill the slot were Dina Merrill, Claire Kelly, and Martha Hyer. Columnist Joe Hyams wrote in September 1957, "There is a resemblance between the Misses Kelly and Hyer. They're both firm-chinned blonds, both the 'simple type' as opposed to the 'sexy type.'" Miss Hyer was more anxious to be accepted on her own merits and said, "She got to the top first so I became a carbon copy. There's no future in that." At the same time, though, Miss Hyer had to admit to a certain degree of enjoyment derived from the similarities. "At one Hollywood award banquet I wore a white gown and had my hair pulled back simply. Crowds parted as if by magic. I got the star treatment—and I liked it." None of the Grace Kelly look-alikes, including Miss Hyer, were to achieve the cinematic success of their famed predecessor. With the retirement from acting of Grace Kelly, the film type that she represented, at least for a time, was no longer seen on the silver screen.

On Friday, March 14, 1958, a son—their heir

With Bing Crosby rehearsing for *High Society*.

At her marriage to Prince Rainier (April 19, 1956).

apparent to the throne of Monaco—was born to Princess Grace. Weighing eight pounds, eleven ounces, the boy was named Albert Alexander Louis Pierre. A 101-gun salute told the excited populace that a son had been born. Monaco was saved from annexation by France.

Grace was reportedly instrumental in closing the Monte Carlo gambling casino on Good Friday, 1958, but would neither confirm nor deny her moralistic efforts. It was further reported that she had never set foot inside the gambling rooms although tourists flocked there in the hope of seeing her.

In 1962 Grace accepted Alfred Hitchcock's offer and signed an agreement to return to moviemaking in the title role of *Marnie* (1964) at Universal. She reversed her stand a few weeks later, however, in the face of strong opposition from her Monegasque subjects who vociferously announced their displeasure at sharing their princess with the world via celluloid. Tippi Hedren, a cool blonde but a wooden actress, was chosen as her replacement. (Miss Hedren had worked for Hitchcock the year prior in *The Birds*.)

In 1963, Grace did a turn before the cameras when she conducted a televised film tour of Monaco. This time, because she served as hostess to millions of viewers who were potential visitors to Monaco, the natives did not object.

A second daughter was born to Princess Grace and Prince Rainier on Monday, February 1, 1965. This child, their last, was named Stephanie Marie Elizabeth. Stephanie was born at Grimaldi Palace as were her sister and brother before her.

In the years that have followed, Caroline has grown to become a beautiful, desirable young lady who has given her parents many headaches with her independent lifestyle. Her name has been linked romantically with several men and boys of international status. When she finally selected Philippe Junot, a French insurance broker (17 years her senior), as her intended spouse, the international news media had fodder for months: Would Caroline and the business-

With Prince Rainier in Paris (September 1956).

man commoner really wed? Caroline's June 1978 wedding to Junot in Monaco, reminiscent in many ways to the highly publicized union of Grace and Prince Rainier (although *much more* private), proved to be the highlight of the 1978 continental social season. Albert, heir apparent to the throne of Monaco, has retained an air of royalty which has pleased his parents. He is now a student at Amherst College in Massachusetts.

There have been various reports over the years that the Kelly-Rainier marriage was shaky at best, but no separation or divorce has been forthcoming. (When the couple celebrated their twentieth anniversary in 1976, there was a seemingly endless array of magazine articles celebrating and evaluating the famed union.) Although the Prince has turned gray of hair and has added considerable poundage, Grace maintains the beauty and poise that endeared her to movie fans twenty-five years ago. Along with Jackie Onassis, Elizabeth Taylor, and Sophia Loren, she remains one of the most sought-after cover article subjects for national magazines.

In the summer of 1973 it was rumored that Grace would make an acting comeback* in a Los Angeles stage revival of her Uncle George Kelly's play, *Behold the Bridegroom.* However, this turned out to be no more than another of the eternal rumors regarding the regal lady. On Monday, April 29, 1974, Princess Grace did make a stage appearance at New York's Lincoln Center to participate in the salute to her old mentor Alfred Hitchcock. She proved to be the hit of the evening. (When the New York publisher Hopkinson and Blake released *The Art of Alfred Hitchcock* by Donald Spoto in 1976, there was a foreword by Grace.)

When not coping with the academic and social affairs of her children, Grace manages a frequent trip to the United States, as when she came to Philadelphia during the bicentennial year for the July 4 holiday. As had become habit, she was besieged with film offers while in the States; one

*On April 22, 1966, Grace was seen on ABC-TV hostessing the telefeature *The Poppy Is Also a Flower,* geared as a charity appeal for United Nations funds.

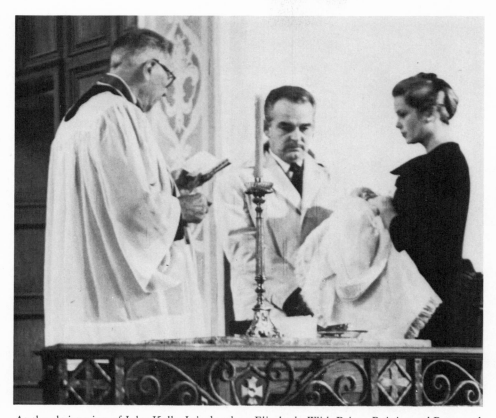

At the christening of John Kelly, Jr.'s daughter Elizabeth. With Prince Rainier and Reverend Augustine J. Schulte in Gladwynne, Pennsylvania (December 1958).

Princess Grace in Paris with local children (October 1959).

that particularly intrigued her was a role in Herb Ross' *The Turning Point* for Twentieth Century-Fox. Vetoing the project the former actress admitted, "I just don't think I can ever get involved in a film again." When she appeared on "The Mike Douglas Show," the regal personality, wearing high black boots, displayed a loss of much of the acquired British accent she somehow had picked up in Philadelphia years before. She noted that daughter Caroline did not seem to be interested in acting, although she liked ballet. On a few occasions, just when the lengthy TV talk teetered on becoming substantial, she told host Douglas, "No comment."

On Monday, September 6, 1976, Grace formally returned to the entertainment world in a special way. She was one of the three performers in a poetry recital, given as part of the Edinburgh International Festival. The evening was entitled "The American Heritage" and was conceived as a tribute to the U.S. Bicentennial. According to

Reuters' news service, "The capacity audience of 300 in Edinburgh's St. Cecilia's Hall gave an enthusiastic reception to [the] readings." Grace's co-performers were Richard Kiley and Britisher Richard Pasco.

The subject material covered the 19th-century American classics as well as this century's offerings by T. S. Eliot, Robert Frost, Carl Sandburg, and Ogden Nash. In her performing, reported Reuters', ". . . [she] seemed completely at home, although she did fluff a couple of her lines. She recovered immediately and only a very attentive listener would have been aware of her mistakes." Kelly gave four performances at the festival, all sold-out events.

Also during 1976 she decided to forge a new link with her past in Hollywood. Her long-time friend and one-time agent, Jay Kanter, now a Twentieth Century-Fox vice-president, persuaded her to join the film company's board of directors. Grace was quite outspoken on her

The royal couple (July 1963).

At a Beverly Hills party with Carol Burnett, Prince Rainier, and Rock Hudson (August 1967).

The royal couple on tour (San Antonio, Texas, in September 1968).

reasons for accepting the $7,500 per annum post:

> There is too much crude sex and violence in movies and television today. I want to help change all that. I want to bring love and peace back to the screen.
>
> I won't be reading scripts nor will I have the power of veto over a script or production, but I hope to use my influence to put things in order.
>
> Because of my responsibilities, my family, and my duties to Prince Rainier, I plan to attend only two board meetings a year.

Early in 1977 Grace supplied the narration for *The Children of Theatre Street,* a feature-length documentary film dealing with Russia's Kirov School of Ballet. Most of the film's proceeds were given to the Princess Grace School for Classical Ballet in Monaco (and to other assorted cultural projects). When *The Children of Theatre Street* opened throughout the United States in late 1977, a good deal of publicity was generated by Princess Grace's appearance. At the opening of the documentary she is seen atop the roof of the Paris Opera House, delivering her introduction which the *Hollywood Reporter* termed "spoken graciously." The well-received picture would be nominated as the Best Documentary of 1977, but lost the Oscar. Princess Grace, however, was given the Film Advisory Board's Award of Excellence plaque in February 1978 for her work as narrator of the film.

When not involved in christening a new Cunard cruise liner (named *Princess* in her honor),

Advertisement for *Once Upon a Time . . . Is Now the Story of Princess Grace* (NBC-TV, May 22, 1977).

or helping to celebrate the anniversary of Loew's Monte Carlo Hotel, or participating in the festivities at the Monte Carlo Circus, the one-time Hollywood star agreed to be the subject of an American TV documentary, *Once Upon a Time . . . Is Now the Story of Princess Grace.*

It was no coincidence that the seventy-five minute special was produced by Twentieth Century-Fox TV. Filming occurred in Monaco, Paris, and other European sites, hostessed by actress Lee Grant. Budd Schulberg, who would write the show, would later ask that his name be removed

With Prince Rainier in the 1970s.

With children Caroline, Albert, and Stephanie, and Prince Rainier in the mid-1970s.

from the credits. The advertisements for the program, telecast on Sunday, May 22, 1977, as part of NBC-TV's "Big Event" showcase, noted that among the interviewees would be Sir Alec Guinness. His segment did not appear on the telecast; the carefully slanted showcase of Princess Grace also failed to have any comments whatsoever from Ray Milland, Bing Crosby, Oleg Cassini, or Jean-Pierre Aumont, each a V.I.P. name in her romantic past. As the usually docile *Hollywood Reporter* would judge, "*Once Upon a Time* is strictly for fairy tales. . . . It is all so perfect that one longs for a little cynicism to at least creep in. . . . 'These are flesh and blood people living flesh and blood lives,' gushes host Lee Grant as she takes us through the make-believe world of a modern princess."

A more meaningful tribute to Grace occurred in June 1977 when the newest issue of the *Ceres Medal* was released by the United Nations Food and Agriculture Organization in Rome. It bore the profile of Princess Grace. The tribute was in recognition for Grace's work in behalf of young people and the Red Cross.

More rewarding than guesting on the televised "Merv Griffin Tennis Tournament" or the "Monte Carlo Circus Festival" was her decision to tour six U.S. cities in February 1978 with a recital of prose and poetry. She again co-starred with Richard Pasco. The presentation, *Birds, Beasts and Flowers,* was devised and staged by John Carroll and was dedicated to the World Wildlife Fund (although the production was not a benefit for the charitable fund). The tour began at the Carnegie Library in Pittsburgh. When the show reached the Hartke Theatre at Catholic University in Washington, D.C., the *New York Times'* Mel Gusow reported:

> Princess Grace looks regal, as she did even before she became royalty. She is a picture-postcard princess, an elegant contrast to the often dowdy monarchs of real life. She has, let it be noted, aged gracefully.
>
> The selections run from the Book of Genesis to Denise Levertov, Shelley, and Keats, seasoned with Paul Gallico and Anonymous. The empha-

sis was on English poets and on short poems. The few prose extracts, such as quotations from Kenneth Clark, were the flattest part of the evening. In no sense was the recital demanding—either on the actors or on the audience. . . .

> Only once did Princess Grace step out of the show's frame and offer us a personal glimpse—a story about a chapel to St. Francis of Assisi in Monaco. The evening is, perhaps, too formal. It is, in fact, carefully composed to show the Princess off to her best advantage. With her silky voice, her poise, and her precise diction, she is eminently suited to read delicate and light verse. . . .

When asked the expected question at each tour stop, Grace responded, "This poetry tour is an evolution, not a change."

Whatever professional and personal future lies ahead for Grace Kelly, there is little doubt that she will remain a headline-maker or that she will continue to remain the subject for analysis on a wide variety of fronts.

In her book *Princess Grace* (1976), author Gwen Robyns offers an intriguing summation of the Grace Kelly phenomenon: "There is a mystique that surrounds Grace and always has from the beginning. It is the act she puts together for survival." Then quoting from an interview with producer John Foreman, Ms. Robyn relates:

> Only Grace could have created Grace Kelly. It must have been a concept in her head. No one else did. No manager, no agent, no producer, not even her family.
>
> She made up the idea of Grace Kelly, and having made it up she was the only one who knew how to make it operate.
>
> She can make Grace Kelly do Grace Kelly things that nobody else can do. She is unique.

The Grace Kelly of today.

FILMOGRAPHY

FOURTEEN HOURS (*20th Century-Fox, 1951*) 92 min.

Producer, Sol C. Siegel; director, Henry Hathaway; based on the story "The Man on the Ledge" by Joel Sayre; screenplay, John Paxton; art directors, Lyle Wheeler, Leland Fuller; music, Alfred Newman; camera, Joe MacDonald; editor, Dorothy Spencer.

Paul Douglas (Dunnigan); Richard Basehart (Robert Cosick); Barbara Bel Geddes (Virginia); Debra Paget (Ruth); Agnes Moorehead (Mrs. Cosick); Robert Keith (Mr. Cosick); Howard Da Silva (Lieutenant Moksar); Jeffrey Hunter (Danny); Martin Gabel (Dr. Strauss); Grace Kelly (Mrs. Fuller); Frank Faylen (Waiter); Jeff Corey (Sergeant Farley); James Millican (Sergeant Boyle); Donald Randolph (Dr. Benson); Willard Waterman (Mr. Harris); Kenneth Harvey (Police Operator); George MacQuarrie (Evangelist); Ann Morrison (Mrs. Dunnigan); Forbes Murray (Police Commissioner); George Putnam (Radio Announcer); Ossie Davis, David Burns, Henry Slate, Harvey Lembeck, Lou Polan (Cab Drivers); Brad Dexter, Shep Menken (Reporters); Joyce Van Patten (Barbara); George Baxter (Attorney).

HIGH NOON (*United Artists, 1952*) 85 min.

Producer, Stanley Kramer; director, Fred Zinnemann; based on the story "The Tin Star" by John W. Cunningham; screenplay, Carl Foreman; music Dmitri Tiomkin; song, Tiomkin, Ned Washington; song sung by Tex Ritter; art director, Rudolph Sternad; set decorator, Emmett Emerson; sound, Jean Speak; camera, Floyd Crosby; editors, Elmo Williams, Harry Gerstad.

Gary Cooper (Will Kane); Thomas Mitchell (Jonas Henderson); Lloyd Bridges (Harvey Pell); Katy Jurado (Helen Ramirez); Grace Kelly (Amy Kane); Otto Kruger (Percy Mettrick); Lon Chaney, Jr. (Martin Howe); Henry "Harry" Morgan (William Fuller); Ian MacDonald (Frank Miller); Eve McVeagh (Mildred Fuller); Harry Shannon (Cooper); Lee Van Cleef (Jack Colby); Bob Wilke (James Pierce); Sheb Woolley (Ben Miller); Tom London (Sam); Ted Stanhope (Station Master); Larry Blake (Gillis); William Phillips (Barber); Jeanne Blackford (Mrs. Henderson); James Millican (Baker); Cliff Clark (Weaver); Ralph Reed (Johnny); William Newell (Drunk); Lucien Prival (Bartender); Guy Beach (Fred); Howland Chamberlin (Hotel Clerk); Virginia Christine (Mrs. Simpson); Morgan Farley (Minister); Virginia Farmer (Mrs. Fletcher); Jack Elam (Charlie); Paul Dubov (Scott); Harry Harvey (Coy); Tim Graham (Sawyer); Nolan Leary (Lewis); Tom Greenway (Ezra); John Doucette (Trumbull); Dick Elliott (Kibbee).

MOGAMBO (*MGM, 1953*) C-115 min.

Producer, Sam Zimbalist; director, John Ford; based on the play by Wilson Collison; screenplay, John Lee Mahin; art director, Alfred Junge; costumes, Helen Rose; second unit directors, Richard Rosson, Yakima Canutt, James C.

Havens; assistant directors, Wingate Smith, Cecil Ford; camera, Robert Surtees, Frederick A. Young; editor, Frank Clarke.

Clark Gable (Victor Marswell); Ava Gardner (Eloise Y. Kelly); Grace Kelly (Linda Nordley); Donald Sinden (Donald Nordley); Philip Stainton (John Brown Pryce); Eric Pohlmann (Leon Boltchak); Laurence Naismith (Skipper); Denis O'Dea (Father Joseph); Asa Etula (Young Native Girl); Wagenia Tribe of Belgian Congo, Samburu Tribe of Kenya Colony, Bahaya Tribe of Tanganyika, M'Beri Tribe of French Equatorial Africa (Themselves).

DIAL M FOR MURDER (*Warner Bros., 1954*) C-88 min.

Producer/director, Alfred Hitchcock; based on the play by Frederick Knott; screenplay, Hitchcock; sets, Edward Carrere, George James Hopkins; music/music director, Dmitri Tiomkin; costumes, Moss Mabry; sound, Oliver S. Garretson; camera, Robert Burks; editor, Rudi Fehr.

Ray Milland (Tony Wendice); Grace Kelly (Margot Wendice); Robert Cummings (Mark Halliday); John Williams (Chief Inspector Hubbard); Anthony Dawson (Captain Swan Lesgate); Leo Britt (The Narrator); Patrick Allen (Pearson); George Leigh (William); George Alderson (The Detective); Robin Hughes (A Police Sergeant); Alfred Hitchcock (Man in Photo).

REAR WINDOW (*Paramount, 1954*) C-112 min.

Producer/director, Alfred Hitchcock; based on the novelette by Cornell Woolrich; screenplay, John Michael Hayes; Technicolor consultant, Richard Mueller; art directors, Hal Pereira, Joseph McMillan Johnson; set decorators, Sam Comer, Ray Mayer; music, Franz Waxman; costumes, Edith Head; assistant director, Herbert Coleman; special effects, John P. Fulton; camera, Robert Burks; editor, George Tomasini.

James Stewart (L. B. "Jeff" Jeffries); Grace Kelly (Lisa Fremont); Wendell Corey (Thomas J. Doyle); Thelma Ritter (Stella); Raymond Burr (Lars Thorwald); Judith Evelyn (Miss Lonely Hearts); Ross Bagdasarian (Song Writer); Georgine Darcy (Miss Torso); Sara Berner (Woman on Fire Escape); Frank Cady (Fire Escape Man); Jesslyn Fax (Miss Hearing Aid); Rand Harper (Honeymooner); Irene Winston (Mrs. Thorwald); Harris Davenport (Newlywed); Marla English, Kathryn Grant (Party Girls); Edwin Parker, Fred Graham (Stunt Detectives); Harry Landers (Young Man); Bess Flowers (Woman with Poodle); James A. Cornell (Man).

THE COUNTRY GIRL (*Paramount, 1954*) 104 min.

Producers, William Perlberg, George Seaton; director, Seaton; based on the play by Clifford Odets; assistant director, Francisco Day; musical sequences staged by Robert Alton; music, Victor Young; songs, Ira Gershwin and Harold Arlen; art director, Hal Pereira; camera, John F. Warren; editor, Ellsworth Hoagland.

Bing Crosby (Frank Elgin); Grace Kelly (Georgie Elgin); William Holden (Bernie Dodd); Anthony Ross (Phil Cook); Gene Reynolds (Larry); Jacqueline Fontaine (Singer/Actress); Eddie Ryder (Ed); Robert Kent (Paul Unger); John W. Reynolds (Henry Johnson); Ida Moore, Ruth Rickaby (Women); Frank Scannell (Bartender); Richard Keene, Jack Kenney, Hal K. Dawson (Actors); Bob Alden (Bellboy); Neva Gilbert (Lady); Chester Jones (Ralph, the Dresser); Jonathan Provost (Jimmie).

THE BRIDGES AT TOKO-RI *(Paramount, 1954)* C-102 min.

Producers, William Perlberg, George Seaton; director, Mark Robson; based on the novel by James A. Michener; screenplay, Valentine Davies; music, Lyn Murray; art directors, Hal Pereira, Henry Bumstead; costumes, Edith Head; Technicolor consultant, Richard Mueller; makeup, Wally Westmore; technical advisor, Commander M. U. Beebe, USN; sound, Hugo Grenzbach, Gene Garvin; camera, Loyal Griggs; aerial camera, Charles G. Clarke; second unit camera, Wallace Kelley, Thomas Tutweiler; editor, Alma Macrorie.

William Holden (Lieutenant Harry Brubaker); Grace Kelly (Nancy Brubaker); Fredric March (Rear Admiral George Tarrant); Mickey Rooney (Mike Forney); Robert Strauss (Beer Barrel); Charles McGraw (Commander Wayne Lee); Keiki Awaji (Kimiko); Earl Holliman (Nestor Gamidge); Richard Shannon (Lieutenant [S.G.] Olds); Willis Bouchey (Captain Evans); Dennis Weaver (Air Intelligence Officer); Marshall Beebe (Pilot); Cheryl Lynn Callaway (Susie); Nadene Ashdown (Kathey Brubaker); Jack Roberts (Quartermaster); Paul Kruger (Captain Parker); Corey Allen, Jim Cronan (Enlisted Men); Bill Ash (Spotter).

GREEN FIRE *(MGM, 1954)* C-100 min.

Producer, Armand Deutsch; director, Andrew Marton; screenplay, Ivan Goff, Ben Roberts; art directors, Cedric Gibbons, Malcolm Brown; camera, Paul Vogel; editor, Harold F. Kress.

Stewart Granger (Rian X. Mitchell); Grace Kelly (Catherine Knowland); Paul Douglas (Vic Leonard); John Ericson (Donald Knowland); Murvyn Vye (El Moro); Jose Torvay (Manuel); Robert Tafur (Father Ripero); Joe Dominguez (Jose); Nacho Galindo (Officer Perez); Charlita (Dolores); Natividad Vacio (Hernandez); Rico Alaniz (Antonio); Paul Marion (Roberto); Bobby Dominguez (Juan); Charles Stevens, Joe Herrera (Bandits); Martin Garralaga (Gonzales); Alberto Morin (Carlos); Rudolfo Hoyos, Jr. (Pedro, the Bartender); Lillian Molieri (Mexican Girl); Marie Delgado, Juli Loffredo, Frances Dominguez, Tina Menard (Women).

TO CATCH A THIEF *(Paramount, 1955)* C-97 min.

Producer/director, Alfred Hitchcock; based on the novel by David Dodge; screenplay, John Michael Hayes; second unit director, Herbert Coleman; art directors, Hal Pereira, Joseph MacMillan Johnson; set decorators, Sam Comer, Arthur Krams; music, Lyn Murray; assistant director, Daniel McCauley; costumes, Edith Head; Technicolor consultant, Richard Mueller; sound, Lewis and John Cope;

special effects, John P. Fulton; process camera, Farciot Edouart; camera, Robert Burks; second unit camera, Wallace Kelley; editor, George Tomasini.

Cary Grant (John Robie); Grace Kelly (Frances Stevens); Jessie Royce Landis (Mrs. Stevens); John Williams (H. H. Hughson); Charles Vanel (Bertani); Brigitte Auber (Danielle); Jean Martinelli (Foussard); Georgette Anys (Germaine); Roland Lesaffre (Claude); Jean Hebey (Mercier); Rene Blancard (Lepic); Wee Willie Davis (Big Man in Kitchen); Edward Manouk (Kitchen Help); Russell Gaige (Mr. Sanford); Marie Stoddard (Mrs. Sanford); Paul "Tiny" Newlan (Vegetable Man in Kitchen); Alfred Hitchcock (Solemn Bus Passenger); Loulette Sablon, Nina Borget (Frenchwomen); Barry Norton, Cosmo Sardo (Frenchmen); George Adrian (Detective); Louis Mercier, Manuel Paris, George A. Nardelli, George Paris (Croupiers); Philip Van Zandt (Jewelry Clerk); Steven Geray (Desk Clerk); Adele St. Maur (Woman with Bird Cage).

THE SWAN *(MGM, 1956)* C-112 min.

Producer, Dore Schary; director, Charles Vidor; based on the play by Ferenc Molnar; screenplay, John Dighton; art directors, Cedric Gibbons, Randall Duell; music, Bronislau Kaper; costumes, Helen Rose; assistant director, Ridgeway Callow; camera, Joseph Ruttenberg, Robert Surtees; editor, John Dunning.

Grace Kelly (Princess Alexandra); Alec Guinness (Prince Albert); Louis Jourdan (Dr. Nicholas Agi); Agnes Moorehead (Queen Maria Dominika); Jessie Royce Landis (Princess Beatrix); Brian Aherne (Father Hyacinth); Leo G. Carroll (Caesar); Estelle Winwood (Symphorosa); Van Dyke Parks (George); Christopher Cook (Arsene); Robert Coote (Captain Wunderlich); Doris Lloyd (Countess Sigenstoyn); Edith Barrett (Beatrix's Maid).

HIGH SOCIETY *(MGM, 1956)* C-107 min.

Producer, Sol C. Siegel; director, Charles Walters; based on the play *The Philadelphia Story* by Philip Barry; screenplay, John Patrick; songs, Cole Porter; music supervisors/adaptors, Johnny Green, Saul Chaplin; music director, Green; orchestrators, Conrad Salinger, Nelson Riddle; additional orchestrators, Robert Franklyn, Albert Senrey; music numbers staged by Charles Walters; art directors, Cedric Gibbons, Hans Peters; set decorators, Edwin B. Willis, Richard Pefferle; costumes, Helen Rose; makeup, William Tuttle; recording supervisor, Dr. Wesley C. Miller; assistant director, Arvid Griffen; special effects, A. Arnold Gillespie; camera, Paul C. Vogel; editor, Ralph E. Winters.

Bing Crosby (C. K. Dexter-Haven); Grace Kelly (Tracy Lord); Frank Sinatra (Mike Connor); Celeste Holm (Liz Imbrie); John Lund (George Kittredge); Louis Calhern (Uncle Willie); Sidney Blackmer (Seth Lord); Margalo Gillmore (Mrs. Seth Lord); Louis Armstrong (Himself); Lydia Reed (Caroline Lord); Gordon Richards (Dexter-Haven's Butler); Richard Garrick (Lord's Butler); Richard Keene (Mac); Ruth Lee, Helen Spring (Matrons); Paul Keast (Editor); Reginald Simpson (Uncle Willie's Butler); Hugh Boswell (Parson).

THE CHILDREN OF THEATRE STREET (*Pepper-corn-Wormser, 1977*) C-90 min.

Producer, Earle Mack; associate producer, Jean Dalrymple; directors, Robert Dornhelm, Mack; screenplay, Beth Gutcheon; artistic director, Oleg Briansky; camera, Karl Kofler; editor, Tina Frese.

Princess Grace (Narrator); featuring the students and faculty of the Vaganova Choreographic Institute, including: Angelina Armeiskaya, Alec Timoushin, Lena Voronzova, Michaela Cerna, and Galina Messenzeva; and Konstantine Zaklinsky of the Kirov Ballet.

ELIZABETH TAYLOR

Cheesecake, 1954-style.

300

CHAPTER 6

Elizabeth Taylor

5' 4"
115 pounds
Black hair
Violet eyes
Pisces

TO ME, ACTING is a matter of absolute concentration. You can laugh and giggle with your friends up to the minute the director says, "Action!" Then you snap your mind into shape and into the character that you're playing and relate to the people that you're acting with and forget everybody else that you've been joking with. This, I suppose, is inside training, as I've never had an acting lesson.

So reasons Elizabeth Taylor, undoubtedly one of the most photographed and discussed personalities of the twentieth century. Since before the age of twelve, she has been in front of the motion picture and still cameras constantly, proving again and again that she is one of the pulchritudinous wonders of this or any era. Interestingly, she generally has the sense not to be overly impressed with her world-famed glamour image. She admitted a few years ago,

I don't think I am a beautiful woman. Ava Gardner is. I think Audrey Hepburn is. But the way I look is all right with me. Because I want to be me. I don't take vitamins or do exercise. I can lose weight when I want to, mainly by just not eating.

301

Over the years her past husbands have made snippy appraisals of their ex-wife, the superstar:

Nicky Hilton: . . . [I] have never seen such beauty in my life. But God, she can be difficult.
Michael Wilding: The real tragedy with Liz is that there is not a man in the world that she cannot have at the snap of her fingers.
Mike Todd: Unbelievable beauty. . . . You know she has a bit of the pioneer spirit to her. I have often seen her pour her own champagne for breakfast.
Eddie Fisher: She tried to help me with my drug problem. Beautiful, of course. . . . Then you had to give her a diamond before breakfast every day.
Richard Burton: There is no guile or hideous scheme known to women that she is unable to employ. She is a great charmer, cajoler, [and] flatterer, and [she's] crafty. And she is breathtakingly beautiful. . . . We love each other but we can't live together.

This cinema femme fatale who was part of MGM's beauty trio (with Lana Turner and Ava Gardner) in the Forties and Fifties has won two Academy Awards, stunning the critics and public alike with her dramatic prowess. As she has confessed, "Acting is hard work and hard work is good for one." She reasons, "If I thought my career had reached a plateau, it would be very dismal," which explains why this celebrated celluloid charmer will probably never retire from the limelight.

In an intriguing investigation of the "real" Elizabeth Taylor, Max Lerner wrote in a *McCall's* magazine article,

She is distant, yet close; flamboyant, yet homey; unconventional, yet highly moral; romantic, but with some solid investments in her portfolio. In short, she is the good-bad girl who gives the audience a sense of breaking the bounds of daily life without casting loose from all moorings.

Today Elizabeth seldom does things in a small or quiet manner. Yet on Saturday, February 27, 1932, the eight-and-a-half-pound daughter of Francis and Sara Taylor was born in London *without* international fanfare. Christened Elizabeth Rosemond, she was preceded by a brother, Howard, born in 1929. Of her newborn daughter who would be hailed ultimately for her classic beauty, Sara Taylor commented, "She was the funniest looking little baby I've ever seen. Her hair was long and black. Her ears were covered with a thick black fuzz. Her nose looked like a tip-tilted button. And her tiny face was so tightly closed, it looked as if it would never unfold."

At the time of their daughter's birth, the Taylors were American residents living in England. Her mother, Sara Warmbrodt, was born in Kansas City, Kansas, and acted professionally with a Los Angeles stock company under the stage name of Sara Sothern. In 1922 she appeared in New York's Times Square Theatre in Channing Pollock's *The Fool,* playing opposite James Kirkwood. After continued dabbling with a theatre career, Sara married Illinois-born Francis Taylor, nephew of millionaire art dealer Howard Taylor. Francis represented his uncle in London and managed a gallery at 35 Old Bond Street.

Elizabeth's first homes were Heathwood in London's Hampstead section and a country residence, Little Swallows, in Kent. In 1935, three-year-old Elizabeth received her first pony, Betty, and began ballet lessons under Madame Vaccani. That same year Elizabeth's first performance occurred when she danced the role of a little angel for Elizabeth, Duchess of York, and

At the age of two.

Eight-year-old Elizabeth with brother Howard and their dog, Spot.

her daughters, the Princesses Elizabeth and Margaret Rose. This comfortable familial lifestyle characterized the girl's first seven years.

Had Elizabeth remained in England, she might never have had a film career. With the outbreak of war imminent in Europe, however, Francis Taylor arranged for his wife and children to join the Warmbrodts in Pasadena, California, in May 1939. During her early weeks in southern California, where most people were movie-conscious and not global politics-oriented, it was suggested on several occasions that Sara have Elizabeth test for the role of Bonnie Blue Butler in *Gone with the Wind* (1939) because of the child's resemblance to star Vivien Leigh. Neither Sara nor Francis considered acting careers for their offspring and the *Gone with the Wind* gambit was vetoed. Years later Sara would comment, "If I had to do it over again, Elizabeth would not be in pictures. I would not allow it. . . . I think she has had so many heartaches she might not have had if she'd been just a girl at home. . . ."

Late in 1939, Francis rejoined his family and opened an art gallery in Hollywood's Chateau Elysee. An early visitor to Taylor's gallery was Andrea Berens who had come to view a display of the British portrait painter Augustus Johns. During her gallery session, Miss Berens was introduced to Sara and Elizabeth who happened to drop by for a visit. Miss Berens was so captivated by Elizabeth that she insisted that the child meet her fiancé, Cheever Cowdin, chairman of the Board of Directors at Universal Pictures.

Cowdin was equally taken by Elizabeth's innate charm and suggested that the child be given a screen test. Before arrangements could be made at Universal, Elizabeth attended her regular voice lesson with Andre De Segurola and had a chance encounter with Carmen Considine, wife of MGM producer John W. Considine, Jr. Elizabeth soon found herself singing for Considine at Metro-Goldwyn-Mayer and then was ushered into the offices of studio chief Louis B. Mayer. After meeting the girl, Mayer, who would be responsible for discovering such child stars as Judy Garland, Freddie Bartholomew, and Margaret O'Brien, bellowed, "Well . . . what are you waiting for? Sign her up! Sign her up!"

Without being subjected to the traditional

screen test, Elizabeth received an MGM offer for a seven-year pact at $100 weekly: Sara and Francis, still quite reluctant to commit their gentle daughter to a film career, rebuffed Considine by informing him that they had promised Universal's Cheever Cowdin a screen test before any commitments were made. Universal doubled MGM's offer and in June 1941 Elizabeth signed with the former studio in spite of the fact that she felt a more positive response at MGM.

In September 1941 Elizabeth spent three bewildering days working on a film titled *Man or Mouse* which starred Hugh Herbert, Guy Kibbee, and Edgar Kennedy. Retitled *There's One Born Every Minute,* the picture was released in August 1942 for a brief, undistinguished run.* By then Elizabeth's contract had been dropped and her days as an actress came to an abrupt halt.

A second "chance encounter" in the summer of 1942 gave Elizabeth another opportunity to score oncamera. MGM was preparing a film version of the Eric Knight novel *Lassie Come Home* (1943) featuring Donald Crisp, Edmund Gwenn, Dame May Whitty, Roddy McDowall, and, of course, Lassie the dog. Producer Samuel Marx and Francis Taylor met while walking their Beverly Hills neighborhood on air raid duty. When Taylor inquired about the progress of Marx's film, the producer reported that the child set to portray Nigel Bruce's granddaughter was too tall to play opposite Master McDowall and would have to be replaced. Francis suggested Elizabeth and the next day a test was arranged which resulted in Elizabeth outdistancing the five other contenders for the role. Elizabeth's seven years of living in England compounded with her love for animals made her a natural selection for the part of Priscilla. She portrayed the part with considerable professionalism for her nine years, displaying a winning quality. However, the canine Lassie still managed to steal the color picture. Elizabeth, at least, received a term contract with the lofty studio.

*In this mini-screwball comedy, Elizabeth was countercast as a brat and, although a nonsinger (as the later *Cynthia,* 1947, would conclusively prove), she was forced to "sing" a duet with Carl "Alfalfa" Switzer. Almost needless to say, in such a bit of miscasting the young Miss Taylor made little impression on anyone at the lot or on the few moviegoers who managed to see the cheapie film.

Since most juvenile vehicles on the Culver City lot were being geared to the talents of contractees Margaret O'Brien and Jackie "Butch" Jenkins, it was decided to loan Elizabeth to Twentieth Century-Fox for the screen version of Charlotte Bronte's *Jane Eyre* (1944). In this literate but rather unmoving version of the classic novel, Elizabeth portrayed Helen Burns, a friend of the young Jane played by Peggy Ann Garner. Elizabeth received no billing for her relatively brief assignment which called for her to endure punishments such as having her hair shorn and standing in a downpour which results in her death from pneumonia.

Back on the home lot, the now seasoned Elizabeth was rushed into the prestigious *The White Cliffs of Dover* (1944), based on the Alice Duer Miller poem and starring Irene Dunne and Alan Marshal. Elizabeth portrayed Betsy, the neighbor child who loves Roddy McDowall. In this paean to England's glory and fortitude, Elizabeth's and Roddy's characters were played by June Lockhart and Peter Lawford in the second half of the film.

Elizabeth's four minor film roles gave her the experience and initiative to pursue her next film role. Producer Pandro S. Berman was preparing Enid Bagnold's 1935 novel *National Velvet* and casting the pivotal role of Velvet Brown proved a problem which was delaying production considerably. The motion picture revolves around the daughter of a rural English butcher (Donald Crisp) who wins a horse called "The Pi" in a raffle and grooms and trains him for England's Grand National Steeplechase in which she rides disguised as a boy.

Elizabeth considered herself a natural choice for the role, listing her age, skill with horses, and English accent as decided assets for producer Berman. Her attributes quickly paled when Berman pointed out that she lacked the proper height, weight, and strength to tackle the demanding role. Elizabeth left Berman's office undaunted and imposed a severe self-regimen which included exercise, increased diet, and plenty of sleep. Within three months she had grown three inches in height and gained fifteen pounds. She won the part!

Production began on Friday, February 4, 1944, under Clarence Brown's direction with Elizabeth in the cinema part that would establish her Hollywood position. *National Velvet* completed post-production in October and went into pre-national release at Radio City Music Hall as the 1944 Christmas attraction. Also featured in the film along with Elizabeth and Crisp were Mickey Rooney, Anne Revere, Reginald Owen, and, in the role of Miss Taylor's older sister, another British refugee, Angela Lansbury.

Of this feature which went on to gross over $4,050,000 in distributors' domestic rentals, Bosley Crowther (*New York Times*) penned, "Mr. Brown has drawn some excellent performances from his cast, especially from little Elizabeth Taylor, who plays the role of the horse-loving girl. Her face is alive with youthful spirit, her voice has the softness of sweet song, and her whole manner in this picture is one of refreshing grace." (Scenes from *National Velvet,* showing Elizabeth and the horse, would be included in the documentary feature *It's Showtime,* 1976.)

In the 1945 Oscar race, Anne Revere captured the Best Supporting Actress Award and Robert J. Kern, also of *National Velvet,* was honored for his editing. Undoubtedly Elizabeth was a strong contender for the Juvenile Oscar which went to her *Jane Eyre* co-star, Peggy Ann Garner, for a stunning performance in *A Tree Grows in Brooklyn.*

At the age of thirteen, when most girls are primarily concerned with adjusting to adolescence, Elizabeth had an MGM contract, a $750 weekly salary, and a smash hit picture, *National Velvet.* Looking back on this period of her life, she would observe, "Being in films then was like the most magical extension of make-believe. It didn't occur to me that it was a career and that I was working for money. I think *Velvet* is still the most exciting film I've ever done. And at the end, to be given the horse on my thirteenth birthday—well, it was one of *the* moments of my life."

Not wishing to break the safe chain of typecasting, Elizabeth was next cast as the teenage lead in *Courage of Lassie,* released in November 1946. The *New York Times* commended the producers for "fashioning a tender and sometimes poignant story about the great love of a dog for its owner," but reprimanded the film-

With Lassie and Frank Morgan in *Courage of Lassie* ('46).

With Mickey Rooney, Donald Crisp, and Anne Revere in *National Velvet* ('44).

makers for adding "a topical twist in which our canine friend becomes a war hero and returns maladjusted. And it is this combination of elemental animal yarn and latter-day heroics which somehow blur this otherwise pretty picture." The *Times* perceptively hit upon the most pertinent asset of Elizabeth's child acting: she was "refreshingly natural." When one recalls the slew of coy, coached, cautious juvenile performers who have marred films and their own careers, one can doubly appreciate the nonchalance of already lilting Elizabeth. *Courage of Lassie* marked the third and final time she would share the screen with an animal co-star.

At this point in her career Elizabeth exerted her own authority with famed studio boss Louis B. Mayer. Rumor on the lot had it that Metro's new youth star would be featured in a film called *Sally in Her Alley* which would require her to sing and dance. Elizabeth and mother Sara made an appointment to meet with Mayer regarding the special lessons which Elizabeth would require. Mayer exploded at what he felt was an audacious suggestion of how he should manage studio affairs of which Elizabeth was only one of very many. His verbal attack was salted with profanity which humiliated Sara. Elizabeth jumped to her mother's defense, screaming, "Don't you dare speak to my mother like that! You and your studio can both go to hell!" With that she bolted from his office in tears. When advised to apologize, Elizabeth refused, feeling that Mayer's inhumanity had provoked her loss of temper. Although her actions amazingly didn't cost her her studio job, Elizabeth refused to enter Mayer's office again—a vow she would keep. Yet decades later she would consent to hostess a segment of *That's Entertainment!*, 1974, a tribute to the glories of MGM.

While Elizabeth was experiencing trauma at the studio, her home life proceeded at a reasonable keel—that is, for the household of a young movie star. She wrote a book entitled *Nibbles and Me*, dealing in unpretentious terms with her abiding passion for chipmunks. On her fourteenth birthday, she was presented with her very own car. A multi-talented young lady, she dabbled in painting and even sold a canvas (more likely for her signature than for the execution of the subject matter). And with the prod-

ding of the studio publicity department, the public was not allowed to forget that in Hollywood there existed that most perfect of creatures: an unspoiled teenage heavenly dream named Elizabeth Taylor. Each day's mail to the Metro lot brought Elizabeth numerous invitations to high school proms, requests for autographed photos, etc. Thanks to her beauty, her naturalness, and the film company's ingenuity and bankroll, Miss Elizabeth Taylor was a household name.

When Elizabeth had been making *There's One Born Every Minute* at Universal, the studio casting director had admonished, "The kid has nothing. . . . Her eyes are too old; she doesn't have the face of a kid." Now, as she approached her fifteenth year, not only was her countenance maturing, but so was her shapely body. No longer a child and not yet an adult, the studio remained wisely cautious in exploiting her presence oncamera, fearful of exhausting her box-office welcome before she developed into a full adult. (Plans to send her to RKO to join Britisher John Mills in a version of John Galsworthy's *The Apple Tree* did not materialize.)

Her next film project was while on loan to Warner Bros., to portray Mary Skinner in *Life with Father* (1947). That studio seemingly spared little expense in transferring the Howard Lindsay-Russel Crouse comedy bonanza from Broadway to the screen. Michael Curtiz directed the Technicolor vehicle in an expansive style, with William Powell (also on loan from MGM) cast as Clarence Day, that irascible 1880s New Yorker who is finally baptized thanks to the love and endurance of his patient spouse, Vinnie (Irene Dunne). Within the context of the rich domestic comedy, Elizabeth's Mary is the country cousin who comes to visit the Day family and promptly begins to flirt with Clarence, Jr. (Jimmy Lydon). Before she and her companion Cora (ZaSu Pitts) depart the big city, Mary coquettishly tries to exert a promise from bewildered Clarence, Jr. that he unflinchingly loves her and that he will be the *first* one to write to her.

When her work ended at Warners, Elizabeth found herself cast in the title role of *Cynthia* back at MGM. Elizabeth portrayed a sickly girl who is overprotected by parents George Murphy and Mary Astor. Elizabeth receives an invitation to the school prom from James Lydon and proves to the family that she can function without their sheltering. *Cynthia* marked Elizabeth's first "adult" screen kiss and MGM milked the occasion for full publicity. Critics generally dismissed the shallow proceedings of *Cynthia* just as they had pronounced its Broadway predecessor, *The Rich Full Life,* a flop in 1945. Elizabeth's performance* was excluded from captious comments as evidenced by Howard Barnes (*New York Herald-Tribune*) who noted, "Miss Taylor does a brilliant job with the title role. In vivid contrast to Hollywood's general conception of the bobby-soxer, she plays an unwilling invalid with grave charm. The scenes in which she has her first taste of the rich, full life are interpreted with subtle authority."

Although *Cynthia* was filmed after *Life with Father,* it was released in July 1947 while her earlier Warner Bros. film was distributed a month later. Metro had some screen plans for Elizabeth that year, but they never materialized. Producer Pandro S. Berman assigned Ted Reeves to script a screen adaptation of W. H. Hudson's extraordinary novel *Green Mansions* with Elizabeth to be cast as Rima the Bird Girl. But the project fumbled and died. (The property was revived in the early Fifties when Metro's Pier Angeli was to star as Rima. Finally in 1959 MGM produced *Green Mansions* with Audrey Hepburn in the lead role.)

Strangely, *Cynthia* would prove to be Elizabeth's last starring role until *Conspirator* in 1950. Meanwhile, the studio utilized her in another bit of ersatz teenage life. The property was *A Date with Judy* (1948) and it was young singing star Jane Powell who had the title role. Elizabeth was cast as Jane's sister Carol, involved in extricating gruff but loveable Dad (Wallace Beery) from an alleged romance with South American dancing instructress Rosita Conchellas (Carmen Miranda). At sixteen,

Elizabeth was a strikingly beautiful young woman, a fact which was reiterated in each frame of her *A Date with Judy* footage. Otis L. Guernsey, Jr. *(New York Herald-Tribune)* confirmed, "The big surprise . . . is Elizabeth Taylor as the petulant dark-eyed banker's daughter. The erstwhile child star of *National Velvet* and other films has been touched by Metro's magic wand and turned into a real, 14-carat, 100-proof siren with a whole new career opening in front of her. . . . Judging from this picture Hedy Lamarr had better watch out with Miss Taylor coming along."

In her nine features within six years Elizabeth passed from child to adolescent to woman without leaving many awkward frames behind in the transition.

MGM dusted off Margery Sharp's novel *The Nutmeg Tree* as a change-of-pace vehicle for the studio's Mrs. Miniver, Greer Garson, who was stagnating in the succession of lofty, soul-suffering creatures she had been portraying on-camera throughout the Forties. The title role in *Julia Misbehaves* (1948) proved to be more detrimental than beneficial to Miss Garson's career. Miss Garson portrayed a fun-loving woman who deserts spouse Walter Pidgeon for a career in London music halls. Eighteen years later she returns for daughter Elizabeth Taylor's wedding. The slapstick comedy finds Greer as part of an acrobatic act, taking a bath oncamera, and tumbling into a puddle of mud. In the midst of these shocking displays of unladylike behavior, daughter Susan Packett (Elizabeth) receives her second screen kiss—this one from Peter Lawford with whom she was slightly infatuated offcamera. Since nearly all the film's action was focused on rambunctious Miss Garson, Elizabeth was shunted to the sidelines, trotted out here and there to look ravishingly pretty and to be saved in the nick of romantic time from marrying the wrong man. While reviewers of the day were disappointed with this Garson-Pidgeon vehicle, they did comment on the pulchritudinous Elizabeth who, stated the *New York Herald-Tribune*'s scribe, "has developed into one of the cinema's reigning queens of beauty and talent."

Her convincing onscreen love scenes prompted MGM to prepare adult properties for their

---

*In *Elizabeth Taylor* (Pyramid, 1973), Foster Hirsch analyzes this film: "As in *Jane Eyre,* Taylor is cast as an ethereal beauty. The part bears no resemblance to Elizabeth Taylor in her latest shrew phase, but it does effectively exploit her early image as a young girl set apart from other kids. The role of lonely Cynthia complemented the Taylor publicity of the time: because she was a famous movie actress, young Liz was isolated from others her own age. Other teenagers were either afraid or jealous of her, and if you believe the *Photoplay* gossip of the time, Elizabeth had trouble getting a date."

blossoming starlet. But first she was rushed into a remake of the Louisa May Alcott classic, *Little Women*. In 1933 RKO had had a hit with Katharine Hepburn, Jean Parker, Frances Dee, and Joan Bennett as the March sisters: Jo, Beth, Meg, and Amy. In the late summer of 1946 David O. Selznick planned to remake the property under Mervyn LeRoy's direction with Jennifer Jones (Jo), Diana Lynn (Amy), Bambi Linn (Beth), Rhonda Fleming (Meg), John Dall (Laurie), and Anne Revere (Marmee). Then, due in part to post-World War II retrenchment and part whimsy, Selznick abandoned the project and sold the rights to Metro. LeRoy was assigned to direct a cast that now included June Allyson (Jo), Peter Lawford (Laurie), Margaret O'Brien (Beth), Janet Leigh (Meg), and Elizabeth as Amy. Topped with a wig of long blonde curls, Elizabeth portrayed the March sister who marries Jo's beau, Laurie. The RKO version was a tough act to follow and MGM's saccharine send-up in color and frills emphasized the soggy elements of the rehashed script.

Shooting on the new *Little Women* concluded in September 1948 and was distributed to theatres as 1949's Easter attraction. In an uncharacteristically silly yet delightful performance, Elizabeth blended into the picture postcard settings, doing her share to recreate the Alcott classic 1940s' style. With this film, Elizabeth terminated her adolescent roles at MGM and moved on to screen womanhood.

Her personal life at this point also took on a new maturity. Heretofore Elizabeth had had arranged dates with young MGM contract actor Marshall Thompson but nothing lasting had materialized in their relationship. During the summer of 1948, sixteen-year-old Elizabeth met twenty-four-year-old athlete Glenn Davis who was about to embark on a tour of duty in Korea. The pair dated over the summer much to the delight of the press and Elizabeth's growing legions of fans. When Davis left for Korea, Elizabeth had his miniature gold football, his All-American sweater, his "A" pin, and a replica of his West Point ring. She explained the ramifications of these possessions with, "We're engaged to be engaged."

In October 1948 Elizabeth received a salary boost to $1,000 a week and sailed for England to begin filming *Conspirator* in which she was co-starred with another Taylor, the adult, still very handsome Robert. The Victor Saville-directed feature had a dual purpose: it was geared to show America and the world that MGM was patriotic in its anti-Communist zeal and that not only were confirmed Reds not human, but they would meet a disastrous end (in this case Robert Taylor as the Communist eventually destroys himself, shattered between his devotion to the Party cause and his love of wife Elizabeth). The other *raison d'être* was to professionally lead Elizabeth from adolescent roles into screen maturity. Since the film, with good cause, would be so rightly overlooked in years to come, a good many devout moviegoers would miss the adroitly handled celluloid transformation of *Cynthia* into adulthood as Melinda Greyton.

Within this sappy, one-dimensional study, Elizabeth is a perky American debutante living in post-war London. Much like many of her earlier screen characterizations, her Melinda is an unpretentious, self-oriented young woman who enjoys the finer things of life and has little time or thought for anything more meaningful than a productive shopping spree. Then she meets Major Michael Curragh (Robert Taylor) who responds to her winning, attractive ways. After they are wed she discovers that her serviceman spouse is actually a Russian agent. A better American than a loyal wife, she realizes she must turn over her husband to the proper authorities. If this brief synopsis of the picture sounds like treacle, the film is far more so, burying the subtle metamorphosis of Elizabeth's screen persona beneath an inept script and Robert Taylor's unfortunately wooden performance.

While making *Conspirator* at the Elstree Studios—part of Metro's corporate policy to diversify its filmmaking abroad and to use up frozen post-World War II funds—Elizabeth's offcamera hours were spent with school lessons, letters to Glenn Davis, and a Parisian shopping spree with her constant chaperone, Sara. While shooting the film at Elstree, Elizabeth developed a crush on British actor Michael Wilding whom she spotted in the commissary. Elizabeth indulged in a slight flirtation with this tall, lean

With Margaret O'Brien, Janet Leigh, and June Allyson in *Little Women* ('49).

With Robert Taylor in *Conspirator* ('50).

At the March 1949 Oscarcast with Glenn Davis.

311

British performer but her heart, for the moment, still belonged to Glenn Davis.

Production on *Conspirator* ended in February 1949 and Elizabeth returned to the United States to celebrate her seventeenth birthday while MGM struggled to assemble the pieces of Elizabeth's first adult role. The studio, now under the aegis of Dore Schary and his message regime, held the picture for thirteen months before releasing it to disappointing reviews in February 1950. (Plans for Elizabeth to co-star with Lana Turner and Margaret O'Brien in a version of Esther Forbes' novel, *The Running of the Tide,* did not materialize.)

While visiting relatives in Florida, Elizabeth became acquainted with twenty-eight-year-old William Pawley, Jr., son of the former ambassador to Brazil. Pawley quickly took over Glenn Davis' position as the man in Elizabeth's life. By June 1949, Elizabeth lost her role in the projected *Quo Vadis** due to several scheduling complications, not the least of which involved the Los Angeles Board of Education's decision to confine Elizabeth's studies to Culver City. In losing a film, Elizabeth gained a fiancé as Pawley presented her with a 3.5-carat diamond ring which she wore over the summer while she filmed *The Big Hangover* (1950) with Van Johnson.

While Elizabeth was consumed with her various romances, the *Harvard Lampoon* took the occasion to remind her that she was a distinguished film celebrity of one sort or another. They announced her as the victor of its annual prize "for so gallantly persisting in her career despite a total inability to act," selecting her as "the most objectionable ingenue." Adding insult to injury they summed up her career to that date by insisting she was one of the two "most objectionable movie children."

In the arena of *l'amour,* Elizabeth was not faring very well. Her career plans were not compatible with Pawley's idea of a dutiful, domesticated, pre-women's-lib wife. The engagement ended and the press took her to task for the first time with the insinuation that she

was nothing more than a temptress and a siren. Innocently commenting on her first press scandal, Elizabeth confessed, "If I were the kind of person they write me up to be, I'd hate myself."

After her romantic break with Pawley, Elizabeth was linked with Howard Hughes,* Roddy McDowall, Vic Damone, Montgomery Clift,** and Pittsburgh Pirate outfielder Ralph Kiner, all of whom she dated before meeting Conrad Nicholson Hilton, Jr. in October 1949. Nicky Hilton, at age twenty-two, was the eldest son of hotel magnate Conrad Hilton. He conducted a six-month whirlwind courtship during which Elizabeth would graduate from high school and have her third engagement announced.

Sara Taylor disclosed in February 1950 that Elizabeth would marry Nicky Hilton, a fact which pleased MGM since their star had just completed Vincente Minnelli's *Father of the Bride,* a sure-fire property. MGM felt the time was right to sneak *Conspirator* and *The Big Hangover* into release and did so with disastrous results critically. Fortunately the press reserved greater coverage for the Saturday, May 6, 1950 afternoon wedding at the Church of the Good Shepherd in Beverly Hills where a crowd of 2,500 gathered to watch Elizabeth and Nicky and their seven hundred invited V.I.P. guests. Elizabeth's gown, designed by Helen Rose and paid for by MGM, was white with lilies of the valley in seed pearls. Covering her head was a misty white veil on a Juliet cap decorated with seed pearls. Elizabeth's bridesmaids were Barbara Thompson (wife of actor Marshall Thompson), Jane Powell, and Ed Sullivan's daughter, Barbara.

While the newlyweds honeymooned in

---

*Elizabeth would remember decades later of Hughes: "He was crazy. Howard promised to buy me my own movie studio if I married him—plus anything else in the world I wanted."

**Elizabeth's love and devotion to the self-destructive, tormented Montgomery Clift would occupy a good deal of her time and energy over the years. Despite his basically homosexual lifestyle, there were times when Taylor hoped she and Clift might someday, somehow wed. The two celebrities seemed to find a good deal of comfort in one another's company, discussing how Hollywood, friends, and family had exploited them. In later years, although Elizabeth did her best to obtain screen employment for Clift, she had outgrown her need for his attention. Her own life was in such a state of turmoil that she had very little time or energy left to devote to his increasingly desperate emotional and physical state.

---

*When MGM filmed *Quo Vadis* (1951) with Robert Taylor and Deborah Kerr in the leads, Elizabeth would be abroad filming but she managed to make an unscheduled appearance in a Coliseum crowd scene, as did a then still undiscovered Sophia Loren.

With Van Johnson, Fay Holden, Percy Waram, Pierre Watkin, Anna Q. Nilsson, and Gene Lockhart in *The Big Hangover* ('50).

With Marietta Canty, Spencer Tracy, Tom Irish, Rusty Tamblyn, and Joan Bennett in *Father of the Bride* ('50).

Europe, MGM released *Father of the Bride* to resoundingly positive notices for the cast headed by Spencer Tracy, Joan Bennett, and Elizabeth. Otis L. Guernsey, Jr. (*New York Herald-Tribune*) observed, "Elizabeth Taylor's good looks aid her in creating the illusion that in each successive scene the audience, like the father, is seeing her for the 'first time.'" Fortunately this time around she had a far more relaxed Mr. Taylor—Don—playing opposite her.

While *Father of the Bride* settled in for a successful box-office run, the Elizabeth-Nicky marriage came to a crashing halt in divorce court eight months after the exchange of vows. The newlyweds' youth and admitted immaturity, coupled with varied backgrounds, careers, and interests, did little to create a firm bond of matrimony. Nicky stated, "I didn't marry a girl. I married an institution."

Of her first marriage Elizabeth later mused, "I fell off my pink cloud with a thud." The couple parted and on Monday, January 29, 1951, after only 205 days of marriage, Elizabeth obtained a divorce.* Regarding her courtroom testimony, Elizabeth noted, "When I divorced Nick, I said on the witness stand that he had told me to go to hell and insulted my mother and insulted me in front of friends. That was absolutely the smallest, weakest grounds possible, and the only ones I would allow my lawyers to disclose. I could have gone into such a multitude of really horrendous things to make what I was doing understandable. But I didn't want anything from Nick. I didn't want alimony. I certainly didn't want to hurt him."

In retrospect it seems even harder to understand or accept just why Schary's hierarchy at MGM displayed such a cavalier attitude toward Elizabeth's career, shunting her from a meaningless vehicle to an important property, then back again to drivel, without any acknowledgment that there was a difference. That she was now the acknowledged top beauty of the lot was undisputed; the company's publicity department did its best to unleash a barrage of releases concerning her regal look, a tactical approach that Louis B. Mayer and his crew had studiously

avoided in the Forties. If one were to chop Elizabeth's career into segments, the period from 1950 (post-*Little Women*) to 1955 (pre-*Giant*) stands as the low spot of her professional career. It is ironical that in this same time frame she was at the height of her young beauty and malleable enough to have been molded into a gorgeous dramatic actress.

Having scored so fortuitously with *Father of the Bride*, MGM could not resist reassembling the cast: Tracy, Bennett, Elizabeth, Don Taylor, Billie Burke, and Moroni Olsen for another go-round at the madcap adventures of Kay Banks Dunstan (Elizabeth), her parents, in-laws, husband, and now a baby. The vehicle was *Father's Little Dividend* (1951) and Vincente Minnelli again put his competent cast through their delightful paces. The project was filmed within twenty-two days. As Minnelli would recall, "We breezed through the shooting with great humor."

MGM quickly assigned Elizabeth to a bit of fluff entitled *Love Is Better Than Ever*, something that definitely was not true in Elizabeth's life. Under the direction of budding talent Stanley Donen she played another small town lass who decides with predatory haste that big city agent Larry Parks is the man for her and that he had better realize it. Once more it was Elizabeth the apprentice vixen who was displayed oncamera. She was grasping and demanded what she wanted no matter what the results or how the other party might feel. Not only was the finished result soppier than even MGM expected, but co-star Larry Parks, who had been riding the crest of success since his two Al Jolson biography films at Columbia in the late Forties, had now been accused and confessed to having been a member of the Communist party. MGM, despite its pleas of pro-Americanism, refused to scrap the paid-for film and decided to shelve it till a more propitious time.

Nasty souls claimed it was type-casting when George Stevens insisted upon borrowing Elizabeth for his Paramount project, *A Place in the Sun*. After shooting was completed (January 3, 1950), it took the film some eighteen months to reach movie screens. *A Place in the Sun* was the title George Stevens used when he filmed Theodore Dreiser's 1925 novel *An American*

---

*Hilton would die on February 6, 1969, of a heart attack; he was then age forty-two.

314

With groom Nicky Hilton (May 6, 1950).

On the set of *Love Is Better Than Ever* ('52) with Francis and Sara Taylor.

With Josephine Hutchinson in *Love Is Better Than Ever*.

316

*Tragedy.** Stevens also changed the characters' names and updated the story which also starred Montgomery Clift and Shelley Winters.

In casting Elizabeth, Stevens observed, "The part calls for not so much a real girl as the girl on the candy-box cover, the beautiful girl in the yellow Cadillac convertible that every American boy, sometime or other, thinks he can marry."

Under Stevens' meticulous, slow-paced direction, *A Place in the Sun* began production in October 1949 and did not reach viewers until August 1951. No one was much surprised by the ecstatic reviews accorded the feature, and Elizabeth was again at a professional peak after a series of recent clinkers. Otis L. Guernsey, Jr. (*New York Herald-Tribune*) reported, "Elizabeth Taylor's delineation of the rich and beauteous Angela also is the top effort of her career.

---

*In 1931 Paramount released *An American Tragedy,* directed by Josef von Sternberg and starring Phillips Holmes, Sylvia Sidney, and Frances Dee, the latter in the role parallel to the one Elizabeth later played.

It is a shaded, tender performance and one in which her passionate and genuine romance avoids the bathos common to young love as it sometimes comes to the screen."

In the 1951 Oscar race, *A Place in the Sun* was nominated as Best Film but lost to MGM's *An American in Paris*. Likewise, nominees Montgomery Clift and Shelley Winters failed to capture the acting awards. George Stevens, however, received an Oscar for his expertise in directing. Other Academy Award winners from the film were screen-writers Michael Wilson and Harry Brown, cinematographer William C. Mellor, costumer Edith Head, musical score composer Franz Waxman, and film editor William Hornbeck.

When greeted by her *A Place in the Sun* notices, Elizabeth was in England filming *Ivanhoe* (1952). (A benevolent MGM determined that a change of scenery would be just the thing for Elizabeth after her divorce.) In the film, based on Sir Walter Scott's panoramic historical novel, Elizabeth played Rebecca, the Jewess, with Robert Taylor in the title role and aristo-

With Montgomery Clift in *A Place in the Sun* ('51).

With Robert Taylor in *Ivanhoe* ('52).

318

cratic Joan Fontaine as the regal Rowena. During her sojourn in England, Elizabeth met Michael Wilding with whom she had flirted a few years earlier while filming *Conspirator*. At thirty-nine, Wilding was nearly twice Elizabeth's age and seemingly possessed the charm, wit, and nimble strength she so admired in a man. By the time *Ivanhoe* had its lavish production values wrapped, Elizabeth publicly admitted her love for Wilding before returning to New York in October 1951.*

By December, Michael was in Hollywood to promote a film and the couple, much to only a few people's surprise, announced their engagement. On Thursday, February 21, 1952, Elizabeth and Michael were married in London's Caxton Hall. Wilding's frequent co-star Anna Neagle and her producer/director husband Herbert Wilcox were witnesses. Helen Rose of MGM designed the bride's attire which consisted of a gray wool suit with a white organdy rolled collar and cuffs. Elizabeth celebrated her twentieth birthday while honeymooning in the French Alps.

During the crush of fresh publicity concerning beauteous Elizabeth, MGM took the opportunity to slip *Love Is Better Than Ever* into release. The studio released the film on a double-bill and it received the "boos" that most everyone had anticipated. Bosley Crowther alerted *New York Times'* readers, "The presence of the new and muchly pictured Mrs. Michael Wilding in the cast of *Love Is Better Than Ever* . . . is the only remotely valid reason . . . for spending an hour and twenty minutes looking at this film." (By this point, alleged Communist Larry Parks was fighting desperately to salvage something of his career by taking stock engagements here and abroad.)

Shortly after her marriage to Wilding, Elizabeth who seemingly held no grudges against the Dore Schary-MGM regime signed a new studio contract. Her then $1,500 weekly salary escalated immediately to $5,000; a year later the pact would be renegotiated yet again, extending the term for five additional years without options

and providing for three films per year. Despite the on-the-lot competition* Elizabeth was riding a crest of studio and public popularity.

With typical Hollywood abandon, Metro thoughtlessly cast her in *The Girl Who Had Everything* (1953). Beyond its wry title, the film offered little; it was a ghastly remake of a 1931 Norma Shearer vehicle entitled *A Free Soul*. During the course of filming under Richard Thorpe's direction (he had guided Elizabeth through *Ivanhoe*), Elizabeth jubilantly announced her pregnancy. On Tuesday, January 6, 1953, Michael Howard Wilding was born via cesarean section at the Santa Monica Hospital. Elizabeth found herself on suspension during the time she took off for the birth of her child. In April, MGM released *The Girl Who Had Everything* to a unanimously negative reaction; even the usually dapper William Powell seemed listless in his supporting role. Elizabeth scarcely noticed the bad reviews as she was so taken with her new maternal role.

The Wildings purchased a $75,000 Hollywood home nestled in the hills and added $50,000 in renovations. The venture caused Elizabeth to cash in $47,000 in bonds and to borrow the remainder of the sum from MGM. The studio agreed and announced that she was set for the romantic interest in *All the Brothers Were Valiant,* an 1880s whaling epic to co-star Robert Taylor and Stewart Granger. A stubborn Elizabeth held out and received another studio suspension while the role was passed to Ann Blyth.

Meanwhile, negotiations fell through on a project that would star Elizabeth and Cary Grant in *Roman Holiday,* directed by Frank Capra. (It would be made at Paramount starring Audrey Hepburn and Gregory Peck under Billy Wilder's direction in 1953 and would win Miss Hepburn an Oscar.) No new projects awaited Elizabeth when production closed down at Paramount on *Elephant Walk* (1954) due to star Vivien Leigh's nervous collapse and subsequent dismissal from the film. Exterior scenes filmed in Ceylon were retained (including long shots of Miss Leigh) by

---

*MGM had wanted Elizabeth and Ava Gardner for *Scaramouche* (1952), but it would be Janet Leigh and Eleanor Parker who joined Stewart Granger and Mel Ferrer in this glossy swashbuckler film.

*Among the beautiful actresses on the lot were Lana Turner, Ava Gardner, Eleanor Parker, Deborah Kerr, Esther Williams, Leslie Caron, Jane Powell, Ann Blyth, Debbie Reynolds, and the about-to-depart Greer Garson, June Allyson, Janet Leigh, and Kathryn Grayson. Grace Kelly had yet to make her meteoric debut.

With husband Michael Wilding in London (February 22, 1952).

With William Powell in *The Girl Who Had Everything* ('53).

replacing Vivien with Elizabeth who accepted the role after refusals by Katharine Hepburn, Jean Simmons, and Olivia de Havilland.

In *Elephant Walk,* Elizabeth played Peter Finch's wife who is caught up in a cross-culture conflict that climaxes with rampaging elephants. The film ended in May 1953 and injury-prone Elizabeth found herself hospitalized when a thin piece of flint became embedded in her eye causing a serious infection.

In June she was out of the hospital and into a shooting schedule for *Rhapsody* (1954) which ended in August and made it into release a month before *Elephant Walk.* Neither film venture gave her the opportunity to do anything but look beautiful in posh settings and lavish wardrobes. Of her *Rhapsody* performance, Bosley Crowther (*New York Times*) annotated, "Miss Taylor never looked lovelier than she does in this high-minded film, which is all wrapped up in music on the starry-eyed classical plane. Her wind-blown black hair frames her features like an ebony aureole, and her large eyes and red lips glistened warmly in the close-ups on the softly lighted screen."

After a European vacation with Michael, Elizabeth remained in England to film *Beau Brummel* (1954) opposite Stewart Granger. Elizabeth replaced originally slated star Eleanor Parker who was on a loan-out to Paramount. Meticulous details went into the Curtis Bernhardt-directed *Beau Brummel,* making it a visual color feast but, like so many MGM historical epics, void of needed drama and viewpoint. Elizabeth appeared briefly in a blonde wig which shoved her performance further into artificiality. Later sequences displayed her own dark tresses to much greater advantage. The critics attacked *Beau Brummel,* especially the British press when the film turned up at the 1954 Royal Command Performance where it was greeted as "Bore Brummel."

Recalling the half-dozen films she made after *A Place in the Sun,* Elizabeth revealed, "All I did was just sort of whistle and hum my way through those films, powdering my nose and getting a great kick out of wearing pretty clothes—dying to wear more makeup, higher heels, lower cut dresses. . . . The first time I ever considered acting when I was young was in *A Place in the*

Sun. . . . I felt I had done well and now maybe MGM would give me a break. It gave me a bit of heart, which was soon lost again—lost under a morass of mediocrity. Not just the scripts. I was mediocre, too." *Beau Brummel,* like *Ivanhoe,* proved that Elizabeth was plagued by a too contemporary image to carry historical drama with reality.

The mediocrity ended—at least by some critics' standards—in April 1954 when Elizabeth began filming *The Last Time I Saw Paris,* taken from F. Scott Fitzgerald's poignant short story, "Babylon Revisited."* To give the tale more poignancy for Fifties audiences, the time frame was changed from the Twenties to post-World War II, and bathos was substituted for pathos. With a cast comprising Elizabeth, Van Johnson (her *The Big Hangover* co-star), Walter Pidgeon, and Donna Reed, it proved to be a high-class soap opera. "The soft soap is smeared so smoothly and that old Jerome Kern [title] tune is played so insistently that it may turn the public's heart to toothpaste" (*New York Times*). On the other hand, there were professional viewers such as Otis L. Guernsey, Jr. (*New York Herald-Tribune*) who praised Elizabeth's performance as Helen Ellswirth: "She is not only a stunning creature but a vibrant one as she flings herself into the role of an impetuous, alluring, pleasure-loving beauty." The film was completed in June and released in November, making it the fourth Elizabeth Taylor project of 1954. Elizabeth took a much-deserved rest which coincided with her second pregnancy. To avoid being placed on suspension—which she could not afford—she added an additional year to her then current studio contract. On Sunday, February 27, 1955—Elizabeth's twenty-third birthday—Christopher Edward Wilding was born at Santa Monica Hospital via cesarean section.

Elizabeth and Michael realized that their first California home would be too cramped for their growing family and menagerie. In addition to Michael and Christopher, the Wildings shared their residence with four dogs, four cats, the

*In 1940, F. Scott Fitzgerald scripted a version of his story for producer Lester Cowan at Columbia, with Shirley Temple scheduled to play the lead role. The project fell through and MGM later bought the screen rights to the Fitzgerald tale.

With Vittorio Gassman in *Rhapsody* ('54).

As Helen Ellswirth in *The Last Time I Saw Paris* ('54).

gelding King Charles from *National Velvet,* and a duck whose favorite perch was Elizabeth's shoulder. The couple purchased a house in Hollywood Canyon for $150,000 and settled in what Elizabeth termed "the most beautiful house I've ever seen."

Her lazy days of quasi-domesticity ended in mid-1955 when she reported to Warner Bros. to begin work on *Giant.* Originally, Grace Kelly had been set for the demanding role of Leslie Benedict, but MGM wanted to keep the currently hot box-office actress busy on the home lot. (In fact, Miss Kelly was assigned the lead in *High Society* opposite Bing Crosby and Frank Sinatra, a part originally intended for Elizabeth.) Thus Elizabeth rejoined her *A Place in the Sun* director George Stevens and a cast that included Rock Hudson, James Dean, and Mercedes McCambridge. In the 1956 Oscar competition, Hudson and Dean were nominated as Best Actor, Mercedes McCambridge as Best Supporting Actress; the film received a nomination as Best Picture, losing to Mike Todd's production of *Around the World in 80 Days.* Only director George Stevens was successful in capturing the Oscar.

Giant was based on Edna Ferber's sweeping novel of the history and growth of Texas and had been in pre-production phases since October 1953. The film covered three decades (1923-1953) in its 198 minutes of screen time and had Elizabeth transformed from a shy eighteen-year-old bride at the beginning to a sophisticated, graying matron—a test of any performer's acting ability. During *Giant's* extensive filming, Elizabeth struck up a close friendship with moody, rebellious James Dean who marked his third major and final film in a role for which Stevens had once considered Richard Burton. Elizabeth also found herself in several explosive situations with painstaking Stevens. In her first encounter with the director she had been a minor and care was taken to keep her protected from the sundry unpleasantries which surfaced on their second professional venture. Speaking of Stevens, Elizabeth stated, "I found out on *Giant. . .* that he tends to like having a patsy or two on a film. Jimmy Dean was one and I was another, but I'll say this for George—he usually picks people who can answer back."

During the evening of Friday, September 30,

1955, cast and crew were watching the day's rushes when word came that reckless James Dean had been killed in an automobile accident. Although Dean had completed his scenes, Elizabeth had not and was required to report to the studio the day after her friend's death to shoot her final footage. It was a traumatic ordeal for the sensitive actress.

Much of *Giant** had been a battle for Elizabeth but her victory came in the form of the laudatory reviews she collected. *Variety* noted, "Miss Taylor, whose talent and emotional ranges have usually seemed limited, turns in a surprisingly clever performance that registers up and down the line. She is tender yet stubborn. Curiously enough, she's far better in the second half of the film, when her hair begins to show some gray, than in the earlier sequences. Portraying a woman of maturity, who has learned to adjust to a different social pattern, Miss Taylor is both engaging and beautiful."

Stevens, in his inimitable style, required some ten months to edit and assemble *Giant.* During the period Elizabeth tackled her next project, *Raintree County* (1957), based on Ross Lockridge, Jr.'s 1,060-page best-selling novel. The project had initially been planned for production in 1948 with Lana Turner or Ava Gardner in the role that eventually became Elizabeth's. However, an austerity program at MGM forced Dore Schary to shelve the big-budgeted historical film temporarily. In 1955 the property was resurrected with a $5.3 million budget which soared to $6 million and the 1839-1892 time span was contracted to 1859-1865. Joining Elizabeth were Montgomery Clift (the self-destructive actor whom Elizabeth protected and sought acting jobs for), Eva Marie Saint, Lee Marvin, Agnes Moorehead, and Walter Abel. Also in the large cast was Tom Drake, Elizabeth's *Courage of Lassie* co-star of a decade earlier.

Clift had taken a home near the Wildings and during the evenings he and Elizabeth often discussed problems dealing with filming and their everyday lives. On Sunday, May 13, 1956, Clift was driving home when he lost control of his car

---

*In September 1956, Elizabeth and Rock Hudson would leave their handprints in the cement at Grauman's Chinese Theatre in Hollywood during the playdate of *Giant.*

With James Dean in *Giant* ('56).

and crashed into a telephone pole. Recalling that hysterical evening, Elizabeth commented, "I rode in the ambulance, and by the time we reached the hospital his head was so swollen that it was almost as wide as his shoulders. His eyes by then had disappeared. His cheeks were level with his nose. The whole thing was like a giant red soccer ball. . . . His jaw had been broken in four places, his nose in two places, and he was badly cut around the eyes. And his upper lip—it was like a spoon had gouged a great big hunk out of his mouth."

Extensive plastic surgery restored Clift's handsome features and added a six-week halt to filming. (Not only was it unfeasible to consider replacing Clift at this late stage in the filming, but Elizabeth refused to consider such an alternative.) Problems, however, were not confined to the *Raintree County* production. On the domestic front, Elizabeth and Michael were in the process of a marital smash-up which could not be rectified by cosmetic surgery. Just as Elizabeth's film assignments rose from B projects to quality scripts, Wilding, who had done some MGM films in the Fifties, saw his career slump

into mediocrity. Supposedly, trouble in the Wilding-Taylor marriage dated back to Christopher's birth early in 1955. What began so happily at Caxton Hall four years, four months, and four weeks earlier ended with a press release on Wednesday, July 18, 1956: "Much careful thought has been given to the step we are taking. It is being done so we can have an opportunity to work out our personal situation. We are in complete accord in making this amicable decision."

Later Elizabeth would reveal to the press, ". . . my marriage with Michael Wilding had become the relationship for which we were much more suited—brother and sister. He's one of the nicest people I've ever known. . . . I wasn't desperate but I was terribly upset. We had both failed—though I didn't blame him and he didn't blame me. . . . I genuinely do not believe in divorce. I know that must sound pretty funny, coming from me." So exited Michael Wilding who would later marry actress Margaret Leighton and still later become Elizabeth's talent agent.

Prior to their separation, the Wildings had spent time with Michael Todd (born June 22, 1907, in Minneapolis) during the early summer

324

of 1956. On the day that her separation was headlined in newspapers, Elizabeth received a call from Todd who was then in Hollywood packaging his *Around the World in 80 Days* (1956) epic. Todd's call instructed Elizabeth where and when to meet him. At the given rendezvous (Benny Thau's MGM office), Todd professed his love for Elizabeth, ending the discussion with, "Don't horse around. You're going to marry me."

A somewhat nonplussed Elizabeth, a superstar in both her public and private life, soon left for Danville, Kentucky, to resume shooting on *Raintree County*. Todd besieged the new love of his life with daily phone calls and flowers. When he traveled to New York on business, he arranged with Elizabeth to spend three weekends with him. The relentless courtship continued when Elizabeth returned to Hollywood in September for final shooting of *Raintree County*.

On Wednesday, October 17, 1956, *Around the World in 80 Days* had its world premiere in New York and Todd and Elizabeth announced their engagement with a diamond ring valued between $92,000 and $100,000. The cameo-packed film went on to win the Oscar, the New York Film Critics Circle Award, and the National Board of Review's Laurel Wreath as Best Film of 1956. Todd's immediate personal prize was Elizabeth who filed for divorce from Wilding on Wednesday, November 14, charging "extreme mental cruelty." At the same time Elizabeth hinted initially about the possibility of retirement. "The blending of a career with marriage does not seem to work out satisfactorily," she noted.

In mid-November, while on vacation with Todd in Florida, she commented, "I may never work again." During this holiday trek, Elizabeth suffered a serious fall on a yacht which resulted in her undergoing a five-hour operation at New York's Harkness Pavilion of Columbia-Presbyterian Medical Center. Several crushed spinal discs were removed and replaced with reconstructed bone from her hip and pelvis. By Monday, January 21, 1957, Elizabeth was released from Harkness and she and Todd flew to Acapulco where Michael Wilding obligingly joined them to obtain a Mexican divorce.

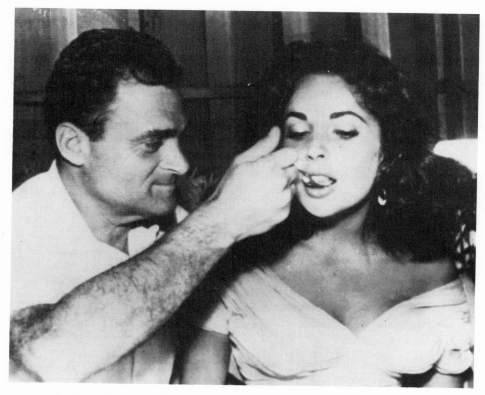

In Puerto Marques, Mexico, with husband Mike Todd (February 2, 1957).

The Wilding-Taylor union was dissolved on January 30, 1957, and Elizabeth and Todd were married on Saturday, February 2. Performing the ceremony was the mayor of Acapulco with Mike Todd, Jr., Cantinflas, and Eddie Fisher as Todd's best men and Debbie Reynolds and Mara Taylor (Howard's wife) as Elizabeth's attendants. For the third time Helen Rose designed Elizabeth's wedding attire which this time consisted of a hydrangea-blue cocktail-length dress and a chiffon scarf over her dark hair. Her jewelry included a matching diamond ring, bracelet, and earrings. For her wedding bouquet, Elizabeth selected white and butterfly orchids and lilies of the valley.

The happy couple embarked on a hectic lifestyle punctuated by special events. On February 27, the new Mrs. Todd celebrated her twenty-fifth birthday and received such gifts as a Renoir painting, a mink coat, and a diamond bracelet. Within a month, Elizabeth announced that she was expecting her third child. At the Oscar presentation in late March, *Around the World in 80 Days* collected five Oscars, while *Giant*, nominated for ten, was trophied only for director George Stevens.

In April, Elizabeth and promoter Todd sailed for Europe to publicize various openings of *Around the World in 80 Days* across the continent. For three months they engaged in rounds of parties and premieres which kept them in the headlines. By mid-July, Elizabeth and Todd returned to the United States where they settled into a twenty-three-room estate at Westport, Connecticut. On July 28 Elizabeth went into premature labor, but her doctors advised against the child's birth at that time. Finally, Elizabeth Frances Todd was delivered by cesarean section on Tuesday, August 6, 1957, at 12:03 P.M. Weighing only four pounds and fourteen ounces, the infant spent her first two months in an oxygen tent.

Meanwhile, Elizabeth's *Raintree County* met with generally disappointing reviews in its initial release, and only grossed $6 million in distributors' domestic rentals. Whereas the film sank, Elizabeth was lauded for her best, most mature performance to date. That cinematic event, however, seemed to pale next to the hoopla crafty Todd planned surrounding the first anniversary

of *Around the World in 80 Days* on October 17. The impresario rented Madison Square Garden and on that Thursday evening staged a birthday gala New York would not soon forget. Everything was handled in a lavish, overblown fashion, including a 24-foot Oscar made of chrysanthemums and a cake made with $15,000 worth of cake mix, 2,000 eggs, and 68 gallons of water that was sectioned into a structure 14 feet high, 35 feet wide, and weighing a ton. Invitations went to 18,000 guests who attended the mobbed party. Souvenir mongers willingly paid waiters who were hawking the supposedly free champagne and programs.

After recovering from a round of bad press concerning his tasteless party, Todd and Elizabeth embarked on November 1 on a round-the-world trip, visiting Honolulu, Sydney, Hong Kong, and Japan. While in Hong Kong, Elizabeth suffered an attack of appendicitis and the Todds promptly returned to Los Angeles. Elizabeth had her appendix removed at Cedars of Lebanon on Tuesday, December 17. A month later the Todds were on the road again, landing in London and moving on to Paris where Elizabeth's long tresses were cut to a short, contemporary wind-blown style by Alexandre. From Paris the pair moved on to Moscow, Prague, Athens, Belgrade, Nice, Madrid, New York, and finally home to Los Angeles. The continent-hopping couple settled in a twelve-room home in Coldwater Canyon in March 1958.

Producer Todd returned to work on preproduction plans for a *Don Quixote* film and Elizabeth celebrated her first Oscar nomination for *Raintree County*. At this point Elizabeth had been absent from the screen for over a year due to Liza's birth and her extensive world travel. After a nervous singing audition for Richard Rodgers, she was passed over for the Nellie Forbush role in Twentieth Century-Fox's screen version of *South Pacific*. (The part went eventually to Mitzi Gaynor.)

Looming in the background at MGM was a screen version of Tennessee Williams' powerfully frank Broadway hit, *Cat on a Hot Tin Roof*, which originally had been purchased for Grace Kelly. By the time the studio fashioned the gingerly conceived script with only the most delicate suggestion of Brick's latent homosexuality,

With her son Michael and Montgomery Clift on the set of *Raintree County* ('57).

With husband Mike Todd and daughter Liza in 1957.

Grace had opted for Monaco and Prince Rainier, leaving the role open for Elizabeth.

Filming began on Wednesday, March 12, 1958, under Richard Brooks' direction. Elizabeth planned *Cat* as her Metro swan song. She feared a plunge back to mediocrity might occur during the remainder of her contract's three-year term. On March 19 Elizabeth contracted a virus which necessitated her absence from shooting. By Friday, March 21, Elizabeth remained in bed with a temperature of 102°F which caused her to cancel plans to fly to New York with Mike Todd where he would be honored the following day by a Friars' Testimonial Dinner at the Waldorf-Astoria Hotel. Accompanying Todd in his Lockheed Lodestar plane—christened "The Lucky Liz"—were Art Cohn, pilot Bill Verner, and co-pilot Tom Barclay. The plane left Burbank under unfavorable weather conditions and experienced moderate icing conditions at 11,000 feet as reported by the pilot at 1:55 A.M. over the CAA communications station. The craft climbed to 13,000 feet and was never heard from again. The scattered wreckage was discovered in the Zuni Mountains of New Mexico at 7,000 feet. State Patrolman Albert Vega stated, "There apparently had been an explosion. The plane was just about all burned out. The bodies were badly burned—beyond identification."

Breaking the news to the ailing Elizabeth were her private physician, Rex Kennamer, and Todd's private secretary, Dick Hanley. When

With Judith Anderson and one of the "no-neck monsters" in *Cat on a Hot Tin Roof* ('58).

Elizabeth saw the two men enter her room, she sensed the inevitable message they carried. After an initial outbreak of hysterical disbelief, Elizabeth was sedated but could not escape the grim reality of her husband's death. To Dr. Kennamer she said, "If only I had been with him. Without him now, I feel like half a pair of scissors. That's what he always used to tell me when he was away from me. I knew I shouldn't have let him go."

Todd was buried* in Jewish Waldheim Cemetery in the Chicago suburb of Forest Park, Illinois, on Tuesday, March 25, amid as much fanfare as would surround one of his productions. Accompanying Elizabeth on board the TWA airliner put at her disposal by Howard Hughes was Metro press agent Bill Lyon, Howard Taylor, Dr. Kennamer, Helen Rose, Dick Hanley, and Eddie Fisher. Debbie Reynolds remained in Los Angeles with Elizabeth's three children.

Michael Todd, Jr. met the plane and accompanied Elizabeth in a limousine to the cemetery where thousands had gathered. Recalling the circus-like atmosphere that bitter cold day of the funeral, Elizabeth later wrote, "After the coffin was lowered into the ground I asked everybody to leave. I knelt and said a prayer and went out by myself. And then the crowd broke loose—the police couldn't hold them back—and rushed at me. My brother Howard was holding me and they started tearing the veil from my hat for souvenirs."

Back in California, Elizabeth was understandably absent from the Oscar presentation where she was nominated as Best Actress for *Raintree County*. Receiving the Oscar was Joanne Woodward for her multi-dimensional performance in Twentieth Century-Fox's *The Three Faces of Eve*.

On Monday, April 14, 1958, a much thinner and weaker Elizabeth Taylor resumed filming of *Cat on a Hot Tin Roof* with co-stars Paul Newman, Burl Ives, Judith Anderson, and Jack Carson.

*One of the more bizarre episodes in celebrity-lore occurred on the weekend of June 25, 1977, a day after Elizabeth had visited the grave site to place red roses and an American flag on it, two days following Todd's birthday. Todd's grave was discovered to have been opened and his remains removed. At first it was suspected that it might be "a far-fetched extortion plan" but the remains were discovered thereafter on the cemetery grounds, leaving the police baffled as to the reason for the "sick" act.

Initially, Elizabeth attempted to cling to the last vestiges of Mike's presence in her life—a shirt he had worn last, his pajamas, the sheets on their bed. Suddenly she was unable to look at his possessions any longer and noted, "You have to watch not to build a shrine."

Todd's estate was estimated at between three and five million dollars, half of which was left in trust for Elizabeth with the other portion going to Michael Todd, Jr. Young Todd planned to continue the Mike Todd Company, Inc., but announced that he would shelve the *Don Quixote* project which the elder Todd had been preparing.

During her mourning period, Elizabeth received condolences from some 100,000 fans as well as journalistic sympathy. The summer of 1958 found Elizabeth in New York en route to Europe. Close family friend Eddie Fisher also "happened" to be in New York and the couple soon found themselves in the headlines. Elizabeth remembered, "Eddie . . . had been one of Mike's best friends, and had idolized Mike to the point of trying to make himself over in his image. I knew Eddie was not very happy. I knew he loved to talk about Mike almost as much as I did. So we went out in public together several times—and all hell broke loose. The press and the public—the whole world—was convinced that I was breaking up a perfectly happy marriage."

Eddie and Debbie—America's uncrowned sweethearts—met in 1953 and were married on September 25, 1955 at Grossinger's resort in the Catskills where Eddie's singing career had begun its upward swing some six years earlier. The couple epitomized youthful ambition with both their careers on the rise. Debbie had landed on top of the ingenue screen heap after MGM's *Singin' in the Rain* (1952) and followed it with a half-dozen lightweight films. Eddie had spent 1951 through 1953 with the armed services and emerged with a contract for a radio program, "Coke Time." His yearly income from radio, TV, clubs, and recording contracts amounted to $700,000. In the second year of their marriage the couple starred in RKO's *Bundle of Joy,* an insipid musical remake of the Ginger Rogers-David Niven film *Bachelor Mother* (1939). On October 21, 1956, Debbie and Eddie became the parents of a daughter Carrie; son Todd was born on February 24, 1958, just twenty-six days before his namesake, Mike Todd, died. Reportedly the Fishers' marriage had taken a severe turn for the worse in 1957. When Debbie discovered she was pregnant with their second child, they remained together.*

Elizabeth and Eddie's New York escape, characterized as a worldly siren leading a naive young man down the path of destruction, involved an evening at the Blue Angel, a weekend trip to Grossinger's, and dining and dancing at the Harwyn Club. Before long Elizabeth cancelled her European vacation plans and Eddie extended his New York business trip from four to fourteen days. Meanwhile, an apparently confused Debbie Reynolds read the headlines and waited patiently in Los Angeles. She released the following statement to the press, "I am still in love with my husband. I hope this separation will iron out the difficulties and we can get together and be happy. I am deeply shocked over what has happened. We were never happier than we have been in the last year."

At the same time Elizabeth had returned to Los Angeles and was busy chatting to ace columnist Hedda Hopper. "You know I don't go about breaking up marriages. Besides you can't break up a happy marriage. Debbie's and Eddie's never has been. I like him very much. I've felt happier and more like a human being for the past two weeks than I have since Mike's death." This same interview contained the infamous, much-quoted Taylor comment, "Mike is dead and I'm alive." The star has since claimed this was a misquote. She said her original statement was to the effect, "Mike is dead and I'm alive and the one person who would want me to try to be happy is Mike."

For some reason Elizabeth felt that what would make her happy was Eddie Fisher. Debbie took divorce action on December 4, 1958, and received her interlocutory decree on February 19, 1959. A month earlier NBC announced that it would axe Fisher's television program in March 1959. Amid a flurry of venomous press, Eliza-

beth found herself number 2 on the Top Ten Moneymaking Stars of 1958. Grosses on *Cat on a Hot Tin Roof* rose to $9.75 million for U.S. and Canadian rentals as the scandal progressed. In late February 1959, Elizabeth received her second Oscar nomination, substantiating the unanimously favorable reviews of her performance as the likeable tigress who woos back her spouse to the marital bed. *Variety* reported, "Elizabeth Taylor has a major credit with her portrayal of Maggie. The frustrations and desires, both as a person and a woman, the warmth and understanding she molds, the loveliness that is more than a well-turned nose—all these are part of a full-accented, perceptive interpretation." Elizabeth felt that " . . . all the publicity surrounding my private life will hurt my chances to win an Oscar." She was correct. The trophy went to Susan Hayward for United Artists' *I Want to Live!*

While married to Todd, Elizabeth had begun studying the tenets of Judaism. On Thursday, March 26, 1959, after extensive preparation, Elizabeth renounced her former Christian Science background in order to become a Jewess. Her Jewish name would be Elisheba Rachel.

On April 1, Eddie opened a six-week performing stint at the Tropicana Hotel in Las Vegas. The crooner and the convert announced their engagement after the show's opening and added that they hoped to be wed in six months. For this to be possible, Debbie would have to consent to a hasty Nevada divorce, eliminating the year-long waiting period in California for the divorce to become final. Debbie finally capitulated and Eddie and Elizabeth were wed on Tuesday, May 12, at the Temple Beth Sholom in Las Vegas. For her fourth wedding, Elizabeth chose a moss-green, cocktail-length chiffon dress designed by film couturier Jean Louis. The actress carried a bouquet of yellow and green orchids. Mike Todd, Jr. was Eddie's best man and Mara Taylor was her sister-in-law's attendant.

Once again Elizabeth hinted at retirement possibilities within eighteen months while she also committed herself to *Suddenly, Last Summer* (1959) at Columbia, and tentatively negotiated with the Mirisch Brothers for *Two for the Seesaw* (1962) and *Irma La Douce* (1963). The latter two screen roles would be in-

*A bit of ironic prophecy occurred in the scenario of Elizabeth's *A Date with Judy.* At one point in the storyline, Elizabeth's character says to volatile Carmen Miranda, "He has two children. How can you break up a marriage? What kind of a woman are you?"

herited by Shirley MacLaine. Summing up her feelings regarding cinema retirement, Elizabeth stated, "My personal life has always been more important to me than anything else. I want to devote my free time to being a wife and mother."

The Fishers devoted their honeymoon to cruising the Mediterranean on the rented yacht *Olnico*. In June they arrived in Spain where Elizabeth consented to play a cameo in the scent-o-vision thriller *Scent of Mystery* (1960) produced by Mike Todd, Jr. Filming then began on *Suddenly, Last Summer* which was on location on the Costa Brava. The major portion of the picture resumed shooting at the Shepperton Studios in London. Under Joseph L. Mankiewicz's shrewd direction, Elizabeth joined a cast that included Katharine Hepburn and Montgomery Clift (once more rescued from professional oblivion by Elizabeth). Gore Vidal and Tennessee Williams fashioned the screenplay from one of Williams' one-act plays, *Garden District*.

The subject matter of *Suddenly, Last Summer* was of a heavy nature with overtones of incest, homosexuality, cannibalism, lobotomy, neurosis, and hysteria leaping from the screen during the 114-minute running time. Columbia released the very adult offering in December 1959 to mixed reviews. *Saturday Review* noted this dichotomous reaction by hailing the motion picture as "fascinating and nauseating, brilliant and immoral." Of Elizabeth's performance, Paul V. Beckley commented in the *New York Herald-Tribune*, " . . . if there were ever any doubts about the ability of Miss Taylor to deliver a flexible and deep performance, this film ought to remove them." In February 1960, Elizabeth and Katharine Hepburn both received nominations as Best Actress as did Doris Day (*Pillow Talk*), Audrey Hepburn (*The Nun's Story*), and Simone Signoret (*Room at the Top*) with the latter actress capturing top honors.

When the much-touted *Cleopatra* project began taking concrete shape at Twentieth Century-Fox, Elizabeth began to express overt interest in playing the seductive title role. Her demands included a $1 million salary, extensive script changes, and a foreign shooting location—all agreed upon by the obliging Fox hierarchy. Initially a tug-of-war existed between Fox

president Spyros Skouras and producer Walter Wanger. Skouras favored Susan Hayward for the role and others mentioned in various publicity releases included Brigitte Bardot, Marilyn Monroe, Jennifer Jones, Kim Novak, Audrey Hepburn, Sophia Loren, Joan Collins, Suzy Parker, and Gina Lollobrigida. Wanger strongly believed that only Elizabeth could cope with the varied demands of the major role. A "final" script reached both Elizabeth and Audrey Hepburn, but the latter had to withdraw when Paramount refused to release her.

At this juncture MGM re-entered the scene by announcing that Elizabeth still owed them one film and that motion picture would be *Butterfield 8*. Unless she completed her contract stipulation, the studio threatened to keep her off the screen for two years. Elizabeth, chained with *Butterfield 8* for only a $125,000 fee, made her own demands to MGM: shooting would be accomplished in New York, Eddie Fisher would receive a role in the film, Helen Rose would do the costumes, Sidney Guilaroff would be her hair stylist, and there must be extensive script changes.

Elizabeth finally began filming "the most pornographic script" she had ever encountered in January 1960.* Although Elizabeth continued to despise the project even after the script was revised, she tackled the role of Gloria Wandrous with renewed professionalism in an effort to rise above the mediocre scenario. *Butterfield 8* also utilized the talents of Laurence Harvey, Mildred Dunnock, Dina Merrill, Betty Field, Kay Medford, Jeffrey Lynn, and Susan Oliver, under the direction of Daniel Mann.

Further delaying her freedom from *Butterfield 8* and MGM were actors' strikes which shut down the production for two months. Once shooting resumed, Elizabeth went through her required paces with the picture's completion her main objective. When *Butterfield 8* concluded, there were no goodbyes to her eighteen-year tenure at MGM.

By July 1960 Elizabeth had signed her

*Said the haughty yet justified Elizabeth, "Doing this picture gripes the hell out of me. . . . It's too commercial, it's in bad taste. Everyone in it is crazy, mixed-up, sick—except for the part Eddie plays. . . . It's the last picture in my contract so I'm doing it, but I don't like it."

As Catherine Holly in *Suddenly, Last Summer* ('59).

With Eddie Fisher in *Butterfield 8* ('60).

Cleopatra contract which stipulated $125,000 for four months' work, $50,000 for each additional week, $3,000 per week living expenses, round-trip transportation for her and her children, and a 16mm print of the film. Reportedly Fisher was paid $1,500 daily to ensure that she would report to the set on time.

Before going to London to begin shooting, Elizabeth enjoyed a cruise of the Greek isles with Eddie. The star and her entourage settled in London's Dorchester Hotel to await the September 30 starting date. Fox had constructed eight-and-a-half acres of ancient Alexandria at the Pinewood Studios during the past two years at a cost of $600,000.

Just as production on this historical extravaganza was about to commence, ailment-prone Elizabeth became ill with a virus which resulted in her temperature soaring to 100⁰ F. Unable to capture any footage of his high-priced star, director Rouben Mamoulian attempted to shoot around her with leads Stephen Boyd (Marc Antony) and Peter Finch (Julius Caesar), but was foiled by inclement weather.

At the end of October, Elizabeth was still feverish and morale on the *Cleopatra* set was at a new low. The delays had cost Fox $2 million but there was indication that conditions would improve. Yet, Elizabeth, for one, became worse. After having a tooth extracted in early November, she rallied only to become seriously ill again on November 14, causing her return to the London clinic. On November 18, producer Wanger announced that the *Cleopatra* set would close down until January 3, 1961, hoping that the arbitrary date would mark the unencumbered resumption of the film. Meanwhile Fox filed a claim for $2.8 million with Lloyd's of London. The insurer countered with a suggestion that Elizabeth was a production liability and should be replaced with Marilyn Monroe. Fox vetoed that suggestion and Elizabeth remained on the payroll. With production stalled, Elizabeth returned to California in November to recuperate. A much healthier Queen of the Nile returned to London early in 1961.

By then the $6 million budget had soared to $9 million and a disgusted Mamoulian resigned with only twelve minutes of film in the can after sixteen months of production. His replacement was Joseph L. Mankiewicz who had guided Elizabeth through *Suddenly, Last Summer.* Mankiewicz took pause to revamp the script. Then all seemed in readiness and filming resumed when Elizabeth was hit by staphylococcus pneumonia on Saturday, March 4, 1961. She hovered between life and death for a week—all duly reported in minute details in the tabloids—during which a tracheotomy was performed to save her life.

Remembering her nightmare, Elizabeth wrote later, "They had a terrible time taking that awful stuff out of my lungs. Four times after the initial time, I stopped breathing. Once I started to go when I was awake. I tried to draw a breath and nothing happened. I could feel the oxygen leaving my whole system. Instead of blood it was like boiling water flowing through my whole body, and it was like tons on my chest and the terrible thing of pulling, sucking, and not being able to get any breath, and finally getting dizzy. There was a scream in my head and the pain as the oxygen started to leave my breath—scorching pain—and then the noise. And I screamed with prayers. I wanted to live. I prayed to God to live."

On Monday, March 27, 1961, Elizabeth left the London Clinic and prepared to return to California for yet another period of recuperation. Part of this recuperation occurred on Tuesday, April 18, at the Santa Monica Civic Auditorium when she received the Oscar for *Butterfield* 8. The film had been released the previous October and critics rallied to attack it while reserving praise for Elizabeth's performance. *Variety* reported, "The picture's major asset is Miss Taylor, who makes what is becoming her annual bid for an Oscar. While the intensity and range of feeling that marked several of her more recent endeavors is slightly reduced in this effort, it is nonetheless a torrid, stinging overall portrayal with one or two brilliantly executed passages within."

A glowing Elizabeth approached the podium to accept the Oscar amid a wild ovation as she was named Best Actress of 1960 over Greer Garson (*Sunrise at Campobello*), Deborah Kerr (*The Sundowners*), Shirley MacLaine (*The Apartment*), and Melina Mercouri (*Never on Sunday*). Of her first Academy Award, Elizabeth

The Oscar winner at a Beverly Hilton Hotel party (April 18, 1961).

responded, "I knew my performance had not deserved it, that it was a sympathy award. I was filled with profound gratitude at being considered by the industry an actress and not a movie star."

While Elizabeth spent her post-Oscar months relaxing and traveling to Russia, the harried *Cleopatra* executives planned a third resumption of shooting. By the summer of 1961 Elizabeth's original co-stars had been replaced by Rex Harrison (Caesar) and Richard Burton (Antony). The massive set in London was scrapped and Alexandria was constructed in Rome where shooting got underway on Monday, September 25, 1961. Again the production was plagued by inclement weather coupled with contract disputes, incomplete sets, and acts of sabotage as when thousands of costumes were discovered ripped apart.

While Elizabeth remained the center of on and off set attention, Eddie Fisher joined the ranks of those dedicated to the star's comfort. His career was all but nonexistent and his record sales sagged badly shortly after his NBC-TV cancellation. Both casual observers and close friends failed to understand the basis of the unique Taylor-Fisher marriage. Elizabeth explained later, "Eddie, who loved Mike, too, was the one man who could understand that my heart would always belong to the memory of Mike. And Eddie, somehow, made Mike seem more alive. Maybe with Eddie I was trying to see if I was alive or dead. Also, for some idiotic reason, I thought that Eddie needed me and I should make *somebody* happy. Anyway, we got married."

Richard Burton had met Elizabeth for the first time at Sunday brunch at the Stewart Grangers' in 1951. Of the nineteen-year-old Elizabeth, the then twenty-six-year-old Burton thought, " . . . she was the most beautiful and sullen creature I had ever met: difficult, unreachable, unmanageable, unobtainable, impenetrable, and—again—difficult."

Their screen careers hadn't crossed before *Cleopatra* in January 1962, and then the result was fireworks—both on and off camera. By February, news of the Burton-Taylor electricity had filtered into several channels. Director Mankiewicz related to producer Wanger, "I have been sitting on a volcano all alone for too long

and I want to give you some facts you ought to know. Elizabeth and Burton are not just playing Antony and Cleopatra."

Once again Eddie and Elizabeth's marital state made headlines. The already married Burton completed the trio, and his wife of thirteen years, Sybil, by whom he had two children, took on a supporting role. On March 21 Eddie flew to New York on business and Sybil returned to London, leaving the co-stars to resume shooting amidst steady rumors of passionate romance. April proved a harrowing month for all concerned with the epic. Shooting concluded in Italy in July 1962 and Burton went to Egypt for two weeks of exterior shots while Elizabeth returned to her residence in Gstaad, Switzerland.

With *Cleopatra* and their respective marriages obviously finished, Elizabeth and Richard attempted to remain apart but found this to be an impossibility. Soon they were filming *The V.I.P.s* (1963) together. Burton had been set for the high-class soap opera and Elizabeth suggested herself for a role originally intended for Sophia Loren. Producer Anatole de Grunwald jumped at the opportunity to reteam *Cleopatra*'s much-publicized lovers. Production on *The V.I.P.s* began in December 1962. Burton remained caught between his duty to Sybil and his love for Elizabeth. On February 9, 1963, he and Sybil celebrated their fourteenth wedding anniversary. Three weeks later he celebrated Elizabeth's thirty-first birthday. By April, Burton and Sybil had formally separated, and, in June, Richard announced, "I want to marry Elizabeth and I will marry her. No ifs, no buts. She wants to marry me. I want to marry her."

That same month *Cleopatra* had its world premiere at New York's Rivoli Theatre. Fox's publicity department kept the film in the public's eye through an extensive pre-release campaign. They wisely feared that a word-of-mouth publicity program would cripple the film at the box office.

What originally began with Joan Collins in the title role of a $2 million remake of DeMille's 1934 epic ended as one of the costliest and most controversial epic films ever made. In its final widescreen color print, *Cleopatra* represented a $40 million expenditure resulting in four hours and three minutes of film. The critics* were divided in their reactions to the feature but unanimous in their reporting that Cleopatra had gotten the best of too contemporary Elizabeth Taylor. Once again Elizabeth failed to shrug off her very twentieth century facade to become the Temptress of the Nile, circa 48 B.C. *Saturday Review* noted, "Elizabeth Taylor . . . is unequal to the demands made on her by Mankiewicz. He has asked for a many-faceted regal portrayal of a powerful woman with a mind of brilliance, a beautiful face, and a demanding body. Elizabeth Taylor has the face, but as a creature of passion she is unconvincing, as a woman of mentality a joke. Mankiewicz, then, was hamstrung from the very beginning by an inadequate performer who, at the same time, provided the *raison d'être* for the gigantic undertaking. Obviously he continued to strive mightily to make a spectacle of intelligence and dignity, but does anyone really want to listen to Elizabeth discuss politics and military matters?" Thanks to audience curiosity about the "immoral" lovebirds performing on-camera and the later television sale of the film, *Cleopatra* eventually moved into the financial black.

Elizabeth and Richard were undaunted by the negative response to *Cleopatra* (and the assorted lawsuits with Fox; all settled out of court). She prepared a television special, *Elizabeth Taylor in London* (there had already been a *Sophia Loren in Rome*), and he began *Becket* with Peter O'Toole. The lushly mounted *The V.I.P.s* was released by MGM in September 1963 and an unfavorable critical reaction was the order for the second time that year. *Variety* reported, "Maybe Miss Taylor needs a sabbatical but there is an ordinariness about her thesping these days which is disconcerting. In *The V.I.P.s* she looks attractive, of course, and shows some moments of fun, fire, and emotion." Yet the craftily entertaining picture grossed $7.5 million in distrib-

utors' domestic rentals and co-star Margaret Rutherford won a Best Supporting Actress Oscar.

With the Sunday, October 6, 1963, airing of her CBS-TV special came a set of warm notices.* They reached Elizabeth in Mexico where Burton was filming *The Night of the Iguana* (1964). Stories about the cast (Burton, Ava Gardner, Deborah Kerr, Sue "Lolita" Lyon) and side-seat observer (Elizabeth) filled newspapers for months, and so overblew the importance of this film based on the Tennessee Williams play, that the movie could in no way live up to the titillating publicity.

Further good news occurred on December 16, 1963, when Sybil received a Mexican divorce on grounds of "abandonment and cruel and inhuman treatment." In January 1964 Elizabeth filed for a Mexican divorce from Fisher which was granted on March 6. Burton and Taylor were in Toronto for Richard's opening of *Hamlet* under Sir John Gielgud's direction. On Sunday, March 15, 1964, Elizabeth and Burton finally became legally man and wife in Montreal. For her fifth set of nuptials Elizabeth attired herself in a yellow daffodil chiffon dress in the empire style with a hyacinth and lily of the valley in a chignon coil in her hair. Her only jewelry was a $93,000 emerald and diamond clip given to her by Burton in Rome during the *Cleopatra* shooting. Serving as Burton's best man was Bob Wilson who had been his *Camelot* dresser on Broadway. Quite knowledgeable and practiced at matrimony, Elizabeth was unattended and unescorted. After the March 16 performance of *Hamlet,* Burton stepped forward after his curtain call and quoted from Act III, Scene I of the play, "We will have no more marriages."

In describing Elizabeth's prior spouses, Richard noted, "Nicky Hilton—a complete mistake; Michael Wilding—handicapped by an enormous difference in ages; Mike Todd—

*England's John Coleman (*The New Statesman*) lambasted Elizabeth in his essay on film star quality and her role in *Cleopatra.* "Whatever it is, and the compressed history of film has seen a variety of offers, Elizabeth Taylor surely lacks it, registers a signal and absolute deficiency in that enigmatic private business that a 'star' can't help disclosing on celluloid. . . ." He added, "Monotony in a split skirt, a pre-Christian Elizabeth Arden with sequinned eyelids and occasions constantly too large for her. Plumply pretty, she gives herself womanfully to the impersonation of the world's prime seductress, yet nary a spark flies."

*Taylor was paid a reported $250,000-$500,000 salary for her video chores. She wore a Yves St. Laurent wardrobe for the occasion and delivered dialogue written by Lou Solomon and S. J. Perelman. On the "leisurely tour" she offered several dramatic readings from classic literature associated with the settings under scrutiny. Reported *Daily Variety*, "Miss Taylor looked good (it is difficult for her to look otherwise), but what impressed one even more was the rich quality of her voice—ordinarily an attribute overlooked because of her visual beauty but emphasized in this case owing to her narrative role."

With daughter Liza ('61).

With Richard Burton "rehearsing" for *Cleopatra* ('63).

As Cleopatra.

339

perfect but dead; Eddie Fisher—deplorable." Richard considered himself Elizabeth's ideal consort and she agreed, "I love not being Elizabeth Taylor, but being Richard's wife. I would be quite content to be his shadow and live through him."

For the first weeks of their marriage Elizabeth existed professionally* through Burton's shadow as he opened *Hamlet* on Broadway at the Lunt-Fontanne Theatre. Yet the crowd of fans crushing the stage door nightly were gathered in hopes of obtaining a glimpse of glamorous Elizabeth. *Hamlet* played for seventeen successful weeks and shattered all previous records that the play had established. Obviously audiences forgave and forgot the scandal.

While Burton had made *Becket* and *The Night of the Iguana* since their *The V.I.P.s* collaboration, Elizabeth had no film offers on her agent's desk. Then came *The Sandpiper* (1965) which would put a million dollars in her pocket and her face on the screen again. Initially

*At one point in 1963, Twentieth Century-Fox had considered Elizabeth for the focal role in *What a Way to Go!* (1964), which eventually starred Shirley MacLaine.

William Wyler was to direct Elizabeth and co-star Burt Lancaster in a Columbia package. Wyler dropped the project to direct *The Collector* (1965) and Lancaster was the next figure to withdraw. Elizabeth quickly engaged Burton as her new co-star and Vincente Minnelli as her director and *The Sandpiper* ended up as a MGM project.

When *Hamlet* closed in August 1964 the Burtons took a cross-country train to California to begin production on *The Sandpiper*. A part of Elizabeth's reading material included Edward Albee's *Who's Afraid of Virginia Woolf?* which had opened on Broadway on October 13, 1962 to thunderous reviews. Elizabeth regarded the role of Martha as the most challenging she had ever encountered and set out to win the opportunity **to portray Albee's three-dimensional shrew on-camera**. The frankness of the play's theme and its language made a film treatment a delicate subject. Fearing that a laundering would destroy the play's import, Albee at first refused to sell the film rights but then capitulated to Warner Bros.' offer of $500,000 in March 1964. Casting rumors for *the* drama of the screen year included

In *The Sandpiper* ('65).

Ingrid Bergman, Bette Davis, Rosalind Russell, and Patricia Neal as Martha, with Cary Grant, James Mason, and Henry Fonda as her battered spouse George. No one seemed to mention the Burtons.

Meanwhile, *The Sandpiper* occupied the Burtons, at first in California for exterior shots and finally in Paris* for interior work. The latter location became necessary for Burton's complex tax situation. In addition to Elizabeth's million, Burton received $500,000. Once, in a moment of conflict with Minnelli over the interpretation of a particular scene, Burton capitulated reportedly with "For the money we will dance!"

The Sandpiper marked a professional reunion for Elizabeth and Minnelli. The director first encountered Elizabeth as a ten-year-old on the Metro lot and later worked with her in *Father of the Bride* (1950) and *Father's Little Dividend* (1951). Unfortunately *The Sandpiper* did not repeat the artistic success of the initial collaboration. No one benefited professionally when the feature reached the screen in July 1965. *Saturday Review* printed, "In spite of the story, in spite of her role, Miss Taylor achieves an almost monumental quality; she is *the* star not walking through a part but employing it as a vehicle. Her acting is of the kind that is convinced rather than convincing." Thanks to the aura still surrounding the names of Taylor and Burton, the ludicrously structured film grossed over $7 million in U.S. and Canadian distributors' rentals, more than paying back its production cost of $5.3 million. Abroad the picture garnered another $7 million in profits!

If Elizabeth professionally belonged to the world, by citizenship she belonged to both England and America. In 1965** she stated, "I like

*In October 1964 Elizabeth and Richard made a transatlantic crossing on the *Queen Elizabeth*. Also making the crossing were Debbie Reynolds and her spouse Harry Karl. The Burtons and the Karls met socially twice during the voyage. When the ship docked, Debbie reported that she and Elizabeth never mentioned Eddie's name. "If you don't forget what's in the past, how can you look forward to the future?" reasoned Debbie.

**In 1965 Elizabeth's book *Elizabeth Taylor: An Informal Memoir* was published, with photographs by Roddy McDowall. Of the 177-page tome, *Library Journal* reported, "It is not a book of secret revelations or public confessions. The material may be familiar, the whole story may be somewhat guarded, but the overall effect is one of honesty. . . . The book is a short one and shows little feeling for language. It is written in a slangy and rather graceless style. Her dedicatory thanks go to Richard Meryman 'for his help and tape recorder' and to Richard Burton 'for marrying me.'"

the British best of all." She was still an American citizen at this time since she had failed to complete her oath of expatriation in Paris a year earlier "to abjure all allegiance and fidelity to the United States of America." She would officially become a British subject in 1971.

With the inferior *The Sandpiper* making money, the Burtons announced that they would star in *Who's Afraid of Virginia Woolf?* which came their way as a Warner Bros. package with Ernest Lehman as producer/scripter and Mike Nichols making his directorial debut in the film medium. Prior to beginning work on *Virginia Woolf,* Burton had filmed *The Spy Who Came in from the Cold* (1965) with Claire Bloom in London while Elizabeth prepared for her upcoming role of Martha. Elizabeth viewed the character as "a desperate woman who has the softness of the underbelly of a baby turtle. She covers it up with the toughness of the shell, which she paints red. Her veneer is bawdy; it's sloppy, it's slouchy, it's snarly. But there are moments when the facade cracks and you see the vulnerability, the infinite pain of this woman inside whom, years ago, life almost died but is still flickering."

Joining the Burtons in the *Virginia Woolf* cast were George Segal and Sandy Dennis as the young couple verbally victimized by George and Martha. Production on the black-and-white drama commenced in July 1965 with three weeks of intense rehearsals before the cameras began rolling. Stage 8 at Warner Bros. turned away studio stars, gossip columnists, and curious onlookers with a simple sign: "CLOSED SET—ABSOLUTELY NO VISITORS." Everything was to remain veiled in secrecy until shortly before the film's release. In becoming Martha, Elizabeth added twenty pounds, a salt-and-pepper wig, a brash walk, and a raucous voice to spout the script's flow of vulgarities. Reflecting on her weeks of filming Martha, Elizabeth essayed later, "Though it was such a complete change from anything else, it was strangely one of the easiest things I've ever done. It was stepping into somebody else's skin who was so remote from my own skin that it was like wearing a mustache and beard and old long wig and cloak. So I had Martha to hide behind, so I'd lost Elizabeth Taylor. There was a freedom that I've never known before in a role."

Rehearsing with Sammy Davis, Jr. and Richard Burton for "The Sammy Davis Show" (January 7, 1966).

As Martha in *Who's Afraid of Virginia Woolf?* ('66).

Production on *Virginia Woolf* finished on Monday, December 13, 1965, and the studio began the long task of assemblage. Early in 1966 the Burtons re-encountered the bygone *Cleopatra* in the form of a $50 million lawsuit initiated by Twentieth Century-Fox. The studio contended that "these two by their irresponsibility and illicit conduct directly or indirectly caused expense of more than $1 million . . . because of the absence of Miss Taylor, which she said was related to her emotional and distraught condition." After twelve days of testimony the matter was allowed to fall into either dissolution or an out-of-court settlement.

Nothing came of the court case as the Burtons left for Oxford, England, in February for a five-night benefit run in Marlowe's *Doctor Faustus* for Oxford University Theatre Centre. Their appearance raised $41,000 for Oxford and the Burtons then departed for Italy and Franco Zeffirelli's film version of *The Taming of the Shrew* (1967).

Originally set to star in the Shakespearean comedy were Marcello Mastroianni and Sophia Loren, but director Zeffirelli changed his mind after viewing Burton's *Hamlet*. In addition to acting Kate and Petruchio, the Burtons co-produced the film and deferred their salaries for a percentage of the gross.

While the Burtons were accomplishing their Shakespearean paces in Italy, *Who's Afraid of Virginia Woolf?* had its New York premiere on Thursday, June 23, 1966. The release of the $7.5 million film was preceded by censorship controversy. When the Production Code Review Board refused its seal two weeks before the premiere, Warner Bros. appealed the decision, listing *Virginia Woolf* as an "exception." With minor deletions, the film passed the Code's criteria and thereafter in release amassed a collection of generous reception notices. Of Elizabeth's performance, *New York Times* critic Stanley Kauffmann commented, "She has shown previously, in some roles, that she could respond to the right director and could at least flagellate herself into an emotional state (as in *Suddenly, Last Summer*). Here, with a director who knows how to get an actor's confidence and knows what to do with it after he gets it, she does the best work of her career, sustained and urgent. Of course, she has an initial advantage. Her acceptance of gray hair and her use of profanity make her seem to be acting even (figuratively) before she begins."

With the added enthusiasm that rave notices bring to performers, the Burtons continued their *Taming of the Shrew* shooting. Richard was on comfortable ground with Shakespeare, but Elizabeth ventured into a new form and style with the film's verse. Explaining their decision to film Shakespeare, Burton stated, "We made *The Taming of the Shrew* because I wanted to act a rough role as far away as possible from those Rex Harrison parts with nice suits and freshly laundered shirts, and my wife because she wanted to talk English for a change. In *Shrew* she shows definite Shakespearean feeling, the only difficulties being some of the Bard's words that are alien to her. For instance, 'how durst thou' is not common talk in California."

During the shooting of *Shrew*, Elizabeth received the shocking news that Montgomery Clift, her long-time friend and frequent co-star, had been found dead in his New York apartment from a heart attack. Elizabeth was set to begin shooting *Reflections in a Golden Eye*, based on the Carson McCullers 1941 novella, with Clift as her co-star. By the time she reported for shooting, producer Ray Stark had filled Clift's role with Marlon Brando, engaged John Huston to direct, and completed the film's major casting with Julie Harris, Brian Keith, and Robert Forster. The pre-production promise of *Reflections in a Golden Eye* (1967) failed to materialize on-screen. Nothing seemed to work.* When shooting ended on *Reflections*, Elizabeth rejoined Burton for another co-starring vehicle, Graham Greene's *The Comedians,* under Peter Glenville's direction. Because the film was such a strong political indictment against the regime in Haiti, Glenville had to shoot on location elsewhere. The company gathered in Dahomey in West Africa for six weeks and followed with additional shooting in Paris and Nice.

The Burtons were thus engaged on the French Riviera the night (April 10, 1967) of the Oscar

---

*A twenty-three-year-old Italian actress, Paola Rosi, substituted for Elizabeth in the nude scenes for *Reflections*. She was hired especially for her walk. Rosi received $200 per day salary and no billing.

presentations for *Virginia Woolf*. The four cast members as well as the director and the film competed for top prizes. An absent Elizabeth received her second Oscar for her moving portrayal of the foul-mouthed Martha and Sandy Dennis captured the Best Supporting Actress trophy for her whimpering Honey. Burton lost his bid to Paul Scofield for *A Man for All Seasons* and Nichols also lost to that film's director, Fred Zinnemann. George Segal was bested by Walter Matthau of *The Fortune Cookie*. *Who's Afraid of Virginia Woolf?* collected additional Oscars for cinematographer Haskell Wexler, art and set decorators Richard Sylbert and George James Hopkins and costume designer Irene Sharaff. The film garnered some $14.5 million in distributors' domestic rentals.

Elizabeth's second Oscar win was clearly deserved and not awarded out of sentiment. The thirty-four-year-old actress allowed her still fresh beauty to be hidden under Martha's foul-mouthed, fiftyish facade and proved unquestionably her abilities as a performer. Ironically after *Virginia Woolf*, Elizabeth would become involved in a series of increasingly specious film projects, all of which succeeded in dragging her from the top ten at the box-office listing.

In a role originally intended for Sophia Loren in *The Comedians* (1967), Elizabeth appeared in support of Burton. *The Comedians* marked the third feature Elizabeth completed for release that year. *The Taming of the Shrew* served as a competent follow-up to her *Virginia Woolf* performance. In addition, her Shakespearean portrayal allowed her to show off her still beautiful face and (buxom) figure which she had concealed in the earlier film. *Time* magazine noted, "In one of her better performances, Taylor makes Kate seem the ideal bawd of Avon—a creature of beauty with a voice shrieking howls and imprecations."

Neither awards nor glowing reviews reached Elizabeth for *Reflections in a Golden Eye* nor *The Comedians*. Arthur Knight commented in *Saturday Review,* "As for Elizabeth Taylor, *Reflections* demonstrated by inversion the contributions of a strong director. Her virulent scenes in *Virginia Woolf* revealed her full capabilities; but when she shrieks 'You son of a bitch!' at Brando in this one, she might still be playing *National Velvet*. The star's sole advantage is that when she sheds her clothes she looks better than anyone else in the picture."

The Comedians combined the political intrigue of Haiti with a love affair involving the Burtons' characters. Elizabeth portrayed another Martha—Martha Pineda—married to Peter Ustinov in the role of the ambassador. All the fire and intensity the Burtons exhibited earlier in *Who's Afraid of Virginia Woolf?* was noticeably absent in *The Comedians* and the acting couple received a deserved critical blasting. In the *Village Voice,* Andrew Sarris noted sadly, "Never before have their mumbling, murmuring, meandering scenes together seemed so boringly inconsequential. They have degenerated in the past few years from a juicy item out of the gossip columns to a dull documentary out of *National Geographic.*"

The Burtons clearly needed a box-office smash to re-establish themselves as drawing powers. Ready for release was *Doctor Faustus* (1968), which they had completed in Rome at the conclusion of *The Taming of the Shrew*. A Columbia release, *Doctor Faustus* starred Burton and members of the Oxford University Dramatic Society with Elizabeth doing a walk-on as nine different embodiments of passion and lust—hardly popular film fare. In listing the serious drawbacks of the project, *Time* magazine stated, "The worst is Elizabeth Taylor, who has a series of walk-ons mostly meant to exemplify lust. Her makeup varies from Greek statuesque to a head-to-toe spray job of aluminum paint. When she welcomes Burton to an eternity of damnation, her eyeball and teeth are dripping pink in what seems to be a hellish combination of conjunctivitis and trench mouth. Mercifully mute throughout, she merely moves in and out of camera range breasting the waves of candle smoke, dry-ice vapor, and vulgarity that swirl through the sets."

Previously, Elizabeth had offered two of her best screen performances in Tennessee Williams vehicles: *Cat on a Hot Tin Roof* and *Suddenly, Last Summer*. Hoping to repeat past successes, Elizabeth entered into *Boom!* (1968), a film version of *The Milk Train Doesn't Stop Here Anymore*. On Broadway the play never launched into a successful run in two attempts in

With Marlon Brando and Brian Keith (with cigarette) in *Reflections in a Golden Eye* ('67).

At Richard Burton's Paris birthday party (December 18, 1967).

345

1963 and 1964. Neither Hermione Baddeley nor Tallulah Bankhead could inject the proper vitality into the role of Flora Goforth, the world's richest woman.

Like Elizabeth's more recent film projects, Tennessee Williams' plays of late have experienced difficulty in living up to earlier promise. *Boom!** might have placed both Elizabeth and Tennessee back on top, but the picture and all of its contributors fell afoul. Critics damned every aspect of the movie and condemned the Burtons' utter self-indulgence in mounting such a vehicle. *Variety* offered in a moment of kind objectivity, "Elizabeth Taylor's delineation is off the mark: instead of an earthy dame, hypochondriac and hyper-emotional, who survived

six wealthy husbands, she plays it like she has just lost the first, who would appear to have taken her away from a roadside truck stop job. The wealth is shown in too nouveau riche a manner. The gowns, jewels, and sets only emphasize the point."

Since their recent co-starring cinema vehicles had reached an all-time low, Elizabeth and Richard investigated separate motion picture projects for their next professional endeavors. Burton chose *Where Eagles Dare* (1969) and Elizabeth allied her talents with Mia Farrow and Robert Mitchum for a bit of mishmash entitled *Secret Ceremony* (1968). This British-filmed project was far from what Elizabeth required at this juncture in her waning career. The role of Leonora in this Joseph Losey-directed vehicle obviously baffled Elizabeth as much as it did the viewing audience. Critic Roger Greenspun (*New York Times*) stated concisely, "As for the inadequacy of Elizabeth Taylor, it approaches sublimity in her misreading of every line." The failure of the film to create any positive box-

*Among the cast of *Boom!* was Noël Coward as The Witch of Capri, a role originally meant for Patricia Neal. Elizabeth's brother Howard made his only film appearance here, playing a bearded skipper of the boat which brings Burton to Flora's island. Howard throws Burton off the boat, forcing him to swim ashore. Howard, Mara, and their five children had been visiting the Burtons on location. Howard took the film role when the actor contracted for the part failed to materialize on time.

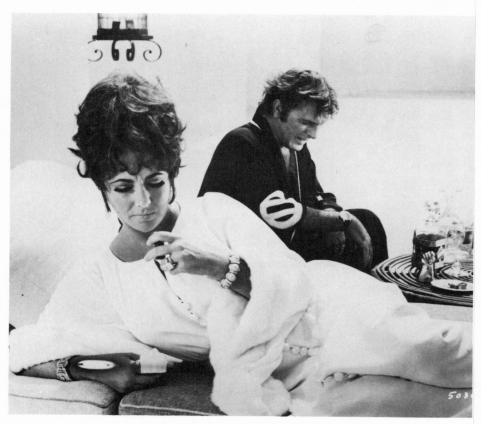

With Richard Burton in *Boom!* ('68).

346

office stir did not deter the NBC network from preparing it for a television airing. NBC snipped fourteen minutes from the film and replaced it with a lawyer and psychiatrist discussing the characters of *Secret Ceremony*. Also cut from the video version was the profanity. The lawyer/psychiatrist voice-overs were used throughout the new version, explaining what NBC felt TV audiences would fail to understand due to Losey's subtle direction. In the metamorphosis, Elizabeth's character suffered a transformation from street hooker to wigmaker (who works at night!) and scenes of Elizabeth working with a wig were spliced into the television version. *Secret Ceremony*, in any of its versions, is best forgotten.

At this point, it appeared that Elizabeth's knack for selecting scripts was no better than MGM's had been in assigning projects to her fifteen years earlier. Her next venture seemed cinematically foolproof. Twentieth Century-Fox paid $500,000 for Frank Gilroy's *The Only Game in Town* prior to its Broadway opening on May 23, 1968. The two-character drama starred Tammy Grimes and Barry Nelson and disappeared after sixteen performances. Slotted to direct the screen adaptation was George Stevens who had extracted exciting performances from Elizabeth in *A Place in the Sun* and *Giant*. Three years earlier the actress and director were nearly reunited for *The Greatest Story Ever Told* with Elizabeth portraying Mary Magdalene. Elizabeth could not reach a satisfactory agreement with the producers and the role was lost.

Signed to complete *The Only Game* cast was Frank Sinatra and shooting was scheduled to begin in September 1968. In July, Elizabeth entered the Fitzroy Nuffield Nursing Home in London for an operation for the removal of her uterus. Although there were no cancer signs, Elizabeth needed to rest, subsequently delaying the start of *The Only Game in Town* until October. Sinatra had a booking at Caesar's Palace in Las Vegas for November and the delay caused his withdrawal. Replacing Sinatra was younger Warren Beatty in his first role since the successful *Bonnie and Clyde* of 1967.

The setting of *The Only Game in Town* was Las Vegas, but the film was set for a Paris location. Burton was concurrently filming *Staircase* (for Twentieth Century-Fox)—which had a London setting—in Paris and the change from Vegas to Paris permitted the Burtons to be together during their respective shooting schedules. This locale also provided a considerable tax break for the pair who each received $1,250,000 for their respective roles. In *Staircase*, Burton and Rex Harrison co-starred as two middle-aged homosexual lovers. But Burton and Harrison remember the ordeal as a cinematic disaster.

Shooting progressed more smoothly on *The Only Game in Town* set until Elizabeth received word that her father had died on Wednesday, November 20. Francis Taylor had suffered strokes in 1965 and 1967. Production halted while Elizabeth and Richard flew to Los Angeles for the burial. Back in Paris, Elizabeth suffered extreme back pains resulting from her 1957 accident to her spine. After an additional ten days of location shooting in Las Vegas, Elizabeth completed her scenes and *The Only Game in Town* finished production by February 1969.

While Twentieth Century-Fox pondered how to best handle the distribution of the feature, Elizabeth entered Cedars of Lebanon Hospital in March for tests and X-rays of her back. This action resulted in a rash of rumors that Elizabeth was afflicted with cancer of the spine. After being discharged from the hospital, Elizabeth and Richard vacationed in Puerto Vallarta before returning to England where Burton was to begin shooting *Anne of the Thousand Days* (1969) for Universal. In 1964 this vehicle had been offered to Elizabeth and Burton by producer Hal B. Wallis but an agreement was never reached at that time. When production commenced under Charles Jarrott's direction, Genevieve Bujold—a decade younger than Elizabeth—assumed the Anne Boleyn role. As she had done in *Quo Vadis* in 1951, Elizabeth donned a costume and mask and appeared in a court dancing scene as an extra. Not to be outdone by her mother, twelve-year-old Liza Todd Burton also appeared in the film as a beggar maid while her eleven-year-old stepsister, Kate Burton, portrayed a serving maid.

Anne of the Thousand Days provided the professional boost that Burton's career needed after *Doctor Faustus, The Comedians, Boom!, Candy!,*

With Warren Beatty in *The Only Game in Town* ('70).

On the set of *Anne of the Thousand Days* ('69) with Richard Burton.

With son Michael in London (August 1969).

349

Staircase, and even the commercially viable but artistically anemic *Where Eagles Dare* (with Clint Eastwood). *Anne of the Thousand Days* was released late in 1969 to qualify for the Oscar race. In his sixth nomination for an Oscar, Burton lost to celluloid gunslinger John Wayne who acquired the Academy Award for his *True Grit* performance.

Prior to the Oscar presentations, Elizabeth and Richard made two television appearances to stir interest in Burton's nomination. On CBS-TV's "60 Minutes" Charles Collingswood, a Puerto Vallarta neighbor, hosted the Burtons for a segment during which they spoke of their marriage, Elizabeth's diamonds, and the pending Oscar race. The following week Burton was a guest on David Frost's interview program. During the first hour Frost chatted with Burton who provided a series of film clips to illustrate his cinematic reminiscences. At an intermission for a commercial, Frost hurried offstage to the private room where Elizabeth was watching the proceedings. He succeeded in bringing Elizabeth out "to say hello." Wearing no makeup and looking very tan, she was quite charming during the taping. When they broke for another commercial Elizabeth complained, "I was conned into this. I was only supposed to come on and say hello. You [Frost] really are a little fink, aren't you?"

Audiences had had three glimpses of Elizabeth on television but no paying audiences had yet seen *The Only Game in Town.* The picture debuted finally in March 1970 and moviegoers stayed away even though the critics exercised greater kindness than they had in evaluating her recent starring films. In *The New Yorker,* Pauline Kael observed, "Miss Taylor has a sweetness and, despite her rather shapeless look, a touching quality of frailty (like some of the women stars of an earlier era, as she gets older she begins to have a defenseless air about her), but the plot makes her ridiculous."

While in Hollywood for the Oscars the Burtons encountered effervescent Lucille Ball at a party and Richard made a comment that he enjoyed the "Here's Lucy" show and would enjoy doing an episode. The shrewd reigning queen of small-screen comedy had a script drawn up and yielded to Elizabeth's requests for Edith Head

for costumes and Sidney Guilaroff for hairstyles. In the domestic comedy episode (aired September 14, 1970, on CBS-TV), Burton disguised himself as a plumber to pass through a lobby full of fans. Lucy spots him and drags him to her suite to fix her faucet. She will not believe him when he tries to drop the disguise. Later Burton inadvertently leaves Elizabeth's precious diamond ring in the pocket of his discarded plumber's clothes. Lucy tries on the ring and—surprise—it becomes stuck. The denouement is typical of the farcical episodes of "Here's Lucy." This show opened the 1970 season and earned a high rating for Miss Ball.

Richard's next film was the moribund thriller *Villain* being shot in London during the autumn of 1970. Dampening this visit to London was a kidnapping threat against Elizabeth made on Thursday, October 1. A deeply upset Elizabeth ventured from her Dorchester Hotel suite on October 6 to attend the wedding of her son Michael Wilding, Jr., age seventeen, to Beth Clutter of Portland, Oregon. The couple was married in Caxton Hall Registry where Elizabeth and Michael Wilding, Sr. had been married nearly twenty years earlier. The Burtons gave the newlyweds a Jaguar and a $70,000 townhouse near their home in London's Hampstead Heath section. Elizabeth clearly stole the limelight when she appeared at the occasion wearing off-white wool trousers with a matching maxi cardigan. Her dark hair fell to her shoulders in a style similar to the groom who wore a maroon velvet caftan and trousers. The bride appeared in a full-length Edwardian white chiffon gown. A garland of daisies and lilies of the valley encircled her short, curly hair. The newlyweds had neither a reception nor a honeymoon.

In November, Elizabeth faced the camera again for her first starring role since the disastrous *The Only Game In Town.* The only difference was her $1 million fee was missing. Elizabeth commented, "I'm taking a percentage and expenses. We all sink or swim together. It makes everyone work harder to bring the picture in. If you win, it's like winning on the red. If you lose, well, it's roulette—but not Russian roulette."

Under Brian Hutton's direction, Elizabeth appeared as Zee Blakely in *X, Y & Zee.* Co-starring were Michael Caine as Elizabeth's husband and Susannah York as the third side of the triangle. While Elizabeth's starring vehicle, released by Columbia in 1972, received a blasting, her acting garnered critical attention. In a lengthy discourse, Foster Hirsch (*New York Times*) observed, "Flecked with echoes and cross-references, the character of Zee is an anthology of the star's career. Zee is the composite Elizabeth Taylor shrew. Liz-Zee specializes in the shriek, the sneer, and the snarl. Eyes flashing, arms flailing, lips curling, nostrils flaring, hair tossing, she enters into verbal battle with the relish of a prize racehorse at the starting gate. Like Martha in *Virginia Woolf*, Zee is an expert in the marital squabble. Like almost all her characters since Martha, Liz's Zee is spectacularly vulgar—she exults in her four-letter dialogue, her repertory of dirty stories, her open hot-bloodedness."

The possibilities of Elizabeth and Richard reteaming to do a film version of *Macbeth* under Roman Polanski's direction loomed as an exciting prospect. Negotiations failed to materialize and Polanski made the *Macbeth* film *sans* the Burtons. A film version of Charles Collingswood's *The Defector* with Elizabeth opposite Gregory Peck also failed to become a celluloid reality, as had her co-starring role with Clint Eastwood in *Two Mules for Sister Sara* (1970), a part later taken by Shirley MacLaine.

Upon completing *X, Y & Zee*, Elizabeth did a bit in the erudite film version of a Dylan Thomas play, *Under Milkwood* (1973), whch featured Burton and Peter O'Toole. Elizabeth's cameo role as the whore, Rosie Probert, delighted neither critics nor audiences. *Newsweek* tersely commented, "Fortunately, Elizabeth Taylor, as Welsh as Cleopatra, plays only a small part, her harsh, yowling cadence a bit of intrusive tourism."

Elizabeth desperately needed another movie vehicle like *Virginia Woolf* and a director like Mike Nichols. Nothing of that calibre occurred. *Hammersmith Is Out* (1972), directed by Peter Ustinov, was a bleak attempt at black comedy which teamed Elizabeth with Burton, Beau Bridges, and actor/director Ustinov. As the slatternly, plumpish waitress, Jimmie Jean Jackson, Elizabeth received salvageable reviews while the film met with general critical dismissal. The *Hollywood Reporter* observed, "Miss Taylor looks gorgeous in Edith Head's costumes and gives one of her best performances in some time, despite the material. There is one scene in particular, when she thinks she is about to die, where she evokes a beautifully deep and tender emotion."

As a re-working of the Faust legend, *Hammersmith Is Out* outraged* a large sector of the audience because of its pointed sexuality, flatulence, and provocative language. The film was shot in May 1971 in Cuernavaca, Mexico, near the Burtons' Puerto Vallarta residence. The Burtons received no up-front salary, working for expenses against a large-percentage deferral pay. *Hammersmith Is Out* resulted in Elizabeth receiving the Silver Bear Award as Best Actress at the 1972 Berlin Film Festival. The film also marked Elizabeth's first cinematic appearance in a bathing suit since *Suddenly, Last Summer* in 1959. Her fluctuating weight during the Sixties was constantly a target for critics and fan magazines which seemed to delight in capturing photos of the ballooning actress.

Of her own appearance, Elizabeth wrote, "I am pretty enough. I try not to look like a slob. I don't have a complex about my looks, but I'm too short of leg, too big in the arms, one too many chins, nose a bit crooked, big feet, big hands, I'm too fat. My best feature is my gray hairs. I have them all named; they're all called Burton." Burton's epithets for his wife included Tubby, Fatty, Elizabeth the Fat, Tiny Tim, Mabel, Maude, Agatha, Cheeky, and Maxie. Elizabeth countered by labeling her hard-drinking, girl-chasing spouse as Ratfink, Man, Mabel, Maude, Agatha, Buster, Boozy, Modesty Blaise, and Obscenity-Lips.

With *Hammersmith Is Out,* the Burtons returned to London for a rest and for the first glimpse of Elizabeth's first grandchild, born to Michael and Beth Wilding. Elizabeth's next birthday became an international event. The cover of *Life* was emblazoned, "LIZ TAYLOR IS 40!" and Burton threw a $45,000 bash in Budapest where he was before the cameras in

*In late 1975, when J. Cornelius Cream was trying to sell *Hammersmith Is Out* to television, he claimed that $50,000-$60,000 was the highest he could ask.

With Beau Bridges in *Hammersmith Is Out* ('72).

Bluebeard with Raquel Welsh, Virna Lisi, and Joey Heatherton. Joining the birthday celebration were 160 close friends, including Michael Caine, Sammy Davis, Jr., Susannah York, Ringo Starr, and Princess Grace of Monaco. Elizabeth appeared in a black evening gown highlighted by several pieces of sparkling jewelry and a lighted candle in her hand.

During the summer of 1972 Elizabeth began filming *Night Watch* (1973) in London while Burton continued his role as Marshal Tito on *Sujetska* in Yugoslavia. *Night Watch* was based on Lucille Fletcher's play which expired after 120 performances with Joan Hackett during the 1971-1972 season. *Night Watch* seemed plagued by accidents and illnesses which caused production delays. Prior to the start of shooting, the production manager became ill forcing the producers to seek a last-minute replacement. Elizabeth, always one to be counted on for a mishap, fell off a set platform and fractured her left index finger. When director Brian Hutton contracted bronchitis, a week's delay in shooting occurred. Finally, the *Night Watch* set closed down for a month when co-star Laurence Harvey underwent emergency abdominal surgery. (It later

developed that Harvey was suffering from terminal cancer.) Elizabeth took this latest delay to join Burton in Yugoslavia where she fell on the steps of a swimming pool, subsequently severing an artery in her left forearm which affected the arm's muscles and nerves. She flew to Switzerland for treatment prior to resuming her *Night Watch* duties.

Elizabeth's personal and professional life had been plagued by countless accidents and illnesses which began to take their toll on her face and figure. Her list of afflictions included disintegrating spinal discs, recurring hemorrhoids, gynecological problems, glandular imbalance, diet-caused anemia, phlebitis, respiratory problems resulting in a tracheotomy, encephalitic attacks, and neurasthenia. *Night Watch* co-star Laurence Harvey commented in his usual piercing manner, "You can't pick her up. There's no place to get a grip on this woman, this sex symbol. This isn't a particularly sexy film, but occasionally we do touch, and when I come near her, she screams."

When *Night Watch* debuted—yet another variation of *Rear Window* (one person is convinced he/she has seen a murder occurring in a neighbor's flat)—no one was thrilled and the Manhattan critics registered three favorable, one mixed, and eleven negative reviews in the rating game. Within the context of the poorly conceived Gothic thriller, she is the unwanted spouse of two succeeding husbands (not a very flattering premise), and tries to trap her errant husband (Harvey) and her disloyal best friend (Billie Whitelaw). As the role of Ellen Wheeler requires Elizabeth to range from normal upper class to a deranged, vengeful murderess, Elizabeth zooms in and out of proper focus on the peculiar characterization. She is as often off the mark as on in this lugubrious whodunit.

The year 1973 also marked the Burtons first and only made-for-television movie. *Divorce; His/Divorce; Hers* were back-to-back films exploring a divorce from the point of view of the husband and the wife. The pair of films were made jointly by ABC-TV and Britain's Harlech TV and televised in the United States on Tuesday and Wednesday, February 6 and 7, 1973. Another critical blasting followed. *Variety* lashed out, "This two-part soupbone made it official: Liz and Dick Burton are the corniest act in show business since the Cherry Sisters." Of Elizabeth's role, *Variety* added, "Miss Taylor wallowed in suds to a point where the many closeups between her ample bazooms failed even in distracting from the nonsense." During the filming of this two-part fiasco, for which the Burtons were very well paid, Elizabeth was enduring another one of her fat periods. To minimize her ungainly figure, the cameras discreetly filmed her sitting behind high tables, or shot her whenever possible from bosom upward. It fooled no one.

After her ill-fated appearance on the small screen, Elizabeth returned to the wide screen in *Ash Wednesday,* filmed from March to June 1973 in Cortina d'Ampezzo and Lake Como, Italy. The director was Larry Peerce who had enjoyed great success with *Goodbye, Columbus* (1969) but had had no commercial popularity thereafter. *Ash Wednesday* featured Elizabeth as a fiftyish American who retreats to Europe for head-to-toe plastic surgery in a wild attempt to recapture the love of her bored, businessman husband (Henry Fonda) who has long since taken a mistress. In the medically complex and financially expensive process, she undergoes a magnificent rejuvenating experience, has an affair with gigolo Helmut Berger, and fails to regain her husband. Like *Night Watch,* the gimmicky *Ash Wednesday,* which gruesomely details gory aspects of the delicate surgery, lost in the review race. Among New York City critics two were favorable, one had mixed feelings, and fourteen offered negative reactions. Offering words of praise was Rex Reed who rejoiced in Elizabeth's physical transformation after what he considered were years of bad scripts, bad directors, and a screeching voice. He observed, "In *Ash Wednesday,* she's subtle, sensitive, glowing with freshness and beauty, fifty pounds lighter in weight; her hair is coiffed simply, her clothes ravishing, her makeup a symphony of perfection."

On the Tuesday eve of Independence Day, 1973, Elizabeth issued the following statement to the press from her suite at New York's Regency Hotel:

> I am convinced it would be a good and constructive idea if Richard and I are separated for a while.
>
> Maybe we loved each other too much—not that I ever believed such a thing was possible.
>
> But we have been in each other's pockets constantly, never being apart except for matters of life and death, and I believe it has caused a temporary breakdown of communications. . . . Wish us well, please, during this most difficult time.

From lawyer Aaron Frosch's splendid home at Quogue, Long Island, Burton responded:

> Perhaps my indifference to Elizabeth's personal problems has triggered off this situation.
>
> Maybe it is something else. Women are strange creatures.
>
> She is a splendid child and I am very fond of the lady. But who knows what goes on in the feminine secret mind. I haven't spoken to her since her extraordinary statement.

With Henry Fonda in *Ash Wednesday* ('73).

The frightful thing is I'm amused by all this. I find the situation wildly fascinating.

Millions of avid readers also found the Taylor/Burton separation fascinating as they scanned the papers daily for the latest intimate news of the marital mix-up of two such VIPs. Of particular speculation was how the Burtons would settle their empire of jewels, art works, and property* should their separation end in divorce.

On Friday, July 20, the Burtons met in Rome and rumors of a reconciliation were touted in global papers. Within ten days, mercurial Elizabeth shattered these possibilities by instructing lawyer Frosch to file a divorce suit on her behalf in Switzerland. Frosch commented to the press, "The grounds will probably be incompatibility or some other such moderate grounds. In other words it won't be adultery. They are very amiable, and no third party exists in either case. Also there are no financial issues to be settled. There is no hysteria, no name calling, and no vilification. There are no issues, no problems, no squabbles." Then why a divorce? Close friends of the Burtons hinted at Richard's excessive drinking and their professional doldrums as the basis of the disintegration of their life together.

In the ensuing months both Elizabeth and Richard made headlines each and every time the photographers could record them appearing in public with a new face. Through long-time pal Peter Lawford, Elizabeth met Los Angeles car dealer Henry Wynberg (age thirty-nine and divorced for seven years). He would spend most of the summer of 1973 at Elizabeth's side following her separation from Burton. The press also linked Elizabeth with Hollywood actor Frank Calganini, a friend of Wynberg's, and independent Hollywood filmmaker Frank Grippo.

Not to be casually outdone by his (ex)wife, Burton raised a bit of journalistic hell on the Oroville, California, set of *The Klansman* in which he co-starred with Lee Marvin and O. J. Simpson. Burton turned his attention to Kim Dinucci, an eighteen-year-old waitress who received a $450 ring from the actor who was thirty years her senior. This tryst quickly faded and Burton began a romance with Ann De Angelo. In spite of their varied romantic endeavors, the Burtons managed to keep in touch during the hectic period of their separation. (She was reunited with him at the Oroville locale for a brief spell.) Burton helped Elizabeth celebrate her forty-second birthday in Puerto Vallarta in February of 1974. A drunken Burton gifted Elizabeth with a cognac-colored diamond ring and matching earrings. Yet these materialistic attempts failed to gloss over the alleged abuses that Burton had supposedly showered upon his wife in recent months.

Ex-mates Eddie Fisher and Sybil Burton expressed their sympathies regarding the termination of Elizabeth and Richard's marriage. Fisher noted, "I am sorry for them both. I know Elizabeth wanted it to work. She tried just as hard when we were married. I respect her for that. I also respect them for pulling out before they hurt each other any more." Sybil, married to actor/singer Jordan Christopher since 1965, commented, "Believe it or not, I feel terrible about it. I have found happiness and I hoped Richard had found his. I won't say it took me by surprise, but I am truly sorry. . . . I think it is very hard to be married to either Richard or Elizabeth, because they are so famous. I think the future may be harder on them than the past, for it will be difficult for both of them to find a mate quite as exciting."

On Wednesday, June 26, 1974, a Swiss court

*The inventory of Elizabeth's jewelry includes the Cartier-Burton diamond, 69.42 carat white gem, as large as a peach pit. Elizabeth's $1 million bid was surpassed by corporate Cartier's bid for $1,055,000. Burton negotiated with Cartier and purchased the diamond; the Krupp diamond (33.19 carats) at $305,000; the La Peregrina pearl, a milky-white pendant purchased for $37,000; an enamel cameo bracelet (given to Elizabeth by director Zeffirelli—supposedly it once belonged to France's Empress Josephine or Napoleon's sister, or both); a ping-pong diamond at .042 carats ($38), received when Elizabeth beat Burton at a game of ping-pong; a $93,000 emerald clip given to Elizabeth by Burton as an engagement present; a platinum wedding ring from Burton; the diamond-and-pearl necklace and earring set from Todd; the diamond-encrusted emerald necklace and matching earrings; the $65,000 40-carat blue sapphire brooch, one inch in length; a diamond belt; a $20 gold piece surrounded by rubies given to Elizabeth by Richard on their tenth wedding anniversary; and a heart-shaped diamond pendant originally given by Emperor Shah Jehan (who built the Taj Mahal) to his wife in 1621, given to Elizabeth on her fortieth birthday by Richard. In addition, Elizabeth also owns a collection of paintings by Degas, Hals, Cassatt, Pissarro, Monet, Modigliani, Renoir, Rouault, Utrillo, and Van Gogh.

granted the Burtons a divorce on the grounds of mutual incompatibility. Elizabeth appeared at the forty-five-minute hearing; Burton's lawyer presented a medical certificate excusing the absent actor from court. Elizabeth received custody of their eleven-year-old daughter, Maria, who had been adopted while the actress was the wife of Fisher.

Three weeks prior to the granting of her divorce Elizabeth arrived at Monte Carlo with a new film entitled *The Driver's Seat* (a.k.a. *Identikit*). Producer Franco Rossellini and director Giuseppe Patroni-Griffi originally offered the film as an official Italian entry in the Cannes Film Festival. When Cannes rejected *The Driver's Seat,* the producer staged the Monaco affair to compete with the festivities in Cannes. Princess Grace and Prince Rainier hosted a premiere for the benefit of the Monaco Red Cross. The motion picture was based on Muriel Spark's novella of a woman's search for the right man to murder her, thus putting an end to her schizophrenia. Before the screening Elizabeth made an appearance in beige chiffon and diamonds to a round of applause. At the film's end, a confused, if not shocked, audience supplied polite applause before hurrying off to a gala party hostessed by Grace Kelly and attended by such luminaries as Franco Zeffirelli, Ursula Andress, Elsa Martinelli, Salvador Dali, Christina Ford, Aristotle Onassis, Stavros Niarchos, the Begum Khan, and Andy Warhol (who had a bit in the film). Agent Freddie Fields succeeded in selling the film to twenty countries, but at that time was unable to snag a distributor in the United States. (Later Paramount expressed interest, but it would be Avco Embassy who would release the picture in late 1975 in the U.S., on a double bill with an unimportant Sophia Loren feature.)

Elizabeth's only appearance on film during 1974 in the United States was as co-host of *That's Entertainment!,** a compilation of outstanding musical moments from her home

*When *That's Entertainment! Part Two* was released in 1976, Elizabeth refused to participate in the ballyhoo for the film. She was miffed that the picture publicized her appearance in the clips, but only used a few brief moments of her Metro footage.

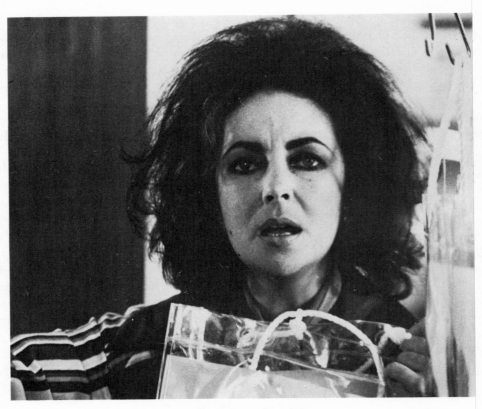

In *The Driver's Seat* ('75).

studio, MGM. Included in the film was a scene of fifteen-year-old Elizabeth singing in *Cynthia*.

Although Elizabeth had no new feature films to make news, her personal life continued to spill out across the press. In October 1974 her son Michael Wilding, Jr. received a divorce from his wife of four years, Beth Ann Clutter. Wilding took up residence in a commune while Miss Clutter returned to her mother's home in Portland, Oregon. Miss Clutter received custody of three-year-old daughter Leyla and planned to study hairdressing and cosmetology in order to support her daughter. In an interview, Beth Ann stated that Elizabeth offered no support for Leyla and had told her (Beth) on the telephone, "Nobody tells me whether I can see my own grandchild. I'll never help you again."

Elizabeth received another bit of shocking news on October 17, 1974, when Burton announced that he planned to marry Princess Elizabeth of Yugoslavia. The already-married princess—a relative of the British royal family—was separated from her second husband and reportedly was seeking a divorce. Burton's romance with the princess faded almost as quickly as it had made the headlines. Replacing the princess in Burton's affections was twenty-four-year-old black actress Jean Bell whom he met while filming *The Klansman* the previous year. Their romance was first chronicled at a party thrown by Terence Young, the director of Burton's new film, *Jackpot* (a Rome-based picture destined never to be completed because of lack of proper financing). Flanked by Princess Elizabeth and Miss Bell, Burton commented to the restaurant's singer, "Please stop those Russian songs. They remind me of my wife who is filming in Russia."

Elizabeth had arrived in Leningrad in late January of 1975 to appear in *The Blue Bird*, the first feature film to be co-produced by American and Soviet moviemakers. Accompanying Elizabeth to Russia were constant companion Henry Wynberg (who was hired to photograph Taylor on the set for some American magazines), her male secretary Raymond, a maid, two Shih-tzu dogs, a Siamese cat, and some 2,800 pounds of luggage. During the on-again, off-again shooting schedule, during which tempers flew, James Coco left and was replaced by Robert Morley, the

American and Soviet crews became less and less diplomatic, costumer Edith Head departed in disgust, and Elizabeth became indisposed. She created a further hiatus in the filming by flying to London where she entered a hospital for ten days to combat the flu. (Later she learned that she had suffered from kidney and liver trouble.) She had lost ten pounds in the hospital which, added to the twenty pounds she had shed before production began, made her look "years younger."

Based on the 1908 fantasy by Maurice Maeterlinck, the famed work had been filmed in Hollywood successfully in 1918 by Maurice Tourneur and then unsuccessfully in a 1940 talkie with Shirley Temple. The new edition had a cast which included Ava Gardner, Jane Fonda, Cicely Tyson, and Russian stars Nadejda Pavlowa, Margareta Terechova, and George Vitzin under the guidance of veteran director George Cukor. The mammoth undertaking completed active production on August 28, 1975, after seven months of shooting and a budget of over $15 million.

Elizabeth, in the quadruple role of Mother, Light, Maternal Love, and Witch, invested in the motion picture and announced she would also receive a percentage* of the box-office gross. A month after the film was through lensing, Elizabeth conducted a press session. At the time she revealed, "We were in Russia because we need their money. They invited us because they want to learn something from our technical expertise, and the Russians were at a disadvantage because the Americans didn't provide the Russians with our best equipment. The American producers Edward Lewis and Paul Maslansky are 'cheapskates.' In five months I did about a week's work."

In describing her main role of Light, who leads two children in search of the bluebird of happiness, Elizabeth stated, "Light can't be saccharine or a Girl Scout leader. In the play she's a goddamn bore, but she will not be a goddamn bore the way I play her. I think I'll put

*She would tell columnist Rex Reed during the hellish filming, "I want to make a percentage on this picture and that's why I'm not walking out. The days of getting a million dollars a film are over. If this film doesn't come out and isn't a big success, I've wasted a year of my life and spent my own money instead of the usual expense I get when I'm working. . . ."

With daughter Liza in 1975.

With director George Cukor on
the set of *The Blue Bird* ('76).

in a few swear words. Everybody's got the wrong image of the film. Give 'em a little cleavage. We can spritz it up."

During her Leningrad filming Elizabeth spoke with Richard Burton many times on joint business and personal matters. Burton was then in Switzerland with Jean Bell, and Henry Wynberg, as usual, was at Elizabeth's side in Russia. On Sunday, August 10, Elizabeth paid for a lavish party in Leningrad to celebrate the completion of her shooting on *The Blue Bird*. During the gala event, Elizabeth received a telegram from Burton requesting that she meet with him in Switzerland on business matters. When Elizabeth flew from Russia, Wynberg accompanied her but soon disappeared after their landing in Geneva.

Miss Taylor met with Burton on Saturday, August 16, at the office of lawyer Morris Solowicz for the business meeting that soon dissolved into a relaxing discussion of old times. That evening the pair met at a friend's villa for a romantic reconciliation. Burton toasted Elizabeth with orange juice and Elizabeth reciprocated with a glass of milk. The couple left separately to tell the news to their respective traveling companions.* Wynberg flew from Geneva the next morning, while the reunited Burtons posed jubilantly for photographer Stanley Bielcki. Of their renewed romance, Burton's New York press representative, John Springer, noted, "One of the big conditions of this reconciliation is that Richard stay away from drink. It's no secret that Elizabeth doesn't like it."

Miss Bell expressed no regrets about Burton's reunion with Elizabeth. "I have known Richard for seven months," she said, "and I still love him. I expected to leave him from the very beginning. Our relationship has been very on and off, and I knew we would never marry." Wynberg's concise reaction for the press was, "It was beautiful while it lasted. I want her to be happy, whether with me, Richard, or anyone. I was her lover. I am still her friend."

News of the reconciliation was emblazoned in New York newspapers on Thursday, August 21, with the *Daily News* headlining, "LIZ AND BURTON TO TRY A RERUN." Press representative John Springer stated at this time, "This is not a trial reconciliation. It is permanent. They are terribly, terribly happy. In fact, I've never heard them sound happier."

The Burtons spent a week together in Switzerland before flying to Israel where it was rumored they would remarry. Their immediate reason for the trip to Tel Aviv was to discuss Burton's forthcoming film, *Abakarov*, with producer-director Wolf Vollmar. (Elizabeth was to participate in the film, playing an aging movie queen. As it developed, neither Taylor nor Burton would grace the project.) During the last evening they spent in Israel, Burton gave a benefit recital at the Jerusalem Theatre. He concluded the program with a quote from poet Gerard Manley Hopkins' "The Leaden Echo and the Golden Echo": "Give beauty back, beauty, beauty, beauty, back to God, beauty's self and

beauty's giver." With that, Elizabeth appeared on stage, dressed in gold, and quietly said, "Shalom."

The Burtons returned to their Swiss home for a relatively quiet September during which their marriage plans remained in abeyance. Burton commented, "We've tried it once before—but we don't know whether we're going to try it again. We've got nothing planned for the moment, at least. It's just a piece of paper, you know."

While the Burtons remained evasive about wedding plans, close friends speculated about the announcement of a remarriage. Former MGM publicity agent and long-time friend of Elizabeth, Bill Lyon, felt, "There must be wedding bells around the corner. Elizabeth's not the sort of person to go on living with someone she's not married to. She has to be married because it represents the kind of permanence she needs."

Few were surprised the following month when newspaper accounts on October 15, 1975, revealed that the Burtons had remarried on Friday, October 10, at a game preserve in Chobe, Botswana, north of South Africa. Performing the simple ceremony was Tswana tribal official Ambrose Masalila and serving as witnesses were game lodge manager Fred Knoessen and an unidentified member of the staff of a charter air company. Elizabeth wore a green dress trimmed with lace and festooned with guinea fowl feathers and Burton appeared in a red open-necked shirt, white slacks, red socks, and white shoes. The pair drove in a four-wheel-drive truck to the banks of the Chobe River some five miles away where the wedding party was joined by two hippos and a rhino. The Burtons reportedly had selected Botswana for their remarriage in order "to be completely and totally alone." The bride was forty-three; the groom forty-nine. (He would buy her a $1,000,000 25-carat pink diamond in Johannesburg; but she would reject the latest generous token stating that the Botswana village where they were remarried "badly needs a hospital and I don't need another ring. . . . Richard doesn't have to spoil me any more." (She did keep the 72-diamond wedding ring designed to match her $260,000 Krupp diamond ring.)

*Elizabeth's parting gift to Wynberg was an expensive Cartier watch. Burton's goodbye to Jean Bell included a "necessary agreement to take care of her." No money was mentioned in the settlement. When Miss Bell later arrived in Los Angeles, she was met by Elizabeth's chauffeur-driven Cadillac.

On Monday, November 10, 1975, Elizabeth hostessed a fiftieth birthday party for Richard at the Dorchester Hotel in London. During the course of the evening the non-drinking Burton remained quiet (almost sullen) and non-festive, a far cry from his gregarious behavior at Elizabeth's fortieth bash in Budapest only three years prior. While the 150 guests drank Don Perignon champagne and Elizabeth sipped Jack Daniels and water, Burton drank mineral water or milk. The festive atmosphere was not the only element absent from Burton's party. Several of the invited guests sent regrets: Princess Margaret of England, Princess Grace, Laurence Olivier, David Niven, Peter O'Toole, and Peter Lawford. Among the celebrities who toasted Burton's fifty years were Lee Remick, Dame Margot Fonteyn, Liza Todd, Michael Wilding, Sr. and Jr.,* and Sir Ralph Richardson. Elizabeth was dressed for the occasion in a tight-fitting black gown accented by diamond hair clips, earrings, pendant, bracelet, and rings.

The Burton reunion was rather short-lived. In January, when he was in Geneva and New York preparing for his stage role in *Equus,* she began a relationship in Switzerland with thirty-five-year-old Peter Darmanin, an advertising executive from Malta. The impetus for this romance was allegedly her fury with Burton's failure to keep away from liquor. Darmanin came and went in Elizabeth's life rather quickly. His souvenirs for the flashy adventure included heavy debts from their luxurious living and a cut eyebrow. "This was done by a half-million-dollar ring," claimed Darmanin, referring to Taylor having hit him with one of her bejeweled hands.

The latest separation between Taylor and Burton became official in early February 1976 when Elizabeth came to New York while Richard was rehearsing for his opening in *Equus.* They both stayed at the Lombardy Hotel, but in separate quarters. Aggravating the situation was Burton's interest in Susan Hunt, the wife of twenty-eight-year-old British racing driver James Hunt. It was not long before Elizabeth asked Burton's stage producer, Alex-

ander Cohen, to cancel the planned party to acknowledge her forty-fourth birthday.

On Friday, February 27, Burton was celebrating (with Ms. Hunt) his glorious reviews in *Equus,* while Elizabeth was back in California with, of all people, Henry Wynberg. At his Beverly Hills home to toast her birthday were Elizabeth and her mother. The movie star's four children phoned from various spots around the world to wish her well. In March of 1976, accompanied by Wynberg, Elizabeth made quite an appearance at the 48th Annual Academy Awards wearing a scarlet strapless gown. At the finale she stepped front and center and stated, "Tonight, saluting the 200th year of this land— the bicentennial year—let us recall that original purpose and reaffirm that necessary dream. Please join me to sing 'America the Beautiful!' " Unfortunately the orchestra played through the patriotic tune with little vocal accompaniment. It seemed that everyone—including Taylor— had forgotten the words!

After a special Washington, D.C., showing, *The Blue Bird* finally opened in mid-May 1976 at the Radio City Music Hall. The critics were less than kind for this heavily edited pageant. Vincent Canby (*New York Times*) suggested that the picture "has about it a kind a lumbering tackiness that I associate with Soviet stage spectacle. . . . " He pinpointed the fault of this co-production as, "You keep seeing two films that want to compete but don't, everyone being polite, accepting compromise, effectively neutered." He added, "What could [director] Mr. [George] Cukor possibly have suggested to Miss Taylor to help her read a line like, 'I am the light that makes men see the radiance in reality'? Keep a straight face, perhaps. The actress has some creditably funny moments as a witch and some none-to-good as a peasant mother who darns socks." On another occasion Canby judged the film "to be the bore of the year to date," a sentiment echoed by critics and audiences throughout the U.S. It was soon withdrawn from release.

Thereafter Taylor remained in a professional lull. There were rumors she would star in *The Ambassador* for producer/director Menaham Golan. The spy drama was to be shot in Israel; but the project fell dormant. An even less likely

*Elizabeth's son Michael plays guitar, flute, and trumpet in the rock group Solar Ben, and via his girlfriend Johanna Lykke-Dahn has become the father of a daughter named Naomi.

concept was to have Elizabeth star on Broadway in a revival of George Bernard Shaw's *Candida.* If these vehicles proved to be merely hopeful dreams, the actress took positive steps with her personal life. She again bid goodbye to Wynberg. (When he was asked if he would make a second reconciliation with her, he replied, "I don't know. I did once. I'm a little confused.") Her new escorts would certainly have made good contestants on "What's My Line?" Portly nutrition expert Dr. Louis A. Scarrone of New York chaperoned Elizabeth in Washington, D.C., and Manhattan. He was replaced by Iranian Ambassador Ardeshir Zahedi, the forty-eight-year-old bachelor. This relationship took a glittering note upward when Taylor flew to Iran in May 1976 as the guest of the Shah and Ambassador Zahedi. When Elizabeth returned to the United States after ten days of luxurious touring of the countryside, the romance had seen its course. In fact, her actions while a guest in Iran had alienated Ardeshir's countrymen. *Zan-E-Ruz,* a popular Iranian woman's journal, wrote of the actress, ". . . [she] is a fattish, short, big-busted woman with poor makeup, and totally out of fashion."

Elizabeth next turned to the political scene. During a big Democratic fund-raising bash at the Waldorf-Astoria Hotel in New York in late June, she made an appearance "trailing clouds of black chiffon and rhinestones." She became the center of attention, stealing the limelight from the soon-to-be-nominated Democratic presidential candidate, Jimmy Carter. Then she swept off to Washington, D.C.

There it was revealed officially to whom she had given her affections. It seemed that in March of 1976, via Lady Frances Ramsbotham, she had met forty-nine-year-old political conservative John William Warner.* Soon Elizabeth and Warner became quite an item as he began accompanying her to fancy New York parties and she spent time at his 2,000-acre Middleburg, Virginia farm.

Burton, who was completing his *Equus* stage

*Warner had been wed to Catherine Mellon from 1957 to 1973; the couple had three children. Thereafter he dated, among others, Barbara Walters and Washington writer Barbara Howard. A lawyer, he had helped in Richard Nixon's presidential campaigns of 1960 and 1968, and in May of 1972 he was elevated from Under-Secretary of the Navy to Secretary of the Navy. In 1974 he accepted the $40,000-a-year post as head of the Bicentennial Committee.

engagement and beginning the filming of *Exorcist II: The Heretic* (1977), had a few comments to make on his latest failed relationship with Elizabeth:

> She is without doubt the woman I have loved most. She has seemed to understand certain needs I have. But I am changing. And, of course, the situation for Elizabeth has changed from what it was when we were first married. . . .

> But what she never truly understood was that I now find myself in a situation similar to menopause. I feel a change in my body. . . . I don't think she could ever accept the change as it came over me. She always wanted me to be a servant to our marriage and a non-drinker. . . . But I'm not a saint. . . .

For her part, before the John Warner relationship became public, Elizabeth told the press about Burton: "It will be very difficult for me to understand how we will survive without each other for the rest of our lives."

One would have thought that the Thursday, July 29, 1976, divorce of Taylor-Burton in Haiti would have ended speculation about their domestic status. But Elizabeth added to the public's curiosity by announcing, "We will still try to meet again. I don't think I can plan for the two of us not being together. . . . Deep down, I had hoped there would have been a reconciliation . . . but . . . I resigned myself to the fact that Richard was probably right—our remarriage had been a mistake. . . . We were just too explosive to get along with each other." As a good-will gesture, Elizabeth offered to give him their yacht (now hers) if he wed "that girl." He gallantly refused.

Burton wed Susan Hunt on August 21 and then went off to Canada to film *Equus* (1977). As for Elizabeth, she had finally agreed to make a new film, *A Little Night Music* (1977), the Stephen Sondheim-Hugh Wheeler Broadway musical of 1973, based on an Ingmar Bergman Swedish film *Smiles of a Summer Night.* Casting and production problems besiege most pictures,

Advertisement for special pre-release engagement of the much-delayed *A Little Night Music* (December 1977).

but an Elizabeth Taylor vehicle always seems to have more than its share of chaos. First Taylor let it be known that she would prefer Bette Davis to play the grand dame of the piece, but Sondheim and producer/director Harold Prince favored Hermione Gingold from the New York and London cast. Miss Gingold was hired. Then British actor Robert Stephens, cast to play Taylor's vis-à-vis, was dismissed. He was informed that the star claimed no "chemistry" existed between the two. He retorted, "Bad chemistry? We're actors, not pharmacists." According to Elizabeth, "The unit manager was the one who spoke to him [Stephens]. If I find out he has put the blame on me, there will be one unit manager less."

The play had been set in Sweden, but due to financing from Austria and West Germany, the locale was changed to Vienna. Since Elizabeth was the one bankable star in this $7.5 million production, she was given royal treatment: a suite at the Hotel Imperial, a seven-passenger Cadillac, and no reprimands when she appeared late on the set. Said veteran performer Hermione Gingold, "I like her. She may be late, but she knows her lines." Prince insisted, "She's been totally cooperative. She seems to have no vanity." The big question in point remained whether her singing would be sufficient for the demands of the film. The last time she had sung on screen was for *A Date with Judy* (1948).

While Elizabeth was filming *A Little Night Music,* Warner saw her in Vienna and they spent time at her Swiss home; later during a filming break, she visited with him in Washington. By October, she had completed work on the musical and he had resigned from his Bicentennial post. Then they announced their engagement. To celebrate the occasion she was given a red, white, and blue ring—it contained a ruby, a diamond,* and a sapphire set in a row, with a star design around each stone.

*Although Elizabeth, for the first time in her career, had given the use of her name to a business—the Elizabeth Taylor Diamond Corp.—the stones for her engagement ring did not come from her outfit. (In 1978 Elizabeth would sue Harry Shuster and Anglo-International Diamond Industries, Inc., which had formed the Taylor firm. According to Elizabeth's suit, the defendants had guaranteed her a $250,000 commission the initial year and a royalty of $200,000 every six months for the privilege of using her name and likeness to promote the company. In her law action she claimed she never received a sou from the defendants.)

Evidentally Phyllis Diller's quip about Elizabeth Taylor—"One more marriage and she'll be listed in the yellow pages"—did not faze the star. On Saturday, December 4, 1976, she and John Warner were wed in a hillside ceremony at his Middleburg, Virginia, farm. For her seventh marriage, she wore a knee-length cashmere dress, "the color of heather." Reverend Neil Morgan conducted the ceremony and among the guests were Warner's son John and daughter Mary, the groom's brother Charles, and his eighty-seven-year-old mother, Mrs. Martha Stuart Warner. Elizabeth told newsmen afterwards, "I have never been so happy. It was a very moving and marvelous moment." For their honeymoon the couple visited Israel, went to her home in Gstaad, Switzerland, and devoted a few days to Kent, England, where she had spent a portion of her childhood.

When not participating in political functions to aid her new husband in his forthcoming Senatorial campaign, Elizabeth managed a few sojourns to the West Coast for filming ventures. She joined with Kirk Douglas, Burt Lancaster, Anthony Hopkins, Helen Hayes, and Linda Blair in *Victory at Entebbe* (ABC-TV, January 13, 1977), one of several made-for-television films dealing with the June 1976 hijacking of a jet plane by Arab terrorists and the bargaining thereafter at Uganda's Entebbe Airport between Israeli leaders and Palestinian extremists. As Edra and Herschel Vilnosky, Elizabeth and Douglas were the anxiety-ridden parents of hostage Blair. The for-the-moment show left little impact with jaded viewers, especially when less than a month later NBC-TV telecast its version of the event with its own star-studded ensemble. However, the project had a special significance for Elizabeth. As would be revealed by Simcha Dinitz, Israel's ambassador to the United States, Taylor had offered to substitute herself for the hostages at the time of the hijack. She had requested to fly to Entebbe to ask Ugandan President Idi Amin to let the prisoners go. All this was detailed at a testimonial dinner for the star in Los Angeles in June 1977.

Because her post-marital acting chores have been of short duration, the press (fan magazines in particular) became worried that the Elizabeth of old might have changed. But she insisted, "I'm

With Anthony Hopkins and Kirk Douglas in *Victory at Entebbe* (ABC-TV, December 13, 1976).

With husband John Warner in 1977.

very much myself. I'm still me, and John's wife." She found time to conduct a mini-seminar in acting at the University of Virginia in Charlottesville. Then in mid-February she appeared in Boston to accept the Harvard Hasty Pudding Woman of the Year Award. She kiddingly told the gathering, "I'm a very private person, [but] I'll answer anything unless I think it's inappropriate." She then held forth on assorted subjects:

On acting: "I learned most from Spencer Tracy. He had a marvelous way of underplaying a character and taught me how to concentrate so I could work intensely."

On filmmaking: "We don't have heroines anymore, but we don't have heroes either. . . . Everything makes me nervous except making films."

Regarding her memorizing technique: "I have a photographic memory. I read my lines three times for the next day's filming and sleep on it. I'm known as one-take Liz."

Regarding her most challenging part: "Martha" in *Who's Afraid of Virginia Woolf?*—"I love parts that aren't me, where I can scream and tear the scenery. I concentrate on my role at the studio, but I shed it like an overcoat when I go home to my personal life."

Just as John Warner has drawn Elizabeth into the world of politics and farming, so she has led him into the arena of show business. When she went to California to film her cameo role in *Winter Kills* (1977),* based on the Richard Condon novel, she was there for a week to play a regal Washington hostess. To portray the U.S. President (a non-speaking role) who escorts her to a formal party the producers chose Warner. Then in March 1977, on ABC-TV, Barbara Walters interviewed the Warners on their Virginia farm. Elizabeth enunciated that she does not "consider myself a movie star and I never have," and as to her future, she wistfully stated, "I love acting. I would hate to feel that I was. . . retired." As to her increasing bouts of chubbiness she responded, "I eat out of contentment."

When Bryan Forbes announced plans to film a sequel to *National Velvet,* entitled *International*

Velvet, (1978), he made overtures to Elizabeth to join the cast which was to feature Tatum O'Neal. However, Taylor declined the bid and Forbes' wife Nanette Newman assumed the part (also rejected by Jean Simmons). Instead, the superstar preferred to continue campaigning for her husband's race for a Republican U.S. senatorial seat in Virginia. Regarding her frantic new way of life, the Oscar winner exclaimed: "The roles of film actress and politician's wife are very similar—and I do enjoy playing character parts. The pace is about the same, but the political scene is more difficult."

For Variety Clubs International (which would name her one of the eight recipients of the Great Lady Award in 1977), Elizabeth agreed to serve as the guest of honor for their 50th Anniversary Dinner, which was taped in Burbank, California, and aired over CBS-TV on Thursday, December 1, 1977. Bob Hope was among the speakers and he quipped, "We're honoring a woman tonight who can lose one earring and upset the world's economy." Among the nostalgic moments during the tribute were a reunion of MGM's *Little Women:* Elizabeth, June Allyson, Margaret O'Brien, and Janet Leigh; as well as a song sung to Taylor by former co-players Tom Drake, Jimmy Lydon, and Roddy McDowall. The *New York Times'* John O'Connor reported of the occasion: "And, through it all, Miss Taylor, noticeably heavier but no less glamorous, manages to look surprised, delighted, or moved for an endless progression of reaction shots. She is the perfect feast for celebrity watchers—prettily arranged and thoroughly insubstantial."

To celebrate the new year, *Harper's Bazaar* magazine in early 1978 selected America's ten most beautiful women. Among those chosen were: Elizabeth, Candice Bergen, Lauren Hutton, Lena Horne, Princess Grace, and Farrah Fawcett-Majors.

In February 1978 Taylor applied for American citizenship. When there was public comment in Virginia that she did this only to bolster the career of her husband, she retorted, "I am not trying to become an American citizen to help my husband. It's because I plan to spend the rest of my life in America." (In the 1978 *Social Register,* John Warner's name has been

*Due to lack of money, *Winter Kills* ceased production. There were plans in mid-1978 to resume filming so that the expensive project could be released.

365

You are cordially invited to
attend a very Special Hollywood Party with

Robert Blake
Debby Boone
Tom Drake
Henry Fonda
Frank Gorshin
Monty Hall

Bob Hope
Rock Hudson
Jimmy Lydon
Roddy McDowell

Paul Newman
Carroll O'Connor
Rowan & Martin
*Plus surprise
star guests and
a celebrity audience*

Sears

ALL STAR TRIBUTE TO
ELIZABETH TAYLOR

SEARS
SPECIAL
EVENT

Tonight
9:00
Channel 2
CBS

The December 1, 1977 (CBS-TV) special.

dropped, reportedly because of his recent marriage to a woman who has been four-times divorced and who is an actress.)

By early 1978 the long-awaited *A Little Night Music* had finally found a distributor in the United States (Roger Corman's New World Pictures), had been re-edited, and had played a test engagement at the Deauville Film Festival. *Variety* complained of the screen version, "Director [Hal] Prince has been too cautious and has failed to give the film sufficient visual flair and movement. . . . Uneven and sometimes slow, the pic has good looks and the name of Elizabeth Taylor for possible playoff use. She is somewhat posey but does sing agreeably." When the motion picture (which had deleted some of the show's original score and added new melodies) bowed inconspicuously in New York in March 1978, the reviewers were stringent in their adverse judgment. ("Perhaps the movie's worst sin is to make the critic feel he must play the role of the piously aggrieved scoutmaster, who has to say a lot of boring, obvious things. . . ."—Vincent Canby, *New York Times*.) Canby referred to "Miss Taylor's game way with a lyric" and added, "There's no reason why Miss Taylor should be photographed so unflatteringly. . . ." The feature, which would win a few prizes for its costuming, disappeared from release engagements rather quickly, neither an artistic nor a commercial success.

Then on June 3, 1978, in Richmond, Virginia, John Warner's political fate (at least for the present) was determined. In a fourteen-hour convention session, Richard D. Obenshain, the former State Republican Chairman and a conservative, achieved the party's nomination for the senatorial seat, defeating Warner et al. According to the *New York Times'* report:

> One sign of spiritous influence was a series of plainly spurious nominations of former husbands of Elizabeth Taylor, the actress, who is married to Mr. Warner and had been regarded as his prime campaign asset through a year of successful crowd-gathering rallies and fund-raisers.

The *Times'* journalist also noted that Warner had spent some $600,000 (about half of which was his own) in the pre-convention nomination bid, and that "since Mr. Warner is not regarded as being available for any other elective office in the commonwealth, his political prospects seemed to have peaked, at least in Virginia."

In recent months it was touted that Elizabeth would return to the acting scene portraying elderly, plump Queen Victoria in a Jack Haley, Jr.-produced TV version of *The Mudlark* (played in the 1950 film by Irene Dunne). Instead, Taylor chose to star with Joseph Bottoms in *Return Engagement*. The ninety-minute fall 1978 show was produced for NBC-TV's "Hallmark Hall of Fame" by Mike Wise and Frank Levy, with Joseph Hardy directing the James Prideaux script.

Although there would now seem to be few fresh professional avenues for the venturesome Elizabeth to attempt, one path she would like to explore is directing. "It fascinates me at this moment in my life even more than acting. The more you enjoy yourself onstage, the less the audience does. The more you cry onstage, the less the audience cries. If you become too self-indulgent, you become too cliquish."

As for her offstage existence, she explains, "I'm living my own life, no one else's. Not Tennessee Williams' or Edward Albee's or William Shakespeare's. I'm living my own interpretation of life and I'm enjoying [it]."

FILMOGRAPHY

THERE'S ONE BORN EVERY MINUTE (*Universal, 1942*) 60 min.

Associate producer, Ken Goldsmith; director, Harold Young; story, Robert B. Hunt; screenplay, Hunt, Brenda Weisberg; art director, Jack Otterson; music director, H. J. Salter; assistant director, Seward Webb; gowns, Vera West; sound, Bernard B. Brown, Charles Carroll; camera, John W. Boyle; editor, Maurice Wright.

Hugh Herbert (Lemuel P. Twine); Peggy Moran (Helen Twine); Tom Brown (Jimmy); Guy Kibbee (Cadwalader); Catharine Doucet (Minerva); Edgar Kennedy (Moe Carson); Scott Jorden (Lester Cadwalader, Jr.); Guss Schilling (Quisenberry); Elizabeth Taylor (Gloria); Charles Halton (Trumbull); Renie Riano (Miss Phipps); Carl "Alfalfa" Switzer (Junior).

LASSIE COME HOME (*MGM, 1943*) C-89 min.

Producer, Samuel Marx; director, Fred M. Wilcox; based on the novel by Eric Knight; screenplay, Hugo Butler; Technicolor consultants, Natalie Kalmus, Henri Jaffa; music, Daniele Amfitheatrof; art directors, Cedric Gibbons, Paul Groesse; set decorators, Edwin B. Willis, Mildred Griffiths; assistant director, Al Raboch; sound, J. Edmondson; special effects, Warren Newcombe; camera, Leonard Smith; editor, Ben Lewis.

Roddy McDowall (Joe Carraclough); Donald Crisp (Sam Carraclough); Edmund Gwenn (Rowlie); Dame May Whitty (Dolly); Lassie (The Dog); Nigel Bruce (Duke of Rudling); Elsa Lanchester (Mrs. Carraclough); Elizabeth Taylor (Priscilla); J. Patrick O'Malley (Hynes); Ben Webster (Dan'l Fadden); Alec Craig (Snickers); John Rogers (Buckles); Arthur Shields (Jock); Alan Napier (Andrew); Roy Parry (Butcher); George Broughton (Allen); Howard Davies (Cobbler); John Power (Miner); Nelson Leigh (Teacher); May Beatty (Fat Woman).

JANE EYRE (*20th Century-Fox, 1944*) 96 min.

Producer, William Goetz; director, Robert Stevenson; based on the novel by Charlotte Brontë; screenplay, Aldous Huxley, Stevenson, John Houseman; production designer, William Pereira; art directors, James Basevi, Wiard B. Ihnen; set decorators, Thomas Little, Ross Dawd; music, Bernard Herrmann; assistant director, Arthur Jacobson; sound, W. D. Flick, Roger Heman; special camera effects, Fred Sersen; camera, George Barnes; editor, Walter Thompson.

Orson Welles (Edward Rochester); Joan Fontaine (Jane Eyre); Margaret O'Brien (Adele); Peggy Ann Garner (Jane as a Child); John Sutton (Dr. Rivers); Sara Allgood (Bessie); Henry Daniell (Brockelhurst); Agnes Moorehead (Mrs. Reed); Aubrey Mather (Colonel Dent); Edith Barrett (Mrs. Fairfax); Barbara Everest (Lady Ingraham); Hillary Brooke (Blanche); Ethel Griffies (Grace Pool); Eily Malyon (Mrs. Sketcher); Ivan Simpson (Mr. Woods); Erskine San-

ford (Mr. Braggs); John Abbott (Mason); Elizabeth Taylor (Helen Burns); Mae Marsh (Leah); Mary Forbes (Mrs. Eshton); Thomas Louden (Sir George Lynn); Gerald Oliver Smith (Footman at Gateshead); Adele Jergens, Ruthe Brady, Billie Seward (Girls at Party); Colin Campbell (Proprietor); Tempe Pigott (Fortune Teller); Billy Bevan (Bookie); Brandon Hurst, Barry Macollum (Trustees); Charles Coleman (Guard).

THE WHITE CLIFFS OF DOVER (*MGM, 1944*) 126 min.

Producer, Sidney Franklin; director, Clarence Brown; based on the poem "The White Cliffs" by Alice Duer Miller; with additional poetry by Robert Nathan; screenplay, Claudine West, Jan Lustig, George Froeschel; music, Herbert Stothart; costumes, Irene; makeup, Jack Dawn; technical advisor, Major Cyril Seys Ramsey-Hill; art directors, Cedric Gibbons, Randall Duell; set decorators, Edwin B. Willis, Jacques Mesereau; sound, Charles E. Wallace; special effects, Arnold Gillespie, Warren Newcombe; camera, George Folsey; editors, Robert J. Kern, Al Jennings.

Irene Dunne (Susan Ashwood); Alan Marshal (Sir John Ashwood); Frank Morgan (Hiram Porter Dunn); Roddy McDowall (John Ashwood II as a Boy); Dame May Whitty (Nanny); C. Aubrey Smith (Colonel); Gladys Cooper (Lady Jean Ashwood); Peter Lawford (John Ashwood II at Age Twenty-Four); Van Johnson (Sam Bennett); John Warburton (Reggie); Jill Esmond (Rosamund); Brenda Forbes (Gwennie); Norma Varden (Mrs. Bland); Elizabeth Taylor (Betsy at Age Ten); June Lockhart (Betsy at Age Eighteen); Charles Irwin (Farmer Kenney); Jean Prescott (Mrs. Kenney); Tom Drake (American Soldier); Isobel Elsom (Mrs. Bancroft); Edmund Breon (Major Bancroft); Miles Mander (Major Loring); Ann Curzon (Miss Lambert); Steven Muller (Gerhard); Norbert Muller (Dietrich); Molly Lamont (Helen); Lumsden Hare (The Vicar); Arthur Shields (Benson); Emily Fitzroy (Spinster in Boarding House); Emily Massey (Elegant Lady in Boarding House); Clifford Brooke (Indian Major in Boarding House); Guy D'Ennery (Curate in Boarding House); Doris Lloyd (Plump Lady in Boarding House); Lal Chand Mehra (Indian Student in Boarding House); Ethel Griffies (Woman on Train); Elton and Eldon Burkett (Twins in Boarding House); Herbert Evans (Footman); Ian Wolfe (Skipper); Alec Craig (Billings); Clyde Cook (Jennings); Bunny Gordon (John at Six Months); Leo Mostovoy (Bandmaster); Arthur Gould-Porter (Captain Portage); Gavin Muir (Captain Griffiths); Charles Coleman (Captain Davis).

NATIONAL VELVET (*MGM, 1944*) C-125 min.

Producer, Pandro S. Berman; director, Clarence Brown; based on the novel by Enid Bagnold; screenplay, Theodore Reeves, Helen Deutsch; music, Herbert Stothart; art directors, Cedric Gibbons, Urie McCleary; set decorators, Edwin B. Willis, Mildred Griffiths; assistant director, Joe Boyle; Technicolor consultant, Natalie Kalmus; sound, Charles E. Wallace; special effects, Warren Newcombe; camera, Leonard Smith; editor, Robert J. Kern.

Mickey Rooney (Mi Taylor); Donald Crisp (Mr. Brown); Elizabeth Taylor (Velvet Brown); Anne Revere (Mrs. Brown); Angela Lansbury (Edwina Brown); Juanita Quigley (Malvelia Brown); Jackie "Butch" Jenkins (Donald Brown); Reginald Owen (Farmer Ede); Terry Kilburn (Ted); Alec Craig (Tim); Eugene Loring (Mr. Taski); Norma Varden (Miss Sims); Arthur Shields (Mr. Hallam); Dennis Hoey (Mr. Greenford the Farmer); Aubrey Mather (Entry Official); Frederic Worlock (Stewart); Arthur Treacher (Man with Umbrella); Harry Allen (Van Driver); Rene Austin, Jane Isbell, Virginia McDowall, Gail Peyton, Iris Kirskey, Bertha Stinchfield, Felicity Bilbrook, Paula Allen, Rhoda Williams, Beverly Billman (Schoolgirls); Stephen Bowson, Harold deBecker, Jr., Richard Haydel, Howard Taylor, Murray Coombs (Schoolboys); Barry Macollum (Townsman); Matthew Boulton (Entry Clerk); Leonard Carey (Pressman); Olaf Hytten (Villager); Gordon Richards (Doctor); Moyna MacGill (Woman); Rose Langdon, William Bailey (Bookies); Eric Wilton (English Bookie); Major Douglas Francis (Track Official); Donald Curtis (American).

COURAGE OF LASSIE (*MGM, 1946*) C-92 min.

Producer, Robert Sisk; director, Fred M. Wilcox; screenplay, Lionel Houser; Technicolor consultants, Natalie Kalmus, Henri Jaffa; co-director of animal sequences, Basil Wrangell; music, Scott Bradley, Bronislau Kaper; art directors, Cedric Gibbons, Paul Youngblood; set decorators, Edwin B. Willis, Paul Huldschinsky; assistant director, Sidney Sidman; sound, Douglas Shearer; camera, Leonard Smith; editor, Conrad Nervig.

Elizabeth Taylor (Kathie Merrick); Frank Morgan (Harry MacBain); Tom Drake (Sergeant Smitty); Selena Royle (Mrs. Merrick); Harry Davenport (Judge Payson); George Cleveland (Old Man); Catherine McLeod (Alice Merrick); Morris Ankrum (Farmer Crews); Arthur Walsh (Freddie Crews); Mitchell Lewis (Farmer Elson); Jane Green (Mrs. Elson); David Holt (Peter Merrick); William Lewin (Sergeant); Minor Watson (Sheriff Grayson); Windy Cook (Youth); Donald Curtis (Charlie); Clancy Cooper (Casey); Byron Foulger (Dr. Coleman); James Flavin (Lieutenant Arnold); Charles Sullivan (Officer Instructor); Addison Richards, Arthur Space (Officers); Robert Emmett O'Connor (Deputy); William "Bill" Phillips (Sergeant Tyler); Douglas Cowan (Sergeant Lewis) Lyle Mulhall (Corporal).

CYNTHIA (*MGM, 1947*) 98 min.

Producer, Edwin H. Knopf; director, Robert Z. Leonard; based on the play *The Rich Full Life* by Vina Delmar; screenplay, Harold Buchman, Charles Kaufman; art directors, Cedric Gibbons, Edward Carfagno; set decorators, Edwin Willis, Paul G. Chamberlain; music, Bronislau Kaper; songs, Johnny Green; assistant director, Marvin

Stuart; sound, Douglas Shearer; camera, Charles Schoenbaum; editor, Irvine Warburton.

Elizabeth Taylor (Cynthia Bishop); George Murphy (Larry Bishop); S. Z. Sakall (Professor Rosenkrantz); Mary Astor (Louise Bishop); Gene Lockhart (Dr. Fred I. Jannings); Spring Byington (Carrie Jannings); James Lydon (Ricky Latham); Scotty Beckett (Will Parker); Carol Brannan (Fredonia Jannings); Anna Q. Nilsson (Miss Brady); Morris Ankrum (Mr. Phillips); Kathleen Howard (McQuillan); Shirley Johns (Stella Regan); Barbara Challis (Alice); Harlan Briggs (J. M. Dingle); Will Wright (Gus Wood).

LIFE WITH FATHER (*Warner Bros., 1947*) C-118 min.

Producer, Robert Buckner; director, Michael Curtiz; based on the play by Howard Lindsay, Russel Crouse; screenplay, Donald Odgen Stewart; art director, Robert Haas; set decorator, George James Hopkins; wardrobe, Milo Anderson; music, Max Steiner; music director, Leo F. Forbstein; assistant director, Robert Vreeland; dialogue director, Herschel Daugherty; technical advisor, Mrs. Clarence Day; makeup, Perc Westmore; sound, C. A. Riggs; montages, James Leicester; special effects, William McGann; special effects director, Ray Foster; camera, Peverell Marley, William V. Skall; editor, George Amy.

William Powell (Clarence Day); Irene Dunne (Vinnie Day); Elizabeth Taylor (Mary Skinner); Edmund Gwenn (Reverend Dr. Lloyd); ZaSu Pitts (Cora); Jimmy Lydon (Clarence, Jr.); Emma Dunn (Margaret); Moroni Olsen (Dr. Humphries); Elisabeth Risdon (Mrs. Whitehead); Derek Scott (Harlan); Johnny Calkins (Whitney); Martin Milner (John); Heather Wilde (Annie); Monte Blue (Policeman); Nancy Duff (Delia); Mary Field (Nora); Queenie Leonard (Maggie); Clara Blandick (Miss Wiggins); Frank Elliott (Dr. Somers); Clara Reid (Scrubwoman); Philo McCullough (Milkman); Lois Bridge (Corsetierre); Douglas Kennedy (Mr. Morley); Phil Van Zandt (Clerk); Russell Arms (Stock Quotation Operator); Michael and Ralph Mineo (Twins); Creighton Hale (Father of Twins); Gertrude Valerie, Hallene Hill, Laura Treadwell, David Cavendish, Henry Sylvester (Churchgoers); Lucille Shamberger (Nursemaid); Arlene Dahl (Girl in Delmonico's).

A DATE WITH JUDY (*MGM, 1948*) C-113 min.

Producer, Joe Pasternak; director, Richard Thorpe; based on the characters created by Alan Leslie; screenplay, Dorothy Cooper, Dorothy Kingsley; Technicolor consultants, Natalie Kalmus, Henri Jaffa; art directors, Cedric Gibbons, Paul Groesse; set decorators, Edwin B. Willis, Richard A. Pefferle; music director, Georgie Stoll; orchestrators, Leo Arnaud, Albert Sendrey, Robert Franklyn; songs, Jimmy McHugh and Harold Adamson; Don Raye and Gene dePaul; Stella Unger and Alec Templeton; assistant director, Jerome Bergman; choreography, Stanley Donen; costumes, Helen Rose; sound, Douglas Shearer, Norwood A. Fenton; special effects, Warren Newcombe; camera, Robert Surtees; editor, Harold F. Kress.

Wallace Beery (Melvin R. Foster); Jane Powell (Judy

Foster); Elizabeth Taylor (Carol Foster); Carmen Miranda (Rosita Conchellas); Xavier Cugat (Cugat); Robert Stack (Stephen Andrews); Selena Royle (Mrs. Foster); Scotty Beckett (Ogden "Oogie" Pringle); Leon Ames (Lucien T. Pringle); George Cleveland (Gramps); Lloyd Corrigan (Pop Scully); Clinton Sundberg (Jameson); Jean McLaren (Mitzie); Jerry Hunter (Randolph Foster); Buddy Howard (Jo-Jo Hoffenpepper); Lillian Yarbo (Nightingale); Eula Guy (Miss Clarke); Francis Pierlot (Professor Green); Rena Lenart (Olga); Sheila Stein (Little Girl in Drug Store); Paul Bradley (Headwaiter); Polly Bailey (Elderly Woman).

JULIA MISBEHAVES (MGM, 1948) 99 min.

Producer, Everett Riskin; director, Jack Conway; based on the novel *The Nutmeg Tree* by Margery Sharp; adaptors, Gina Kaus, Monckton Hoffe; screenplay, William Ludwig, Harry Ruskin, Arthur Wimperis; art directors, Cedric Gibbons, Daniel B. Cathcart; set decorators, Edwin B. Wallis, Jack Moore; music, Adolph Deutsch; songs, Jerry Seelen and Hal Borne; assistant director, Marvin Stuart; costumes, Irene; makeup, Jack Dawn; sound, Douglas Shearer, Charles E. Wallace; special effects, Warren Newcombe; camera, Joseph Ruttenberg; editor, John Dunning.

Greer Garson (Julia Packett); Walter Pidgeon (William Packett); Peter Lawford (Ritchie); Cesar Romero (Fred); Elizabeth Taylor (Susan Packett); Lucile Watson (Mrs. Packett); Nigel Bruce (Colonel Willowbrook); Mary Boland (Mrs. Gennochio); Reginald Owen (Bennie Hawkins); Ian Wolfe (Hobson); Phyllis Morris (Daisy); Edmund Breon (Jamie); Fritz Feld (Pepito); Marcelle Corday (Gabby); Veda Ann Borg (Louise); Aubrey Mather (Vicar); Henry Stephenson (Lord Pennystone); Winifred Harris (Lady Pennystone); Ted DeWayne, Henry Monzello, William Snyder, Ray Saunders, Michael Kent (Acrobatic Troupe); Elspeth Dudgeon (Woman in Pawn Shop); James Logan (Moving Man); Victor Wood (Postman); Jimmy Aubrey (Drunk); Mitchell Lewis (Train Official); Lola Albright, Gail Langford, Joi Lansing, Patricia Walker, Shirley Ballard, Ruth Hall (Mannequins); Art Foster, George Goldsmith, Dave Thursby (English Sailors); Alphonse Martell (Frenchman in Theatre).

LITTLE WOMEN (MGM, 1949) C-121 min.

Producer/director, Mervyn LeRoy; based on the novel by Louisa May Alcott; screenplay, Andrew Solt, Sarah Y. Mason, Victor Heerman; Technicolor consultants, Natalie Kalmus, Henri Jaffa; art directors, Cedric Gibbons, Paul Groesse; set decorators, Edwin B. Willis, Jack D. Moore; music, Adolph Deutsch; assistant director, Al Raboch; makeup, Jack Dawn; costumes, Walter Plunkett; sound, Douglas Shearer, A. Norman Fenton; special effects, Warren Newcombe; camera, Robert Planck; editor, Ralph E. Winters.

June Allyson (Jo); Peter Lawford (Laurie); Margaret O'Brien (Beth); Elizabeth Taylor (Amy); Janet Leigh (Meg); Rossano Brazzi (Professor Bhaer); Mary Astor (Marmee); Lucile Watson (Aunt March); Sir C. Aubrey Smith (Mr. Laurence); Elizabeth Patterson (Hannah); Leon Ames (Mr. March); Harry Davenport (Dr. Barnes);

Richard Stapley (John Brooke); Connie Gilchrist (Mrs. Kirke); Ellen Corby (Sophie); Will Wright (Storekeeper); Olin Howlin (Schoolteacher).

CONSPIRATOR (MGM, 1950) 85 min.

Producer, Arthur Hornblow, Jr.; director, Victor Saville; based on the novel by Humphrey Slater; screenplay, Sally Benson; music, John Wooldridge; art director, Alfred Junge; sound, A. W. Watkins; camera, Freddie Young; editor, Frank Clarke.

Robert Taylor (Major Michael Curragh); Elizabeth Taylor (Melinda Greyton); Robert Flemyng (Captain Hugh Ladholme); Harold Wartender (Colonel Hammerbrook); Honor Blackman (Joyce); Majorie Fielding (Aunt Jessica); Thora Hird (Broader); Wilfred Hyde-White (Lord Pennistone); Marie Ney (Lady Pennistone); Jack Allen (Raglan); Helen Haye (Lady Witheringham); Cicely Paget-Bowman (Mrs. Hammerbrook); Karel Stepanek (Radek); Nicholas Bruce (Alek); Cyril Smith (Detective Inspector).

THE BIG HANGOVER (MGM, 1950) 82 min.

Producer/director, Norman Krasna; based on the story "Mike and Ike" by Krasna; screenplay, Krasna; art directors, Cedric Gibbons, Paul Groesse; set decorators, Edwin B. Willis, Henry W. Grace; music, Adolph Deutsch; women's costumes, Helen Rose; special effects, Warren Newcombe; camera, George Folsey; editor, Frederick Y. Smith.

Van Johnson (David Maldon); Elizabeth Taylor (Mary Belney); Percy Waram (John Belney); Fay Holden (Martha Belney); Edgar Buchanan (Uncle Fred Mahoney); Selena Royle (Kate Mahoney); Gene Lockhart (Charles Parkford); Leon Ames (Carl Bellcap); Rosemary De Camp (Claire Bellcap); Philip Ahn (Doctor Lee); Pierre Watkin (Samuel C. Lang); Russell Hicks (Steve Hughes); Gordon Richards (Williams); Kathleen Lockhart (Mrs. Parkford); Matt Moore (David Rumlie); Anna Q. Nilsson (Helen Lang); Tristram Coffin (Jenkins); Brett King (Intern); Dino Bolognose, Cosmo Sardo (Waiters); Cliff Clark (Albert Johnson); Louise Lorimer (Mrs. Johnson); Bess Flowers (Mrs. Hughes).

FATHER OF THE BRIDE (MGM, 1950) 93 min.

Producer, Pandro S. Berman; director, Vincente Minnelli; based on the novel by Edward Streeter; screenplay, Frances Goodrich, Albert Hackett; music, Adolph Deutsch; art directors, Cedric Gibbons, Leonid Vasian; set decorators, Edwin B. Willis, Keogh Gleason; costumes, Helen Rose, Walter Plunkett; assistant director, Marvin Stuart; makeup, Jack Dawn; sound, Douglas Shearer; camera, John Alton; editor, Ferris Webster.

Spencer Tracy (Stanley T. Banks); Joan Bennett (Ellie Banks); Elizabeth Taylor (Kay Banks); Don Taylor (Buckley Dunstan); Billie Burke (Mrs. Doris Dunstan); Leo G. Carroll (Mr. Massoula); Moroni Olsen (Herbert Dunstan); Melville Cooper (Mr. Tringle); Taylor Holmes (Warner); Paul Harvey (Reverend A. I. Galsworthy); Frank Orth (Joe); Rusty Tamblyn (Tommy Banks); Tom Irish (Ben Banks); Marietta Canty (Delilah); Willard Waterman (Dixon); Nancy Valentine (Fliss), Mary Jane Smith (Effie); Jacqueline Duval (Peg); Fay Baker (Miss

Bellamy); Frank Hyers (Duffy); Chris Drake, Floyd Taylor, Don Anderson, William Mahan, Walter Kelly, Peter Thompson, Carleton Carpenter (Ushers); Lucille Barnes, Erin Selwyn, Janet Fay, Wendy Waldron (Bridesmaids); Douglas Spencer (Organist); Roger Moore, Sherry Hall, Mickey McCardle (Ad-libs); Stuart Holmes, Anne Kunde, Ella Ethridge, William Bailey, Dorothy Phillips (Bits in Dream Sequence); Dick Alexander (Mover with Chandelier); Dewey Robinson (Mover with Lamp); William "Bill" Phillips (Movers' Foreman); John Walsh (Western Union Boy).

FATHER'S LITTLE DIVIDEND (MGM, 1951) 82 min.

Producer, Pandro S. Berman; director, Vincente Minnelli; based on characters created by Edward Streeter; screenplay, Frances Goodrich, Albert Hackett; music, Albert Sendrey; music director, Georgie Stoll; art directors, Cedric Gibbons, Leonid Vasian; set decorators, Edwin Willis, Keogh Gleason; women's costumes, Helen Rose; sound, Douglas Shearer; camera, John Alton; editor, Ferris Webster.

Spencer Tracy (Stanley Banks); Joan Bennett (Ellie Banks); Elizabeth Taylor (Kay Dunstan); Don Taylor (Buckley Dunstan); Billie Burke (Doris Dunstan); Moroni Olsen (Herbert Dunstan); Frank Faylen (Policeman); Marietta Canty (Delilah); Rusty Tamblyn (Tommy Banks); Tom Irish (Ben Banks); Hayden Rorke (Dr. Andrew Nordell); Paul Harvey (Reverend Galsworthy); Donald Clark (The Dividend); Beverly Thompson (Nurse); Dabbs Greer (Taxi Driver); Robert B. Williams (Motorcycle Cop); Harry Hines (Old Man); Frank Sully (Diaper Man); Janet Fay, Nancy Valentine, Wendy Waldron, Erin Selwyn, Jacqueline Duval (Bridesmaids); George Bruggeman (Gym Instructor); Lon Poff (Elderly Man on Porch).

A PLACE IN THE SUN (Paramount, 1951) 122 min.

Producer/director, George Stevens; based on the novel *An American Tragedy* by Theodore Dreiser; screenplay, Michael Wilson, Harry Brown; art directors, Hans Dreier, Walter Tyler; costumes, Edith Head; music, Franz Waxman; camera, William C. Mellor; editor, William Hornbeck.

Montgomery Clift (George Eastman); Elizabeth Taylor (Angela Vickers); Shelley Winters (Alice Tripp); Anne Revere (Hannah Eastman); Keefe Brasselle (Earl Eastman); Fred Clark (Bellows); Raymond Burr (Marlowe); Herbert Heyes (Charles Eastman); Shepperd Strudwick (Anthony Vickers); Frieda Inescort (Mrs. Vickers); Kathryn Givney (Mrs. Louise Eastman); Walter Sande (Jansen); Ted de Corsia (Judge); John Ridgely (Coroner); Lois Chartrand (Marsha); William R. Murphy (Mr. Whiting); Douglas Spencer (Boatkeeper); Charles Dayton (Kelly); Paul Frees (Morrison); Josephine Whittell (Secretary to Charles Eastman); Frank Yaconelli (Truck Driver); Ralph A. Dunn (Policeman); Bob Anderson (Eagle Scout); Mary Kent (Mrs. Roberts the Landlady); Lisa Golm (Maid); Ezelle Poule (Receptionist); Jay Morley (Executive); Kathleen Freeman (Martha); Wallace Scott (Factory Guard); Eric Wilton (Butler); Al Ferguson (Bailiff); Gertrude Astor, Lula Mae Bohrman (Women); Major Sam Harris (Man);

Harold NcNulty (Jury Foreman); Ian Wolfe (Dr. Wyeland); Carmencita Johnson (Girl).

QUO VADIS (MGM, 1951) C-171 min.

Producer, Sam Zimbalist; director, Mervyn LeRoy; based on the novel by Henryk Sienkiewicz; screenplay, John Lee Mahin, S. N. Behrman, Sonya Levien; art directors, William A. Horning, Cedric Gibbons, Edward Carfagno; music, Miklos Rozsa; choreography, Marta Obolensky, Auriel Millos; camera, Robert Surtees, William V. Skall; editor, Ralph E. Winters.

Robert Taylor (Marcus Vinicius); Deborah Kerr (Lygia); Leo Genn (Petronius); Peter Ustinov (Nero); Patricia Laffan (Poppaea); Finlay Currie (Peter); Abraham Sofaer (Paul); Marina Berti (Eunice); Buddy Baer (Ursus); Felix Aylmer (Plautius); Nora Swinburne (Pomponia); Ralph Truman (Tigellinus); Norman Wooland (Nerva); Peter Miles (Nazarius); Geoffrey Dunn (Terpnos); Nicholas Hannen (Seneca); D. A. Clarke-Smith (Phaon); Rosalie Crutchley (Acte); John Ruddock (Chilo); Arthur Walge (Croton); Elspeth March (Miriam); Strelsa Brown (Rufia); Alfredo Varelli (Lucan); Roberto Ottaviano (Flavius); William Tubbs (Anaxander); Pietro Tordi (Galba); Lia De Leo (Pedicurist); Sophia Loren (Extra); Elizabeth Taylor (Guest); Walter Pidgeon (Narrator).

CALLAWAY WENT THATAWAY (MGM, 1951) 81 min.

Producers/directors/story/screenplay, Norman Panama and Melvin Frank; art directors, Cedric Gibbons, Eddie Imazu; music, Marlin Skiles; camera, Ray June; editor, Cotton Warburton.

Fred MacMurray (Mike Frye); Dorothy McGuire (Deborah Patterson); Howard Keel (Stretch Barnes/Smoky Callaway); Jesse White (George Markham); Fay Roope (Tom Lorrison); Natalie Schafer (Martha Lorrison); Douglas Kennedy (Drunk); Elisabeth Fraser (Marie); Johnny Indrisano (Johnny Tarranto); Stan Freberg (Marvin); Don Haggerty (Director); Clark Gable, Elizabeth Taylor, Esther Williams (Guest Stars); Dorothy Andre (Girl); Kay Scott, Margie Liszt (Phone Girls); Glenn Strange (Black Norton); Mae Clarke (Mother); Hugh Beaumont (Mr. Adkins); Earle Hodgins (Doorman).

LOVE IS BETTER THAN EVER (MGM, 1952) 81 min.

Producer, William H. Wright; director, Stanley Donen; story/screenplay, Ruth Brooks Flippen; art directors, Cedric Gibbons, Gabriel Scognamillio; music/music director, Lennie Hayton; camera, Harold Rosson; editor, George Boemler.

Larry Parks (Jud Parker); Elizabeth Taylor (Anastacia Macaboy); Josephine Hutchinson (Mrs. Macaboy); Tom Tully (Mr. Macaboy); Ann Doran (Mrs. Levoy); Elinor Donahue (Pattie Marie Levoy); Kathleen Freeman (Mrs. Kahrney); Doreen McCann (Albertina Kahrney); Alex Gerry (Hamlet); Dick Wessel (Smittie); Gene Kelly (Guest Star); Richard Karlan (Siddo); Dave Willock (Davey); Frank Hyers (Bernie); Bertil Unger (Randie Dean); Nancy Saunders (Pauline); Margaret Lloyd (Mrs. Culpepper); George Matkovich (Cahoogit); Lucille Curtis (Mother);

Mae Clarke (Mrs. Ireland); William "Bill" Phillips (Mr. Khourney); Ann Tyrell (Mrs. Whitney); Gail Bonney (Mrs. Oelschlager); Tom Hanlon (Announcer).

IVANHOE *(MGM, 1952)* C-106 min.

Producer, Pandro S. Berman; director, Richard Thorpe; based on the novel by Sir Walter Scott; screenplay, Noel Langley; adaptor, Aeneas MacKenzie; art director, Alfred Junge; costumes, Roger Furse; makeup, Charles Parker; music, Miklos Rosza; sound, A. W. Watkins; camera effects, Tom Howard; camera, Freddie Young; editor, Frank Clarke.

Robert Taylor (Ivanhoe); Elizabeth Taylor (Rebecca); Joan Fontaine (Rowena); George Sanders (De Bois-Guilbert); Emlyn Williams (Wamba); Robert Douglas (Sir Hugh De Bracy); Finlay Currie (Cedric); Felix Aylmer (Isaac); Francis DeWolff (Font De Bouef); Guy Rolfe (Prince John); Norman Wooland (King Richard); Basil Sydney (Waldemar Fitzurse); Harold Warrender (Locksley); Patrick Lovell (Philip de Malworsin); Roderick Lovell (Ralph de Vipoint); Sebastian Cabot (Clerk of Copmondurst); John Reedclock (Hundebert); Michael Brennan (Baldwin); Megs Jenkins (Servant to Isaac); Valentine Dyall (Norman Guard); Lionel Harris (Roger of Bermondsley); Earl Jaffe (Austrian Monk).

THE GIRL WHO HAD EVERYTHING *(MGM, 1953)* 69 min.

Producer, Armand Deutsch; director, Richard Thorpe; based on the novel *A Free Soul* by Adela Rogers St. John and the play by Willard Mack; screenplay, Art Cohn; art directors, Cedric Gibbons, Randall Duell; music, Andre Previn; costumes, Helen Rose; camera, Paul Vogel; editor, Ben Lewis.

Elizabeth Taylor (Jean Latimer); Fernando Lamas (Victor Y. Ramondi); William Powell (Steve Latimer); Gig Young (Vance Court); James Whitmore (Charles "Chico" Menlow); Robert Burton (John Ashmond); William Walker (Julian); Harry Bartell (Joe); Elmer Petersen (Himself); Dan Riss (Counsel); Paul Harvey (Senator Drummond); Dean Miller (Radio Announcer); Emory Parnell (Auctioneer); Earle Hodgins (Spotter); Frank Dae (Old Man Kinkaid); John McKee (Secretary); Anthony Warde, Philip Van Zandt (Colleagues); James Horne, Perry Sheehan, Dee Turnell, Sally Musick (Guests in Town House); Jack Sterling (Cab Driver); Pat O'Malley, A. Cameron Grant, George Brand (Senate Board Members).

RHAPSODY *(MGM, 1954)* C-115 min.

Producer, Lawrence Weingarten; director, Charles Vidor; based on the novel *Maurice Guest* by Henry Handel Richardson; screenplay, Fay Kanin, Michael Kanin; adaptors, Ruth Goetz, Augustus Goetz; art directors, Cedric Gibbons, Paul Groesse; set decorators, Edwin B. Willis, Hugh Hunt; music adaptor, Bronislau Kaper; women's costumes, Helen Rose; assistant director, Ridgeway Callow; special effects, A. Arnold Gillespie, Warren Newcombe; camera, Robert Planck; editor, John Dunning.

Elizabeth Taylor (Louise Durant); Vittorio Gassman (Paul Bronte); John Ericson (James Guest); Louis Calhern (Nicholas Durant); Michael Chekhov (Professor Schu-

man); Barbara Bates (Effie Cahill); Richard Hageman (Bruno Furst); Richard Lupino (Otto Krafft); Celia Lovsky (Frau Sigerlist); Stuart Whitman (Dove); Madge Blake (Mrs. Cahill); Jack Raine (Edmund Streller); Brigit Nielsen (Madeleine); Jacqueline Duval (Yvonne); Norma Nevens (Student/Pianist).

ELEPHANT WALK *(Paramount, 1954)* C-102 min.

Producer, Irving Asher; director, William Dieterle; based on the novel by Robert Standish; screenplay, John Lee Mahin; art directors, Hal Pereira, Joseph MacMillan Johnson; set decorators, Sam Comer, Grace Gregory; Technicolor consultant, Richard Mueller; assistant director, Francisco Day; choreography, Ram Gopal; music, Franz Waxman; costumes, Edith Head; special effects, John P. Fulton, Paul Lerpae; process camera, Farciot Edouart; camera, Loyal Griggs; editor, George Tomasini.

Elizabeth Taylor (Ruth Wiley); Dana Andrews (Dick Carver); Peter Finch (John Wiley); Abraham Sofaer (Appuhamy); Noel Drayton (Atkinson the Planter); Abner Biberman (Dr. Pereira); Rosalind Ivan (Mrs. Lakin); Barry Bernard (Strawson the Planter); Philip Tonge (Ralph the Planter); Edward Ashley (Gregory the Planter); Leo Britt (Chisholm the Planter); Mylee Haulani (Rayna); Jack Raine (Norbert the Planter); Victor Millan (Koru the Servant); Norma Varden (Mrs. Beezely); Carlos Rivero (Car Servant); Delmar Costello (Native Patient); Satini Pualioa (Foreman); Vivien Leigh (Ruth Wiley—Ceylon Long Shots); Madhyma Lanka Mandala Dancers (Themselves).

BEAU BRUMMELL *(MGM, 1954)* C-113 min.

Producer, Sam Zimbalist; director, Curtis Bernhardt; based on the play by Clyde Fitch; screenplay, Karl Tunberg; art director, Alfred Junge; music, Richard Addinsell; costumes, Elizabeth Haffenden; camera effects, Tom Howard; camera, Oswald Morris; editor, Frank Clarke.

Stewart Granger (Beau Brummell); Elizabeth Taylor (Lady Patricia); Peter Ustinov (Prince of Wales); Robert Morley (King George III); James Donald (Lord Edwin Mercer); James Hayter (Mortimer); Rosemary Harris (Mrs. Fitzherbert); Paul Rogers (William Pitt); Noel Willman (Lord Byron); Peter Dyneley (Midger); Charles Carson (Sir Geoffrey Baker); Ernest Clark (Dr. Warren); Peter Bull (Mr. Fox); Mark Dignam (Mr. Burke); Desmond Roberts (Colonel); David Horne (Thurslow); Ralph Truman (Sir Ralph Sidley); Elwyn Brook-Jones (Mr. Tupp); George De Warfaz (Dr. Dubois); Henry Oscar (Dr. Willis); Harold Kasket (Mayor); Maurice Kaufman (Lord Alvanley); D. A. Clarke-Smith (Sir John Wyatt); Gordon Phillott (Roper, Sr.); Francis Drake (Roper, Jr.); Thomas Gallagher (Bruiser); Alexander Gauge (Newspaper Man); Dennis Shaw (Dog Man); Finlay Currie (Robert MacIver); John Chandos (Silva); Ann Hanslip (Lady Manley); Andrew Osborne (Lord Mindon); Bessie Love (Maid); Kenneth Hyde, Clement McCallin (Footmen).

THE LAST TIME I SAW PARIS *(MGM, 1954)* C-116 min.

Producer, Jack Cummings; director, Richard Brooks; based on the story "Babylon Revisited" by F. Scott Fitzgerald; screenplay, Julius J. and Philip G. Epstein, Brooks; assistant director, William Shanks; music, Conrad Salinger; song, Jerome Kern and Oscar Hammerstein II; art directors, Cedric Gibbons, Randall Duell; set decorators, Edwin B. Willis and Jack D. Moore; costumes, Helen Rose; special effects, A. Arnold Gillespie; camera, Joseph Ruttenberg; editor, John Dunning.

Elizabeth Taylor (Helen Ellswirth); Van Johnson (Charles Wills); Walter Pidgeon (James Ellswirth); Donna Reed (Marie Ellswirth); Eva Gabor (Lorraine Quarl); Kurt Kasznar (Maurice); George Dolenz (Claude Matine); Roger Moore (Paul); Sandy Descher (Vicki); Celia Lovsky (Mama); Peter Leeds (Barney); John Doucette (Campbell); Odette (Singer); Luis Urbina, Gilda Fontana (Flamenco Dance Team); Christian Pasques (Boy); Ed Hinton, Richard Emory, Steve Wayne (American Officers); Loulette Sablon (Nurse); Jean Heremans (Leon); Josette Deegan, Mary Ann Hawkins (Two Girls Fighting); Matt Moore, Paul Power, Harry Cody (English Men); Ann Codee (Another Nurse); Gene Coogan (Gendarme).

GIANT (*Warner Bros., 1956*) C-198 min.

Producers, George Stevens, Henry Ginsberg; director, Stevens; based on the novel by Edna Ferber; screenplay, Fred Guiol, Ivan Moffat; music/music director, Dmitri Tiomkin; songs, Paul Francis Webster and Tiomkin; costumes, Marjorie Best, Moss Mabry; assistant director, Joe Rickards; production designers, Boris Leven, Ralph Hurst; camera, William C. Mellor; editors, William Hornbeck, Fred Bohanan, Phil Anderson.

Elizabeth Taylor (Leslie Lynnton Benedict); Rock Hudson (Bick Benedict); James Dean (Jett Rink); Mercedes McCambridge (Luz Benedict); Chill Wills (Uncle Bawley); Jane Withers (Vashti Snythe); Robert Nichols (Pinky Snythe); Dennis Hopper (Jordan Benedict III); Elsa Cardenas (Juana); Fran Bennett (Judy Benedict); Carroll Baker (Luz Benedict II); Earl Holliman (Bob Dace); Paul Fix (Dr. Horace Lynnton); Judith Evelyn (Mrs. Horace Lynnton); Carolyn Craig (Lacey Lynnton); Rod Taylor (Sir David Karfrey); Alexander Scourby (Old Polo); Sal Mineo (Angel Obregon II); Monte Hale (Bale Clinch); Mary Ann Edwards (Adarene Clinch); Napoleon Whiting (Swazey); Charles Watts (Whiteside); Maurice Jara (Dr. Guerra); Victor Millan (Angel Obregon I); Pilar Del Rey (Mrs. Obregon); Felipe Turich (Gomez); Sheb Wooley (Gabe Target); Francisco Villalobos (Mexican Priest); Noreen Nash (Lona Lane); Guy Teague (Harper); Max Terhune (Dr. Walker); Ray Bennett (Dr. Borneholm); Barbara Barie (Mary Lou Decker); Slim Talbot (Clay Hodgins); Tex Driscoll (Clay Hodgins, Sr.); Juney Ellis (Essie Lou Hodgins); Ray Whitley (Watts).

RAINTREE COUNTY (*MGM, 1957*) C-187 min.*

Producer, David Lewis; associate producer, Millard Kaufman; director, Edward Dmytryk; based on the novel by Ross Lockridge, Jr.; screenplay, Kaufman; costumes, Walter Plunkett; assistant director, Ridgeway Callow; music, Johnny Green; songs, Paul Francis Webster and Green; art directors, William A. Horning, Urie McCleary; set decorators, Edwin B. Willis, Hugh Hunt; special effects,

Warren Newcombe; camera, Robert Surtees; editor, John Dunning.

Montgomery Clift (John Wickliff Shawnessy); Elizabeth Taylor (Susanna Drake); Eva Marie Saint (Nell Gaither); Nigel Patrick (Professor Jerusalem Webster Stiles); Lee Marvin (Orville "Flash" Perkins); Rod Taylor (Garwood B. Jones); Agnes Moorehead (Ellen Shawnessy); Walter Abel (T. D. Shawnessy); Jarma Lewis (Barbara Drake); Tom Drake (Bobby Drake); Rhys Williams (Ezra Gray); Russell Collins (Niles Foster); DeForrest Kelley (Southern Officer); Myrna Hansen (Lydia Gray); Oliver Blake (Jake the Bartender); John Eldredge (Cousin Sam); Isabelle Cooley (Soona); Ruth Attaway (Parthenia); Eileene Stevens (Miss Roman); Rosalind Hayes (Bessie); Don Burnett (Tom Conway); Michael Dugan (Nat Franklin); Michael Dante (Jesse Gardner); James Griffith (Bourbon Voice).

*Eventually edited to a 180-minute version for general distribution.

CAT ON A HOT TIN ROOF (*MGM, 1958*) C-108 min.

Producer, Lawrence Weingarten; director, Richard Brooks; based on the play by Tennessee Williams; screenplay, Brooks, James Poe; art directors, William A. Horning, Urie McCleary; set decorators, Henry Grace, Robert Priestly; assistant director, William Shanks; Miss Taylor's wardrobe, Helen Rose; makeup, William Tuttle; color consultant, Charles K. Hagedon; sound, Dr. Wesley C. Miller; special effects, Lee LeBlanc; camera, William Daniels; editor, Ferris Webster.

Elizabeth Taylor (Maggie Pollitt); Paul Newman (Brick Pollitt); Burl Ives (Big Daddy Pollitt); Jack Carson (Gooper Pollitt); Judith Anderson (Big Mama Pollitt); Madeleine Sherwood (Mae Pollitt); Larry Gates (Dr. Baugh); Vaughn Taylor (Deacon Davis); Vince Townsend, Jr. (Lacy); Zelda Cleaver (Sookey); Brian Corcoran (Boy Pollitt); Hugh Corcoran (Buster Pollitt); Rusty Stevens (Sonny Pollitt); Patty Ann Gerrity (Dixie Pollitt); Deborah Miller (Trixie Pollitt); Tony Merrill, Jeane Wood (Party Guests); Bobby Johnson (Groom).

SUDDENLY, LAST SUMMER (*Columbia, 1959*) 114 min.

Producer, Sam Spiegel; director, Joseph L. Mankiewicz; based on the one-act play by Tennessee Williams; screenplay, Gore Vidal, Williams; music, Buxton Orr, Malcolm Arnold; music director, Orr; production designer, Oliver Messel; art director, William Kellner; set decorator, Scot Slimon; assistant director, Bluey Hill; makeup, David Aylott; sound, Peter Thornton, A. G. Ambler, John Cox; camera, Jack Hildyard; editors, William W. Hornbeck, Thomas G. Stanford.

Elizabeth Taylor (Catherine Holly); Katharine Hepburn (Mrs. Venable); Montgomery Clift (Dr. Cukrowicz); Albert Dekker (Dr. Hockstader); Mercedes McCambridge (Mrs. Holly); Gary Raymond (George Holly); Mavis Villiers (Miss Foxhill); Patricia Marmont (Nurse Benson); Joan Young (Sister Felicity); Maria Britneva (Lucy); Sheila

Robbins (Hockstader's Secretary); David Cameron (Young Blonde Intern).

SCENT OF MYSTERY (*Mike Todd, Jr.,1960*) C-125 min.

Producer, Michael Todd, Jr.; associate producer, Ned Mann; director, Jack Cardiff; story, Kelley Roos; screenplay, William Roos; additional situations, Gerald Kersh; music, Mario Nascimbene; additional music, Jordan Ramin, Harold Adamson; music director, Franco Ferrara; assistant director, Piero Musetta; wardrobe, Charles Simminger; makeup, Neville Smallwood; production supervisor/art director, Vincent Korda; set decorator, Dario Simoni; sound, Joe Kane; special effects, Cliff Richardson; camera, John Von Kotze; second unit camera, John Drake; editor, James Newcom.

Denholm Elliott (Oliver Larker); Peter Lorre (Smiley); Beverly Bentley (The Decoy); Paul Lukas (Baron Saradin); Liam Redmond (Johnny Gin); Leo McKern (Tommy Kennedy); Peter Arne (Fleming); Diana Dors (Girl in Bikini); Mary Laura Wood (Margharita); Juan Olaguivel (Lorry Operator); Maurice Marsac (Storekeeper); Judith Furse (Artist); Billie Miller (Miss Miller); Michael Trubshawe (Englishman); Elizabeth Taylor (Sally Kennedy).

BUTTERFIELD 8 (*MGM, 1960*) C-109 min.

Producer, Pandro S. Berman; director, Daniel Mann; based on the novel by John O'Hara; screenplay, Charles Schnee, John Michael Hayes; art directors, George W. Davis, Urie McCleary; set decorators, Gene Callahan, J. C. Delaney; music, Bronislau Kaper; costumes, Helen Rose; assistant directors, Hank Moonjean, John Clarke Bowman; color consultant, Charles K. Hagedon; camera, Joseph Ruttenberg; editor, Ralph E. Winters.

Elizabeth Taylor (Gloria Wandrous); Laurence Harvey (Weston Liggett); Eddie Fisher (Steve Carpenter); Dina Merrill (Emily Liggett); Mildred Dunnock (Mrs. Wandrous); Betty Field (Mrs. Fanny Thurber); Jeffrey Lynn (Bingham Smith); Kay Medford (Happy); Susan Oliver (Norma); George Voskovec (Dr. Tredman); Virginia Downing (Clerk); Carmen Matthews (Mrs. Jescott); Whitfield Connor (Anderson); Dan Bergin (Elevator Man); Vernon Dowling (Cabbie); Samuel Schwartz (Doorman); Rudy Bond (Big Man); Victor Harrison (Irate Man); Beau Tilden (Chauffeur); Don Burns (Photographer); Richard X. Slattery (State Trooper); Philip Faversham (Man).

CLEOPATRA (*20th Century-Fox, 1963*) C-243 min.*

Producer, Walter Wanger; director, Joseph L. Mankiewicz; based on the histories by Plutarch, Suetonius, Appian, and other ancient sources, and *The Life and Times of Cleopatra* by C. M. Franzero; screenplay, Mankiewicz, Ranald MacDougall, Sidney Buchman; assistant director, Fred R. Simpson; production designer, John De Cuirt; art directors, Jack Martin Smith, Hilyard Brown, Herman Blumenthal, Elven Webb, Maurice Pelling, Boris Juraga; set decorators, Walter M. Scott, Paul S. Fox, Ray Moyer; costumes for Miss Taylor by Irene Sharaff; costumes, Vittorio Nino Novarese, Renie; music, Alex North; associate music director, Lionel Newman; choreography, Hermes Pan; sound, Fred Hines, James Corcoran; camera effects, L. B. Abbott, Emil Kosa, Jr.; camera, Leon Shamroy; second unit camera, Claude Renoir, Piero Portalupi; editor, Dorothy Spencer.

Elizabeth Taylor (Cleopatra); Richard Burton (Mark Antony); Rex Harrison (Julius Caesar); Pamela Brown (High Priestess); George Cole (Flavius); Hume Cronyn (Sosigenes); Cesare Danova (Apollodorus); Kenneth Haigh (Brutus); Andrew Keir (Agrippa); Martin Landau (Rufio); Roddy McDowall (Octavian); Robert Stephens (Germanicus); Francesca Annis (Eiras); Gregoire Aslan (Pothinos); Martin Benson (Ramos); Herbert Berghof (Theodotos); John Cairney (Phoebus); Jacqui Chan (Lotos); Isabelle Cooley (Charmian); John Doucette (Achillas); Andrew Faulds (Canidius); Michael Gwynn (Cimber); Michael Hordern (Cicero); John Hoyt (Cassius); Marne Maitland (Euphranor); Carroll O'Connor (Casca); Richard O'Sullivan (Ptolemy); Gwen Watford (Calpurnia); Douglas Wilmer (Decimus); Marina Berti (Queen at Tarsus); John Karlsen (High Priest); Loris Loddi (Cesarion at Age Four); Jean Marsh (Octavia); Gin Mart (Marcellus); Furio Meniconi (Mithridates); Kenneth Nash (Caesarion at Age Twelve); Del Russell (Caesarion at Age Seven); John Valva (Valvus).

THE V.I.P.s (*MGM, 1963*) C-119 min.

Producer, Anatole de Grunwald; associate producer, Roy Parkinson; director, Anthony Asquith; screenplay, Terence Rattigan; art director, William Kellner; set decorator, Pamela Cornell; assistant director, Kip Gowans; gowns, Hubert de Givenchy, Pierre Cardin; music, Miklos Rozsa; production advisor, Margaret Booth; Miss Taylor's makeup, Dave Aylott; Miss Taylor's hairstyles, Vivienne Walker Zavitz; sound, Cyril Swern; camera, Jack Hildyard; editor, Frank Clarke.

Elizabeth Taylor (Frances Andros); Richard Burton (Paul Andros); Louis Jourdan (Marc Champselle); Elsa Martinelli (Gloria Gritti); Margaret Rutherford (Duchess of Brighton); Maggie Smith (Miss Mead); Rod Taylor (Les Mangam); Orson Welles (Max Buda); Linda Christian (Miriam Marshall); Dennis Price (Commander Millbank); Richard Wattis (Sanders); Ronald Fraser (Joslin); David Frost (Reporter); Robert Coote (John Coburn); Joan Benham (Miss Potter); Michael Hordern (Airport Director); Lance Percival (BOAC Official); Martin Miller (Dr. Schwutzbacher); Peter Sallis (Doctor); Stringer Davis (Hotel Waiter); Clifton Jones (Jamaican Passenger); Moyra Fraser, Jill Carson (Air Hostesses); Joyce Carey (Mrs. Damer); Griffiths Davis (Porter); Maggie McGrath (Waitress); Frank Williams (Assistant to Airport Director); Rosemary Dorken, Pamela Buckley (Airport Announcers); Ray Austin (Rolls Royce Chauffeur); Angus Lennie (Meteorological Man); Duncan Lewis (Hotel Receptionist); Richard Briers (Met. Official); Virginia Bedard, Cal McCord (Visitors); Ann Castle (Lady Reporter); Clifford Mollison (Mr. River the Hotel Manager).

THE SANDPIPER (*MGM, 1965*) C-117 min.

Producer, Martin Ransohoff; associate producer, John Calley; director, Vincente Minnelli; story, Ransohoff; adaptors, Irene Kamp, Louis Kamp; screenplay, Dalton

Trumbo, Michael Wilson; art directors, George W. Davis, Urie McCleary; set decorators, Henry Grace, Keogh Gleason; music, Johnny Mandel; song, Paul Francis Webster and Mandel; assistant director, William McGarry; titles, Herb Rosenthal; Laura's paintings by Elizabeth Duquette; Redwood sculpture by Edmund Kara; coordinator of Big Sur scene, Eduardo Tirella; sound, Franklin Milton; camera, Milton Krasner; wildlife camera, Richard Borden; editor, David Bretherton.

Elizabeth Taylor (Laura Reynolds); Richard Burton (Dr. Edward Hewitt); Eva Marie Saint (Claire Hewitt); Charles Bronson (Cos Erickson); Robert Webber (Ward Hendricks); James Edwards (Larry Brant); Torin Thatcher (Judge Thompson); Tom Drake (Walter Robinson); Doug Henderson (Phil Sutcliff); Morgan Mason (Danny Reynolds).

WHO'S AFRAID OF VIRGINIA WOOLF? (*Warner Bros.*, 1966) 132 min.

Producer, Ernest Lehman; director, Mike Nichols; based on the play by Edward Albee; screenplay, Lehman; assistant director, Bud Grace; production designer, Richard Sylbert; set decorator, George James Hopkins; music/music director, Alex North; costumes, Irene Sharaff; sound, M. A. Merrick; production advisor, Doane Harrison; camera, Haskell Wexler; editor, Sam O'Steen.

Elizabeth Taylor (Martha); Richard Burton (George); George Segal (Nick); Sandy Dennis (Honey).

THE TAMING OF THE SHREW (*Columbia*, 1967) C-122 min.

Executive producer, Richard McWhorter; producers, Richard Burton, Elizabeth Taylor, Franco Zeffirelli; director, Zeffirelli; based on the play by William Shakespeare; adaptors, Paul Dehn, Suso Cecchi D'Amico, Zeffirelli; production designer, John De Cuir; art directors, Giuseppe Mariani, Elven Webb; set decorators, Dario Simoni, Carlo Gervasi; music, Nino Rota; music director, Carlo Savina; costumes for Miss Taylor by Irene Sharaff; costumes, Danilo Donati; assistant directors, Carlo Lastricati, Rinaldo Ricci, Albino Cocco; sound, David Hildyard, Aldo De Martino; special effects, Augie Lehman; camera, Oswald Morris, Luciano Trasatti; editor, Peter Taylor.

Elizabeth Taylor (Katharina); Richard Burton (Petruchio); Cyril Cusack (Grumio); Michael Hordern (Baptista); Alfred Lynch (Tranio); Alan Webb (Gremio); Victor Spinetti (Hortensio); Roy Holden (Biondello); Mark Dignam (Vincentio); Bice Valori (The Widow); Natasha Pyne (Bianca); Michael York (Lucentio); Giancarlo Cobelli (The Priest); Vernon Dobtcheff (Pedant); Ken Parry (Tailor); Anthony Gardner (Haberdasher); Alberto Bonucci (Nathaniel); Gianni Magni (Curtis); Lino Capolicchio (Gregory); Roberto Antonelli (Philip); and Tina Perna, Milena Vucotich, Alfred Bianchini, Valentino Bacchi.

REFLECTIONS IN A GOLDEN EYE (*Warner Bros.-Seven Arts*, 1967) C-109 min.

Producer, Ray Stark; associate producer, C. O. Erickson; director, John Huston; based on the novel by Carson McCullers; screenplay, Chapman Mortimer, Gladys Hill; music, Toshiro Mayuzumi; music director, Marcus Dods; production designer, Stephen Grimes; art director, Bruno Avesani; set decorator, William Kiernan; costumes, Dorothy Jeakins; assistant director, Vanao Caruso; sound, Basil Fenton-Smith, John Cox, Leslie Hodgson; camera, Aldo Tonti; editor, Russell Loyd.

Elizabeth Taylor (Leonora Penderton); Marlon Brando (Major Weldon Penderton); Brian Keith (Lieutenant Colonel Morris Langdon); Julie Harris (Alison Langdon); Robert Forster (Private Williams); Zorro David (Anacleto); Irvin Dugan (Captain Weincheck); Gordon Mitchell (Stables Sergeant); Fay Sparks (Susie).

THE COMEDIANS (*MGM, 1967*) C-156 min.

Producer/director, Peter Glenville; based on the novel by Graham Greene; screenplay, Greene; art director, François de Lamothe; set decorator, Robert Christides; music/music director, Laurence Rosenthal; assistant director, Jean-Michel Lacor; sound, Jonathan Bates; camera, Henri Decae; editor, Françoise Javet.

Richard Burton (Brown); Alec Guinness (Major Jones); Elizabeth Taylor (Martha Pineda); Peter Ustinov (Ambassador Pineda); Paul Ford (Mr. Smith); Lillian Gish (Mrs. Smith); George Stanford Brown (Henri Philipot); Roscoe Lee Browne (Petit Pierre); Gloria Foster (Madame Philipot); James Earl Jones (Dr. Magiot); Zakes Mokae (Michel); Raymond St. Jacques (Captain Concasseur); Douta Seck (Joseph); Cicely Tyson (Marie Therese).

DOCTOR FAUSTUS (*Columbia*, 1968) C-93 min.

Producers, Richard Burton, Richard McWhorter; directors, Burton, Nevill Coghill; based on the play *The Tragical History of Doctor Faustus* by Christopher Marlowe; adaptor, Coghill; assistant director, Gus Agosti; production designer, John De Cuir; art director, Boris Juraga; set decorator, Dario Simoni; music director, Mario Nascimbene; costumes, Peter Hall; choreography, Jacqueline Harvey; titles, National Screen Service; sound, David Hildyard, John Aldred; camera, Gabor Pogany; editor, John Shirley.

Richard Burton (Doctor Faustus); Andreas Teuber (Mephistopheles); Elizabeth Taylor (Helen of Troy); Ian Marten (Emperor); Elizabeth O'Donovan (Empress); David McIntosh (Lucifer); Jeremy Eccles (Beelzebub); Ram Chopra (Valdes); Richard Carwardine (Cornelius); Richard Heffer, Hugh Williams (Scholars); Gwydion Thomas (Scholar/Lechery); Nicholas Loukes (Cardinal/Pride); Richard Durden-Smith (Knight); Patrick Barwise (Wagner); Adrian Benjamin (Pope); Jeremy Chandler (Attendant at Emperor's Court); Angus McIntosh (Rector Magnificus); Ambrose Coghill (Professor/Envy); Julian Wontner, Richard Harrison, Nevill Coghill (Professors); Michael Menaugh (Good Angel); John Sandbach (Boy-turned-into-Hind); Sebastian Walker (Idiot); R. Peverello (Wrath); Maria Aitken (Sloth); Valerie James (Idleness); Bridget Coghill, Petronella Pulsford, Susan Watson (Gluttony); Jacqueline Harvey, Sheila Dawson, Carolyn Bennitt (Dancers); Jane Wilford (Nun/Court Lady).

BOOM! (*Universal*, 1968) C-113 min.

Producers, John Heyman, Norman Priggen; associate producer, Lester Persky; director, Joseph Losey; based on the story "Man, Bring This Up Road" and the play *The Milk Train Doesn't Stop Here Anymore* by Tennessee Williams; screenplay, Williams; assistant director, Carlo Lastricati; production designer, Richard MacDonald; music, John Barry; Indian music, Nazirali Jairazbnoy, Viram Jasani; song, John Dankworth, Don Black; costumes, Tiziani; sound, Leslie Hammond, Gerry Humphreys; camera, Douglas Slocombe; editor, Reginald Beck.

Elizabeth Taylor (Flora "Sissy" Goforth); Richard Burton (Chris Flanders); Noël Coward (The Witch of Capri); Joanna Shinkus (Blackie); Michael Dunn (Rudy); Romolo Valli (Dr. Lullo); Fernando Piazza (Etti); Veronica Wells (Simonetta); Claudye Ettori (Manicurist); Howard Taylor (Journalist); Gens Bloch (Photographer); Franco Pesce (Villager).

SECRET CEREMONY (*Universal, 1968*) C-109 min.

Producers, John Heyman, Norman Priggen; director, Joseph Losey; based on the story by Marco Denevi; screenplay, George Tabori; music, Richard Rodney Bennett; makeup, Alex Garfath; assistant director, Richard Dalton; production designer, Richard MacDonald; art director, John Clark; set decorator, Jill Oxley; Miss Taylor's wardrobe, Marc Bohan, Christian Dior; costumes, Susan Yelland; sound, Leslie Hammond; camera, Gerald Fisher; editor, Reginald Beck.

Elizabeth Taylor (Leonora); Mia Farrow (Cenci); Robert Mitchum (Albert); Peggy Ashcroft (Hannah); Pamela Brown (Hilda). When re-edited for television, the narrative was placed within the framework of a discussion between psychiatrists: Michael Strong (Dr. Walter Stevens); Robert Douglas (Sir Alex Gordon).

ANNE OF THE THOUSAND DAYS (*Universal, 1969*) C-145 min.

Producer, Hal B. Wallis; associate producer, Richard Mc-Whorter; director, Charles Jarrott; based on the play by Maxwell Anderson; adaptor, Richard Sokolove; screenplay, John Hale, Bridget Boland; production designer, Maurice Carter; art director, Lionel Couch; set decorator, Peter Howitt; music, Georges Delerue; costumes, Margaret Furse; choreography, Mary Skeaping; assistant director, Simon Relph; technical advisor, Patrick McLoughlin; horse master, Jeremy Taylor; sound, John Aldred; camera, Arthur Ibbetson; editor, Richard Marden.

Richard Burton (King Henry VIII); Genevieve Bujold (Anne Boleyn); Irene Papas (Queen Katherine of Aragon); Anthony Quayle (Cardinal); John Colicos (Thomas Cromwell); Michael Hordern (Thomas Boleyn); Katharine Blake (Elizabeth Boleyn); Peter Jeffrey (Norfolk); Joseph O'Connor (Fisher); William Squire (Thomas More); Esmond Knight (Kingston); Nora Swinburne (Lady Kingston); Vernon Dobtcheff (Mendoza); Brook Williams (Brereton); Gary Bond (Smeaton); T. P. McKenna (Norris); Denis Quilley (Weston); Terry Wilson (Harry Percy); Lesly Pateson (Jane Seymour); Nicola Pagett (Princess Mary); June Ellis (Bess); Kynaston Reeves (Willoughby); Marne Maitland (Compeggio); Cyril Luckham (Prior Houghton); Amanda Walter, Charlotte Selwyn, Elizabeth Counsell (Anne's Ladies-in-Waiting); Juliet Kempson, Fiona Hartford, Lilian Hutchins, Ann Tirard (Katherine's Ladies-in-Waiting); Amanda Jane Smythe (Child Elizabeth); Elizabeth Taylor (Courtesan); Kate Burton (Serving Maid); Liza Todd Burton (Beggar Maid).

THE ONLY GAME IN TOWN (*20th Century-Fox, 1970*) C-113 min.

Producer, Fred Kohlmar; director, George Stevens; based on the play by Frank D. Gilroy; screenplay, Gilroy; assistant directors, Robert Doudell, Jean-Michel Lacor; art directors, Herman Blumenthal, Auguste Capelier; set decorators, Walter M. Scott, Jerry Wunderlich; music/music director, Maurice Jarre; costumes, Mia Fonssagrives, Vicki Tiel; sound, Jo de Bretagne, David Dockendorf; special camera effects, L. B. Abbott, Art Cruickshank; editors, John W. Holmes, William Sande, Pat Shade.

Elizabeth Taylor (Fran Walker); Warren Beatty (Joe Grady); Charles Braswell (Thomas Lockwood); Hank Henry (Tony); Olga Valery (Woman with Purple Wig).

X, Y & ZEE (*Columbia, 1972*) C-110 min.

Executive producer, Elliott Kastner; producers, Jay Kanter, Alan Ladd, Jr.; director, Brian G. Hutton; screenplay, Edna O'Brien; music, Stanley Myers; songs, Rick Wakeman and Dave Lambert, John Mayer; art director, Peter Mullins; set decorator, Arthur Taksen; costumes, Beatrice Dawson; makeup, Alex Garfath; assistant director, Colin Brewer; sound, Cyril Swern, Bob Jones; camera, Billy Williams; editor, Jim Clark.

Elizabeth Taylor (Zee Blakeley); Michael Caine (Robert Blakeley); Susannah York (Stella); Margaret Leighton (Gladys); John Standing (Gordon); Mary Larkin (Rita); Michael Cashman (Gavin); Gino Melvazzi (Headwaiter); Julian West (Oscar); Hilary West (Shaun).

HAMMERSMITH IS OUT (*Cinerama, 1972*) C-114 min.

Executive producer, Frank Beetson; producer, Alex Lucas; director, Peter Ustinov; screenplay, Stanford Whitmore; set decorator, Robert Benton; music, Dominic Frontiere; assistant director, Newton Arnold; camera, Richard H. Kline; editor, David Blewitt.

Elizabeth Taylor (Jimmie Jean Jackson); Richard Burton (Hammersmith); Peter Ustinov (Doctor); Beau Bridges (Billy Breedlove); Leon Ames (General Sam Pembroke); Leon Askin (Dr. Krodt); John Schuck (Henry Joe); George Raft (Guido Scartucci); Marjorie Eaton (Princess); Lisa Jak (Kiddo); Linda Gaye Scott (Miss Quim); Mel Berger (Fat Man); Anthony Holland (Oldham); Brook Williams (Peter Rutter); Carl Donn (Cleopatra); Jose Espinosa (Duke); Stan Ross (Inmate).

UNDER MILKWOOD (*Altura Films International, 1973*) C-88 min.

Producers, Hugh French, Jules Buck; associate producer, John Comfort; director, Andrew Sinclair; based on the radio play by Dylan Thomas; screenplay, Sinclair; assistant director, Dominic Fulford; art director, Geoffrey Tozer; music Brian Gascoigne; sound, Cyril Collick; camera, Bob Huke; editor, Willy Kemplen.

Richard Burton (First Voice); Elizabeth Taylor (Rosie Probert); Peter O'Toole (Captain Cat); Glynis Johns

(Myfanwy Price); Vivien Merchant (Mrs. Pugh); Sian Phillips (Mrs. Ogmore-Pritchard); Victor Spinetti (Mog Edwards); Ryan Davies (Second Voice); Angharad Rees (Gossamer Beynon); Ray Smith (Mr. Waldo); Michael Forrest (Sinbad Sailor); Ann Beach (Polly Garter); Glynn Edwards (Mr. Cherry Owen); Bridget Turner (Mrs. Cherry Owen); Talfryn Thomas (Mr. Pugh); Wim Wylton (Mr. Willy Nilly); Bronwen Williams (Mrs. Willy Nilly); Jeg Wynn Owen (Lily Smalls); Hubert Rees (Butcher Beynon); Mary Jones (Mrs. Beynon); Aubrey Richards (Reverend Eli Jenkins); Mark Jones (Evans the Death); David Jason (Nogood Boyo); Richard Davies (Mr. Pritchard); Maudie Edwards (Mrs. Utah Watkins); Dudley Jones (Dai Bread); Dorothea Phillips (Mrs. Dai Bread One); Ruth Madoc (Mrs. Dai Bread Two); T. H. Evans (Old Man); Gwyneth Owen, Lucy Griffiths, Angela Brinkworth (Neighbors).

NIGHT WATCH (*Avco Embassy, 1973*) C-98 min.

Producers, Martin Poll, George W. George, Barnard Straus; associate producer, David White; director, Brian G. Hutton; based on the play by Lucille Fletcher; screenplay, Tony Williamson; additional dialogue, Evan Jones; music, John Cameron; art director, Peter Murton; set decorator, Peter James; sound, Jonathan Bates; Billie Williams; editor, John Jympson.

Elizabeth Taylor (Ellen Wheeler); Laurence Harvey (John Wheeler); Billie Whitelaw (Sarah Cooke); Robert Lang (Appleby); Tony Britton (Tony); Bill Dean (Inspector Walker); Michael Danvers-Walker (Sergeant Norris); Rosario Serrano (Dolores); Pauline Jameson (Secretary); Linda Hayden (Girl in Car); Kevin Colson (Carl); Laon Maybanke (Florist).

DIVORCE; HIS/DIVORCE; HERS (*ABC-TV, 1973*) C-150 min.

Executive producer, John Heyman; producers, Terence Baker, Gareth Wigen; director, Waris Hussein; teleplay, John Hopkins; music, Stanley Myers; Miss Taylor's costumes, Edith Head; production designer, Roy Stannard; camera, Ernst Wild, Gabor Pogany; editor, John Bloom.

Elizabeth Taylor (Jane Reynolds); Richard Burton (Martin Reynolds); Carrie Nye (Diana Proctor); Barry Foster (Donald Trenton); Gabriele Ferzetti (Turi Livicci); Daniella Surina (Franca); Mark Colleano (Tommy Reynolds); Eva Griffith (Judith Reynolds); Thomas Baptiste (Minister); Ronald Radd (Angus McIntyre); and Rudolph Walker, Rosalyn Vandor.

ASH WEDNESDAY (*Paramount, 1973*) C-99 min.

Producer, Dominick Dunne; director, Larry Peerce; screenplay, Jean-Claude Tramont; assistant directors, Steven Barnett, Tony Brandt; costumes, Edith Head; music/music director, Maurice Jarre; titles, Wayne Fitzgerald; technical adviser, Dr. Rodolphe Troques; sound, Basil Fenton-Smith; camera, Ennio Guarnieri; editor, Marion Rothman.

Elizabeth Taylor (Barbara Sawyer); Henry Fonda (Mark Sawyer); Helmut Berger (Erich); Keith Baxter (David); Maurice Teynac (Dr. Lambert); Margaret Blye (Kate); Monique Von Vooren (German Woman); Henning

Schlueter (Bridge Player); Dino Mele (Mario); Kathy van Lypps (Mandy); Dina Sassoli (Nurse Ilse); Carlo Puri (Paolo); Andrea Esterhazy (Comte d'Arnoud); Jill Pratt (Simone); Irina Wassilchikoff (Silvana Del Campo); Maximillian Windisch-Graetz (Viet Hartung); Sandra Johnson (Sandy); Maria Grazia Marescalchi (Saleslady).

THAT'S ENTERTAINMENT! (*MGM/United Artists, 1974*) C-132 min.

Executive producer, Daniel Melnick; producer/director/script, Jack Haley, Jr.; music supervisor, Jesse Kaye; additional music adaptor, Henry Mancini; assistant directors, Richard Bremerkamp, David Silver, Claude Binyon, Jr.; film librarian, Mort Feinstein; sound, Hal Watkins, Aaron Rochin, Lyle Burbridge, Harry W. Tetrick, William L. McCaughey; cameras, Gene Polito, Ernest Laszlo, Russell Metty, Ennio Guarieri, Allan Green; opticals, Robert Hoag, Jim Liles; editors, Bud Friedgen, David E. Blewitt.

Narrators: Fred Astaire, Bing Crosby, Gene Kelly, Peter Lawford, Liza Minnelli, Donald O'Connor, Debbie Reynolds, Mickey Rooney, Frank Sinatra, James Stewart, Elizabeth Taylor.

THE DRIVER'S SEAT (a.k.a. IDENTIKIT) (*Avco Embassy, 1975*) C-101 min.

Producer, Franco Rossellini; director, Giuseppe Patroni-Griffi; based on the novel by Muriel Spark; screenplay, Raffaele La Capria, Griffi; music, Franco Mannino; art director, Mario Ceroli; costumes, Gabriella Pescucci; camera, Vittorio Storaro.

Elizabeth Taylor (Lise); Ian Bannen (Bill); Guido Mannari (Carlo); Mona Washbourne (Mrs. Fiedke); Maxence Mailfort (Richard); and Andy Warhol.

THE BLUE BIRD (*Twentieth Century-Fox, 1976*) C-100 min.

Producer, Paul Maslansky; executive producer, Edward Lewis; co-producers, Lee Savin, Paul Radin; director, George Cukor, based on the novel by Maurice Maeterlinck; screenplay, Hugh Whitemore, Alfred Hayes, Alexel Kapler; production designer, Brian Wildsmith; art director, Valery Urkevich; set decorator, Yevgeny Starikovitch, Edward Isaev, Tamara Polyanskoya; assistant directors, Mike Gowans, Yevgeny Tatarsky, Liliana Markova, Stirlin Harris; music, Irwin Kostal, Lionel Newman; lyrics, Tony Harrison; sound, Theodore Soderberg, Gordon Everett, Gregory Elbert, John Bramaill; camera, Freddie Young, Jonas Gritzus; editors, Ernest Walter, Tatyana Shapiro, Stanford C. Allen.

Elizabeth Taylor (Mother/Witch/Light/Maternal Love); Jane Fonda (Night); Ava Gardner (Luxury); Cicely Tyson (Cat); Robert Morley (Father Time); Harry Andrews (Oak); Todd Lookinland (Tyltyl); Patsy Kensit (Mytyl); Will Geer (Grandfather); Mona Washbourne (Grandmother); George Cole (Dog); Richard Pearson (Bread); Nadejda Pavlowa (The Blue Bird); George Vitzin (Sugar); Margareta Terechova (Milk); Oleg Popov (Fat Laughter); Leonid Nevedomsky (Father); Valentina Ganilaee Ganibalova (Water); Yevgeny Scherbakov (Fire); Pheona McLellan (Sick Girl).

VICTORY AT ENTEBBE (*ABC-TV, 1977*) C-119 min.

Executive producer, David L. Wolper; producer, Robert Guenette; associate producer, Albert J. Simon; director, Marvin Chomsky; teleplay, Ernest Kinoy; production designer, Edward Stephenson; set decorator, Charles Rutherford; costumes, Jack Martell; assistant directors, Peter Bogart, James Benjamin; music, Charles Fox; sound, Larry Stephens; camera, James Kilgore; editors, David Saxon, Jim McElroy.

Anthony Hopkins (Prime Minister Yitzhak Rabin); Burt Lancaster (Defense Minister Shimon Peres); Harris Yulin (General Don Shomron); Stephen Gierasch (Chief of Staff Mordechai Gur); Helmut Berger (Chief Terrorist Wilfried Bose); Richard Dreyfuss (Lieutenant Colonel Yehonatan Netanyahu); Helen Hayes (Mrs. Wise); Linda Blair (Chana); Elizabeth Taylor (Edra Vilnosky); Kirk Douglas (Herschel Vilnosky); David Groh (Benjamin Wise); Christian Marquand (Michel Bacos); Jessica Walter (Passenger Nomi Haroun); Julius Harris (Idi Amin Dada); Theodore Bikel (Yakov Scholomo).

WINTER KILLS (*Stirling Gold, 1977*—Incomplete)

Executive producers, Leonard J. Goldberg, Robert Sterling; producer, Fred Caruso; director, William Richert; based on the novel by Richard Condon; screenplay, Richert; art directors, Bob Boyle, Norm Newberry; set decorator, Art Parker; Camera, Vilmos Zsigmond.

With: Jeff Bridges, John Huston, Anthony Perkins, Eli Wallach, Sterling Hayden, Richard Boone, Elizabeth Taylor, Toshiro Mifune, Dorothy Malone, Tomas Milian, and John Warner.

A LITTLE NIGHT MUSIC (*New World Pictures, 1978*) C-124 min.

Executive producer, Heinz Lazek; producer, Elliott Kastner; director, Harold Prince; based on the musical play by Stephen Sondheim and Hugh Wheeler, suggested by the Ingmar Bergman film *Smiles of a Summer Night*; screenplay, Wheeler; songs, Sondheim; costumes, Florence Klotz; choreography, Patricia Birch; music director, Paul Gemignani; music scorer/supervisor, Jonathan Tunick; art directors, Herta Pischinger, Thomas Riccabona; assistant directors, Gerhard von Halem, David Wimbury, Claudio Schreiber, Keith Rotman; sound mixer, David Hildyard; camera, Arthur Ibbetson; editor, John Jympson. .

Elizabeth Taylor (Desiree Armfeldt); Diana Rigg (Charlotte Mittelheim); Len Cariou (Frederick Egerman); Lesley-Anne Down (Anne Egerman); Hermione Gingold (Mme. Armfeldt); Laurence Guittard (Carl-Magnus Mittelheim); Christopher Guard (Erich Egerman); Chloe Franks (Fredericka Armfeldt); Heinz Marecek (Kurt); Leslie Dunlop (Petra); Jonathan Tunick (Conductor); Hubert Tscheppe (Franz); Rudolf Schrympf (Band Conductor); Franz Schussler (Mayor); Johanna Schussler (Mayoress); Jean Sincere (Box-Office Lady in Theatre); Dagmar Koller, Ruth Brinkman (Ladies); Anna Veigl (Concierge); Stefan Paryla (Uniformed Sergeant); Eva Divorska, Lisa De Cohen (Whores); Kurt Martynow (Major Domo); Gerty Barek (Cook); James De Groat (Footman).

Glamour à la MGM.

CHAPTER 7

LANA TURNER

5'3½"
110 pounds
Blonde hair
Blue eyes
Aquarius

LANA TURNER IS one of the last of the beautiful, irrepressible, magical Hollywood *stars* still attracting the world's attention. For decades, she has been the focal point of an exhausting array of gossip and scandals. While her hectic private existence would have probably driven the average filmgoer into exile due to public disgust or to the grave through sheer energy output, Lana has sashayed onward. It required only one scandal to wreck permanently the career of Fatty Arbuckle, one exposed diary to hurl Mary Astor into a career dungeon, one publicized orgy to cast Lionel Atwill into poverty row banishment. Not so with Lana.

Why? Lana Turner is, again, a *star*—a very unique one. She is a gorgeous dispenser of the class that once made Hollywood the glamour mecca of the world. She attained her status as a sweater-girl starlet, a World War II pin-up queen, and an MGM sex goddess not through her acting prowess, but through her physical magnetism. Occasionally Lana would surprise even her devout followers by turning in a well-wrought dramatic performance, as in *The Postman Always Rings Twice* (1946), *The Bad and the Beautiful* (1952), or *Peyton Place* (1957) (for

Refining the movie fledgling, Hollywood-style ('37).

which she was Oscar-nominated). For a woman who has reaped international huzzahs for her ability to sport beautiful clothes and celebrated hair-dyes, acting is simply above and beyond the call of duty.

However, to introduce the questions of "Can she act?" "Could she act?" or "Will she ever start acting?" in examining the career of Lana Turner is to misread her appeal. There is simply far more to the Turner charisma than her celluloid skills. As Hollywood watchdog Adela Rogers St. John noted some years back, "Look, let's not get mixed up about the real Lana Turner. She was always a movie star and loved it. Her personal life and movie star life *are one.*"

In a moment of shrewd insight, Lana once described her life as having been "a series of emergencies." Indeed it has. Her life began about as opposite as possible from the glamorous high-living of a Hollywood superstar. Julia Jean Mildred Frances Turner was born on Sunday, February 8, 1920,* in Wallace, Idaho, a tiny, grimy mining town. Her father, Virgil Turner, was a gypsy-like worker (born in Alabama) who met Mildred Frances Cowan at a Saturday night dance in Wallace. Elopement to Missouri quickly followed, and then a return to Wallace when Mildred became expectant. Into such beginnings came Lana Turner.

As Lana grew up, nicknamed Judy, the Turner family trekked from mining hovel to mining shack, with Virgil frequently resorting to gambling and bootlegging to keep his family solvent. When the girl was eight, the family loaded up their Star automobile (then reputed to be the cheapest of second-hand cars) and headed for San Francisco. They based themselves in Daly City outside the metropolis, and Virgil landed a stevedore job. He supplemented his income by shooting craps behind the cargo he unloaded on the docks. Mrs. Turner at times worked as a model, and Lana's first public appearance reputedly came when she was three. She ran up onto the stage to her modeling mom and performed an impromptu dance.

Mr. Turner's ne'er-do-well personality enchanted his daughter, but aggravated his wife. Mildred decided to take steps to start her own lifestyle and at the same time to safeguard her daughter's welfare. She took a job in a beauty parlor, told Virgil she was through with him, and boarded her child with a Modesto, California, family. Lana at first had a difficult time recognizing this as concern. She missed her father greatly and would later recall that her step-family treated her "as a scullery maid."

On the evening of December 14, 1930, Virgil Turner became involved in an all-night crap-shooting contest in the basement of the *San Francisco Chronicle* at Fifth and Mission Streets. The next day, police found the thirty-six-year-old man dead of a fractured skull on a street corner several miles away in Butchertown. His murderer was never apprehended. As Lana would relate years later, "The shock I suffered then may be a valid excuse for me now—may explain things I do not myself understand." A stunned Mrs. Turner called her daughter back to her. Lana continued to grow up in poverty, moving from San Francisco to Sacramento and back again as her mother attempted to get a firm foothold in the beautician trade.

Mystery clouds the adolescent years of Lana Turner. At some point, Mildred became close friends with one Gladys Heath. When Mrs. Heath moved to Los Angeles, the Turner family decided to move south along with her. Lana herself simply refers to the enigmatic Mrs. Heath as "a wonderful friend," with no further elucidation. At any rate, the women took an apartment near Hollywood High School where Lana was enrolled. Gladys and Mildred continued beautician work. Judy rapidly became the talk of her school, where her rapidly developing physique made her perfect movie material and the intended conquest of all male students. Her pulchritude was far more impressive than her studies, and she was soon flunking math and cutting classes to hobnob in the neighborhood malt shop.

The famous Schwab's Drug Store, contrary to

*Lana now gives the year as 1921, insisting that MGM changed the birth year to 1920 to make her seem older.

As Cynthia Potter in *Love Finds Andy Hardy* ('38).

The emerging sex symbol in the late 1930s.

Hollywood scripture, was *not* the locale for Lana's cinema discovery. Actually she was spotted in an ice cream parlor* across from Hollywood High. While her typing teacher marked her absent from class one morning in January 1936, Judy snared the attention of Billy Wilkerson, publisher/founder of the *Hollywood Reporter.* After posing the grand old question, "How'd ya like to be in pictures?" Wilkerson escorted the interested sixteen-year-old to Zeppo Marx's talent agency. Marx was impressed by the shapely novice. However, no producer appeared to share his or Wilkerson's interest.

Finally an offer came. David O. Selznick was producing *A Star Is Born* (1937) for United Artists release. With William Wellman directing the now classic tale of Hollywood, Judy made her debut in a thirty-second crowd-scene bit at a bar. Nobody noticed her and Selznick laughed when Marx tried to convince him to place her under contract. RKO and Twentieth Century-Fox gave similar vetoes. Judy decided to seek employment elsewhere and accepted a salesgirl post in a Hollywood dress shop.

The selling job did not last long. Before *A Star Is Born* was released, Solly Baiano of the Marx agency called her and packaged the girl in a select group he was promoting to casting officials. It was Warner Bros., where Bette Davis, Paul Muni, James Cagney, Edward G. Robinson, Errol Flynn, Kay Francis, Pat O'Brien and Olivia de Havilland were the top draws, that finally made an offer.

The interested party at the Burbank studio was Mervyn LeRoy, responsible for such film classics as *Little Caesar* (1931) and *I Am a Fugitive from a Chain Gang* (1932). The producer/director was preparing to film *They Won't Forget,* the graphic account of Southern prejudice based on Ward Greene's book *Death in the Deep South.* Claude Rains was starring as the flamboyant attorney. The proceedings required a young woman to be the focal point of the early segment of the motion picture. She would have four scenes: in a classroom, at a drugstore soda counter, in the crowded street, and back in the schoolroom with some lines of dialogue.

*Today it is the site of a gas station.

Throughout her sequences she would wear one outfit: a form-fitting skirt, a tight-clinging wool sweater, high spiked heels, and a beret. Most important, the segments required the young actress to sashay with an obvious abundance of sex appeal. She had to slink down a street with appropriate breast-bouncing and derriere-swaying, and end up being murdered (registering shock as her assailant approaches her). With her already come-hither look, and 35-23-35 figure, Judy Turner appeared perfect for the provocative bit role of Mary Clay. LeRoy recognized as soon as the scene was shot that Judy had "it," and on February 22, 1937, signed her to a personal contract at $50 a week.

As usual, LeRoy was astute. Audience reaction to Lana's onscreen stroll was enormous, even if the young actress was less impressed. "I was one of those photogenic accidents. I was a fifteen-(sic) year-old kid with a bosom and a backside strolling across the scene for less than a minute." The passion of her fan mail encouraged Warner Bros. to concoct a publicity campaign extolling "The Sweater Girl," whom they endlessly posed seductively for cheesecake glossies and planted in nightclubs as bait for press photographers. By the time *They Won't Forget* ("a brilliant sociological drama" reported the *New York Times*) was released in June 1937, LeRoy had made sure the actress had changed her name from the pedestrian Judy to the more alluring Lana, and had given her featured billing in the picture.

LeRoy began making professional moves to insure Lana's continued career climb. He assigned her to a bit role in Warner Bros.' *The Great Garrick* (1937), a costumed romance set in the 1750s, starring Brian Aherne as the fabled actor and placing Olivia de Havilland, the studio's top ingenue, in the female stellar spot. Lana's chore was to be Auber, the scullery maid. The picture, directed by James Whale of *Frankenstein* repute, laid a very expensive box-office bomb. Studio chieftain Jack L. Warner was so incensed at its failure that he reputedly banned Whale from the lot.

At this juncture, producer Samuel Goldwyn (who had seen a screening of *They Won't Forget*) decided he must have Lana for a small role in his forthcoming *The Adventures of Marco Polo* (1938). He borrowed her to play the black-

386

haired handmaiden of Binnie Barnes. In this trouble-plagued production, Robert E. Sherwood wrote a screenplay that intended to be tongue-in-cheek but instead seemed ludicrous; Gary Cooper was miscast as the thirteenth-century adventurer; Sigrid Gurie made very little impact in the romantic lead; John Carradine was ousted from the role of the chief villain when the bigger box-office bait Basil Rathbone became available; and director John Cromwell quit after five days of filming. He was replaced by Archie Mayo. Lana had two short scenes midway through the ruptured storyline as the flirtatious maiden who dallies with raucous Lord Kaidu (Alan Hale) much to the annoyance of his domineering spouse (Barnes). It was an assignment any of the Goldwyn Girls could have played with ease.

Back at Burbank, powerful Jack L. Warner had decided that his studio had no berth for Lana. "She hasn't got it; she's just a kid," he told LeRoy. It just so happened that LeRoy was sim-ilarly displeased with Warner and was shifting his headquarters to Culver City—to the regime of Louis B. Mayer, patriarch of Metro-Goldwyn-Mayer. When Mervyn LeRoy took his business there, he took Lana with him. "She *wanted* to be in the movies," recalled LeRoy. "She did what a director told her to do and learned fast. I sold her to MGM in a deal arranged by Benny Thau." Hence, by early 1938, Lana—now a bright red-head—was part of the awesome talent package assembled under the talisman of Metro's Leo the Lion.

"Why, when we were at MGM," Lana proudly related years later, "we worked years before anybody called us stars. Louis B. Mayer brought us along in little parts—even *Love Finds Andy Hardy*. Then, if we showed promise, he would put us opposite the established stars—like Clark Gable, Robert Taylor, Spencer Tracy—who could lend us the power of their names. Then, when we became established, he would co-star the rising young players with us. Believe me,

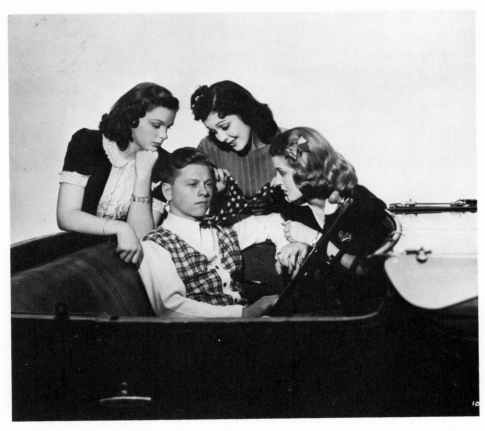

Publicity pose for *Love Finds Andy Hardy* with Judy Garland, Mickey Rooney, and Ann Rutherford.

387

when the time came for you to move from the featured players' building into the building of the stars' dressing rooms, it was a thrilling event in your life. It was like entering a new kingdom in which you were the queen."

For a lady never touted as the most expressive or intelligent of motion picture actresses, Lana Turner described the MGM training ground remarkably well. She immediately began the very rapid rise from featured player to queen of that beautiful kingdom of stardom which she has occupied to this day.

Lana arrived at the Metro facilities just as an opening had sadly occurred in the celebrated constellation. While Greta Garbo, Joan Crawford, and Norma Shearer (rapidly losing favor since the 1936 death of her husband, studio-executive Irving Thalberg) were still reigning supreme, Jean Harlow, the wonderful platinum bombshell, had died tragically in June of 1937. As such, the studio was pursuing new blonde hopefuls, looking for a fresh shape to fill the high heels of the late actress. It was the Harlow shadow that first drew Lana into the inside circle of MGM and first introduced her to the "king" of Hollywood, Clark Gable. Years later, Gable told interviewer Dorothy O'Leary of his initial meeting with a young woman who would soon become his top romantic screen partner.

It was back in 1938, shortly after the untimely and unfortunate death of Jean Harlow. I remember I was making *Too Hot to Handle* when the front office telephoned one day and told me they—the mysterious and omnipotent *they*—thought they had a possible candidate to replace Harlow. Well, not exactly a replacement, but a girl who was glamorous and could be groomed for the same type of role. Would I test with her? . . .

On my first day I arrived for the appointed reading test and was frankly amazed by the girl who was there. She was so young—practically a child. Her mother was along, probably for moral support, for the girl was obviously nervous, although she

had already been signed to a contract by MGM.

She had been given the script for a scene from *Red Dust,* which I had made six years before. We did a run-through, and I felt sorry for the kid. She was beautiful, but was no actress. Not in the true sense of the word. She couldn't read lines; she didn't make them mean anything. It was obvious she was an amateur, untutored in the projection of mood, in getting a role over to an audience.

This was Lana Turner. . . .

Yes, that was Lana Turner, a most beautiful girl with an unhoned acting ability. Immediate superstardom was by no means possible, as evidenced by her reading of the "Vantine" Harlow role. So Metro enrolled her in the studio school to supplement her scanty education where, as Lana recalls, "I spent most of my time fending off learning and fending off Mickey Rooney." She then began the slow ascent to stardom that Metro carefully observed, constantly gauging her appeal and growth as an actress and a screen personality.

Lana's first film for MGM as a contract player was *Love Finds Andy Hardy* (1938). This was the fourth entry in the very popular Hardy family series and a virtual proving ground for young starlets. Star Mickey Rooney was teamed not only with series regular Ann Rutherford as Polly Benedict, but with Lana* and a newcomer named Judy Garland.

As was Lana's custom, she was rapidly winning wide-eyed attention from the studio per-

*In his very in-depth *The Films of Lana Turner* (1976), author Lou Valentino offers a chronology of projects that were considered for Lana but for one reason or another never starred the actress or were shelved: *Having Wonderful Time* (1938); *I Take This Woman* (1938); *Snug Harbor* (1938); *Idiot's Delight* (1938); *Thunder Afloat* (1939); *The Rains Came* (1939); *Living in a Big Way* (1939); *20 Little Working Girls* (1940); *Tropical Hurricane* (1940); *Bethel Merriday* (1940); *Witch in the Wilderness* (1940); *Presenting Lily Mars* (1940); *The Harvey Girls* (1941); *They Live by Night* (1941); *Flying Blonde* (1941); *Best Foot Forward* (1942); *The Petty Girl* (1942); *The Hard Way* (1942); *Cry Havoc* (1942); *Jenny Was a Lady* (1943); *Music for Millions* (1943); *Frankie from Frisco* (1943); *Midnight in Bombay* (1943); *Easy to Wed* (1943); *Josephine* (1945); *Lucky Baldwin* (1946); *Coquette* (1946); *Forever Amber* (1947); *Madame Bovary* (1949); *The Reformer and the Redhead* (1949); *Born Yesterday* (1949); *Nothing Doing*

sonnel, even before completing her first role there before a camera. Men ogled the "kid," while ladies tended to automatically dislike the beautiful specimen. However, Lana immediately displayed a likeable, unaffected personality that won over most of the co-workers with whom she came into contact. MGM costumer Sheila O'Brien in an interview with David Chierichetti for *Film Fan Monthly* recalled this Turner trait:

> The first day on *Love Finds Andy Hardy,* I took one look at Lana and Judy Garland, and I was sure I'd love Judy and dislike Lana. By the lunch break, I felt just the opposite. Judy was always going around the set stirring up trouble and Lana was just as sweet as she could be. She was so considerate, she'd always hang her costume up instead of dropping it on the floor for me to pick up like a lot of ladies I could name. At the end of the day when I'd take all the costumes up to Wardrobe to be pressed, she'd grab half of them and trudge up there with me. During the lunch hour, we'd sneak off the lot and go shopping at Sears' or Penney's. Or we'd sneak off of the stage and grab a cigarette.

In this release, Lana was one of two dates that Mickey Rooney was to escort to a Christmas eve dance (although the other gal was Miss Rutherford, he ended up with Miss Garland!). Turner was displayed as a simplistic miss whose chief hobby was kissing. Critics were quickly to dismiss the on-the-rise Lana as far too beautiful to

(1949); *To Please a Lady* (1949); *Three Guys Named Mike* (1949); *Kiss of a Millionaire* (1949); *A Letter from the President* (1949); *Interrupted Melody* (1949); *The Lonesome Gal* (1949); *Why Should I Cry?* (1952); *Battle Circus* (1952); *One More Time* (1952); *Helen of Troy* (1953); *My Most Intimate Friend* (1953); *The King's General* (1953); *Weekend at Las Vegas* (1953); *The Cobweb* (1954); *Tracey Cromwell* (1954); *Rosalinda* (1954); *Deep in My Heart* (1954); *Magnificent Matador* (1954); *My Man Godfrey* (1956); *Love Is a Long Goodbye* (1956); *Miss Plymouth Comes Across* (1956); *The Sound and the Fury* (1957); *Pylon* (1957); *Anatomy of a Murder* (1958); *Streets of Montmartre* (1959); *The Colonel's Lady* (1960); *The Chalk Garden* (1960); *Not All Cats Are Gray* (1963); *The Marriage of a Star* (1966); *North to Brindisi* (1966); *The Tangled Web* (1967); *Let Me Count the Ways* (1967); *Sex and the Married Man* (1967); *Shocking!* (1971); *Deadlock* (1975); *Horror Hotel* (1976).

pass as the unsophisticated teenager she was cast to play in the folksy feature. Still, *Love Finds Andy Hardy* provides a nice setting in which to observe Lana, especially on a behind-the-camera basis. While Judy Garland worshippers have been quick to defend their tarnished idol by blaming lusty MGM for ruining her with exhausting work schedules that drove her to dissipation, Lana faced the same routine and became "Queen of the Nightclubs" to boot. To the amazement of her confreres, Lana would report at dawn to the studio, bounce through a twelve-hour work day, and then dash from the set to change clothes and freshen her makeup before starting her nightclub rounds. Yet, as one stunned observer noted, ". . . while she partied almost nightly, she was never late for her early morning studio call."

The brand of youthful sex appeal that Lana emanated was greatly in demand by filmmakers of the Thirties and her fortunes began to rise at MGM. But there were occasional set-backs. Her role as Miss Rutherford, a divorcée, was nearly all deleted in *The Chaser* (1938), a quickie starring Dennis O'Keefe. When it was released in August 1938, she could be spotted only in an office scene reading a magazine (she was garbed most chicly). Her footage had been declared extraneous to the plotline, and it remained for starlet Ann Morriss to be the distaff focal point of the picture.

However, there were sure signs that Lana was catching on with the public in *Rich Man, Poor Girl* (1938). She was billed fifth under Robert Young, Ruth Hussey, Lew Ayres, and Guy Kibbee but above Rita Johnson, an ingenue then enrolled in the same MGM stardom indoctrination program as Lana. As Helen Thayer, the rumba-loving, wisecracking sister of Hussey, Lana was promoted in the film's advertising as that "kissing bug" of Andy Hardy.

The careful grooming continued. *Dramatic School,* a prestigious holiday release of 1938, starred two-time Oscar winner Luise Rainer in one of her final Hollywood films. It co-starred Paulette Goddard who was soon to begin the same type of glamour-girl career at Paramount as Lana would enjoy at MGM (though Paulette was a better actress). In the Mervyn LeRoy-produced *Dramatic School,* Lana appeared as

Mado, a rather grasping acting school student who has no love for rival Rainer. Then came the role of Rosalie, a gangster's moll, in another MGM series picture, *Calling Dr. Kildare* (1939). Here her character becomes smitten with the young title character (played by Lew Ayres), hoping to protect her brother falsely accused of a crime. As one magazine reviewer would point out, "Lana Turner goes glamourous on us, and she needn't take a back seat to any of the other glamour girls."

Lana's following was growing steadily, as her beauty won admirers in the cinemas and her nightclub hopping won rapt attention from the columnists. MGM decided to award her with her first lead, but, ever cautious, presented it via a *B* picture, *These Glamour Girls* (1939). Lew Ayres and Tom Brown provided the masculine charm, but the film is memorable mainly because it features a stock company of second lead and player contract leading ladies, including Metro's own Ann Rutherford and Marsha Hunt, Warner Bros.' Anita Louise and Jane Bryan, and Mary Beth Hughes; the latter became a princess of program films at Twentieth Century-Fox in the early Forties.

Like nearly all of Hollywood and the country, Lana was caught up in the *Gone with the Wind* sweepstakes and the studio urged that she audition for the demanding role of Scarlett O'Hara, along with such seasoned performers as Paulette Goddard, Joan Bennett, and Frances Dee. While Lana certainly looked fetching in her Southern belle test wardrobe, her audition revealed that she had very little grasp of the complexities of Margaret Mitchell's devious heroine.

Then came a film which had dual meaning in Lana's life. *Dancing Co-Ed* (1939) was Lana's introduction to top billing and the meeting ground for her first husband. The man in question was twenty-nine-year-old Artie Shaw, the popular bandleader/clarinetist and Hollywood playboy, trademarked by his flagrantly intellectual aura. In *Dancing Co-Ed*, Lana played Patty Morgan, a Monarch Pictures starlet who is "spotted" on a Midwestern college campus so she can be discovered by a hoopla-raising studio. Lana was pleasant in this forgettable entry which was more than can be said for Mr. Shaw's emoting. Sheila O'Brien was again Lana's cos-

tume mistress for this film. She recalls of her friend, "When she was making a picture with Artie Shaw, she couldn't stand him. He was so bad, we could barely hold our laughter until we got outside where he couldn't hear."

Lana might have had close ties to her natural mother, but when Louella Parsons, eagle-eyed Queen Mother of the gossip columns, offered the starlet her ample shoulder to cry on, Lana accepted. Perhaps the story of the first Turner marriage can be best related by quoting Miss Parsons' account as offered in her tome, *Tell It to Louella* (1961):

> This is what Lana told me. "I had a date with Greg [Bautzer, a Los Angeles attorney] and he called to say he couldn't keep it. Some kind of legal business. I got mad and decided I'd go out anyway and I thought of someone who'd make Greg mad—and jealous. So I called Artie."
>
> "Then what happened?"
>
> "About midnight Artie said it would be nice if we got married. I said it would be nice too. The next thing we knew, we were on our way to Las Vegas."
>
> She wired her mother from that city to say she was married, but did not mention to whom. Mrs. Turner called Bautzer and learned quite quickly that it wasn't he. She learned it was Artie Shaw in the next day's papers.

Someone else who learned the news the next day grieved tremendously over the event. It was young Judy Garland who imagined that she was in love with Shaw and that now her life held no meaning. She reasoned that it was just another example of the ugly duckling girl with the big voice being rejected. Having lost out to such a beautiful competitor as Lana allegedly scarred Judy for life.

From the start of their impromptu marriage in the early morning hours of Tuesday, February 13, 1940, the union was doomed. Thrice-married Shaw promptly began playing a Pygmalion act with his newest bride, inundating Lana with

With Lee Bowman in *Dancing Co-Ed* ('39).

thick books, classical records, and art gallery visits. Before long, restless Lana confided to Louella Parsons, "I know that I ought to be interested in those things. After all, I didn't have too much education. But, you know something, Louella, all they did was make me sleepy."

The Turner-Shaw marriage dissolved on Thursday, September 12, 1940. The official reason for the split was that Lana could not accommodate Artie's sprawling intellectual appetite. The unofficial rumor was that MGM studio boss Louis B. Mayer was fearful that his increasingly valuable box-office commodity might become indisposed by having a baby. There were even rumors that he persuaded Lana to have an abortion without Shaw's knowledge, thus leading to the final argument between the couple. If this story is true, it must have upset Lana terribly, because pal Sheila O'Brien related, "She wanted to get married and have a baby. She was always talking about babies." In fact, even though Sheila knew Lana hated Shaw initially, "the next thing you know she went off and married him because she thought that was how she'd have her baby." Lana recuperated from the divorce by visiting Honolulu accompanied by twenty-one pieces of luggage. The Royal Hawaiian Hotel honored her visit by adding "Baked Potato a la Lana" to its restaurant menu. (Artie Shaw would continue onward with his matrimonial sweepstakes. Among his eight wives have been Ava Gardner; Kathleen Winsor, author of *Forever Amber;* Betty Kern, daughter of Jerome; and actress Evelyn Keyes to whom he is still wed.)

Whatever the facts behind the fractured marriage, Lana faced business as usual at Metro. *Two Girls on Broadway* (1940) cast her as the younger sister of Joan Blondell, both smitten with hoofer George Murphy. This was the third Turner film to be directed by S. Sylvan Simon. In this reworking of *Broadway Melody* (1929) Lana had occasion to display her more than adequate dancing ability. As Lou Valentino points out in *The Films of Lana Turner,* the film "bears con-

With George Murphy and Joan Blondell in *Two Girls on Broadway* ('40).

clusive evidence that had Metro chosen to continue her training along those lines, she could have had a very prominent musical career. . . . The grace and precision of the Turner-Murphy team is worth the entire weight of *Two Girls on Broadway,* especially in the dazzling 'My Wonderful One' production number. . . . " Then came *We Who Are Young* (1940), a Dalton Trumbo account of a destitute couple (Lana and John Shelton) adrift in Manhattan. *PM* newspaper praised Lana's performance as Margy Brooks, claiming that she "not only proves herself a good actress; she does something even more consoling. She proves that not only bad girls are well set up. Even in cotton house dresses she proves that." Far more typical of Lana's reception by the critics could be found in Bosley Crowther's *New York Times* review of the same feature, which appeared the day of her divorce from Shaw. Crowther wrote that Lana was "blissfully easy to watch, so long as she doesn't talk or make an attempt to act."

Then came a big career boost for Lana, one that elevated her to the next plateau of MGM gloss. Robert Z. "Pop" Leonard was directing *Ziegfeld Girl* (1941), the studio's mammoth musical loaded with tunes and Busby Berkeley choreography, and starring James Stewart, Judy Garland, Hedy Lamarr, and Tony Martin, with Jackie Cooper, Ian Hunter, Dan Dailey, Edward Everett Horton, and Eve Arden in the supporting rank. As reddish blonde Sheila Regan, Lana received fourth billing, under Stewart, Garland, and Lamarr. Lana's role was initially not as full as her co-stars' assignments, but Leonard saw promise in her and continually enlarged her part. "By the end of the picture," says Lana, "they added a drunk scene and a death scene. It was the first time anyone realized I could play something beside a co-ed."

With its classic "You Stepped Out of a Dream" number, gorgeous orchestrations, and Leonard's opulent know-how, *Ziegfeld Girl* includes the scene in which Lana's walk down a flight of stairs becomes a thing of beauty—and a classic movie vignette. Theodore Strauss in the

On the set of *Ziegfeld Girl* ('41).

393

New York Times exulted of the picture: "The girls, especially Lana Turner, who must have been born on Olympus, are breathtaking . . . it is the perilously lovely Miss Turner who gets this department's bouquet for a surprisingly solid performance as the little girl from Brooklyn." *Ziegfeld Girl* launched Lana into MGM's big money, big promotion pictures, and perhaps this explains why it remains Miss Turner's favorite celluloid credit.

Next to Clark Gable and Mickey Rooney, Spencer Tracy, a powerhouse "actor's actor" with two Oscars to his credit, was Metro's top male star. Tracy was usually flanked with the most beautiful of the Metro leading ladies to supplement his supposed lack of screen sex appeal; Harlow, Loy, and Lamarr had all co-starred with Spencer. It was with great trepidation that Tracy—replacing a previously announced Robert Donat—accepted the dual challenge of playing *Dr. Jekyll and Mr. Hyde* (1941) as directed by Victor Fleming. Like the great majority he still vividly recalled Fredric March's Oscar-winning performance in the 1932 version of the Robert Louis Stevenson novel and feared that he could not compete against such a standard of performance. It would lead the usually subdued performer to lend an exaggerated tone to his character interpretations, one of the few times in his lengthy career when his acting could be called "hammy." There were other casting problems with this feature. Swedish import Ingrid Bergman had originally been cast as Dr. Jekyll's fiancée, Beatrix Emery, but the Scandinavian actress decided that the role of the ill-fated dancehall performer Ivy Peterson would be more of an acting challenge for her. Thus to oblige Miss Bergman, Lana's assignment was changed from Ivy to that of Beatrix, the too delicate lady. Lana's best moments come in the perverted dream Tracy enjoys during his transformation. Therein he flagellates the ladies in Marquis de Sade fashion. This racy scene is often snipped when aired on prime time television.

From Tracy, the next promotion was to Gable, and Lana got him in *Honky Tonk* (1941). So torrid was the teaming that the crisp Jack Conway direction and great supporting cast (Frank Morgan, Claire Trevor, Marjorie Main, Albert Dekker) went all but unnoticed. As *Variety* would report of this romantic Western, "The major power in *Honky Tonk* is in the love scenes between Gable and Miss Turner. These sequences should get wide word of mouth and women [will] make the matinees look like a give-away day in a department store. For the men, plus the flash of Miss Turner in black undies and opera length hose, there's enough action and gunplay to also make them willing customers." As the ads promised, "Clark Gable Kisses Lana Turner and It's Screen History." Boudoir scenes, Gable nearly pounding down Lana's door, and eleven Gable-Turner kisses in the 105-minute feature made *Honky Tonk* responsible for, as *Life* magazine phrased it, "the birth of a new starring team, the hottest, most electric combination of movie personalities since Boyer and Lamarr." As was predicted, *Honky Tonk* was a sizeable box-office winner and fully proved that Lana was the new sex star of MGM—and of all Hollywood.

While a Gable-Turner love affair became the subject of much speculation, the couple never had anything more than a friendly working relationship. (As Lana would state, "Ours was a closeness without intimacy. There was a dear loving for him but never an affair. No way.") Mrs. Gable, better known as actress Carole Lombard,* saw to that. Before production began, Carole, having heard the gossip attesting that Lana seduced most of her leading men, invaded the sanctum of Louis B. Mayer and demanded insurance that Lana would not trifle with Clark's affections. Mayer assured Miss Lombard that chastity would prevail—and it did. Gable meanwhile modified his 1938 critique of Lana: "Again I was surprised by this girl. . . . This time, pleasantly surprised. She was so much better an actress. Gone was the amateur . . . she had

---

*Years later Lana would reveal of the filming of *Honky Tonk*, "We rehearsed our first love scene—ours was a wonderful chemical rapport which came over on film—and suddenly I turned around and froze. There was beloved Carole Lombard, Mrs. Gable! She seldom came on the set but I guess she wanted to see who the new kid was. Well, it's one thing to work with a King but quite another to have his Lady there. I retreated to my dressing room and when director Jack Conway came to say we were ready to shoot, I wailed, 'I can't!' Whether Jack told Clark, I don't know. I just know that while I sat in my dressing room suffering, beautiful Carole disappeared."

learned so much about acting since our first meeting back in 1938."

True, Lana's emoting had improved since her inclusion on the Metro payroll. Unfortunately she did not develop the full personality and charm that had made Jean Harlow so beloved a star, or approach the dramatic abilities that would place Grace Kelly in such esteem in the mid-Fifties. Lana would remain a remarkably attractive figure with just enough acting acumen to keep her talent from obscuring her gorgeous appearance.

idol—"It's TNT—For Taylor 'N' Turner"—but most agreed that Van Heflin was the film's main interest with his Oscar-winning characterization of Taylor's drunken advisor.

As Lana soared professionally, so did she romantically. Columnists had a full-time job speculating on her company-keeping with such actors as Victor Mature and Robert Stack, drummer Gene Krupa, singer Tony Martin (freshly divorced from Alice Faye), bandleader Tommy Dorsey, and Dorsey's ace drummer, Buddy Rich.

With Clark Gable in *Honky Tonk* ('41).

A happy reunion followed for Lana as she was to be directed by her old mentor, Mervyn LeRoy. The film was *Johnny Eager* (1942) and the co-star was Robert Taylor, fond of playing tough gangster roles (like the title character) to elude the "pretty boy" image that haunted him. Lana did well* with her role of Lisbeth Bard, the society girl whom Taylor frames and then predictably falls in love with, in spite of the one-dimensional note in which the part was written. Once again the publicity department made much of the teaming** of Lana with another male

*Jeanine Basinger in *Lana Turner* (1976) would estimate, "*Johnny Eager* is poorly paced and poorly written—but it has one asset in addition to Heflin-Lana Turner. She is on the screen a minimum of time, but her presence haunts the scenes in which she does appear. Every time a door opens, the audience hopes she will enter, so they can have another look at her, swathed in mink from head to toe, her blonde hair spread over the fur in masses of curls. Turner tackles her scenes of desperation and near-madness with all she's got. She makes up in emotional intensity what she lacks in technical skill."

**It was due to a sad string of coincidences that Turner and Taylor never were rematched on camera. Actually he was to be among *The Three Musketeers* (1948), to appear in *The Cobweb* (1955), and still later to co-star in *By Love Possessed* (1961). But previous commitments prevented these rematch occasions with Lana.

MGM's Lana Turner in the early Forties.

Also included among the 150-plus males whom Lana dated during this era was Howard Hughes, who saw Lana off and on until 1946. The story goes that, at one point, Lana felt so secure that she would ensnare the elusive billionaire that she had all her linens monogrammed "HH." When Lana confronted Hughes with this fact after he had finally told her marriage was out of the question, Howard shrugged and said, "Marry Huntington Hartford!"

Lana's next teaming with Clark Gable, *Somewhere I'll Find You* (1942), became memorable for less than happy circumstances. The picture began shooting about a month after Pearl Harbor. To launch the project on a well-publicized start, Lana invited the press to view her "Victory Bob" haircut.

When *Somewhere* was in the midst of shooting, one of Hollywood's great tragedies occurred. Carole Lombard, en route back home after a bond-selling trek, was killed in a plane crash on Table Mountain near Las Vegas on January 16.

Gable was horribly shaken by the tragedy. After the funeral and burial of his wife at Forest Lawn, he went into dismal seclusion on the Encino ranch Carole had purchased from Raoul Walsh, and *Somewhere*'s set was closed down. For a time it appeared that the film would have to be scrapped. But as with *Saratoga* (1937), where Jean Harlow died before completing her scenes with Gable, the show went miserably on. Gable returned to the set on February 23. Lana was so upset for Gable that she could hardly stand to be near him when not before the cameras. With all the built-in publicity, the film did very well with the public and the stars were lauded as "the screen's most provocative lovers" (*Newsweek*) and "the most popular lovemakers on the screen today" (*New York Herald-Tribune*). All this was despite the film being a rather feeble love story, with war correspondent Gable constantly re-encountering his beloved Lana all over the combat globe.

Before *Somewhere I'll Find You* was released,

396

With costume designer Irene at MGM in late 1942.

397

Gable had enlisted in the Air Force. His last words from Carole via telegram were "Pappy, you'd better join this man's army." Hence, after two pictures, the Gable-Turner love team temporarily dissolved, not to mesh again until well after an aging, shattered Gable began his slow adjustment to post-war, post-Lombard life.

Lana also changed her status before *Somewhere I'll Find You* reached the theatres—she remarried. Husband number two was Joseph Stephen Crane, a twenty-seven-year-old tobacco heir and wanderer who had introduced himself to Lana in the Hollywood Mocambo nightclub. A month after the meeting, on Friday, July 17, 1942, the same Las Vegas judge, E. Marshall, who had married Lana and Shaw, married the star and her latest. Domestic relationships between the actress and Crane proceeded quietly until December of that year, when Lana jubilantly announced that she was pregnant. Then Crane's first wife suddenly announced that her divorce from Crane would not be legally final until January 19, 1943! The results upstaged the war news on front pages as Lana annulled her marriage, led reporters to believe she would not rewed Crane, and then did remarry him in Tijuana, Mexico, on Sunday, March 14 (only after Crane had allegedly attempted suicide with sleeping pills). Crane's comment after the remarriage was, "Everything is going to be all right."

On Sunday, July 25, 1943, Cheryl Christine Crane was born. She was an RH baby who required blood transfusions during her first few weeks until all her blood was changed. She was to be Lana's only child.

Besides her continuing motion picture work, Lana, like many other stars of the Forties, fre-

With husband Stephen Crane and eight-week-old daughter Cheryl in 1943.

quently guested on radio,* where there was ample opportunity to earn easy money, plug one's latest films, and even learn some acting tips. Perhaps Miss Turner's most memorable guest spot on radio occurred on Thursday, November 4, 1943, when she was the featured attraction on the "Abbott and Costello" program. A few hours before air time, Lou Costello learned that his infant son, Lou, Jr., one week before his first birthday, had crawled from his playpen, fallen into the swimming pool, and drowned. Costello, who had just that morning bought the baby a teddy bear, was grievously shocked but, in a daze, insisted on doing the show despite fill-in offers from Jimmy Durante, Red Skelton, and Mickey Rooney. As the shattered Costello fluffed dialogue lines and lost his place in the script, Lana became so emotional that she could scarcely utter her lines. It was only after the broadcast that the studio audience learned, from a weeping Bud Abbott, the very sad story behind that performance.

Stephen Crane soon became an Army private, leaving Lana to continue her career. In 1943 she appeared in three Metro releases but in only one stellar role. In the fluffy, slapstick *Slightly Dangerous* she was the soda jerk who attempts to pass herself off as the daughter of tycoon Walter Brennan (the latter in an unusually distinguished, well-scrubbed assignment—he actually wore his teeth!). Lana's chief contribution to the project was the "Turner chassis." MGM's portrait artist, Eric Carpenter, photographed Lana in a series of cheesecake poses during the filming

of *Slightly Dangerous*. The resultant poses—especially the one of Lana in a captivating black-sequinned gown—not only graced the ad campaign for the film, but provided the basis for the pin-up poses used for G.I. consumption during World War II. *The Youngest Profession* used Lana as tinsel in a cameo assignment, grouping her with guest stars Walter Pidgeon, Greer Garson, Robert Taylor, and William Powell as targets of intense autograph-seeker Virginia Weidler. In *Du Barry Was a Lady*, a Red Skelton-Lucille Ball Technicolor vehicle, Lana has a fifteen-second walk-on during the "I Love an Esquire Girl" production number.

If her career was running a steady course, her personal life was not. In April of 1944 Lana sued Private Crane for divorce, the official decree being granted on Monday, August 21, 1944. Divorcing a soldier was not the best publicity, and Louis B. Mayer was doubly worried—her single release of 1944 was *Marriage Is a Private Affair*, in which, as Theo Scofield West, Lana breathlessly chases other men while hubby John Hodiak is fighting the Axis in the South Pacific. But the film drew less attention than did her new string of romances, including a rekindling with old chum Victor Mature and a liaison with 4-F Frank Sinatra.

There were two Turner releases in 1945. The first, *Keep Your Powder Dry*, cast her with Laraine Day and Susan Peters as WACs in training. The picture, directed by Edward Buzzell, was a well-decorated nothing, but it was obvious that impoverished plotlines did as little to impede Lana's screen popularity as her less-than-sparkling acting. Next came *Week-End at the Waldorf*, an all-time box-office champ that was released just after the long-prayed-for V-J Day and proved irresistible fare to glamour-craving returning veterans and their sweethearts.

Again directed by Lana's *Ziegfeld Girl* mentor, "Pop" Leonard, the picture was a reworking of Vicki Baum's *Grand Hotel*, which had become Metro's all-star classic in 1932. In this revision, Garbo's ballerina Grusinskya became Ginger Rogers' actress, John Barrymore's dashing jewel thief became Walter Pidgeon's flirtatious war correspondent, Wallace Beery's Prussian businessman became Edward Arnold's American magnate, Lionel Barrymore's dying old Kringe-

*Among her dramatic show roles were: "Lux Radio Theatre" in *They Drive by Night* (June 2, 1941) with George Raft and Lucille Ball; "Lux Radio Theatre" in *The Devil and Miss Jones* (January 19, 1942) with Lionel Barrymore; "Screen Guild Players" in *Mr. and Mrs. Smith* (February 8, 1942) with Errol Flynn; "Lux Radio Theatre" in *Crossroads* (March 29, 1943) with Jean-Pierre Aumont; "Philip Morris Playhouse" in *The Talk of the Town* (October 1, 1943); "Lux Radio Theatre" in *Slightly Dangerous* (October 25, 1943) with Victor Mature; "The Star and the Story" in *Lucky Partners* (May 7, 1944) with Walter Pidgeon; "Screen Guild Players" in *Once Upon a Honeymoon* (November 20, 1944) with John Hodiak; "Suspense" (May 3, 1945); "Lux Radio Theatre" in *Honky Tonk* (April 11, 1946) with John Hodiak; "Screen Guild Players" in *Marriage Is a Private Affair* (June 17, 1946) with John Hodiak; "Academy Award Theatre" in *Vivacious Lady* (August 14, 1946); "Screen Guild Players" in *The Postman Always Rings Twice* (June 23, 1947) with John Garfield; "Lux Radio Theatre" in *Green Dolphin Street* (September 19, 1949) with Van Heflin and Peter Lawford; "Screen Guild Players" in *Homecoming* (October 6, 1949) with Clark Gable; "Suspense" (December 15, 1949).

With Eugene Pallette in *Slightly Dangerous* ('43).

lein was transformed into Van Johnson's young soldier (facing a possibly fatal operation to remove shrapnel from the area of his heart), and Joan Crawford's seductive stenographer Flaemmchen became Lana's seductive stenographer, Bunny Smith. She is a girl who "travels from 10th Avenue to Park . . . on curves!" With added gloss like Xavier Cugat's orchestra, *Week-End at the Waldorf*, in keeping with the postwar jubilation, contained a far happier finale than its predecessor. Pidgeon and Rogers are facing matrimony and Lana walks out on tycoon Arnold to stand by freckled Johnson as he goes to his operation.

By the close of 1945 Lana was nearing the top of the Metro payroll, earning $4,500 weekly. Joan Crawford had gone to Warner Bros., and Garbo and Shearer had retired. Titian-haired Greer Garson was regarded as queen of the women's pictures on the lot, while a dark-haired newcomer named Ava Gardner was only beginning her career climb at Metro. Lana, as one of the top female attractions on the lot, was given regal treatment. She was awarded a beau-

tiful dressing room, and received such bonuses as a nurse to stand by (at her request) whenever she was not feeling well.

Of course, life-hungry Lana continued reigning as queen of the gossip columns. By the close of 1945, Lana was madly enraptured with Turhan Bey, Universal's Viennese "victory sex symbol" who had won a following while the major domestic stars were off at war. "My romance with Turhan is the most beautiful thing in my life," sighed Lana to Louella, who ran this testimonial in her column. A wedding was planned for August 1946 before a party at the home of Ann Rutherford gave rise to the events that scrapped this love affair.

At the party, Steve Crane was present and made some slighting remarks about his ex's new romance. A fight resulted. Bey left the get-together with a scratched face and Crane went home with a black eye. Two weeks later Bey told Lana over the phone, "I'll talk to you tomorrow," and never called back. In fact, he soon abandoned Hollywood and eventually returned to his native land. Meanwhile, Miss Parsons publicly chastised Bey, accusing him of fracturing the heart of poor Lana (who already was being escorted about town by the likes of Rory Calhoun, Peter Shaw, and Robert Hutton). Religious differences later became the official reason for the split between Lana and Turhan.

Louella's pity earned more sympathizers for Lana than it might have earlier, for in May of 1946 there arrived at the theatres Lana's best screen performance in the classic sex tragedy, *The Postman Always Rings Twice*. Due to censorship guidelines, the James M. Cain novel had been considered unfilmable in Hollywood.* But screenwriters Harry Ruskin and Niven Busch managed to fashion a script that retained the basic elements of the sordid tale of a young wife who seduces a wanderer into killing her older,

*this **One** Complete Cream – is all **you** need...*

Lana Turner

appearing in
"MARRIAGE IS A
PRIVATE AFFAIR"
a Metro-Goldwyn-Mayer
Picture

How does Lana Turner do it?
So busy . . . bond-selling, film-making . . . yet always so
lovely! . . . She's found that this one cream does *everything* for skin
beauty. Yes, Woodbury Complete Beauty Cream gives you
complete skin care—*takes just 3 minutes* . . .

The product endorser ('44).

*There had been a 1936 Broadway stage version with Richard Barthelmess, Mary Phillips, and Joseph Greenwald. The 1939 French film version, *Le Dernier Tournant*, starred Fernand Gravet, Corinne Luchaire, and Michel Simon, and the 1942 Italian motion picture version, *Ossessione*, featured Massimo Girotti, Clara Calamai, and Elio Marcuzzo.

boring husband. The more lurid incidents of the plot were filtered out from the scenario.

As Cora Smith, the ever-white-clad murderess, Lana was actually superb. It was a case of the perfect actress playing her perfect role, and Lana was totally alluring and fascinatingly lethal in her most famous screen characterization. Another reason for this exceptional performance was the inspiration supplied by her co-star, Warner Bros.' John Garfield. He became Lana's favorite leading man, and she has often voiced high praise of him. "He had terrific magnetism. The lines just bounced back and forth between us in *The Postman Always Rings Twice*. It kept a gal on her toes." With a splendid supporting cast that included Cecil Kellaway, Hume Cronyn, Leon Ames, Alan Reed, and Audrey Totter (then being groomed by MGM as a junior Lana), *Postman* received superlative reviews and enjoyed a substantial box-office profit. The *New York Times* reported, "It gives Lana Turner and John Garfield the best roles of their careers. . . . Too much cannot be said for the principals. Mr. Garfield reflects to life the crude and confused young hobo who stumbles aimlessly into a fatal trap and Miss Turner is remarkably effective as the cheap and uncertain blonde who has a pathetic notion to 'be somebody' and a pitiful notion that she can realize it through crime." *Life* selected *Postman* as its "Movie of the Week," writing, "There is plenty of suspense, and whenever Turner and Garfield take over the screen, [there are] more fireworks than on the fourth of July."

The director of this 113-minute black-and-white melodrama was veteran Tay Garnett. He recorded his thoughts on Lana in his autobiography *Light Your Torches and Pull Up Your Tights* (1973), "Lana, more than any other actress, including Marilyn Monroe, has been publicized as a sex symbol. Actually, she is as soft as a baby rabbit, as sweet as cotton candy, and as frustrated as a maternal woman can be; she has always wanted a houseful of children, but since her daughter Cheryl's birth, motherhood has been denied Lana because of an RH negative blood factor. Lana, the envy of a million women, envies a million women—those with a household full of youngsters."

Some years later in a *Saturday Evening Post* article, she reflected on her trademark *Postman* role:

With Pierre Watkin and Natalie Schafer in *Keep Your Powder Dry* ('45).

With Franklyn Farnum (man to right of Lana) in *Week-End at the Waldorf* ('45).

It may seem strange that I should choose the part of a completely bad woman as my favorite. The fact is, playing a "wicked woman" makes the audience more aware of you as an actress. This role gave me something to work with. Cora was not the usual heroine. . . . I thought I understood the odd, twisted reasoning that made her yearn for a small piece of property out in the hills—for what she considered respectability and security—and yet, at the same time, led her to do things which ruined her chance of getting what she wanted.

I liked the all-white wardrobe Cora wore and the way she did her hair. But the high point in my enjoyment of this role came after the film was completed. Then James Cain presented me with a leatherbound first edition of *The Postman Always Rings Twice*, bearing the message, "For my dear Lana, thank you for giving a performance that was even finer than I expected."

While *Postman* was proving to be a box-office bonanza, Lana was involved in another romance, this time crooner Frank Sinatra who was in the midst of separating from his wife, Nancy. He was then under contract to MGM who guaranteed him a rich future in the next few years. The studio did its best to keep the Turner-Sinatra mutual admiration society quiet, but the two uninhibited individuals refused to remain under wraps. However, by the time (October 1946) the romance rumors were filtering through the gossip columns, Lana and Frank had gone their separate ways. She told Louella Parsons, "I am not in love with Frank and he is not in love with me. I have never in my life broken up a home."

After *Postman* it was hoped that Lana would have a follow-up picture that would consolidate her acting reputation. Otto Preminger, who would later prove to be her nemesis, tried to give her the opportunity. When Twentieth Century-Fox suspended production of *Forever Amber* in mid-1946 and Preminger was assigned to take over direction of the epic, he suggested that Lana would make an excellent replacement for Peggy Cummins as Amber St. Clair. Studio head Darryl F. Zanuck said no; but Preminger was persistent. He invited both Lana and Zanuck to a dinner party. He told the Metro actress who was eager for the part, "It's up to you now." As Preminger recently recalled, "She did her best. She flirted shamelessly with Zanuck, at one point even sitting on his lap. But he would not change his mind." Linda Darnell was cast in the plum role.

Instead, she went into *Green Dolphin Street* (1947), an awesomely boring tale in which she tried to rob her gentle sister (Donna Reed) of the man (Richard Hart) she loves. Her other co-star was Van Heflin and the accent was on costumes, of which there were many. The highlight of the 141-minute feature was an earthquake (during which Lana gives birth to a baby!), not as dramatic as that of *San Francisco*, but definitely a relief from the low-keyed tenor of the Samson Raphaelson scenario. *Cass Timberlane* (1947) was adapted from the Sinclair Lewis novel and co-starred Lana with Spencer Tracy, she the young woman he impulsively weds and then finds unsatisfied. Both leading roles were difficult to play effectively; Tracy succeeded as the judge; Lana did not as Virginia Marshland. (At least she was a feast for the eyes. As Kate Cameron wrote in the New York *Daily News*, "There is no doubt about it, Lana Turner screens more beautifully than any other blonde in Hollywood. In *Cass Timberlane*, she literally illumines the Music Hall screen with a glow that is soft, warm, and altogether feminine.") Thankfully there was a seasoned supporting cast including Zachary Scott, Mary Astor, and Josephine Hutchinson to shore up the gaps of the melodrama.

At about this time MGM purchased *Raintree County* via a contest they sponsored. They planned to have Lana, Ava Gardner, Janet Leigh, Robert Walker, Van Heflin, and/or Richard Hart play the leading roles. Due to the tremendous expenses of producing this Civil War story, it was shelved until 1957 when Elizabeth Taylor, Eva Marie Saint, and Montgomery Clift were starred in the epic.

While Lana's recent celluloid offerings left a great deal to be desired even by her indulgent fans, the actress managed to retain her heady

With director Tay Garnett scene-shooting *The Postman Always Rings Twice* ('46).

With Hume Cronyn and John Garfield in *The Postman Always Rings Twice*.

popularity through her romances. The man of the moment was Tyrone Power, then in the midst of arduously attempting to put his career back in gear at Twentieth Century-Fox after his war service in the Marines. Since Power was still wed to French actress Annabella, the columnists played up that the handsome couple were just "good friends." Few were naive enough to believe that status. Most of Hollywood applauded the union, and the ever wide-eyed Louella Parsons termed the romance "the deepest emotional experience of Lana's life. . . . I believe that for the first time she felt something that was more than glandular, that she didn't love just an aspect of the man, but the whole man."

The passionate Power/Turner liaison lasted for about eighteen months, and the two appeared to enjoy each other's company immensely with Lana even taking up athletics to please her outgoing beau. At one point she was so impassioned for the presence of Power, that she abandoned the *Green Dolphin Street* sound

stages to fly off to Mexico City to be near her beloved. Almost needless to say, the Metro hierarchy was not pleased, but was nearly powerless to stop the hedonistic Lana. All predicted marriage as soon as Power could untangle himself from Annabella, and prophesied that the pair would become the new "King" and "Queen" of Hollywood. But it was not to be. Power soon became acquainted with the luscious Linda Christian and switched his affections for Lana to Linda. A grave depression overtook Lana. Louella Parsons even noted, "I feel this is where Lana's self-destructive impulses took over." However, the malaise wore away. By the time Tyrone wed Miss Christian in a fan-frenzied church ceremony in Italy, Lana would already have remarried.

At any rate, about the time of her sad split with Power (a situation that drew endorsements from both MGM and Fox executives), Lana was set to again co-star with Gable. Originally the stars were to be reunited in a film project en-

405

titled *Lucky Baldwin*, but the studio switched the couple to a picture called *Homecoming* (1948), with Mervyn LeRoy directing. Gable was not the same man Lana had met in 1938. His war experiences and lingering sorrow over Carole Lombard's demise had lured him into heavy drinking and dissipation. These days he was not always in the best of shape on the set, getting "the shakes" and requiring short camera set-ups and constant retakes. Still, LeRoy was able to relate to both performers, bringing out the talent

interrupted marriage is somewhat old hat, yet it is too recent to be good nostalgia." Voted one of 1948's ten *worst* films by the New York critics, *Homecoming* nevertheless magnetized audiences, ever enthralled by the Gable/Turner charisma despite the weakness of the plot.

During *Homecoming*, Gable made this official comment, "It remained for *Homecoming* for me to realize that now Lana is a real actress. A professional. She knows what she's doing. She knows what she wants to get over in a role or

With Richard Hart in *Green Dolphin Street* ('47).

that was dry-rotting in Gable and embedded in Lana. Unfortunately, *Homecoming* had a too mundane plot, dealing with a society physician (Gable) at war romancing a WAC (Lana). When she dies of injuries suffered at the Battle of the Bulge, he is left free and clear to return a better person to his wife at home, Anne Baxter. Complained *Modern Screen* magazine, "Perhaps the main flaw in the Gable/Turner number is its lack of timeliness. The story of the war-

scene—and does it. She has poise. She's sure of herself in her work."

At one point, MGM was convinced enough of the continuing value of the Turner/Gable screen teaming that they considered bidding for the screen rights to the Broadway hit comedy *Born Yesterday*. But the vehicle was sold to Columbia Pictures for a 1950 film starring Judy Holliday and Broderick Crawford. It won an Oscar for Miss Holliday.

Another 1948 release of Lana's, *The Three Musketeers,* caused a well-publicized hassle when Lana originally accepted a suspension rather than play Milady Countess de Winter. She later changed her mind, joining a cast including Gene Kelly, June Allyson, Van Heflin, Angela Lansbury, Frank Morgan, Vincent Price, and a squad of other boisterously decorative performers. George Sidney directed this latest celluloid version of the Dumas adventure, focusing on the colorful decor rather than the spirit of the cloak-

the air of a company-mannered Mae West. And she makes love to her victims with elegant high school hauteur. But wait till you see her as the luckless and tragic lady locked up in the London tower, with lightning flashing on her pale beauty! Take it away, makeup man!"

Meanwhile, 1948 heard wedding bells encoring for Lana. She had spent the 1947 Christmas season at the Round Top, Connecticut, home of Henry J. Topping, a millionaire then separated from wife number three, actress

With Spencer Tracy in *Cass Timberlane* ('47).

and-rapier melodrama. Lana's icy portrayal of Milady Countess de Winter inspired the following lament from the *New York Times:* "Completely fantastic . . . is Miss Turner as the villainess, the ambitious Lady de Winter, who does the boudoir business for the boss. Loaded with blonde hair and jewels, with twelve-gallon hats and ostrich plumes, and poured into her satin dresses with a good bit of Turner to spare, she walks through the palaces and salons with

Arline Judge. "Bob" and Lana soon became inseparable. Three days after Arline won an uncontested Bridgeport, Connecticut, divorce, on Monday, April 26, 1948, Lana and her latest took the vows in the Bel Air palace of her promoter Billy Wilkerson. The actress had a $30,000 trousseau for the occasion. The officiate was Reverend Stewart P. MacLennan, who informed the press after the ceremony: "Lana is such a sweet girl! There is a spiritual quality

In *The Three Musketeers* ('48).

about her." While honeymooning in Europe, news leaked that Lana was pregnant. However, the pregnancy terminated in a miscarriage, the first of two she would suffer as Mrs. Topping.

Lana later revealed that she married Topping for "security," and indeed she did begin enjoying a two-year absence from the screen shortly after the wedding. While she was free from the rigors of filmmaking, she became involved in assorted adventures that titillated the readers of the fan magazines. One account related an evening of strong drink and a showing of a stag film, *The Book Salesman*, after which the host and hostess allegedly invited their guests to view them at play in the swimming pool. On another occasion, the Toppings attended the Mocambo nightclub to hear Billy Daniels sing. Topping invited the entertainer back to the house afterward and retired, at which time Lana and Billy left the guests to visit the den. A pajama-clad Topping wandered in at an inappropriate moment and a fistfight allegedly ensued. With other gossip to their credit, the Toppings finally

separated in September of 1951. Shortly thereafter Lana went to the Hollywood Presbyterian Hospital with a lacerated arm that she blamed on a shower door. The official divorce decree did not materialize until Saturday, November 15, 1952.

The movies had meanwhile lured Lana back and in February 1950 she went before the cameras in *A Life of Her Own*. The title seemed very appropriate for the thirty-year-old actress who was earning $5,000 weekly. Not only had there been extensive scripting problems (trying to skirt around the censorship code), but the role of the male lead proved hard to cast. James Mason was set for the part but backed out, claiming his British background clashed with the characterization. Wendell Corey was then borrowed from Paramount but he left the production and at his request MGM engaged Ray Milland to play opposite Lana. Celebrated women's director George Cukor was in charge and did give Lana's acting some fine edges in a maudlin romance (she loves married million-

With daughter Cheryl in 1949.

aire Milland who has a crippled wife). The original ending for the feature had Lana committing suicide, but after screening the product, Metro tacked on a new finale in which the "heroine" was permitted to face life without the one man she adores. The best emoting in the lacklustre film came from Ann Dvorak as a suicide-prone older model.

Some five months after Lana completed *A Life of Her Own*, she began filming *Mr. Imperium*, a

release ahead of this dud. Once again it was the supporting players who enlivened the storyline, herein Marjorie Main and Debbie Reynolds.

Despite the disappointment of *Mr. Imperium*, MGM signed Lana to a new long-term contract on December 31, 1951. Evidently the studio had taken to heart the enduring public enthusiasm for the long-reigning sex goddess. It was in the early 1950s that Geoffrey McBain wrote in *Cosmopolitan* magazine:

With Ann Dvorak in *A Life of Her Own* ('50).

frothy love story in color, showcasing Metropolitan opera star Ezio Pinza, who had done so well on Broadway in *South Pacific*. The multi-hued scenery included Palm Springs and the Italian Riviera, but could not flesh out the wispy tale of Prince Ezio being smitten with an American club singer. (Lana's song "My Love and My Mule" was dubbed by Trudy Erwin.) MGM was so disappointed with the results that it shelved the feature for well over a year, allowing Pinza's next feature, *Strictly Dishonorable*, to go into

What is a Lana Turner? *Who* is a Lana Turner? Lana Turner is a name in lights on a thousand grubby Main Streets. Lana Turner is a long, low, libidinous whistle on the wetted lips of America. She is the four-by-six glossy that serves as barracks wallpaper from Tokyo to Heidelberg and in the cabins of all the ships at sea. She is the pick-up a guy will never stop hoping to make until senility overtakes him. She is the girl a girl can always think she is, until the house lights come up. She is love with a stranger; the girl you didn't marry; the chapter Havelock Ellis forgot to write; and she is yours whenever you want her, for forty cents plus tax. . . . She is, in short, a Hollywood press release come to life.

Lana next began work on her most expensive, highly-promoted film in years—*The Merry Widow* (1952), the third version of the Franz Lehar operetta. Metro spared few expenses on this project. They hired Paul Francis Webster to pen some new lyrics, William Ludwig and Sonya Levien to rewrite the libretto, and Curtis Bernhardt to direct. Even Lana did her part to make the film a winner, and by dieting and corsets reduced her waistline from 23″ to 21″. For all the efforts, the new *The Merry Widow* was something of a flub. It lacked the character of Erich von Stroheim's 1925 silent version, and Lana and co-star Fernando Lamas could not dispense the array of charm of Maurice Chevalier and Jeanette MacDonald who had brightened the 1934 version. Lana's vocals were dubbed by Trudy Erwin. As predicted, *The Merry Widow* was a treat to the eye but little else. The *New York Times* remarked, "Considerate of Miss Turner's talents, they have only called upon her to do such things as be interested, haughty, and wear superb costumes, including an assortment of lacy step-ins that generously reveal her legs."

If *The Merry Widow* did less for Lana professionally than the studio had expected (financially it was a success), it did provide her with a new escort and romance—Fernando Lamas. The couple soon became the most talked-about duo in Hollywood, and MGM decided to plan a future project to showcase their handsome contract stars.

First, however, came the film that many feel contains Lana's best performance—*The Bad and the Beautiful* (1952). She played Georgia Lorrison, the daughter of a dead screen actor, an actress who rises from a hard-drinking wastrel to a top cinema star under the tutelage of producer and heel Kirk Douglas. The story is related in flashback, with producer Walter Pidgeon

calling together director Barry Sullivan, writer Dick Powell, and star Lana to try to persuade them to again work for Douglas who has done them all dirty while promoting them to top-money talents. In Lana's case, Douglas rescues her from a morbid existence of drinking and playing records of her late father droning Shakespearean verse (the voice belonging to Louis Calhern) and builds her into an adulated star. Then Douglas deserts her in a moment of top triumph to take a cheap broad to his mansion for a romp. When Lana discovers this, she races to her car, driving away in a fit of hysteria. It proved to be one of the most famous scenes of all Hollywood pictures.

Years after the completion of this landmark film, Lana related that she and director Vincente Minnelli were not at all chummy during production. When the time came to film the hysterical scene, Lana asked Minnelli what she was to do. He airily replied, "I haven't a clue." Hence, Lana had to improvise and direct herself in the most memorable vignette of her film career.

While many rightfully jumped on a Turner bandwagon to promote Lana's name into the Oscar sweepstakes,* the press was not entirely in accord with the praise. The ever-reserved *New York Times* complained, "Frankly, she is no more convincing as the drunken extra than she is as the star. She is an actress playing an actress, and neither one is real. A howling act in a wildly racing auto—pure bunk—is the top of her speed." Nevertheless, *The Bad and the Beautiful* was a great hit for Lana with the public. It remains one of the most watchable of her many screen performances.

As life went on for Lana, so did romantic partners. Even the casual film enthusiast could repeat the fact that Lana had won a $216,000 divorce settlement from Bob Topping; that in October 1952 Frank Sinatra had come home and either found Lana and Ava Gardner com-

*Jeanine Basinger would assess in *Lana Turner*, ". . . [she] is excellent in *The Bad and the Beautiful*. For once a glamorous movie star is played by one. [That same year Bette Davis appeared in Twentieth Century-Fox's *The Star*, detailing the plight of a has-been screen legend]. She understands the role, and she makes it hers. None of the sex symbols who have been touted as actresses—not Hayworth or Gardner or Taylor or Monroe—has ever given such a fine performance. Yet she was not even nominated for an Oscar."

With Kirk Douglas in *The Bad and the Beautiful* ('52).

paring his lovemaking to that of Artie Shaw or, as crazy rumor persisted, in bed together; and that more recently muscle-bulging actor Lex "Tarzan" Barker had supplanted Fernando Lamas in Lana's affections. Lamas did not take the altered relationship like a gentleman. At a party in the home of Marion Davies, Lamas tore into Lana, condemning her drinking, openly sneering at her lovemaking acumen, and climaxing with the opinion that if Lana "must be intimate with Barker, she not be so in public."

Hollywood gasped at Fernando's critique, and Metro, who had just merrily fashioned a new Turner/Lamas vehicle, *Latin Lovers* (1953), desperately rushed in Ricardo Montalban to replace the volcanic Lamas. (Lamas had already recorded several songs for the film.) The Mervyn LeRoy-directed release was memorable only because it presented a relaxed and happy Lana being guided by a familiar and favorite director.

While Lex Barker (born Alexander Crichlow Barker on May 8, 1919, in Rye, New York) had played the Great White Ape with his clean-cut features, perfect English, and inferior ape call in only five RKO releases, the shadow of Tarzan loomed over him. This, along with a broken marriage to Arlene Dahl, made him anxious to work in Europe, where he hoped to land some non-jungle roles and to take advantage of the tax shelter available to Americans working in Europe for eighteen consecutive months. Lana herself at this point saw little reason to stay in the U.S. MGM had been the scene of a coup in 1951, when Louis B. Mayer was ousted by the forces of Dore Schary. Like most of her confreres remaining from the golden age, Lana had little love for the dry, economy-loving new breed and missed the coddling of dethroned potentate Mayer. Hence Lana accompanied Lex to Europe, and in Italy made a film for Metro, *Flame and the Flesh*, released in the States in 1954. Audiences, already addicted to television,* could

*Appropriately Lana's TV debut occurred as part of Ed Sullivan's salute to MGM's 30th anniversary. On the February 14, 1954, telecast of "Toast of the Town," Lana was seen performing

With Ricardo Montalban in *Latin Lovers* ('53).

not get excited about Lana donning a black wig and seducing Carlos Thompson from his betrothed (Pier Angeli). Actually the public was more intrigued with the magazine accounts of the shared life in Naples of Lana and Lex. The couple would legalize their union in Turin, Italy, on Monday, September 7, 1953, remarrying in Hollywood that December.

At MGM, Ava Gardner, a personal friend of Lana's, was winning the major portion of publicity, especially after her handling of the original Harlow role in the *Red Dust* remake, *Mogambo* (1953), in which she co-starred with Clark Gable and Grace Kelly. The studio planned to reteam Clark and Ava in *Betrayed* (1954) to be shot in the Netherlands and England. But with Lana already living abroad, it made more sense to cast her as Carla Van Owen and economically work her into another contracted picture. The European CinemaScope shooting allowed Lana to remain within her tax deal. However, the dull script, a tired, fifty-four-year-old Gable, and an unbecoming brunette hair-dye, that only reminded audiences that Lana was maturing, did nothing to boost the once-torrid team to new prominence. *Variety* termed *Betrayed* "a confused, often dull meller burdened with a running time of one hour and 47 minutes [sic]." Most people felt that Victor Mature, as "The Scarf," was the one vital force in the picture. *Betrayed* proved to be an off-key swan song not only to the Gable-Turner teaming, but to Gable's MGM years. (His long-term pact expired with this picture.)

When Lana returned to Hollywood, things were no better. Television was still cutting into film profits, and Metro was not renewing options. There was little time remaining on her studio contract, and her next film made one wish it had already lapsed. This was *The Prodigal*

(1955), a supremely tinny attempt to cash in on the success of Twentieth Century-Fox's *The Robe* (1953) and *Demetrius and the Gladiators* (1954). In a series of decadent costumes and hair styles that must be seen to be truly believed, Lana portrayed the wicked Samarra, worshipper of the Love Goddess and seducer of Edmund Purdom's handsome prodigal son. The ads outdid themselves: "SEE a Myriad of Thrills . . . Unparalleled Wonder and Splendor! Pagan Priestess in the Temple of Love. . . . Revolt of the Slaves and Their Orgy of Vengeance! The Vulture Pit, an Awesome Sight! . . ." The film bore the signs of the desperate MGM mentality (the Temple site was built over the old Esther Williams swimming tank). *The Prodigal* deserved and received unanimously rotten reviews, and Lana herself quipped, "It played two weeks in Pomona. It shoulda played Disneyland."

To obtain a return on their maintenance of the great Turner, Metro hurriedly lent her services to other studios before her option lapsed. Thus Lana visited Warner Bros. at a $300,000 fee to co-star with John Wayne in a World War II actioner, *The Sea Chase* (1955), filmed largely at Kaelakekua Bay in Kailua, Hawaii. It was a most luscious Lana who paraded in this spy melodrama. One critic observed that Turner boarded the German vessel "with a cruise wardrobe that will have all the lady spies in town asking their governments for more charge accounts." Most agreed that it was certainly bizarre casting to have such typically American products as Wayne and Turner cast as Germans. (Fortunately neither performer attempted a Rhineland accent).

Lana then returned to her home lot for *Diane*, a project once considered in the 1930s for Greta Garbo. It would not be released until 1956.

In the interim she went to Twentieth Century-Fox to join with Richard Burton in *The Rains of Ranchipur* (1955), a CinemaScope color remake of *The Rains Came*. (Ava Gardner and Rita Hayworth had been other contenders for the Turner role, according to director Jean Negulesco.) As it developed the Turner-Burton teaming was not exciting, far less so even than the cool pairing of Tyrone Power and Myrna Loy in the 1939 original film. Even many of the special effects sequences from the initial version

---

the "Madame Cremation" number which Judy Garland had performed in *The Ziegfeld Follies* (1946). Thereafter Lana's video appearances included the 28th (1956), the 30th (1958), and 38th (1966) Oscar shows; a Milton Berle special (October 11, 1959), where among other tunes she sang "Just Turn Me Loose on Broadway" which Bette Davis had originated on stage in 1952; "The Carol Burnett Show" (January 1968) in which she danced to "Greensleeves"; and "The Survivors" series in 1969 (see *infra*). She made her first late evening TV talk program appearance on "The Johnny Carson Show" (May 17, 1972). The next day, May 18, 1972, she was engaged in a ninety-minute interview with David Frost on his video talk session.

With Brian Smith in *Betrayed* ('54).

With Richard Davalos and John Wayne in *The Sea Chase* ('55).

415

were woven into the second. Lana's character here underwent some changes from the Loy edition. She is now an American wed to a titled Englishman (Michael Rennie) and at the finale is allowed to survive. While few critics had kind words for this $4 million "epic," many Turner devotees consider this feature to display Lana of the Fifties at her loveliest.

Within a month after the January 1956 release of *Diane*, Turner ended her MGM pact. This quickly forgotten costume drama served only to demonstrate how faded the Turner star and the Metro product had become. After eighteen years of safeguarding and promotion by the wizards of Culver City, Lana left the lot. It was as if Olympus was losing its famed gods; in the space of a few years such luminaries as Clark Gable, Walter Pidgeon, Ava Gardner, and Lana all departed the facility.

While Lana's film career was in descent, she distracted herself by being (for a time) a very contented Mrs. Lex Barker. She resided in a Brentwood mansion boasting two-dozen rooms and featuring a projection hall, a private beauty parlor and ice cream fountain, a giant swimming pool, a dozen telephones, and such touches as a $25,000 tea service that could accommodate sixty guests. Barker had meanwhile signed an acting contract with Universal-International, where he was managing to earn roles that required more than loincloths. The couple spent their free time in Acapulco. Trouble began to dominate the Turner/Barker love match when he became increasingly concerned over her riotous spending. She had departed MGM, leaving him the sole breadwinner, but she still lived as if she were reaping a $200,000 a year income. Barker at one point ordered her to stick to a $1,500 a month budget, but with no tangible results. When he requested a business agent to try to solve Lana's lavish spending habits, the manager's reply was, "That woman doesn't need a manager; she should have a keeper." A separation in 1956 finally interrupted the once blissful union. A final divorce decree was issued on Tuesday, July 23, 1957. Barker's Universal contract expired along with the marriage and he quickly slid into obscurity. (Little was heard of Barker during the last fifteen years of his life. On May 11, 1973, he collapsed in midtown Manhattan and was pronounced dead at the Lenox Hill Hospital. The ex-star had been wed five times.)

Hardly anyone in Hollywood could have predicted in early 1957 that Lana Turner, of all people, would be nominated for a Best Actress Oscar in that year's sweepstakes. However, so much better was Lana's performance as Constance MacKenzie* in Twentieth Century-Fox's blockbuster *Peyton Place* (1957) than anything she had done in years, that Lana did indeed find herself among the heralded actresses of the season. With Mark Robson's tasteful direction, a John Michael Hayes scenario that gave dignity to Grace Metalious' best seller, a lilting Franz Waxman music score, sumptuous, crisp photography by William Mellor, and a cast including professionals like Hope Lange, Lloyd Nolan, Arthur Kennedy, and Betty Field, *Peyton Place* led the very discriminating National Board of Review to judge the picture "an example of how a fine motion picture can be made out of a cheap and dirty book."

Lana did handle the demanding role** of Constance most admirably, being restrained and at times powerful as the scandal-besieged mother in that nasty New England town. Like Dorothy Malone of the ABC teleseries that began in 1964, Lana managed to make Constance the dominating figure of the drama. She was especially impressive in the scenes with daughter Allison (Diane Varsi), just as Miss Malone would be with Mia Farrow. With even the approval of the *New York Times*, who opined that she did "remarkably well," Lana faced Oscar competition from Deborah Kerr (*Heaven Knows, Mr. Allison*), Anna Magnani (*Wild Is the Wind*),

*Susan Hayward had considered accepting the role, but dropped out of the project.
**Valentino would note in *The Films of Lana Turner*, "On April 15, 1957, Louella Parsons' 'exclusive' of the day informed movie fans that Hollywood's erstwhile Sweater Girl was about to undertake her first role as the mother of a teenager. . . . Turner fans did not take the news lightly, of course. First and foremost, it seemed to indicate the end of Lana's gilt-edged glamour days and that henceforth she would be destined exclusively for maternal roles. None of the movies' celebrated World War II Love Goddesses had yet succumbed to playing the mother of a teenager and, at thirty-six, Lana was still younger than all of the others." Ms. Basinger in *Lana Turner* would observe, "Wearing her hair in a tight French twist and pursing her lips, Turner represses her own native sensuality. She creates the opposite of herself, a woman who goes cold and suspicious at a moment's notice, an 'all-men-are-alike' lady."

With Richard Burton in *The Rains of Ranchipur* ('55).

With Roger Moore and Marisa Pavan in *Diane* ('56).

417

In *Peyton Place* ('57).

418

Elizabeth Taylor (*Raintree County*), and Joanne Woodward (*The Three Faces of Eve*). Miss Woodward took the prize. It would be Lana's only Academy nomination to date.

From a new high in her acting, Lana then spiraled to a new low in her personal life. Unlike Jean Harlow, who tired of her tinselly image and was attracted to men of intellectual aura, Lana had long made clear that her libido swelled for the he-man mold of escort. In 1957, she began dating Johnny Stompanato, a thirty-two-year-

Chandler). It was harmless frou-frou that benefited from a few, rousing love scenes between the co-stars—especially one adjacent to a bathtub. It was to be the first of several pictures for Lana with Universal-International.

Meanwhile Lana continued her fling with Stompanato. She went to England to star in Paramount's *Another Time, Another Place* (1958), shot for Turner's production company, Lanturn Productions, in a joint venture with an English firm. Location footage was shot in the fishing

With Richard Denning and Jeff Chandler in *The Lady Takes a Flyer* ('58).

old gigolo whose main claim to fame was being a "pal" of gangster Mickey Cohen. With daughter Cheryl away at Ojai's Happy Valley School, Lana began having an affair with Stompanato which the latter interpreted as a precursor to marriage.

The Lady Takes a Flyer (1958) had actually been filmed before *Peyton Place*, but was not released till early 1958. She is the flying instructress who falls in love with (equally attractive) ex-Air Force Colonel Mike Dandridge (Jeff

village of Polperro in Cornwall with soundstage work at London's Elstree Studios. Her co-players were Barry Sullivan, Glynis Johns, and a young Sean Connery. It would prove to be mushy soap opera, cheaply made, and a credit to no participant.

Stompanato followed Lana to England. Industry gossips began to whisper horrible stories of Johnny threatening Lana with a scarred face or worse whenever she made an attempt to dis-

With Terrence Longdon in *Another Time, Another Place* ('58).

courage him. It was frighteningly clear that the hoodlum was determined to become Lana's husband at any cost. Still, Lana appeared to enjoy her beau's company, and columnists shook their heads when the couple spent eight sunny weeks in Acapulco—strictly at Lana's expense.

The disaster that climaxed this affair is one of Hollywood's goriest and saddest scandals. Fourteen-year-old Cheryl came home from school at Easter time of 1958 and was met by her mother and Stompanato. As the police story later reported it, Cheryl was awakened by shouting in her mother's bedroom. Stompanato was yelling "I'll get you if it takes a day, a week, or a year! I'll cut you up! I'll stomp you! And if I can't do it myself, I'll find someone who can!" The frightened adolescent raced to the kitchen, grabbed a ten-inch butcher knife, ran to the bedroom with the words "You don't have to take that, Mama!" and on April 4, 1958 (Good Friday evening) stabbed Stompanato, killing him.

This, of course, is just one (the official) version of the death of the fabled Johnny Stompanato. Famed lawyer Jerry Giesler managed to keep the more scurrilous tidbits to a minimum during the sensationalistic trial.

When the police arrived after the murder, both mother and daughter received the right to a phone call. Lana called attorney Giesler and Cheryl telephoned her father, Stephen Crane. Both ladies went to police headquarters, where Cheryl was kept in prison. The news spread like wildfire. By the time Lana returned home, rushing to the privacy of her bedroom with its blood-soaked pink carpet, her lawn was blanketed by reporters, fans, necrophiles, and worse. As *Newsweek* magazine reported, Lana's "wild sobs could be heard by people on the lawn out front."

Johnny Stompanato was buried in a tiny country cemetery in Woodstock, Illinois. It was the end of his troubles, but the beginning of Lana's, as she relived the miserable experience over and over in court. Photographs of a make-up-free, weeping Lana won mass circulation as she cried in the witness chair and tried to protect her daughter. Giesler performed a magnificent feat of counseling and the jury eventually

420

With Terry Burnham and Karen Dicker in *Imitation of Life* ('59).

brought in a verdict of "justifiable homicide." When this was read, an unidentified man arose and shouted that the reason for murder was jealousy between Lana and Cheryl* for Johnny. The outcry had little effect on the announced legal decision but did provide the pulps with material for years afterwards, as had the dozens of Lana's ardent love letters which Mickey

*In the Stompanato case, Cheryl Crane became a ward of the juvenile court after the justifiable homicide verdict. Cheryl lived at the home of her maternal grandmother, Mrs. Mildred Turner, until two years later, when her father and mother transferred her, with the court order of Judge Allen T. Lynch, to the El Retiro Institution in the Sylmar section of San Fernando Valley. Rumor stated that she was placed there because the parents feared an elopement with Robert Martin Gunn, a twenty-two-year-old drive-in restaurant employee, but it was denied by Lana. "Anyone with a girl in the thirteen- to sixteen-year age bracket realizes some of the problems that arise, and in Cheryl's case she suffered a severe shock two years ago that isn't easily overcome. This institution is to help girls who need that extra bit of help." El Retiro was surrounded by a twelve-foot wall and contained about forty girl inmates. Lana and Crane paid $35.49 per day for Cheryl's stay there. Despite security precautions, Cheryl twice escaped from the institution. She is today an attractive, unmarried lady who is successfully employed in Stephen Crane's restaurant business.

Harold Robbins wrote a fictionalized account of the case entitled *Where Love Has Gone.* In the 1964 film version, Susan Hayward played the "Lana Turner" part, with Joey Heatherton as her daughter.

Cohen had sold to the *Los Angeles Herald Examiner.* All of these terrible tragedies caused Lana to take stock of herself, but amazingly did not the slightest bit of damage to her box-office power.

Despite all the sensationalistic publicity concerning Lana's latest indiscretion (or perhaps because of it), Universal made a deal with the actress that through one film insured her with a hefty income for the rest of her life. Guaranteed a percentage of the profits, Lana starred for Universal in *Imitation of Life* (1959), the remake of the 1934 picture which had starred Claudette Colbert. The glossy new color version changed the plot to make Lana an actress and not a businesswoman, but retained the basic story— a young black girl (Susan Kohner) uses her light complexion to elude bigotry and to break her mother's (Juanita Moore) heart. With 125 minutes of almost unrelieved soap-opera misery, *Imitation of Life* contains as a morbid climax the most elaborately weepy funeral ever filmed, with Mahalia Jackson wailing "Trouble of the World" while most of Lana's co-stars (John

Gavin, Sandra Dee) sniffle and a church crammed with extras floods with supporting tears. The morbid picture, coupled with Lana's morbid publicity and Ross Hunter's glittery production values, made *Imitation of Life* must-viewing for most 1959 audiences. It grossed $6.5 million in just U.S. and Canadian distributors' gross rentals. As such, the star made a bundle from the receipts. Lana later stated, "I thank God for *Imitation of Life*. Just that one picture has provided an income that should be able to keep me for the rest of my life."

Lana was next scheduled to play the leading female role in *Anatomy of a Murder* (1959) but she and autocratic director Otto Preminger had a difference of opinion. Reportedly the feud centered around her wardrobe for the film. Preminger's costume co-ordinator (and later wife) Hope Bryce had selected in a Beverly Hills shop a pair of slacks in which Lana's character, Laura Manion, would appear for the Columbia release. However, Lana's agent, Paul Kohner, passed down word that Jean Louis would design any and all of Turner's outfits. An oversized tiff ensued and Lana was replaced by Lee Remick. To this day Lana has nothing but high contempt for Preminger and enjoys venting her disgust.

Then, with another share-the-profits arrangement, Lana made a second melodrama for Ross Hunter's production unit at Universal. *Portrait in Black* (1960) was based on a 1947 Broadway play—with Claire Luce—that had once been considered as a project for Joan Crawford. It was an extremely well-mounted thriller in which wealthy San Franciscan Lana persuades sensual physician Anthony Quinn, her lover, to do away with crippled husband Lloyd Nolan. The intriguing cast included Sandra Dee and John Saxon for the teenage set, and, for nostalgia purposes, Anna May Wong and Virginia Grey. The reworking of the *Postman* theme again proved good business, helping Lana to fill her bank account, which she confessed had mysteriously shrunk. "Where did the rest go? I don't know, but it went. Chalk it up to bad management, or just not having the sense to save. Before, I never owned a thing, except the house I was living in at the time." Lana began wisely investing the money, heeding experts' advice on real estate purchases and other investments.

After two solid years of good behavior, Lana wed for the fifth time on Sunday, November 27, 1960. The bridegroom was Fred May, a forty-three-year-old horse breeder/trainer/owner who operated from a Chino, California, ranch. He wed his forty-year-old spouse at the Miramar Hotel in Santa Monica, and for a time the marriage seemed very happy. Nevertheless, a Mexican divorce ended this union on Monday, October 15, 1962, but the couple did and do remain good friends. "I know it sounds corny, but Fred and I seem to understand each other better since we were divorced. We see each other quite a bit. I think he's grown a great deal since our marriage, and I think I have changed too."

The over-forty Lana was in many ways a new woman. Away from the big studio system, she was able to more often speak her mind. She reached her new maturity beautifully, and here and there in the Sixties accepted screen roles that treated her with proper charm and supplied her with a fitting stipend. *By Love Possessed* (1961), released by United Artists and based on the James Gould Cozzens novel, saw her having an affair with Efrem Zimbalist, Jr., the law partner of her crippled husband Jason Robards, Jr. Back at MGM, she was lovely if a bit matronly and stiff in a good Bob Hope comedy, *Bachelor in Paradise* (1961), which allowed her to dance the Bossa Nova. Less can be said about the insipid *Who's Got the Action?* (1962), a silly farce in which she played the wife of a bookie (Dean Martin). There were tremendous production problems on Columbia's *Love Has Many Faces* which did not see release until February 1965. Lana endured long bouts of illness, feuded with the filmmakers, feared that co-players Ruth Roman and Stefanie Powers were getting too much footage, and wondered if the venture had been worth it. Filmed in Acapulco and New Mexico, the Alexander Singer-directed venture focused lovingly on Lana's million-dollar wardrobe (by Edith Head) and the physique of Hugh O'Brian as a male hooker. In a hilariously symbolic finale that was filmed with a straight face, Lana is gored by a bull and nearly expires at the local hospital.

Still, in many ways, Lana was the old Lana too, and on Tuesday, June 22, 1965, she wed her sixth husband, thirty-four-year-old Robert Eaton, who

422

On the set of *By Love Possessed* ('61).

With Efrem Zimbalist, Jr. in *By Love Possessed*.

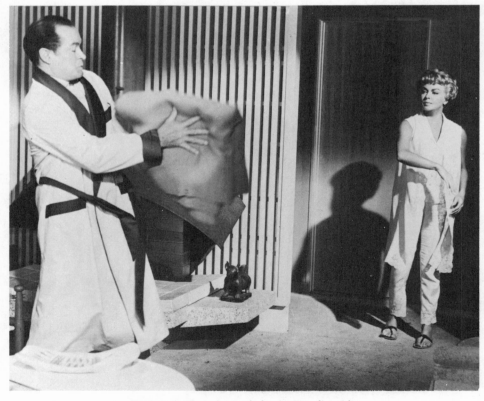

With Bob Hope in *Bachelor in Paradise* ('61).

With Dean Martin in *Who's Got the Action?* ('62).

With Hugh O'Brian in *Love Has Many Faces* ('65).

With Keir Dullea in *Madame X* ('66).

had dreams of becoming a film producer. Not long after the marriage, Lana returned to Universal to star as *Madame X* (1966),* the old weeper which allowed her to age twenty years, win Italy's Best Actress award, and earn another hefty salary via a share-the-profits arrangement with producer Ross Hunter. (It was co-produced with Lana's company, Eltee Productions.) The latest version of *Madame X*, hokey but well-executed, was very popular but caused critic Pauline Kael to pen, "She's not Madame X, she's brand X; she's not an actress, she's a commodity."

For a time after Lana completed *Madame X*, the Universal lot maintained the elaborate bungalow she occupied there as a tourist attraction. Patrons of their famous studio tour paraded through the cottage, photographing sights like her bedroom and makeup mirror.

Lana also did her patriotic bit by making a trip to buoy fighting men's spirits in Vietnam. Upon her arrival she hurt her ankle, and immediately medics of all ages began debating over who was to treat her. As Lana sighed, "You know what they wanted and I know what they wanted. They all wanted to hold LT's foot."

Meanwhile, Robert Eaton was still intent on becoming a film producer, so Lana humored him and, by adding her name to his assets, made it possible for her spouse to produce a hideous concoction entitled *The Big Cube* (1969). Shot in Mexico, the film cast Lana as an aging actress with a weird daughter, and also exploited the talents of George Chakiris, Richard Egan, Dan O'Herlihy, and a singing group called The Finks. The film (one reviewer called it "an unqualified idiot's delight") was quickly and mercifully forgotten, and perhaps added to the reasons for the Eatons' divorce on Tuesday, April 1, 1969. Eaton obviously did not take the divorce at all well. He thereafter penned an atrocious novel entitled *The Body Brokers*, which dealt with a forty-five-year-old actress and her deranged daughter who get away with throwing a man over a cliff because he would not bed mother and daughter

*Producer Hunter and Lana had originally planned a remake of *The Dark Angel*, but could not obtain the screen rights.

simultaneously. The book drew scarcely more attention than it deserved.

Certainly, the book failed to disturb Lana. By the time it appeared, she was remarried! Husband number seven was Ronald Dante, a thirty-nine-year-old nightclub hypnotist. On Thursday, May 8, 1969, they were wed in Las Vegas, where Dante was appearing at the Pussycat A-Go-Go They soon returned to Lana's hilltop Hollywood home, where Dante worked on a book on hypnotherapy when not driving his motorcycle about the Los Angeles hills or buying another fur jacket or Brazilian fertility symbol. "When I leave in the morning for work," the bride informed the press, "my darling is sleeping. I try to be so quiet getting my panties out of the drawer, getting my dress off the hanger. He opens his eyes and says, 'Goodbye, dear, have a good day at the office.' That's our private kind of love joke."

Lana was not daily heading for an office, but she certainly was heading for a joke. When Harold Robbins' novel *Where Love Has Gone* had appeared in 1962, Lana was insistent that

she would never speak to him again. Still, by 1967, peace was made in the form of a contract for Lana to star in Robbins' projected epic tele-series, "The Survivors." This was probably the most dismal professional episode in Lana's career to date. As she said at the time of the debacle, "If we were to film what really has happened behind the cameras, no one would believe it."

In keeping with the epic plans, Universal assigned William Frye to produce the series, and provided him with the highest series budget in the history of television—$8,000,000 for the 1969-1970 season. $200,000 was spent on the set, $100,000 for wardrobes (half of which went to tailor Lana alone), and chunks of the remainder for star recruitment (Lana, George Hamilton, Ralph Bellamy, and Kevin McCarthy). Two months of location-shooting on the Riviera and $1,000,000 worth of expenses accumulated *before* the first episode was even completed.

There developed personality problems to

In *The Big Cube* ('69).

In the teleseries "The Survivors" (ABC-TV, '69).

equal those of a financial sort. Lana was not pleased with her jewelry, and took producer Frye to task about it. Depending on whom one believes, Frye either told her he could not be bothered or called the star a bitch. Whatever his comment, Lana slapped him across the face and Frye retaliated by slapping Lana twice! Another producer came and went in the tidal waves of ego before veteran Walter Doniger got production finally running in a forward direction, describing his post as like "having a cocktail party on the wing of an airplane."

Lana's role was that of Tracy Carlyle Hastings, "a wife and mother who is prepared to stop at nothing to protect the reputation and future of her son by another man." She found the hazards of television production upsetting ("Oh baby, I still ask myself, how the hell did I get into this?") and compensated for the ruffled feathers by demanding royal treatment. She warned co-star Kevin McCarthy never to upstage her ("Don't ever play those games with me or I'll just stop the scene and you'll be standing there with egg on your face!"), lambasted the writers ("They get so damn poetic in that writers' room!"), and

waged a victorious war for a limousine to be on constant call ("Television provides cars for no one. No one! But since I've been in my position I've always had limousines. Now I'm the only one on the lot who has a limousine and it took quite a bit of doing!"). The company was thereafter treated to the sight of Lana being chauffeured back to her dressing room, one block from the sound stage, whenever she needed to use the bathroom.

Despite all its publicity and private wars, "The Survivors" finally appeared on ABC-TV on Tuesday, September 29, 1970. Several weeks later it was withdrawn, an industry embarrassment labeled by *Time* magazine as "just possibly the worst decision of Lana's forty-five-movie, seven-husband career . . . the most overpriced and troubled TV series ever."*

In the meantime, Lana's marriage to Dante

*In 1971 Universal TV would seek to recoup a portion of its enormous investment in the series by spending some $200,000 to reassemble footage from the show and splice in new scenes. The only principal from the original project to participate in the new filming would be Ralph Bellamy. As supervised by Howard Tatelman, the repackaged entry was entitled *The Last of the Powerseekers*.

showed signs of being her most overpriced and troubled marriage ever. In late 1969, after six months of connubial union, they separated, and it was well-publicized that Lana was suing her mate for defrauding her of $35,000. Divorce was delayed when Dante threatened to proclaim intimate facts about Lana of a slanderous nature, and over two years would pass before a divorce settlement was resolved.

She's paying all she can for secrecy. But the price just went up.

The Last of the Powerseekers

Lana Turner. George Hamilton
Jan Michael Vincent

8pm Movie

KTLA 5

TV ad for the feature film version of the teleseries "The Survivors."

In early 1970 Lana agreed to put her name on two thousand mini-spas for women in the U.S. and foreign countries, including England and Japan. Her explanation for endorsing the "Lana Turner Mini-Spas" was, "I'll do anything I can to promote good health." The venture never came to fruition.

"The Survivors" did Lana no good at all as far as career impetus goes. At another time in show-business history, Lana might have been swallowed up by the apathy of the discriminating new-breed audience. However, by 1970, the nostalgia craze had taken root and was affecting almost everybody. Many of the most enthusiastic of the nostalgia buffs were young people who were just discovering the actors, actresses, and singers of yesterday. In 1971, the summer stock producers Lee Guber and Shelly Gross an-

nounced that Lana Turner would appear under their management in her first live performance ever on stage in the sophisticated but rather stuffy comedy *40 Carats*. The role was that of Ann Stanley,* a forty-year-old, tres chic divorced businesswoman who is ardently pursued by a handsome young man half her age.

Explaining her reasons for tackling her first play on the legitimate boards, Lana stated, "I saw Barbara Rush do it [in stock] a couple of years ago. Had anyone told me that I'd play it, I'd say, 'You're out of your mother's skull.' But I was tired of inactivity. The kind of films that are done lately, I just refuse to do. I won't do junk and I won't do nudity and it's not healthy being an actor unemployed. I didn't just jump at *40 Carats*. I took time to think it over. Plus I got a very lovely deal." (Lana reaped $17,500 per week, plus hairdresser, secretary, car, chauffeur, and choice of hotel suites. The management also enticed her by providing the role with fifteen costume changes, a few of which she did provide from her past movies.)

When Lana opened at Shady Grove Music Fair near Bethesda, Maryland, on Tuesday, June 8, 1971, the house was packed and a wildly open display of love for the superstar was evident. The enchanted patrons applauded each entrance, exit, and costume change she made, and the more long-standing fans clapped rapidly when Lana says in the play that she is only thirty-six. (They applauded again when she admitted in the play to being forty.) After a thunderous standing ovation, Lana ran from the in-the-round stage back to her dressing room, and gurgled to her mother, press agent, and a *New York Times* reporter, "I was ready to take the gaspipe. I felt like a parade horse walking around that ring. I felt I should have a baton. Did I make any sense?" So flustered was Lana by this first in her career that she was unable to deliver a curtain speech she wanted to make to the first night well-wishers.

Not all went well at Shady Grove. There were a number of missed performances on Lana's part. She herself explained that, during her fourth performance, "I twisted my right knee

*Played on Broadway on 1968 by Julie Harris, later replaced by June Allyson, and then by Zsa Zsa Gabor.

429

going up the blooming ramps in the first act. But I did the show and the matinee and the evening show the next day, Saturday. . . . Sunday, when I got out of bed, I couldn't walk. . . . My understudy went on three nights. . . ."

At any rate, Lana went on to play *40 Carats* in the Guber/Gross tents in Maryland, Pennsylvania, and New York. During the tour, she gave many interviews and spoke on a number of subjects, including maturity ("You find you really don't need those fifteen mink coats because you can only wear one at a time"), future ambitions ("I've always wanted to find my own private island and I hear Greece has over a thousand. Who knows? Maybe I'll find a millionaire too"), and her belief in reincarnation ("I feel I was a member of an Egyptian royal family at one period. Not any of that Cleopatra jazz, but royal. Also—and this may sound strange—I was once an American Indian").

While Lana's credible appearance in *40 Carats* made her eligible for the starring spot in the 1973 screen version (and she would have been excellent), no solid offers materialized. The role of Ann Stanley went to Liv Ullmann, who was too young for the part, but not wholly to blame for that box-office disappointment from Columbia Pictures.

After completing the grueling tour, Lana returned to California. She by now had sold her Malibu beach home and ranch, and was residing in what she described as a "beautiful, beautiful penthouse in Malibu." She then proceeded to untangle herself once and for all from Dante, from whom she had been separated for over two years. On Wednesday, January 26, 1972, a legal decree of divorce finally was issued and Dante received a settlement of about $200,000. No record was ever filed as to whether Lana retrieved the $35,000 of which the hypnotist reportedly defrauded her. (In mid-1974, Dante was arrested on the charge of "having tried to hire an assassin to kill a rival hypnotist." The court ordered thirty days of psychiatric tests to determine if he was mentally competent to stand trial, considering his mental faculties might have been damaged by drugs.)

So Lana Turner settled down to a relatively quiet life, close to her mother in Malibu, and keeping in contact with her businesswoman daughter. Gossipers noted that when Lana did make a rare appearance at a party or premiere, her escort was always Taylor Pero, introduced as her "secretary/companion." In late 1973, anxious for any kind of screen work, Lana accepted the lead in a London-made thriller, eventually titled *Persecution* (1974). She was cast as a crippled murderess; her co-stars were Trevor Howard, Ralph Bates, and Olga Georges-Picot. The film, plagued by financing problems, received little distribution and was called by Lana "the worst film I've ever made."

Meanwhile in New York, press agent/show-business historian John Springer had been conducting a series of evenings at the city's Town Hall paying homage to "Legendary Ladies" of the screen. The programs generally consisted of film clips from the star's films, followed by an appearance from the star herself to answer audience questions. Bette Davis, Joan Crawford, Sylvia Sidney, Myrna Loy, and Rosalind Russell had previously appeared. And now Springer arranged for Lana Turner to have *her* night of glory before the Town Hall audience.

The choice of Lana was considered offbeat but, to almost everybody's pleasant surprise, was the most successful. On Sunday, April 13, 1975, at 8:15 the program began. For two hours (including intermission), the audience applauded and cheered clips from seventeen of Lana's films, including her stroll from *They Won't Forget*, a scene with Clark Gable and Marjorie Main from *Honky Tonk*, several sequences from *The Postman Always Rings Twice*, her staircase scene from *Ziegfeld Girl*, and many others, including *Imitation of Life* and *Madame X*. Finally, after the famous driving scene from *The Bad and the Beautiful*, Lana made her entrance, wearing a white gown by Don Werle, and won the longest standing ovation of the series to date. With a nervous smile she looked out at the packed house and sighed, "So! This is tonight!"

In the ensuing question-and-answer period Lana again debunked the myth of Schwab's Drug Store, and again credited a malt shop across from Hollywood High ("where I could sneak after cutting typing class") as her discovery spot. She referred to Mervyn LeRoy as a "great gentleman," and said of her scene of infamy in *They Won't Forget*, "I did just what they told me. I

In *Persecution* ('74).

431

STARTS TODAY

LANA TURNER
IN HER MOST DRAMATIC ROLE SINCE "MADAME X"

IN

SHEBA

PG

GENERAL CINEMA CORPORATION
PARKWOOD
293-4753 · 3315 W. COLONIAL

GENERAL CINEMA CORPORATION
SEMINOLE
838-7222 · CASSELBERRY

COLONIAL
DRIVE-IN THEATRE

Twin Theatre · 898-6401
CONWAY 2
2680 E. Conway Road · Orlando

10-4-74

Advertisement for *Persecution* (a.k.a. *Sheba*).

couldn't think of any part of my anatomy as being so important. When I saw the picture with my mother, I was embarrassed and slid down in my seat." She lamented her accolade of "Sweater Girl," saying, "It seems like every sexy, young-looking broad had to have a title and mine became the 'Sweater Girl.' I never found out who was responsible for that, but if I ever find out. . . ." Despite her poo-pooing of that title, Lana did invigorate the crowd by gesturing towards her 35-inch bust and attesting, "They're still mine!"

As to her co-workers, Lana made some candid reflections. She giggled about a love scene she had with "King" Gable in *Homecoming* that terminated when her chewing gum got entangled in his dentures, and again paid tribute to John Garfield, "He was shy, vibrant, and intelligent and so ahead of his time." She claimed to be unaware that Bette Davis was after her *Postman* role ("My role! I never knew that and Bette and I are friends"), and appeared grateful to have been "blessed with my sensitive directors," though she admitted that Vincente Minnelli rattled her

during *The Bad and the Beautiful* and that she despised Otto Preminger. Surprisingly, she answered a question about her affair with Tyrone Power, stating, "I cared very deeply for him. Ty and I shared a wonderful year and a half but there was no question of marrying since he was still married to Annabella." She also remarked on the press ("Some I regard as the vultures they are and some, a few, I respect. I've had my hatchet jobs"), hailed daughter Cheryl ("Oh, my lovely daughter. God, I'm so proud of her. I call her Miss Executive"), and dismissed the question as to whether there were any male stars she would have liked to have worked with by grinning and saying, "When you've had the best. . . ." The audience laughed knowingly and Lana purred "Shame on you!" to her throng.

When the inevitable question of whether or not she would change her life was asked, Lana answered, "Would I do it all again? Yes, yes, yes, because my life is truly controlled by destiny. If I could have changed it I would have but I don't believe that way." The evening concluded with bouquets of flowers, another standing ovation, and Lana shaking hands with front row observers. Her later evaluation of the evening was, "They were lovely, but the only parts I really enjoyed were when the little devil in me could have some fun with the answers."

Afterward, Lana was the honored guest at a party hosted by producer/director John Bowab, her guiding light of *40 Carats*. She said of her present life, now centered in a Century City co-op, "I have a few close friends and thousands of acquaintances, and my personal life will just sound dull if I tell you about it. I was queen of the nightclubs when I was eighteen, but I'd rather sit home with my color TV now." She said she hoped to work in movies again, but only if the script is worthy. "There are some good women left who aren't on crutches, and the writers should be writing for us. I'm not about to open a bar or boutique!" (She made no mention of her mini-spas.) Lana did remind all that she did not need to work, with her wise real estate holdings ("Each time it's paid off"), and touted her race horse, Gray Host, now retired to lucrative stud service. "So, listen, if I don't get any work, I'll just depend on my stud—I mean, of course, my horse."

In *Bittersweet Love* ('76).

Lana hoped her Town Hall evening would bring in some movie offers. In August of 1975 *Variety* announced that Lana would star in *Deadlock*, a suspense yarn to be jointly produced by Dioscouri and Leejo Productions, but the financing for the project never materialized. In late 1975 she accepted a stage offer to co-star with Louis Jourdan in *The Pleasure of His Company* at the Chicago Arlington Park Theatre. Shortly before Christmas, the press reported that a performance had to be terminated after the first act one evening because Lana was ill, but the next night she was back, delighting her audiences.

In mid-April 1976, Lana returned to film-making. She would claim that the project intrigued her because David Miller was signed to direct the venture. Evidently she held no ill feelings against him for *Diane*, their last movie together. The picture was initially called *And Jill Came Tumbling Down* and was then retitled *Birthmark*. When it was released by Avco Embassy at Thanksgiving time, 1976, it was known as *Bittersweet Love*. As the *Hollywood Reporter* would analyze, it "is a lush, romantic film that attempts to blend new and old movie images. The new is treating a racy theme, incest, although committed innocently, and the old, presenting aspects of what used to be called a 'woman's picture,' the indiscretion committed by a woman in her youth, which has come back to haunt her in her maturity.... Lana Turner is that woman and she parades the dazzling gowns and jewelry that gave women's pictures their special cachet."

Bittersweet Love was promoted with the ad campaign, "At last . . . a love story that Hollywood had never dared to make." But, as the *New York Times* and other reviewers agreed, the problem with the film is "that despite the earnestness of the cast, inspiration seems to have died with the posing of the problem. Right to the end, the young couple [Meredith Baxter Birney and Scott Hylands] remain two Nice People who have been given a Terrible Problem. What they haven't been given is sufficient depth of character to make anyone care long or profoundly about them."

The film served as a pointed reminder of how time had eroded Lana's once lofty marquee power. For this entry she was billed below the title, and although she was garbed and adorned with outfits and jewelry to make any woman envious, the cinematographer did her mature looks no justice. (To be fair, no one in the cast was photographed favorably, neither the young leads, nor the mature set: Lana, Celeste Holm, Robert Alda, and Robert Lansing.) Then, too, Lana had some pretty excruciating dialogue to deliver—which she did with all the conviction she could muster. At one point she explains to her ex-lover (Lansing) who fathered her daughter, "Do you think I didn't think about an abortion? But that was 1944 and this is now.... I didn't want to bleed to death in some back room."

Other segments of the scenario did their best to make light of Lana's character; it was as if the scripters had a (sub)conscious desire to belittle the veteran actress. For example, when Lansing is discussing Lana with his wife (Holm) he remarks of his one-time romance, "I can't even remember what she looked like. . . . It was all so goddamn insignificant." Perhaps the stunning blow to the viewer's effort to maintain a focal interest in Lana (who actually has a rather subordinate part) occurs near the finale when Meredith Baxter Birney whines to Lana, "What you did with Michael's [Hylands] father thirty years ago isn't any of my business. I don't want to know about it."

Lana, never very much at ease on live television, even made a nervous appearance on "The Dinah Shore Show" to promote *Bittersweet Love*. It was a project that should have been made for television.

Anxious to keep active* in the show-business world of the 1970s, Lana again returned to stage work. In the summer of 1977 she toured in the fantasy-comedy romance *Bell, Book and Candle*, playing an assortment of extremely lucrative East Coast and Mid-West straw-hat playdates. Although the vehicle had long since worn thin (and had proved to be a very poor showcase in the 1958 film for Kim Novak), Lana gave her fans what they wanted, a close inspection of a still glamorous living legend. Some of the critics

*Rumors that she might co-star in the mini-TV version of Harold Robbins' 79 *Park Avenue* proved unfounded.

Lana as a TV "Film Festival" star.

who viewed the proceedings went out of their way to be catty (miffed, so the story goes, because Turner's contract with producer/director/co-player Harold J. Kennedy forbade interviews with her), "Not only is Turner incapable of magic but, far worse, she hasn't even an understudy's notion of what she's supposed to be doing on stage. She spends most of the evening examining the hem of her skirt. Or screwing her earrings. Or patting her blonde concrete hair" (Kevin Kelly, *Boston Globe*). More to the point were Elaine Matas' comments in the Hazleton, Pennsylvania, *Standard-Speaker*: "As the curtain was raised, the large crowd greeted Miss Turner with thunderous applause. . . . The 'Sweater Girl' in the 1940s, Miss Turner has retained her shapely figure and is as beautiful as ever. Sighs of adoration came from the audience as lights were turned on the stage to reveal the leading lady. It is a pleasure to watch the charm and grace of Miss Turner as she practically glides across the stage." As the love-hungry witch, Gilliam Holroyd, Lana extracted the proper response from summertime theatregoers.

Plans for Lana to tour England and the continent with an evening of film clips and answering audience questions did not materialize. However, in January 1978 it was announced that she would co-star in Jack Webb's telefeature *Little Mo*, playing the mother of the late tennis star Maureen Connolly. So eager was Turner to return to the filmmaking scene that she withdrew from the opening engagements (in Palm Beach, Florida, and Atlanta, Georgia) of a new *Bell, Book and Candle* tour (being replaced in Florida by Carroll Baker). But by the time that filming got underway for the three-hour project, Lana had already withdrawn from the venture. Allegedly she was ill with flu, but Hollywood observers claim there were differences of opinion between the Sex Goddess and the TV producers concerning costuming, makeup, and shooting schedule. Anne Baxter was quickly hired to replace Lana in a cast that included Glynnis O'Connor, Michael Learned, Claude Akins, Martin Milner, and Leslie Nielsen, with direction by Daniel Heller. The resilient Miss Turner returned to the stage and in April performed for three weeks in Dallas, Texas, in *Bell, Book and Candle*.

Lana's escorts and dates over recent years have encompassed such diverse types as Ronald Ziegler, ex-President Richard Nixon's former press agent, and, more recently, Charles Evans, New York businessman and brother of producer Robert Evans. The forty-four-year-old Evans had previously been seen with Barbra Streisand before hair-stylist Jon Peters entered her life. Said a "friend" of Lana's at the time, "All Lana wants now is quiet and solitude in her life. She wants a man she can really settle down with. And despite the fact Chuck is eleven years younger, that's where he is at." Plans for the couple to wed in the summer of 1976 never materialized and today Lana is again a free agent.

Looking back over the romantic trail left by Turner in her five-decade sojourn in Hollywood, pal Ava Gardner blurted forth, "Honey, when it comes to men, Lana and I are the world's lousiest pickers." Recent rumors that the relationship of Lana and her long-time personal manager, thirty-seven-year-old ex-singer Taylor Pero, was more social than professional proved to be based on an unfounded fabrication of public newspapers. Turner, who has gained quite a degree of class over the years, has this to say of her famed romance record:

> You know why I've been married so many times? Take the seven men. I could have lived with any of them, other than the father of my daughter, without that piece of paper. But I want it right on the table. I want it legal. I gotta marry 'em. Better I shouldn't, maybe, but I did, and each one had its own individual hurt. I'm not bitter, but you know, to love and to be loved are two very different things. I always thought I was being loved for myself. It was only later I found out I wasn't. If they're clever and if they give me the right story, I take the bait. Then I get kicked in the teeth again.
>
> I'm so gullible. I'm so goddamn gullible. And I'm sick of me being gullible.

FILMOGRAPHY

A STAR IS BORN *(United Artists, 1937)* C-111 min.

Producer, David O. Selznick; director, William Wellman; story, Wellman, Robert Carson; screenplay, Dorothy Parker, Alan Campbell, Carson; music, Max Steiner; assistant director, Eric Stacey; art director, Lyle Wheeler; set decorator, Edward Boyle; Technicolor consultant, Natalie Kalmus; costumes, Omar Kiam; camera, W. Howard Greene; editors, Hal C. Kern, Anson Stevenson.

Janet Gaynor (Esther Blodgett [Vickie Lester]); Fredric March (Norman Maine); Adolphe Menjou (Oliver Niles); Andy Devine (Danny McGuire); May Robson (Lettie); Lionel Stander (Libby); Owen Moore (Casey Burke); Elizabeth Jenns (Anita Regis); J. C. Nugent (Theodore Blodgett); Clara Blandick (Aunt Mattie); A. W. Sweatt (Alex); Peggy Wood (Central Casting Receptionist); Franklin Pangborn (Billy Moon); Edgar Kennedy (Pop Randall); Adrian Rosley, Arthur Hoyt (Makeup Men); Edwin Maxwell (Voice Coach); Guinn "Big Boy" Williams (Posture Coach); Vince Barnett (Bernie); Paul Stanton (Academy Award Speaker); Robert Emmett O'Connor (Bartender at Santa Anita); Olin Howland (Rustic); Irving Bacon (Station Agent); Clarence Wilson (Justice of the Peace); Jonathan Hale (Night Court Judge); Francis Ford, Kenneth Howell, Chris-Pin Martin (Prisoners); Robert Homans (Bailiff); Marshall Neilan (Bert); Dr. Leonard Walker (Orchestra Leader at Hollywood Bowl); Fred "Snowflake" Toones (Black Prisoner); Gayne Whitman (Announcer at Chinese Theatre); Dennis O'Keefe, Claude King, David Newell, Eddie Kane (People at Burke's Party); Carole Landis, Lana Turner (Extras at Santa Anita); Jed Prouty (Artie Carver); George Chandler (Delivery Boy); Trixie Friganza, Jane Barnes (Waitresses).

THEY WON'T FORGET *(Warner Bros., 1937)* 95 min.

Producer/director, Mervyn LeRoy; based on the novel *Death in the Deep South* by Ward Greene; screenplay, Robert Rossen, Aben Kandel; art director, Robert Haas; music/music arranger, Adolph Deutsch; music director, Leo F. Forbstein; camera, Arthur Edeson; editor, Thomas Richards.

Claude Rains (Andrew J. Griffin); Gloria Dickson (Sybil Hale); Edward Norris (Robert Perry Hale); Otto Kruger (Michael Gleason); Allyn Joslyn (William P. Brock); Lana Turner (Mary Clay); Linda Perry (Imogene Mayfield); Elisha Cook, Jr. (Joe Turner); Cy Kendall (Detective Laneart); Clinton Rosemond (Tump Redwine); E. Alyn Warren (Carlyle P. Buxton); Elisabeth Risdon (Mrs. Dale); Clifford Soubier (Jim Timberlake); Granville Bates (Pindar); Ann Shoemaker (Mrs. Mountford); Paul Everton (Governor Thomas Mountford); Donald Briggs (Harmon Drake); Sibyl Harris (Mrs. Clay); Eddie Acuff (Fred, the Soda Jerk); Frank Faylen (Bill Price); Raymond Brown (Foster); Leonard Mudie (Judge Moore); Trevor Bardette (Shattock Clay); Elliott Sullivan (Luther Clay); Wilmer Hines (Ransome Clay); John Dilson (Briggs, the Detective); Harry Davenport, Edward McWade, Harry Beresford (Veterans); Thomas Jackson, George Lloyd (Detectives); Earl Dwire (Jury Foreman); Peter Potter, John Ridgely, Jerry Fletcher (Boys in Poolroom); Robert Cummings, Sr. (Whippel, the Banker); I. Stanford Jolley, Henry Hall (Courtroom Extras); Tom Wilson (Farmer); Forbes Murray (Doughty, the Publisher); Tom Brower, Harry Hollingsworth (Turnkeys).

THE GREAT GARRICK *(Warner Bros., 1937)* 89 min.

Producer/supervisor, Mervyn LeRoy; director, James Whale; based on the story "Ladies and Gentlemen" by Ernst Vajda; screenplay, Vajda; music director, Leo F. Forbstein; music, Adolph Deutsch; art director, Anton Grot; assistant director, Sherry Shourds; costumes, Milo Anderson; camera, Ernest Haller; editor, Warren Low.

Brian Aherne (David Garrick); Olivia de Havilland (Germaine De La Corbe); Edward Everett Horton (Tubby); Melville Cooper (M. Picard); Luis Alberni (Basset); Lionel Atwill (Beaumarchais); Marie Wilson (Nicolle); Lana Turner (Auber); Linda Perry (Molle); Craig Reynolds (Janin); Dorothy Tree (Madame Moreau); Chester Clute (Moreau); Etienne Girardot (Jean Cabot); Albert Dekker (Le Brun); Milton Owen (Captain Thierre); Trevor Bardette (Noverre, the Blacksmith); E. E. Clive (Vendor); Harry Davenport (Innkeeper of Turk's Head); Paul Everton (Innkeeper of the Adam and Eve); Jack Norton (Drunken Gentleman); *Hamlet* sequence: Leyland Hodgson (Man in Box); Fritz Leiber (Horatio); Fritz Leiber, Jr. (Fortinbras); Corbet Morris (Osric); Olaf Hytten (Ambassador); Constance Tellissier (Woman in Box); Connie Leon (Woman in Audience); Elspeth Dudgeon (Old Witch); Ben Weldon (Blacksmith).

THE ADVENTURES OF MARCO POLO *(United Artists, 1938)* 104 min.

Producer, Samuel Goldwyn; associate producer, George Haight; director, Archie Mayo; story, N. A. Pogson; screenplay, Robert E. Sherwood; music, Hugo Friedhofer; music director, Alfred Newman; art director, Richard Day; set decorator, Julia Heron; assistant director, Walter Mayo, costumes, Omar Kiam; sound, Thomas T. Moulton; special effects, James Basevi; camera, Rudolph Maté; editor, Fred Allen.

Gary Cooper (Marco Polo); Sigrid Gurie (Princess Kukachin); Basil Rathbone (Ahmed); Ernest Truex (Binguccio); Alan Hale (Kaidu); George Barbier (Kublai Khan); Binnie Barnes (Nazama); Lana Turner (Nazama's Maid); Stanley Fields (Bayan); Harold Huber (Toctai); H. B. Warner (Chen Tsu); Eugene Hoo (Chen Tsu's Son); Helen Quan (Chen Tsu's Daughter); Soo Young (Chen Tsu's Wife); Mrs. Ng (Chen Tsu's Mother); Lotus Liu (Visahka); Ferdinand Gottschalk (Persian Ambassador); Henry Kolker (Nicolo Polo); Hale Hamilton (Maffeo

Polo); Robert Greig (Chamberlain); Reginald Barlow (Giuseppe); Ward Bond (Mongol Guard); James Leong (Tartar Warrior); Dick Alexander (Ahmed's Aide); Jason Robards, Sr. (Messenger); Gloria Youngblood, Diana Moncardo, Dora Young, Mia Schioka (Court Girls).

LOVE FINDS ANDY HARDY *(MGM, 1938)* 90 min.

Producer, Carey Wilson; director, George B. Seitz; based on characters created by Aurania Rouverol; screenplay, William Ludwig; songs, Mack Gordon and Harry Revel; Roger Edens; wardrobe, Jeanne; sound, Douglas Shearer; camera, Lester White; editor, Ben Lewis.

Lewis Stone (Judge Hardy); Mickey Rooney (Andy Hardy); Judy Garland (Betsy Booth); Cecilia Parker (Marian Hardy); Fay Holden (Mrs. Hardy); Ann Rutherford (Polly Benedict); Betsy Ross Clarke (Aunt Milly); Lana Turner (Cynthia Potter); Marie Blake (Augusta); Don Castle (Dennis Hunt); Gene Reynolds (Jimmy MacMahon); Mary Howard (Mrs. Tompkins); Frank Darien (Bill Collector); George Breakston (Beezy); Raymond Hatton (Peter Dugan).

THE CHASER *(MGM, 1938)* 75 min.

Producer, Frank Davis; director, Edwin L. Marin; story, Chandler Sprague, Howard Emmett Rogers; screenplay, Everett Freeman, Harry Ruskin, Bella and Samuel Spewack; wardrobe, Dolly Tree; art directors, Cedric Gibbons, Randall Duell; set decorator, Edwin B. Willis; assistant director, Richard Green; camera, Charles Lawton, Jr.; editor, George Boemler.

Dennis O'Keefe (Thomas Z. Brandon); Ann Morriss (Dorothy Mason); Lewis Stone (Dr. Prescott); Nat Pendleton (Floppy Phil); Henry O'Neill (Calhoun); Ruth Gillette (Mrs. Olson); John Qualen (Lars); Robert Emmett Keane (Simon Kelly); Jack Mulhall (Joe); Irving Bacon (Harvey); Pierre Watkin (Mr. Beaumont); Barbara Pepper (Mabel); Lana Turner, (Miss Rutherford, in the Office).

RICH MAN, POOR GIRL *(MGM, 1938)* 72 min.

Producer, Edward Chodorov; director, Reinhold Schunzel; based on the play *White Collars* by Edith Ellis; screenplay, Joseph A. Fields, Jerome Chodorov; art directors, Cedric Gibbons, Gabriel Scognamillo; set decorator, Edwin B. Willis; music, Dr. William Axt; wardrobe, Dolly Tree; sound, Douglas Shearer; camera, Ray June; editor, Frank E. Hull.

Robert Young (Bill Harrison); Ruth Hussey (Joan Thayer); Lew Ayres (Henry Thayer); Guy Kibbee (Phillip Thayer); Lana Turner (Helen Thayer); Rita Johnson (Sally Harrison); Don Castle (Frank Thayer); Sarah Padden (Mrs. Thayer); Gordon Jones (Tom Grogan); Virginia Grey (Selma Willis); Marie Blake (Mrs. Gussler); Dorothy Tennant (Woman in Shoe Store); Edwin Maxwell (Manager of Shoe Store); Barbara Bedford (Kate); Mitchell Lewis (Man Who Yells); Jules Cowles (Man with Radio); Francisco Maran (Maitre d'Hotel).

DRAMATIC SCHOOL *(MGM, 1938)* 80 min.

Producer, Mervyn LeRoy; director, Robert B. Sinclair; based on the play *School of Drama* by Hans Szekely, Zoltan Egyed; screenplay, Ernst Vajda, Mary McCall, Jr.; art directors, Cedric Gibbons, Gabriel Scognamillo; set decorator,

Edwin B. Willis; gowns, Adrian; Music, Franz Waxman; sound, Douglas Shearer; camera, William Daniels; editor, Frederick Y. Smith.

Luise Rainer (Louise Mauban); Paulette Goddard (Nana); Alan Marshal (Andre D'Abbencourt); John Hubbard (Roul Fleury); Genevieve Tobin (Gina Bertier); Melville Cooper (Boulin); Henry Stephenson (Monsieur Pasquel, Sr., the Director); Lana Turner (Mado); Virginia Grey (Simone); Gale Sondergaard (Therese Charlot); Erik Rhodes (Georges Mounier); Ann Rutherford (Yvonne); Hans Conried (Remy); Rand Brooks (Pasquel, Jr.); Jean Chatburn (Mimi); Marie Blake (Annette); Frank Puglia (Alphonse); Cecilia Callejo (La Brasiliana); Margaret Dumont (Pantomimic Teacher); Dorothy Granger (Fat Girl); Maurice Cass (Verdier, the Composer); Marek Windheim (Greneuil, the Librettist); Minerva Urecal (Rose, Boulin's Secretary); Priscilla Totten, Mimi Doyle, Maxine Marx, Carol Parker, Ocean Claypool, Ruth Alder, Dick Haymes, Rick Vallin, George Travell, Eric Effron, Louis Adlon, Roy Bush, Jack Daniels, Edward Arnold, Jr. (Students).

CALLING DR. KILDARE *(MGM, 1939)* 86 min.

Producer, Lou Ostrow; director, Harold S. Bucquet; based on characters created by Max Brand; story, Brand; screenplay, Harry Ruskin, Willis Goldbeck; art directors, Cedric Gibbons, Gabriel Scognamillo; set decorator, Edwin B. Willis; music, David Snell; wardrobe, Dolly Tree; sound, Douglas Shearer; camera, Alfred Gilks, Lester White; editor, Robert Kern.

Lew Ayres (Dr. James Kildare); Lionel Barrymore (Dr. Leonard Gillespie); Laraine Day (Mary Lamont); Lana Turner (Rosalie); Samuel S. Hinds (Dr. Stephen Kildare); Lynne Carver (Alice Raymond); Nat Pendleton (Wayman); Emma Dunn (Mrs. Martha Kildare); Walter Kingsford (Dr. Walter Carew); Harlan Briggs (John Galt); Henry Hunter (Harry Galt); Marie Blake (Sally); Phillip Terry (Bates); Roger Converse (Joiner); Donald Barry (Collins); Bobs Watson (Tommy Benson); Margaret Bert (Mrs. Benson); Alma Kruger (Molly Byrd); George Offerman, Jr. (Nick); Reed Hadley (Tom Crandall); Aileen Pringle (Mrs. Thatcher); Dorothy Adams (Mother); Anne Todd (Jenny); Elspeth Dudgeon (Old Lady in Hall); Horace McMahon (Fog Horn).

THESE GLAMOUR GIRLS *(MGM, 1939)* 78 min.

Producer, Sam Zimbalist; director, S. Sylvan Simon; story, Jane Hall; screenplay, Hall, Marion Parsonnet; art directors, Cedric Gibbons, Harry McAfee; set decorator, Edwin B. Willis; wardrobe, Dolly Tree; music, Edward Ward, David Snell; vocal/orchestral arranger, Wally Heglin; song, Ward, Bob Wright, Chet Forrest; sound, Douglas Shearer; camera, Alfred Gilks; editor, Harold F. Kress.

Lew Ayres (Philip S. Griswold); Lana Turner (Jane Thomas); Tom Brown (Homer Ten Eyck); Richard Carlson (Joe); Jane Bryan (Carol Christy); Anita Louise (Daphne Graves); Marsha Hunt (Betty Ainsbrudge); Ann Rutherford (Mary Rose Wilston); Mary Beth Hughes (Ann); Owen Davis, Jr. (Greg Smith); Sumner Getchell (Blimpy); Peter Hayes (Skel); Don Castle (Jack); Tom Collins (Tommy Torgler); Ernest Truex (Grad); Nella Walker

(Mrs. Graves); Henry Kolker (Mr. Griswold); Dennie Moore (Mavis).

DANCING CO-ED *(MGM, 1939)* 84 min.

Producer, Edgar Selwyn; director, S. Sylvan Simon; story, Albert Treynor; screenplay, Albert Manheimer; song, Ernest Lecuona, Carmen Lombardo, Charles O'Flynn; choreography, George King; music, Edward Ward, David Snell; art directors, Cedric Gibbons, Harry McAfee; set decorator, Edwin B. Willis; wardrobe, Dolly Tree; sound, Douglas Shearer; camera, Alfred Gilks; editor, W. Donn Hayes.

Lana Turner (Patty Morgan); Richard Carlson (Pug Braddock); Artie Shaw (Himself); Ann Rutherford (Eve); Lee Bowman (Freddie Tobin); Leon Errol (Pop Sam Morgan); Roscoe Karns (Joe Drews); Monty Woolley (Professor Lange); Thurston Hall (H. W. Workman); Walter Kingsford (President Cavendish); Mary Field (Miss May); Chester Clute (Braddock); Edythe Elliott (Housemother); Benny Baker (Evans); Bert Moorhouse, Lee Phelps (Stooges); Mary Beth Hughes (Toddy); Johnny Day (Assistant Stage Director); June Preisser (Ticky James); Wayne "Tiny" Whitt (Fat Student); Hal Le Seuer (Steve); Maxine Marx (Girl); Laura Treadwell (Dean of Women); Veronica Lake, Dick Winslow (Couple on Motorcycle); Robert Walker (Boy); Edward Arnold, Jr. (Student).

British release title: *Every Other Inch a Lady.*

TWO GIRLS ON BROADWAY *(MGM, 1940)* 73 min.

Producer, Jack Cummings; director, S. Sylvan Simon; story, Edmund Goulding; screenplay, Joseph Fields, Jerome Chodorov; art directors, Cedric Gibbons, Stan Rogers; set decorator, Edwin B. Willis; music presentation, Merrill Pye; music director, Georgie Stoll; music arranger, Walter Ruick; orchestrators, Leo Arnaud, George Bassman; choreography, Bobby Connolly, Eddie Larkin; songs, Nacio Herb Brown, Arthur Freed, and Roger Edens; Harry Revel and Ted Fetter; wardrobe, Dolly Tree; sound, Douglas Shearer; camera, George Folsey; editor, Blanche Sewell.

Lana Turner (Pat Mahoney); Joan Blondell (Molly Mahoney); George Murphy (Eddie Kerns); Kent Taylor ("Chat" Chatsworth); Richard Lane (Buddy Bartell); Wallace Ford (Jed Marlowe); Otto Hahn (Ito); Chester Clute (Salesman); Lloyd Corrigan (Judge); Don Wilson (Announcer); George Meader (McChesney); May McAvoy (Secretary); Charles Wagenheim, Cyril Ring (Assistants); Hillary Brooke, Carole Wayne (Girls); Harry Lash, J. Anthony Hughes, Lester Dorr, Arthur O'Connell (Reporters); Dick Elliott (Watchman); Jimmy Conlin (Poem Vendor); Lee Murray (Newsboy); Jessie Arnold (Another Secretary).

British relase title: *Choose Your Partner.*

WE WHO ARE YOUNG *(MGM, 1940)* 80 min.

Producer, Seymour Nebenzahl; director, Harold S. Bucquet; story/screenplay, Dalton Trumbo; art directors, Cedric Gibbons, Wade B. Rubottom; set decorator, Edwin B. Willis; music, Bronislau Kaper; wardrobe, Dolly Tree; sound, Douglas Shearer; camera, Karl Freund; editor, Howard O'Neill.

Lana Turner (Margy Brooks); John Shelton (William Brooks); Gene Lockhart (C. B. Beamis); Jonathan Hale (William Braddock); Grant Mitchell (Jones); Henry Armetta (Tony); Irene Seidner (Mrs. Weinstock); Clarence Wilson (R. Glassford); Charles Lane (Perkins); Hal K. Dawson (Salesman); Richard Crane (Bellboy); John Butler (Peabody); Horace McMahon (Foreman); Ian Wolfe (Judge); Dorothy Adams (Nurse); Don Castle, Jack Rice (Clerks); Harry Hayden (Examiner); Bill Lally, Edgar Dearing, Ralph Dunn (Policemen); Hal Price (Bartender).

ZIEGFELD GIRL *(MGM, 1941)* 131 min.*

Producer, Pandro S. Berman; director, Robert Z. Leonard; story, William Anthony McGuire; screenplay, Marguerite Roberts, Sonya Levien; music, Herbert Stothart; music director, Georgie Stoll; vocal arrangers/orchestrators, Leo Arnaud, George Bassman, Conrad Salinger; musical presentation, Merrill Pye; music number staged by Busby Berkeley; songs, Roger Edens; Joseph McCarthy and Harry Carroll; Ralph Freed and Edens; Gus Kahn and Nacio Herb Brown; John Schonberger, Richard Coburn, and Vincent Rose; Edward Gallagher and Al Shean; Walter Donaldson; Harold Adamson and Donaldson; Antonio and Rosario; art directors, Cedric Gibbons, Daniel B. Cathcart; set decorator, Edwin B. Willis; gowns/costumes, Adrian; makeup, Jack Dawn; sound, Douglas Shearer; camera, Ray June; editor, Blanche Sewell.

James Stewart (Gilbert Young); Judy Garland (Susan Gallagher); Hedy Lamarr (Sandra Kolter); Lana Turner (Sheila Regan); Tony Martin (Frank Merton); Jackie Cooper (Jerry Regan); Ian Hunter (Geoffrey Collis); Charles Winninger (Pop Gallagher); Edward Everett Horton (Noble Sage); Paul Kelly (John Slayton); Eve Arden (Patsy Dixon); Dan Dailey (Jimmy Walters); Al Shean (Himself); Fay Holden (Mrs. Regan); Felix Bressart (Mischa); Rose Hobart (Mrs. Merton); Bernard Nedell (Nick Capalini); Ed McNamara (Mr. Regan); Mae Busch (Jenny); Josephine Whittell (Perkins); Rene Riano (Annie); Six Hits and a Miss (Singers); Elliott Sullivan, James Flavin (Truckers); Joyce Compton (Miss Sawyer); Ruth Tobey (Betty Regan); Bess Flowers (Palm Beach Casino Patron); Jean Wallace, Myrna Dell, Georgia Carroll, Louise La Planche, Virginia Cruzon, Alaine Brandes, Patricia Dane, Irma Wilson, Leslie Brooks, Madeline Martin, Vivien Mason, Harriet Bennett, Nina Bissell, Frances Gladwin (Ziegfeld Girls); Antonio and Rosario (Specialty Dancers).

*In Sepia.

DR. JEKYLL AND MR. HYDE *(MGM, 1941)* 127 min.

Producer/director, Victor Fleming; based on the novel by Robert Louis Stevenson; screenplay, John Lee Mahin; music, Franz Waxman; choreography, Ernst Matray; art directors, Cedric Gibbons, Daniel B. Cathcart; set decorator, Edwin B. Willis; gowns, Adrian; men's wardrobe, Gile Steele; sound, Douglas Shearer; special effects, Warren Newcombe; montage, Peter Ballbusch; camera, Joseph Ruttenberg; editor, Harold Kress.

Spencer Tracy (Dr. Harry Jekyll/Mr. Hyde); Ingrid Bergman (Ivy Peterson); Lana Turner (Beatrix Emery); Donald Crisp (Sir Charles Emery); Ian Hunter (Dr. John Lanyon); Barton MacLane (Sam Higgins); C. Aubrey Smith (The

Bishop); Peter Godfrey (Poole); Sara Allgood (Mrs. Higgins); Frederic Worlock (Dr. Heath); William Tannen (Intern Fenwick); Frances Robinson (Marcia); Denis Green (Freddie); Billy Bevan (Mr. Weller); Forrester Harvey (Old Prouty); Lumsden Hare (Colonel Weymouth); Lawrence Grant (Dr. Courtland); John Barclay (Constable); Doris Lloyd (Mrs. Marley); Gwen Gaze (Mrs. French); Hillary Brooke (Mrs. Arnold); Mary Field (Wife).

HONKY TONK (MGM, 1941) 105 min.

Producer, Pandro S. Berman; director, Jack Conway; screenplay, Marguerite Roberts, John Sanford; music, Franz Waxman; art directors, Cedric Gibbons, Eddie Imazu; set decorator, Edwin B. Willis; gowns, Kalloch; men's costumes, Gile Steele; sound, Douglas Shearer; camera, Harold Rosson; editor, Blanche Sewell.

Clark Gable (Candy Johnson); Lana Turner (Elizabeth Cotton); Frank Morgan (Judge Cotton); Claire Trevor (Gold Dust Nelson); Marjorie Main (Reverend Mrs. Varner); Albert Dekker (Brazos Hearn); Chill Wills (The Sniper); Henry O'Neill (Daniel Wells); John Maxwell (Kendall); Morgan Wallace (Adams); Douglas Wood (Governor Wilson); Betty Blythe (Mrs. Wilson); Hooper Atchley (Senator Ford); Harry Worth (Harry Gates); Veda Ann Borg (Pearl); Dorothy Granger (Saloon Girl); Sheila Darcy (Louise); Cy Kendall (Man with Tar); Erville Alderson (Man with Rail); John Farrell (Man with Feathers); Don Barclay (Man with Gun); Ray Teal (Poker Player); Esther Muir (Blonde on Train); Francis X. Bushman, Jr., Art Miles (Dealers); Demetrius Alexis (Tug); Anne O'Neal (Nurse); Russell Hicks (Dr. Otis); Henry Roquemore (Butcher); John Carr (Brazos' Henchman); Art Belasco, Frank Mills, Ralph Peters, Eddie Gribbon, Syd Saylor, Harry Semels (Pallbearers); Fay Holderness (Bricklayer); Eddy Waller (Train Conductor); Will Wright, Alan Bridge, Lee Phelps (Men in Meeting House); Heinie Conklin (Dental Patient).

JOHNNY EAGER (MGM, 1942) 107 min.

Producer, John W. Considine, Jr.; director, Mervyn LeRoy; story, James Edward Grant; screenplay, John Lee Mahin, Grant; art directors, Cedric Gibbons, Stan Rogers; set decorator, Edwin B. Willis; music, Bronislau Kaper; gowns, Kalloch; sound, Douglas Shearer; camera, Harold Rosson; editor, Albert Akst.

Robert Taylor (Johnny Eager); Lana Turner (Lisbeth Bard); Edward Arnold (John Benson Farrell); Van Heflin (Jeff Hartnett); Robert Sterling (Jimmy Courtney); Patricia Dane (Garnet); Glenda Farrell (Mae Blythe); Barry Nelson (Lew Rankin); Henry O'Neill (A. J. Verne); Charles Dingle (A. Frazier Marco); Cy Kendall (Bill Halligan); Don Costello (Billiken); Paul Stewart (Julio); Diana Lewis (Judy Sanford); Lou Lubin (Benjy); Connie Gilchrist (Peg Fowler); Robin Raymond (Matilda Fowler); Cliff Danielson (Floyd Markham); Joseph Downing (Ryan); Byron Shoras (Officer Joe Agridowski); Nestor Paiva (Tony); Douglass Newland (Cop); Edward Earle, Alonzo Pirce (Men); Charles Thomas (Bus Conductor); Emory Parnell (Traffic Cop); Joyce Bryant (Woman); Elliott Sullivan (Ed).

SOMEWHERE I'LL FIND YOU (MGM, 1942) 108 min.

Producer, Pandro S. Berman; director, Wesley Ruggles; story, Charles Hoffman; adaptor, Walter Reisch; screenplay, Marguerite Roberts; music, Bronislau Kaper; art directors, Cedric Gibbons, Malcolm Brown; set decorators, Edwin B. Willis, Hugh Hunt; gowns, Kalloch; sound, Douglas Shearer; camera, Harold Rosson; editor, Frank E. Hull.

Clark Gable (Jonathan Davis); Lana Turner (Paula Lane); Robert Sterling (Kirk Davis); Reginald Owen (Willie Manning); Lee Patrick (Eve Manning); Charles Dingle (George L. Stafford); Tamara Shayne (Mama Lugovska); Leonid Kinskey (Dorloff); Molly Lamont (Nurse Winifred); Patricia Dane (Crystal McReagan); Sara Haden (Miss Coulter); Richard Kean (Professor Anatole); Francis Sayles (Pearcley); Tom O'Grady (Bartender); Donald Kerr (Waiter); Gayne Whitman (Penny's Companion); Grady Sutton (Young Man); Dorothy Morris (Girl); Keye Luke (Thomas Chang); Miles Mander (Floyd Kirsten); Eleanor Soohoo (Ming); Allen Jung (Sam Porto); Douglas Fowley (Captain); Benny Inocencio (Felipe Morel); Van Johnson (Lieutenant Halls); Angel Cruz (Manuel Ortega); Keenan Wynn (Sergeant Purdy); Frank Faylen (Slim); J. Lewis Smith (Pete Brady); Lee Tung-Foo (Chinese Doctor); Diana Lewis (Penny); Rags Ragland (Charlie).

SLIGHTLY DANGEROUS (MGM, 1943) 94 min.

Producer, Pandro S. Berman; director, Wesley Ruggles; story, Ian McLellan Hunter, Aileen Hamilton; screenplay, Charles Lederer, George Oppenheimer; (uncredited) gag consultant, Buster Keaton; art directors, Cedric Gibbons, Malcolm Brown; set decorators, Edwin B. Willis, Mildred Griffiths; costumes, Irene; music, Bronislau Kaper; sound, Douglas Shearer; camera, Harold Rosson; editor, Frank E. Hull.

Lana Turner (Peggy Evans |Carol Burden| |narrator|); Robert Young (Bob Stuart); Walter Brennan (Cornelius Burden); Dame May Whitty (Baba); Eugene Pallette (Durstin); Howard Freeman (Mr. Quill); Ward Bond (Jimmy); Ray Collins (Snodgrass); Pamela Blake (Mitzi, the Soda Jerk); Florence Bates (Amanda); Millard Mitchell (Baldwin, Durstin's Assistant); Alan Mowbray (English Gentlemen); Paul Stanton (Stanhope, Burden's Lawyer); James Ford (Reggie, Amanda's Escort); Cliff Clark (Detective); Mimi Doyle (Miss Kingsway, Durstin's Secretary); Spencer Charters (Claudius, Owner of Swade Cafe); Robin Raymond (Girl); Pat West (Man Getting on Bus); Frances Rafferty, Kay Medford (Pretty Girls Getting Off Bus); Ann Doran (Salesgirl, Jumbo Split Scene); Almira Sessions (Landlady); Edward Earle (Employee); Eddie Acuff, Murray Alper (Sailors); Bobby Blake (Boy on Porch).

THE YOUNGEST PROFESSION (MGM, 1943) 82 min.

Producer, B. F. Ziedman; director, Edward Buzzell; based on the book by Lillian Day; screenplay, George Oppenheimer, Charles Lederer, Leonard Spigelgass; costumes, Irene, Howard Shoup; art directors, Cedric Gibbons, Edward Carfagno; set decorators, Edwin B. Willis, Helen Conway; music, David Snell; assistant director, Julian Silberstein; sound, Willhelm W. Brockway; camera, Charles Lawton; editor, Ralph Winters.

Virginia Weidler (Jean Lyons); Edward Arnold (Burton V. Lyons); John Carroll (Dr. Hercules); Jean Porter (Patricia Drew); Marta Linden (Mrs. Edith Lyons); Dick Simmons (Douglas Sutton); Ann Ayars (Susan Thayer); Agnes Moorehead (Miss Featherstone); Marcia Mae Jones (Vera Bailey); Raymond Roe (Schuyler); Scotty Beckett (Junior Lyons); Jessie Grayson (Lilybud); Greer Garson, Walter Pidgeon, William Powell, Robert Taylor, Lana Turner (Guest Stars); Beverly Tyler (Thyra Winters); Patricia Roe (Polly); Marjorie Gateson (Mrs. Drew); Thurston Hall (Mr. Drew); Aileen Pringle (Miss Farwood); Nora Lane (Hilda); Dorothy Christy (Sally); Mary Vallee (Mary); Gloria Tucker (Gladys); Jane Isbell (Jane); Hazel Dawn (Hazel); Beverly Boyd (Beverly); Randa Allen (Randa); Ann MacLean (Ann); Gloria Mackey (Gloria); Bobby Stebbins (Richard); Shirley Coates, Mary McCarty (Girls); Ann Codee (Sandra's Maid); Edward Buzzell (Man in Theatre); Sara Haden (Salvation Army Lass); Dorothy Morris (Secretary); Ray Teal (Taxi Driver).

DU BARRY WAS A LADY *(MGM, 1943)* C-101 min.

Producer, Arthur Freed; director, Roy Del Ruth; based on the play by B. G. De Sylva and Herbert Fields; screenplay, Irving Brecher; songs, Cole Porter; Lew Brown, Ralph Freed, and Roger Edens; Freed, Brown, and Burton Lane; Freed and Lane; E. Y. Harburg, Freed, and Lane; Edens; music adaptor, Edens; choreography, Charles Walters; art director, Cedric Gibbons; costumes, Irene, Howard Shoup, Gile Steele; camera, Karl Freund; editor, Blanche Sewell.

Lucille Ball (May Daly/Mme. Du Barry); Red Skelton (Louie Blore/King Louis); Gene Kelly (Alec Howe/Black Arrow); Douglass Dumbrille (Willie/Duc De Rigor); Rags Ragland (Charlie/Dauphin); Donald Meek (Mr. Jones/Duc De Choiseul); George Givot (Cheezy/De Roquefort); Zero Mostel (Rami, the Swami/Cagliostro); Tommy Dorsey & His Band (Themselves); Virginia O'Brien (Ginny); Louise Beavers (Niagara); Charles Coleman (Doorman); Dick Haymes (Dorsey Singer); Cecil Cunningham, Harry Hayden (Couple); Clara Blandick (Old Lady); Marie Blake (Woman); Andrew Tombes (Escort); Don Wilson (Announcer's Voice); Dick Alexander, Art Miles, Paul "Tiny" Newlan (Men); Chester Clute (Doctor); Kay Williams, Kay Aldridge, Hazel Brooks (Girls); Lana Turner (Guest Star); Jo Stafford (Singer).

MARRIAGE IS A PRIVATE AFFAIR *(MGM, 1944)* 116 min.

Producer, Pandro S. Berman; director, Robert Z. Leonard; based on the novel by Judith Kelly; screenplay, David Hertz, Lenore Coffee; art directors, Cedric Gibbons, Hubert B. Hobson; set decorators, Edwin B. Willis, Richard Pefferle; costume supervisor, Irene; assistant director, William Lewis; music, Bronislau Kaper; sound, William Brockway; camera, Ray June; editor, George White.

Lana Turner (Theo Scofield West); James Craig (Captain Miles Lancing); John Hodiak (Lieutenant Tom West); Frances Gifford (Sissy Mortimer); Hugh Marlowe (Joseph I. Murdock); Natalie Schafer (Mrs. Selworth); Herbert Rudley (Ted Mortimer); Paul Cavanagh (Mr. Selworth); Morris Ankrum (Ed Scofield); Jane Green (Martha); John Warburton (Chris); Byron Foulger (Ned Bolton); Tom Drake (Bill Rice); Shirley Patterson (Mary Saunders); Reverend Neal Dodd (Minister); Nana Bryant (Nurse); Alexander D'Arcy (Senora Guizman); Virginia Brissac (Mrs. Courtland West); Addison Richards (Colonel Ryder); Keenan Wynn (Major Bob Wilton); Eve Whitney (Maid of Honor); Hazel Brooks, Ann Lundeen, Linda Deane, Lynn Arlen, Beryl McCutcheon, Elizabeth Daily (Bridesmaids); Sam McDaniel (Black Porter); Bruce Kellogg (Young Lieutenant); George Meeker (Josie); Douglas Morrow (Lieutenant Colonel); Ann Codee (Saleswoman); Eula Guy (Maid); Charles Coleman (Butler); Arthur Space (Drunk).

KEEP YOUR POWDER DRY *(MGM, 1945)* 93 min.

Producer, George Haight; director, Edward Buzzell; screenplay, Mary C. McCall, Jr., George Bruce; art directors, Cedric Gibbons, Leonid Vasian; set decorators, Edwin B. Willis, Ralph S. Hurst; technical advisor, First Lieutenant Louise V. White; costumes, Irene, Marion Keyes; assistant director, Horace Hough; music, David Snell; sound, Richard Stevens; camera, Ray June; editor, Frank E. Hull.

Lana Turner (Valerie Parks); Laraine Day (Leigh Rand); Susan Peters (Ann Darrison); Agnes Moorehead (Lieutenant Colonel Spottiswood); Bill Johnson (Captain Bill Barclay); Natalie Schafer (Harriett Corwin); Lee Patrick (Gladys Hopkins); Marta Linden (Captain Sanders); June Lockhart (Sarah Swanson); Edith Leach (Mary Carter); Jess Barker (Junior Vanderheusen); Michael Kirby (Captain John Darrison); Henry O'Neill (Brigadier General Rand); Tim Murdock (Captain Mannering); Sondra Rodgers (WAC Hodgekins); Marjorie Davies (WAC Polhemus); Rex Evans (Marco Cummings); Pierre Watkin (Mr. Lorrison); Shirley Patterson (WAC Brooks); Barbara Sears (WAC McBride); George Peters (Lieutenant); Marie Blake, Claire Rochelle (WAC Corporals); Elizabeth Russell (WAC Sergeant); Dorothy Ackers, Claire Whitney (Fitters); Ruth Lee (Instructor); Ray Teal (Army Captain); Early Cantrell (WAC Company commander); Charlotte Hunter, Margaret Kays, Jetsy Parker, Jane Ray, Beth Renner, Melba Snowden, Bobbie Woods, Judi Blacque, Marilyn Christine, Rita Dunn, Jeanne Frances, Jean French (WACS).

WEEK-END AT THE WALDORF *(MGM, 1945)* 130 min.

Producer, Arthur Hornblow, Jr.; director, Robert Z. Leonard; suggested by the play *Grand Hotel* by Vicki Baum; adaptor, Guy Bolton; screenplay, Sam and Bella Spewack; art directors, Cedric Gibbons, Daniel B. Cathcart; set decorators, Edwin B. Willis, Jack Bonar; choreography, Charles Walters; music/music director, Johnny Green; orchestrator, Ted Duncan; vocal arranger, Kay Thompson; songs, Sammy Fain, Ted Koehler, and Pepe Guizar; costume supervisor, Irene; assistant director, William Lewis; sound, Douglas Shearer; special effects, Warren Newcombe; camera, Robert Planck; editor, Robert J. Mern.

Ginger Rogers (Irene Malvern); Walter Pidgeon (Chip Collyer); Van Johnson (Captain James Hollis); Lana

Turner (Bunny Smith); Robert Benchley (Randy Morton); Edward Arnold (Martin X. Edley); Leon Ames (Henry Burton); Warner Anderson (Dr. Campbell); Phyllis Thaxter (Cynthia Drew); Keenan Wynn (Oliver Webson); Porter Hall (Stevens); Samuel S. Hinds (Mr. Jessup); George Zucco (Bey of Aribajan); Xavier Cugat & His Orchestra (Themselves); Lina Romay (Juanita); Bob Graham (Singer); Michael Kirby (Lieutenant John Rand); Cora Sue Collins (Jane Rand); Rosemary DeCamp (Anna); Jacqueline DeWitt (Kate Douglas); Frank Puglia (Emile); Charles Wilson (Hi Johns); Irving Bacon (Sam Skelly); Miles Mander (British Secretary); Nana Bryant (Mrs. H. Davenport Drew); Russell Hicks (McPherson); Ludmilla Pitoeff (Irma); Naomi Childers (Night Maid); Moroni Olsen (House Detective Blake); William Halligan (Chief Jennings); John Wengraf (Alix); Ruth Lee (The Woman); William Hall (Cassidy, the Doorman); Jack Luden, Mel Shubert (Clerks); Ruth Warren, Jean Carpenter (Telephone Operators); Bryon Foulger (Barber); Harry Barris (Anna's Boyfriend); Dorothy Christy (Cashier); Bess Flowers, Ella Ethridge, Franklyn Farnum (Guests).

THE POSTMAN ALWAYS RINGS TWICE *(MGM, 1946)* 113 min.

Producer, Carey Wilson; director, Tay Garnett; based on the novel by James M. Cain; screenplay, Harry Ruskin, Niven Busch; art directors, Cedric Gibbons, Randall Duell; set decorator, Edwin B. Willis; costume supervisor, Irene; music, George Bassman; orchestrator, Ted Duncan; assistant director, Bill Lewis; sound, Douglas Shearer; camera, Sidney Wagner; editor, George White.

Lana Turner (Cora Smith); John Garfield (Frank Chambers); Cecil Kellaway (Nick Smith); Hume Cronyn (Arthur Keats); Leon Ames (District Attorney Kyle Sackett); Audrey Totter (Madge Gorland); Alan Reed (Ezra Liam Kennedy); Jeff York (Blair); Charles Williams (Doctor); Cameron Grant (Willie); Wally Cassell (Ben); Morris Ankrum, William Halligan (Judges); Garry Owen (Truck Driver); Edgar Sherrod (Man); Edward Earle (Doctor); Byron Foulger (Picnic Manager); Sondra Morgan (Matron); Philip Ahlm, John Allan, Harold Miller, Reginald Simpson (Photographers); Paula Ray (Woman); Tom Dillon (Father McConnell); James Farley (Warden); Joel Friedkin (John X. McHugh).

GREEN DOLPHIN STREET *(MGM, 1947)* 141 min.

Producer, Carey Wilson; director, Victor Saville; based on the novel by Elizabeth Goudge; screenplay, Samson Raphaelson; art directors, Cedric Gibbons, Malcolm Brown; set decorator, Edwin B. Willis; costume supervisor, Irene; music, Bronislau Kaper; assistant director, Norman Elzer; sound, Standish J. Lambert, Michael Steinore; special effects, Warren Newcombe, A. Arnold Gillespie; camera, George Folsey; editor, George White.

Lana Turner (Marianne Patourel); Van Heflin (Timothy Haslam); Donna Reed (Marguerite Patourel); Richard Hart (William Ozanne); Frank Morgan (Dr. Edmund Ozanne); Edmund Gwenn (Octavius Patourel); Dame May Whitty (Mother Superior); Reginald Owen (Captain O'Hara); Gladys Cooper (Sophie Patourel); Moyna MacGill

(Mrs. Metivier); Linda Christian (Hin-Moa); Bernie Gozier (Jacky-Pato); Pat Aherne (Kapua-Manga); Al Kikume (Native); Edith Leslie (Sister Angelique); Gigi Perreau (Veronica at Age Four); Douglas Walton (Sir Charles Maloney); Leslie Dennison (Captain Hartley); Lumsden Hare (Anderson); William Fawcett (Nat); Wyndham Standing (Government General); Lucille Curtis (Mrs. Samuel Kelly); Carol Nugent (Veronica at Age Seven); James Leong (Chinese Longshoreman); Guy Kingsford (Young Fisherman); Ramsey Ames (Corinne); Tetsu Komai (Chinaman); Patricia Emery (Niece).

CASS TIMBERLANE *(MGM, 1947)* 119 min.

Producer, Arthur Hornblow, Jr.; director, George Sidney; based on the novel by Sinclair Lewis; screenplay, Donald Ogden Stewart; adaptors, Stewart, Sonya Levien; costumes, Irene; art directors, Cedric Gibbons, Daniel Cathcart; set decorators, Edwin B. Willis, Richard Pefferle; music, Roy Webb; music director, Constantin Bakaleinikoff; assistant director, George Ryan; sound, Douglas Shearer, Frank B. MacKenzie; special effects, Warren Newcombe, A. Arnold Gillespie; camera, Robert Planck; editor, John Dunning.

Spencer Tracy (Cass Timberlane); Lana Turner (Virginia Marshland); Zachary Scott (Brad Criley); Tom Drake (Jamie Wargate); Mary Astor (Queenie Havock); Albert Dekker (Boone Havock); Margaret Lindsay (Chris Grau); John Litel (Webb Wargate); Mona Barrie (Avis Elderman); Josephine Hutchinson (Lillian Drover); Selena Royle (Louise Wargate); Richard Gaines (Dennis Thane); John Alexander (Dr. Roy Drover); Cameron Mitchell (Eino Roskinen); Howard Freeman (Hervey Plint); Jessie Grayson (Mrs. Higbie); Griff Barnett (Herman); Guy Beach (George Hame); Cliff Clark (Humber Bellile); Milburn Stone (Nestor Purdwin); Almira Sessions (Zilda Hatter); Tim Ryan (Charlie Ellis); Bess Flowers (Mary Ann Milligan); Lester Dorr (Salesman); Roy Gordon (Critic); Mitchell Kowall (Doorman); Arno Frey (Waiter); Manuel Paris, Albert Pollet (Frenchmen at Party); Buz Buckley (Newsboy); Ed Oliver (Pianist); Emmett Vogan (Beehouse); Walter Pidgeon (Man at Cocktail Party).

HOMECOMING *(MGM, 1948)* 113 min.

Producer, Sidney Franklin; associate producer, Gottfried Reinhardt; director, Mervyn LeRoy; story, Sidney Kingsley; adaptor, Jan Lustig; screenplay, Paul Osborn; art directors, Cedric Gibbons, Randall Duell; set decorators, Edwin B. Willis, Henry W. Grace; music, Bronislau Kaper; music director, Charles Previn; assistant director, Norman Elzer; makeup, Jack Dawn; costumes, Helen Rose; technical advisor, Paul Lund; sound, Douglas Shearer, Norwood A. Fenton; special effects, Warren Newcombe, A. Arnold Gillespie; camera, Harold Rosson; editor, John Dunning.

Clark Gable (Ulysses Delby Johnson); Lana Turner (Lieutenant Jane "Snapshot" McCall); Anne Baxter (Penny Johnson); John Hodiak (Dr. Robert Sunday); Ray Collins (Lieutenant Colonel Avery Silver); Gladys Cooper (Mrs. Kirby); Cameron Mitchell (Monkevickz); Art Baker (Williams); Lurene Tuttle (Miss Stoker); Jessie Grayson (Sarah); J. Louis Johnson (Sol); Bill Self (Junior Lieutenant); Jeff Corey (Cigarette Smoker); Thomas E. Breen

(Young Man); Wheaton Chambers (Doctor); Phil Dunham (Elevator Operator); Frank Mayo, Roger Moore, Dan Quigg, Broderick O'Farrell, George Sherwood, Charles Miller, Nolan Leary (Doctors); Joseph Crehan (Colonel Morgan C.O.); Bert Moorhouse, David Newell (Surgeons); Anne Nagel, William Forrest, Dorothy Christy (Guests); Danielle Day (Young French Girl); Geraldine Wall (Head Nurse); Olga Borget (Newswoman); Edwin Cooper (Head Surgeon); William Tannen (Attendant); Leo Vandervelde (Page Boy); Ralph Montgomery, Robert Skelton (GIs); Arthur O'Connell (Driver); Alan Hale, Jr. (M.P.); Marshall Thompson (Sergeant McKeen).

THE THREE MUSKETEERS *(MGM, 1948)* C-126 min.

Producer, Pandro S. Berman; director, George Sidney; based on the novel by Alexandre Dumas; screenplay, Robert Ardrey; Technicolor consultants, Natalie Kalmus, Henri Jaffa; art directors, Cedric Gibbons, Malcolm Brown; set decorators, Edwin B. Willis, Henry W. Grace; music Herbert Stothart; orchestrator, Albert Sendrey; music director, Charles Previn; assistant director, George Rhein; makeup, Jack Dawn; costumes, Walter Plunkett; sound, Douglas Shearer, Conrad Kahn; special effects, Warren Newcombe; montage, Peter Ballbusch; camera, Robert Planck; editors, Robert J. Kern, George Boemler.

Lana Turner (Milady Countess Charlotte de Winter); Gene Kelly (D'Artagnan); June Allyson (Constance Bonacieux); Van Heflin (Robert Athos); Angela Lansbury (Queen Anne); Frank Morgan (King Louis XIII); Vincent Price (Richelieu, the Prime Minister); Keenan Wynn (Planchet); John Sutton (George, Duke of Buckingham); Gig Young (Porthos); Robert Coote (Aramis); Reginald Owen (de Treville); Ian Keith (de Rochefort); Patricia Medina (Kitty); Richard Stapley (Albert); Byron Foulger (Bonacieux); Sol Gross (Jussac); Robert Warwick (D'Artagnan, Sr.); Marie Windsor (Dark-eyed Lady-in-Waiting); Ruth Robinson (Mother of D'Artagnan); Tom Tyler (Traveler); Fred Coby, Leonard Penn (Musketeers); Kirk Alyn, John Holland (Friends of Aramis); Francis McDonald (Fisherman); Reginald Sheffield (Subaltern); Wilson Benge, Alec Harford (Valets); Harry Wilson (Kidnapper); Dave Sharpe (Double for Gene Kelly); Mickey Simpson (Executioner); Frank Hagney (Executioner of Lyons).

A LIFE OF HER OWN *(MGM, 1950)* 108 min.

Producer, Voldemar Vetluguin; director, George Cukor; screenplay, Isobel Lennart; art directors, Cedric Gibbons, Arthur Lonergan; set decorators, Edwin B. Willis, Henry W. Grace; gowns, Helen Rose; makeup, William Tuttle; music, Bronislau Kaper; music director, Johnny Green; sound, Douglas Shearer; camera, George Folsey; editor, George White.

Lana Turner (Lily Brannel James); Ray Milland (Steve Harleigh); Tom Ewell (Tom Caraway); Louis Calhern (Jim Leversoe); Ann Dvorak (Mary Ashlon); Barry Sullivan (Lee Gorrance); Margaret Phillips (Nora Harleigh); Jean Hagen (Maggie Collins); Phyllis Kirk (Jerry); Sara Haden (Smitty); Hermes Pan (Lily's Dance Partner); Carol Brannan (Model); Tom Seidel (Bob Collins); Beth Douglas,

Roberta Johnson, Alice Wallace, Bunny Waters, Pat Davies, Dorothy Abbott, Bridget Carr, Charlene Hardey, Marlene Hoyt (Stock Models); Dorothy Tree (Caraway's Secretary); Maura Murphy (*Vogue* Receptionist); Kathleen Freeman (Peg); Beverly Garland (Girl at Party); Frankie Darro (Bellboy); Paul Kramer (Airport Gateman).

MR. IMPERIUM *(MGM, 1951)* C-87 min.

Producer, Edwin H. Knopf; director, Don Hartman; based on the play by Knopf; screenplay, Knopf, Hartman; music director, Johnny Green; music, Bronislau Kaper; songs, Ray Gilbert and Augustin Lara; Harold Arlen and Dorothy Fields; art directors, Cedric Gibbons, Paul Groesse; set decorators, Edwin B. Willis, Richard Pefferle; color consultants, Henri Jaffa, James Gooch; costumes, Walter Plunkett; makeup, William Tuttle; sound, Douglas Shearer; camera, George J. Folsey; editors, George White, William Gulick.

Lana Turner (Fredda Barlo); Ezio Pinza (Mr. Imperium); Marjorie Main (Mrs. Cabot); Barry Sullivan (Paul Hunter); Sir Cedric Hardwicke (Bernand); Keenan Wynn (Motor Cop); Debbie Reynolds (Gwen); Ann Codee (Anna Pelan); Wilton Graff (Andrew Bolton); Giacomo Spadoni (Giovanni); Chick Chandler (George Hoskins); Joseph Vitale (Bearded Man); Mae Clarke (Secretary); Jimmy Cross (Assistant Director); Don Haggerty (Director); Arthur Walsh, Allan Ray, Wilson Wood, Bobby Troup (Band Specialties); Cliff Clark (Restaurant Proprietor); Matt Moore (Gateman).

British release title: *You Belong to My Heart.*

THE MERRY WIDOW *(MGM, 1952)* C-105 min.

Producer, Joe Pasternak; director, Curtis Bernhardt; based on the operetta by Franz Lehar, Victor Leon, Leo Stein; screenplay, Sonya Levien, William Ludwig; music, Lehar; new lyrics, Paul Francis Webster; music numbers created and staged by Jack Cole; music director, Jay Blackton; art directors, Cedric Gibbons, Paul Groesse; set decorators, Edwin B. Willis, Arthur Krams; costumes, Helen Rose, Gile Steele; makeup, William Tuttle; color consultants, Henri Jaffa, Alvord Eiseman; special effects, A. Arnold Gillespie, Warren Newcombe; camera, Robert Surtees; editor, Conrad A. Nervig.

Lana Turner (Crystal Radek); Fernando Lamas (Count Danilo); Una Merkel (Kitty Riley); Richard Haydn (Baron Popoff); Thomas Gomez (King of Marshovia); John Abbott (Marshovian Ambassador); Marcel Dalio (Police Sergeant); King Donovan (Nitki); Robert Coote (Marquis De Crillon); Sujata (Gypsy Girl); Lisa Ferraday (Marcella); Shepard Menken (Kunjany); Ludwig Stossel (Major Domo).

THE BAD AND THE BEAUTIFUL *(MGM, 1952)* 118 min.

Producer, John Houseman; director, Vincente Minnelli; story, George Bradshaw; screenplay, Charles Schnee; music, David Raksin; assistant director, Jerry Thorpe; art directors, Cedric Gibbons, Edward Carfagno; set decorators, Edwin B. Willis, Keogh Gleason; costumes, Helen Rose; makeup, William Tuttle; sound, Douglas Shearer; special effects, A. Arnold Gillespie, Warren Newcombe; camera, Robert Surtees; editor, Conrad A. Nervig.

Lana Turner (Georgia Lorrison); Kirk Douglas (Jonathan Shields); Walter Pidgeon (Harry Pebbel); Dick Powell (James Lee Bartlow); Barry Sullivan (Fred Amiel); Gloria Grahame (Rosemary Bartlow); Gilbert Roland (Victor "Gaucho" Ribera); Leo G. Carroll (Henry Whitfield); Vanessa Brown (Kay Amiel); Paul Stewart (Syd Murphy); Sammy White (Gus); Elaine Stewart (Lila); Jonathan Cott (Assistant Director); Ivan Triessault (Von Ellstein); Kathleen Freeman (Miss March); Marietta Canty (Ida); Lucille Knoch (Blonde); Steve Forrest (Leading Man); Perry Sheehan (Secretary); Robert Burton (McDill); Francis X. Bushman (Eulogist); Harold Miller (Man); George Lewis (Lionel Donovan); Madge Blake (Mrs. Rosser); William Tannen, Dabbs Greer, Frank Scannell, and Sara Spencer (Reporters); Stanley Andrews (Sheriff); William "Bill" Phillips (Assistant Director); Karen Verne (Rosa); Barbara Thatcher, Sharon Saunders, Erin Selwyn (Girls); Peggy King (Singer); Ben Astor (Joe); Bess Flowers (Joe's Friend at Party); Major Sam Harris (Party Guest); Norma Salina, Janet Comeford, Kathy Qualen (Bobby Soxers); Louis Calhern (Voice on the Recording).

LATIN LOVERS *(MGM, 1953)* C-104 min.

Producer, Joe Pasternak; director, Mervyn LeRoy; screenplay, Isobel Lennart; art directors, Cedric Gibbons, Gabriel Scognamillo; set decorators, Edwin B. Willis, Jacques Mapes; music, Nicholas Brodszky; songs, Brodszky, Leo Robin; music director, George Stoll; choreography, Frank Veloz; orchestrator, Pete Rugolo; assistant director, Arvid Griffen; women's costumes, Helen Rose; men's costumes, Herschel McCoy; makeup, William Tuttle; color consultants, Henri Jaffa, Alvord Eiseman; sound, Douglas Shearer; special effects, A. Arnold Gillespie, Warren Newcombe; camera, Joseph Ruttenberg; editor, John McSweeney, Jr.

Lana Turner (Nora Taylor); Ricardo Montalban (Roberto Santos); John Lund (Paul Chevron); Louis Calhern (Grandfather Santos); Jean Hagen (Anne Kellwood); Eduard Franz (Dr. Lionel Y. Newman); Beulah Bondi (Woman Analyst); Joaquin Garay (Zeca); Archer MacDonald (Howard G. Hubbell); Dorothy Neumann (Mrs. Newman); Robert Burton (Mr. Cumberly); Rita Moreno (Christina); Beatrice Gray (Receptionist); Lois Kimbrell (Secretary); Matt Moore (Man); Gloria Noble, Lynn Sousa, Suzanne Alexander (Brazilian Girls); Tristram Coffin (Paul's Business Associate); Melba Meredith (Mrs. Costa); Paul Maxey (Mr. Costa).

FLAME AND THE FLESH *(MGM, 1954)* C-104 min.

Producer, Joe Pasternak; director, Richard Thorpe; based on the novel by Auguste Bailly; screenplay, Helen Deutsch; color consultant, Joan Bridge; music director, George Stoll; songs, Nicholas Brodsky, Jack Lawrence; art director, Alfred Junge; sound, A. W. Watkins; camera, Christopher Challis; editors, Albert Akst, Ray Poulton.

Lana Turner (Madeline); Pier Angeli (Lisa); Carlos Thompson (Nino); Bonar Colleano (Ciccio); Charles Goldner (Mondari); Peter Illing (Peppe); Rosalie Cautch-ley (Francesca); Marne Maitland (Filiberto); Eric Pohlmann (Marina Proprietor); Catherina Ferraz (Dressmaker); Alexis De Gallier (Playboy).

BETRAYED *(MGM, 1954)* C-111 min.

Producer/director, Gottfried Reinhardt; screenplay, Ronald Millar, George Froeschel; music, Walter Goehr; song, Goehr, Ronald Millar; Miss Turner's costumes, Balmain-Paris; art director, Alfred Junge; sound, A.W. Watkins; camera, Freddie Young; editors, John Dunning, Raymond Poulton.

Clark Gable (Colonel P. Deventer); Lana Turner (Carla Van Owen); Victor Mature ("The Scarf"); Louis Calhern (General Ten Eyck); O. E. Hasse (Colonel Helmuth Dietrich); Wilfrid Hyde-White (General Charles Larraby); Ian Carmichael (Captain Jackie Lawson); Niall MacGinnis (Blackie); Nora Swinburne ("The Scarf's" Mother); Roland Culver (General Warsleigh); Leslie Weston (Pop); Christopher Rhodes (Chris); Lilly Kann (Jan's Grandmother); Brian Smith (Jan); Anton Diffring (Captain Von Stranger).

THE PRODIGAL *(MGM, 1955)* C-117 min.

Producer, Charles Schnee; director, Richard Thorpe; story by Joe Breen, Jr., Samuel James Larson; adapted from the Bible; screenplay, Maurice Zimm; music, Bronislau Kaper; costumes, Herschel McCoy; art directors, Cedric Gibbons, Randall Duell; set decorators, Edwin B. Willis, Henry Grace; makeup, William Tuttle; assistant director, Arvid Griffen; sound, Wesley C. Miller; special effects, A. Arnold Gillespie, Warren Newcombe; camera, Joseph Ruttenberg; editor, Harold F. Kress.

Lana Turner (Samarra); Edmund Purdom (Micah); Louis Calhern (Nahreeb); Audrey Dalton (Ruth); James Mitchell (Asham); Neville Brand (Rhakim); Walter Hampden (Eli); Taina Elg (Elissa); Francis L. Sullivan (Bosra); Joseph Wiseman (Carmish); Sandra Descher (Yasmin); John Dehner (Joram); Cecil Kellaway (Governor); Philip Tonge (Barber/Surgeon); Henry Daniell (Ramadi); Paul Cavanagh (Tobiah); Dayton Lummis (Caleb); Tracey Roberts (Tahra); Jarma Lewis (Uba); Jay Novello (Merchant); Dorothy Adams (Carpenter's Wife); Peter DeBear (Carpenter's Son); Phyllis Graffeo (Miriam); Patricia Iannone (Deborah); Eugene Mazzola (David); George Sawaya (Kavak); Richard Devon (Risafe); Ann Cameron (Lahla); Gloria Dea (Faradine); John Rosser (Lirhan); Charles Wagenheim; (Zubeir); Gordon Richards (Scribe); Paul Bryar (Townsman); Rex Lease (Purveyor); George Lewis (Guard); Almira Sessions (Old Lady); Chuck Roberson (Chieftain); Tom Steele (Slave); Gloria Stone (Mouse); Linda Danson (Owl); Joanne Dale (Bunny); Lucille Maracini (Ram); Lila Zali (Monkey); Diane Gump (Fox); Patricia Jackson (Lion); John Damler (Jailer).

THE SEA CHASE *(Warner Bros., 1955)* C-117 min.

Producer/director, John Farrow; based on the novel by Andrew Geer; screenplay, James Warner Bellah, John Twist; assistant directors, Emmett Emerson, Russell Llewellyn; art director, Franz Bachelin; set decorator, William Wallace; wardrobe, Moss Mabry; makeup, Gordon Bau; music, Roy Webb; orchestrators, Maurice DePackh,

Leonid Raab; sound, Francis J. Scheid; camera, William Clothier; editor, William Ziegler.

John Wayne (Karl Erlich); Lana Turner (Elsa Keller); Lyle Bettger (Kirchner); David Farrar (Commander Napier); Tab Hunter (Cadet Wesser); James Arness (Schlieter); Wilton Graff (Hepke); Dick Davalos (Cadet Walter Stemme); John Qualen (Chief Schmidt); Paul Fix (Max Heinz); Luis Van Rooten (Matz); Peter Whitney (Bachman); Alan Hale, Jr. (Wentz); Lowell Gilmore (Captain Evans); John Doucette (Bo'sun); Alan Lee (Brounck); Claude Akins (Winkler); Adam Williams (Kruger); Gil Perkins (Baldhead); Fred Stromsoe (Mueller); James Lilburn, Tony Travers, John Indrisano, Joey Ray (Sub Lieutenants); Cameron Grant (Kruse); Gavin Muir (Officer-of-the-Watch); Gloria Dea, Josephine Para, Lucita, (Spanish Girls); Isabel Dwan, Theresa Tudor Renata Huy (Frauleins); John Sheffield (Patron in Dining Room).

THE RAINS OF RANCHIPUR *(Twentieth Century-Fox, 1955)* C-104 min.

Producer, Frank Ross; director, Jean Negulesco; based on the novel *The Rains Came* by Louis Bromfield; screenplay, Merle Miller; art directors, Lyle R. Wheeler, Addison Hehr; set decorators, Walter M. Scott, Paul S. Fox; makeup, Ben Nye; assistant director, Eli Dunn; music, Hugo Friedhofer; music director, Lionel Newman; orchestrator, Maurice DePackh; choreography, Stephen Papich; sound, Alfred Bruzlin, Harry M. Leonard; special effects, Ray Kellogg; camera, Milton Krasner; editor, Dorothy Spencer.

Lana Turner (Edwina Esketh); Richard Burton (Dr. Safti); Fred MacMurray (Tom Ransome); Joan Caulfield (Fern Simon); Michael Rennie (Lord Esketh); Eugenie Leontovich (Maharani); Gladys Hurlbut (Mrs. Simon); Madge Kennedy (Mrs. Smiley); Carlo Rizzo (Mr. Adoani); Beatrice Kraft (Oriental Dancer); Paul H. Frees (Sundar); King Calder (Mr. Smiley); Argentina Brunetti (Mrs. Adoani); John Banner (Ranchid); Ivis Goulding (Louise); Ram Singh (Major Domo); Lou Krugman (Courier); Rama Bai (Lachmaania); Naji Gabbay (Wagonlit Porter); Jugat Bhatia (Headhunter); Major Sam Harris (Officer at Party); Ram Chandra (Satter); Trade Wyler (Guest); Elizabeth Prudhomme (Nurse Patel); Phyllis Johannes (Nurse Gupta); George Brand (Mr. Simon).

DIANE *(MGM, 1956)* C-110

Producer, Edwin H. Knopf; director, David Miller; based on the novel *Diane de Poitiers* by John Erskine; screenplay, Christopher Isherwood; art directors, Cedric Gibbons, Hans Peters; set decorators, Edwin B. Willis, Henry Grace; costumes, Walter Plunkett; makeup, William Tuttle; assistant director, Ridgeway Callow; music, Miklos Rozsa; sound, Dr. Wesley C. Miller; special effects, A. Arnold Gillespie, Warren Newcombe; camera, Robert Planck; editor, John McSweeney, Jr.

Lana Turner (Diane de Poitiers); Pedro Armendariz (King Francis I); Roger Moore (Prince Henri); Marisa Pavan (Catherine de Medici); Sir Cedric Hardwicke (Ruggieri); Torin Thatcher (Count de Breze); Taina Elg (Alys); John Lupton (Regnault); Henry Daniell (Gondi); Ronald

Green (The Dauphin); Sean McClory (Count Montgomery); Geoffrey Toone (Duke of Savoy); Michael Ansara (Count Ridolfi); Paul Cavanagh (Lord Bonnivet); Melville Cooper (Court Physician); Christopher Dark (Gian Carlo); Marc Cavell (Piero); Gene Reynolds (Montecuculli); John O'Malley (Marechal de Chabannes); Peter Gray (Sardini); Mickey Maga (Charles); Ian Wolfe (Lord Tremouille); Ronald Anton (Francis); Percy Helton (Court Jester); Jamie Farr (Mute Squire); Charles Keane (Captain); James Drury (Lieutenant); Vesey O'Davoren (Valet); Stuart Whitman (Henri's Squire); Wes Christensen, Glase Lohman (Guards); Milton Parsons, James Logan, James Fairfax (Suitors); Bob Dix (Young Officer).

PEYTON PLACE *(Twentieth Century-Fox, 1957)* C-157 min.

Producer, Jerry Wald; director, Mark Robson; based on the novel by Grace Metalious; screenplay, John Michael Hayes; art directors, Lyle R. Wheeler, Jack Martin Smith; set decorators, Walter M. Scott, Bertram Granger; executive wardrobe designer; Charles LeMaire; costumes, Adele Palmer; makeup, Ben Nye; assistant director, Hal Herman; music, Franz Waxman; orchestrator, Edward B. Powell; sound, E. Clayton Ward, Frank Moran; special camera effects, L. B. Abbott; camera, William Mellor; editor, David Bretherton.

Lana Turner (Constance MacKenzie); Hope Lange (Selena Cross); Lee Philips (Michael Rossi); Lloyd Nolan (Dr. Matthew Swain); Diane Varsi (Allison); Arthur Kennedy (Lucas Cross); Russ Tamblyn (Norman Page); Terry Moore (Betty Anderson); Barry Coe (Rodney Harrington); David Nelson (Ted Carter); Betty Field (Nellie Cross); Mildred Dunnock (Mrs. Thornton); Leon Ames (Harrington); Lorne Greene (Prosecutor); Robert H. Harris (Seth Bushwell); Tami Connor (Margie); Staats Cotsworth (Charles Partridge); Peg Hillias (Marion Partridge); Erin O'Brien-Moore (Mrs. Page); Scotty Morrow (Joey Cross); Bill Lundmark (Paul Cross); Alan Reed, Jr. (Matt); Kip King (Pee Wee); Ray Montgomery (Naval Officer); Jim Brandt (Messenger); John Doucette (Army Sergeant); Harry Carter (Court Clerk).

THE LADY TAKES A FLYER *(Universal, 1958)* C-93 min.

Producer, William Alland; director, Jack Arnold; story, Edmund H. North; screenplay, Danny Arnold; art directors, Alexander Golitzen, Richard H. Riedel; set decorators, Russell A. Gausman, Oliver Emert; technical advisor, Jack Ford; gowns, Bill Thomas; music, Herman Stein; music supervisor, Joseph Gershenson; assistant director, David Silver; sound, Leslie I. Carey, Corson Jowett; special camera, Clifford Stine; camera, Irving Glassberg; edtior, Sherman Todd.

Lana Turner (Maggie Colby); Jeff Chandler (Mike Dandridge); Richard Denning (Al Reynolds); Andra Martin (Nikki Taylor); Chuck Connors (Phil Donahue); Reta Shaw (Nurse Kennedy); Alan Hale, Jr. (Frank Henshaw); Jerry Paris (Willie Ridgley); Dee J. Thompson (Collie Minor); Nestor Paiva (Childreth); James Doherty (Tower Officer).

ANOTHER TIME, ANOTHER PLACE (*Paramount, 1958*) 98 min.

Producer, Joseph Kaufman; associate producer, Smedley Aston; director, Lewis Allen; based on the novel *Weep No More* by Lenore Coffee; screenplay, Stanley Mann; music, Douglas Gamley; music director, Muir Mathieson; song, Jay Livingston, Ray Evans; production designer, Tom Monahan; assistant director, Rene Dupont; wardrobe, Laura Nightingale; sound, Gerry Turner, J. B. Smith; camera, Jack Hildyard; editor. Geoffrey Foot.

Lana Turner (Sara Scott); Barry Sullivan (Carter Reynolds); Glynis John (Kay Trevor); Sean Connery (Mark Trevor); Terrence Longdon (Alan Thompson); Sidney James (Jake Klein); Martin Stephens (Brian Trevor); Doris Hare (Mrs. Bunker); Julian Somers (Hotel Manager); John Le Mesurier (Dr. Aldridge); Cameron Hall (Alfy); Jane Welsh (Jonesy); Robin Bailey (Captain Barnes); Bill Fraser (R. E. Sergeant).

IMITATION OF LIFE (*Universal, 1959*) C-125 min.

Producer, Ross Hunter; director, Douglas Sirk; based on the novel by Fannie Hurst; screenplay, Eleanore Griffin, Allan Scott; art directors, Alexander Golitzen, Richard Riedel; set decorators, Russell A. Gausman, Julia Heron; costumes, Jean Louis, Bill Thomas; makeup, Bud Westmore; assistant director, Frank Shaw, Wilson Shyer; songs, Sammy Fain and Paul Francis Webster; Arnold Hughes and Frederick Herbert; backgound music, Frank Skinner; music supervisor, Joseph Gershenson; sound, Leslie I. Carey, Joe Lapis; Russell Metty; editor, Milton Carruth.

Lana Turner (Lora Meredith); John Gavin (Steve Archer); Sandra Dee (Susie at Age Sixteen); Dan O'Herlihy (David Edwards); Susan Kohner (Sarah Jane at Age Eighteen); Robert Alda (Allen Loomis); Juanita· Moore (Annie Johnson); Terry Burnham (Susie at Age Six); Mahalia Jackson (Herself); Karin Dicker (Sarah Jane at Age Eight); John Vivyan (Young Man); Lee Goodman (Photographer); Ann Robinson (Show Girl); Troy Donahue (Frankie); Sandra Gould (Receptionist); David Tomack (Burly Man); Maida Severn (Teacher); Edwin Parker (Policeman); Forbes Murray, Leota Lorraine, Chuckie Bradley (Bits); George Barrows (Furniture Mover).

PORTRAIT IN BLACK (*Universal, 1960*) C-112 min.

Producer, Ross Hunter; director, Michael Gordon; based on the play by Ivan Goff, Ben Roberts; screenplay, Goff, Roberts; art director, Richard H. Riedel; set decorator, Julia Heron; music, Frank Skinner; music theme, Buddy Pepper, Inez James; music supervisor, Joseph Gershenson; Miss Turner's gowns, Jean Louis; assistant director, Phil Bowles; makeup, Bud Westmore; sound, Waldon O. Watson, Henry Wilkinson; camera, Russell Metty; editor, Milton Carruth.

Lana Turner (Sheila Cabot); Anthony Quinn (Dr. David Rivera); Sandra Dee (Catherine Cabot); John Saxon (Blake Richards); Richard Basehart (Howard Mason); Lloyd Nolan (Matthew Cabot); Ray Walston (Cob O'Brien); Virginia Grey (Miss Lee); Anna May Wong (Tani); Dennis Kohler (Peter Cabot); Paul Birch (Detective); John Wengraf (Dr. Kessler); Richard Norris (Mr. Corbin); James Nolan, Robert Lieb (Detectives); John McNamara

(Minister); Charles Thompson (Sid); George Womack (Foreman); Henry Quan (Headwaiter); Elizabeth Chan (Chinese Dancer); Harold Goodwin, Jack Bryan (Patrolmen).

BY LOVE POSSESSED (*United Artists, 1961*) C-115 min.

Producer, Walter Mirisch; director, John Sturges; based on the novel by James Gould Cozzens; screenplay, John Dennis [Charles Schnee], Isobel Lennart, Bill Roberts, Ketti Frings; music/music director, Elmer Bernstein; song, Bernstein, Sammy Cahn; assistant director, Sam Nelson; wardrobe, Bill Thomas; makeup, Del Armstrong, Layne Britton; art director, Malcolm Brown; sound, Franklin Hansen; camera, Russell Metty; editor, Ferris Webster.

Lana Turner (Marjorie Penrose); Efrem Zimbalist, Jr. (Arthur Winner); Jason Robards, Jr. (Julius Penrose); Barbara Bel Geddes (Clarissa Winner); George Hamilton (Warren Winner); Susan Kohner (Helen Detweiler); Thomas Mitchell (Noah Tuttle); Everett Sloane (Reggie); Yvonne Craig (Veronica Kovacs); Jean Willes (Junie McCarthy); Frank Maxwell (Jerry Brophy); Gilbert Green (Mr. Woolf); Carroll O'Connor (Bernie Breck).

BACHELOR IN PARADISE (*MGM, 1961*) C-109 min.

Producer, Ted Richmond; director, Jack Arnold; based on the story by Vera Caspary; screenplay, Valentine Davies, Hal Kanter; music, Henry Mancini; title song, Mancini, Mack David; art directors, George W. Davis, Hans Peters; set decorators, Henry Grace, Keogh Gleason; color consultant, Charles K. Hagedon; assistant director, Eric Von Stroheim, Jr.; wardrobe, Helen Rose; makeup, Del Armstrong; sound, Franklin Milton; camera, Joseph Ruttenberg; editor, Richard W. Farrell.

Bob Hope (Adam J. Niles); Lana Turner (Rosemary Howard); Janis Paige (Dolores Jynson); Jim Hutton (Larry Delavane); Paula Prentiss (Linda Delavane); Don Porter (Thomas W. Jynson); Virginia Grey (Camille Quinlaw); Agnes Moorehead (Judge Peterson); Florence Sundstrom (Mrs. Pickering); Clinton Sundberg (Rodney Jones); John McGiver (Austin Palfrey); Alan Hewitt (Backett); Reta Shaw (Mrs. Brown); Mary Treen (Housewife); Tracy Stratford ("Mrs. McGonigle"); Robert B. Williams (Fireman); Joy Monroe (Voluptuous Girl); Lisa Seagram (Beautiful Girl); Robert Hopkins, Rodney Bell, Herbert Lytton, Robert Carson (Attorneys).

WHO'S GOT THE ACTION? (*Paramount, 1962*) C-93 min.

Producer, Jack Rose; director, Daniel Mann; based on the novel *Four Horseplayers Are Missing* by Alexander Rose; screenplay, Jack Rose; music/music director, George Duning; art director, Arthur Lonergan; assistant director, Artie Jacobson; wardrobe, Edith Head; makeup, Del Armstrong; camera, Joseph Ruttenberg; editor, Howard Smith.

Dean Martin (Steve Flood); Lana Turner (Melanie Flood); Eddie Albert (Clint Morgan); Nita Talbot (Saturday Knight); Walter Matthau (Tony Gagoots); Margo (Roza); Paul Ford (Judge Boatwright); Lewis Charles

(Clutch); John McGiver (Judge Fogel); Dan Tobin (Mr. Sanford); Alexander Rose (Mr. Goody); Jack Albertson (Officer Hodges); George Dee (Waiter); Alphonse Martell (Maitre D'); Hillary Yates (Hoxie); Joseph Vitale (Bartender); Eddie Quillan (Dingo, the Phone Repairman); Ralph Montgomery (Street Cleaner); Charles LaRocca (Doorman); Wilbur Mack (Groom/Octogenarian); Len Hendry, Lee Sabinson (Lawyers); House Peters, Jr. (Cop in Elevator); June Wilkinson (Bride).

LOVE HAS MANY FACES (*Columbia, 1965*) C-105 min.

Producer, Jerry Bresler; director, Alexander Singer; screenplay, Marguerite Roberts; music, David Raksin; title song, Raskin, Mack David; Miss Turner's wardrobe, Edith Head; art director, Alfred Sweeney; set decorator, Noldi Schreck; assistant director, Richard Moder; makeup, Ben Lane, Del Armstrong, Del Acavedo; sound, Charles J. Rice, Jesus Gonzales; camera, Joseph Ruttenberg; editor, Alma Macrorie.

Lana Turner (Kit Jordon); Cliff Robertson (Pete Jordon); Hugh O'Brian (Hank Walker); Ruth Roman (Margot Eliot); Stefanie Powers (Carol Lambert); Virginia Grey (Irene Talbot); Ron Husmann (Chuck Austin); Enrique Lucero (Lieutenant Riccardo Andrade); Carlos Montalban (Don Julian); Jaime Bravo (Manuel Perez); Fannie Schiller (Maria); Rene Dupreyon (Ramos).

MADAME X (*Universal, 1966*) C-99 min.

Producer, Ross Hunter; director, David Lowell Rich; based on the play by Alexandre Bisson; screenplay, Jean Holloway; art directors, Alexander Golitzen, George Webb; set decorators, John McCarthy, Howard Bristol; Miss Turner's and Miss Bennett's gowns, Jean Louis; wardrobe, Kathleen McCandless; makeup, Bud Westmore; assistant director, Doug Green; music, Frank Skinner; music supervisor, Joseph Gershenson; sound, Waldon O. Watson, Clarence Self; camera, Russell Metty; editor, Milton Carruth.

Lana Turner (Holly Anderson); John Forsythe (Clay Anderson); Ricardo Montalban (Phil Benton); Burgess Meredith (Dan Sullivan); Constance Bennett (Estelle); Keir Dullea (Clay, Jr. as an Adult); Teddy Quinn (Clay, Jr. as a Child); John Van Dreelen (Christian Torben); Virginia Grey (Mimsy); Warren Stevens (Michael Spalding); Carl Benton Reid (Judge); Frank Maxwell (Dr. Evans); Karen Verne (Nurse Riborg); Joe De Santis (Carter); Frank Marth (Combs); Bing Russell (Sergeant Riley); Teno Pollick (Manuel Lopez); Jeff Burton (Bromley).

THE BIG CUBE (*Warner Bros.-Seven Arts, 1969*) C-98 min.

Producer, Lindsley Parsons; director, Tito Davison; story, Davison, Edmundo Baez; screenplay, William Douglas Lansford; art director, Manuel Fontanals; assistant director, Winfield Sanchez; music, Val Johns; song, Johns, Howard Finkelstein; gowns, Travilla; makeup, Ann Guerrero, Rosa Guerrero; sound, James L. Fields; camera, Gabriel Figueroa; editor Carlos Savage, Jr.

Lana Turner (Adriana); George Chakiris (Johnny);

Richard Egan (Frederick); Daniel O'Herlihy (Charles); Karin Mossberg (Lisa); Pamela Rodgers (Bibi); Carlos East (Lalo); Augusto Benedico (Doctor); Victor Junco (Delacroix); Norma Herrera (Stella); Pedro Galvan (Dean); The Finks (Themselves); Regina Torne (Queen Bee).

THE LAST OF THE POWERSEEKERS (*Universal TV, 1971*) C-100 min.*

Associate producers, John Wilder, Michael Gleason; producer, Harry Tatelman; directors, Walter Doniger, Josef Leytes, Paul Henreid; based on characters created by Harold Robbins, Richard De Roy, Wilder, Gleason; teleplay, Wilder, Gleason, Norman Katkov, Richard Bluel, J. M. Richards; executive story consultant, De Roy; art director, Howard E. Johnson; set decorators, John McCarthy, Joseph Stone; music supervisor, Stanley Wilson; music, Michel Colombier; assistant director, Kenny Williams; gowns, Luis Estevez; costume consultant, William Hamilton; makeup, Bud Westmore; sound, Terry Kellum, Lyle Cain; camera, William Margulies, Jean Rabier; editorial supervisor, Richard Belding; editor, Gene Palmer.

George Hamilton (Duncan Carlyle); Kevin McCarthy (Philip Hastings); Ralph Bellamy (Baylor Carlyle); Lana Turner (Tracy Carlyle Hastings); Louis Hayward (Jonathan Carlyle); Diana Muldaur (Belle Wheeler); Jan-Michael Vincent (Jeffrey Hastings); Richard Eastham (Anthony Mathesson, III); Louise Sorel (Jean Vale); Pamela Tiffin (Rosemary); Schell Rasten (Max Schiffman); Barlett Robinson (Emory Sherman); Carlos Romero (Carlos); Alyce May (Nora); Byron Webster (Dr. William Osborne); Dee Carroll (Martha); Harvey Gardner (Cabbie); Michael Bell (Corbett); William Bramley (Sergeant Grady); Gail Bonney (Duncan's Nurse); Joanna Cameron (Belinda Hastings); Gregoire Aslan (Mr. Bertalot); Yvonne Furneaux (Miss Rabier); George Mikell (Mr. Mikell); John Rico (Armand St. Verre); Rudolph Walker (Mr. Nyesi); Elizabeth White (French Nurse); Catherine Busson (Nurse Leah).

*Assembled from the footage of the teleseries "The Survivors" (ABC-TV, 1969).

PERSECUTION (*Fanfare, 1974*) (a.k.a. SHEBA) C-92 min.*

Producer, Kevin Francis; associate producer, Hugh Attwooll; director, Don Chaffey; story/screenplay, Robert B. Hutton, Rosemary Wootten; additional scenes and dialogue, Frederick Warner; art directors, Jack Shampan, Peter Williams; assistant director, Anthony Waye; Miss Turner's costumes, Anthony Mendleson; Miss Turner's makeup, Roy Ashton; music, Paul Ferris; sound, Jack Brommage; camera, Kenneth Talbot; editor, Michael Campbell.

Lana Turner (Carrie Masters); Trevor Howard (Paul Bellamy); Ralph Bates (David Masters); Olga Georges-Picot (Monique Kalfon); Suzan Farmer (Janie Masters); Mark Weavers (Young David); Patrick Allen (Robert Masters); Jennifer Guy (Waitress); Shelagh Fraser (Mrs. Banks); Ronald Howard (Dr. Ross); John Ryan (Gardener).

*Cut to 88 minutes.

BITTERSWEET LOVE *(Avco Embassy, 1976)* C-92 min.
Producers, Joseph Zappala, Gene Slott, Joel B. Michaels; director, David Miller; screenplay, Adrian Morrall, D. A. Kellogg; music, Ken Wannberg; orchestrator, Albert Woodbury; art director, Vince Cresciman; Miss Turner's makeup, Michael Germaine; makeup Jerry Soucie; sound, Michael Evje; sound effects, Rich Harrison; camera, Stephen Katz; editor, Bill Butler.

Lana Turner (Claire); Robert Lansing (Howard); Celeste Holm (Marian); Robert Alda (Ben); Scott Hylands (Michael); Meredith Baxter Birney (Patricia); Gail Strickland (Roz); Richard Masur (Alex); Denise DeMirjian (Nurse Morrison); John Friedrich (Josh); Amanda Gavin (Judy); Jerome Guardino (Psychiatrist); Jac Jozefson, Jr. (Mr. Schate); Vince Milana (Dr. Green); Erik Nelson (Minister); Elizabeth Rogers (Joan); Adriana Shaw (Mara); Gretchen Sloate (Blonde); Ann Sweeny (Josie); Patricia Tidy (Martha).

ABOUT THE STAFF

JAMES ROBERT PARISH, Los Angeles-based free-lance writer, was born in Cambridge, Massachusetts. He attended the University of Pennsylvania and graduated as a Phi Beta Kappa with a degree in English. He is a graduate of the University of Pennsylvania Law School and had been the president of Entertainment Copyright Research Co., Inc., as well as a reporter for Manhattan film trade papers. Among the books that he is author of are *The Great Movie Series, The Fox Girls, Hollywood's Great Love Teams,* and *The Jeanette MacDonald Story.* He is the co-author of *The MGM Stock Company, The Debonairs,* and *Film Directors Guide: The U.S.* and many other books on the media. Mr. Parish is also a contributor to national magazines.

GREGORY W. MANK is a graduate of Mount St. Mary's College, with a B.A. in English. He has written several articles for *Films in Review* and *Film Fan Monthly* and has been associated with Mr. Parish on *Hollywood Players: The Forties, Hollywood Players: The Thirties, The Tough Guys, Great Child Stars,* and others. Mr. Mank lives in Pennsylvania with his wife Barbara and daughter Jessica, and is active in theatre as a performer and a teacher.

DON E. STANKE in the past few years has interviewed more than forty American film and stage personalities and has had career articles published on most of them in cinema journals. Interviewing and writing is avocational, since Mr. Stanke is a full-time administrator with a San Francisco firm. With Mr. Parish, he is the co-author of *The Glamour Girls, The Debonairs, The Swashbucklers, The All-Americans, and The Leading Ladies,* and has contributed to *The Real Stars #2, The Tough Guys, Hollywood Players: The Thirties,* and *The Child Stars.*

JOHN ROBERT COCCHI was born in Brooklyn where he currently resides. He is one of Amer-ica's most respected film researchers. He is the New York editor of *Boxoffice* magazine. He was research associate on *The American Movies Reference Book: The Sound Era, The Fox Girls, Good Dames, The Swashbucklers,* and many others. He has written cinema history articles for *Film Fan Monthly, Screen Facts,* and *Films in Review.* He is the author of *The Western Picture Quiz Book* and is co-founder of one of New York City's leading film societies.

RICHARD G. PICCHIARINI is a free-lance theatre and film researcher ensconced on New York's Upper West Side. He has contributed frequently to *Playbill* magazine and is the author of *A History of the Tony Awards: 1947-77.* Recently absent from the stage, he has a long array of regional acting credits as well as having appeared in an off-off Broadway production of *Hamlet* in 1974. Among other works, he has contributed to *The Great Western Pictures* by Mr. Parish and Michael R. Pitts.

PETER SANDERSON was born in Milton, Massachusetts, and attended Thayer Academy in nearby Braintree. He earned his B.A. in 1973 and his M.A. in 1976 at Columbia University, and is currently completing his doctorate in English literature at Columbia. He has long had a great interest in the cinema as well as in the theatre and opera.

New York-born FLORENCE SOLOMON attended Hunter College and then joined Ligon Johnson's copyright research office. Later she was director for research at Entertainment Copyright Research Co., Inc., and is currently a reference supervisor at ASCAP's Index Division. Ms. Solomon has collaborated on such works as *The American Movies Reference Book, TV Movies, Film Actors Guide: Western Europe,* and many others. She is the niece of the noted sculptor, the late Sir Jacob Epstein.

Index

Numbers in italics indicate pages showing photographs of the individuals and movies mentioned. If the letter "n" follows a page number, the reference is to a footnote on the indicated page.

452

461

462

472